lex100.com

Editor-in-chief/Chairman: John Pritchard

Content editor: Daniel Coyne
Consultant editor: Teresa Sandon
Editorial assistant: Lily Waddell
Managing director: David Goulthorpe
Head of sales: Amy McDermott
Business development manager: Marie Eldridge
Content development director: Annette Sheppard
Head of content development: Hannah Randall
Content development editors: Rebecca Clark, Oliver Cross, Sian Goodwin, William Inglis, Lucy Jefkins, Max King, Andrew McKenzie, Stephanie Nash, Leigh Rose, Claire Slater, Taylor Small, Ryan Smith
Advertising content development co-ordinator: Harry Milburn
Digital content development co-ordinator: Cameron Shears
Technical director: Michael Pocock
Data management and electronic publishing: Sasha Morgan, Alexander Sivirentsev, Anders Wennerwik

Printed and bound by: LegoPrint S.p.A., Italy

The Lex 100 is published by Legalease
188-190 Fleet Street, London EC4A 2AG

© Legalease Limited and John Pritchard 2016

ISBN: 978 1 906854 32 4

Contents

Editor's welcome

Welcome to the 12th edition of **The Lex 100** – and we're bigger and better than ever.

The year may change but our work doesn't – **Lex** has once again published the most in-depth survey of trainee solicitors across the land, gathering anonymous feedback on their training contract experiences to compile a trusted, well-sourced review of 173 different law firms in the UK.

This spring, over 3,000 trainees completed our online survey, and the detailed insight which they have provided has been collated and edited by the **Lex 100** team to form the firm profiles contained in these pages.

Trainees score the **Lex 100** firms in 13 different categories, ranging from job satisfaction, client contact and work quality, to vacation schemes and international secondments for those firms who offer such placements.

The trainees also provided qualitative feedback, and you will see that we have quoted their responses frequently to bring you as many trainee views as possible.

First, see the **Lex 100 Winners** pages (**p69-84**) for the standout performers of 2016/17, and then read on to peruse the individual firm profiles.

The featured firm profiles (**p89-407**) also contain information from *The Legal 500*, our sister publication. The combination of **Lex**'s trainee feedback and the information on firm performances sourced by *The Legal 500* serves as a great introduction to the training contract providers in the market.

Our **law school** and **career clinic** pages (**p9-67**) explain step-by-step how to progress from student to qualified lawyer, and this year we have added an article on the Qualified Lawyers Transfer Scheme for foreign-qualified lawyers seeking to gain solicitor status in England and Wales.

Don't forget to head to **lex100.com**, where our useful **firm comparison tool** allows users to filter **The Lex 100** survey results according to their own criteria and preferences. We also bring you all the essential legal market news relevant to aspiring lawyers.

We are on facebook and twitter, and you can sign up to our weekly newsletter from our homepage – please get in touch if you have any queries about **The Lex 100**.

We wish you the best of luck for this academic year, and we hope you find **The Lex 100** to be a useful resource!

Daniel Coyne,
Editor, The Lex 100
daniel.coyne@legalease.co.uk
t: @TheLex100
f: The Lex 100

Welcome to the firms

You want to fight for truth and justice… you want to help neglected children… or you want to wield power in corporate boardrooms… for whatever reason, you think you want to be a lawyer. But pursuing a legal career can take you down many different paths…

The life of a corporate lawyer at Linklaters bears little resemblance to the life of a family practitioner at Penningtons Manches, which in turn is nothing like the day-to-day business of a bloodstock lawyer at Prettys or a personal injury solicitor at Irwin Mitchell. Just as the work is different, so too are the people. And the firms themselves, while sharing the common goal of business success, are also dissimilar in style and outlook. On these pages we aim to give you a thumbnail sketch of the various types of firm available to you as you look for a training contract. Readers should be aware that we are generalising to a certain extent, and you should always investigate each firm as much as you can to get a sense of individual flavour and personality. Always check individual firms for trainee numbers and salary details. Although we have, of course, done some of the legwork for you – see the individual firms' pages in the main section of the book.

Magic Circle

An elite group of London's largest and most profitable corporate law firms, comprising Allen & Overy, Clifford Chance, Freshfields Bruckhaus Deringer, Linklaters and Slaughter and May. These are huge firms with hundreds of partners and annual UK trainee intakes of between 85 and 120 candidates. They advise the world's leading companies and banks on their most challenging deals and transactions. They have sleek, impressive offices with fantastic facilities and they offer thorough training, international travel and exposure to major clients and deals. However, they are also known for long hours and high stress levels, and they tend to offer less client contact and 'real' work than smaller firms. To make up for this, the salary and bonuses are at the top end of the scale. If you see yourself as a high-flying corporate or finance lawyer, juggling big deals and huge sums of money, and are prepared to put in the hours, then these are the firms for you.

Large global/City firms

This wide-ranging group of firms offers a similar approach and philosophy to the Magic Circle. We include here practices such as Ashurst, Baker & McKenzie, DLA Piper, Jones Day, Hogan Lovells, Herbert Smith Freehills, Norton Rose Fulbright, Simmons & Simmons, Pinsent Masons and CMS Cameron McKenna. Work still has a definite corporate/commercial focus, clients are household names and deals are big. Trainee numbers are generally smaller, but you'll still be part of a large group, with perhaps an intake of around 60 trainees each year. The hours and stress levels might not be on a par with the Magic Circle firms, but the pay might not be quite as

> **Magic Circle firms advise the world's leading companies, and have sleek offices with fantastic facilities… they are also known for long hours and high stress levels.**

high either. A training contract at this type of firm can offer many of the rewards of City training, with perhaps slightly less of a stressful, hothouse environment.

US firms

It is only relatively recently that US firms have started to offer training contracts in London, and they appear to present an enticing combination of high salaries and large corporate deals, with plenty of hands-on experience and a smaller, more manageable number of trainees (typically between five and 15). Firms such as Covington & Burling, Skadden, Arps, Slate, Meagher & Flom, Shearman & Sterling, White & Case and Cleary Gottlieb Steen & Hamilton are all praised for thorough training in an environment where there is no room to hide, but plenty of space to shine. On the downside, hours can be long, with eye-watering billable targets and stress levels to match.

Large national/regional firms

Another group of commercial firms, handling high-quality work and offering anywhere between 12 and 50 trainee places each year. We include here practices such as Addleshaw Goddard (with offices in Manchester, Leeds and London), East Anglia practice Mills & Reeve and Bristol-based Burges Salmon. You should be offered a good spread of work at firms like these, and the bias will still be corporate/commercial, with decent litigation and property practices too. These firms are among the highest payers outside London, and offer an excellent alternative to the City.

Mid-sized London firms

This group covers a variety of firms with a number of specialist areas. Examples include Watson, Farley & Williams (particularly well known for shipping work); Olswang (strengths in media, technology and property); Bird & Bird (leading reputation in IP and IT); and Macfarlanes and Travers Smith (corporate boutiques). Typically there will be between 15 and 40 trainees, allowing room to shine but providing you with plenty of ready-made friends. There is often more one-to-one supervision from partners and more client contact.

Smaller London firms

The smaller London firms can provide an excellent training environment, with early responsibility, hands-on work and often your own caseload. You will get exposure to the main areas of corporate, property and litigation, but should also get to experience some of the niche practice areas in which these smaller firms excel. One main downside to these firms can be the slightly higher levels of uncertainty over retention rates, so check out recent stats. Firms falling into this category generally have between ten and 20 trainees. Farrer & Co (strong in media and family); Lewis Silkin (advertising and employment specialists); Penningtons Manches (family law) and Bristows (IP) are examples of this type of firm. If you want a different kind of training experience to the commercial firms mentioned above, you could consider a legal aid specialist such as Hodge Jones & Allen, where a large proportion of work is publicly funded. This type of firm gives trainees the opportunity to experience areas of law such as human rights, crime, family and clinical negligence, in a more socially conscious environment.

Leading regional firms

Outside London there is a huge range of firms to choose from. Many will be leaders in their fields, with both local and national (sometimes international) clients. The larger examples will have between ten and 30 trainees and should offer a good balance of structured training, significant work and hands-on experience. Not to mention pretty decent hours, a short commute (depending on where you choose to live) and a good work/life balance. Some of these firms are based in one city, such as Walker Morris (Leeds), while others have several locations, eg Freeths (bases including Birmingham, Leicester and Nottingham).

Smaller regional firms

If the idea of a large, competitive group of trainees makes you want to run a mile, and you'd rather get stuck into real work as soon as possible, then a smaller regional firm will often provide excellent client contact combined with a relaxed working atmosphere and reasonable hours. Firms such as Reading-based Boyes Turner and Southampton-based Paris Smith have fewer than ten trainees, and regularly feature in our **Lex 100 Winners'** tables for manageable stress levels or work/life balance. They also show the positive side of legal training – where it is possible to obtain thorough, hands-on experience in a variety of practice areas without saying goodbye to your social life. ■

Law School

The LPC – The Lex Lowdown

The Legal Practice Course is the final mandatory qualification required before commencing a training contract. It's also a considerable financial commitment, especially following the 2012 hike in tuition fees. For that reason, you are well-advised to do as much research as you can – so read on!

If you've made the decision to pursue a career as a solicitor, the next step for a graduate is to enrol on the LPC (except for non-Law students who must first take the GDL conversion course). There are several different courses and providers in the market, but all of them cover the same core content required by the profession's standards body, the Solicitors Regulation Authority.

Legal obligation

The LPC is an integral part of the process of becoming a solicitor in England and Wales. It is a vocational course and is supposed to prepare you for life at any law firm, from niche family practice to international commercial giant. Your application to study the LPC needs to be made the year before you intend to start the course. This will typically be during your final year if you are a law undergraduate. For those taking the conversion route into law (non-law graduates), your application will usually be made during the year you complete the graduate diploma in law (GDL).

Costly endeavour

At the moment, there are roughly 40 LPC providers, all vying with each other to tempt you to spend a year at their institution. The cost of doing the LPC full time ranges from around £7,500 to over £14,000, and in return you will be taught everything (well, nearly everything) you'll need to know to become a practising solicitor. For those who have already secured a training contract, course fees may be paid by your future employer, and some firms also stump up maintenance grants. If your future firm isn't that generous, you can try your hand at obtaining cash elsewhere. For example, the Law Society publicises various bursary schemes – but be warned, the competition is incredibly fierce. Perhaps also consider taking the LPC part-time, which will provide you with enough spare time to continuing earning some money and therefore help to ease the financial burden. Funds are only available for the most deserving and committed. There is also a diversity access scheme for talented people whose route

to becoming a solicitor is made difficult because of a disability or social circumstances. The application for both schemes usually commences in February. See the Junior Lawyers Division (JLD) of the Law Society website (www.lawsociety.org.uk) for more details.

> ‘ **The best way to find out about life as a solicitor is to do some legal work experience** 🖊

Are you sure?

Without the financial security of knowing you have a training contract at the end of the LPC, there are some difficult questions to be answered before you fire off your application to law school. The Law Society sets out some important points to reflect on (see box, 'Thinking it over'). Once you've considered these elements, there are some other things to think about, namely: how do you go about choosing which law school you want to attend, and how can you really be sure that law is the career for you? Well, the second part's the easy(ish) bit. The best way to find out about life as a solicitor is to do some legal work experience, through firm vacation schemes and open days, and also by talking with those currently training or practising as lawyers. If you are debating between qualifying as a solicitor or a barrister, then it's also worthwhile undertaking a 'mini-pupillage' at a set of chambers to get a flavour of the Bar.

Choosing a provider

Most LPC providers maintain close links with law firms, which can be of huge benefit to students as these firms will be feeding some of their knowledge and experience of practice into the study programme.

Thinking it over

Spending upwards of £7,500 on anything is a huge decision to make, so if you are thinking about applying for the LPC, the matter shouldn't be taken lightly. The Junior Lawyers Division (JLD) of the Law Society urges prospective LPC applicants to be mindful of the following points before applying:

- Successful completion of the LPC does not guarantee a training contract;
- If you don't have an offer of a training contract before starting the LPC, you should assess how realistic your chances are of getting one;
- Not all firms will pay for the LPC (and GDL if applicable) if you are offered a training contract. And those that do pay course fees may not do so retrospectively if you are offered a training contract whilst enrolled at law school;
- Not all lawyers are rich, very few are. Even once qualified, the debt payments continue and most lawyers are still paying off debt years after qualification;
- Consider part-time or part-time study options as well as the Chartered Institute of Legal Executives (CILEX) route to qualification as a solicitor. Although the CILEX route may take longer, it will be a less expensive route to qualification; and
- Speak to people currently on the LPC, or those who have recently completed it, about the difficulties in obtaining a training contract.

There are many ways in which providers work together with firms; it may be through designing bespoke courses for particular firms, or by making arrangements whereby certain firms will come in to give students careers advice, or to provide training in commercial awareness. So if you haven't already secured a training contract, it would be worth spending some time researching whether a particular provider has connections with any firm (or firms) you are interested in training at.

However, those candidates who already have training contracts lined up before they start law school may not have an option as to which law school they attend. A firm may stipulate that future trainees only attend an institution which offers certain subjects. Indeed, bespoke courses are on the rise. Several firms have an agreement with BPP Law School, so all their future trainees (who haven't already completed the LPC) undertake a specially designed LPC at BPP. Many other firms have opted for customised courses at The University of Law, meaning that students will take an LPC specifically tailored to life at their future firm. This means that students will be taught in firm-specific groups and get the chance to work on precedents (i.e. draft documents) used in real matters handled by their future employers.

The debunking of a myth

The Graduate Diploma in Law explained.

While attending numerous law fairs last autumn, the Lex team was struck by the number of students voicing uncertainty and concern about the law conversion course and how candidates who have sat it may be perceived by employers. This article will hopefully offer a bit more information on what the conversion course is, and calm fears that it may be anything other than a respected, well-worn pathway into the legal profession.

Though the legal industry is undergoing considerable changes by offering different routes for young people to enter the profession, the most common route to solicitor or barrister status remains the tried-and-tested pathway of getting a good degree and enrolling at a law school. On this journey, aspiring lawyers will pursue many fiercely fought-over opportunities to bolster their CVs, strengthen their skills and stand out from the crowd. From the initial steps of attending law fairs and conducting career research, to taking up voluntary work and applying for vacation schemes and mini-pupillages, there is a lot to consider. For the purposes of this article, however, we will begin by keeping it simple and focus just on the compulsory qualifications required, and the two main routes from graduate to lawyer.

Law graduates

Those who graduate with a qualifying law degree (QLD), which covers the essential foundations as required by the profession's regulators, are ready to proceed straight to the 'vocational stage' of the process. At this stage, two different courses cater for the two different branches of the profession. Enrolling on the Legal Practice Course (LPC) prepares students for a solicitor training contract, while taking the Bar Professional Training Course (BPTC) is the final preparatory stage required before commencing a pupillage to become a barrister.

Non-law graduates

For non-law graduates, an extra mandatory stage is required before one can enrol on either of the vocational courses described above. This extra stage is a course called the Graduate Diploma in Law (GDL), which must be completed before commencing the LPC or BPTC.

Now let's explain the non-law route in detail...

What is the GDL?

The GDL (sometimes referred to as the Common Professional Examination, or CPE) enables non-law graduates to in effect 'catch up' on the legal knowledge developed by undergraduates with QLDs. All GDL courses must cover the seven key areas of law required for the LPC/BPTC. These are: contract, criminal, tort, equity and trusts, land law, European Union law and public law. Different providers vary in how they structure their syllabuses, and there will also be additional modules as part of the qualification, but this core content is mandatory for all.

According to the Law Society's 2013 Annual Statistics Report, 4,437 people in total were directly admitted to the Roll of Solicitors in 2012-13. Of these, 3,307 were law graduates and 1,130 were non-law graduates. Therefore, roughly a quarter of all direct entrants to the ranks of solicitors that year came through the GDL. A minority, but a large one, and a well-established pathway to becoming a solicitor. As for the other half of the profession, the Bar Standards Board was unable to provide us with the relevant statistics for those called to the Bar, but there is no reason to suggest it will be markedly different (see Martin Pascoe QC's quote below).

The providers

Soon you will be hearing from two students currently enrolled on the GDL, one of whom is pursuing pupillage while the other has a coveted Magic Circle training contract already in her grasp. First up, let's hear from Jayne Jeffcott, head of students at the University of Law which is one of the UK's leading providers of specialist legal education.

Jeffcott believes that the GDL is an "incredibly valuable way to enter the profession". She goes on to stress several ways in which taking the GDL route can be advantageous. When moving on to take the similarly-intensive LPC or BPTC, Jeffcott cites the "natural progression" GDL students will have taken: "the methodology of our practically-focused courses is engrained and very recent, so GDL students are used to the high volume of study and tend to hit the ground running far quicker than the law graduates who come in."

Beyond offering ideal preparation for the rigours of law school, GDL students should also be confident in the different skills and experience that they are able to offer. Jeffcott offers encouragement to non-law graduates, saying: "don't be defensive about the fact that you haven't done an undergraduate Law degree. Instead, stress how this makes you a different sort of candidate with different skills and an alternative undergraduate experience." Nobody does the GDL on a whim, she adds, and "because of the cost and the work involved, the students who do the GDL tend to be focused and incredibly committed. Employers understand this."

The employers
Interviews we have conducted support Jeffcott's assertion, with employers keen to stress their appreciation of the GDL course.

Martin Pascoe QC, head of the pupillage committee at South Square chambers, tells us: "South Square greatly benefits, as do our clients, from having barristers with diverse skills and experiences because they have taken different routes to the Bar. A number of our barristers have degrees in Law, some have taken non-Law degrees and then sat the CPE/GDL and others have started their career in another sector before coming into the law. We select our pupils from a mix of backgrounds so the route candidates take to the Bar is not relevant. What is important for pupillage is an excellent academic record and the potential to become an outstanding commercial barrister."

When asked if non-law graduate applicants could ever be at a disadvantage when applying for training contracts, Sarah Cockburn, the senior graduate recruitment manager at Magic Circle firm Allen & Overy, says "no, in fact approximately half of A&O's trainees did not study Law as their first degree."

Similarly, Burges Salmon recruitment advisor Frances Bennett also states that approximately half of the firm's trainee recruits came through the GDL route, and elaborates on why such candidates are

valued: "Studying a subject other than law can offer you different perspectives and helps to develop a variety of skills. In reality, once you start to practice law it is unlikely you will refer back to material that you studied in your law degree or GDL so for us it doesn't matter which route you have come from. We like to have a variety of experiences and backgrounds in our trainee intake and students who have not studied law may have developed slightly different skills to law students."

> **' GDL students should be confident in the different skills and experience that they are able to offer ,**

The students
Who are these students, then? Who enrols on the GDL, and why do they choose to do so? What are their thoughts on the course and how does it compare to their undergraduate studies? Again, these are all common questions heard at law fairs. Of course, the boring broad answer is to say that it varies according to each individual, but rather more helpfully we have spoken to two current GDL students to gather their thoughts.

James Fireman is a current GDL student who plans to progress to the BPTC and obtain a pupillage. He studied Politics and International Relations at the University of Manchester and, explaining law's attraction, says: "I really liked political philosophy and the moral debates. I liked the thought-provoking side of what is wrong and what is right. It offers a foundation for the moral arguments found within law and therefore I always felt that a career in law was an option." James did a couple of mini-pupillages in his second year and this confirmed his desire to become a barrister, as it offered "a real insight into the ways in which a lawyer deals with their clients, and also the court proceedings themselves."

As for the GDL itself, James stresses the intensity of the one-year programme: "It's set out in a way where you can very clearly organise your time, but you have to be very organised and strict with yourself. It is all there for you and outlined step-by-step, but if you miss something you will have no idea what's going on in the workshop. It's very important that you keep up-to-date with what's going on in order to make the most of it. This year I've had to be very organised!"

Hattie Jones commenced the GDL in September 2014 and will then tackle the LPC afterwards, having accepted a training contract offer from Clifford Chance in March. Hattie completed a BA in Japanese a year early at Cambridge. Always interested in a career in law, she used that extra time wisely by sitting one year of the undergraduate law course. She then did a Masters in Criminology and Criminal Justice.

Like James, she mentions the considerable demands which the GDL brings: "The work load is fairly time-intensive. The content is not massively complicated, and we go through it at speed so it is simplified down quite a lot. But there is a lot of work." When asked what advice she would offer prospective GDL students, Hattie highlights one key difference with undergraduate level, saying that "the course itself is very structured in terms of working from manuals rather than the traditionally broader undergraduate approach."

One common concern among students – at all stages – considering a career in law is that there is a 'type': a certain student with a particular background and a set of narrow experiences whom all recruiters want to see walk in through the interview room door. Those we have spoken to here suggest this is not the case. Employers value variety amongst their workforce, and students from different academic backgrounds are sought after. Jeffcott builds on this, saying: "name a degree subject and I've probably taught them". She cites English and History as two of the more common degree subjects but notes a rise in the number of scientists, linguists and mathematicians making the switch, along with career changers who have worked alongside legal professionals and been inspired to go back to school.

That switch is, of course, a big decision to make, and a considerable financial commitment for already debt-laden students to take on. While GDL fees have remained relatively constant in real terms, the tripling of undergraduate tuition fees has had a knock on effect and is likely to be a main factor in enrolment numbers for the GDL reducing nationwide. More than ever, those who do convert are sure of their decision and are completely committed to a legal career.

> **More than ever, those who do convert are sure of their decision and are completely committed to a legal career**

Before making the commitment students will naturally have thought about their decision very carefully and have made it an informed one. An ideal starting point will be to head to your careers centre and, like the proactive students who prompted the writing of this article, your university's law fair.

There is plenty of encouragement and support to be found for those planning to enrol on the GDL. Providers enthuse about the course and the calibre of students it attracts. Employers actively seek to recruit candidates from a wide range of backgrounds, and therefore value those who have obtained alternative academic tuition at undergraduate level. Students enrolled on the course have done their research, spoken to industry professionals and decided that, despite the extra costs a year of studying brings, the GDL is for them. If you are a non-law undergraduate and want to become a solicitor or a barrister, the option is there for you.

The Qualified Lawyers Transfer Scheme

If you're a disillusioned barrister or a foreign lawyer keen to broaden your capabilities, the QLTS enables you to change direction and qualify as a solicitor in England & Wales.

Overseas lawyers seeking to qualify as a solicitor in England & Wales must successfully complete the Qualified Lawyers Transfer Scheme (QLTS).

The QLTS is the mandatory award required of qualified lawyers from other jurisdictions wishing to qualify as a solicitor in England & Wales. The scheme also applies to barristers in England & Wales who would like to qualify as solicitors, though it should be noted that they must have first completed pupillage before taking the QLTS.

To enrol on the QLTS you must be a qualified, practising lawyer in your home jurisdiction, and this jurisdiction must be recognised by the Solicitors Regulation Authority (SRA). You need to have followed the full route to qualification in your home jurisdiction.

The scheme is run by the SRA and was introduced on 1 September 2010. The SRA assesses the character and suitability of all those applying for solicitor status. If you pass this test, it's then on to the exam itself.

The assessment, structured in two parts, tests applicants for the knowledge and skills which solicitors must possess at the moment of qualification. Applicants must first pass Part One before taking on Part Two of the assessment.

Part One of the assessment is the six-hour, 180-question Multiple Choice Test (MCT) which assesses the candidate's core knowledge and understanding of the law in England & Wales. The MCT covers 11 areas of the law.

Part Two is called the Objective Structured Clinical Examination (OSCE). As part of the OSCE, candidates are examined on their client interview, advocacy, research, writing and drafting skills.

More details on the QLTS examination can be found at www.sra.org.uk/solicitors/qlts/key-features.page.

Exemptions may be offered to barristers qualified in England & Wales, lawyers from Scotland and Northern Ireland, and, in certain cases, lawyers from elsewhere in the European Economic Area.

There are no formal English language assessments within the QLTS, though candidates will naturally require excellent English skills in order to pass.

Kaplan is the sole assessor of the QLTS, and as such is not permitted to offer training courses for the scheme. There are several other providers running QLTS training courses, though none are directly authorised by the SRA and such training is therefore unregulated, so do your research.

Note to foreign law students: Foreign law students wishing to become a lawyer in England and Wales are required to take the GDL and then the LPC/BPTC. If you feel that your academic qualifications make you eligible for a partial exemption, you can apply for a Certificate of Academic Standing to bypass the GDL.

LPC providers

Here is a list of institutions authorised to provide the Legal Practice Course, as stated on the Solicitors Regulation Authority website (www.sra.org.uk). Correct at the time of going to print.

Anglia Ruskin University

BPP Law School: London, Leeds, Manchester, Bristol, Birmingham, Liverpool, Cambridge

Birmingham City University

Bournemouth University

Cardiff Law School

City Law School

De Montfort University

Leeds Beckett University

Liverpool John Moores University

London Metropolitan University

Manchester Metropolitan University

Northumbria University

Nottingham Trent University

Staffordshire University

Swansea University

University of Central Lancashire

University of Derby

University of Hertfordshire

University of Huddersfield

University of Law: Birmingham, Bristol, Chester, Guildford, Leeds, London, Manchester (see p22 for further details)

University of Lincoln

University of Sheffield

University of South Wales

University of Sunderland

University of the West of England, Bristol

University of West London

University of Westminster (see p24 for further details)

University of Wolverhampton

Eight things every training contract applicant should know

Advice from The University of Law on the best approach.

The deadline for training contract applications for many law firms is at the end of July. But it's never too early to start making your plans and preparing for a key task in progressing your legal career.

1. Don't apply to every law firm in Britain

Not only does it eat time to apply to too many law firms, but the associated mass copy and pasting gives candidates' applications an impersonal feel. Far better to select a group of firms which appeal to you – and specialise in areas of law that you would like to work in – and then target them specifically. So if, for example, you have an interest in international corporate law, media law and litigation, pick a handful of firms of varying sizes which specialise in each area and focus all your research on them. Don't worry if your list contains an unlikely assortment of outfits – no one else will see it – or if it changes as you conduct your research. The important thing is to have a starting point.

2. Figure out what makes the firms you're applying to different from their competitors

Law firms can appear, at face value, to be near-identical institutions differentiated only by their branding. But look under the bonnet at their annual financial results and you often discover major differences. A guiding principle for UK corporate firms is that the most high-value work is done by the Magic Circle of Slaughter and May, Clifford Chance, Linklaters, Freshfields Bruckhaus Deringer and Allen & Overy, with levels of legal complexity generally dropping as you move down the top 50. But there are many exceptions to this rule, with some smaller firms boasting market-leading niche expertise in a particular specialty. Candidates who know where all firms fit into this legal market hierarchy – and the current state their chosen firms find themselves in relative to rivals during changing times – have a major advantage.

3. Understand the bigger picture

The quickest way to get a handle on how the legal profession is developing is to read one of the books that have been published on it recently. Steve Weiner's *21st Century Solicitor* and Richard Susskind's *Tomorrow's Lawyers* are both highly readable, up-to-date reflections on the developing legal market that can be digested in a couple of days. And if you're really in a hurry, you could always read one of the many reviews of these books in the legal press that are available online.

4. Explain why you want to spend your life practising law

When it comes to the detail of the application form itself, the first thing candidates need to do – after accurately filling out their personal information without making any spelling mistakes, of course – is to articulate why they want to be lawyers. On one hand, this involves explaining why you enjoy law. There should be, hopefully, plenty of experiences from university to draw upon here. As you do, it's important to angle these experiences to the practise of law, rather than simply the study of the subject. This is where pro bono experience is invaluable.

5. Explain why you want to spend your life doing other things professionally

The second limb of explaining why you want to be a lawyer involves demonstrating your understanding of the limits of the law, and why you will need other attributes to succeed at the firm you're applying to. For corporate firms – which account for a large proportion of training contracts – this means showing that you are commercially aware.

6. Get the tone right

Many training contract application forms include one light-hearted question among the heavier stuff. For example, DLA Piper asks its applicants to 'Describe an unusual situation you have found yourself in, humorous or otherwise.' What firms are partially doing here is gauging how well candidates would fit in as members of a team working in an office environment – where, even in law firms, there are plenty of relaxed moments. As a result, it's important to get the tone of your answer right. Try too hard to be hilarious and you risk getting your application binned on the grounds of being a potential village idiot. But respond in a way lacking any humour and there is a danger of coming across as an automaton who might not relate well to colleagues and clients.

7. Avoid extra-curricular overload

The key to answering the traditional application form question about your outside interests and activities is again to consider what the law firm wants to discover by asking it. To an extent, the question is an attempt to gear the hiring process to recruit more interesting people, but perhaps more importantly it's a way of finding out how capable a candidate is at juggling lots of different things at the same time. For example, someone who keeps up a healthy range of extra-curricular activities while also obtaining a good degree result is probably well-organised and able to handle stress well. These are key attributes for a lawyer. So, rather than present yourself as someone with a spectacular breadth of interests, it's better to show that you are simply a person who is inclined to lead a balanced, interesting life.

8. Recognise that the application form is just the beginning

A related, and final, point is to be genuine in your application answers. You are, after all, aiming to set yourself up for the next stage of the process: an interview. Presenting yourself as someone you are not may, on occasion, help aspiring lawyers get through the first application sift, but inauthenticity tends to unravel in the high pressure environment of face-to-face questions from senior lawyers. Law firms, most of all, want graduates who are confident enough to be themselves.

How law students can improve their employability

The University of Law (ULaw)'s director of employability, John Watkins, hones in on some of the behavioural traits that could hold law students back.

The first is an assumption by the academic high-achievers, who tend to be drawn to law, that teamwork is a straightforward task that they don't have to learn.

'Students tend to make assumptions about their capacity for teamwork,' Watkins explains. 'What they often don't realise is that the transition into the work place is a big one. There will be a broad range of ages, and people with very differing attitudes and capabilities.'

Working well with these other individuals isn't something that you learn overnight, adds Watkins, particularly when students have spent most of their lives hanging out with people who are pretty similar to themselves.

Another challenge faced by students when entering the workplace is the type of feedback that they expect. In an educational environment, feedback is all about the quality of work that is submitted. But as an employee, feedback tends to revolve around behaviour because quality of work is largely taken for granted.

'How do you relate to other people? Do you have a pleasant manner? What is your mood like under pressure? These factors often shape people's careers far more than they are willing to accept. As a result, preparing students to accept this sort of feedback, and to respond to it, is really important.'

Then there are things like IT skills and presentation ability. For many, these aren't aspects of the working world that are particularly keenly anticipated.

'The assumption in the digital age is that graduates can do anything IT-related, but they often come up short on the more complex office packages. For an employer this can be frustrating and also costly. Similarly, you'd much rather take on someone who has had some experience of delivering presentations in a formal setting.'

All this is certainly a shift from the good old days when Watkins, a former accountant, was starting out himself in the early 90s. He remembers:

'20 years ago people left university and jobs were plentiful. Mistakes at an early stage didn't have huge consequences. Now they can affect the whole direction that your career takes.'

Watkins predicts that employability will become a hot topic for universities to weave into syllabuses rather than continuing to teach it as a standalone extra. At ULaw, the LLB includes compulsory employability classes that are built into its three-year curriculum.

Where law differs from other subjects is through its unique pro bono culture and the possibility to incorporate free legal advice into formal learning through the clinical legal education model. ULaw offers one of the UK's largest and most varied pro bono programmes with over 2,900 opportunities.

'The pro bono schemes at ULaw are an excellent place for individuals to test those employability skills. Real-life contact with clients can create some really awkward scenarios, but it is a perfect training ground. It shows that the workplace can be challenging and, with the right supervision, you can get some fantastic results.'

The best law students tend to combine a healthy dollop of pro bono with diligence in their academic work while setting aside enough time to immerse themselves in firms' recruitment programmes. Watkins advocates a more analytical approach than is often taken.

'If your ultimate aim is to understand an organisation, a key objective is to understand how that organisation works and what its strategies are. So, rather than simply looking at law fairs as an exercise in handing out freebies, think seriously about why the firms are there, consider their recruitment criteria and then set about ensuring your CV matches what is being looked for.'

ULaw alumni profile: Solomon Wifa

The University of Law (ULaw) alumnus Solomon Wifa can lay claim to helping get a man off death row in Jamaica as well as becoming the youngest-ever managing partner of the London office of international firm O'Melveny & Myers.

A law qualification gives you many invaluable life skills – almost like a toolkit to use not just professionally but personally too. It provides you with transferable skills to take into most situations and helps you to look at those situations more dispassionately, analysing both the risks and benefits.

I also believed that a law degree would allow me to do anything I wanted. It would open doors. I didn't think all these years on that I would still be a solicitor; I imagined I would have moved into more of a business role – a law degree gives you those transferable skills, which is what interested me.

I studied the LPC over two years part-time at ULaw's Guildford centre, graduating in 1997. I absolutely loved the campus and the course, and have made lifelong friends from my time there. The space and serenity of the campus was ideal for me, escaping the big city to a calmer place to focus and learn.

I enjoyed and highly valued the practical element of the course and soon realised that I wanted to be closer to the clients, and I realised I was interested in law aligned with business rather than the Bar.

A qualification in law has been fundamental to achieving my career ambitions. Having studied at the most respected institution meant that I experienced law at the most prestigious level. I knew I wanted to be a solicitor and that I wanted to work at the business end of law, so it was important to me to make sure I had the transferable skills in order to fulfil this commercial element.

As an undergraduate I also worked nights for extra cash as a night porter at The Langham Hotel in London. I worked in the day in the office as a paralegal and then back to my night porter duties at the hotel. Looking back I don't know how I did it but it was absolutely worth it. They liked me and while there I got the opportunity to work on a case with SJ Berwin. Following this, I was lucky enough to be offered a paralegal position with them and this led to a training contract. Don't leave any stone unturned, think laterally and network, because you never know where it might take you.

My biggest career highlight was getting a condemned prisoner off death row in Jamaica. I was a young lawyer doing some pro bono work at SJ Berwin and never in a million years would I have imagined working on a case like that. We succeeded in having his sentence commuted and, to this day, I have a model boat made out of match sticks in my office sent as a gift from the client, called *Cruising Glory* – every day this boat reminds me to take a step back and put things into perspective.

My advice to law students starting out is to persevere. When I was studying at ULaw, I must have completed over 300 applications and was knocked back from about 99% of them. It is hard at this time, especially in such a competitive field, so it must be something you 100% have your heart set on – don't go into it half-hearted, be resolute. Also, be strategic – go for what interests you, what you're passionate about and what you know – that way you will shine through.

I recently joined Willkie Farr & Gallagher to help build up the firm's European private equity platform. Previous to this, I was managing partner at O'Melveny & Myers's London office, which kept me very busy, travelling all over the world. When I joined O'Melveny, we were small and I loved being part of something that had the potential to grow.

Promoting diversity is very important to me. I would love to see greater diversity across all levels of the profession. It is encouraging to see more women and ethnic minorities entering the industry but this is not as representative higher up the chain.

The University of Law

The University of Law

Braboeuf Manor, Portsmouth Road, Guildford GU3 1HA

Whether your ambition is to work as a lawyer or in wider business, studying at The University of Law (ULaw) will ensure you'll get the best possible start to your career. We're the UK's largest law school with nine locations nationwide and an award-winning Careers and Employability Service. Our innovative business-focused postgraduate courses are designed and taught by lawyers with real commercial experience and have a strong emphasis on building the practical skills that today's employers are looking for. As a ULaw student, you will have access to the country's largest and most varied pro bono programme. Offering over 2,900 opportunities to put your legal skills into practice. Not to mention the UK's largest legal mentoring programme, with the support of almost 500 practising lawyers. Our record speaks for itself: in 2015 more ULaw graduates secured training contracts than from any other law college.

Graduate Diploma in Law (full-time/part-time/i-GDL)

Our GDL is designed to build knowledge and skills that more than match a law degree. Academic training is built around real-life examples with research assignments that directly reflect the way you'll work as a lawyer. Our unique Ethics and Professional Legal Practice module equips you with the professional skills you'll need as a modern lawyer. Study your GDL at ULaw and upgrade to a Graduate LLB at no extra cost.

Legal Practice Course (full-time/part-time/i-LLM LPC)

We're confident that our LPC is the best preparation for entering legal practice by offering you the skills to succeed in the business world. Future lawyers and business leaders need a wealth of skills to prepare them for today's market place. Our client-focused LPC enables you to develop the commercial awareness, critical thinking, project management and networking skills that will prepare you for the challenges ahead. Study our LPC and you can gain an MSc in Law, Business and Management or LLM in Professional Legal Practice at no extra cost. An online option is also available leading to an LLM.

Bar Professional Training Course (full-time/part-time)

Our BPTC is uniquely structured to mirror the real-life experience of a barrister in practice. We're the only legal training provider offering a 'live' selection process designed to attract the brightest students. Learn from qualified tutors with unparalleled experience in delivering high-quality advocacy training. Most of your learning will be in small groups with plenty of opportunities via practitioner evenings, mock trials, court visits, mooting, negotiating and advocacy competitions, and pro bono.

Online LLM in Legal Practice: (conflict resolution) or (intellectual property)

Study one of our Masters programmes and develop in-depth knowledge and specialist skills in your chosen study area of either conflict resolution or intellectual property.

Online MSc in Law, Governance, Risk and Compliance

Build international legal and GRC knowledge with our career-enhancing Masters qualification, in collaboration with the International Compliance Association (ICA).

Events

We run events of all types, including open days, law fairs and insight days. Check them out at www.law.ac.uk/events.

Contact
Admissions
Phone: 0800 289997
International: +44 1483 216000
Email: admissions@law.ac.uk

www.law.ac.uk/postgraduate

Why The University of Law?

Emily McKinnell LPC student

What made you choose ULaw?
I chose ULaw because of its excellent reputation and convenient location. The open day was very informative and engaging, and solidified my decision to attend ULaw. It gave me the opportunity to have a real insight into the life of a ULaw student and an opportunity to ask any questions about the course, workload and teaching modes. I think the defining factor is the tutors: they are the lifeblood of ULaw. They are enthusiastic, personable and devoted to helping their students. They are always available to answer questions, lend a listening ear or help you in a moment of exam stress. They dedicate their time to ensuring that all their students are fulfilling their potential.

What are your career ambitions?
Throughout my first year at ULaw I was applying for training contracts. ULaw's careers department was excellent in helping me achieve this goal. They read through my CV, helped me tailor applications and prepped me for interviews. The careers service was an invaluable asset and I believe was a major contributing factor in helping me secure a training contract.

Any highlights of your time at ULaw?
It is hard to put a finger on just one highlight, as I have had so many fantastic opportunities. Despite the rigorous nature of the courses offered at ULaw, there is still a heavy emphasis placed on socialising and having fun. There are clubs and societies, such as football, netball, rugby and choir, and social events organised, including the Christmas and Summer balls and the ULaw annual pub quiz. Ultimately, all of these experiences at ULaw have led me to make friends for life.

Do you think studying law can help you really make a difference?
The short answer is yes. On a higher level, law is a gateway for change in society and a vehicle for justice. It is clear to see how a long and successful career in law would enable someone to contribute positive change to society. However, on a much smaller level, it is possible to make some difference right from the beginning of the GDL or LPC through the many volunteering and pro bono schemes offered by ULaw, such as at the National Centre of Domestic Violence and the Citizens Advice Bureau. The ability to make a difference starts on the first day of term!

What are you passionate about?
The areas of law I have been most interested in during my time at ULaw are land and property law, and contract and commercial law. The structure of the GDL and LPC has enabled me to pursue these interests and tailor my learning to these areas. I am pursing these interests in my professional life by undertaking

> **'On a higher level, law is a gateway for change in society and a vehicle for justice.'**

my training contract in a firm which specialise in corporate real estate and construction.

Outside law, I have a love of music and drama. I was a member of the ULaw choir and recently played the part of Nancy in a production of Oliver! I am also very interested in current affairs and politics, and have undertaken work experience in the House of Commons and the House of Lords.

Tell us an interesting fact about yourself
I am named after Emmeline Pankhurst.

Westminster Law School

4-12 Little Titchfield Street, London W1W 7UW

Westminster Law School is based in Little Titchfield Street in the heart of London. As one of London's leading providers of legal education, we're well known for our highly practical approach to teaching and learning. Our modern facilities provide a friendly, diverse and international environment to study law.

The school offers a range of full-time and part-time undergraduate and postgraduate courses, as well as a number of highly regarded short and professional courses.

LPC/LLM in Legal Practice course

Our LLM Legal Practice incorporates both the LPC and an LLM in one award. Students enrolling onto this course have the option either to:

- Complete the LPC on its own
- Complete the LPC and convert this to an LLM by completing an additional dissertation

Our LPC/LLM in Legal Practice equips you with all the skills and knowledge needed to be a highly successful lawyer. Our approach is friendly and supportive, with small, interactive group work, allowing you to benefit from individual guidance and support. Using high-quality teaching materials, sessions are set within a balanced timetable and replicate the tasks undertaken in practice.

A distinctive feature of the course is the broad range of electives offered, reflecting areas of practice from high-street to city firms. We are the only LPC provider currently authorised to refer students taking the Immigration elective for exemption from Level One of the Legal Service Commission's (LSC) Immigration and Asylum Accreditation Scheme.

Students on the course benefit from:

- The expert knowledge and high-quality teaching of our team of solicitors
- A personal tutor to support and guide you throughout the course
- A dedicated LPC resource room equipped with reference, computer and printing facilities and supported by an on-site administrator
- Flexible course content – tailor your course towards commercial or private client practice from a choice of 12 electives.

- Strong links with legal professionals who provide mentoring, or work shadowing and work experience placements
- Opportunities to develop your employability, including working with real clients through pro bono projects such as land registration adjudication
- Tailored careers support including help with CVs and cover letters, interview and psychometric test practice workshops and an annual legal careers fair
- Highly competitive course fees with course materials, texts and manuals

Undergraduate degrees

- European Legal Studies LLB Honours
- Law with French Law LLB Honours
- Law LLB Honours
- MLaw Integrated Master's in Law

Graduate Diploma in Law (GDL)

This intensive conversion course is designed for non-law graduates of any discipline, or overseas law graduates who wish to qualify as either barristers or solicitors. The course begins with a two-week introduction to the English legal system and the legal profession. You will then study the seven foundation subjects.

We have been successfully running this conversion course since 1977 and our students have taken a variety of first degrees at a wide range of universities. Our teaching team contains a rich mix of those who are professionally qualified and others who are active researchers.

Contact
Admissions
Phone: 020 7915 5511
Email: course-enquiries@westminster.ac.uk

UNIVERSITY OF WESTMINSTER⌗

www.westminster.ac.uk

A day in the life of...

... Katie Sills

Katie graduated from the GDL in 2011 and the LPC in 2012

The main reason for choosing to study here was a combination of the location and price, and the university and the course absolutely lived up to my expectations.

I had heard about how tough the LPC was (and it is), but the lecturers were brilliant at structuring the course in a way that was easy to process and they offered assistance whenever it was needed. Unlike a number of other providers, Westminster also delivers the majority of lectures live, which I found particularly helpful as it gave me the opportunity to interact and ask questions.

It was very easy to settle in and make new friends. Westminster is a very welcoming university and everyone (lecturers and students) seems to bond very quickly, despite the array of cultural backgrounds. In my case, I also think it helped that there was an organised mixer at the local pub at the beginning of the course, as we all got to know one another in a much more relaxed setting.

And without a doubt, it was the people that made the course for me. The lecturers are first rate and everyone on the course was very supportive. I also enjoyed the student law (pro bono) clinic as it gave me the opportunity to work on a real-life case under excellent supervision. This definitely broadened my understanding of law in practice and prepared me for work experience placements.

The relationship with lecturers and tutors was fantastic. All of the lecturers are extremely approachable and are always available to help you out. You can tell that they are genuinely interested in your wellbeing, as they go out of their way to highlight job opportunities, offer advice and read over your training contract applications.

They are all very knowledgeable about their chosen areas and are passionate about teaching. Consequently, I found that even the driest subjects became interesting and they helped me to excel in everything.

Being a student in London, there is a never-ending selection of restaurants, bars and events to choose from. With regard to studying law, there's so much history and relevance in the city. The courts are easily accessible and it is much easier to find work experience to help boost your CV.

The social life at university is what you make of it. While Westminster does have a students' union and a vast array of activities to join, I tended to socialise with those on my course. The GDL and LPC are both very intense and I found that I quickly built up strong social relationships with my peers, many of whom will remain friends for life.

The standard set by Westminster is very high and, consequently, it has prepared me well.

Westminster provides an extremely supportive network, which pushed me to explore different channels.

> 'Westminster provides an extremely supportive network, which pushed me to explore different channels.'

To anyone thinking of applying for a law course at the University of Westminster, I would give one piece of advice – do it! I could not recommend the university enough. Westminster is a very forward-thinking university which, on top of the outstanding teaching, offers numerous law fairs, career events and student advisors to help with networking and applications. You are genuinely treated as an individual and given the time and attention that you need to help you to succeed, both while at university and in the future.

Career clinic

Training contract application deadlines

ʌNORTON ROSE FULBRIGHT

Our thanks to **Norton Rose Fulbright** for sponsoring this page

DECEMBER 2016
(31) Ashurst LLP *(first deadline)*
Morrison & Foerster (UK) LLP

JANUARY 2017
Mishcon de Reya

(3) Nabarro LLP

(13) Jones Day

(15) Osborne Clarke
Simmons & Simmons

(27) PwC

(29) Norton Rose Fulbright *(finalists and graduates)*

(31) Bristows LLP *(February/March interviews)*
Cooley (UK) LLP
Hogan Lovells International LLP *(non-law)*
Roythornes Solicitors
Taylor Vinters

FEBRUARY 2017
(28) Bond Dickinson LLP

MARCH 2017
(31) Dentons *(non-law)*

APRIL 2017
(1) Browne Jacobson LLP

(30) Taylor Wessing LLP

SUMMER 2017
Charles Russell Speechlys

JUNE 2017
Bates Wells Braithwaite

(1) Foot Anstey LLP

(2) Thrings LLP

(30) Brabners LLP
Hogan Lovells International LLP *(law)*
Irwin Mitchell LLP
O'Melveny
Pemberton Greenish
Reed Smith LLP
Shoosmiths LLP

JULY 2017
DLA Piper UK LLP

(7) DWF LLP

Norton Rose Fulbright

Norton Rose Fulbright is a global law firm. We provide the world's preeminent corporations and financial institutions with a full business law service. We have 3,800 lawyers and legal staff based in more than 50 cities across Europe, the United States, Canada, Latin America, Asia, Australia, Africa, the Middle East and Central Asia.

Recognised for our industry focus, we are strong across all the key industry sectors: financial institutions; energy; infrastructure, mining and commodities; transport; technology and innovation as well as life sciences and healthcare.

A view from our offices

(14) Kirkland & Ellis International LLP

(15) Akin Gump Strauss Hauer & Feld

(16) Norton Rose Fulbright *(penultimate-year undergraduates (law), finalists, graduates (law and non-law))*

(17) Covington & Burling LLP

(23) Leathes Prior

(28) Watson Farley & Williams LLP

(30) Berwin Leighton Paisner LLP

(31) Addleshaw Goddard LLP
Anthony Collins Solicitors
Ashfords LLP
Ashurst LLP *(second deadline)*
Birketts LLP
Blaser Mills
Bristows LLP *(August interviews)*
Burges Salmon

Cleary Gottlieb Steen & Hamilton
Debevoise & Plimpton LLP
Dentons *(law)*
Farrer & Co
Fieldfisher
Gibson, Dunn & Crutcher LLP
Hill Dickinson LLP
Holman Fenwick Willan
Ince & Co LLP
K&L Gates LLP
Kennedys Law LLP
King & Wood Mallesons
Macfarlanes LLP
Mayer Brown International LLP
Memery Crystal
Michelmores LLP
Mills & Reeve LLP
Morgan, Lewis & Bockius
Olswang
Penningtons Manches LLP
RPC
Russell-Cooke LLP
Shearman & Sterling LLP

Skadden, Arps, Slate, Meagher and Flom (UK) LLP
Stephenson Harwood
Travers Smith LLP
Wedlake Bell LLP
Weil, Gotshal & Manges
White & Case LLP

AUGUST 2017
(19) Maples Teesdale LLP *(for 2018 contracts)*

See website/contact firm
Allen & Overy
Baker & McKenzie LLP
Burness Paull LLP
CMS Cameron McKenna LLP
Clyde & Co LLP
Dechert LLP
Latham & Watkins
Slaughter and May
Stephens & Scown LLP

Norton Rose Fulbright

Wherever we are, we operate in accordance with our global business principles of quality, unity and integrity. We aim to provide the highest possible standard of legal service in each of our offices and to maintain that level of quality at every point of contact.

For further information about the firm, please see p304.

Website: www.nortonrosefulbright.com

Our canteen

Vacation scheme application deadlines

TaylorWessing

Our thanks to **Taylor Wessing** for sponsoring this page

For further information about the firm, please see p380

From 1 October 2016
Simmons & Simmons *(Winter; first come, first served)*

From 15 October 2016
Simmons & Simmons *(Summer; first come, first served)*

28 October 2016
Jones Day *(Winter)*

30 October 2016
Norton Rose Fulbright *(Winter: finalists and graduates)*

31 October 2016
Berwin Leighton Paisner LLP *(Winter)*

2 November 2016
White & Case LLP *(Winter)*

4 November 2016
Burges Salmon *(Winter)*
Shearman & Sterling LLP *(Winter)*

6 November 2016
Ashurst LLP *(Winter)*

12 November 2016
Stephenson Harwood *(Winter)*

16 December 2016
Jones Day *(Spring)*

30 December 2016
Addleshaw Goddard LLP *(Spring, Summer)*

31 December 2016
Dentons *(Spring, Summer)*
Morrison & Foerster (UK) LLP
Dechert LLP *(Spring)*

January 2017
Bates Wells Braithwaite *(Spring, Summer)*
Mishcon de Reya

From 1 January 2017
Simmons & Simmons *(Spring; first come, first served)*

3 January 2017
Nabarro LLP

8 January 2017
Ashurst LLP *(Spring, Summer)*
Norton Rose Fulbright *(Summer: penultimate-year undergraduates and finalists)*

12 January 2017
Burges Salmon *(Spring, Summer)*
Skadden, Arps, Slate, Meagher and Flom (UK) LLP *(Spring, Summer)*

13 January 2017
Jones Day
Kirkland & Ellis International LLP
Weil, Gotshal & Manges *(Spring, Summer)*

15 January 2017
Debevoise & Plimpton LLP
Fieldfisher *(Spring, Summer)*
Irwin Mitchell LLP
Olswang
Osborne Clarke

20 January 2017
Shearman & Sterling LLP *(Spring, Summer)*

27 January 2017
DWF LLP
PwC
Watson Farley & Williams LLP *(Spring, Summer)*

30 January 2017
Taylor Wessing LLP

31 January 2017
Akin Gump Strauss Hauer & Feld
Berwin Leighton Paisner LLP *(Spring, Summer)*
Birketts LLP
Charles Russell Speechlys
Cooley (UK) LLP
Covington & Burling LLP
Dechert LLP *(Summer)*
Hill Dickinson LLP
Ince & Co LLP *(Spring)*
K&L Gates LLP
Kennedys Law LLP
King & Wood Mallesons *(Spring, Summer)*
Leathes Prior *(Spring, Summer)*

Macfarlanes LLP *(Spring, Summer)*
Mills & Reeve LLP
Morgan, Lewis & Bockius
O'Melveny
Penningtons Manches LLP
RPC
Reed Smith LLP
Stephenson Harwood *(Spring, Summer)*
Travers Smith LLP *(Summer)*
Wedlake Bell LLP
White & Case LLP *(Spring, Summer)*

February 2017
Gibson, Dunn & Crutcher LLP
Shoosmiths LLP

1 February 2017
Browne Jacobson LLP

14 February 2017
Holman Fenwick Willan *(Spring)*

28 February 2017
Ashfords LLP
Bond Dickinson LLP
Michelmores LLP
Roythornes Solicitors

11 March 2017
Anthony Collins Solicitors

April 2017
Stephens & Scown LLP

1 April 2017
Foot Anstey LLP

30 April 2017
Blaser Mills

31 July 2017
Holman Fenwick Willan

Rolling application
Travers Smith LLP *(Winter)*

See website/contact firm
Allen & Overy
Baker & McKenzie LLP
Bristows LLP
Burness Paull LLP
CMS Cameron McKenna LLP
Cleary Gottlieb Steen & Hamilton
Clyde & Co LLP
DLA Piper UK LLP
Farrer & Co *(Spring, Summer)*
Hogan Lovells International LLP
Latham & Watkins
Mishcon de Reya *(Winter)*
Slaughter and May

Your training timetable

Law students (second year undergraduate) and non-law students (final year)

NB This timetable refers mainly to law firms which recruit two years in advance. Check with individual firms for specific application dates and deadlines.

 Research law firms, attend law fairs, read glossy brochures, apply for winter vacation schemes; non-law students apply for Graduate Diploma in Law (GDL)

 Attend vacation scheme; alternatively, relax and enjoy your Christmas holidays

 Apply for Easter vacation schemes

 Apply for summer vacation schemes

 Attend vacation scheme; alternatively, relax and enjoy your Easter holidays

 Apply for training contracts and attend interviews

 Continue to apply for training contracts and attend interviews. Attend vacation scheme or take an enjoyable trip abroad to talk about at interview – it's more interesting than doing three vacation schemes back-to-back

 Start final year of degree (law students)/start GDL (non-law students)

 Apply for Legal Practice Course (LPC)

 Start LPC

 Start training contract – good luck!

 Qualify!

Vacation schemes

What they are and why they are worth pursuing...

As pre-training contract legal experience goes, vacation schemes are the big one. Now well-established and ubiquitous in the industry, vacation schemes are a great way to experience first-hand life at a law firm, and to see if the employer, and career, matches your interests. It's also an opportunity to impress and enhance your prospects, with several vac schemes also offering training contract interviews at the end of the placement. All that said, it still requires giving up two weeks' precious holidays, during which you will have other commitments including, perhaps ironically, working hard towards securing the impressive academic grades so valued by law firms! So in signing up for a vacation scheme, what exactly are you getting in return?

The legal job market is highly competitive and these days it is not enough to simply have a solid academic background. Recruiters are looking for much more than a 2(1) and AAB at A-level, and with so many applicants to choose from, students face an incredible amount of pressure to impress in the search for training contracts. This has resulted in an increase in the number of students taking part in vacation schemes, meaning it can be as difficult to get a vacation placement as it is to bag a training contract!

Nowadays it is seen as the norm for law students to give up at least two weeks of their holidays to gain work experience, with some students taking part in as many as four vacation schemes over the summer. Is this really necessary? The answer has to be yes – in moderation. It is beneficial to you in helping you choose the type of firm which suits you, and it will look good on your application form – showing employers that you are serious about a career in the law and willing to put yourself out during the precious holidays. Firms also take vac schemes very seriously too, and guaranteed training contract interviews at the end of these schemes are now increasingly common. Some firms are also moving towards recruiting their trainees solely through their vac scheme pools. "Don't underestimate the value that firms place on these schemes", says one recruitment head, "and make sure that you do your research, you're clear about

why you want the vacation scheme, you've demonstrated the skills that they're looking for and your application is free from typos. But also remember that this is a great opportunity for you to find out more about your shortlisted firms, their cultures and values, and importantly whether they are the right fit for you."

The benefits of work experience for any job are obvious, but it is particularly important for a legal career where there are so many different types of law firm and practice areas to choose from, and where so much time and money goes into training. Maybe

> **The legal job market is highly competitive and these days it is not enough to simply have a solid academic background**

you've always dreamed of being a real estate lawyer, but do you know what a real estate lawyer actually does? Maybe the thought of criminal law entices you, but you may be a fortnight's work experience away from falling in love with M&A. Many vacation schemes allow you to spend time in the departments in which you have an interest, so you can find out if you're going to hate it after the first week, before it's too late.

So what do the vac schemers themselves say? Firstly, take a look at the 'why did you choose this firm over any others?' question in our trainee survey, and see for yourself how many trainees cite their vacation scheme as an important reason for making their training contract choice. One person who completed a vac scheme and will soon train at the same firm says that "many firms treat vacation schemes as extended interviews to determine if candidates can complement their businesses. Although this may sound intimidating, to the contrary, a scheme is the perfect opportunity to showcase your abilities, personality and enthusiasm. Remember too, firms do actually wish to attract the best candidates! It's likely by being selected for a vacation scheme you're already in contention, so have confidence and enjoy yourself!" Wise words worth remembering on your first day.

And what if you haven't managed to get yourself on any vacation scheme? Don't give up – you could always try offering your services to firms for free (even for a couple of days at a time) – or approach your local law centre where you'll witness real legal problems and advice administered first-hand. These approaches show potential employers that you have imagination and are serious about a career in the law. If all else fails, head off for some voluntary work (at home or abroad) and gain some real-life experience, while learning more about yourself at the same time. It will also give you something different to talk about at your interview.

> ' **Many vacation schemes allow you to spend time in the departments in which you have an interest, so you can find out if you're going to hate it after the first week, before it's too late** '

The application process

Write the best covering letters, CVs and application forms – and put yourself at the front of the queue...

It's an arduous process applying for training contracts – but with sensible preparation, a dose of common sense and a touch of luck (not to mention decent academic results!) it needn't seem such an uphill struggle. There are plenty of little things you can do to make life easier for yourself.

First impressions count

Hard to believe, but many applicants still fall at the first and most obvious hurdle: spelling and grammar on application forms. You may be heading for a First from a top university and be captain of the rugby team, but if you can't spell the word 'liaise' on your application form, you'll be drop-kicked straight into the rubbish bin.

Recruiters tell us time and time again that applications, whether paper or online, are simply not up to scratch, even from seemingly top candidates. 'The reason for most of our rejections is poor spelling and grammar', bemoans a graduate recruiter at a major US firm in London. 'As a lawyer, you will want your advice to be trusted by the client; if the first thing they see is a typo, even if the advice is spot on, it will introduce a level of doubt. Attention to detail is a must.'

If possible, download the form or print it off and work on a draft copy. Make sure you spell-check it (by eye as well as using a spell-checker) and then paste it back into the online application. If the form states how many lines / words you can use per question, stay within those limits. If the firm prints off the forms, anything written beyond the limit may not be read.

Easy as ABC

Probably the single biggest bugbear among recruiters is stating the wrong firm on the application, i.e. 'I'd like to work at Allen & Overy because...' on a form for Irwin Mitchell. Silly, we know, but frighteningly common, especially when making multiple applications. And the use of mailmerge covering letters and cut-and-paste online applications has inflamed the problem. Remember that every firm you are applying to wants to see evidence that you have selected that firm as the place where you wish to pursue your career, so make your application specific. A graduate recruitment insider at a US firm in London says: 'If we cannot see why you have applied to us over all of the other London offices of US-based firms, we cannot take your application further.'

It sounds obvious, but one of the most common pieces of advice from recruiters is: read, re-read and re-read your application(s) again. Better still, get someone else to read them – it's easy to read what you expect to see rather than what is really there. 'Spelling and grammar errors are non-negotiable for a law firm and provide recruiters with an easy reason to reject a candidate, regardless of their other attributes,' cautions Caroline Lindner, trainee recruitment manager at Norton Rose Fulbright. Words are a lawyer's stock-in-trade, and if your written English isn't up to scratch, you are unlikely to be invited for an interview; the firm may well take the view that if you can't use words accurately, you simply won't function in this profession.

It cannot be stressed enough that poor presentation (whether written or verbal) is simply not going to be tolerated by firms. After all, when you do finally make it, clients will take your knowledge of the law as read: you will be judged equally on your presentation skills and ability to communicate.

Problem areas

We know it's no walk in the park. It's not easy selling yourself on two sides of A4 or an online form with endless, predictable questions. The sections which most trouble students are those which demand a demonstration of competency, e.g. 'Outline a situation where you have overcome a barrier and achieved a required outcome'. 'Students tend to be too descriptive and not analytical enough', says one university careers adviser. Of course, such self-analysis does not always come easy. Testing life experiences, let alone corporate

Helpful hints (from the graduate recruiters themselves)

- Use the correct name and spelling of the firm and individual to whom you are applying;
- Check all spelling and grammar;
- Do use spell check, but guard against Americanisms or words used out of context;
- Follow instructions to the letter;
- Give the form the time it deserves, don't rush it;
- Use simple and straightforward language – big words sound pompous and silly;
- Take questions at face value and answer exactly what is being asked, not what you think is being asked – it's unlikely to be a trick;
- Contact the firm if a question is obscure and seek clarification;
- Guard against sloppy and casual language, particularly when applying online;
- Draw evidence of your skills from all your experience, not just the past year (but drop the Brownie badges);
- Try to be analytical as well as descriptive in your answers;
- Don't undersell yourself – giving examples of how you have met deadlines, prioritised matters or how you get along with people is not showing off – it's important for firms to know these things about you;
- Don't get too philosophical – keep your answers relevant to the business of being a lawyer;
- Find out deadlines well in advance – don't waste your time, or the firm's time, by applying late;
- Always read through the completed form carefully before sending. Better still, get someone else to read it for you
- Don't submit the form until you're entirely happy with it. Most systems will not allow you to recall the form if you have made a mistake.

lingo, are not necessarily going to be at your fingertips. Furthermore, you need to walk the line between self-analysis and being overly introspective, so try not to be too philosophical. Also bear in mind that referring to something you did when you were two years old will probably be taken as irrelevant!

Most careers services offer help with preparing CVs and completing application forms, as well as providing general interview preparation. They typically offer guidance on how to answer a range of fairly standard questions such as 'What are your strengths? What are your weaknesses? What has been your greatest achievement?', as well as hypothetical questions and competency-based questions, such as 'describe a situation where you worked in a team' and 'describe a situation in which you solved a problem'.

'From memory of being a graduate myself years ago,' recalls one old-hand in the recruitment sector, 'I used to be stumped by some of these questions. But don't think if you haven't done glamorous teamwork like climbing to the top of Mount Kilimanjaro, it doesn't

count. It's worth looking through all your experiences and extra-curricular activities to analyse what you have gained from them – really think about where you are getting your evidence from. Also, it's easy to be short-sighted so don't just focus on the past six or 12 months. Try to analyse experiences that really mean something to you – it's easier to sound convincing if you are passionate about your subject – and never make things up – it will be painfully obvious and embarrassing when you're found out!'

Other problem areas are the obscure or quirky questions, such as 'which character in fiction do you resemble and why?' Students commonly assume that these are 'trick' questions, designed to catch them out and unveil say, a passion for trashy novels. But firms deny the use or the value of trickery – they maintain that more out-of-the-ordinary questions are just another way of seeking evidence of relevant skills, such as leadership. The bottom line is, if you're not sure what a question is asking of you, feel free to ring the firm concerned and ask. All the recruiters we spoke to would rather you call than answer incorrectly.

And it is crucial to ensure that you answer the question being asked. It sounds obvious, but take a question at face value and answer it as thoroughly as you would an exam question. Oh, and if you're asked to complete a form in black ink, use black and not the sparkly glitter pen you thought looked more appealing!

Technical glitch

By far the preferred method of recruitment today is via online applications. But that comes with its own problems. Some systems are badly designed, and it is extremely frustrating when candidates are automatically thrown out if they do not have a 2(1) or are non-EU citizens, for example. There is no opportunity for explanations and it gives a highly negative impression of the firm.

The other common mistake is the use by applicants of sloppy or casual language, ie email or text talk. Under no circumstances should you write, 'I'd like to wk @ Simmons coz....' The firm will expect the same standard of presentation on the form as they would for a hard copy, so do not be tempted to use a chatty, email style or abbreviated words. Our advice is to adapt each application carefully to the firm you are currently applying to and read through each online application as you would a paper one. And a bit of a plea on behalf of a graduate recruiter who has to read nearly 3,000 forms a year – 'Do keep things concise, and make the answers easy to read and interesting!'

Timing is everything

There is a consensus among careers advisers that firms do not fully appreciate the time constraints students are under, and how difficult it is to fit application form filling into a busy schedule. It's understandable that more than a bit of cut-and-pasting goes on. 'Interviews used to be a friendly chat for an hour or so on campus, end of story. Now firms want students to give up a day or more, at their offices, in term time. But they also want people with a 2(1)!' comments David Ainscough deputy director of the University of Cambridge Careers Service. 'We try to persuade firms to interview at the university or during vacations. Students who may be pressured to sacrifice academic work should consult their tutor, who will be writing their references, can often exert influence on firms, and will want to help their pupils to manage their time sensibly.'

Sounds like a little mutual understanding between firms and students is needed. Recruiters: students are under huge pressures these days; cranking up the timetable does nobody any favours. Applicants: less is more; apply to fewer firms but make each application count. Try to find out as much as possible about the firms in advance so you can really target your applications to the firms that appear to suit you.

Assessment days

A day of high-pressure evaluation at a law firm also gives you a platform to show off your skills.

These days, over 80% of the UK's top 100 commercial firms use assessments of one form or another. So what will you actually have to do during an assessment day? Well, it really varies from firm to firm, but our findings indicate that written case studies, group exercises, and verbal reasoning tests are all popular choices. Popular for the firms, that is...

Mental agility

A written case study will typically feature something linked to the firm's business. For example, you might be given a true case scenario or real client problem and be asked how you would advise the client. But non-law students shouldn't worry themselves too much about the legal aspects of the task. As a university careers adviser says – even if the problem does have a legal framework, it is unlikely that the firm is looking for deep legal knowledge. 'They look for people who approach things in the right way,' she explains. 'A lot of students get very concerned because they think they have to know the law off by heart.' However, even if the task doesn't have a legal basis, it will usually have a commercial slant and firms certainly look for commercial awareness. Our advice, therefore, is read, read, read! By regularly reading the FT, the business pages and the legal press you will start to build up a clearer picture of the commercial world. Approach the case study logically, and make sure you follow the instructions properly – you need to demonstrate clearly the reasons for having reached your conclusion.

Physical challenge

But what about the dreaded group exercise? Firms like to focus on testing different attributes, but these challenges can actually be fun. That said, it's important to remember that you are being assessed during this kind of exercise. Above all, firms want you to show an ability to think on your feet. You need to display both confidence and negotiating prowess. However, a careers adviser at a university's careers service cautions students to not talk themselves out of a job: 'A student may feel they have to talk all the time, but this is not the case. Firms look for people who can work well in a

team and thus help the whole group to achieve their task. This involves a blend of skills such as leadership, the ability to draw other people into the discussion, effective questioning and time management'.

Another important quality is enthusiasm; get involved and embrace what is asked of you. You will probably be involved in a group negotiation exercise of some kind. If such a thought makes you want

> **❛ Firms like to focus on testing different attributes, but these challenges can actually be fun ❜**

to hide in a cupboard and weep quietly, then maybe the law isn't for you. Or perhaps you should think about joining the university's debating society, where you'll get plenty of practice before you are asked to perform before a potential employer. University careers services and websites can offer guidance on likely scenarios, providing simple examples of the type of case study that might be given to you, either individually or to solve as a group. Enquire as to what help is available, and prepare.

Testing times

Verbal reasoning tests are widely used. They assess not only that you can write grammatically correct sentences, but also that you can understand the meaning of a written passage. 'We get so many people with well-written applications and a good 2(1) that we need to find a way to make a distinction between them', says one graduate recruiter. As the written word is an essential tool for any solicitor, what better way to assess future trainees than by using verbal reasoning 'to find out whether candidates can correctly make deductions, assumptions and recognise inferences

Fail to prepare, prepare to fail

Recruiters' tips for preparation:

- Do your homework! The better prepared you are, the more confident you will feel. Find out as much as you can about the firm, its ethos, clients, and recent cases.
- Re-read your application. Be prepared to show that you have thought about why you applied to the firm and that you can describe why it appeals to you.
- Expand your commercial knowledge by reading the business and legal press. If you're asked about business deals, it's no good saying that you've been out of the country. Read up on these things – the FT does a summary of deals at the weekend. It's also good to have consistency of knowledge, not just what's been going on in the last couple of days. And remember, firms don't want to just test your memory – they want to see commercial application as well as awareness.
- Visit your careers centre – it will have lots of information about assessment days and usually some sample tests.
- Don't be afraid to speak out in university seminars and tutorials. Start practising now and it will come more naturally in an assessment group exercise.
- Contact the firm's graduate recruitment team if you have any queries about times, location or dress code.
- Plan your travel time and route to the assessment.

The day itself:

- Dress for success: always dress modestly and smartly (a suit is best). Remember it's a professional, business-like image you want to portray.
- Always arrive on time, or preferably a bit early, to give yourself time to calm down/go to the loo etc.
- Even if you get a bad feeling from one of the exercises, keep going and don't give up – give it 100% throughout.
- Don't be afraid to be nervous – if you're shaking you won't necessarily be judged on it!
- Body language and speech are important: don't slouch or mumble and avoid verbal tics such as 'like', 'you know' and 'sort of'. Try and maintain eye contact when appropriate. A firm handshake is best, but try not to break any bones.
- Try to think on your feet and give honest, heartfelt opinions – if your heart's not in it, you won't shine.
- Don't be blasé – enthusiasm and a smile are key attributes and will get you a long way.

– all important in the work of a lawyer,' says Clare Harris, associate director of legal resourcing at Hogan Lovells. There are an enormous number of different types of tests, some much more complicated than others. So does practice make perfect? 'If a student knows they will be tested as part of the selection procedure, I would suggest that they have a go at some practice tests', says one university careers adviser. 'Not only will this give them an idea of what to expect but it will also allow them to practise completing the test under time pressure'.

Of course this will be a pressurised day and you are bound to be nervous, but within that try to relax and also be confident in your abilities!

A-Z guide to commercial enlightenment

If you're planning on becoming a lawyer it's best that you get to grips with the relevant jargon. It will soon become second nature and none of it is particularly difficult, but it's still worth swotting up ahead of an interview to avoid being stumped by any unforeseen acronyms.

ABS (Alternative Business Structure) – The model by which non-law companies are able to invest in law firms and provide legal services, following the implementation of the Legal Services Act 2007.

ANTITRUST – Laws to discourage anti-competitive behaviour among companies, such as monopolies, cartels and restrictive practices. The term originates from the US, where cartels formed 'trusts' in order to bully smaller companies.

ARBITRATION V MEDIATION V LITIGATION – All are methods of resolving disputes, therefore known collectively as Dispute Resolution. Only litigation involves going to court. Arbitration is an attempt to reach agreement (arbitration agreement) using an umpire and is legally binding. Mediation is a less formal, voluntary process and there is no legally binding outcome.

ASSOCIATE V ASSISTANT – Both are qualified solicitors who have not yet been elevated to the firm's partnership. Associate is an Americanism and is sometimes used as a middle-ground promotion between assistant and partner.

BENCH – The judges or magistrates in a court.

BEST FRIENDS – Law firms with no formal links or financial ties but who give each other first preference when referring work. Usually an international arrangement between firms in different jurisdictions.

BILLABLE HOURS – Also known as chargeable time, it is the legal work undertaken that can justifiably be charged to the client, eg would not include redrafting a document chewed in the photocopier.

BRIEF – The document of instructions from a solicitor to a barrister. Includes facts of the case and outlines what the solicitor would like the barrister do to.

BOND – Similar to a loan, the bond is an IOU issued by a company or government in return for money provided by investors (bondholders). One of many methods of raising capital, it is a form of debt.

CSR (CORPORATE SOCIAL RESPONSIBILITY) – How firms manage their business processes to produce an overall positive impact on society, including areas such as environmental impact management, corporate governance, diversity and the way in which the firm responds to the needs of the wider community.

CALLED TO THE BAR – The ceremony whereby members of the Inns of Court become qualified barristers.

CHAMBERS – The rooms (offices) occupied by a group of barristers who share overheads.

COUNSEL – Another term for barrister.

DATA ROOM – A room set up during a corporate transaction where the purchaser's advisers can conduct due diligence on the target company's accounts and activities.

DEBT – Money borrowed by companies, such as loans or bonds.

DERIVATIVES – A spin-off of financial products such as shares or bonds. Derivatives include futures and options.

DUE DILIGENCE – The detailed study of information about a company, such as its accounts and activities, prior to an acquisition or take-over.

EQUITY – Shares in a company.

EQUITY PARTNER V NON-EQUITY PARTNER – Equity partners collectively own the firm because they have bought a share of the business and therefore receive a cut of the profits. Non-equity partners have been professionally promoted but have not yet bought a share in the business and receive only a salary.

FEE-EARNER – Anyone who conducts legal work that can be charged to a client. Includes trainees, paralegals and legal executives, but not secretaries.

FIRM – A business model comprising a partnership of individuals (partners). Contrasts with a company comprising directors, executives and a chairman. Most law businesses are firms rather than companies. Increasingly, many are becoming LLPs (see below).

FLOTATION – The admission of a new company to a stock exchange, so that its shares can be traded publicly. See IPO.

GDL (GRADUATE DIPLOMA IN LAW) – also known as the Common Professional Examination (CPE). A one-year conversion course to law for non-law graduates.

HOSTILE BID – An attempt to acquire a company without the approval of the target's shareholders/owners.

IPO (INITIAL PUBLIC OFFERING) – The offer of a company's shares on a stock market. Also known as a flotation, it occurs when the privately owned shares in a company become publicly traded for the first time.

IN-HOUSE LAWYER – A solicitor (or sometimes, a barrister) working for a company or public body instead of a law firm or set of chambers.

INNS OF COURT – Four administrative bodies within the Bar – Inner Temple, Middle Temple, Gray's Inn and Lincoln's Inn. Each barrister and student barrister must belong to one.

IP (INTELLECTUAL PROPERTY) – An umbrella term covering copyright, patent and trade mark law. An area of the law which serves to protect a company or individual's products or work from unauthorised use.

JUNIOR – How you will feel for much of your training contract! Also, the secondary barrister at trial, i.e. Senior/Lead counsel and Junior counsel (see L below).

LLP (LIMITED LIABILITY PARTNERSHIP) – . A halfway house between a partnership and a limited company. Limits the partners' personal liability in the event of debt.

LEAD COUNSEL V JUNIOR COUNSEL – Lead counsel is the barrister who leads the advocacy in court, i.e. makes the opening speech, often a QC (see below). The junior assists with the case and advocacy and, despite the name, is also very experienced.

LEGAL SERVICES ACT 2007 – An Act of Parliament that liberalises the market for legal services in England and Wales. Implemented in 2011, the act allows non-lawyers to own and operate law firms for the first time (see 'Alternative Business

Structures'), and enables companies such as banks and even supermarkets to provide legal advice in some areas, such as wills and conveyancing.

LOCKSTEP – The different pay levels awarded to partners, dependent on years of service rather than legal ability. Contrasts with the US system of 'eat what you kill', where pay is equated to number of hours billed.

M&A (MERGERS AND ACQUISITIONS) – The area of legal practice specialising in advising companies on merging with, or buying, other companies. Comprises the bulk of corporate work.

MAGIC CIRCLE – Colloquial term referring to five UK law firms that have historically led the market in terms of corporate work, size and profits – Allen & Overy LLP; Clifford Chance LLP; Freshfields Bruckhaus Deringer; Linklaters; Slaughter and May.

MANAGING PARTNER V SENIOR PARTNER – The MP is the main boss of a law firm and runs the business internally; in large firms, the MP is too busy to do fee-earning work. The SP is a firm ambassador, focusing on client relationships externally and combines the role with fee-earning.

NQ (NEWLY-QUALIFIED) – Refers to a lawyer in their first year of qualified legal practice, ie a lawyer who has successfully completed their training contract and has been admitted by the Law Society as a qualified solicitor.

OF-COUNSEL – American term for certain senior lawyers who are not partners.

PEP (PROFITS PER EQUITY PARTNER) – A partner's annual share of their firm's profits.

PPP/PFI (PUBLIC PRIVATE PARTNERSHIP/ PRIVATE FINANCE INITIATIVE) – Forms of funding, typically for major public infrastructure such as roads, hospitals and prisons. Funding and operation is a collaboration between the government and private sector companies.

PQE (POST-QUALIFICATION EXPERIENCE) – The number of years in legal practice since qualifying as a lawyer.

PARALEGAL – A legal assistant who is not a qualified solicitor or barrister. Typically has some legal training or experience.

PRIVATE EQUITY – An area of legal practice advising on the funding (through shares or loans) provided by specialist organisations to unquoted companies.

PRIVATE PRACTICE – Working in a law firm or as a sole practitioner, rather than in-house at a company or in the public sector.

PRO BONO – Latin term meaning 'for the good'. Legal advice and assistance provided voluntarily and without charge.

PUPIL – Trainee barrister working at a set of chambers.

PUPILMASTER – Fully-qualified barrister who supervises the pupil.

QC (QUEEN'S COUNSEL) – A senior barrister who has been selected by the Lord Chancellor to qualify for this most senior rank. Also known as a 'Silk' due to robe worn in court.

RAINMAKER – A hot-shot lawyer who brings lots of deals and money into the firm, and generally 'makes things happen'.

RIGHTS OF AUDIENCE – Suitably qualified to undertake advocacy in court.

SECURITIES – Forms of investment in a company, can either be shares (equity) or bonds (debt).

SECURITISATION – A method of raising finance by obtaining loans that are 'secured' against a particular asset of the company (asset-backed loan). The loans go into a Special Purpose Vehicle and therefore do not appear on the company's balance sheet.

SET – A group of barristers trading under a common name. Another word for Chambers.

SOLICITOR ADVOCATE – A solicitor with special qualifications to allow him/her rights of audience in court. Avoids the requirement to hire a barrister.

TMT (TELECOMS, MEDIA AND TECHNOLOGY) – An area of legal practice or law firm department, specialising in advising companies and individuals working in these sectors.

TENANT – A qualified barrister with permanent rooms in a set of chambers.

TRADE MARK ATTORNEY – Professionals (Registered Trade Mark Agents – not solicitors or barristers) who specialise in advising clients on trade mark rights. May work in-house in companies or in private practice.

VANILLA – Or plain vanilla. Finance terminology meaning no unusual features. E.g. plain vanilla options or swaps.

VENTURE CAPITAL – Money provided by specialist organisations to invest in companies not listed on the stock exchange. Sometimes referred to as private equity and can be used to fund MBO/MBIs, for example.

WET AND DRY SHIPPING – Both are specialist areas of legal practice. Wet shipping (also known as admiralty) involves advice on collisions, damage and salvage. Dry shipping is advice on carriage of goods contracts (charterparties) and cargo claims.

WHITE-COLLAR CRIME – Crime involving business and finance irregularities, such as fraud and tax evasion.

Asset management

Who are asset managers and what legal services do they require?
Asset managers are firms of skilled financial professionals who invest capital on behalf of a wide variety of market participants, including pension funds, endowments, family offices and certain private individuals. They use sophisticated investment techniques and invest in a wide variety of asset classes. The asset management sector performs a crucial economic function by pooling capital so that it can be allocated efficiently, while also offering investors access to financial expertise and investment opportunities that might not otherwise be available to them.

Simmons & Simmons LLP offers a full suite of legal services to its asset management clients, including providing advice on fund formation, the creation of new share classes, corporate transactions and finance transactions, as well as specialist tax, litigation and employment advice. Simmons & Simmons also offers asset managers multi-jurisdictional contentious and non-contentious regulatory advice, which helps them to navigate the increasingly complex regulatory environment that has developed following the global financial crisis.

Hedge fund managers

Hedge fund managers have traditionally sought to generate absolute returns, which simply means that they aim to be profitable in both rising and falling markets. Hedge fund managers use advanced risk management and investment techniques to generate these returns, although different funds adopt different trading strategies.

The fees hedge fund managers charge are often referred to as 'two and 20', or an annual management fee of 2% of assets under management (AUM) and a performance fee of 20% of any profits that are generated.

For regulatory and tax reasons, hedge funds are typically structured as 'master-feeders'. This simply means that US investors will invest in a limited partnership 'feeder fund' and non-US investors will invest in an offshore corporate 'feeder fund'. Both of these funds will then invest in a so-called 'master fund', which is itself usually an offshore company. It is the assets of the so-called 'master fund' that are then invested in stocks, bonds, derivatives or other assets.

Private equity fund managers

Broadly, the term 'private equity' refers to medium to long-term investments that are made in unlisted companies (or in publicly listed companies which are subsequently taken private). However, there are many different types of private equity investment manager, from venture capitalists who invest in early-stage companies with high-growth potential, to large private equity houses that provide equity financing for management buyouts (MBO), management buyins (MBI), 'public-to-privates' and other transactions.

Private equity funds are typically structured as limited partnerships. In the UK, a limited partnership structure is used instead of a traditional partnership because it allows the liability of the investors in the fund (ie the limited partners) to be limited to the amount they have committed to invest in the fund. In contrast, the liability of the general partner to the fund will be unlimited.

What are the key skills required?

Lawyers who know their clients' businesses and understand their commercial motivations are more likely to be able to develop long-term, collaborative relationships with them, and this is certainly true of the firm's asset management clients.

What does the day-to-day work involve?

The type of work that a lawyer in the asset management sector will be involved with varies significantly by practice area:

Financial services – funds

Specialist fund lawyers may help skilled traders or investment bankers launch a new hedge fund or private equity fund of their own, or they may assist an existing asset manager to launch a new fund or to create a new share class for an existing fund.

Financial services – non-contentious regulatory

Non-contentious regulatory lawyers help asset managers to comply with the increasingly onerous regulatory obligations that have been introduced following the global financial crisis. This may include advising on new pieces of regulation as they come into force, or it may involve helping a fund or manager to comply with existing rules to which they are subject.

Financial markets litigation – contentious regulatory

Contentious regulatory work for asset management clients often involves responding to requests for information from regulators, including the Financial Conduct Authority in the UK or the Securities and Exchange Commission in the US. Trainee work may involve detailed analysis of trading data or electronic communications (such as emails and Bloomberg chats) as well as interviewing traders, portfolio managers or investment analysts to understand why particular investment decisions were taken.

Corporate

Simmons & Simmons' corporate lawyers advise the firm's asset management clients on all aspects of their corporate transactions, from large-scale acquisitions by private equity firms to hedge fund group restructurings. Trainees in the corporate department will be involved with a wide range of tasks, from helping to draft share purchase agreements and other agreements to assisting with verification, which is the process of ensuring that all of the statements made by a company in an offering document are accurate.

Financial transactions

Our lawyers advise on all types of transactions undertaken by asset managers, including advising on investments made by private equity, infrastructure and real estate funds and the financing and exits undertaken in relation to these funds.

Corporate tax

Tax lawyers work closely with funds lawyers and corporate lawyers, advising on all aspects of domestic and international tax, to ensure that deals undertaken by our asset management clients are structured in a tax-compliant and efficient manner. Trainees

Simmons & Simmons

working in tax may be asked to research specific points of UK tax law or to manage the process of obtaining local tax advice.

What have been the key recent developments in the area in the past 12 months?

The key trend in the asset management sector in the last 12 months has undoubtedly been increasing levels of regulation. The asset management industry, which has traditionally been lightly regulated, has been subject to greater scrutiny following the global financial crisis and, as a result, asset managers are now facing much more onerous regulatory obligations. In addition, uncertainty about the future regulatory framework has been increased by the Brexit vote.

Simmons & Simmons

Simmons & Simmons is a leading international legal practice with over 1,500 staff worldwide, including over 250 partners, and a total legal staff of over 800. Our current client base includes a significant number of the current FTSE 100 and Fortune Global 500 companies, investment banks and many of the world's largest financial conglomerates. We provide services from offices based in Europe, the Middle East and Asia. We view the world through the lens of our key sectors: asset management and investment funds, financial institutions and technology, media and telecommunications.

For further information about the firm, please see p356.
Website: www.simmons-simmons.com

Banking and finance

Caroline Gershon, an associate in the banking and finance practice at Weil, Gotshal & Manges, gives an insight

What is banking?

Banking has been, for the last few years, and remains today, the focus of a great deal of attention, scrutiny and criticism, and is central not just to the British economy but to the global economy. This dramatic backdrop to banking today makes it an exciting, challenging and stimulating area of law to practise. Banking can take the form of lending money to blue-chip companies to finance new business plans, issuing high-yield bonds or helping investors acquire whole businesses. The lawyer's role in this field is varied and dynamic, acting both for borrowers and lenders to create, negotiate and deliver a bespoke financing package to suit a myriad of circumstances.

The banking practice at Weil

At Weil, a large proportion of the work of the banking group involves acting on leveraged buy-outs, whereby a company or business is acquired by a private equity firm using a high level of borrowed funds (debt). Weil's role is to negotiate the loan documentation and associated security package on behalf of either the borrower or lender and manage the ongoing relationship between the parties as it develops over the life of the loan.

The firm not only acts on deals where new money is being lent, but on deals to restructure or refinance existing debt, where the borrower may be in financial difficulty and unable to repay their loans, or, may wish to put in place new finance arrangements which are more closely aligned to their new business plan.

A typical Weil deal will require the lending of hundreds of millions of pounds by the largest financial institutions to top private equity institutions and it is unusual for a transaction to only involve the UK, as many clients and businesses operate internationally. This gives lawyers the opportunity to work with clients and lawyers from countries across the globe, in particular places where Weil has international offices. Frequently, this process is co-ordinated and driven by the team in London, which can be very rewarding.

One of the most interesting elements of a Weil banking transaction is working with the clients to structure the financing. In the past few years traditional European banks have taken a more conservative view on lending, which in turn has led private equity institutions to explore other avenues of financing and innovative ways of structuring deals. This is always with a view to obtaining the best pricing and greatest flexibility for the business that is being financed. Financing options in Europe range from traditional European loans, to high-yield bonds, to accessing the US loan market. With a strong capital markets team and a close working relationship with the Weil New York office, the London banking team is particularly well placed to advise clients on a full range of different options.

Another interesting feature of banking work, which is virtually unique to the discipline, is the requirement to understand the business of the borrower, and this is true regardless of whether you represent the borrower or the lender on any given matter. This is because a loan agreement lasts for several years, unlike many other complex commercial contracts which seek to address one specific event (for example a sale and purchase agreement). During the life of a loan, a business is developing, and therefore the loan agreement should aim to contemplate as many of those business changes as possible. This is fascinating and the result is that banking lawyers develop strong commercial awareness and business acumen.

Working culture and life

Weil is an incredibly friendly firm and it prides itself on having a relaxed, open-door policy. Due to the nature of the transactions the firm work on, both in terms of complexity and timing, trainees and junior lawyers have the opportunity to take on a high level of responsibility and get involved as an active part of the deal team. This will involve drafting documentation, dealing directly with the lawyers representing the other parties, instructing overseas counsel and significant client contact from day one.

One of the best things about being a banking lawyer is that there is no such thing as a typical day: you could find yourself attending a kick-off meeting to discuss a new deal with a client, drafting documents and participating in conference calls with local and overseas lawyers on an ongoing matter, heading to a client's offices to obtain signatures to close a deal, researching a point of law to address a particularly complex or new legal problem, or preparing a client pitch for new business for the firm – the list is endless! The work is very varied and therefore a flexible attitude, willingness to learn and enthusiasm for participating are absolutely essential in order to thrive in an area of law that can require long and intense but rewarding hours.

Banking lawyers are typically sociable individuals due to the high level of teamwork and client contact involved in their work and they need to have the confidence to take on early responsibility, a good head for business and a keen eye for detail. Common sense is also a must, as well as excellent transaction management skills and a high level of ambition and drive to get a deal completed successfully and secure the best outcome for your client. Since the lender/borrower relationship exists beyond the original deal and survives for several years, it is essential to maintain a good relationship with the other parties to a transaction and their counsel, so excellent negotiation and persuasion skills are vital.

Weil, Gotshal & Manges

The banking department at Weil works both on stand-alone finance matters and alongside the other transactional practice groups at the firm for clients including Advent International, CVC, Goldman Sachs and JPMorgan.

For further information about the firm, please see p400.
Website: www.weil.com

Corporate

Gary MacDonald is a partner in the corporate and banking team at DWF LLP in Edinburgh

What is corporate law?

Corporate law involves advisory and transactional work for business organisations and for individuals with business interests. Corporate lawyers advise on a variety of areas, including mergers and acquisitions, stock market flotations and fundraisings, restructurings and reorganisations, investments and joint ventures.

Corporate law encompasses a surprisingly broad range of work, which is generally centred around the drafting and negotiation of contracts and advising on matters of company law. It is usually non-contentious and therefore corporate lawyers rarely spend any time in court.

Key skills for corporate lawyers

Commercial awareness and a real understanding of the business world are paramount in corporate law. It is important that you understand the commercial issues and challenges which are particular to your client, as well as general issues affecting the sectors in which it operates.

Good drafting skills are essential, as is attention to detail. You will also be required to think on your feet during negotiations and sometimes work to demanding timetables.

Project management is also a key part of the job. Often you will be overseeing projects which involve input from a number of other specialist lawyers within your firm. It is important to make sure that they understand what is required of them and deliver to the deadlines you set. Your job will often involve pulling together all of this input and ensuring its consistency and accuracy.

As with any area of law, communication and people skills are key. You will work with a broad range of clients. Some will have been involved in numerous corporate transactions, but others will be relative novices. You will need to be adaptable, and ensure that you pitch your advice at the right level. You will also need to get used to dealing with senior individuals within commercial organisations who are confident, and who know exactly what they expect from their legal advisers. This can be challenging, but also professionally very rewarding.

Realities of the job

The average working hours of a corporate lawyer vary. As a deal nears completion, there is no doubt that a corporate lawyer's hours get longer and can involve late-night working. This is because, as the deal nears completion, there will be a push to agree outstanding points and documents. Corporate transactions are commonly very strategically important to the parties involved and deadlines are often demanding.

One of the most satisfying things about being a corporate lawyer is reaping the benefits of the work you put in. There is a great sense of achievement which comes with completing a transaction and seeing a project through from start to finish. High-profile deals also often attract press coverage for the parties and lawyers involved.

Day-to-day work

On a typical day, there is a balance of client work and internal matters to deal with – that balance can vary. Often corporate lawyers will be leading transactions, dealing with the negotiation of the principal documents and dealing with other professionals involved in the transaction. Corporate partners usually act as the internal project leader, both co-ordinating input from other legal disciplines (there can be many specialists needed) and acting as the main client liaison.

Corporate lawyers may work on a number of deals simultaneously. Equally, a large deal may occupy most of a lawyer's time for a period of several months.

The type of work that trainees are likely to get involved in consists of assisting with initial research at the beginning of a transaction, working on due diligence (asking questions of the seller or answering a buyer's questions – in either case so that the buyer gains a full understanding of what they are buying) and drafting documentation, including simple agreements, board minutes, shareholder resolutions and Companies House forms. A trainee will also often have the opportunity to sit in on negotiations as a transaction progresses.

Corporate lawyers are also responsible for business development, which includes both the maintenance of relationships with existing clients (it sounds straightforward but actually takes work because many clients' corporate transactions are few and far between) and the development of new business.

Developments in corporate

In the years following the 2007/08 credit crunch, deal activity declined due to lack of available finance and because businesses were cautious about the economic environment. Many companies concentrated on sustaining their business rather than looking for opportunities to grow and expand.

The recent upturn in the economy has meant a significant increase in corporate activity and consequently an increasing number and range of opportunities for corporate lawyers. This has included an increase in the number of flotations on UK stock markets, as well as significant interest from many overseas companies in investing in UK businesses. Corporate lawyers are busy again, and getting busier!

DWF LLP

DWF is a UK business law firm with an international reach. Our legal experts combine real commercial understanding and deep sector knowledge to help clients anticipate issues, create opportunities and achieve the outcomes they need.

DWF was ranked second for the quality of its legal advice in the 2012 Client Satisfaction Report by *Legal Week*.

The firm employs over 2,450 people, including 296 partners and 1,520 fee-earners.

For further information about the firm, please see p186.
Website: www.dwf.law

Dispute resolution

Caroline Edwards is a dispute resolution partner and member of the firm's International Board at Travers Smith LLP

Thinking *Silk* meets *The Good Wife*? Well, sort of! For unpredictability, the need to think on your feet and the excitement of a legal and tactical battle both in and out of court, you certainly need to look no further. However, there is a lot more to dispute resolution than your favourite legal TV drama might suggest.

Most dispute resolution departments focus on handling civil and commercial disputes between individuals, groups, companies or organisations. They could be based here or overseas. The possible range of subject matter is limitless and although many disputes ultimately boil down to an argument between two parties to a contract, no two cases are ever identical. There are also many occasions where the dispute is not about a contract at all – allegations of fraud and defamation are prime examples. You will find that firms vary in the extent to which their dispute resolution department deals with more specialist categories such as employment disputes and competition, and other regulatory investigations.

While a litigator might represent a client in court proceedings or in arbitration, this does not happen in every case. In fact, one of the most important skills of a good litigator is the ability to enable your client to resolve its dispute in the best and most cost-effective way possible, which may mean not going to court at all. Litigators are therefore regularly involved at the very outset of a dispute and use a range of settlement strategies to bring a case to a satisfactory conclusion, well before the client needs to step into the court room.

What makes a good litigator?

To be a good litigator, not only do you need a sound understanding of the law, but you must be able to apply your knowledge to the commercial realities of the situation and come up with a strategy which you will then need to communicate clearly and effectively to your clients. Good communication and drafting skills are also vital when working with barristers and witnesses to prepare your client's case, and when dealing with the other side.

An exciting and key role for the solicitor in dispute resolution is to play the detective. To build your client's case, you need to spot the strengths in your own evidence and the weaknesses in the other side's case, often hidden among a very large volume of documents. A forensic eye and attention to detail are therefore important attributes, as is the ability to step back from the detail and see the overall game plan. Finally, being organised will help you to keep on top of your caseload as there are often many elements of a case to juggle at the same time and you are likely to be handling a number of matters simultaneously, all with differing issues and deadlines.

The good and the bad

There is no such thing as a 'typical day' in dispute resolution and, in fact, it is the variety of the work which makes it such an attractive option. There is also plenty of scope to be given responsibility for aspects of a case, or even a whole matter, right from the start. In any one day you might be working on several different cases, all at varying stages of the litigation process. You might be attending court or a conference with counsel, meeting a client for the first time to discuss a new matter, or a witness to go through their evidence; you might be reviewing documents to find a 'smoking gun' or drafting a settlement proposal to the other side.

Like any job, there are elements of a litigator's workload which can be stressful (for example, preparing an urgent injunction application on behalf of an enthusiastic but elusive client) or dull (such as wading through thousands of documents to work out what should be disclosed). However, the sheer variety of the work, the teamwork involved in preparing a case, and the satisfaction of getting a good result for the client make being a litigator extremely rewarding.

In terms of managing a caseload, the timetable determined by the court (or tribunal or regulator) on your cases will help you to anticipate when you are likely to be busiest, but there are always unexpected developments so you need to be flexible and adept at working under time pressure.

Dispute resolution in 2016

Commercial litigation continues to be a thriving and diverse practice area. The largest and most high-profile cases of 2016 see litigating parties ranging from overseas billionaires and financial institutions, to high-street retailers and property companies. While the aftermath of the credit crunch continues to live on in the courts, we have also seen a rise in group litigation, as well as an increase in follow-on damages claims which follow findings of EU competition infringements, and in professional negligence and fraud cases. For example, we are acting for Hewlett-Packard group companies in relation to fraud and professional negligence claims arising out of the US$11bn acquisition of Autonomy Corporation plc in 2011, and we have been representing Icelandic bank Kaupthing hf in proceedings launched by Vincent Tchenguiz and others claiming £2.2bn and alleging conspiracy to injure by unlawful means.

Regulatory investigations and enforcement action have come to form a significant part of the workload of all of the top law firms in London. With the FX manipulation story competing for headlines with the LIBOR scandal, we can foresee no let-up to the substantial amount of legal work generated by these issues, from regulatory investigations to litigation, both domestically and internationally. Travers Smith has been involved in all of the high-profile investigations, for example we advised the Oversight Committee of the Bank of England (together with Lord Grabiner QC) in connection with its investigation into the role of bank officials in relation to conduct issues in the foreign exchange market.

The ongoing reforms to civil procedure have given rise to new challenges as the courts grapple with their stricter case and costs management powers. The prospect of further increases to court fees, changes to the structure of the civil courts system and additional reforms to costs management are all developments we are watching with interest.

Meanwhile, at the time of writing, Britain is only just beginning to come to terms with its referendum decision to leave the EU. While we do not anticipate any immediate downturn in commercial litigation in this country (and indeed, it may increase), the uncertainty which pervades at this time is likely to impact on parties' appetite for risk and their sense of urgency to resolve disputes.

TRAVERS SMITH

Travers Smith LLP

Travers Smith is an award-winning independent law firm. We concentrate on being the best at what we do and have a reputation for excellence in all the fields of law in which we practise. We take our work, but not ourselves, seriously. Entrepreneurial and efficient, we focus on the results we can achieve for our clients rather than the points we can score along the way. This approach has attracted a long and loyal list of clients to the firm. Our lawyers undertake high-quality, and often high-profile, work within a collegiate and supportive environment which benefits both our lawyers and our clients alike. Over half of the firm's work has an international dimension – to service this we have an office in Paris, as well as close working relationships with other independent law firms around the world that share our high standards.

We have a thriving and expanding dispute resolution team which punches well above its weight, gaining instructions to act in some of the largest and most complex pieces of litigation in the City, and producing outstanding results for our clients. We are also highly regarded in the field of regulatory investigations and enforcement work.

For further information about the firm, please see p388.
Website: www.traverssmith.com

Employment and pensions

Elizabeth Parkin, solicitor in employment, Birmingham, and Heather Chandler, partner in pensions, Milton Keynes at Shoosmiths LLP share the ins and outs

Employment

Employment law covers a wide range of areas and involves both contentious and non-contentious work. Broadly speaking, it encompasses any area of the law that relates to the employment of individuals. This can involve not only advising on areas such as redundancies, dismissals and grievance situations, but also supporting corporate and commercial lawyers involved in the sale and purchase of businesses and advice on property matters (for example where there is a change in ownership of a building or services being provided to a property).

Employment lawyers need to be able to offer commercial advice, as well as advising on the legal aspects of an issue. Employment law can be extremely technical, and employment lawyers need to be able to break down these technical rules in order to advise clients on the risks involved in particular courses of action, as well as offering innovative solutions. Along with this ability to offer commercial advice, employment lawyers also need to be personable, as there is a high level of interaction with clients directly and their HR departments. Attention to detail is a necessity, especially as matters can often lead to litigation.

As employment law covers a wide range of topics, employment lawyers have to ensure that they keep up-to-date with the most recent case law and legislative changes. A high level of organisation and dedication is needed to ensure that they are able to offer the most up-to-date advice to their clients. Individuals need to be good at working to tight deadlines, as clients seeking employment advice often require a quick response and therefore employment law is a fast-paced area to work in. It can also be demanding due to the variety of issues that clients need advice on. Saying this, a high level of client contact and variety of work makes employment law an interesting, challenging and enjoyable area to work in.

One of the key areas of development in employment law has been the procedural changes to the tribunal process. In an effort to reduce costs and increase efficiency, tribunals are now using judges sitting alone (rather than in a panel of three) for standard unfair dismissal claims. The most significant change is in relation to the introduction of fees in the tribunal system, which came into force in 2013. The Government introduced a system whereby (subject to means testing) fees are charged to use the employment tribunal for submission of claims, certain applications and the substantive hearing. The tribunal also has the power to order an unsuccessful party to reimburse the fee to the successful party. The hope was that it would dissuade vexatious employees from bringing unreasonable claims. However, the change has been the subject of legal challenge on whether it prevents access to justice. It has had a noticeable impact on the number of claims submitted, but has not netted quite the level of revenue anticipated. It will be interesting to see whether the fees remain following the judicial review process.

Pensions

Pensions law involves setting up and helping trustees and employers operate pension schemes either trust or contract based, referencing those relevant areas of law. Clients range from corporations, charities and other not-for-profit organisations, to individual trustees, lay or professional.

We advise on issues of compliance with legislation and the regulatory regime applicable. Whilst not usually contentious, the pensions ombudsman handles disputes through a paper process. There is also a pensions regulator and a regime of notifications and compliance with that office to manage. In rare circumstances we have cases referred to counsel and/or the courts. We work closely with employment lawyers on contract interpretation and also on executive termination issues where compensation for loss of pension benefits may be a significant factor.

The sale or purchase of a business or company will often have a pensions dimension and advice will be required on the contractual obligations of the seller and the purchaser around any existing pension schemes, what future pension provision is required and any compliance risks a purchaser may be acquiring. There are a number of types of pension scheme but final salary schemes (also called defined benefit schemes) are the type most likely to give rise to issues. These schemes promise benefits linked to salary and length of service and have to be funded. Pension funds/schemes are some of the largest investors globally and management of the investments and the obligations around keeping a scheme in funds to the levels statute requires is something on which we advise regularly, together with actuaries and investment managers.

We draft documentation daily, from deeds to letters, and attend meetings with trustees assisting with the day-to-day running of schemes. We also deliver training to clients so can be in and out of the office. We act both pro actively to tell clients about issues they need to be aware of and what actions they may need to take, as well as reactively to requests to assist with projects like merging two pension schemes, or amending the terms of a schemes. Part of our role is to work with other professionals who also work with pensions schemes such as actuaries, accountants, investment managers and auditors. Communicating with a wide range of individuals with different experience of pensions is also part of our daily work.

Good communication skills are key to being a good pensions lawyer as well as having a good and consistent attention to detail when required. It is also important to be able to understand commercial issues and advise clients in a pragmatic way, helping them to assess and mitigate risk. Much of what we do involves problem solving and it's a key skill to be able to logically pull together lots of complex points and documents and come up with an integrated view. Being a pensions lawyer is therefore intellectually challenging, requiring pragmatic and creative thinking.

Pensions law has been subject to rapid change over the last decade, most recently the auto enrolment regime which came into effect from October 2012. It requires employers to pay towards pension provision for all their employees at a minimum level. This compulsion is new and there are a number of steps to take and issues to resolve to comply. There is also significant cross-over with employment law and practice involved.

Shoosmiths LLP

We are close to our clients, constantly listening, thriving on their challenges, bringing the energy, ideas and results they need.

We are a full-service law firm with teams in commercial, corporate, employment, real estate, intellectual property, banking, planning, and dispute resolution. Through our Access Legal consumer brand, we also offer private client, personal injury, medical negligence, and conveyancing. We have ten offices across the UK and more than 700 lawyers.

For further information about the firm, please see p352.
Website: www.shoosmiths.co.uk

Insurance and reinsurance

Lee Bacon is a partner and Marta Jarque Branguli a senior associate in the insurance and reinsurance group at Clyde & Co LLP, both specialising in litigation and arbitration arising from international insurance and reinsurance placements

What is insurance and reinsurance?

Put to one side everything you think you know about insurance – car, home, travel – all, frankly, a little uninspiring albeit hugely important. Think instead of one of the largest sectors of the global financial services market and unarguably the sector that has best navigated the financial crisis.

Insurance is about risk – and specifically the pooling of risk. The development of insurance has been a crucial component of economic development. From the earliest days of underwriting trading voyages to India and China from Lloyd's coffee shop in Georgian London, to the underwriting of multibillion-dollar construction projects, it is difficult to identify an area of economic activity that has not been underpinned by the risk transfer provided by insurance.

Insurance is an extremely broad market but broadly consists of two main types of cover: (a) property insurance (which covers damage to an insured's own property of whatever type) and may include loss of revenue insurance (which covers a financial loss accruing to an insured); and (b) liability insurance (which covers an insured in the event of claims made against it by a third party).

You may also have heard of 'reinsurance' and specifically by reference to Lloyd's of London – the insurance market based within the iconic Richard Rogers building in the City of London. 'Reinsurance' is the structure by which insurers can pass some or all of their risk to other insurance counterparties – hence 're'-insurance.

Re/insurance law and practice

The practice of re/insurance law is extremely wide and encompasses both contentious and non-contentious matters.

Non-contentious work includes the negotiation and drafting of insurance/reinsurance contracts (policies) and structures; M&A work; regulatory issues; and general commercial/corporate work. While in practice it is very similar to the same work types for non-insurer industries, because of the way insurance companies are regulated, financed and operated such work requires specialist industry knowledge. With insurers and reinsurers forming some of the world's largest companies, such deals are often huge in scale and complexity.

It is perhaps on the contentious side, however, that the scope of the practice of re/insurance law is at its most diverse. Indeed the majority of commercial disputes before the English courts and main arbitral bodies are funded in some way or another by insurers.

Global practice

The insurance and reinsurance sector demands specialism on a global scale.

Clyde & Co offers the broadest international coverage of any insurance law firm with an impressive footprint which covers the Middle East, Asia, South America, Europe and the US. We represent domestic and international clients on matters of both regional and international scale. We are a truly global law firm, constantly aiming to match our insurance clients' global presence in locations where they require us.

In practice, for example, businesses which are based overseas will often be insured with a London firm and the largest insurance disputes will often have an international angle to them.

Key issues in today's economy

Re/insurance is a largely stable market and this stability is one of its strengths. It has a long history, and in England a long-developed body of law, the principles of which have recently been reformulated in statute by the Insurance Act 2015, the biggest legislative change in insurance law for over 100 years.

As business becomes more global, a key issue continues to be the opportunities presented by new markets and the challenges of underwriting exposures in an increasingly interconnected world. In 2016, key issues for re/insurers include developing solutions to handle the increasing cyber risk, developing new products to stay relevant in the face of challenges faced by global clients such as exposures created by reputational damage, the impact of Brexit and the challenges and opportunities presented by new technologies such as blockchain.

Growing industry

The London re/insurance market has always had an international focus, and this tradition has only expanded in line with the wider effects of globalisation so as to allow London to have retained its market leading position.

A strong recent trend is the development of so-called global programmes pursuant to which a large multinational corporate will seek to wrapup many of its exposures in one combined global policy rather than relying on disparate policies in each jurisdiction. Such covers raise complex regulatory and legal difficulties.

Secondly, the re/insurance market has weathered the financial crisis better than other financial service sectors and because of this it has seen an influx of new capital – from the traditional banking sources, private equity and latterly hedge funds. This influx of capacity increases the competitiveness of the market, leading to more call for innovative and risk-bearing products. That said, the downturn in investment income following the financial crisis has also been a driver for insurers to improve underwriting and claims performance, as risk spreading through diversification and achieving economies of scale through merger. The insurance industry has always prided itself on its ability to innovate and offer new products and solutions to meet changes in demand.

Day-to-day work

It is difficult to generalise as to the day-to-day work of a lawyer in a re/insurance practice. A solicitor focusing on insurance and reinsurance coverage disputes concerning the most complex and international placements may have only one or two large matters at any one time and have to swiftly become a mini-expert on the underlying subject matter. Conversely, a specialist professional indemnity solicitor may spend most of their time working on the defence of a larger number of claims against solicitors or accountants. However, the underlying subject matter for even this specialism will vary greatly.

Therefore, a Monday can be spent drafting a pleading in defence of a claim against a fellow solicitor. Tuesday, there can be a conference call with lawyers in Chile discussing the scope of cover of a property insurance policy. Wednesday can bring an interview with a coffee trader suspected of aiding the mysterious disappearance of a shipment, with Thursday engaged in considering a 'bloodstock' claim following an injury to a racehorse, and the week culminating on Friday drafting a mediation agreement for a banking liability claim.

CLYDE&CO

Key skills required

In order to succeed in the insurance industry you must have a real understanding of the client's business needs. Commercial awareness is key to understanding and solving the issues and challenges that the clients are facing. As well as a sound understanding of the law, good communication and people skills are vital as you will be working with a broad range of clients. Of course, as with any litigation the review and collation of evidence is crucial and this requires hard work and attention to detail. Preparing complex and detailed submissions in often tight deadlines means that you will have to be well organised and remain calm under pressure.

Looking forward

Insurance is a growing industry. Emerging markets need insurance to get investment and so as consumption continues to grow, the insurance market will grow, resulting in opportunities for emerging market insurers. This will cause a shift in power from the developed market towards emerging economies and emerging market insurers.

Clyde & Co LLP

Clyde & Co is a global law firm headquartered in London, with 40 offices (and counting) on six continents. Insurance and reinsurance is at the heart of what we do and our continuing international expansion has largely been driven by responding to the needs of our client base in the sector. What this means in practice is that we are often involved in the most complex and challenging work across the globe. Because of our focus on insurance we also have leading teams across the breadth of industry sectors including corporate insurance and all the main insurance lines.

For further information about the firm, please see p170.
Website: www.clydeco.com

Intellectual property

Liz Cohen is a partner and Claire Phipps-Jones an associate in the IP litigation team at Bristows LLP

What is intellectual property (IP) law?
It's the global Samsung v Apple smartphone wars, the 'understated and extreme simplicity' of Apple's iPad, the disappearance of The Pirate Bay, the reason why anyone can publish the football fixtures, the law preventing you from 'jailbreaking' your games console, the reason that you don't buy your Predator football boots from 'Adidos' and can't wear a Topshop T-shirt with Rihanna's face on it, the secret behind the distinct taste of Coca-cola and your love of seedless grapes, to name but a few!

Intellectual property law protects those rights that are intangible intellectual creations. The obvious rights covering most of the examples referred to above are patents (protecting inventions), trade marks (brands), designs (3D shape/conformation) and copyright (in relation to literary and artistic works), but there are other rights such as database rights, confidential information, trade secrets and plant variety rights.

There are many opportunities in IP, and your work can involve any part of the lifecycle of an IP right. This can include involvement in the creation and registration of rights, for example, or in the drafting and processing of patent/trade mark applications with registries in the UK and abroad. It can also entail assisting in transactions involving IP rights to allow a rights holder to exploit and make money from its right, for example, by drafting and negotiating R&D agreements, or dealing with the transfer or licensing of IP rights in corporate transactions. Of course, it can also involve litigating IP rights when it all goes wrong!

Useful/key skills which are needed
Practising IP can involve contentious and non-contentious work, with most firms having combined departments. However, firms with a greater focus on IP, such as Bristows, separate out such work into various departments by IP right and/or whether the work is litigious.

Working in IP involves working with clients ranging from individual inventors, artists, musicians, designers and writers to massive global corporations. A particularly meticulous nature and love of language is of assistance when involved in, for example, the drafting of an IP right or non-contentious transactional work, where it is necessary to map out the possible future consequences of one's choice of words. An ability to understand and apply legal principles to sometimes complex situations with an eye on your client's industry and commercial drivers is a crucial skill when identifying a suitable strategy in litigation or in possible settlement negotiations.

In the case of litigation, the job also involves liaising with patent and trade mark attorneys (who are generally responsible for registering IP rights and will have made various submissions on the validity of a given right in order for it to be granted), experts in the relevant industry (in particular with regard to whether an invention was new and non-obvious when it was applied for, or perhaps to assist in determining what a patent claim actually means to those in the industry and whether an allegedly infringing product actually infringes), barristers and in many cases lawyers from other jurisdictions to ensure alignment of the approach taken in proceedings across the globe. This obviously requires good communication skills, both oral and written.

Day-to-day work
In the patent litigation department at Bristows, your day largely depends on the stage of each of the various litigation projects that you are working on. It can involve initial meetings or calls with clients to discuss a case and its prospects, drafting pleadings, considering prior art (earlier publications that can be used to invalidate a patent), reviewing documents to determine whether they are relevant and need to be disclosed, preparing a product or process description with the client (which involves drafting a detailed description of the product or process that is alleged to be infringing), meetings with experts, conferences with counsel to discuss and prepare the case for trial, and obviously days in court. Alongside which there is always correspondence with the opposing side, calls

and correspondence with the client to keep them well informed and obtain instructions, and often calls with foreign counsel to ensure alignment in various jurisdictions.

It is not unusual to have a number of cases each at a different stage, so managing you time is vital to ensure that all deadlines are met. Of course, there is often other work, such as preparing freedom to operate advice including infringement and validity opinions, for example, considering whether a client's proposed new commercial product may potentially infringe an existing patent held by a third party prior to launch. This can involve reviewing not only the new product, but conducting searches of and reporting on potentially relevant patents.

You may also be involved in patent licensing and settlement negotiations, although at Bristows such agreements would largely have significant input from our commercial IP/IT team, which specialises in transactional IP.

Developments in this area in the past 12 months
The joy of working in IP is the dynamic subject matter of your work. The scope of patented inventions obviously moves on with time, so what was a hot topic in terms of patent litigation a decade ago is likely to be old news now. The current hot topics in patent litigation continue to be telecoms and life sciences. In addition, the recent referendum and the resulting Brexit will result in some interesting issues in relation to IP legislation, which is currently derived from European treaties, directives and regulations.

The advent of the internet and the digital age means that written, audio and visual information has never been more accessible, resulting in some very interesting new issues regarding the responsibility for infringement and policing of copyright and trade marks online. The role of internet service providers (ISPs), search engines and sites such as eBay remains a popular subject of trade mark litigation.

BRISTOWS

Bristows LLP

Bristows is an independent, full-service law firm based in London with an international client base that includes some of the world's leading innovative companies. We are particularly well known for our work in the TMT and life sciences sectors and representing businesses with significant IP and technology assets.

Recognised for groundbreaking and complex work, we distinguish ourselves through the depth of our knowledge in each of our disciplines. A high proportion of Bristows' lawyers have specialist backgrounds, including technical degrees, PhDs and practical experience related to the industries we represent. This enables our clients to call on a rare blend of legal and commercial understanding.

For further information about the firm, please see p142.
Website: www.bristows.com

Mergers and acquisitions

Matt Anson graduated in law from the University of Wales. Now an associate in the M&A department of Shearman & Sterling (London) LLP, he shares his experience

What is mergers and acquisition law?
In broad terms, M&A practice is concerned with the sale and purchase of companies and/or their assets. The transactions we advise on range from relatively simple acquisitions or disposals of private companies based solely in the UK, to larger and more complex deals which involve a number of jurisdictions and companies that have their securities traded publicly. Although the size and scope of the deals we advise on varies, the work we undertake is typically complex and is almost always cross-border.

The level of client contact at Shearman means that over time you really get to know the businesses that you provide advice to; spending time getting to know a client is a gratifying part of the job and something which our clients really value. M&A is also a great way to get to know other lawyers in the firm as the nature of our work dictates that we work closely with other specialist teams including tax, real estate, employment and our regulatory team. We also work cross-border with lawyers in our international offices and with local counsel around the world.

At Shearman, our M&A team encompasses a range of corporate law, including both public and private M&A as well as private equity deals. Such varied deals ensure that we learn a range of different skills and can add value to a host of different clients. Associates in the team naturally tend to specialise in an area as they get more senior; but as a junior associate I'm currently happy to try my hand at a mixture of transactions.

Useful/key skills
The M&A team at Shearman is a busy, transactional team so the usual qualities of a good lawyer come in handy, such as: attention to detail, time management, commercial awareness, team work and a good attitude.

Good organisation skills are crucial since a large part of any transactional lawyer's day is project management. It is also vital to ensure that advice is commercially focused – being able to tailor your advice to a client's specific needs is a key skill. It follows that putting in the effort to acquire an understanding of our clients' businesses pays dividends over time.

Like any area where tight deadlines are involved, the ability to cope with pressure and stay calm when things start getting busy is important, too. Ultimately though, this is something people tend to get better at the longer they have been doing the job.

Realities of the job
The fact that M&A is such a broad area means that the work is pretty varied and, at Shearman in particular, it's an area of practice where client contact is a part of life from trainee level. The subject matter of the transactions you work on provides natural variety to the work too (you can be negotiating the purchase agreement for a football club one week, and drafting documents for the merger of two telephone companies the next).

You will work long hours sometimes, but the work is interesting and there is a real buzz from 'getting the deal done'. For many clients the transaction we advise them on will be a landmark event which (when it's completed) really adds to the sense of accomplishment.

Day-to-day work
There isn't really a 'typical' day, but from an early stage you can expect to be involved in due diligence (the process by which the target business or company is investigated by a prospective buyer) and drafting transaction documents (from the corporate authorisations required to the sale and purchase agreement). You will also spend part of your time managing logistics and instructing local counsel where required.

Ensuring you keep up with developments is – as it is for all lawyers – very important, and Shearman & Sterling's comprehensive training programme makes it easy to keep up to date. Shearman provides a wide spectrum of training (which includes technical legal sessions, 'soft' skills sessions and seminars with leading academics).

Developments in this area in the past 12 months

Like many firms in the City, we have noticed an appreciable increase in M&A activity in the last 12 months. What has been particularly interesting is the impact this has had on negotiations; sellers have found themselves in a stronger position and, as a result, they are often able to negotiate more favourable treatment in the transaction documents (eg, by securing a 'locked box' transaction instead of selling on the basis of completion accounts, or by providing less extensive warranty protection than they otherwise might have done).

SHEARMAN & STERLING LLP

Shearman & Sterling (London) LLP

Shearman & Sterling has been advising many of the world's leading corporations and financial institutions, governments and governmental organisations for more than 135 years. The firm is committed to providing legal advice that is insightful and valuable to its clients. This has resulted in groundbreaking transactions in all major regions of the world.

Together, the firm's lawyers work across practices and jurisdictions to provide the highest quality legal services, bringing their collective experience to bear on the issues that clients face.

For further information about the firm, please see p348.
Website: www. shearman.com

Private equity

David Arnold, a partner at Kirkland & Ellis International LLP, gives us his perspective

Solicitors practising in the area of private equity law are principally divided into two categories: (i) those advising private equity funds in connection with 'raising a fund', ie the arrangements between the fund manager and the investors in the fund; and (ii) advising private equity funds investing the fund and selling its investments, most commonly being the acquiring and disposal of companies and any legal issues that arise during the time they own a company. This page focuses on the work of the second category.

A private equity fund is a type of investment fund set up by a private equity firm (the fund manager), which invests other people's money, such as that of pension funds, insurance companies and sovereign wealth funds, by buying and owning businesses. Typically, a private equity firm will buy a majority of the shares of a private company (being a company whose shares are not traded on a stock exchange), control the company and put the firm's representatives on the management board. The private equity firm will hold that company for usually between about two to five years, during which time it will seek to provide operational input to improve and grow the business of the company, following which it will look to sell the company, hopefully at a profit, and return the proceeds to the investors in the fund. A private equity firm will usually not only use the money in the fund to acquire a target company, but will try to 'leverage' its returns by also using debt finance provided either by a bank or an alternative provider of finance (such as a credit fund or the bond market).

What do private equity lawyers do?

On a typical private equity acquisition, one law firm acts for the private equity fund that is buying the company; another firm acts for the seller; a third for the bank or other institution that is providing finance to the private equity fund; and a fourth firm advises the company's senior management team.

Solicitors work on up to five or six deals at a time – all at various stages of completion – and a transaction typically lasts three to six months. In the preliminary stages of a potential deal, private equity solicitors are instructed by the client to carry out an initial analysis of a company. Once a client decides to proceed with the acquisition, many lawyers and advisors are involved in the due diligence process, which is designed to flag up any risks or issues that might affect the value of the company. Towards the end of the process, solicitors work through the contractual arrangements with the seller, with the senior management team of the target company, and arrange the financing.

The number of lawyers working in a team will vary vastly depending on the complexity of the deal and whether the client is the bank or other provider of finance, the senior management team, the sellers or the buyers – there is more work involved when buying a company, particularly at the due diligence stage, than when advising a seller or the senior management team.

Successful private equity lawyers develop long-standing relationships with private equity firms, and will continue to advise the same private equity firm repeatedly on different acquisitions and disposals, or fund raises, as the case may be. For lawyers involved in mergers and acquisitions generally, having private equity clients is therefore a very good source of business as private equity firms are, by definition, serial users of lawyers capable of doing mergers and acquisitions.

Realities of the job

Private equity solicitors can expect to travel overseas; the amount of travel depends on the firm you join and where the clients are based. The work is cyclical and the hours can be long and involve working weekends leading up to key deadlines and the completion of a deal: some working days are 9.00am to 5.00pm; some are 8.00am to midnight or later. Many private equity deals are competitive auctions so lawyers are often busiest in the run-up to the auction bid dates, when the client is in a race against other buyers. The variability of the hours can be tough but the variety of interesting work makes up for it: you may be buying companies as varied as Odeon cinemas, Alton Towers or Aston Martin. The best aspect of this practice area is working with such motivated clients; private equity is a young, meritocratic industry with many clients in their 30s and 40s. The relationship between lawyers and clients is long-standing and based on trust so it is important to build those relationships socially.

Good private equity lawyers will have strong commercial acumen and numerical skills, a genuine interest in the underlying business of their clients, and probably most importantly good people skills – for working in teams and building long, trust-based relationships with clients. From a purely legal perspective, they will mostly be working with contract law and company law issues, but will also develop a good grounding in many other areas of law such as tax, antitrust and employment law issues.

Trainees will assist with due diligence, help to implement usually complex corporate structures, and will work closely with the huge amount of documents needed to close a transaction. There are opportunities for early responsibility for trainees, and on a large transaction there are plenty of discreet tasks that can be given to trainees.

Developments in private equity

Private equity was badly affected at the beginning of the recession following the 2008 global financial crash because of general economic uncertainty and a lack of available finance from banks. However it did not take long for activity levels to pick up again, and private equity investors are among the most innovative of deal doers and will find ways of making the most of investment opportunities, even in difficult markets. Some of the more prevalent developments in private equity over the past few years have included:

(i) The emergence of alternative providers of debt finance beyond the large investment banks. As banks had their balance sheets shrunk following the financial crash, and came under increasing pressure to maintain higher levels of regulatory capital, their ability to lend into private equity deals has shrunk. They have been replaced to a large extent by alternative providers of finance, such as specialist credit funds.

KIRKLAND & ELLIS

(ii) Increased European-wide regulation on private equity funds raising capital from institutional investors in Europe, and subsequently investing in Europe. This has put increased cost and red tape on raising funds, and certain limitations on what a private equity firm can do with an investment after making an acquisition.

(iii) An increase in the number of private equity firms becoming 'multiple asset managers', which means raising investment funds which don't just focus on typical private equity-style investments, but also on other investment strategies (such as investing in real estate or credit).

Kirkland & Ellis International LLP

Kirkland & Ellis is an international law firm with more than 1,700 lawyers representing global clients in offices worldwide. In London it is renowned for providing multidisciplinary advice to a wide range of leading private equity clients.

For further information about the firm, please see p254.
Website: info@kirkland.com

Real estate

Megan Caulfield, a third-seat trainee at Ashurst LLP, reflects on her experiences in the department during the first seat of her training contract

What is real estate law?
Real estate law is a lot more fast-paced and exciting than most law students will remember from their time at university! At Ashurst the work is transactional, high-profile and often involves a political element which makes for an interesting area of work.

Generally the real estate department is split into four areas: real estate development, real estate investment, construction and planning. At Ashurst the work mainly involves commercial property.

In the real estate team, work is often split between property development and investment: development varying from renovation to re-leasing and investment focusing on the buying and selling of real estate as assets. Trainees will undoubtedly be referring back to their land law notes. Starting a seat in real estate with an understanding of the basic concepts such as leases, licences and easements, for example, would be a good start. As with most areas of law there are also a lot of contract law principles involved in a real estate transaction. Trainees will be expected to draft agreements and review leases. There is also a cross-over with tax law and trainees will be required to get to grips with the stamp duty land tax forms which are submitted to HMRC.

Work in the construction team is heavily contract based. Work will involve assistance with the drafting of contracts for employing contractors to carry out the construction of a new building or refurbishment of an existing one.

Planning is a niche and complex area of law which can have a crucial impact upon the deliverability of construction or development projects. Without the correct planning permission being granted, such projects or development cannot go ahead. The work has an administrative law focus and will involve local government law just as much as land law. Matters vary from assisting developers in seeking planning permission or disputes where planning permission has been refused to corporate support or due diligence.

What are the key skills needed to be a real estate trainee?
Real estate trainees will learn to be organised very quickly. While this applies to lawyers generally, in real estate you will often balance a number of matters as opposed to just one transaction. This will also require you to be disciplined in managing the deals you are working on and have good time management skills.

Trainees must always take the initiative and be proactive in assisting fee-earners. There is always something you can be assisting with. The more involved you get in a transaction, the more responsibility you will get and therefore, the more you will learn from it. Trainees are also likely to get a significant amount of client contact, especially as you become more confident and experienced as the seat progresses. This will allow you to develop your communication skills and your own style of working.

Benefits of working in real estate

Real estate is an incredibly interesting and diverse area to work in. The tangible nature of the work allows you to get to grips with some difficult concepts and also makes it very rewarding when you can see the work that you have been involved in shaping the London landscape. Real estate work is also becoming increasingly international, with foreign investors and developers being particularly interested in the City of London.

Real estate is a department in which you will assist other areas of the firm, from corporate to finance to projects. This allows you to get a good understanding of the work done across the entire firm. The varied and evolving area of law means that a real estate lawyer is quick to adapt and can manage tasks, no matter how daunting and challenging they first appear.

Ashurst LLP

With 25 offices in 15 countries and a number of referral relationships we offer the reach and insight of a global network, combined with the knowledge and understanding of local markets. Our 400 partners and further 1,200 lawyers work across ten different time zones, responding to our clients wherever and whenever they need us.

Our clients are at the heart of our thinking, our ambition is to be our clients' most incisive partner. You will see we have a prestigious client base, with whom we build strong partnerships working closely together on large and complex multi-jurisdictional transactions to deliver incisive and insightful commercial solutions. Our global reach provides opportunities for our people to work in numerous jurisdictions with leading international organisations across the world.

You will enjoy an inclusive culture which genuinely values the breadth of individual perspectives and contributions that we gain from having a diverse workforce. As part of a truly collaborative team working in partnership together with openness and respect across offices, geographies and specialisms, we support each other to achieve great things for our clients. We take exactly the same approach with our people: we're interested in understanding each other, finding new and better ways to bring out each individual's talents, and simply enjoying the interaction with other high-calibre, down-to-earth people. It's a strong, shared culture that will enable you to apply your intellect, develop yourself and thrive as an international lawyer.

For further information about the firm, please see p110.
Website: www.ashurst.com

Shipping

Paul Herring is a qualified solicitor at Ince & Co

Shipping law is the law related to shipping and international trade by sea/river. It might appear to be a very niche area of practice, but, in fact, it's incredibly diverse and many of the leading contract law authorities are shipping cases (*The Moorcock*, *Heron II*, *Wagon Mound No.2* and *The Happy Day*, to name just a few). In shipping law, while the focus is on a particular sector, clients face as wide a range of legal issues as in any other.

There are both contentious and non-contentious sides to working in shipping law. On the contentious side, shipping litigation can develop out of contractual disputes – for example, disputes related to charterparty (ship hire) contracts, ship building contracts, contracts for the carriage of cargo, towage and salvage contracts. The first three of these are often referred to as dry shipping disputes. Shipping litigation can also arise out of maritime incidents – such as collisions, groundings, an engine breakdown, the total loss of a ship or oil pollution. These may be tortious claims (such as between two ships following a collision) or contractual claims (such as a cargo owner claiming for their lost or damaged cargo). Claims arising from such incidents are sometimes referred to as wet shipping disputes.

On the non-contentious side, the work ranges from advising on the financing of ship building and sale/purchase, to regulatory advice, as the shipping industry faces ever-increasing intervention by governments.

Many of the contracts used in the shipping industry have seemingly peculiar and unusual terms that have been refined and developed over a long time. Years of accumulated case law have clarified and elucidated the meanings of key words and phrases. There are some weird and wonderful rules which would seem quite alien to other areas of law.

Given the technical nature of the industry, cases often have a technical side and require significant amounts of expert evidence. For example, following a collision, you might seek input from a Master Mariner as to what he or she would have done in the circumstances facing the actual ship's captain. Where there has been an engine breakdown, you might seek advice from an engineer on how the ship should have been maintained and why it broke down. This opportunity to delve into technical issues lends a further dimension to the role of a shipping solicitor and cases can often challenge a solicitor's understanding of the technical detail.

Shipping is naturally a global industry and this can make for some extremely wide-ranging jurisdictional issues. It also means that as a shipping lawyer you can find yourself engaging with clients, lawyers and experts in many different countries and learning about the idiosyncrasies of different jurisdictions. Dealing with claims in other jurisdictions can be surprising and exciting, throwing up novel issues and presenting new and interesting challenges. It can also provide the opportunity for travel.

The shipping industry is a 24-hour business; running seven days a week, 365 days a year, transporting goods all over the world. It is certainly the case that time is money in this business. As such, shipping solicitors sometimes work anti-social hours and to urgent deadlines; for example, in the immediate aftermath of an incident where salvage services may need to be arranged or actions taken to minimise the impact on the environment, or when a ship is arrested and security must be provided urgently in order to secure her release. The benefit of this is that the work is often very interesting and provides you with a real sense of being on the cutting edge, giving advice in real time.

A good shipping lawyer understands their clients' industries, and new trainees will learn to adapt their legal knowledge to their clients' needs as they gain experience in the job. Being commercially aware is extremely important as, in many cases, the client will be uninterested in the strict legal answer and will want a solution that caters for the commercial pressures and circumstances. It is often our job to juggle commercial pressures with getting the law right and ensuring that our clients' position is properly protected.

Day-to-day work

Every day is different; on any given day a junior litigation solicitor is likely to handle a number of claims at different stages of progression.

For example, you might be preparing for a collision liability hearing where the Admiralty Court will decide the percentage of blame between two ships involved in a collision. This could involve drafting pleadings or reviewing counsel's drafts, drafting witness statements, and working with experts. It might also involve preparing court bundles. You might review an initial incoming claim for clients – for example, a claim for damages for delay (known as demurrage) after a ship has been delayed in port. You might be asked to write an advice on the merits of defending a cargo claim received by a ship owner. You are likely to be liaising with lawyers and experts abroad – perhaps taking a supervisory role in relation to proceedings abroad, particularly where there are high-value and multiple claims following a significant incident. You might also be dealing with an urgent casualty – mobilising an in-house Master Mariner to attend on board the ship and interview the relevant crew members. The solicitor usually takes the desk role and co-ordinates the process, fielding information, analysing press articles, sending reports to clients and taking a bird's eye view.

Some claims will be busy and substantial, whereas others may be small or perhaps slow moving. This means that there is often a lot of variety in the work you are doing. On smaller claims, trainee solicitors can take on more responsibility. As trainees become more experienced and develop the tools of their trade, they will tend to take on an increased number of cases and handle higher value or more complicated disputes.

INCE & CO | INTERNATIONAL LAW FIRM

Ince & Co

With 140 years of experience, Ince & Co is one of the oldest law firms in the City. Thanks to a world-leading reputation initially built on shipping and insurance, over the decades the firm has successfully explored new territory and established expertise across a number of other related industries, including aviation, energy and offshore and international trade. Ince & Co is a truly international firm with offices in Beijing, Dubai, Hamburg, Hong Kong, Le Havre, London, Monaco, Paris, Piraeus, Shanghai and Singapore.

The firm has up to six places available on both its 2018 trainee intake and its 2016 trainee recruitment placement scheme.

For further information about the firm, please see p230.
Website: http://graduates.incelaw.com

The Lex 100 Winners

The best-performing firms from the 2016 trainee survey

The Lex 100 Winners – methodology

Which firm offers the best quality of work? Which is the most stress-free? And where will you get to deal with real walking, talking clients? Our tables show the **Lex 100 Winners** – the highest scoring firms in each of our thirteen categories, as rated by their trainees.

Methodology
For the purposes of this section, we took the twenty highest average scores in each survey category to produce our tables.

Because the difference in scores between the firms was sometimes negligible, full average scores are shown here, e.g. 87.6, rather than the rounded-up scores (88%) which appear in the main section of the book. Even so, some firms received exactly the same score, so their position in the table is equal, and in some instances the tables therefore have more than twenty firms.

When assessing the tables we performed recommended statistical tests to ensure that the analysis was valid, representative and robust. We used our professional judgement to exclude what we perceived to be outlying or unrepresentative elements in the data.

Readers should also be aware that our survey covered a very wide range of firms, from global giants with hundreds of trainees to niche and regional firms with only a handful of trainees, so in these tables we are not attempting to compare like with like. If readers wish to do this (e.g. to compare scores for work/life balance at the Magic Circle firms), they should refer to the scores on the individual firms' pages.

Also see page 87 for the full survey methodology.

Job satisfaction

How would you rate your overall job satisfaction?

Nockolds Solicitors	91.5
Debevoise & Plimpton LLP	91.3
Farrer & Co	90.4
Foot Anstey LLP	89.7
Michelmores LLP	89.7
Blaser Mills	88.4
Woodfines LLP	87.9
Royds Withy King	87.4
Forsters LLP	87.0
Arnold & Porter (UK) LLP	87.0
Osborne Clarke	86.8
Cooley (UK) LLP	86.3
Hodge Jones & Allen LLP	86.1
Anthony Collins Solicitors	85.8
Burges Salmon	85.5
Taylor Wessing LLP	85.2
Eversheds LLP	85.1
Holman Fenwick Willan	85.1
Roythornes Solicitors	85.1
Shoosmiths LLP	85.0

Analysis

The three leading firms in this category couldn't be more diverse, demonstrating that job satisfaction means many different things to different people. Working at Hertfordshire's **Nockolds Solicitors** 'feels like being part of a large family' and trainees are 'encouraged to carry out a lot of work at an early stage'. Trainees at US firm **Debevoise & Plimpton** have a 'higher level of responsibility, make a significant contribution, are valued and treated with respect', while the current cohort at **Farrer & Co** 'feel very lucky' and enjoy 'better hours, friendlier people and more interesting work' then some of their peers. **Foot Anstey**'s trainees 'aren't just a number and get to play a vital role in transactions', with one stating: 'I'm always left thinking I made the right choice'. Similarly, the current intake at **Michelmores** is 'given much more significant responsibility and encouraged to develop our professional career in many different ways'. At **Blaser Mills** the 'working hours are balanced and there is a lot of client contact, which is great'. Also scoring highly for job satisfaction are Cambridge's **Woodfines**, where trainees experience 'varied and engaging seats' and **Royds Withy King**, which provides 'good exposure and client contact'. The training at **Forsters** compares 'fantastically' with other firms as one trainee says 'some friends even envy the experience I am having', and at **Arnold & Porter** 'even the busiest partners will make time to sit down with you and discuss your work'.

Firm living up to expectations

How far has the firm lived up to your expectations?

Farrer & Co	92.6
Blaser Mills	92.4
Kingsley Napley LLP	91.6
Nockolds Solicitors	91.5
Debevoise & Plimpton LLP	91.3
Foot Anstey LLP	90.4
Osborne Clarke	90.3
Michelmores LLP	89.7
Taylor Wessing LLP	89.7
Burges Salmon	88.8
Cooley (UK) LLP	88.8
Forsters LLP	88.7
Cartmell Shepherd	88.0
Birketts LLP	87.7
Payne Hicks Beach	87.2
Covington & Burling LLP	87.2
Boyes Turner	87.2
Shoosmiths LLP	87.2
Arnold & Porter (UK) LLP	87.0
Eversheds LLP	86.8

Analysis

Law firms invest a great deal of time and money into attracting the best candidates, producing glossy brochures and snazzy websites to project their image. But does the picture painted equate to reality? On the whole, yes, particularly among the leading firms in this category. Many of the trainees at long-established **Farrer & Co** chose the firm for its 'top-class reputation' and have not been disappointed, particularly in respect of quality of work, clients and training, while at **Blaser Mills**, trainees have found that the welcoming atmosphere and friendliness of staff permeates right through the firm. Trainees at **Kingsley Napley** describe a 'friendly, inclusive atmosphere' where 'office doors are open, including those of the partners', while those starting at **Nockolds Solicitors** have found 'the glowing review given by current trainees' has lived up to expectations. **Debevoise & Plimpton** is a 'very friendly firm, doing world-class work in some interesting areas'; **Foot Anstey** is 'very aspirational and this came across in its marketing and graduate recruitment materials'; and **Osborne Clarke** 'really does live up to everything it claimed to be – a very friendly firm, with big ambitions and really exciting work'. Promises of client contact, responsibility, 'City-type work' and work/life balance made by **Michelmores** 'came across as something the firm had committed to rather than just being marketing and it has all been true', says one trainee. **Taylor Wessing** 'prides itself on being an innovative, forward-thinking and efficient law firm which was appealing and is actually engrained in everyday life', while at **Burges Salmon** 'everyone I met was very 'human' and it has remained this way throughout'.

Quality of work

How would you rate the quality of work you are given?

Blaser Mills	93.4
Debevoise & Plimpton LLP	91.3
Foot Anstey LLP	90.4
Farrer & Co	90.4
EMW Law LLP	90.3
Skadden, Arps, Slate, Meagher & Flom (UK) LLP	90.3
Akin Gump Strauss Hauer & Feld	90.2
Payne Hicks Beach	89.7
Osborne Clarke	89.1
Hodge Jones & Allen LLP	89.0
Sidley Austin LLP	88.9
Forbes Solicitors	88.7
Gateley Plc	88.4
Milbank, Tweed, Hadley & McCloy LLP	88.3
Michelmores LLP	88.3
Cartmell Shepherd	88.0
Cleary Gottlieb Steen & Hamilton	87.9
Kirkland & Ellis International LLP	87.5
Royds Withy King	87.4
Freeths	87.3
Burges Salmon	87.3

Analysis

Of all the factors to consider when choosing a training contract, work quality is key. Thankfully, tales of trainees chained to photocopiers for months on end are a thing of the past due to strict training guidelines for solicitors but, that said, firms do vary considerably in the type and amount of work given to trainees. Earning top spot in this category, **Blaser Mills** provides 'excellent opportunities to develop and grow both professionally and personally'. **Debevoise & Plimpton**'s 'trainees get involved and take a lead with certain work streams' and the work is 'interesting and sophisticated'. **Foot Anstey**'s trainees 'aren't just a number and get to play a vital role in transactions', while the current intake at **Farrer & Co** has 'more exposure to wider transactions and clients'. A trainee at **EMW Law** has 'the opportunity to run my own files and get involved in a lot of high profile, nitty-gritty work', and trainees at US firms **Skadden, Arps, Slate, Meagher & Flom** and **Akin Gump Strauss Hauer & Feld** report that 'most work requires actual thought and intelligent drafting' and 'there is a steep learning curve, but it's incredibly rewarding', respectively. **Payne Hicks Beach** scores highly for its 'better quality of work'; **Osborne Clarke** gives trainees 'plenty of responsibility and exciting projects to handle'; and at **Hodge Jones & Allen** the 'quality of work is extremely high'.

Client contact

How would you rate your amount of client contact?

Forbes Solicitors	94.4
Nockolds Solicitors	94.0
Spearing Waite LLP	92.1
Hodge Jones & Allen LLP	91.8
McMillan Williams	89.7
TLT	89.4
Warner Goodman LLP	89.3
Anthony Collins Solicitors	88.6
Mundays LLP	88.5
EMW Law LLP	87.4
Arnold & Porter (UK) LLP	87.0
Prettys	86.7
FBC Manby Bowdler LLP	86.2
Woodfines LLP	85.9
Blaser Mills	85.4
Penningtons Manches LLP	85.0
Kingsley Napley LLP	85.0
Mills & Reeve LLP	85.0
Blandy & Blandy LLP	84.8
Maples Teesdale LLP	84.7
Foot Anstey	84.7
Michelmores LLP	84.7

Analysis

Client contact is high on the wish list of many applicants and while the perception that large firms equate with less client exposure is not always true, our table does reveal that smaller firms score well in this category. **Forbes Solicitors** in the North West is 'local yet large enough to offer a good range of work' and we hear that dealing directly with clients 'makes me feel like the work is worthwhile'. Trainees at **Nockolds Solicitors** have 'much more client contact than some peers in other firms' and run their own files, while **Spearing Waite** encourages 'hands-on experience, lots of client contact and a lot more responsibility', as does **Hodge Jones & Allen**, where trainees are 'treated like adults' and given 'extremely high' levels of client contact, responsibility and supervision. When asked what the best thing is about **McMillan Williams**, trainees rate it as the 'level of exposure we are given in terms of client meetings, case work and responsibility'. Training highlights at national firm **TLT** have included 'being the primary contact for large clients' and 'being asked to pick up the phone to the client to advise them', while at **Warner Goodman** one responding trainee appreciated 'getting good feedback from my clients on my first file in my name'. At Birmingham-based **Anthony Collins Solicitors**, 'trainees often have their own caseload and deal with clients directly, which is something that sets the firm apart', and **Mundays**' trainees 'feel like part of a team – rather than a small cog'. One trainee at **EMW Law** had 'more client contact and responsibility than any other trainee I know'.

Stress levels

How stressful do you find your job?

Lester Aldridge LLP	76.4
Wilkin Chapman LLP	76.1
Riverview Law	73.7
Pemberton Greenish	72.5
Brabners LLP	72.2
Farrer & Co	71.9
SAS Daniels LLP	69.9
Baker & McKenzie LLP	69.7
Michelmores LLP	69.7
Reed Smith LLP	69.1
Nockolds Solicitors	69.0
Sullivan & Cromwell LLP	68.2
Foot Anstey LLP	67.6
Anthony Collins Solicitors	67.2
Stephens Scown LLP	67.0
Charles Russell Speechlys	66.9
Osborne Clarke	66.8
Birketts LLP	66.7
Skadden, Arps, Slate, Meagher & Flom (UK) LLP	66.5
Forbes Solicitors	65.8

Analysis

As with any well-paid profession, it is inevitable that life as a lawyer will bring its share of stress from time to time; but as a trainee, this should be limited to rare occasions of deadline pressure, or an approaching hearing, for example, and not a constant state of anxiety. Trainees are employed to learn and develop, not to provide cheap labour and carry the weight of a legal matter on their shoulders. All the firms listed in this category scored highly for lack of stress and comprehensive support. **Lester Aldridge**, for example, has a 'great learning process' and 'colleagues are always here to provide help and guidance whilst also allowing freedom to do and learn'. At **Wilkin Chapman**, the 'standard of work is good, and the stress levels are far better than at other firms', while the 'classic levels of stress and pressure definitely don't exist' at **Riverview Law**, where 'support is never-ending'. **Pemberton Greenish** stands out for 'friendliness and the supportiveness of staff' and **Brabners** is praised for its 'shorter hours and less stressful, friendlier and more relaxed environment'. Trainees at **Farrer & Co** welcome the 'top-class training' and 'partner supervision and availability which is great here'; **SAS Daniels** provides 'more time with partners' and trainees 'feel much more relaxed and at ease assisting a partner with their work' as well as running their own files. **Baker & McKenzie** 'gives you a lot more responsibility and support as a trainee to help you develop as a lawyer'. Trainees at **Michelmores** report a 'friendly, encouraging and genuinely helpful environment', while **Reed Smith** is also reported to have a 'close-knit team environment'.

Work/life balance

How happy are you with your work/life balance?

Nockolds Solicitors	**94.0**
Anthony Collins Solicitors	**92.9**
Thomas Cooper LLP	**91.7**
Riverview Law	**91.4**
Lester Aldridge LLP	**91.4**
RadcliffesLeBrasseur	**90.5**
Coffin Mew LLP	**89.8**
Forsters LLP	**89.5**
Foot Anstey LLP	**89.0**
Prettys	**88.4**
Collyer Bristow LLP	**87.5**
Blandy & Blandy LLP	**87.3**
Spearing Waite LLP	**87.1**
Mundays LLP	**86.8**
Royds Withy King	**86.4**
Pitmans LLP	**85.9**
K&L Gates LLP	**85.9**
Pemberton Greenish	**85.9**
Thrings LLP	**85.6**
Farrer & Co	**85.4**
Wilsons	**85.4**

Analysis

While some trainees thrive on the typically long hours of City work (and the high pay that goes with it), many others seek a balance between their work and play. Although some firms do promote respectable working hours, the very nature of legal work means that it is not a nine-to-five profession. However, firms scoring highly in this category do not demand persistent unsocial hours, such as **Nockolds Solicitors**, which repeatedly receives a 'glowing review' in this regard; **Anthony Collins Solicitors**, which has 'better working hours' than some rivals; and **Thomas Cooper**, where 'our hours are excellent – we're usually out of the office by 6-6.30pm'. Other firms earning praise include **Riverview Law**, which is a 'fun and relaxed place to work and offers an excellent work/life balance' and **Lester Aldridge**, where several trainees cite the firm's work/life balance as the reason for joining the firm. At **RadcliffesLeBrasseur**, 'there is a culture of hard work but trainees and other fee earners will rarely still be in the office after 6.30pm' and similarly, **Coffin Mew** has 'very good hours – I can leave at 5pm if I want to'. One of the few London-headquartered firms in our top-ten, **Forsters** provides an 'excellent balance between the City and working at a provincial firm' in that it 'offers interesting and important work while at the same time allowing employees to have a good work/life balance'. **Foot Anstey** has a 'genuine focus on work/life balance for its employees' and East Anglia's **Prettys** gives trainees a 'high level of responsibility whilst also maintaining a good work/life balance'.

Friendliness of the firm

How would you rate the friendliness of the firm?

Birketts LLP	**96.7**
Osborne Clarke	**96.4**
Debevoise & Plimpton LLP	**96.3**
Foot Anstey LLP	**96.2**
Farrer & Co	**96.1**
Gateley Plc	**95.5**
Blaser Mills	**95.4**
Royds Withy King	**95.4**
Trethowans LLP	**95.1**
Eversheds LLP	**94.9**
Spearing Waite LLP	**94.6**
Forsters LLP	**94.5**
Bird & Bird LLP	**94.3**
Bristows LLP	**94.3**
Nockolds Solicitors	**94.0**
Michelmores LLP	**94.0**
Woodfines LLP	**93.9**
Riverview Law	**93.7**
Travers Smith LLP	**93.6**
Sullivan & Cromwell LLP	**93.2**

Analysis

It doesn't matter how high the salary, prestige of the clients or quality of work, a pleasant working environment is key to enjoying your career and the 'camaraderie vibe' of a firm should not be overlooked. Topping the league in this category, trainees at **Birketts** consistently cite 'friendliness' as a key reason for joining the firm, which has a 'genuinely friendly culture in all four offices'. **Osborne Clarke** scores highly for its 'friendly, open culture' and 'the open-plan office really sculpts and shapes the firm's attitude – there's little hierarchy'. **Debevoise & Plimpton** trainees highlight the 'very friendly people' and 'whilst clearly exceptional lawyers, they are all very approachable', as are colleagues at **Foot Anstey**, which boasts 'friendly and down-to-earth lawyers who are very forthcoming'. Despite a prestigious client base at **Farrer & Co** (including royalty), trainees have found it an 'incredibly friendly firm from the offset' where 'trainees and fee-earners treat each other with respect'. National firm **Gateley Plc** has a 'great reputation as a firm with a friendly working environment' and similarly, **Blaser Mills** is 'a friendly firm with an open-door policy'. One trainee chose South West firm **Royds Withy King** because it 'didn't just claim its culture was friendly – it actually is and trainees are given a lot of support'. **Trethowans** is 'a very friendly place to work' and 'it is great to know that there is no such thing as a silly question', while **Eversheds** is praised for 'the value it places on individuals, no matter what their role is within the firm' and it is said to be a 'very 'unstuffy' law firm'.

Social life

How good is your firm's social life?

Nockolds Solicitors	**94.0**
Leathes Prior	**90.1**
Boyes Turner	**89.7**
Burges Salmon	**89.4**
Gateley Plc	**88.4**
Jones Day	**87.7**
Travers Smith LLP	**87.7**
Freeths	**87.7**
Burness Paull LLP	**87.6**
Spearing Waite LLP	**87.1**
Cooley (UK) LLP	**86.3**
Michelmores LLP	**86.1**
Farrer & Co	**86.1**
Bird & Bird LLP	**85.9**
Baker & McKenzie LLP	**85.0**
Muckle LLP	**84.4**
Devonshires Solicitors LLP	**84.3**
Forsters LLP	**83.7**
Forbes Solicitors	**83.0**
RPC	**82.5**

Analysis

Of course, all work and no play makes for an unhappy trainee. Most law firms appreciate the business benefits of a collegiate workforce who bond over a vol-au-vent and glass of prosecco once in a while. Some firms provide a raft of regular social opportunities, whether for business development purposes or just for staff morale, while at others there is little but the events trainees organise themselves. **Nockolds Solicitors** leads the way once again, this time for its 'great social events', while **Leathes Prior** provides 'good additional training opportunities as well as lots of social events and activities to get involved in'. **Boyes Turner** is 'more social and friendly' than others, say trainees; **Burges Salmon** is 'really good at offering social events, sporting activities and weekends away, etc'; and **Gateley Plc** has a 'strong social and charitable aspect'. At **Jones Day**, the 'best thing about the firm is the social life: it is great here if you want to work hard and play harder', while fellow City firm **Travers Smith** is a 'more sociable place than most'. National firm **Freeths** attracts praise as a 'particularly social firm' that provides 'good exposure to networking events', while Scotland's **Burness Paull** has 'more firm-organised social events' – 'my friends are jealous of where I am', states a current trainee. Concluding the top ten is Leicester's **Spearing Waite**, where 'the firm's dedication and loyalty to its staff is exceptional'.

Vacation schemes

If you did a vacation scheme with your firm, how would you rate it?

Forsters LLP	98.7
Burges Salmon	97.6
Roythornes Solicitors	96.7
Nabarro LLP	96.6
Sullivan & Cromwell LLP	94.8
Cleary Gottlieb Steen & Hamilton	94.8
Farrer & Co	94.7
Covington & Burling LLP	94.7
Boyes Turner	94.7
Gowling WLG	94.1
Osborne Clarke	94.0
Debevoise & Plimpton LLP	93.3
Jones Day	92.6
Latham & Watkins	92.4
Wedlake Bell LLP	92.4
Travers Smith LLP	92.3
Blaser Mills	91.7
Bird & Bird LLP	91.7
Milbank, Tweed, Hadley & McCloy LLP	91.7
Pinsent Masons LLP	91.6
Baker & McKenzie LLP	91.6

Analysis

The quality of vacation schemes varies wildly across the market, with some deployed to showcase a firm and others used to directly source future trainees. Certainly, the more vacation schemes you can bag, the greater your ability to choose the right firm or, indeed, discover whether a legal career is really for you. The firms listed here all stood out for the quality of their vac schemes. The scheme at **Forsters** provided a 'good sense that it was a very friendly firm with a decent level of training and a good work/life balance' and one trainee 'knew by lunchtime that day that it was the place for me'. A respondent from **Burges Salmon** 'thoroughly enjoyed the vacation scheme and all contact with the firm during the recruitment process' while a trainee at **Roythornes Solicitors** chose the firm due to the 'overwhelmingly positive experience I had on the vacation scheme'. **Nabarro** lived up to its 'really friendly, down-to-earth reputation on the summer scheme'; **Sullivan & Cromwell** 'stood out' during its vacation scheme 'as having an incredibly friendly environment with extremely smart people that I wanted to learn from'; and trainees at **Cleary Gottlieb Steen & Hamilton** 'enjoyed the vac scheme the most' compared to others. **Farrer & Co** draws praise for the 'genuine work given, even as a vac scheme student' and **Covington & Burling**'s current cohort 'really enjoyed' their vacation scheme, as did trainees at **Boyes Turner**. National heavyweight **Gowling WLG** was chosen by several trainees following an impressive vac scheme, which conveyed the 'friendly and unstuffy' culture of the firm.

Confident of being kept on

How confident are you that you will be kept on at the end of your training contract?

Michelmores LLP	91.9
Sullivan & Cromwell LLP	91.5
Burges Salmon	90.6
Riverview Law	90.3
Weil, Gotshal & Manges	89.8
TLT	88.2
Bristows LLP	88.2
Slaughter and May	88.1
Latham & Watkins	87.8
Kirkland & Ellis International LLP	87.5
Linklaters LLP	86.2
White & Case LLP	85.6
Lester Aldridge LLP	85.4
Herbert Smith Freehills LLP	85.3
Forbes Solicitors	84.4
Debevoise & Plimpton LLP	84.3
Covington & Burling LLP	84.3
Farrer & Co	84.0
Coffin Mew LLP	83.8
Foot Anstey LLP	83.6

Analysis

You've only just cleared the hurdle of gaining a training contract and survived your first few weeks as a trainee, when thoughts soon turn to the likelihood of a job offer on qualification. It is notoriously difficult to predict the newly qualified (NQ) retention rates of firms when selecting a training contract because they are so dependent on a firm's future business needs and the economic climate. However, current trainees at **Michelmores** 'feel passionate about the opportunities for the future', while those at **Sullivan & Cromwell** highlight the investment the firm makes in each trainee. **Burges Salmon** trainees cite the firm's 'encouraging retention rate' as a reason for choosing it, and at law and compliance firm **Riverview Law** trainees are eligible for its Leadership Programme which trains future managers of the firm. The retention rates and 'excellent long-term career prospects' are factors for choosing **Weil, Gotshal & Manges** and at **TLT** trainees feel they have 'better prospects of being kept on' compared to peers at other firms. **Bristows** 'all but guarantees a job offer on qualification', says one trainee, while the 'future career opportunities' is another good reason for choosing **Slaughter and May**. **Latham & Watkins'** trainees report that they feel invested in, particularly in respect of overseas opportunities including retreats, client interaction and secondments. At fellow US firm **Kirkland & Ellis**, trainees are 'treated like an NQ' and given the 'opportunity to carve out your career', while the firm has a 'serious commitment to junior lawyers'.

Financial remuneration

How satisfied are you with your financial remuneration?

Sullivan & Cromwell LLP	94.8
Latham & Watkins	93.5
Cooley (UK) LLP	92.9
Kirkland & Ellis International LLP	91.3
White & Case LLP	90.6
Skadden, Arps, Slate, Meagher & Flom (UK) LLP	90.3
Milbank, Tweed, Hadley & McCloy LLP	90.0
Weil, Gotshal & Manges	89.8
Burges Salmon	89.4
Gibson, Dunn & Crutcher LLP	88.9
Cleary Gottlieb Steen & Hamilton	88.8
Osborne Clarke	88.7
Morgan, Lewis & Bockius	88.5
O'Melveny	87.5
Shearman & Sterling LLP	87.2
Covington & Burling LLP	87.2
Arnold & Porter (UK) LLP	87.0
Allen & Overy	86.7
Sidley Austin LLP	86.4
Hogan Lovells International LLP	86.4

Analysis

It's no surprise that the US-based international firms dominate our top-ten in this category, with US firms in London paying as much as 40% more to newly-qualified solicitors than UK counterparts. There is more to life than the dollar, but if remuneration is what motivates you, consider a training contract at **Sullivan & Cromwell**, where 'our pay is better' than rivals, or perhaps **Latham & Watkins**, where there are 'longer hours, but higher pay and more responsibility given' compared to some other City firms. At **Cooley** 'the remuneration is very generous and we recently received a salary increase', while at **Kirkland & Ellis International**, trainees cite pay and friendliness among the best attributes of the firm. The training contract at **White & Case** is popular for its international opportunities and 'good salaries for trainees', while many choose **Skadden, Arps, Slate, Meagher & Flom** for its 'reputation, quality of work, small trainee intake and good qualification salary'. **Milbank, Tweed, Hadley & McCloy** has the 'best overall package' and **Weil, Gotshal & Manges** offers 'higher remuneration, a smaller intake and cutting-edge work'. The only non-US origin firm in our top ten is Bristol-headquartered **Burges Salmon**, rated as the 'best firm outside London in terms of quality of work, remuneration and location' and just clinching a top-ten place this year is **Gibson, Dunn & Crutcher**.

Diversity

How would you rate the level of diversity at your firm?

Debevoise & Plimpton LLP	96.3
Baker & McKenzie LLP	94.5
Covington & Burling LLP	92.9
Osborne Clarke	92.6
Latham & Watkins	91.6
Sullivan & Cromwell LLP	91.5
Forsters LLP	91.2
Eversheds LLP	91.1
SAS Daniels LLP	90.9
Michelmores LLP	90.4
Birketts LLP	90.4
Anthony Collins Solicitors	90.1
Woodfines LLP	89.9
PwC	89.8
Foot Anstey LLP	89.7
Pinsent Masons LLP	89.4
Bristows LLP	88.9
Forbes Solicitors	88.7
Akin Gump Strauss Hauer & Feld	88.5
Milbank, Tweed, Hadley & McCloy LLP	88.3
Farrer & Co	88.3

Analysis

The legal profession continues to be heavily criticised for a lack of diversity among professional staff, despite initiatives that span back as far as the last decade. Efforts to recruit trainees from all ethnic groups and social classes have been ramped up in recent years since major clients began to list diversity and social responsibility among criteria when choosing their legal providers. **Debevoise & Plimpton** leads the way in this category and is widely praised by trainees for its friendliness and inclusivity. At global giant **Baker & McKenzie**, trainees chose the firm because it 'gave applicants of whatever background an equal chance' and for its 'LGBT diversity'. Highlights of working at **Covington & Burling** include its 'unique personalities and diversity' and 'friendly and inclusive environment'; and likewise, **Osborne Clarke** boasts a 'very open and inclusive environment'. At **Latham & Watkins**, the 'genuinely nice people to work with' are 'very friendly, approachable and inclusive' and **Sullivan & Cromwell** and **Forsters** are also praised by trainees for similar attributes. **Eversheds** 'genuinely lives up to its claim of being a workplace that values its staff and has been successful in fostering a positive attitude towards inclusiveness at all levels'. North West firm **SAS Daniels** stands out, say trainees, for friendliness and collegiate culture, while **Michelmores** is 'very friendly and inclusive, and just a nice place to work'.

International secondments

How would you rate the international secondment opportunities available?

Holman Fenwick Willan	96.7
White & Case LLP	96.1
Watson Farley & Williams LLP	95.4
Sullivan & Cromwell LLP	93.2
Herbert Smith Freehills LLP	92.2
Thomas Cooper LLP	91.7
Baker & McKenzie LLP	89.7
Cleary Gottlieb Steen & Hamilton	88.8
Stephenson Harwood	87.8
CMS Cameron McKenna LLP	87.4
Eversheds LLP	86.8
DLA Piper UK LLP	84.6
Norton Rose Fulbright	84.6
Morgan, Lewis & Bockius	84.5
Latham & Watkins	82.0
Trowers & Hamlins LLP	81.8
Vinson & Elkins RLLP	78.9
Hogan Lovells International LLP	78.1
Shearman & Sterling LLP	77.2
Freshfields Bruckhaus Deringer LLP	77.0

Analysis

The opportunity to work overseas can be the holy grail for many prospective trainees and without doubt it is a huge selling point for UK and US-based firms with a growing network of international offices. Note however, that an address list the size of the Eurovision Song Contest does not guarantee secondments to all offices, just certain key destinations, if at all. At **Holman Fenwick Willan**, 'the international opportunities are second-to-none' and trainee secondment abroad is 'guaranteed', as it is at **White & Case**, where the 'truly global profile of the firm is very attractive and the guaranteed foreign seat is a fantastic opportunity'. The 'international scope' of **Watson Farley & Williams** is of significant appeal and those who have completed an international seat found it 'fantastic – made to feel part of the team from day one and given increased responsibility'. **Sullivan & Cromwell**'s trainees' highlights to date include 'finding out that I get to go to the New York office on secondment' and at **Herbert Smith Freehills** trainees appreciate the 'international opportunities and work in emerging markets and Africa'. Trainees at shipping firm **Thomas Cooper** describe their international seats as 'amazing' and 'an excellent personal and professional experience', while at global heavyweight **Baker & McKenzie** there is 'great exposure to international work that is beneficial for my profile' and in a 'great variety of potential locations'. **Cleary Gottlieb Steen & Hamilton** and **Stephenson Harwood** offer an 'international dimension' and 'very appealing overseas secondments' respectively, while at **CMS Cameron McKenna**, trainees report that 'gaining experience in a foreign office of the firm was a great experience, both culturally and in terms of technical development'.

The Lex 100 survey

The 2016 survey of trainees at law firms

The Lex 100 survey – methodology

We sent online surveys to graduate recruitment managers at the UK's largest law firms. 173 successfully took part and distributed our survey to their trainees. Once again, we had a fantastic response and ended up with over 3,000 completed surveys, which provided us with a particularly robust sample to analyse. The data from the surveys was processed and analysed by the editor of this publication.

We asked current trainees to rate their firm with a score from 0 to 10 (10 being the best possible score) in thirteen different categories:

1   Satisfied in your job?
2   Firm living up to expectations?
3   High quality of work?
4   Enough client contact?
5   Stress-free?
6   Happy work/life balance?
7   Friendly firm?
8   Great social life?
9   Good vacation scheme?
10   Confident you'll being kept on?
11   Good remuneration?
12   Diverse firm?
13   Good international secondments?

When assessing the responses, we analysed the data against market norms and performed recommended statistical tests to ensure the analysis was valid, representative and robust. We used our professional judgement to exclude what we perceived to be outlying or unrepresentative elements in the data.

We then gave each firm a score out of one hundred for each category, based on the average score from the total trainees' responses. These scores are shown alongside 'The Lex 100 verdict', where we piece together trainee responses to compile an overview of the feedback offered.

We also asked the trainees for more detailed information about their experiences and their firm under the headings:

1   Why did you choose this firm over any others?
2   Best thing about the firm?
3   Worst thing about the firm?
4   Best moments of your training?
5   Worst moment of your training?

A representative sample of what the trainees' answers is found on the second page of the featured firm profiles.

In keeping with Lex tradition, we also asked respondents which fictional character their firm would be. We were really happy to receive some creative and amusing answers to this question, which range from Albus Dumbledore to Yoda! For each firm we have tried to name the character most frequently mentioned together with the comments which seemed most representative of the firm in question. This is of course just a bit of fun and we hope that both firms and candidates will take it in the spirit intended!

This section is split into two parts, with the first tranche of firms providing valuable additional information including the application process, vacation schemes, and key firm stats.

Please also head to **lex100.com** for instant access to these firms' application forms.

The Lex 100 survey

Featured firms:
extended profiles

Addleshaw Goddard LLP

Milton Gate, 60 Chiswell Street, London EC1Y 4AG

Survey results *(marks out of 100%)*

Satisfied in your job?	79
Firm living up to expectations?	83
High quality of work?	78
Enough client contact?	74
Stress-free?	55
Happy work/life balance?	67
Friendly firm?	88
Great social life?	77
Good vacation scheme?	81
Confident you'll be kept on?	80
Good remuneration?	64
Diverse firm?	84
Good international secondments?	64

 verdict

Addleshaw Goddard is a 'national mid-tier firm with great clients', and is praised by trainees for offering 'good-quality work coupled with a better work/life balance than at comparable firms'. Elaborating on the latter point, respondents cited the firm's 'respect for family life and support for colleagues with children', adding that 'HR is really accommodating'. Some of the current trainee cohort were former mature students and paralegals, and the firm earns plaudits for considering 'non-standard trainees'. As for the quality of work, feedback suggests that trainees are entrusted with 'complex and high-value cases'. Examples of recent work include 'representing a FTSE 100 company in an international arbitration', 'being involved in the Berezovsky estate settlement discussions' and 'playing a relatively major role on a £100m+ transaction'. Though mentioned less frequently, some complaints are reserved for trainees being used as 'an additional clerical resource', and instances of 'file admin' and 'bundling until midnight' do occur. Despite the 'friendliness of the staff', there are additional grumbles about the 'lack of organised social events for trainees'. However, trainees laud Addleshaw Goddard's pro bono credentials, as 'the charity committee puts on various events and fundraisers which people tend to get behind'. Respondents identify a confidence among those working at the firm. One cites the 'ambitions for future growth' as a deciding factor in choosing to join Addleshaw Goddard, while another mentions colleagues' 'belief in the firm and the direction it's going in'. To embark upon a training contract at a national firm that has 'an excellent reputation, and lives up to it', apply to Addleshaw Goddard.

If the firm were a fictional character it would be...

The Flash (DC Comics) – goes above and beyond to get the job done but still knows how to have fun

The firm

Addleshaw Goddard possesses an impressive client base, routinely representing FTSE 100 companies. The firm has offices in London, Leeds and Manchester as well is in the major international business hubs of Singapore, Dubai, Doha, Muscat and Hong Kong. Sector focuses include energy, financial services and property. Addleshaw Goddard posted a 5% rise in revenue for 2015/16.

The deals

Handled a significant amount of work for British Airways, including advising it on the wet lease of two Boeing 737-700 aircraft from Danish airline Jet Time; advised KPMG as administrators of De Stefano Property Group, including facilitating the sale of a large property portfolio to Catalyst Capital; advised Hitachi Rail Europe on First Great Western's procurement of rolling stock for the West of England; led for Peel Group on the sale of a 50% investment in MediaCityUK to Legal & General; acted for Alix Partners as administrators of a care home group on the sale of three care homes based in North Wales.

The clients

Adidas; Advance Global Capital; Department for Transport; HSBC; Harper Collins; Laing O'Rourke; Nationwide; Tata Chemicals; Vueling; West Bromwich Building Society.

The star performers

Top-ranking departments according to *The Legal 500* (see legal500.com for more details)
Banking and finance; Banking litigation; Construction; Corporate and commercial; Corporate tax; Education; Employment; Energy; Health; IT and telecoms; Insolvency and corporate recovery; Intellectual property; Local government; Media and entertainment; Pensions; Personal tax, trusts and probate; Professional negligence: claimant; Project finance and PFI; Property litigation; Transport.

- **Why did you choose this firm over any others?** 'I wanted to work for a leading law firm based in Leeds'; 'had a reputation for giving trainees quality work'; 'I thoroughly enjoyed the vacation scheme'; 'quality of client base'; 'friendly environment'; 'increased international opportunities'; 'the non-hierarchical structure'; 'genuinely nice people who are invested in your progression'; 'good level of responsibility'; 'the down-to-earth attitude of all the people I encountered'; 'reputation in the market'

- **Best thing about the firm?** 'The collegiate atmosphere'; 'good set of clients'; 'people are nice'; 'friendly and open atmosphere'; 'the open-plan office means you have good relationships with colleagues in various teams and at various levels'; 'the culture is genuinely open and friendly'; 'headline clients'; 'the people'; 'high-profile work'; 'exposure to interesting variety of work'; 'wide availability of junior support'

- **Worst thing about the firm?** 'The volume of graduate recruitment events trainees are expected to organise'; 'induction training'; 'IT systems'; 'departments can be quite separate from one another'; 'seat move process'; 'the social aspects could be better – we work well together but don't invest in team-building'; 'working London hours for regional salary'; 'limited international secondment opportunities'

- **Best moment?** 'Working on real estate finance'; 'getting to go to court to see a trial I have worked on'; 'being trusted to run matters independently'; 'completing the final tranche of sales on an international transaction'; 'going on secondment to our Hong Kong office'; 'running completions by myself'; 'working on a big case that was all over the news, and knowing the outcome before the press'

- **Worst moment?** 'Bibling'; 'the few all-nighters in corporate were a bit of a low point'; 'having my requests to gain experience of particular types of work ignored'; 'the first few weeks' settling in period'; 'seat move disappointment'; 'poorly delivered external PSC courses'; 'working on a Sunday'; 'finding out I had forgotten to send an urgent email'

A day in the life of...

... Chris Reardon trainee, Addleshaw Goddard LLP

Departments to date: Infrastructure, projects and energy; commercial and business support and restructuring

University: York   **Degree and class:** English literature 2(1)

9.15am: I arrive in the office and check my emails with a cup of coffee. I draw up two to-do lists – one prioritising tasks for the day and another with tasks for the week.

9.30am: I am currently working on a deal for the sale of a large solar power farm for one of our clients. I dial in to a conference call with our client and the buyers, to give an update on the progress we have made in relation to the share purchase agreement. I take notes to record any action points that will require my attention following the call – this time it is ensuring that the buyer receives a 'punch list' (a list of tasks that need to be completed to satisfy the terms of a construction contract) ahead of a site visit the following week.

11.15am: I attend a training session being led by one of our partners who specialises in rail infrastructure projects. The training meeting is one of a series of meetings to provide updates on the sorts of legal and regulatory issues our key clients in the rail sector face.

12.30pm: I head down to the AG restaurant to grab some lunch with the other trainees. This is always a good opportunity to find out about what is going on elsewhere in the firm.

1.15pm: Back at my desk, I check my emails and see that an agreement relating to a big deal which is due to complete next week has been finalised. I update my index of documents to be produced for the completion accordingly, making a note of which contracts have yet to be agreed by both parties and are not ready to be added to the suite of final documents. I update my supervisor on the progress and instruct our print room to produce bound engrossments of the contract, ready for signing and dating.

2.30pm: I have some post-completion tasks from a deal that completed a few weeks ago. I use the index of completion documents to put together a list of contracts and supporting documents to go into an e-bible for each party. I then send this off to my PA who produces a contents page using my list and instructs our print room to produce the bibles.

3.30pm: I am offered the chance to accompany one of our partners in the team to a client meeting. The purpose of the meeting is to negotiate some terms of a crucial project document with the other side and their lawyers via conference call. I take notes on the outcome of each point, recording which are resolved and which require further attention. After the call, we discuss the outcome of the negotiation with the client. I then produce a note summarising the meeting and circulate it to the members of our team involved.

5.30pm: I receive the e-bibles I requested and check them for accuracy, before sending them out to the client and the other side via courier.

6.00pm: Following my visit to AG's weekly pro bono legal advice centre, which I volunteer at once a month, I produce a letter to the housing department of a local council on behalf of one of our visitors. I email the letter

> 'The training meeting is to provide updates on the sorts of legal and regulatory issues our key clients in the rail sector face.'

across to the visitor for their approval and sign off prior to posting, with an update on their case to date.

6.45pm: With all my major jobs for the day complete, I record my time and head out. I join some friends in a nearby pub for a drink, before heading home.

http://graduates.addleshawgoddard.com

About the firm

Address: Milton Gate, 60 Chiswell Street, London EC1Y 4AG
Telephone: 020 7606 8855
Website: www.addleshawgoddard.com/en
Email: graduate@addleshawgoddard.com
Twitter: @AGgrads

Senior partner: Charles Penney
Managing partner: John Joyce

Other offices: Dubai, Hong Kong, Japan, Leeds, Manchester, Oman, Qatar, Singapore.

Who we are: Addleshaw Goddard is a premium business law firm with international reach and exceptional breadth of services.

What we do: Addleshaw Goddard is a leading advisor to FTSE 100 companies across its business divisions – corporate and commercial, finance and projects, litigation, real estate and international.

What we're looking for: Graduates who are capable of achieving a 2(1) and can demonstrate commercial awareness, teamwork, motivation and drive. Applications from law and non-law graduates are welcomed.

What you'll do: During each six-month seat there will be regular two-way performance reviews with the supervising partner or solicitor. Trainees may have the opportunity to spend a seat in one of the firm's other offices and there are a number of secondments to clients available.

Perks: Gym membership, season ticket loan, subsidised restaurant, pension and private healthcare.

Sponsorship: GDL and LPC fees are paid, plus a maintenance grant of £7,000 (London) or £4,500 (elsewhere in the UK).

Facts and figures

Total partners: 177
Other fee-earners: 620
Total trainees: 70

Trainee places available for 2019: 30
Applications received pa: 2,000
Percentage interviewed: 20%

First year salary: £37,000 (London), £25,000 (Leeds and Manchester)

Turnover in 2015: £192.5m (+12% from 2014)
Profits per equity partner: £491,000 (+26%)
(see legalbusiness.co.uk for full financial information)

Application process

Apply to: Samantha Hill – graduate resourcing advisor.
How: Online application form via website.
When: By 31st July 2017 for 2019 contracts
What's involved: Application form, first stage interview and assessment centre

Vacation schemes
Spring/summer: Apply by 31 December 2016.

ADDLESHAW
GODDARD

Akin Gump Strauss Hauer & Feld

Eighth Floor, Ten Bishops Square, London E1 6EG

Lex 100 Winner

See categories below
and tables from page 69

Survey results *(marks out of 100%)*

Satisfied in your job?	82
Firm living up to expectations?	82
High quality of work?	(90)
Enough client contact?	74
Stress-free?	64
Happy work/life balance?	79
Friendly firm?	84
Great social life?	64
Good vacation scheme?	79
Confident you'll be kept on?	75
Good remuneration?	79
Diverse firm?	(89)
Good international secondments?	45

 **verdict**

This year marks Akin Gump Strauss Hauer & Feld's *Lex 100* survey debut. The US firm hired the majority of what was Bingham McCutchen's London office in 2014, including its trainees, and then added to this with the inauguration of its own training contract and the arrival of the first London trainee intake in September 2015. Respondents praise the firm's 'high-quality work' and 'reputation for excellence', while first-years cite the 'sector focus' and 'type of work' as major attractions, with one elaborating: 'I've always been interested in the financial side of law, and the firm's strength in financial restructuring drew me in'. The firm is a **Lex 100 Winner** in the diversity and work quality categories. The 'occasional long hours' are 'similar to other US and Magic Circle firms', and this can produce an 'expectation that, regardless of whether you are on holiday or it is the weekend, you are always in contact and ready to work'. To compensate for this is the 'top salary'. The 'small intake' leads to Akin Gump's trainees 'being treated in many respects as an associate from day one'. As a result 'there is a steep learning curve, but it is incredibly rewarding', as evidenced by highlight moments including 'being the client contact for a transaction', 'handling a complicated restructuring in Brazil almost single-handedly' and 'suggesting a new solution to an associate that was then used for a deal'. While 'being the most junior lawyer in a very high-calibre team is sometimes daunting', trainees appreciate that 'everyone is very welcoming' and they 'integrate into the teams very quickly'. To take on 'challenging work' while 'learning from some of the best people in their field', apply to Akin Gump Strauss Hauer & Feld.

If the firm were a fictional character it would be...

Jason Bourne – works under the radar, is the best at what it does and enjoys considerable autonomy from headquarters

The firm

Akin Gump's first London trainee intake arrived in September 2015, following the firm's City expansion. Headquartered in Washington D.C, Akin Gump has 20 offices across North America, Europe, the Middle East and Asia, and advises on a range of corporate and financial matters. Well-known practice areas include financial restructuring, capital markets, investment funds and tax.

The deals

Recently acted for the par and secondary holders of private placement notes on the €2bn financial restructuring and subsequent bankruptcy of Royal Imtech; advised investors on North West Electricity Networks' £305m fixed rate and RPI-linked notes issuance; acted for Lukoil on a $1bn project financing to develop the Shah Deniz gas field off the coast of Azerbaijan; advised borrower Omnium Telecom Algérie on two syndicated loans; advised Fitch ratings on the review of securitisation structures, principally UK RMBS.

The clients

BlueCrest; Damovo; ExxonMobil; Finisterre Capital; Harman International Industries; LEO Pharma; Lukoil; Soma Oil & Gas; Systematica Investments; VimpelCom.

The star performers

Top-ranking departments according to *The Legal 500* (see legal500.com for more details)
Bank lending – investment grade debt and syndicated loans; Banking litigation: investment and retail; Commercial litigation; Corporate restructuring and insolvency; Corporate tax; Debt capital markets; EU and competition; Emerging markets; Financial services (contentious); Financial services (non-contentious/ regulatory); International arbitration; Investment funds: hedge funds; M&A: upper mid-market and premium deals, £250m+; Oil and gas; Private equity: transactions: Large-cap deal capability; Private funds; Securitisation.

- **Why did you choose this firm over any others?** 'A positive vacation scheme experience'; 'the client base'; 'friendliness'; 'remuneration'; 'I was looking for the US firm mentality'; 'clients'; 'people I met during interviews'; 'high-quality work'; 'reputation for excellence'; 'small trainee intake'; 'sector focus'; 'challenging work'; 'the firm's strength in financial restructuring drew me in'

- **Best thing about the firm?** 'Everyone is passionate about their work as well as being very welcoming'; 'the people'; 'the type of work'; 'the emphasis on work/life balance'; 'salary'; 'reputation'; 'people'; 'being treated in many respects as an associate from day one'; 'learning from some of the best people in their field'

- **Worst thing about the firm?** 'Occasional long hours'; 'poor opportunities for international secondments'; 'the choice of seats is limited compared to a large full-service firm'; 'the expectation that, regardless of whether you are on holiday or it is the weekend, you are always in contact and ready to work'

- **Best moment?** 'Giving a presentation on penalty clauses'; 'getting very positive feedback from my supervisor on the mid-seat review meeting'; 'completing challenging tasks and getting positive feedback'; 'trip to Paris by Eurostar to interview clients was memorable'; 'handling a complicated restructuring in Brazil almost single-handedly'; 'integrating into the team very quickly'

- **Worst moment?** 'Making mistakes when working on important client deals'; 'being the most junior lawyer in a very high-calibre team is sometimes daunting'; 'the PSC exams at the beginning of the training contract'

A day in the life of...

... Rupert Cullen second-year trainee solicitor, Akin Gump LLP

Departments to date: Litigation, financial restructuring, tax, corporate (current)

University: University of Cambridge

Degree and class: Classics (First class)

9.00am: I arrive at the office, located where the City meets hipster Shoreditch – every other shop is an independent coffee outlet, so we are never short of breakfast options. I respond to any emails which have come in from the US overnight and take a few minutes to read the *Financial Times*. The deals I am working on for our investment fund clients will often be front-page news, and I have the inside track!

9.30am: Today is the firm's monthly corporate breakfast, an opportunity for the corporate, energy and tax teams to meet up over croissants and bacon rolls to discuss any interesting new matters and legal issues. It is also a chance for the partners to discuss the firm's strategy with more junior lawyers. This time, the focus is on both the challenges and opportunities presented by Brexit.

10.30am: I catch up with one of the corporate partners about a document review which the firm is undertaking to see if a client investing into the UK needs to take any action with respect to the new 'persons with significant control' regime, which came into force in April. Because the teams at Akin Gump are small, trainees have the opportunity to work in close contact with partners from day one. I spend the rest of the morning working on the review and helping to draft a memorandum setting out its conclusions.

12.30pm: I now attend one of the firm's lunchtime training sessions – these are often delivered by partners who are among the best practitioners in their field, or by external speakers such as leading commercial QCs. On this occasion, we hear about the latest developments in the restructuring of distressed debt. Other recent topics have included construction litigation, schemes of arrangement and the implications of Blockchain.

1.30pm: Shortly after lunch, I join a call with a client and our colleagues from the New York office to discuss the progress of a transaction. I have assisted with the preparatory work and am encouraged to contribute – our training contract offers plenty of chances to take on responsibilities that might come only after qualification at other firms.

2.30pm: Checking my emails, I see that another department is looking for a trainee to make a trip to Brazil at short notice. In the course of my training contract I have had my share of trips away from the office (including a week spent at the offices of a Paris investment fund) but this time I am busy and regretfully decline. I spend the next few hours preparing the first draft of a set of board minutes concerning the acquisition of a foreign company by a UK entity.

4.30pm: Later, I help to submit an application to incorporate a new UK company to sit within a client's investment structure. I have been involved in planning this structure from its earliest stages and it gives me a warm glow to see it turning from a PowerPoint presentation into a reality.

6.30pm: With the UK company well on its way to incorporation, I move on to the next item on

> **'Trainees have the opportunity to work in close contact with partners from day one.'**

my list, reviewing and drafting amendments to a non-disclosure agreement. We are frequently sent these to comment on by fund clients, and for a trainee they are good drafting practice – like snowflakes, they are all similar but never exactly alike.

7.30pm: Before heading home, I unwind in the Health and Wellbeing Centre located in the basement of Ten Bishops Square.

www.akingump.com/en/careers/uk-students

About the firm

Address: Eighth Floor, Ten Bishops Square, London E1 6EG
Telephone: 020 7012 9600   **Fax:** 020 7012 9601
Website: www.akingump.com
Email: graduaterecruitment@akingump.com
Twitter: @akin_gump

Senior partner: James Roome
Managing partner: Sebastian Rice

Other offices: Abu Dhabi, Beijing, Dallas, Dubai, Fort Worth, Frankfurt, Geneva, Hong Kong, Houston, Irvine, Longview, Los Angeles, Moscow, New York, Philadelphia, San Antonia, San Francisco, Singapore, Washington DC.

Who we are: Akin Gump's London office is the hub of the firm's international offices, practising at the top of its markets. Clients range from corporations and financial institutions to foreign governments and individuals.

What we do: Practices include: financial restructuring; corporate transactions; finance; energy; debt and equity capital markets; financial services regulatory; disputes; construction; investment funds; EU; competition; and tax.

What we're looking for: We hire the best and the brightest. We look for exceptional and consistent academic achievement combined with evidence of a driven outlook through extracurricular achievements. You should demonstrate intellectual curiosity, be solution-driven and keen for early responsibility.

What you'll do: Our London office is an exciting and inspiring environment to train in. By focusing on a smaller intake we maintain flexibility and seek to grow through our junior lawyer retention. Seats are tailored to three-or six-month durations to provide a breadth of experience.

Perks: Health insurance, income protection insurance, life insurance, travel insurance, dental insurance, season ticket loan, annual eye exam.

Sponsorship: GDL and LPC fees are paid in addition to a maintenance grant of £8,000 per year of study.

Facts and figures

Total partners: 37
Other fee-earners: 54
Total trainees: 8

Trainee places available for 2019: Up to 4
Applications received pa: 300
Percentage interviewed: 15%

First year salary: £43,000
Second year salary: £48,000
Newly qualified salary: £112,500

Application process

Apply to: Victoria Widdows – director of international legal recruiting and development.
How: Online application via website.
When: By 15 July 2017 for September 2019 training contracts.
What's involved: Face-to-face interviews with members of the graduate recruitment panel.

Vacation schemes

Summer: July (apply by 31 January 2017)

Allen & Overy

One Bishops Square, London E1 6AD

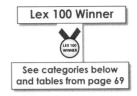

Lex 100 Winner

LEX 100 WINNER

See categories below
and tables from page 69

Survey results *(marks out of 100%)*

Satisfied in your job?	78
Firm living up to expectations?	81
High quality of work?	80
Enough client contact?	76
Stress-free?	63
Happy work/life balance?	52
Friendly firm?	86
Great social life?	77
Good vacation scheme?	87
Confident you'll be kept on?	81
Good remuneration?	87
Diverse firm?	83
Good international secondments?	75

 **verdict**

For those attracted by the 'prestige and work that comes with being Magic Circle', Allen & Overy takes some beating. The firm offers trainees the chance to work alongside 'some of the brightest legal minds' at the 'leading firm in banking and finance law'. Though 'at times trainees do repetitive tasks', the 'responsibility given to trainees' ensures 'opportunities to get involved with cutting-edge deals' across 'several world-leading departments'. Highlight moments enjoyed by trainees include 'working on a large bank recapitalisation' and 'attending a roundtable discussion with a key client and having all my research presented'. The flip side to working at a leading corporate firm is 'the unpredictability and length of the hours', and this has resulted in 'several very late nights in the run up to a closing' and 'trying to spot spelling mistakes in my own work at 2am'. Still, trainees report that the prestige of working on 'high-profile deals' regularly makes up for this, as does the trainee salary which is worth a **Lex 100 Winner** award. As one respondent commented, 'we work on market-defining transactions, and it's great when your mum and dad have heard of the clients you've acted for!' There is a 'steep learning curve' at A&O, but the feedback consistently praises the 'fantastic support'. A client secondment allowed one trainee to 'see the commercial drivers behind deals', while another respondent evaluated their international seat as an 'amazing experience' which showcased the 'benefits of being part of such a seamless network'. For 'access to market-leading deals' at a firm with an 'excellent reputation' and 'international outlook', consider Allen & Overy.

If the firm were a fictional character it would be...

Desmond Hume (Lost) – has performed a number of impressive feats down the years yet still has flashes of inspiration regarding the future

The firm

Allen & Overy is a recognised global leader for its work in the finance and projects spaces. The Magic Circle firm has offices across Europe, Asia, the Middle East, Africa and the Americas, and routinely advises governments, financial institutions and international conglomerates across the full range of legal services.

The deals

Worked for the lenders, including Bank of America, on the financing to support Royal Dutch Shell's £47bn purchase of BG Group; advised the lending syndicate on the $75bn acquisition financing of Anheuser-Busch InBev's takeover of SAB Miller; advised Barclays on the $6.5bn BHP Billiton multi-currency hybrid bond issue; advised Deutsche Bank on a €400m guaranteed notes offering; acted for Credit Agricole on the €1.25bn Alpha Trains structured financing.

The clients

Aviva; Bank of Tokyo-Mitsubishi UFJ; Bombardier; Four Seasons Health Group; Goldman Sachs; Lone Star; News UK; RBS; Saudi Electricity Company; Turkcell.

The star performers

Top-ranking departments according to *The Legal 500* (see legal500.com for more details)
Acquisition finance; Asset financing and leasing; Bank lending – investment grade debt and syndicated loans; Corporate restructuring and insolvency; Debt capital markets; Derivatives and structured products; Emerging markets; Employee share schemes; Employment: employers; High yield; Infrastructure (including PFI and PPP); Islamic finance; Mining and minerals; Oil and gas; Pensions (non-contentious); Pensions dispute resolution; Power (including electricity, nuclear and renewables); Rail; Securitisation; Trade finance; Water.

- **Why did you choose this firm over any others?** 'I felt like people were being themselves in the workplace'; 'the most global Magic Circle firm'; 'best banking firm in the world, with a great international presence'; 'competitive salary'; 'great office'; 'friendly culture'; 'provides an optimal environment for you to showcase your skills'; 'experience at interview'; 'I really enjoyed my vacation scheme'; 'forward-thinking'; 'meeting trainees and associates at a campus event'

- **Best thing about the firm?** 'The quality of the work'; 'at times I have been doing junior associate-level work'; 'the amount of support available to trainees'; 'friendly, intelligent people that I work with'; 'people eager to help your personal development'; 'the facilities in the London office are exceptional'; 'the rooftop bar'; 'six-week qualification leave'; 'the breadth of departments and offices'; 'A&O encourages you to create links across the firm'

- **Worst thing about the firm?** 'Good trainee salary but stagnates at associate level'; 'inability to make weekday plans'; 'sometimes the feeling that we have little control over the training process'; 'lack of transparency in respect of administrative decisions'; 'very long working hours'; 'the internal reviews'; 'the work/life balance only seems to get worse as you progress'

- **Best moment?** 'Attending an arbitration hearing'; 'secondment to New York'; 'working directly with a partner on a time-pressured signing and closing'; 'being involved in market-leading deals reported in the news'; 'signing my first big leveraged deal'; 'attending a hearing at the Privy Council'; 'high-quality research tasks'; 'getting positive feedback from clients'; 'closing my first deal'

- **Worst moment?** '24 hours straight in the office'; 'stress during a closing'; 'the first month is pretty difficult as you don't know how basic things work'; 'working late on Christmas Eve'; 'not getting on with my supervisor'; 'finding out all the sleeping pods were full at 5am'; 'a mid-seat review which I did not agree with'; 'the mundane tasks in the transactional seats'

A day in the life of…

… Shalina Daved trainee, Allen & Overy LLP

Departments to date: General securities group in the international capital markets department; banking, financial and regulatory litigation; and regulatory and asset management.
University: University of Nottingham; University of Cambridge
Degree and class: BA Law with German – First Class Honours; LLM – First Class

8.00am: I take part in the 'body circuits' class at the gym in our building which is extremely well equipped. There is a wide range of classes and best of all, membership is free.

9.15am: I pop into Lavanda – our subsidised Italian cafe/bar on the sixth floor-to get breakfast and a coffee and head to my desk to log in and read the *FT*'s morning news roundup.

9.30am: I attend our fortnightly departmental meeting where each member of the team presents the matters they are working on. This provides a good overview of the range of work the department deals with. One of the partners discusses a key sectoral development – today, on the regulation of payment systems in the UK.

10.10pm: In light of 'Brexit', the prospect of the UK losing access to the single market and assuming 'third country' status, we are assisting clients with contingency planning. I read the advice that has come in from our European offices and identify potential gaps on which we require further analysis.

12.30pm: All trainees in the department are tasked with keeping track of developments in financial services regulation. I am responsible for bank structural reform and bank recovery and resolution. I check weekly newsletters for any updates.

1.15pm: A&O is set in an amazing location, right behind Spitalfields market and next to Shoreditch. There is a huge range of restaurants, cafes and bars on our doorstep. As it is sunny, a few fellow trainees and I head out to eat at one of the street food stalls in Spitalfields.

2.15pm: We are working with the corporate department on an acquisition of a company which has entities all around the globe. We are responsible for obtaining regulatory approval of the transaction from regulators in each of the relevant jurisdictions. I prepare for our weekly call with counsel on the other side.

3.00pm: We attend the conference call with the target company's counsel. I am asked to lead on what is required from the other side for my allocated jurisdictions which include Denmark and Hong Kong.

3.30pm: Following the call, I create an action list of what both sides need to follow up on prior to next week. I speak to Danish counsel in relation to the Danish Financial Services Authority's requirements and call the client regarding outstanding information.

5.15pm: As part of my pro bono project on the role of the rule of law in Parliament, the trainees and associate involved meet to discuss our findings and next steps. A fellow trainee and I

have been invited to an All-Party Parliamentary Group on the Rule of Law meeting so it is off to the House of Commons next week! Allen & Overy has excellent global and local pro bono initiatives ranging from human rights work, advising at legal advice centres, mentoring programmes and working with children from local schools.

> **'As part of my pro bono project, the trainees and associate involved meet to discuss our findings and next steps.'**

6.00pm: We are advising an individual who wishes to set up an investment firm in a third country and provide its services to UK clients. I continue researching which of the investment firm's anticipated activities would require authorisation in the UK and whether the investment firm falls within any exceptions or exclusions.

7.30pm: I make a to-do list for the morning and, together with other trainees, head up to get dinner from the tenth floor restaurant which boasts views of the city skyline.

www.aograduate.com

About the firm

Address: One Bishops Square, London E1 6AD
Telephone: 020 3088 3399
Website: www.aograduate.com
Email: graduate.recruitment@allenovery.com
Facebook: www.facebook.com/AllenOveryGrads
Twitter: @allenoverygrads

Senior partner: Wim Dejonghe
Managing partner: Andrew Ballheimer

Other offices: Abu Dhabi, Amsterdam, Antwerp, Bangkok, Barcelona, Beijing, Belfast, Bratislava, Brussels, Bucharest*, Budapest, Casablanca, Doha, Dubai, Düsseldorf, Frankfurt, Hamburg, Hanoi, Ho Chi Minh City, Hong Kong, Istanbul, Jakarta*, Johannesburg, London, Luxembourg, Madrid, Milan, Munich, Moscow, New York, Paris, Perth, Prague, Riyadh*, Rome, São Paulo, Seoul, Shanghai, Singapore, Sydney, Tokyo, Warsaw, Washington DC and Yangon. *Associated office

Who we are: Allen & Overy LLP is an international law firm with approximately 5,200 people in 44 offices worldwide.

What we do: Clients include many of the world's top organisations. We are renowned for the high quality of our banking, corporate and international capital markets advice.

What we're looking for: Candidates must be predicted or have achieved a 2(1) degree and 340 UCAS points (AAB), or equivalent, and have a genuine interest in law. Evidence of a global mindset, teamwork, resilience and commercial awareness are also important.

What you'll do: Trainees spend a year in at least two of our core areas of banking, corporate and international capital markets.

Perks: Working at Allen & Overy offers an exceptional range of benefits, including life insurance, pension scheme, an interest-free season ticket loan, on-site gym and sports hall, medical, dental and physiotherapy service, beauty treatment centre, dry cleaners, music rooms, multi-faith prayer rooms and two restaurants.

Sponsorship: We pay fees for GDL/LPC and a maintenance grant for the GDL (£7,000 outside London; £8,000 in London) and £7,000 for the LPC. Future joiners will study the bespoke A&O LPC (MA with business) at BPP in London.

Facts and figures

Total partners: 530 (approx worldwide)
Other fee-earners: 2,700
Total trainees: 180

Trainee places available for 2019: 90

First year: £42,000

Turnover in 2015: £1,281m (+4% from 2014)
Profits per equity partner: £1.21m (+8% from 2014)
(see legalbusiness.co.uk for full financial information)

Application process

Apply to: Graduate recruitment.
How: Online at www.aograduate.com.
When: Both law and non-law students should apply from October 2016. Please visit our website for full details.
What's involved: Two interviews.

Vacation schemes

Allen and Overy offers 75 vacation placements across the year from all degree disciplines. For full details about eligibility requirements and application deadlines, please visit our website at www.aograduate.com.

ALLEN & OVERY

Anthony Collins Solicitors

134 Edmund Street, Birmingham B3 2ES

Lex 100 Winner

LEX 100 WINNER

See categories below
and tables from page 69

Survey results *(marks out of 100%)*

Satisfied in your job? **86**

Firm living up to expectations? **84**

High quality of work? **87**

Enough client contact? **89**

Stress-free? **67**

Happy work/life balance? **93**

Friendly firm? **91**

Great social life? **73**

Confident you'll be kept on? **71**

Good remuneration? **71**

Diverse firm? **90**

 **verdict**

As a firm which undertakes 'high-quality and very interesting work for charity and third sector clients', Anthony Collins Solicitors encourages trainees to represent clients who are 'passionate about what they do and actively trying to improve their communities or to help those less fortunate'. With 'the largest charities client base outside of London', the firm is 'still growing fast and expanding into new sectors' making it a 'very exciting time to be a trainee'. This will have contributed to the firm earning a **Lex 100 Winner** medal for job satisfaction, along with four other gongs. This is reflected in stand-out moments which include 'attending a client meeting with top-level executives and being able to hold conversations with them' and 'participating in a mediation process in my first month'. Some respondents have lamented that Anthony Collins 'doesn't promote itself enough' and that 'it is often underappreciated how much high-quality and high-profile work we undertake', though one respondent mentions how the firm has built up an 'excellent reputation over a short period of time' in the Birmingham market. While there can be instances of 'photocopying numerous documents' and 'not enough fee-earning work', feedback indicates a 'high level of responsibility and client contact'. This 'client exposure' is coupled with working alongside 'friendly and approachable' colleagues who 'make an effort to get to know you from day one'. To work at a firm that is 'valued for its outstanding client service' and that advises companies making a 'positive contribution' to society, apply to Anthony Collins Solicitors.

If the firm were a fictional character it would be...

Little John (Robin Hood) – an unexpected giant with a sharp wit and a big heart, it works with others to bring relief to the disadvantaged

The firm

Established in 1973, Anthony Collins Solicitors represents a broad array of clients from its Birmingham base. The firm represents individuals and businesses and has a strong sector focus which includes education, faith communities, housing and local government. The firm has more than 130 lawyers, including over 25 partners.

The deals

Helped Salford City Council with employment issues as they set up a new independent housing association, Salix Homes; acted for Affinity Sutton on its new £600m contract with Osborne Property Services; advised Gloucester City Council on the transfer of 4,800 homes to Gloucester City Homes; handled the dissolution of the civil partnership of a public figure; secured a six-figure settlement for a client who sustained a head injury but was not given a CT scan, despite the claimant's family reporting abnormal behaviour to the health authorities.

The clients

Affinity Sutton; Chartered Institute for the Management of Sport; Cheshire West and Chester Council; Derwent Living; Friends of the Elderly; Knowsley Housing Trust; MIND; Salford City Council; Sense; Torus Group.

The star performers

Top-ranking departments according to *The Legal 500* (see legal500.com for more details)
Charities and not-for-profit; Clinical negligence: claimant; Commercial litigation; Commercial property; Construction; Court of Protection; Employment; Family; Local government; Personal injury: claimant; Personal tax, trusts and probate; Property litigation; Social housing.

- **Why did you choose this firm over any others?** 'The culture of the firm'; 'public child law is championed by the firm'; 'to work alongside people who wanted to make a difference and not just churn out numbers'; 'it fitted in with my personal views on social responsibility'; 'the desire to go the extra mile for all of its clients'; 'the friendly and supportive working environment'

- **Best thing about the firm?** 'The firm's ethos and purpose in working for organisations such as charities and third sector clients'; 'the work/life balance'; 'you're encouraged to challenge ideas and propose solutions'; 'I am treated like a valued member of the team'; 'the ability to work with clients who are passionate about what they do'

- **Worst thing about the firm?** 'The perception of other people that we are a religious firm'; 'the split between the commercial and private client teams'; 'it doesn't promote itself enough'; 'it is often underappreciated how much high-quality and high-profile work we undertake'

- **Best moment?** 'Being given the opportunity to attend a panel interview for a legal services tender with two partners and playing an active role in the delivery of the presentation'; 'researching a narrow area of law and advising the sector leads at partnership level as to how the firm should respond to a government policy announcement'

- **Worst moment?** 'It is not great when you make a mistake'; 'working late nights due to the tight timescales in an adjudication process'; 'photocopying numerous documents'

A day in the life of...

... Amy Callahan-Page first-year trainee, Anthony Collins Solicitors LLP

Departments to date: Contentious construction, personal injury, clinical negligence
University: University of Birmingham
Degree and class: Law LLB Hons 2(1)

8.45am: I arrive at the office with time to grab a drink and have a chat with colleagues before starting the working day.

9.00am: I review my emails, calendar and task list to determine what needs to be completed today. I am managing some files myself and am also given specific tasks on more complex files, so it is important to always be aware of deadlines and priorities. My first job is to draft a letter of instruction to a hepatologist (liver expert), asking them to complete a condition and prognosis report on our client's liver injury.

9.45am: I head off to court with a senior fee-earner, counsel and our clients to attend a court approval hearing. At the hearing the judge (thankfully!) approves a multimillion-pound settlement that has been agreed out of court on one of our clinical negligence cases. I take a detailed note of the claimant's and defendant's submissions and the judge's decision. After the hearing there are hugs of thanks all around from our client's mother!

11.00am: Back at the office I spend some time contacting clients to give them an update on their case and the next steps that we will be taking. As this is a private client seat, it is particularly important we keep in touch with our clients and ensure they understand the legal process and what we are doing to progress their claims.

11.30pm: I call a witness on a personal injury case, and ask him questions to prompt him to talk me through what he witnessed at the scene of a road traffic accident. I take thorough notes so I can draft his witness statement and advise him of the requirements for being a witness in the case. The training here is very hands on and it offers a considerable amount of independence and responsibility.

12.00pm: I draft the witness statement, ensuring that the statement is compliant with the Civil Procedure Rules and that it accurately reflects what the witness has told me.

1.00pm: It's lunchtime, so I meet with another trainee for a bite to eat and a catch up. We head out into the city centre, which is conveniently located on our doorstep and try to decide where to go!

2.00pm: Back in the office, I spend some time undertaking medical research to assist us on a new case, where a pharmacy gave our client an incorrect prescription of medication. In particular, I research the potential long-term consequences and side effects from the drug.

3.30pm: It's time to attend our monthly trainee forum. The trainees meet regularly to discuss their seats, arrange trainee social events and organise charity fundraising activities. We also invite guest speakers from different departments to talk to us about the

work that they do, or to deliver training on new and interesting legal developments.

4.15pm: I get back to my desk to see that we have had a number of new client enquiries. I call one prospective client to find out more about their situation to determine whether we would be able to assist them; having regular

> **'Having regular client contact is one of the things I really enjoy about training at ACS.'**

client contact is one of the things I really enjoy about training at ACS. I advise them on what they would need to prove to bring a claim, and explain limitation dates. I then draft a letter to them to confirm my advice in writing.

4.45pm: I spend some time researching kidney trauma experts and drafting letters of approach to determine if they would be able to act as an expert on a case.

5.15pm: It's the end of the day and everyone is encouraged to leave on time, so I head off to a local networking event with some of the other trainees.

About the firm

Address: 134 Edmund Street, Birmingham B3 2ES
Telephone: 0121 200 3242
Website: www.anthonycollins.com
Email: trainingcontract@anthonycollins.com

Senior partner: Peter Hubbard

Who we are: Anthony Collins Solicitors LLP is a law firm with a clear purpose – to 'improve lives, communities and society'.

What we do: We provide advice and support to help our clients achieve their goals across our specialist sectors – social housing, local government, education, social business, health and social care, charities and private individuals.

What we're looking for: At Anthony Collins Solicitors we don't just look for technical expertise. We want people who bring a wider skill set to our firm. Emotional intelligence and a desire to collaborate are key qualities that we look for.

What you'll do: Our trainees are encouraged to take an integral role in the team and are exposed to high-quality work from day one.

Perks: Travel loan, BHSF fund, quarterly office lunch, dress-down Fridays, BTSS membership.

Facts and figures

Total partners: 26
Other fee-earners: 114
Total trainees: 9

Trainee places available for 2019: 10
Applications received pa: 250
Percentage interviewed: 20%

First year salary: £22,000
Second year salary: £24,000
Newly qualified salary: £35,000

Application process

Apply to: Vicky Paterson.
How: Via the vacancy section on the website.
When: By 31 July 2017 for 2019 contracts.
What's involved: Psychometric testing, interview, assessment centre.

Vacation schemes

Summer: July 2017 (appy by 11 March).

Ashfords LLP

Ashford House, Grenadier Road, Exeter EX1 3LH

Survey results *(marks out of 100%)*

Satisfied in your job?	78
Firm living up to expectations?	78
High quality of work?	82
Enough client contact?	74
Stress-free?	56
Happy work/life balance?	77
Friendly firm?	86
Great social life?	72
Good vacation scheme?	74
Confident you'll be kept on?	77
Good remuneration?	66
Diverse firm?	79

 verdict

Several Ashfords trainees told us of their eagerness to work in the South West, and that the firm enjoys a 'strong reputation in the region'. This reputation reflects a firm with a 'commercial focus' that undertakes a 'range of work' on behalf of 'high-calibre clients'. Trainees 'get a lot of responsibility' and are tasked with 'hands-on work', with one stating that 'I have been allowed to run my own files and progress matters without micro-management'. This 'excellent exposure to work' is balanced by trainees being 'supported fully throughout their tasks'. Work highlights of the current intake include 'travelling to London to advise a very wealthy client on their visa application', 'attending a mediation with the client and my supervising partner' and 'the pride in reaching financial close on a million-pound renewables project'. It is felt that 'remuneration could be slightly better' as the salary is 'generally a little less than at comparable firms', but one respondent adds that this has 'improved in recent years'. The firm is praised for having a 'good work/life balance', which means that trainees 'can still have a life outside of work'. On the downside, the most common gripe is reserved for the 'lack of transparency around available seats', with trainees sometimes informed of their next rotation 'less than six weeks before the seat is due to start'. Despite this frustration, the 'wide variety of seats on offer' is a clear attraction. More broadly, the 'friendly yet professional atmosphere' at Ashfords and the 'welcoming attitude' of senior colleagues puts new recruits at ease, and is even said to engender a 'family feel' at the firm. To work at an 'ambitious' firm with 'strong leadership' where you can advise a 'good range of household-name clients', remember Ashfords.

If the firm were a fictional character it would be...

Dorothea (Middlemarch) – energetic, idealistic and never satisfied with its lot

The firm

Ashfords has over 70 partners based across its six offices in Bristol, Exeter, Taunton, Plymouth, Tiverton and London. A leader in the South West, the firm was shortlisted for National/Regional Firm of the Year at the *Legal Business* Awards 2016. Corporate, real estate, energy and private client are just some of the firm's leading practice areas.

The deals

Acted for Pennon Group on the £100m acquisition of the entire issued share capital of Bournemouth Water; advised Santander UK on its refinancing of Seasalt and its associated companies; represented New Directions Holdings in High Court proceedings concerning the enforcement of restrictive covenants against former employees; assisted Welland Bio Power with the construction and operation of a new renewable energy facility; advised Exeter City Council on a twelve-acre mixed-use regeneration scheme.

The clients

Cornish Mutual; Eden Ventures; The Environment Agency; Exeter Finance; Lloyds Bank; Sensus UK; Sovereign Housing Association; Viridor Waste Management; Wandsworth Borough Council; Welland Bio Power.

The star performers

Top-ranking departments according to *The Legal 500* (see legal500.com for more details)
Commercial property; Construction; Contentious trusts and probate; Corporate tax; Crime: fraud; EU and competition; Employment; Energy; Health and safety; Insolvency and corporate recovery; Intellectual property; Local government; Personal injury: defendant; Personal tax, trusts and probate; Project finance and PFI; Property litigation; Social housing; Sport; TMT: IT and telecoms; Transport: shipping.

- **Why did you choose this firm over any others?** 'The supportive environment'; 'good level of work/life balance'; 'the friendly people at the assessment day'; 'reputation for good-quality work'; 'Bristol location'; 'reputation as a welcoming and inclusive firm'; 'South West location'; 'they provided a range of seat options'; 'the wide range of areas covered'; 'the open-plan seating policy'

- **Best thing about the firm?** 'Professional atmosphere'; 'the people'; 'the high level of work in a friendly environment'; the quality of the training is outstanding'; there is always someone to ask for help'; 'the firm has a definite character of inclusiveness'; 'opportunities for networking'; 'everybody takes the time to get to know you'

- **Worst thing about the firm?** 'Communication as to seats'; 'the business park location is not very sociable'; 'I can have very quiet periods in terms of my workload where I do not gain useful experience'; 'sometimes I would prefer more direct supervision'; 'remuneration could be slightly better'

- **Best moment?** 'I really enjoyed my time on client secondment where I gained a wealth of commercial experience'; 'being accepted as an NQ in my favourite department of the firm'; 'being involved in highly complex projects'; 'sitting in on client negotiations'; 'being given a matter of my own to run with'; 'getting very positive feedback'

- **Worst moment?** 'Advocacy practice workshop'; 'having to work through the night with clients in America'; 'the lack of client contact in one particular seat'; 'heavy workload while a colleague was on annual leave'; 'paginating documents in the wrong order'; 'sending a document off to court with the wrong parties detailed in the heading'

A day in the life of...

... **Lee Ward** second-seat trainee, Ashfords LLP

Departments to date: Planning, projects. Lee has been with Ashfords for three years, having started his career with Ashfords as a paralegal in the construction department.

8.00am: Today starts slightly differently as I attend a golf networking event hosted by Old Mill, a local accountancy firm. The event is attended by a number of professionals from firms such as Charles Stanley, Barclays and Expedite. The event consists of 45 minutes of practice in the driving range followed by breakfast. The views overlooking the driving range are a great way to start the day.

10.15am: I usually arrive at the office at around 8.45am but today I get in at around 10.15am. Ashfords is very encouraging (even at junior level) when it comes to networking and building good client relations so was happy for me to attend the networking event. When I arrive I check my emails to see if anything urgent has come in overnight. The office is open-plan so while checking my emails I chat with my supervisor about a Brexit debate hosted by Ashfords the evening before.

10.25am: I exchange emails with the other trainees relating to the vacation scheme social we are planning for next month.

10.30am: The projects department can be quite high-paced and I'm approached by a solicitor in the team who has asked me to draft some supporting documents for a project we're involved in for the procurement of domiciliary care and community support. The project is relatively complex and has a value of £110m.

12.15pm: After drafting the documents I discuss them with the solicitor and we work together to finalise everything before she sends the documents out to the client.

1.00pm: I break for lunch and head upstairs to the third-floor gym. After 40 minutes I call it a day, and head to the onsite café to pick up some lunch. The other trainees are all eating lunch together so I join them for the last 20 minutes before returning to my desk. Last year Ashfords' charity of the year was Mind, a mental health charity, so Ashfords is keen to promote a good work/life balance and support employee wellbeing through various initiatives which include lunchtime yoga classes, Mind workshops and free use of the onsite gym.

2.00pm: I'd been working on a contractual analysis report earlier in the week so I pick this up again in the afternoon. The project relates to an anaerobic digestion plant which was procured by way of an engineering, procurement and construction contract. In particular I'm focusing on the payment provisions contained within the contract.

4.00pm: I receive a call from a partner in our London office who explains that his client will be arriving at the Exeter office at 4.30pm to execute contracts for a project they have been working on together. The final versions are emailed to me and I prepare the contracts for signing. We agree that during the meeting,

the partner will dial in so he can discuss the contracts with the client and supervise the proper execution of the documents.

4.30pm: I meet with the client downstairs and show him to a meeting room where we run through the contracts. During this time I 'dial in' the London partner who discusses last-minute

> '**Ashfords is very encouraging (even at junior level) when it comes to networking and building good client relations.**'

changes which have been made and once the client is happy we execute the documents.

5.30pm: After the meeting I telephone the London partner for a debrief. I then arrange for the executed documents to be couriered to our London office the next day.

6.15pm: I make a list of things which need to be actioned for the next day; in particular I note that we have been asked to provide some follow up advice on whether a local council can delegate any function it may have to collect and dispose of waste. After this I head home for the evening.

www.ashfords.co.uk/trainees

About the firm

Address: Ashford House, Grenadier Rd, Exeter EX1 3LH
Telephone: 01392 333634
Website: www.ashfords.co.uk
Email: traineerecruitment@ashfords.co.uk
Twitter: @AshfordsTrainee

Senior partner: Mark Lomas
CEO: Garry Mackay

Other offices: Bristol, London, Plymouth, Taunton, Tiverton

Who we are: Ashfords is a top 100 law firm that provides legal and professional services to businesses and individuals throughout the UK and abroad.

What we do: Our three divisions (business services, real estate and infrastructure, and private client) cover a wide range of practice areas, including: corporate, commercial property, projects, employment, IP, trusts and estates, and many more.

What we're looking for: Someone that is very motivated and ready to immerse themselves in real client matters, providing our clients with the benefit of a fresh and expert approach.

What you'll do: We have a clear career model with structured development to support you at each stage. Trainees have access to development on an individual, firm-wide and departmental level to help achieve career ambitions.

Perks: Annual benefits include: 20 days' paid leave (increases to 25 on qualification), birthday day off, additional Ashfords Christmas day off, holiday purchase scheme, free in-house gym (Exeter office), 5% non-contributory pension, membership of The Junior Lawyers Division, cycle scheme, annual bonus scheme.

Sponsorship: Full course bursary given for the LPC when you study at any University of Law. All PSC courses and practice certificate fees are paid by the firm.

Facts and figures

Total partners: 77
Other fee-earners: 274
Total trainees: 28

Trainee places available for 2019: 15
Applications received pa: 550
Percentage interviewed: 12

First year salary: Competitive
Second year salary: Competitive
Newly qualified salary: Competitive

Turnover in 2015: £35.4m (+11% from 2014)
Profits per equity partner: £261,000 (+14%)
(see legalbusiness.co.uk for full financial information)

Application process

How: Online application form.
When: By 31 July 2017.
What's involved: Online application form followed by assessment centre: partner interview, group exercise and written exercise.

Vacation schemes

Summer: June/July 2017 (apply by 28 February 2017).

ashfords

Ashurst LLP

Broadwalk House, 5 Appold Street, London EC2A 2HA

Survey results *(marks out of 100%)*

Satisfied in your job?	77
Firm living up to expectations?	78
High quality of work?	77
Enough client contact?	73
Stress-free?	60
Happy work/life balance?	60
Friendly firm?	87
Great social life?	76
Good vacation scheme?	89
Confident you'll be kept on?	77
Good remuneration?	76
Diverse firm?	80
Good international secondments?	60

 **verdict**

Current trainees were motivated to apply to Ashurst because the firm conducts 'Magic Circle-quality work' while recruiting a 'trainee intake which is comparatively small'. This enables Ashurst to 'deliver a better training experience' which 'cannot be matched by other firms of its size'. Highlight moments include 'working on a £47bn deal', 'assisting with preparation for and attending a judicial review hearing in the RCJ' and 'being given recognition in front of the client by the partner for coming up with the new structure that saved a deal'. Respondents state that 'Ashurst is particularly strong in the corporate space' and that 'the energy department is well respected'. These areas of work are supplemented by the firm's 'strong international presence', though there are a few complaints that there are not enough international secondments and that the 'application system lacks transparency'. As can perhaps be expected of a major City firm, 'long hours' can mean 'sleeping in the office' and 'a week of 3am finishes', though it is said that 'it is not constant and you are recognised for your commitment'. You can count on a 'very good support network' and a 'friendly working environment', and the 'team socials and drinks' will help you to unwind. Additionally, 'partners are just as approachable for questions as the juniors' and there is also 'no social divide between support staff and fee-earners', all of which contributes to Ashurst's 'famously personable and friendly atmosphere'. To experience a 'well-rounded training contract' at a firm which will 'invest a lot' in you, consider applying to Ashurst.

If the firm were a fictional character it would be...

Tony Stark (Iron Man) – successful and forward-thinking with great ideas, but still up for a laugh

The firm

City heavyweight Ashurst earns respect for its broad corporate and projects departments, and is a popular choice for blue-chip clients. The firm has recently withdrawn from Italy and Sweden but still has offices across Asia-Pacific, Europe, the Middle East and North America. Ashurst earned nominations for both Energy & Infrastructure and Corporate Team of the Year at the *Legal Business* Awards 2016. The firm is set to relocate from Appold Street to Spitalfields in 2019.

The deals

Advised BP Gas Marketing on the purchase of gas from Ithaca Energy; advised Avenue Capital on its proposed acquisition of a €2bn non-performing loan portfolio from Ulster Bank; assisted Petropavlovsk with its $335m convertible bond refinancing; handled a €516m CLO for arranger Morgan Stanley; advised Barclays and Denmark's export credit agency on the £138m financing of the 27.8MW Cramlington biomass plant in Northumberland.

The clients

Abu Dhabi Islamic Bank; Bank of America Merrill Lynch; BlueBay; Honda Motor Europe; Informa; Mitsui & Co; National Express; RBS; Vedanta Resources; Xchanging Plc.

The star performers

Top-ranking departments according to *The Legal 500* (see legal500.com for more details)

Acquisition finance; Bank lending – investment grade debt and syndicated loans; Commodities: derivatives; Commodities: physicals; Corporate restructuring and insolvency; Debt capital markets; Derivatives and structured products; Emerging markets; Employee share schemes; Employment: employers; Infrastructure (including PFI and PPP); Islamic finance; Mining and minerals; Oil and gas; Pensions dispute resolution; Pensions (non-contentious); Power (including electricity, nuclear and renewables); Rail; Securitisation.

- **Why did you choose this firm over any others?** 'Overall work/life balance'; 'reputation for friendliness'; 'approachable senior staff'; 'quality of work'; 'a friendly and more relaxed atmosphere; 'the low number of trainees means better work'; 'George Harrison wrote a song about one of the founders'; 'I had a great time on the vacation scheme'; 'variety of seat choices'; 'international outlook'; 'gets top City work'

- **Best thing about the firm?** 'As long as you meet deadlines and get things done, it does not matter much whether you work at home or leave the office'; 'working very hard to promote diversity'; 'genuinely a nice place to work'; 'there is a froyo machine'; 'quality of work'; 'supervisors are generally friendly'

- **Worst thing about the firm?** 'IT systems often suffer problems at annoying moments'; 'the printers'; 'seat rotation process could be a lot more transparent'; 'the office facilities'; 'no gym'; 'poor people management'; 'London office located in two buildings'; 'the hours are not always materially different enough from bigger firms to warrant the discrepancy in pay'

- **Best moment?** 'Attending massive closing meetings after weeks of late nights'; 'completing my first transaction'; 'I have often found myself doing NQ-level work'; 'co-authoring a memo with a partner, which was then sent to a client'; 'general day-to-day banter'; 'attending a week-long arbitration, followed by dinner with the client and counsel'; 'being given my own file to run'; 'celebrating a deal until 5am'

- **Worst moment?** 'A client taking out their stress on me'; 'not securing my first-choice seat for my final seat'; 'when I thought I lost a key document belonging to a client'; 'receiving an aggressive email from a lawyer at another firm'; 'long hours spent proofreading'

A day in the life of...

... Joanna Green trainee, Ashurst LLP
Departments to date: Disputes, real estate
University: Nottingham
Degree and class: Law with South East Asian Law, 2(1)

8.45am: I like getting in a little earlier than most of the department to tick some small jobs off my list before the day's emails start flowing in. Due to the number of matters that we work on at one time in real estate there is always a steady flow of emails to keep on top of.

9.15am: One of the main tasks that I have for today is drafting CPSE replies for a property that one of our clients is selling. As the client only recently bought the property, I dig out the CPSE replies that we received and use these to help inform my replies. I make a note of any queries that I have ready to ask our client's agent.

10.30am: I get a call from a client who is looking for some more information on an email that I sent yesterday afternoon. I explain the outstanding points on the electricity easement and gas deed and we discuss the practicalities of the deeds in relation to the site layout.

11.00am: I have nearly finished drafting the CPSE replies when a calendar invite pops up on my computer reminding me that I have a meeting with a colleague from the tax department to run through an SDLT return that I prepared earlier in the week.

12.30pm: I grab some lunch from the mini Writs, and eat at my desk while having a

read through some of the legal updates we receive on a daily basis. Having eaten my lunch, I make a quick call to the cashier desk to see if a payment I've requested from a client has been received so I can pay their stamp duty land tax and submit the relevant tax return to HMRC.

1.10pm: I jump in a cab and head to a local primary school with a number of other lawyers and support staff from across the firm. We visit this school on a weekly basis to read with Year 6 students, helping them to develop their comprehension skills. The students have put in a lot of effort this year and it is very rewarding to see how far they have come.

2.30pm: I check my BlackBerry on the way back to the office and can see that an associate has had the chance to run through some documents that I have drafted. Once back in the office I pop over to the associate's office and we run through his comments. I then update the documents and send them to our client to see if they are happy for us to circulate the documents to the new tenant's solicitor.

3.30pm: My supervisor has invited me to join a call which he is having on a new matter. After the call my supervisor talks me through the documents that we will need to draft and we give the property litigation team a ring for

their advice on a point that was raised during our conversation with the client.

4.30pm: I have received the first draft of a substation lease and have been asked to review the document. I mark up the document with my comments ready to discuss these with the senior associate who has been liaising with the client on this matter.

> **'We visit a school on a weekly basis to read with Year 6 students, helping them to develop their comprehension skills.'**

6.00pm: I have a few things on my list that I want to get out before the end of the day. In particular, I have four Land Registry forms to submit in relation to a pro bono matter that I have been assisting on.

7.00pm: Once these jobs are done, I make a quick list of what needs to be done tomorrow, and ask my supervisor if there's anything else I can help with before I go. I register my time for any work that I haven't logged throughout the day, turn my computer off and head upstairs to a networking event with a group of vacation scheme students.

About the firm

Address: Broadwalk House, 5 Appold Street, London EC2A 2HA
Telephone: 020 7638 1111   **Fax:** 020 7638 1112
Website: www.ashurst.com
Email: gradrec@ashurst.com
Facebook: www.facebook.com/AshurstTrainees

Managing partner: Paul Jenkins

Other offices: Abu Dhabi, Beijing, Brisbane, Brussels, Canberra, Dubai, Frankfurt, Glasgow (support office), Hong Kong, Jakarta (associated office), Jeddah (associated office), Madrid, Melbourne, Milan, Munich, New York, Paris, Perth, Port Moresby, Shanghai, Singapore, Sydney, Tokyo, Washington DC.

Who we are: With 25 offices in 15 countries and a number of referral relationships we offer the reach and insight of a global network, combined with the knowledge and understanding of local markets.

What we do: Our clients are at the heart of our thinking; our ambition is to be our clients' most incisive partner. You will see we have a prestigious client base, with whom we build strong partnerships working closely together on large and complex multi-jurisdictional transactions to deliver incisive and insightful commercial solutions. Our global reach provides opportunities for our people to work in numerous jurisdictions.

Facts and figures

Total partners: 410
Other fee-earners: 1,300
Total trainees: 90

Trainee places available for 2019: 45
Applications received pa: 1,500
Percentage interviewed: 10-15%

First year salary: £41,000
Second year salary: £46,000
Newly qualified salary: £70,000

What we're looking for: We expect a lot of ourselves – and so, as you would expect, you will need to be comfortable with challenges and pressure. You should also be able to express yourself confidently on paper and out loud, whether that's among your team or in a client's boardroom.

What you'll do: A training contract at Ashurst will move your mind beyond technical knowledge of the law. Ultimately, we want to help you become a thought leader with a reputation for clear, perceptive and influential advice – a professional in whom governments and leading businesses the world over can place their trust.

Perks: Private medical insurance, life assurance, income protection, pension, season ticket loan (interest-free), dental insurance, ISA savings account, wine club, technology purchase plan, holiday purchase, travel insurance, reduced rate gym membership, childcare vouchers, cycle to work scheme, give as you earn, onsite services including doctor, dentist, physiotherapist and masseuse. 25 days' holiday (plus bank holidays), staff restaurant.

Sponsorship: For the GDL and LPC, we offer scholarships that cover your course fees and provide £8,000 per year towards the cost of maintenance (£7,000 if you choose to study the GDL outside London).

Application process

Apply to: Hammad Akhtar, graduate recruitment partner.
How: Online application form.
When: 1 October-31 December 2016; 1 May-31 July 2017.
What's involved: Written case study on the interview day, competency-based interview with a member of graduate recruitment, scenario-based interview with two partners from our trainee interviewing committee.

Vacation schemes

Winter: 12-16 December 2016 (apply by 6 November 2016)
Spring: 3-7 April 2017 (apply by 8 January 2017)
Summer: 26 June-14 July;
24 July-18 August 2017 (apply 8 January 2017)

Baker & McKenzie LLP

100 New Bridge Street, London EC4V 6JA

See categories below and tables from page 69

Survey results *(marks out of 100%)*

Satisfied in your job?	82
Firm living up to expectations?	84
High quality of work?	85
Enough client contact?	79
Stress-free?	70
Happy work/life balance?	74
Friendly firm?	91
Great social life?	85
Good vacation scheme?	92
Confident you'll be kept on?	81
Good remuneration?	84
Diverse firm?	95
Good international secondments?	90

 **verdict**

Baker & McKenzie is a 'truly international' firm with over 70 offices in nearly 50 countries, with trainees unsurprisingly citing the 'unrivalled global opportunities' as a major attraction. These opportunities include undertaking 'some really interesting cross-border work' from the London office, and there are also chances to complete international secondments in any one of a 'great variety of potential locations'. The firm is named a **Lex 100 Winner** in the international secondments category, and also triumphs in four other areas. The firm offers 'access to top-level clients' across a 'broad range of departments'. One respondent praises the 'top disputes team', while another trainee appreciates how 'specialist departments (such as pensions and intellectual property) do not just provide corporate support but have their own clients and work streams'. There can be some 'long hours' at the firm, and the 'work/life balance in corporate departments' can make 'planning life outside the office challenging'. That said, you can look forward to some great work moments, with recent examples including 'project managing large aspects of a due diligence transaction in eight jurisdictions', and 'being involved in a high-profile mediation'. There are some minor gripes about 'the buffet lunches' and 'IT systems', and there is one complaint that 'the trainee Christmas party is not subsidised by the firm'. On the plus side, the 'comprehensive training at the start of each seat' is lauded, as is the fact that 'Bakers does all its PSC training in-house'. To train at an international firm which offers a 'significant amount of direct client contact', add Baker & McKenzie to your shortlist.

If the firm were a fictional character it would be...

Dora the Explorer – travels around the world while always speaking the local language

The firm

Baker & McKenzie is one of the largest firms in the world, and currently has 77 offices in 47 countries. Befitting its massive size and reach, the firm specialises in handling huge transactions, often with a multi-jurisdictional focus. The London office is highly regarded for its tax, competition and employment law capabilities. London revenue jumped 9% last year while headcount remained flat.

The deals

Advised CSL on matters arising from its $275m acquisition of Novartis' global influenza vaccine business; represented EDF during the CMA's energy market investigation; advised Unilever on its acquisition of Procter & Gamble's Camay and Zest businesses, including a large factory in Mexico City; handled Bain Capital's acquisition of Davigel from Nestlé; advised Landesbank Baden-Württemberg in proceedings involving credit derivative transactions.

The clients

Accenture; British American Tobacco; CVC; Coca-Cola European Partners; Europa Capital; Fedex; Invesco Real Estate; Macquarie Group; Shell UK; Towers Watson.

The star performers

Top-ranking departments according to *The Legal 500* (see legal500.com for more details)
Banking litigation: investment and retail; Brand management; Commercial contracts; Corporate crime (including fraud, bribery and corruption); Corporate tax; Customs and excise; Data protection; Debt capital markets; EU and competition; Emerging markets; Environment; Equity capital markets; Fraud: civil; IT and telecoms; Pharmaceuticals and biotechnology; Private equity: transactions: Large-cap deal capability; Product liability: defendant; Real estate funds; Trade finance; VAT and indirect tax.

- **Why did you choose this firm over any others?** 'LGBT diversity'; 'international opportunities'; 'flexibility in seat choices'; 'partners I met at interview'; 'small trainee intake'; 'friendly vacation scheme'; 'global firm with local lawyers'; 'wide range of practice areas'; 'top disputes team'; 'I felt the firm gave applicants of whatever background an equal chance'

- **Best thing about the firm?** 'No egos here'; 'sports teams'; 'charity events'; 'colleagues are amiable'; 'two senior partners in the corporate finance department often go to the shop on a Friday afternoon and buy drinks for the whole team'; 'trainees are very close-knit'; 'they try to ensure that everyone sits where they would like'

- **Worst thing about the firm?** 'The buffet lunches'; 'the office could use a lick of paint'; 'when you have to stay late'; 'IT systems'; 'decisions being made without consulting the relevant people'; 'the international nature of the firm can bring some interesting work but it can also bring some really administrative work'

- **Best moment?** 'Leading a client call'; 'achieving a really good settlement for a client'; 'the trainee revue at the firm Christmas party'; 'getting invited to a San Francisco group meeting'; 'client secondment'; 'bi-monthly Friday night drinks'; 'secondment to Sydney'; 'achieving a favourable outcome for our client'; 'developing my research and analytical skills'

- **Worst moment?** 'Missing a deadline'; 'issues with signings'; 'photocopying documents at 4am'; 'being ridiculously busy in the build-up to Christmas'; 'waiting to find out which seat I was going to be put in'; 'collating signature pages at 2am for the third night in a row'

A day in the life of...

... John Hall third-seat trainee, Baker & McKenzie LLP

Departments to date: Corporate (private equity and funds), IT/commercial
University: Leeds
Degree and class: History, 2(1)

9.30am: After having a look at my BlackBerry on my commute to check what I have ahead of me for the day, I grab a coffee from the canteen and make my way into the employment department. I have a quick chat with a few of the associates in the team on my way in – everyone is looking forward to our summer social event next week, a rounders match in Hyde Park against the pensions department!

10.00am: I drop in to catch up with an associate who I've been assisting on a large case. The case is a claim which is due to go to tribunal in around a month's time, so we are in the process of collating the final documents for the tribunal bundle and preparing witness statements. I have been asked to attend a call with one of the witnesses for our side and take a first cut at drafting her witness statement. The call lasts about an hour – I then return to my room to discuss the approach I should take with my supervisor and begin my drafting.

12.45pm: The employment department schedules weekly lunches for the whole department to gather and discuss the various pieces of work that are keeping us all busy, as well as recent legal developments that are of interest. Employment law is quite dynamic, with new case law that could shape the advice we give to our clients arriving on a near-weekly basis! It's my turn to give a short presentation to the department on the case I'm working on.

2.00pm: Once the lunch is over, I send round an instruction email to six of my colleagues based in our overseas offices. One of our clients needs assistance with the varying regulations surrounding criminal background checks in six key jurisdictions. Our London office is often responsible for co-ordinating this kind of project and it gives trainees a great chance to build relationships beyond the UK. I set a reminder in my diary to discuss the responses we receive with the senior associate managing the project – trainees can expect to be heavily involved in collating and shaping the final work product we will send to the client.

4.30pm: A new email comes in from graduate recruitment about the vacation scheme students who will be arriving next week. One will be sitting in our team so I and the other trainees agree to introduce ourselves over coffee on Monday. We discuss as a group how the student could get involved in our ongoing pieces of work.

5.30pm: Some new documents have just been sent over by the client who is involved in the large case that we are working on. I review the documents and notice that some urgent work is required to protect our client's commercially sensitive information. I mark up where I think some changes should be made on the documents and run them by the associate before carrying them out and storing the new versions in our disclosure folder.

'Employment law is quite dynamic, with new case law that could shape the advice we give to our clients arriving on a near-weekly basis!'

6.30pm: I grab my sports bag and head down to reception to meet up with some fellow trainees and associates – we all play football for the firm's team so we're heading down to Battersea for a match in the London Legal League. While the season is underway, we play on a weekly basis and as well as being a good way to unwind after a day's work, the matches offer a great chance to socialise and get to know lawyers from outside your own department.

www.bakermckenzie.com/londongraduates

About the firm

Address: 100 New Bridge Street, London EC4V 6JA
Telephone: 020 7919 1000   **Fax:** 020 7919 1999
Website: www.bakermckenzie.com/londongraduates
Email: londongraduates@bakermckenzie.com
Facebook: www.facebook.com/BakerMcKenzieGraduates

Managing partner: Alex Chadwick

Other offices: Over 75 offices in nearly 50 countries.

Who we are: A leading global law firm with a presence in virtually every important financial and commercial centre.

What we do: We deliver high-quality local solutions across a broad range of practices and global advice in conjunction with our international offices. Our client base consists primarily of venture capital funds, investment banks, technology powerhouses and household-name brands.

What we're looking for: We are looking for trainees who are stimulated by intellectual challenge and respect and enjoy the diversity of cultural, social and academic backgrounds found in the firm. Effective communication skills, together with the ability to be creative and practical problem solvers, team players and to have a sense of humour, are qualities which will help them stand out from the crowd.

What you'll do: The two-year training contract comprises four six-month seats which include a corporate and a contentious seat, usually within our highly regarded dispute resolution department, together with the possibility of a secondment abroad or with a client.

Perks: Permanent health insurance, life insurance, private medical insurance, group personal pension, subsidised gym membership, season ticket loan, subsidised staff restaurant.

Sponsorship: We pay fees and a maintenance grant for the GDL and LPC. Those studying towards the GDL receive a £6,000 maintenance grant, and those studying for the LPC will receive an £8,000 maintenance grant.

Facts and figures

Total partners: 90 (London only)
Other fee-earners: 271 (London only)
Total trainees: 62 (London only)

Trainee places available for 2019: 30
Applications received pa: 2,000

First year salary: £45,000
Second year salary: £49,000
Newly qualified salary: £72,000

Application process

Apply to: The graduate recruitment team.
How: Online via our website.
When: Vacation scheme (spring and summer) and training contract for 2019 – see website for deadlines.
What's involved: Online application form, online tests and video interview. Successful applicants will be invited to an assessment centre consisting of: a group exercise, partner interview/case study and associate interview.

Vacation schemes

Spring: Spring 2017
Summer: Summer 2017

BAKER & McKENZIE

Bates Wells Braithwaite

10 Queen Street Place, London EC4R 1BE

Survey results *(marks out of 100%)*

Satisfied in your job?	78
Firm living up to expectations?	83
High quality of work?	83
Enough client contact?	75
Stress-free?	53
Happy work/life balance?	69
Friendly firm?	86
Great social life?	69
Good vacation scheme?	68
Confident you'll be kept on?	58
Good remuneration?	59
Diverse firm?	82

 verdict

With a 'strong social ethos' and an emphasis on 'client contact', Bates Wells Braithwaite is a 'growing' City firm with considerable 'scope for future expansion and success' in the market. The firm is a 'socially responsible business' at the cutting edge of developments in the charity and social enterprise sector. Trainees are given the opportunity to specialise and pursue their own areas of 'personal interest' such as faith-based, environment, technology and education. They are immersed in 'diverse work' and are rewarded with 'high levels of responsibility' and 'quality training'. The firm provides a 'welcoming atmosphere' where trainees will gain hands-on experience taking 'genuinely interesting' projects through to completion. While 'late hours' are inevitable on important cases, and one respondent reported working late for 'three weeks straight', the firm 'strives to maintain a healthy work/life balance' as it recognises that trainees have a life 'beyond the walls of the office'. 'Public interest' and 'common good' are at the heart of BWB's work, and the firm offers newcomers 'lots of high-quality client-based work'. Top first-year trainee moments include: 'taking the lead on running a significant case for an important client', 'tabling an amendment in parliament and having it discussed in the House of Lords' and 'receiving praise for work'. The supervisors are both 'encouraging and supportive' and there isn't a shortage of 'inspiring people' to work with. For the staff at BWB, it is 'more than a job – people here really believe in making a positive impact on society'. Those looking for 'excellent client contact' at a socially responsible firm should further research the Bates Wells Braithwaite training contract.

If the firm were a fictional character it would be...

Marshall Eriksen (How I Met Your Mother) – principled and pragmatic, and not your typical lawyer

The firm

From its single office in central London, Bates Wells Braithwaite handles market-leading third sector work, representing a huge swathe of charities and public sector clients. This focus is supplemented by the firm's busy commercial, employment and real estate departments. Bates Wells Braithwaite employs over 30 partners and more than 100 lawyers in total.

The deals

Defended *The Sunday Times* and two journalists in libel and malicious falsehood claims brought by Peter Cruddas; advised the Independent Parliamentary Standards Authority in connection with a complaint made against a high-profile political figure, which involved potential criminal and civil proceedings; assisted with Bromley College and Greenwich College's merger; advised the English National Opera on the removal of its chief executive and also negotiated the departure of its artistic director; acted for the Advertising Standards Authority in defending a judicial review application by UK Services Support.

The clients

ActionAid; the British Film Institute; Caffe Nero; Endemol; Euromoney Institutional Investor; Nikon UK; the Royal College of Nursing; the Royal Society of Arts; Thomson Directories; University of the Arts London.

The star performers

Top-ranking departments according to *The Legal 500* (see legal500.com for more details)
Administrative and public law; Brand management; Charities and not-for-profit; Commercial contracts; Commercial property: general; Education: institutions; Education: schools; Electoral; Employment: employers; Employment: senior executives; Immigration: business; Immigration: human rights, appeals and overstay; Local government; M&A: smaller deals, up to £50m; Media and entertainment (including media finance); Partnership; Professional discipline; Property litigation; Reputation management.

- **Why did you choose this firm over any others?** 'Strong social ethos'; 'strength in my areas of interest'; 'the standard of work referred to trainees'; 'it continues to be at the forefront of developments in the charity and social enterprise sector'; 'sector specialisms related to my own interest in public law and not-for-profits'; 'seemed to be a good size for high-quality work'

- **Best thing about the firm?** 'It really is trying to chart a course to support the public interest and the common good'; 'even when there is more pressure than normal and a lot of work to do, colleagues are friendly, supportive and understanding'; 'opportunities to take proper responsibility for a project and seeing it through'

- **Worst thing about the firm?** 'Outdated policies that don't match where the firm is or where it is going'

- **Best moment?** 'Corresponding with the Charity Commission for a year before finally convincing them that an absolutely awesome organisation should be a registered charity'; 'taking the lead on running an important case for an important client'; 'receiving praise for my work'

- **Worst moment?** 'Getting to court without noticing the papers I was about to file had been photocopied one-sided'; 'working late on one particular large deal for three weeks straight'; 'getting feedback that felt unaddressable'

A day in the life of...

... Alex Jameson second-year trainee, Bates Wells Braithwaite
Departments to date: Dispute resolution, corporate and commercial, employment, charity and social enterprise, real estate
University: Hull   **Degree and class:** Law 2(1)

9.00am: I arrive in the office and settle down at my desk to check my emails while I eat breakfast. Coffee, croissant and tangerine-esque orange variant. Breakfast of champions. The office is open plan with a large kitchen and atrium in the middle where colleagues often meet through the day to catch up.

9.20am: A calendar entry pops up to remind me to undertake a weekly case-law check. A judgment has come in on a Court of Appeal case I was monitoring, so I prepare a note of the salient points to discuss with my supervisor.

9.30am: The team has a catch up each week to find out what our colleagues are working on and where assistance is needed. This is my opportunity to get involved in various matters.

10.00am: A partner has a conference with counsel this morning. I prepared the instructions so have been asked to come and take a note. After some final preparation, we take a taxi to the Strand for a pre-meeting and coffee with the client we'd been corresponding with as I put together the instructions. It was great to meet the client face to face.

12.00pm: The conference went well and we are back in the office. I'm told the note isn't urgent, but the partner would like me to draft a letter to the other side based on counsel's advice regarding their withholding documents, so I get to work on that. Buoyed by leading counsel's advice, I come up with something quite robust and send it on for review.

1.00pm: It's a nice day, so instead of heading up to our roof terrace a few of us make the short stroll across Southwark Bridge and pick up lunch at Borough Market.

2.00pm: I pop over to my supervisor's desk to discuss the case update. They would like me to type up a note to send around the department that we can then send to our clients.

2.30pm: I begin typing up the note from this morning, but get interrupted by an urgent email. We have been bringing a high-profile class action on behalf of some 80 individuals, and the other side has applied to court to extend a deadline. After a brief discussion with the partner I get to work on drafting a response objecting to the application which is great exposure for me as a trainee.

3.00pm: Coffee. We have IPad coffee machines in the office. Back to that letter.

3.30pm: The partner and I discuss my letter and we share thoughts on tactics. After a few minor tweaks, I send it to court and other parties, along with an update to the clients.

4.00pm: I complete a couple of short research tasks for solicitors in the department, and find time to finish my note of the morning's conference. I spend the rest of the afternoon working on a pro bono matter. We are encouraged to pursue work that is of particular interest to us and are given the time and support to do this. BWB is a B Corporation, an independently-awarded certification which recognises that the firm values people and the

> **'We are encouraged to pursue work that is of particular interest to us and are given the time and support to do this.'**

community as much as it does making a profit. This particular matter is a review of a music publishing agreement for a songwriter. One of the recently qualified solicitors, acting as my mentor, has agreed to check my work and we review. There are a few things I'd missed, but nothing fundamental and it's all part of my training.

6.00pm: I check the week's tasks are all done and dusted, and type up a list of things I need to do next week.

6.30pm: It is Friday. A group of us head to the pub and enjoy the rest of the evening.

www.bwbllp.com/training-contracts

About the firm

Address: 10 Queen Street Place, London EC4R 1BE
Telephone: 020 7551 7777
Website: www.bwbllp.com
Email: training@bwbllp.com
Facebook: www.facebook.com/BatesWellsBraithwaite
Twitter: www.twitter.com/BWBllp

Managing partner: Martin Bunch

Who we are: BWB is a City law firm servicing a wide range of commercial and statutory organisations, charities and social enterprises. BWB is the first UK law firm to certify as a B Corp.

What we do: BWB has one of the leading charity and social enterprise teams in the country, along with a fast-growing corporate and commercial practice. Our clients include third-sector organisations, commercial organisations, regulators and individuals.

What we're looking for: The firm is looking for trainees with not only an excellent academic record and the ability to communicate clearly and effectively, but most importantly it is looking for trainees who positively want to join a firm such as Bates Wells Braithwaite.

What you'll do: Two six-month seats in the first year and three four-month seats in the second year. The firm runs a programme of internal seminars specifically addressed to trainees and operates a mentoring scheme.

Perks: These include a firm pension scheme with match funding provided; profit-sharing scheme; interest-free season ticket loan; permanent health insurance; subsidised gym memberships; wellbeing weeks and classes; cycle to work scheme; volunteering scheme; introducer schemes (client and recruitment); option to purchase additional leave.

Sponsorship: The firm will provide full financial support for both the GDL and LPC course. Fees will only be paid for courses that commence after the offer of a training contract has been made.

Facts and figures

Total partners: 34
Other fee-earners: 58
Total trainees: 9

Trainee places available for 2019: 6
Applications received pa: 750
Percentage interviewed: 5%

First year salary: £34,000
Second year salary: £36,000
Newly qualified salary: £57,000

Application process

Apply to: Hayley Ferraro, senior graduate recruitment and HR advisor.
How: Online via the website.
When: By June 2017 for 2019 contracts.
What's involved: Assessment day.

Vacation schemes

Spring: Apply by January 2017.
Summer: Apply by January 2017.

Bates Wells Braithwaite

Berwin Leighton Paisner LLP

Adelaide House, London Bridge, London EC4R 9HA

Survey results *(marks out of 100%)*

Satisfied in your job?	78
Firm living up to expectations?	82
High quality of work?	81
Enough client contact?	79
Stress-free?	59
Happy work/life balance?	64
Friendly firm?	87
Great social life?	76
Good vacation scheme?	89
Confident you'll be kept on?	77
Good remuneration?	76
Diverse firm?	85
Good international secondments?	70

 **verdict**

Many respondents cite Berwin Leighton Paisner's 'property focus' as a major attraction, and the City firm certainly commands an 'impressive client base' befitting its status as 'the best real estate firm in the country'. This 'highly-respected practice', which includes the 'top-rated land and planning departments', affords trainees the chance to work on 'high-quality projects', such as 'assisting a partner on a £100m deal', 'helping to close a huge corporate reorganisation in my first seat' and 'finally closing the structuring and financing of a European deal after many nights spent at my desk'. As the latter example suggests, there will be periods of 'long hours', and one respondent wrote that 'working on a difficult deal meant staying into the early hours of the morning on several days'. More favourable comments were centred on the 'great vacation scheme'. One trainee appreciated how 'friendly and welcoming everyone was', while another stated that 'partners went out of their way to give me good work'. BLP has a 'great reputation for excellent training and taking care of its lawyers'. Its bespoke LPC programme is considered 'comprehensive', and the 'positive working environment' at the firm cultivates a 'friendly and inclusive culture'. There are concerns about the 'lack of transparency on qualification', particularly as 'retention rates have been disappointing for recent cohorts', yet the firm is also said to 'take care of its lawyers'. Other plus points are the 'fantastic opportunities' for international and client secondments, and that after the working day, the 'social events are always good fun'. To embark upon a training contract at a firm offering 'client contact from day one', consider Berwin Leighton Paisner.

If the firm were a fictional character it would be...

Archimedes (The Sword in the Stone) – an understated character, constantly whispering wise words in the ear of the client

The firm

Berwin Leighton Paisner is acclaimed for its real estate expertise, encompassing the commercial property, construction, property litigation and planning departments. The firm also offers high-quality commercial and private client services. The firm announced the opening of a Myanmar office in November 2015, its fourth in Asia and 14th globally. BLP was nominated for Legal Technology Team of the Year at the *Legal Business* Awards 2016.

The deals

Acted for Goldman Sachs on developing its listed futures business; advised Ncondezi Energy on an agreement with Shanghai Electric Power Company to develop a coal-fired power plant in Mozambique; advising Amber Infrastructure and Aviva Investors as the funders on the £110m financing of 12 schools as part of the Priority Schools Building Programme; acting for National Grid on the UK's first EU-funded carbon capture and storage project; acting for key client Thames Water in a £55m dispute brought by the Canal & River Trust regarding Thames Water's right to abstract water from the River Lee.

The clients

3i Infrastructure Partners; Battersea Cats and Dogs Home; Bombardier; Credit Suisse; Goldman Sachs; Haversham Holdings; Lloyds; Patron Capital; Rothschild (Singapore); Tesco.

The star performers

Top-ranking departments according to *The Legal 500* (see legal500.com for more details)
Acquisition finance; Asset financing and leasing; Bank lending (investment grade debt and syndicated loans); Charities and not-for-profit; Contentious trusts and probate; Corporate restructuring and insolvency; Derivates and structured products; Emerging markets; Employee share schemes; Employment: employers; Health and safety; Infrastructure (including PFI and PPP); Mining and minerals; Oil and gas; Pensions (non-contentious); Personal tax, trusts and probate; Rail; Securitisation; Water.

- **Why did you choose this firm over any others?** 'Open-door policy'; 'friendly atmosphere'; 'good clients'; 'quality of training'; 'fantastic tax department'; 'industry-leading real estate practice'; 'I really enjoyed my vacation scheme'; 'high rankings in many departments'; 'a high calibre of work'; 'strong UK practice'; 'reputation for excellent training'; 'sector focus'; 'Magic Circle work without Magic Circle hours'

- **Best thing about the firm?** 'Real estate offering'; 'a good level of work without having to give up any semblance of a social life'; 'office location – right next to the River Thames and with great views – often quite distracting!'; 'the people'; 'client contact from day one'; 'high-quality projects'; 'great client exposure'

- **Worst thing about the firm?** 'Culture differences between departments'; 'there is not always recognition of what other departments bring to the firm'; 'retention rates'; 'the qualification process is stressful'; 'the toilets'; 'printers always breaking'; 'very real estate-centric'; 'there could be more international secondment opportunities'

- **Best moment?** 'Getting two job offers on qualification'; 'completing a matter in the tax department and everyone was very appreciative of the work I had contributed'; 'the work and client contact in real estate'; 'working directly with clients'; 'holding a three-hour one-to-one client meeting in my fourth seat'; 'closing a $100m financing in four days'

- **Worst moment?** 'Staying late for drafting'; 'being scolded by a partner'; 'drafting boards minutes at 4am'; 'six weeks of due diligence'; 'not meeting a deadline'; 'nerves on the first day'; 'having to deal with some very unpleasant clients'; 'verification of admission documents'

A day in the life of...

... Adrian Kwok first-seat trainee, Berwin Leighton Paisner LLP

Departments to date: Structured debt and capital markets
University: King's College London
Degree: Hispanic Studies with English

8.45am: I usually get to the office early to check emails that have come in overnight and review my to-do list. I then head down to Alibi (the firm's canteen) for breakfast with fellow trainees.

9.30am: I receive an email from a partner regarding an issuance of variable funding notes. I have been asked to update the documents list and prepare revised drafts of the transaction documents. I look through the briefing note, which is useful for learning about the transaction structure and what the transaction documents set out to achieve. I then work on the documents for the rest of the morning and sit down with the partner to discuss what I have prepared. This is a great learning experience as I am able to appreciate the subtle nuances of the transaction from her comments on the documents. After revising the drafts, the documents are ready for circulation to the client.

1.00pm: It is a sunny day today so I have made plans with trainees and associates in my department to go to Borough Food Market for lunch and coffee.

2.00pm: We have been instructed by a lender in a real estate financing project. As the project approaches completion, it is my responsibility to update the conditions precedent checklist on a daily basis so all parties are clear about the status of each item on the list. I will now join a partner on a call with the borrower's legal counsel to negotiate provisions of the security documents and discuss outstanding items on the list. Afterwards, I review the notes I took during the call to discuss the next steps with the partner and draft an email to update the client.

4.30pm: I will be assisting a partner and an associate on several ISDA negotiations over the next few weeks, and the partner has arranged for me to take part in a training session. The training introduces the main provisions of the ISDA master agreement and the key negotiation areas when acting for hedge providers and other counterparties. It is great to have the chance to learn about such a technical and intricate area of law, and the training gives me good insight into the secondment opportunities to leading financial institutions that the firm offers to trainees.

6.15pm: After a busy day, I touch base with the associates and partners to update them on my progress and check whether there is anything else I can help with. After ensuring that all work for today has been completed, I return to my desk to quickly look through my emails and make a to-do list for tomorrow.

'The training gives me good insight into the secondment opportunities to leading financial institutions that the firm offers to trainees.'

6.45pm: I send a message to a couple of friends I met on the LPC to see whether they are up for dinner and a few drinks tonight. They oblige and I set off for the Oyster Shed, a riverside bar within five minutes' walk from the office that looks out across the Thames.

www.blplaw.com/trainee

About the firm

Address: Adelaide House, London Bridge, London EC4R 9HA
Telephone: 020 3400 1000
Fax: 020 3400 1111
Website: www.blplaw.com/trainee
Email: traineerecruit@blplaw.com
Facebook: Berwin Leighton Paisner Graduates
Twitter: @BLPTrainees

Managing partner: Lisa Mayhew

Other offices: Abu Dhabi, Beijing, Berlin, Brussels, Dubai, Frankfurt, Hong Kong, Manchester, Moscow, Paris, Singapore, Tel Aviv, Yangon.

Who we are: We support clients from 14 international offices. Our clients include 50 Global Fortune 500 or FTSE 100 companies.

What we do: We have particular strengths in real estate, corporate, finance and tax, and a strong litigation and dispute resolution capability.

What we're looking for: In addition to talented individuals with brilliant minds and bright attitudes, we are looking for people who can take complex, often pressurised, commercial situations in their stride. The sort of people our clients want on their side and will ask for by name.

What you'll do: When recruiting trainees, our focus is on quality rather than quantity. As a result, our trainees are rewarded with a high degree of responsibility and involvement, underpinned by an exceptional standard of training and support. BLP has always prided itself on providing the right environment for people to grow.

Perks: Generous flexible benefits package, season ticket loan, ride to work scheme.

Sponsorship: CPE/GDL and LLM+ fees paid and £7,200 maintenance per course.

Facts and figures

Total UK partners: 152
Other UK fee-earners: 465
Total trainees: 83

Trainee places available for 2019: 40-45
Applications received pa: Approx 2,500
Percentage interviewed: Approx 10%

First year: £40,000
Second year: £45,000
Newly qualified: £66,000

Application process

How: Online application via www.blplaw.com/trainee.
When: By 30 July 2017 for 2019 training contracts.
What's involved: Online application; online test; assessment centre; vacation scheme (if applied for); final round interview with two partners.

Vacation schemes

Winter: December (apply by 31 October 2016).
Spring: April (apply by 31 January 2017).
Summer: June to August (apply by 31 January 2017)

Birketts LLP

24-26 Museum Street, Ipswich IP1 1HZ

Lex 100 Winner

See categories below
and tables from page 69

Survey results *(marks out of 100%)*

Satisfied in your job?	85
Firm living up to expectations?	88
High quality of work?	87
Enough client contact?	83
Stress-free?	67
Happy work/life balance?	82
Friendly firm?	97
Great social life?	79
Good vacation scheme?	84
Confident you'll be kept on?	75
Good remuneration?	63
Diverse firm?	90

 verdict

Birketts' trainees praise its 'excellent reputation', 'friendly atmosphere' and 'regional presence' in Cambridgeshire, Essex, Norfolk and Suffolk. The firm 'excels in all core practice areas and give trainees experience working in different parts of the law'. The 'client base' was also a 'massive pull' for one trainee. Many current trainees applied after completing work experience where they witnessed the 'friendly culture promoted by the partners' who are willing to 'spend large chunks of their days' with those on work experience and make time to offer trainees 'first-class training'. Looking at the 'long-term picture', Birketts is seen as a 'quickly expanding' firm with a 'good reputation' for giving newcomers a 'variety of tasks' and 'helpful feedback'. Trainees are given 'hands-on experience and responsibility from an early stage', and are 'regularly talking with clients directly with the appropriate support from supervisors'. The firm offer 'an excellent quality of life without having to sacrifice the high-quality work', and has earned four **Lex 100 Winner** medals. There are 'departmental gatherings' and other social events within the firm. Recent trainees' successes include 'working directly with the partners on a large corporate transaction', 'instructing my very own client for the first time by myself' and 'playing a key part at each stage of a client's claim and attending the hearing where the client won his case'. Despite a few complaints about some 'late-night photocopying' and the 'overwhelming responsibility', trainees praise the 'level of respect' they are given from day one. Take a closer look at Birketts if you are looking for a firm whose partners 'really care about your development'.

If the firm were a fictional character it would be...

The Avengers – the team continues to grow as it achieves great results

The firm

Top 100 firm Birketts posted record revenues for the 2015/16 financial year, announcing a 9.8% rise in turnover to £38.7m. The firm is headquartered in Ipswich, with additional offices in Norwich, Cambridge and Chelmsford. The dispute resolution, private client and real estate practices are all ranked highly by *The Legal 500*.

The deals

Acted for Kingsley Healthcare on a £200m fundraising investment; defended Powerscourt Services against a multi-million pound fraud claim; advised Port Technology Holdings on IP aspects of the exploitation of its personal data store and subsequent disputes; advised adjacent property owners on the redevelopment of Tottenham Hotspur FC's stadium; advised Muntons on a £53.4m asset-based finance facility.

The clients

Archant; Barclays Bank; Breckland District Council; Cromwell Manor Services; Greene King plc; Hitachi Capital UK; Larking Gowen; Norwich Airport; Partizan Films; Patisserie Valerie.

The star performers

Top-ranking departments according to *The Legal 500* (see legal500.com for more details)
Agriculture and estates; Charities and not-for-profit; Commercial litigation; Construction; Corporate and commercial; Crime: fraud; Debt recovery; Education; Employment; Environment; Family; Health; Immigration; Insolvency and corporate recovery; Licensing; Personal tax, trusts and probate; Planning; Property litigation; Social housing; Transport and shipping.

- **Why did you choose this firm over any others?** 'My week's work experience at the firm'; 'location was important, so that I could stay living at home'; 'wide range of practice areas'; 'local reputation'; 'I wanted to train with a large regional firm'; 'the high retention rates'; 'excellent work/life balance'

- **Best thing about the firm?** 'Everyone is friendly and approachable'; 'I have been given responsibility'; 'client contact'; 'partner involvement in your development'; 'I always feel like I can ask for help'; 'I appreciate being supervised by highly skilled and talented fee-earners'; 'the level of respect that trainees are given'; 'I am frequently given feedback'

- **Worst thing about the firm?** 'When mice were discovered'; 'moving seats to another office located in a different county';

'a lack of networking opportunities for trainees'; 'some late nights'

- **Best moment?** 'Completing my first purchase of land on behalf of a client'; 'being left to run some files after meeting with the clients'; 'attending the Olympic velodrome for a day-long client event and having the opportunity to cycle on the track'; 'being able to observe a barrister present a case you played a part in putting together'

- **Worst moment?** 'Having to stay until 1am on a corporate deal'; 'copying bundles late one Friday evening'; 'being given a task with no guidance'; 'desperately trying to collate client evidence'; 'bundling huge amounts of confidential documents'; 'making a really embarrassing mistake'

A day in the life of…

… **Anna Wills** first-year trainee, Birketts LLP

Departments to date: Private client, agriculture

University: University of East Anglia

Degree and class: Law, 2(1)

I am a trainee solicitor at Birketts LLP and I am currently in my second seat working in the agriculture team at the firm's Norwich office. One of the best things about being a trainee is that no two days are the same but here is a standard day…

A typical morning: My first job of the day is to check my emails and review my to-do list which I update every day before I go home. I find that this means that I can get started as soon as I get in, but not before a cup of tea!

I have written down a few points that I need to ask my supervisor and I ask him when I see that he has a moment.

After talking to my supervisor I am given a file to work on that requires drafting a deed of variation to an existing lease and drafting a new lease, as well as a letter of explanation for the client. Drafting can take a while and it is essential that the documents match up so I initially draft at my desk and then pop into a private room so that I can proof read away from all distractions.

A typical afternoon: After drafting the documents I ask a colleague a few points that I need clarification on and update my drafting accordingly. We also discuss the team meeting at lunch (including that we

hope that there is cake) and review the agenda. Today we have our team meeting. This is a chance for all four offices to get together (normally via video conference) to talk about how we are doing as a team and if there are any issues that are impacting our practice. Today Brexit was discussed in detail with everyone agreeing that no one knows what is going to happen so we will make the best of the situation.

A colleague asks me to find some urgent planning permission notices which have been revealed by a local search. This involves talking to the local council to ensure that we receive the documents in time.

I receive a call from a case worker at the Land Registry who informs me that they are dealing with a first registration application that I made. They ask me a number of questions which I am able to answer and I type up my attendance note once the call has ended.

My supervising partner asks me to do some research on SDLT provisions and I confer with a tax colleague to get some suggestions as to where to start.

I give my supervisor an update as to where we are in regard to finalising a deed of variation for a farm business tenancy and he

advises me to chase the other side to approve our draft. I also hand over the documents that I have drafted today for my supervisor to review. We make an appointment for the following day once he has had a chance to consider them.

> **'Today Brexit was discussed in detail with everyone agreeing that no one knows what is going to happen.'**

A typical evening: I ensure that all my emails throughout the day have been filed both electronically and on the paper file and I make a to-do list for the following day.

I am part of a rounders team for the firm and we go to a local tournament which is a great way to network in an informal setting. I'm not a natural, but I am assured that it is the taking part which counts!

www.birketts/careers/graduates.aspx

About the firm

Address: 24-26 Museum Street, Ipswich IP1 1HZ
Telephone: 01473 232300   **Fax:** 01473 230524
Website: www.birketts.co.uk
Email: suzannah-rogers@birketts.co.uk
Facebook: www.facebook.com/birketts-llp-graduates
Twitter: @birkettsllp

Senior partner: James Austin

Other offices: Cambridge, Norwich, Chelmsford

Who we are: Birketts is an ambitious, full-service, top 100 UK law firm with a rich heritage, advising businesses, institutions and individuals in the UK and internationally.

What we do: Our business is divided into four main disciplines – corporate/commercial, commercial property, litigation/dispute resolution and private client.

What we're looking for: Applications are welcome from both law and non-law students. Applicants should have a minimum of a 2(1) degree and good A Level results (minimum B,B,B or equivalent), strong interpersonal skills and a common sense approach.

What you'll do: Our training contract comprises four seats, with each one lasting six months. You are likely to spend time in corporate, commercial property and private client teams as well as the firm's specialist practice areas e.g. employment, shipping, tax and agriculture.

Perks: Staff profit share, life assurance (x 4 salary), contributory pension scheme, private medical insurance (after probation), permanent health insurance, interest-free season ticket loan, subsidised gym membership, cycle to work scheme (salary sacrifice), childcare vouchers, social events throughout the year, eye-care vouchers.

Sponsorship: LPC fees

Facts and figures

Total partners: 59
Other fee-earners: 222
Total trainees: 16

Trainee places available for 2019: 10-12
Applications received pa: 300
Percentage interviewed: c20-30%

First year salary: £23,500
Second year salary: £24,500
Newly qualified salary: £36,000-£37,500

Turnover in 2015: £34.9m (+10% from 2014)
Profits per equity partner: £258,000 (+2%)
(see legalbusiness.co.uk for full financial information)

Application process

Apply to: Suzannah Rogers – recruitment officer
How: Via our careers/graduates page: http://www.birketts.co.uk/careers/graduates
When: Between 1 February 2017-31 July 2017 for training contracts commencing 2019.
What's involved: You will be interviewed at the office to which you have applied by two partners and the interview will last approximately 45 minutes. At the interview you will be asked to present for 5-10 minutes on a topic of your choice.

Vacation schemes

Summer: June 2017 (apply by 31 January 2017)

Birketts

Blaser Mills

40 Oxford Road, High Wycombe HP11 2EE

Lex 100 Winner

See categories below
and tables from page 69

Survey results *(marks out of 100%)*

Satisfied in your job? **88**

Firm living up to expectations? **92**

High quality of work? **93**

Enough client contact? **85**

Stress-free? **54**

Happy work/life balance? **78**

Friendly firm? **95**

Great social life? **65**

Good vacation scheme? **92**

Confident you'll be kept on? **63**

Good remuneration? **54**

Diverse firm? **84**

 verdict

A 'very dynamic, up-and-coming firm', Blaser Mills is a 'regional firm that is expanding'. The 'all-round open-door policy' means trainees 'feel comfortable and valued'. This 'reputable medium-sized firm offers both a wide range of work and a high level of client contact and individual responsibility'. From the secretaries to the managing partner, people are 'incredibly friendly and approachable', a trait which has helped the firm to secure six **Lex 100 Winner** medals, including for friendliness and job satisfaction. Trainees have enjoyed 'getting praise from one of the toughest supervisors', 'representing the firm at a once-in-a-lifetime hearing at the Royal Courts of Justice' or simply 'building their confidence' day-by-day. With 'no hand-holding', trainees are able to 'get a lot of hands-on experience' from day one and are 'treated with respect'. There is the 'right amount of responsibility and freedom', which 'increases over time'. The 'working hours are manageable' as the firm is 'conscious of the importance of work/life balance'. Bug bears include parking arrangements and 'seat requests not necessarily being listened to'. Trainees should expect a 'massive learning curve' and 'plenty of hard work' as they will be 'involved in the day-to-day running of files from the start'. The 'friendly firm' provides the 'kind of environment people want to train in' with 'excellent opportunities'. Also, there are 'lots of experienced lawyers in a variety of areas', and Blaser Mills is 'committed to getting the best out of its trainees' by encouraging them to 'develop both professionally and personally'. If you like the idea of plenty of responsibility from day one, then Blaser Mills is a good firm to keep in mind.

If the firm were a fictional character it would be...

Tintin – friendly, honourable and a proven problem-solver

The firm

Blaser Mills has a team of over 75 lawyers based across six offices in the South East region. The firm has built up considerable expertise in family, private client and personal injury cases. The firm also has a highly-regarded criminal law practice.

The deals

Acting in the Operation Elveden corruption probe; handling several murder and immigration cases; acts for severely injured claimants in multi-defendant claims; advised on acquisitions for development and property companies, as well as on the sale and purchase of hotels.

The clients

Blaser Mills represents both individuals and corporate clients on a range of contentious and non-contentious matters. This includes the pursuit of damages on behalf of claimants, as well as various commercial and contractual deals for small to mid-size companies.

The star performers

Top-ranking departments according to *The Legal 500* (see legal500.com for more details)
Commercial litigation; Commercial property; Crime: general; Debt recovery; Employment; Family; Personal injury: claimant; Personal tax, trusts and probate; Property litigation.

- **Why did you choose this firm over any others?** 'Opportunity to have a large say in what seats you do'; 'open-door policy throughout the firm'; 'responsibility given to trainees'; 'opportunities to progress within the firm'; 'broad range of practice areas'; 'multi-practice and expanding'; 'the firm has a very good reputation'; 'it has a reputation in the South East as a very dynamic, up-and-coming firm'

- **Best thing about the firm?** 'The ability to talk to anyone in the firm'; 'my supervisor and other partners within the firm are always very approachable and happy to help when they can'; 'everyone is very welcoming'; 'lots of experienced lawyers in a variety of different areas'; 'colleagues are incredibly friendly and approachable'

- **Worst thing about the firm?** 'Financial remuneration'; 'there is little information about retention rates provided to trainees'; 'the offices are large and spread out so I don't feel I know

many colleagues in other locations, apart from the trainees'; 'seat allocations and information about qualifying jobs being offered are left until relatively late'

- **Best moment?** 'Completing my first sale and purchase in the residential property team'; 'settling my first case'; 'successfully defending an application in a County Court against an experienced barrister'; 'receiving an email from a client showing her appreciation for all the hard work I had put into her file'; 'the opportunity to undertake a full 12 months in an area of law that I want to qualify into'

- **Worst moment?** 'Reading a case file which took two whole days'; 'panicking in what should have been a basic application before a district judge'; 'when a completion came very close to the wire and we weren't sure if it would happen'; 'initially finding out I was doing an area of law that I did not have any interest in'

A day in the life of...

... Mohsin Shabbir second-year trainee, Blaser Mills LLP

Departments to date: Corporate and commercial, family and divorce (private), personal and serious injury
University: University of Kent, Canterbury
Degree and class: LLB Law, 2(1)

8.30am: I am fortunate to live relatively close to our new head office in High Wycombe, so my morning commute is not too strenuous. A cup of tea is a must and it allows to me to speak to my colleagues before I settle down at my desk. Part of my morning routine is checking through my emails and listing all the tasks that I need to do for the day. I meet with my supervisor to talk through my to-do list and identify what tasks need to be prioritised, making sure I build in the various meetings with clients that my supervisor has scheduled.

9.15am: My first task is to draft a letter before action for an international client in relation to breach of contract and IP infringement. I really enjoy drafting these as it allows me to conduct some research, identify the main issues and get involved with some quasi-contentious work in a largely non-contentious team.

10.00am: My supervisor and I have a meeting with a client in relation to a bank debenture. Our client is seeking independent legal advice in relation to the debenture. I had reviewed the documentation with my supervisor a few days previously and had prepared an advice note in advance of the meeting. My supervisor explains the finer points of the debenture to the client and goes through the advice note. Client meetings are great for learning not only about technical legal issues, but also understanding how they impact clients in a business sense.

11.00am: I am assisting my supervisor with the sale of a company and he has asked me to set up a virtual data room (VDR) in order to upload the documents onto a secure and encrypted platform. I organise the electronic disclosure bundle and arrange the VDR. Invites for the VDR are sent out to the buyer's solicitors.

12.00pm: I meet with my supervisor for a conference call with our LLP client. Having met the client and been involved in telephone and email exchanges with them, I feel I play an integral role. This call is to review the draft shareholders' agreement that we have prepared for our client's new venture. A few minor changes are required but our client is keen to sign the documentation as soon as possible. I edit the draft shareholders' agreement, making the changes. The draft is then submitted to the client for final thoughts.

1.00pm: Lunchtime typically involves a short walk with two of my department colleagues to grab a sandwich and get some fresh air. It is encouraged to go out and have a lunch break so that you come back refreshed and ready for the afternoon.

3.00pm: My supervisor and I meet a new client. They have an interesting and complex set of issues and I am asked to take an attendance note of the meeting, which we'll refer to when actioning our client's instructions.

4.15pm: Debrief with my supervisor. Our new client's immediate and most pressing

> '**Having met the client and been involved in telephone and email exchanges with them, I feel I play an integral role.**'

requirement is responding to a letter purporting breach of contract and director's duties. I am asked to begin drafting our client's outline argument and researching the relevant law for review tomorrow morning.

5.30pm: I make the amendments and submit the letter by email to our international client for their approval. I am not likely to receive any approval to send the letter until the morning due to the different time-zones.

6.00pm: I leave the office and head to Egham, Surrey where I have organised a five-a-side football match with my firm against a firm of accountants that we regularly meet with. After the match we head to the pub for a general catch-up, a few drinks and some food.

www.blasermills.co.uk

About the firm

Address: 40 Oxford Road, High Wycombe HP11 2EE
Telephone: 020 3814 2020
Website: www.blasermills.co.uk
Email: enquiries@blasermills.co.uk
LinkedIn: www.linkedin.com/company/blaser-mills
Twitter: @BlaserMills

Senior partner: Alka Kharbanda
Managing partner: Jonathan Lilley

Other offices: Amersham, Harrow, London, Rickmansworth, Staines

Who we are: Blaser Mills is a leading law firm based in the South East with 18 partners and over 65 lawyers.

What we do: We are a full-service firm, offering a comprehensive range of legal services to businesses and private individuals. We act for blue-chip companies that are household names as well as SMEs, entrepreneurs and not-for-profit organisations.

What we're looking for: We don't have a 'one size fits all' criteria for what we look for in a trainee. We believe that different areas of work require different skills and our lawyers are as individual as the clients that we represent. However, our successful trainees have often had one or more of the following attributes: good academic background, enquiring interest in the wider world, ability to work under pressure, excellent communication skills, commercial awareness, analytical ability, sense of humour, attention to detail, energy, resilience and ambition.

What you'll do: Training starts in September with a full induction day that introduces you to the firm. You will need to hit the ground running though, as you start work in your first seat from the second day. You will have four varied seats of six months each, giving you the opportunity to gain experience across a range of legal disciplines. You will be allocated a training supervisor that will offer you a degree of direction, but encourages you to use your initiative and gain independence throughout your time at the firm.

Perks: Trainees are enrolled into our pension scheme and are given life cover from day one. Throughout the traineeship, trainees are encouraged to join young professionals networking groups, seminars and events to continually develop themselves professionally.

Facts and figures

Total partners: 18
Other fee-earners: 49
Total trainees: 10

Trainee places available for 2019: 4-6
Applications received pa: 300
Percentage interviewed: circa 5%

First year salary: £22,000
Second year salary: £23,000
Newly qualified salary: £N/A

Application process

How: Online, through the Apply4law portal
When: 31 July 2017
What's involved: Assessment day, including written exercises, group exercises and interviews.

Vacation schemes

Summer: July/August and deadline of 30 April 2017.

Bond Dickinson LLP

4 More London Riverside, London SE1 2AU

Survey results *(marks out of 100%)*

Satisfied in your job?	81
Firm living up to expectations?	81
High quality of work?	83
Enough client contact?	69
Stress-free?	62
Happy work/life balance?	81
Friendly firm?	89
Great social life?	77
Good vacation scheme?	85
Confident you'll be kept on?	82
Good remuneration?	72
Diverse firm?	82

 verdict

Bond Dickinson has a 'supportive and friendly atmosphere'; partners are 'interested in getting to know trainees' and 'want them to succeed'. The firm has 'bags of ambition and talks a strong game', with 'respected clients, personality and friendliness'. Bond Dickinson makes sure 'trainees get the best possible experience' and although there is a 'lack of international opportunities', the firm is 'expanding' and has a 'vision to grow'. Top trainee moments include playing a 'vital role in completing a deal worth in excess of £60m', 'attending a sentencing hearing in the Magistrates Court' and being the point of contact for a 'property transaction of £10m'. The training is 'tailored to the individual' by supervisors who put an emphasis on 'investing time, knowledge and effort in helping trainees improve and reach their potential both as lawyers and as people'. Trainees are 'not expected to work late if it is not required for the job' and are 'encouraged to bring ideas to the table'. The firm has a 'national reach' while still maintaining a 'local identity' and trainees are 'exposed to high-level work early on', and 'decent levels of responsibility'. Trainees also receive a 'huge confidence boost' when 'good work doesn't go unnoticed' as part of working within a 'wider team', which is a 'very supportive' environment to work in. For those 'striving to achieve quality and excellence while managing to remain human', Bond Dickinson is a great choice.

If the firm were a fictional character it would be...

Mr Benn – quite old school, yet is able to adapt to any situation

The firm

Bond Dickinson possesses a wide market reach in the UK with eight offices in England and Scotland, and it bolstered its international credentials in June 2016 by forming an exclusive strategic alliance with US firm Womble Carlyle Sandridge & Rice. Corporate tax, property litigation, employment and IP are traditional firm strengths. Bond Dickinson was shortlisted for National/Regional Firm of the Year at the *Legal Business* Awards 2016.

The deals

Provided strategic planning advice to Bellway Homes as part of a consortium in connection with a 1600-unit development; defended Darlington Borough Council in equal pay litigation brought by multiple claimants; acted for Atom Bank on its £135m equity fundraising, which involved investments from several banks and investment management companies; assisted with the £150m refinancing of a sub-group of Grainger plc; acted for Churchill Property Services on the £4.4m sale of a freehold site in Aycliffe Business Park, which includes 40 occupied units.

The clients

British Association of Oral Surgeons; British Gas; IBM; The National Trust; Old Mutual Wealth; Post Office; Procter & Gamble; Sainsbury's; Santander; University of Durham.

The star performers

Top-ranking departments according to *The Legal 500* (see legal500.com for more details)

Agriculture and estates; Charities and not-for-profit; Commercial litigation; Commercial property; Construction; Contentious trusts and probate; Corporate tax; Debt recovery; Education; Employment; Environment; Health and safety; IT and telecoms; Licensing; Pensions; Personal tax, trusts and probate; Planning; Professional negligence; Property litigation; Social housing.

- **Why did you choose this firm over any others?** 'Genuinely friendly atmosphere'; 'opportunity to practice in the niche area of law in which I am interested'; 'strong presence at graduate recruitment events'; 'high-quality work and clients'; 'great location in Newcastle'; 'high level of client contact'; 'good work/life balance'; 'informative and enjoyable vacation scheme'; 'open-minded approach to career-changers'

- **Best thing about the firm?** 'Open-door policy'; 'good work/life balance'; 'good-quality work'; 'friendly environment'; 'great level of responsibility'; 'friendly atmosphere'; 'everyone strives to achieve quality and excellence'; 'supportive working atmosphere'; 'its friendliness and inclusivity'; 'other partners are interested in getting to know you'

- **Worst thing about the firm?** 'No kettles on the floors'; 'small amount of formal training'; 'some relationships between offices can be negative'; 'work can be a bit basic on a slow day'; 'uneven spread of each type of work across offices'; 'lack of dialogue about seat rotation'; 'the lack of sinks to wash plates'

- **Best moment?** 'Attending an employment tribunal where the other side was a litigant in person'; 'experiencing sentencing hearing in the Magistrates Court'; 'getting really great feedback on something I thought had been unnoticed'; 'the opportunity to undertake a commercial secondment'; 'playing a significant part in completing a deal worth in excess of £60m'

- **Worst moment?** 'Spending three months of a seat feeling I wasn't making a contribution to my team due to lack of work'; 'managing the huge amount of extra-curricular tasks that are expected to be picked up by trainees'; 'the frustration of not knowing the practice area'; 'spending a week assessing a claim and drafting a response when it wasn't actually needed'

A day in the life of...

... Rebecca Butler trainee solicitor, Bond Dickinson LLP

Departments to date: Commercial, commercial disputes
University: University of Plymouth, University of Law – Bristol
Degree and class: LLB (Hons) Law 2(1)

8.00am: I read the news.

8.30am: I arrive at the office. I check my emails, review my calendar and catch up with my supervisor.

9.05am: I continue preparing the documentation to appoint Law of Property Act receivers. I finalise the validation report and letters of acceptance for my supervisor's approval.

9.45am: We have a work experience student in our department. I introduce them to the team, allocate a desk and provide them with various tasks.

10.00am: During my seat within commercial disputes, I have been given a high level of responsibility, interesting technical work and the opportunity to build direct client relationships. I attend a client meeting with my supervisor to discuss the ongoing issues relating to a private nuisance. I take notes, ensuring I have a record of our action points.

11.15am: I return to my desk, dictate the attendance note and draft a letter to the

other side putting them on notice of our intention to obtain a Norwich Pharmacal Order.

12.15pm: I catch up with the work experience student, supervise and provide feedback. I allocate them further tasks for the afternoon.

12.30pm: I go out to lunch with a colleague.

1.30pm: I return from lunch and have an email from one of the solicitors in the team requesting a financial status search on three companies. I conduct the search, draft a note of the company's structure and monitor the companies for future insolvency alerts.

2.00pm: My supervisor receives a request from a client regarding a tenant breaching their obligations pursuant to a lease. I review the lease. I draft a letter referring to the breached covenants and possibility of an injunction. I send the letter to my supervisor for authorisation and then to our client for consideration.

3.45pm: I start to review documentation and draft a memorandum in relation to a breach

of contract query received from a large real estate client.

4.50pm: I review the further tasks undertaken by the work experience student, provide feedback and have a Q&A session.

> '**I have been given a high level of responsibility, interesting technical work and the opportunity to build direct client relationships.**'

5.20pm: After checking I have completed everything on my to-do list for the day, I finalise my time recording on our time management system.

5.30pm: One great benefit to our office location: I go for a run around the Plymouth seafront, tracking my time on Strava!

www.bonddickinson.com

About the firm

Address: 4 More London Riverside, London SE1 2AU
Telephone: 0845 415 0000   **Fax:** 0845 415 6900
Website: www.bonddickinson.com
Email: graduates@bonddickinson.com
Twitter: @BondDTrainees

Chairman: Nick Page
Managing partner: Jonathan Blair

Other offices: Aberdeen, Bristol, Leeds, London, Newcastle, Plymouth and Southampton.

Who we are: Bond Dickinson, a dynamic UK law firm, provides a comprehensive legal service to our clients in a wide range of legal sectors across seven UK cities. Following a successful merger in 2013, Bond Dickinson continues to increase its business by growing its presence across the UK, strengthening client relationships, winning new business and investing in more highly skilled and ambitious people. Anyone at the start of their legal career would be joining us in a period of expansion and excitement.

What we do: We are a full-service law firm with a focus on eight major sectors: energy, waste and natural resources; retail and fast-moving consumer goods (FMCG); real estate; financial institutions; chemicals and manufacturing; transport and infrastructure; private wealth; and insurance. We also continue to expand our technology; hospitality and leisure; and education sectors.

What we're looking for: At Bond Dickinson we look for intellectually able, motivated and enthusiastic graduates from any discipline. Successful applicants will understand the need to provide practical, commercial advice to clients. You will share the firm's commitment to self-development and teamwork and its desire to provide clients with services that match their highest expectations.

What you'll do: We look at our trainee recruitment as a long-term investment. Trainees at Bond Dickinson will have an opportunity to spend six months in four business groups, gaining a real breadth of experience. This is your training contract and it's up to you to make the most of it. We offer fantastic opportunities to develop your legal career. Your personal preferences are taken into serious consideration during the seat rotation process

Perks: Flexible benefits, including travel loan, pension, discounted car parking schemes.

Sponsorship: Full sponsorship for LPC and GDL and maintenance grant.

Facts and figures

Total partners: 138
Other fee-earners: 700
Total trainees: 55

Trainee places available for 2019: 30

First year salary: TBC
Second year salary: TBC

Turnover in 2015: £107m (+8% from 2014)
Profits per equity partner: £284,000 (+26% from 2014)
(see legalbusiness.co.uk for full financial information)

Application process

Apply to: Joanne Smallwood.
How: Online application at www.bonddickinson.com.
When: By 28 February 2017 for 2019 training contracts.
What's involved: Online application, aptitude and ability tests, assessment day, presentation, panel interview.

Vacation schemes
Summer: June and July schemes are available in 2017.
Apply by 28 February 2017 at
www.bonddickinson.com.

Brabners LLP

Horton House, Exchange Flags, Liverpool L2 3YL

Survey results *(marks out of 100%)*

Satisfied in your job?	78
Firm living up to expectations?	81
High quality of work?	74
Enough client contact?	69
Stress-free?	72
Happy work/life balance?	85
Friendly firm?	86
Great social life?	76
Good vacation scheme?	56
Confident you'll be kept on?	73
Good remuneration?	68
Diverse firm?	82

 verdict

Brabners combines a 'strong presence in the North West' with a 'fantastic reputation for carrying out quality work'. Indeed, the firm 'specialises in areas which are in demand and growing', and is commended by one trainee for its 'strength in corporate and sports law'. Though the firm naturally has a 'strong North West focus', respondents enthuse that Brabners also 'has the ability to obtain work from national clients'. You can look forward to a 'good amount of responsibility from the start', as 'trainees at Brabners are given the freedom to chart their own path'. Stand-out trainee moments to date include 'representing a client at a case management hearing in my first seat', 'finalising a settlement agreement with a partner from the other side' and 'completing a corporate sale transaction that had taken over my life for the best part of a fortnight, and going out with the clients after to celebrate'. One criticism shared with us is that the amount of client contact 'can vary between seats', and this might explain 'some of the basic administration tasks' which trainees can be handed. Still, trainees' opinions are 'sought and valued by other fee-earners' so there is scope to 'develop your profile within the firm'. There can be long hours on occasion, which can lead to 'working until past midnight to meet a key deadline', but on the whole Brabners offers a 'good work/life balance'. Working with 'approachable and friendly' colleagues makes for a 'relaxed environment' which has earned a **Lex 100 Winner** award for low stress levels, and it is therefore 'easy to ask questions if you are unsure about anything'. To train at a North West firm alongside 'solicitors who are regarded as leaders in their field', consider applying to Brabners.

If the firm were a fictional character it would be...

Charlie Bucket (Charlie and the Chocolate Factory) – has a strong moral compass and outsmarts others by staying true to itself

The firm

Brabners' three offices in the North West region combine to offer a range of services in the private client, real estate, corporate and commercial and TMT sectors. This well-regarded firm is also a member of two international networks, enabling its client reach to extend across 35 countries throughout Europe.

The deals

Advised Restore on its £55.7m purchase of Wincanton's records management business; advised Grange Motors on the disposal of a site in the Lake District National Park; advised Cold Move on the carve-out and sale of a cold storage and logistics business; acted for Urban Sleep on the £41.6m sale of its portfolio of student accommodation to Empiric; advised rugby league club Salford Red Devils on several disputes.

The clients

Alpha Technology; Axa; Begbies Traynor; Business Growth Fund; England Golf; Impellam Group; Inteb Sustainability; JD Wetherspoon; Nando's; Peel Ports Group.

The star performers

Top-ranking departments according to *The Legal 500* (see legal500.com for more details)
Agriculture and estates; Banking and finance; Charities and not-for-profit; Commercial litigation; Contentious trusts and probate; Corporate and commercial; Corporate tax; Crime: general; Debt recovery; Employment; Family; Health; Intellectual property; Licensing; Media and entertainment; Personal tax, trusts and probate; Property litigation; Social housing; Sport; Transport.

- **Why did you choose this firm over any others?** 'Offered high-quality work without sacrificing work/life balance'; 'I was looking to join a North West firm that has a strong reputation for corporate/commercial work'; 'potential for growth'; 'excellent reputation for its work with SMEs'; 'the recruitment process is partner-driven'; 'the firm takes an interest in each employee as an individual'; 'the training was highly recommended'

- **Best thing about the firm?** 'Located in a thriving city'; 'friendly staff'; 'you are given the opportunity to work on really complex areas of law'; 'the firm takes an interest in how we are getting on'; 'it really believes in work/life balance'; 'everybody is treated on the same level'

- **Worst thing about the firm?** 'There should be better dialogue between the firm's three offices'; 'limited number of seats which means there is not much choice'; 'there could be more client contact'; 'workplace politics'; 'not the prettiest office'; 'no international opportunities'; 'limited administrative resources'

- **Best moment?** 'Receiving praise after researching a complex area of pensions law'; 'being given the independence to progress matters and files on my own'; 'I attended mediation with my supervising partner which was a fantastic experience'; 'winning a case for our client in the High Court'; 'ego-massaging praise after working on a difficult matter'

- **Worst moment?** 'My mid-seat appraisal was pretty critical and that was hard to take'; 'getting into the office at 7am in order to redraft an agreement'; 'nearly missing a court deadline'; 'working late to find the last train home cancelled'; 'photocopying and preparing bundles'; 'daily administration letters to clients'; 'organising property deeds for a large client'

Why Brabners LLP?

Brabners LLP has expanded rapidly in recent years, enabling us to provide a greater range of services and increased strength and depth. We recruit and retain a team of highly motivated and skilled professionals and support staff, committed to delivering effective, client-focused legal services. Our proactive approach is constructive, committed and down to earth, and we work closely with our clients to provide commercially realistic solutions to their legal problems.

Brabners LLP is one of the few law firms that holds 'Investor in People' status and we place great emphasis on the structure and progression of our training programme. The programme is continually re-appraised to ensure that it meets the requirements of each trainee solicitor.

Brabners LLP is consistently listed as an award winner in *The Lex 100* student guide to the UK's premier law firms.

As a firm we strongly believe that trainees have a place within our teams and encourage them to contribute to the work of their teams by allocating them responsibility from the outset. In each of your four seats you will spend time with a partner or senior lawyer, although you may also assist other fee-earners within the department. Your work will be closely monitored by your principal who will give support, guidance and assistance. Trainees are encouraged to discuss with their principal any problems they encounter as

part of our strong 'open-door' policy which encourages trainees to seek help whenever they need it. We recognise and encourage an eagerness to learn and consider a genuine ambition to succeed to be an attribute. We willingly devote the time required to ensure our trainees achieve their goals.

We strongly believe a wide range of disciplines should be experienced before a decision to specialise is made. Our comprehensive training and development programme includes all that is required by the SRA and also provides an induction course and ongoing in-house training and development.

Personal development appraisals are conducted at three and six monthly intervals to ensure that trainee progress is valuable and informed. Training and staff development in the firm is the responsibility of our director of training, Dr Tony Harvey, and the training programme is overseen by the firm's trainee partners, Rupert Gill and Helen Marriott (Liverpool), Sam Mabon and Lydia Edgar (Manchester).

Life as a trainee with us is not all work and we encourage a positive work/life balance. Our offices maintain a friendly and social environment, something envied by many larger firms. Brabners LLP's social life will play a great part in your life as a trainee and our trainees are encouraged to organise regular social events, including the annual staff conference, and our annual pro bono

activities frequently raise in excess of £30,000 for the charity chosen by our staff. Brabners LLP colleagues regularly socialise after office hours, with Liverpool and Manchester having vibrant young professional scenes in which trainees soon become involved. We are active participants in a football league and regularly engage in other sports with other

> 'Trainees are encouraged to discuss with their principal any problems they encounter as part of our strong "open door" policy.'

professionals. Officers of the regional JLDs are frequently Brabners LLP trainees.

It is our practice to select six trainees each year, three based in Liverpool and three in Manchester. We seek to recruit people who have great potential to succeed. We are not looking for clones, but individuals with varying personalities, who offer and receive a great deal of benefit from their time with us. You should be able to demonstrate intelligence, intuition, humour, approachability and commitment and have some connection with, or interest in, the North West. We prefer candidates to have achieved, or to be forecast to achieve, a good 2(1) degree but, ultimately, our assessment of you is based on our belief in your ability.

www.brabners.com

About the firm

Address: Horton House, Exchange Flags, Liverpool L2 3YL
Telephone: 0151 600 3000 **Fax:** 0151 227 3185
Website: www.brabners.com
Email: trainees@brabners.com

Chief executive: Janet Pickevance
Managing partner: Mark Brandwood

Other offices: Liverpool, Manchester, Preston.

Who we are: One of the top North West commercial firms, Brabners LLP, in Liverpool, Manchester and Preston, has the experience, talent and prestige of a firm with a 200-plus-year history. Brabners LLP is a dynamic, client-led specialist in the provision of excellent legal services to clients ranging from large plcs to private individuals.

What we do: The firm carries out a wide range of specialist legal services and its client base includes plcs, public sector bodies, banks and other commercial, corporate and professional businesses. Brabners LLP is organised into client-focused departments: banking, corporate, commercial (including media and sports law), employment, litigation, property (including construction), social housing and private client (including family).

What we're looking for: Graduates and those undertaking the GDL or LPC who can demonstrate intelligence, intuition, humour, approachability and commitment.

What you'll do: The LLP is one of the few law firms that holds Investor in People status and has a comprehensive training and development programme. The LLP was listed in the *Sunday Times* Best 100 UK Employers to work for in 2006-11. Trainees are given a high degree of responsibility and are an integral part of the culture of the firm. Each trainee will have partner-level supervision. Personal development appraisals are conducted at three and six-monthly intervals to ensure that trainee progress is valuable and informed. The training programme is overseen by the firm's director of training, Dr Tony Harvey, and each centre has a designated trainee partner. It is not all hard work and the firm has an excellent social programme.

Sponsorship: LPC fees (full).

Facts and figures

Total partners: 70
Other fee-earners: 150
Total trainees: 12

Trainee places available for 2019: 6

First year salary: Not less than £22,000

Turnover in 2015: £30m (+0% from 2014)
Profits per equity partner: £236,000 (-4%)
(see legalbusiness.co.uk for full financial information)

Application process

Apply to: Dr Tony Harvey, director of training, risk and compliance.
How: Online application.
When: Apply by 30 June 2017 for contracts starting September 2019.
What's involved: Interview/assessment day.

Brabners

Bristows LLP

100 Victoria Embankment, London EC4Y 0DH

Lex 100 Winner

See categories below
and tables from page 69

Survey results *(marks out of 100%)*

Satisfied in your job?	81
Firm living up to expectations?	80
High quality of work?	80
Enough client contact?	70
Stress-free?	59
Happy work/life balance?	79
Friendly firm?	94
Great social life?	81
Good vacation scheme?	86
Confident you'll be kept on?	88
Good remuneration?	82
Diverse firm?	89

 verdict

Bristows has a 'reputation for very high-quality intellectual property work'. In a 'booming sector of the law', the firm prides itself as a City firm 'without the cut-throat competitive environment'. The 'big-name and impressive client list' were important factors for many current trainees. The London-based firm is full of 'very friendly, welcoming and intelligent people'. As there is only a 'small intake of trainees', the 'personal approach' results in a 'friendly culture' and Bristows becomes a 'very big family'. The firm's three **Lex 100 Winner** awards are for friendliness, confidence of being kept on and diversity levels. One respondent reported, 'I am given real work to do and never feel like I am being exploited'. Trainees are 'exposed to challenging and varied work' that is 'super-interesting from the first week'. Everyone is 'very approachable' and you are 'not seen as just a trainee but a valued member of the team as you are involved and listened to in discussions'. Trainees are made to 'feel equal' and even when 'the office is manic, everyone still has time for the trainees'. Top trainee moments include 'working on really high-profile trials', 'winning interim applications three times in a row' and 'completing a deal'. The 'sociable hours' are appreciated and the firm is described as a 'breath of fresh air' where trainees 'look forward to coming into work every day'. 'Job satisfaction' is evident but trainees report that there isn't 'much control over the first seat'. Although one respondent remarked there wasn't 'anything really negative', one thing that 'could be improved' is more 'client contact'. Those looking to work at a collegiate firm with a market-leading reputation in TMT and IP should take a closer look at Bristows.

If the firm were a fictional character it would be...

The Doctor (Doctor Who) – has strong historic roots, but is completely at ease with the developments and technologies of the future

The firm

London-based Bristows continues to command a market-leading reputation in the TMT and IP areas, and also operates an impressive corporate practice, advising clients on property transactions and smaller M&A deals. The firm remains independent but collaborates effectively with lawyers across the US, Europe and Asia.

The deals

Successfully defended Google against Streetmap in a High Court claim for abuse of dominant position; represented Samsung in regards to a major patent dispute with Unwired Planet, which involved the consideration of the competition law issue of patent 'privateering'; advised LaSalle Investment Management on the sale of the assets of its LaSalle Garden Centre Fund; advised Nicoventures on the branding and marketing of its electronic cigarette products; acted for P&O Cruises on TV sponsorship and product placement deals.

The clients

AstraZeneca; Capgemini; Genomics England; Intercontinental Hotels Group; Marks & Spencer; Ofcom; Pearl Diver Capital; Royal Mail; Samsung; WPP.

The star performers

Top-ranking departments according to *The Legal 500* (see legal500.com for more details)
Brand management; Charities and not-for-profit; Commercial contracts; Commercial litigation; Commercial property: general; Commercial property: investment; Competition litigation; Data protection; EU and competition; Employment: employers; IT and telecoms; Intellectual property; M&A: smaller deals, up to £50m; Media and entertainment (including media finance); PATMA: Trade mark attorneys; Partnership; Pharmaceuticals and biotechnology.

- **Why did you choose this firm over any others?** 'Everyone I spoke to during the recruitment process was very nice and friendly'; 'forefront of IP'; 'size of trainee intake'; 'sector expertise'; 'treats its employees very well'; 'big-name clients'; 'interesting work with a scientific or technical twist'; 'excellent working environment'; 'personal approach'; 'good working hours'; 'the opportunity to work with some of the brightest minds in the legal world'

- **Best thing about the firm?** 'The quality of work'; 'everyone is really good at what they do'; 'a lot of people care about your development'; 'everyone knows everyone which helps to create good links within the firm'; 'good selection of biscuits in the meeting rooms'; 'the interesting clients'; 'excellent work from a very junior level'; 'very pleasant working environment'

- **Worst thing about the firm?** 'You don't have as much control over seat choices as you might get at other firms'; 'the coffee in the client meeting rooms is dire'; 'limited feedback'; 'it isn't always that transparent'; 'communication between departments'; 'international secondments are not possible'; 'not being able to have an input on the first seat'

- **Best moment?** 'Getting invited along to a client dinner'; 'attending a settlement meeting for a matter which was the first I'd worked on in which I really felt I'd made a contribution'; 'working on two trials'; 'working in a team spanning the whole department to complete a deal'; 'hearing a chairman of a plc read a speech I had prepared at the AGM'

- **Worst moment?** 'Serving documents at the wrong office'; 'a few late nights of bundling'; 'doing disclosure-related admin late at night'; 'patents can be tough for non-scientists'; 'my taxi almost being hit by an unmarked police car travelling at high speed as I was being driven to a client to drop off some documents'

A day in the life of...

... Constance Crawford second-year trainee, Bristows LLP

Departments to date: Real estate, regulatory, IP litigation
University: University of Bristol
Degree and class: Biochemistry (BSc), 1st

9.00am: I arrive at Bristows and grab a quick coffee from the hub, our staff common room, before settling down to read through the emails which have come in overnight and check my calendar and to-do list for the day. In the IP litigation department, I sit with Dominic Adair, one of the partners.

9.20am: I get a call from one of the associates I have been working with on an industrial patent case asking me to check a reference in the Civil Procedure Rules. I carry out some research on Westlaw and write up my findings in a short note. This research will assist the associate in negotiating an order for directions with the other side.

10.00am: I have been writing an article for publication in a patent journal, which summarises how recent case law has been developing a new concept in patent law known as plausibility. The deadline is fast approaching, so I spend some time editing and proof-reading my latest draft before sending it to the partner for review.

11.15am: One of the other trainees is preparing for trial, so two of us help her by checking that the bundles have been copied correctly and taking them to chambers.

11.45am: I'm involved in a full day meeting with counsel tomorrow so I spend some time preparing. I read the latest round of correspondence between the parties relating to a dispute about confidentiality, review a number of our client's disclosure documents and make a note of the pertinent issues they raise so that I have them to hand and make sure I have printed all the documents we might need.

12.30pm: There's an internal patent litigation seminar over lunch where associates and trainees provide updates on recent case law and any procedural developments that the group needs to be aware of. Accompanied by the usual sandwich lunch, these informal sessions are a great way to learn about relevant changes in the law while getting to know other colleagues that you might not have worked with yet.

2.00pm: I attend a call with an expert who will be assisting us with the life sciences case I work on. The team is in the process of drafting the expert's report and to this end, we discuss a number of scientific publications referred to in the patent that might help us convince the judge that our patent is valid.

3.45pm: I get an urgent email from an associate working on a large telecoms case asking me to file an application at the High Court. After taking instructions and making sure I have enough copies, I hurry to court to file the application before the counters close.

4.15pm: One of the deadlines for the service of fact evidence is only a week away in the life sciences case I work on and the partner has asked me to review the latest draft of a witness statement and start organising the exhibits. One of the pieces of evidence we intend to rely on comes from the client's disclosure documents and so I set about identifying the

> ' I get an urgent email from an associate working on a large telecoms case asking me to file an application at the High Court.'

correct document and checking that it doesn't contain anything adverse to our case.

6.30pm: The last thing on my to-do list for the day is to draft an email to the client involved in the telecoms litigation, providing a summary of all the correspondence which has been exchanged between the parties that day. Once I've done that, I prepare my to-do list for the next day.

7.00pm: I leave the office and make my way across town for a yoga class.

training.bristows.com

About the firm

Address: 100 Victoria Embankment, London EC4Y 0DH
Telephone: 020 7400 8000
Website: www.bristows.com
Email: trainee.recruitment@bristows.com
Twitter: @bristowsgrad

Senior partner: Philip Westmacott
Managing partners: Mark Watts, Theo Savvides

Who we are: Bristows LLP is a medium-sized firm that handles the kind of work normally associated with only the largest firms. Established over 175 years ago, we have a client list that includes leading businesses from a variety of innovative sectors including life science and TMT.

What we do: Our core practice areas are intellectual property; information technology and data protection; corporate; commercial disputes; real estate; regulatory; EU and competition; media and marketing; employment and tax.

What we're looking for: We are extremely selective because we are looking for people who will be our future partners. As part of such a select and high-calibre intake, we will give you real responsibility earlier than you might expect.

What you'll do: During the two years' training, you will spend time in each of our main departments developing your skills and knowledge. You will also work closely with our partners and associates. Part of your training may involve a secondment to one of a number of leading clients.

Perks: Life assurance; pension scheme; private medical insurance; permanent health insurance; travel insurance; eye care; health assessment; employee assistance programme; cycle-to-work scheme; childcare voucher scheme; season ticket loan; discounted gym membership; onsite cafe/deli.

Sponsorship: GDL and LPC fees paid in full, plus a maintenance grant of £8,000 for each course.

Facts and figures

Total partners: 38
Other fee-earners: 120
Total trainees: 19

Trainee places available for 2019: 10
Applications received pa: 1,500
Percentage interviewed: 5%

First year salary: £38,000
Second year salary: £41,000
Newly qualified salary: £60,000

Turnover in 2015: £38.1m (+12% from 2014)
Profits per equity partner: £392,000 (+8%)
(see legalbusiness.co.uk for full financial information)

Application process

Apply to: May Worvill – graduate resourcing manager.
How: Online application form.
When: By 31 January for February/March interviews; by 31 July for August interviews.
What's involved: A video interview, two panel interviews and a written exercise.

Vacation schemes

For opportunities to spend time with the firm during winter, spring and summer, please see website for details.

BRISTOWS

Browne Jacobson LLP

Mowbray House, Castle Meadow Road, Nottingham NG2 1BJ

Survey results *(marks out of 100%)*

Satisfied in your job?	80
Firm living up to expectations?	82
High quality of work?	79
Enough client contact?	73
Stress-free?	54
Happy work/life balance?	75
Friendly firm?	86
Great social life?	65
Good vacation scheme?	70
Confident you'll be kept on?	83
Good remuneration?	70
Diverse firm?	81

 verdict

Browne Jacobson's 'strong reputation' for a 'mix of public and private sector work' is a 'big pull' for most trainees. The insurance, public sector and real estate practices are some of Browne Jacobson's well-known specialisms. This national firm is 'committed to training and progression', and is a 'growing firm with a growing reputation' with the accompanying 'big-name clients'. There is a 'good level of hands-on supervision', 'client exposure' and a 'decent level of responsibility' on offer for Browne Jacobson's trainees, as there is only one trainee assigned per team in each office. Within the team there are 'some great lawyers who will offer informal mentoring' and are 'willing to go the extra mile to ensure that the trainees are developing'. Also, it has been noticed that the 'lack of hierarchy' means the 'partners are approachable' and trainees can 'learn a lot when working with them'. This 'down-to-earth firm' puts an emphasis on giving trainees the 'room to grow and develop within each seat'. There is 'no pressure to stay late when it is unnecessary' but trainees can still face a 'huge culture shock' and 'inconsistent work levels which can be hard to time-manage'. Best moments for trainees include 'running files under appropriate supervision', 'attending a three-week trial at the Royal Courts of Justice with a partner and a QC' and 'completing a complex piece of work without any adjustments'. Browne Jacobson is a great choice for those looking for a firm that is 'going places' while maintaining a 'friendly atmosphere'.

If the firm were a fictional character it would be...

Meredith Grey (Grey's Anatomy) – determined and highly successful, values friendships and understands the importance of a good work/life balance

The firm

Nottingham-headquartered Browne Jacobson has undergone impressive growth in recent years. Turnover has increased sharply and a wider network of offices has expanded the firm's reach across the UK. It is a full-service firm with leading insurance, public sector and real estate practices. It was recognised for its strong performance by being shortlisted for the National/Regional Firm of the Year trophy at the *Legal Business* Awards 2016.

The deals

Advised Lloyds Development Capital on the acquisition of a minority stake in Aspin Group; advised Fogarty Group on asset-based facilities provided by Close Brothers to finance its future development; advised Cheshire East Council on the procurement process to find a partner to deliver a range of geo-thermal and other energy projects in the Cheshire region; advised Serco Leisure Operating Limited on the design and build contracts related to its procurement of a series of leisure facilities across the UK; advised new client Metropolitan Housing Trust on the acquisition of 61 new homes in Nottinghamshire from private developers.

The clients

Boots Alliance; City of Lincoln Council; East Midlands Housing Group; England and Wales Cricket Board; Havenwood Construction; Hiscox; KPMG; Sir Robert McAlpine; Ted Baker; Willmott Dixon.

The star performers

Top-ranking departments according to *The Legal 500* (see legal500.com for more details)
Charities and not-for-profit; Clinical negligence: defendant; Commercial litigation; Commercial property; Construction; Education; Environment; Health and safety; IT and telecoms; Insolvency and corporate recovery; Intellectual property; Local government; Personal injury: defendant; Personal tax, trusts and probate; Planning; Private finance initiative; Professional negligence; Property litigation; Social housing; Sport.

- **Why did you choose this firm over any others?** 'Experience at the open day and assessment centre'; 'reputation for good public sector work'; 'the respected IP practice'; 'national reach'; 'sizeable firm based outside of London'; 'unique client base'; 'I liked the open-plan feel of the offices'

- **Best thing about the firm?** 'People are incredibly smart and knowledgeable'; 'it's not stuck up itself'; 'big-name clients'; 'even the partners will make you tea'; 'the café is very good'; 'one trainee per team per office'; 'many seats offer good client contact'; 'really nice new laptops'; 'high number of blue-chip clients'; 'very impressive London office'

- **Worst thing about the firm?** 'IT could be improved'; 'poor PSC courses'; 'sometimes a lack of openness and dialogue around training and NQ opportunities'; 'still very Nottingham-focused'; 'the London office is quiet and lacks personality'; 'very little going on socially'; 'administrative processes are cumbersome and unwieldy'

- **Best moment?** 'Taking witness statements on my own'; 'attending a settlement meeting'; 'attending two trials in one month where I got to work closely with the client'; 'assisting on a case which could be heard in the Supreme Court'; 'going to visit a client at his large country house to take witness statements from the neighbours in relation to a planning dispute'; 'winning a pro bono case for a disabled client'

- **Worst moment?** 'Forgetting to save a document before the computer crashed'; 'sometimes a lack of supervision'; 'last-minute bundling work'; 'lots of pressure when there were many deadlines at once'; 'missing out on going to the Court of Appeal due to a scheduling conflict'; 'taxi ride from London to Nottingham'

A day in the life of...

... Katherine Utton first-year trainee, Browne Jacobson LLP

Departments to date: Education, employment
University: Lancaster
Degree and class: Criminology and philosophy 2(1)

8.30am: I start the day by checking my emails to see if anything has come in over the weekend. I also check the latest education news stories to see if there is anything relevant to our clients. I notice that there is a story on including overtime in holiday calculations so I email the team to let them know I will draft an update to send out to our clients.

9.00am: I am advising a client on settlement negotiations and I have a message asking me to call them with an update. I have been involved in this tribunal claim from an early stage, and as my colleague has been away for the last week I have been handling the negotiations (with supervision). She confirms she is happy for me to continue running the file so I update them on the latest offer we received and we discuss how they want to proceed.

9.30am: I have relayed my client's instructions to the representative on the other side, so now I can make a start on the rest of my to-do list. Before I start I check the quick-call messages and note that an academy is seeking some advice on an employment issue. I have advised this academy before, on a different matter, so I volunteer to call the client back to discuss. I really like quick-call queries because you are encouraged to deal with clients directly and the issues are always really varied.

10.00am: Time for my weekly catch-up with my supervisor. Although I sit next to my supervisor we have a weekly catch-up so that he can keep an eye on what work I am doing. It really is a very supportive environment for a trainee, which helps give you the confidence to ask questions without feeling stupid!

10.30am: My supervisor has just updated me on one of the files I am helping him with and asked me to think about what steps we need to take next. As a trainee you are always encouraged to think about a case as a whole, rather than just being given individual tasks to do. We are trying to negotiate a settlement for our client, so I draft a without prejudice letter for him to review. He makes a couple of amends and I then send it out.

12.30pm: It's time for lunch, so I head downstairs to our café (No.44). We are really lucky to have some great chefs and the food is always delicious. No.44 is always busy and is a great place for catching up with the other trainees. One thing I really like about being a trainee is having other people that you can share your experiences with and it is really good to be able to talk things through – particularly when it comes to seat change!

1.30pm: Earlier this week I attended a preliminary hearing for a client. I have already updated them on the outcome, but I want to tidy up my own notes before saving them to the file. I also check the orders that were made and update my diary with the key dates.

3.00pm: A colleague comes over to ask me about a presentation I did for the team last week, as she is currently trying to advise a client on a similar point. Even as a trainee you are expected to be able to contribute and give

> **'I really like quick-call queries because you are encouraged to deal with clients directly and the issues are always really varied.'**

your own views on matters, so I talk her through my research and reasons behind my advice.

3.30pm: I spend the next couple of hours drafting a settlement agreement for a client. There are some specific confidentiality clauses that the client wants to include so I spend some time making sure the wording is as clear and concise as possible. Once I have had it reviewed by my supervisor I am able to send it to the client for approval.

5.30pm: I check the quick-call messages again and make sure nothing urgent has come in. There is never any requirement to stay later than you need, so once I confirm there is nothing outstanding I head home.

www.brownejacobson.com/careers

About the firm

Address: Mowbray House, Castle Meadow Road, Nottingham NG2 1BJ
Telephone: 0808 178 9064 **Fax:** 0115 947 5246
Website: www.brownejacobson.com/careers
Email: traineeapplications@brownejacobson.com
Twitter: @brownejtrainees

Senior partner: Derek Bambury
Managing partner: Iain Blatherwick

Other offices: Birmingham, London, Manchester, Exeter.

Who we are: We are a full-service firm with an impressive client portfolio, including blue-chip corporates, local and owner-managed businesses, NHS trusts, insurers, and education and public sector organisations.

What we do: We offer a comprehensive range of quality legal services, with expertise across a number of key specialisms, including retail, technology, financial services, education, health, local and central government, brands, international and insurance.

What we're looking for: We are looking for commercially minded law and non-law graduates who can bring with them enthusiasm,

tenacity, commitment and a passion for delivering exceptional service, combined with a flexible and friendly attitude. For more information about life as a trainee visit their blog at www.traineetalk.co.uk.

What you'll do: Trainees start with an induction, a fast-track professional skills course and then go on to undertake an extensive internal trainee development programme. They spend four periods of six months in some of the principle areas of the firm, gaining an overview of the practice. Trainees get great training, a friendly and supportive working environment and real career opportunities. They are also given quality work and exposure to clients from early on, but are supported in achieving results and recognised for their contribution. Training contracts are based in Nottingham and Birmingham although, on occasion, opportunities may arise in our other offices.

Perks: We offer a flexible benefits package with life assurance, income protection and a pension as standard, plus private medical care, dental care, travel insurance, critical illness cover, childcare vouchers, Ride2Work and discounted shopping.

Sponsorship: LPC/GDL tuition fees paid, plus £5,000 maintenance grant. These will not be paid retrospectively.

Facts and figures

Total partners: 109
Other fee-earners: 343
Total trainees: 19

Trainee places available for 2019: 20
Applications received pa: 800
Percentage interviewed: 10%

First year salary: £25,500
Second year salary: £26,500
Newly qualified salary: Market rate

Turnover in 2015: £58.9m (+17% from 2014)
Profits per equity partner: £412,000 (+24%)
(see legalbusiness.co.uk for full financial information)

Application process

Apply to: Recruitment team.
How: Apply online at www.brownejacobsoncareers.com.
When: By 1 April 2017 for 2019 training contracts.
What's involved: Psychometric testing, telephone interview, assessment centre (group exercises and interview).

Vacation schemes

Summer: June 2017 (apply online by 1 February 2017).

brownejacobson LLP

Burges Salmon

One Glass Wharf, Bristol BS2 0ZX

Survey results *(marks out of 100%)*

Satisfied in your job? 85

Firm living up to expectations? 89

High quality of work? 87

Enough client contact? 75

Stress-free? 56

Happy work/life balance? 75

Friendly firm? 92

Great social life? 89

Good vacation scheme? 98

Confident you'll be kept on? 91

Good remuneration? 89

Diverse firm? 83

 **verdict**

Burges Salmon's six-seat training contract is one of the stand-out reasons many trainees chose to apply to the Bristol-based firm. Plus it offers 'London-quality work without the commute' and with a 'West Country work/life balance'. There is 'one core office' where trainees get to meet a 'huge amount of people quickly' and there is 'seamless communication across the departments'. Trainees are placed in a 'position of trust' where 'consideration is given to their ideas and reasoning'. There is a 'friendly culture' and people are 'smiling and up for banter'. Recent newcomers champion the 'quality of the lawyers' and identify the firm as 'great to work for', and **Lex 100 Winner** awards have been secured for living up to expectations, job satisfaction, plus five other categories. This 'friendly firm' has a 'clear strategy' and an 'excellent training programme to help ease trainees in' rather than 'dumping them in at the deep end'. 'Rewarding moments' for new trainees include 'finalising a huge real estate deal with a private client', 'taking a leading role in a workshop for a large number of clients' and 'assisting with the completion of a very complex loan agreement only three months into my training contract'. There are a few grumbles about 'staying past midnight to prepare trial bundles' but on the whole the firm provides decidedly 'reasonable hours' for its trainees. A client secondment was described as an 'invaluable experience with maximum responsibility and client exposure'. This 'ambitious firm' has a 'strong position in the market', and for those keen to take on quality work across a range of departments, applying to Burges Salmon is a 'no brainer'.

If the firm were a fictional character it would be...

Jon Snow (A Game of Thrones) – out beyond the wall but still a lead character, with a great story and some excellent character traits

The firm

Bristol-headquartered Burges Salmon continues to perform exceptionally. Turnover was up 8% for 2015/16, with profit per equity partner jumping 7% over the same financial year. A strong alternative to the London set, the firm has respected corporate, private client and TMT departments. Burges Salmon was named Real Estate Team of the Year at the *Legal Business Awards 2016*.

The deals

Advised the Department of Transport on the restructuring of the Highways Agency and its pension provisions; acted for FirstGroup on its successful bid for the TransPennine Express Franchise; defended Celtic Energy in a Serious Fraud Office (SFO) investigation into the transfer of its freehold interest in mines to a group of BVI-registered companies; advised Gravis Capital Partners on the £96m recapitalisation of Agrivert; advised the Department for Education on the establishment of a corporate vehicle to deliver the social care and education services of Slough Borough Council.

The clients

Bank of Ireland; John Lewis Partnership; Mapfre; Merseyrail; Mulberry; National Trust; The Nuclear Decommissioning Authority; South Eastern Railway; UBS; the University of Bristol.

The star performers

Top-ranking departments according to *The Legal 500* (see legal500.com for more details)
Agriculture and estates; Banking and finance; Commercial litigation; Contentious trusts and probate; Corporate and commercial; Corporate tax; Crime: fraud; EU and competition; Employment; Energy; Family; Health and safety; Immigration; Insolvency and corporate recovery; Licensing; Local government; Pensions; Professional negligence; Project finance and PFI; Rail.

- **Why did you choose this firm over any others?** 'Located in Bristol'; 'six-seat training programme'; 'the quality of the training'; 'getting a good impression of my interviewers'; 'the cake'; 'some niche practice areas'; 'colleagues are at the top of the profession in many fields'; 'great vacation scheme'; 'encouraging retention rate'; 'the alternative ethos that subtly permeates the firm'; 'top-quality work coupled with reasonable hours'

- **Best thing about the firm?** 'There is no expectation to stay late when there is no urgent work to complete'; 'the support provided'; 'collegiate nature'; 'no mergers so far'; 'everyone is based under one roof'; 'the cake trolley on a Friday'; 'the blend of excellence and kindness'

- **Worst thing about the firm?** 'Lack of control over the workload'; 'there are not many secondment opportunities'; 'inconsistency in expectations between departments'; 'mixed quality of catering'; 'stuffiness'; 'an overly sedate nature at times'; 'the technology needs updating slightly'; 'printers always seem to break'

- **Best moment?** 'Receiving a thank you email from a partner for my work on a transaction'; 'getting experience in court'; 'being heavily involved in a complex matter'; 'an all-day completion lunch with a five-course meal and champagne at Claridge's afterwards'; 'going on client secondment'; 'attending a property conference with three partners'

- **Worst moment?** 'Reviewing a room full of files as part of a disclosure exercise'; 'being thrown in at the deep end early on in my first seat'; 'rearranging evening plans to work late'; 'getting three hours sleep one night during a completion'; 'having my seat changed at the last minute by email, with no discussion'

A day in the life of...

... Rayann Fearon first-year trainee, Burges Salmon LLP

Departments to date: Disputes, client secondment (projects), pensions

University: University of Leicester

Degree and class: Law, 2(1)

7.15am: I meet with a fellow first-year trainee and head to an exercise class that takes place a short walk from the office. I enjoy being part of a large intake as we often catch up outside work for dinner, coffee and in this case exercise!

8.40am: I live very close to the office in an area called Old Market. I have positioned myself very close to the office to ensure an easy commute. Before heading to my desk I grab some breakfast from our restaurant.

9.00am: I have a brief catch-up with my supervisor and discuss some client emails from the previous night, confirming any 'actions' where appropriate. I check my to-do list and order tasks based on priority. I am heading to a corporate finance networking event this evening, so I need to plan my day around that, ensuring I complete any urgent work prior to my departure. I catch up with a vacation scheme student we have sitting in the department who has been helping out on a matter that I am working on and discuss next steps.

9.30am: Once a week the team has departmental 'prayers' which allows everyone to discuss the work they have on, their capacity to take on more, and any interesting events they may be attending.

9.45am: I am currently in the pensions department which undertakes a variety of work including: trustee advisory; company advisory; public sector; regulatory; corporate support; and incentives. I am assisting with a matter relating to a client who is currently undergoing a tender process to change supplier of core services. Having reviewed the suppliers' proposals, provided summary reports and completed the scoring matrix for the client I am now preparing a note for my supervisor to pre-empt and assist with any queries that may arise from the client off the back of this work.

12.00pm: I have been asked to look at a small piece of technical research relating to incentives to assist the corporate department with a query from a client. Incentives is a smaller element of the wider pensions team and is very interesting as it incorporates a mixture of corporate, tax and employment within the work.

1.15pm: I meet with some of the trainees and go for lunch in the restaurant. The trainees tend to eat lunch together when they can to catch up and see how everyone is getting on in their respective departments.

2.30pm: I have received a request from the client I am working with in relation to the tender about some further work they would like to be completed to assist with the shortlisting process. This involves reviewing the tender proposals and compiling a comparative table summarising their key services. I discuss my ideas with my supervisor and make a start.

5.00pm: I have a brief catch up with my supervisor where I discuss the work that I have completed and receive some feedback. We decide on next steps and how I should progress this with the client.

> '**I am looking forward to meeting some experienced banking professionals to discuss the sector in a more informal setting.**'

5.30pm: I review my calendar and prepare my to-do list for tomorrow. I am meeting another trainee and some solicitors at the firm to head out to the networking event. I am still unclear as to where I would like to qualify but I know I have an interest in banking. Therefore, I am looking forward to meeting some experienced banking professionals to discuss the sector in a more informal setting.

7.30pm: After the networking event, I head for tapas with another trainee by the harbourside. Bristol has such a wide range of delicious restaurants – I am slowly making my way through the list!

About the firm

Address: One Glass Wharf, Bristol BS2 0ZX
Telephone: 0117 939 2000 **Fax:** 0117 902 4400
Website: www.burges-salmon.com
Facebook: www.facebook.com/burgessalmontrainee
Twitter: @BurgesSalmonTS

Senior partner: Alan Barr
Managing partner: Peter Morris

Other offices: London

Who we are: Burges Salmon is an independent UK law firm with a unique model and culture.

What we do: Our main departments include corporate and financial institutions, dispute resolution, projects, real estate and private client.

What we're looking for: We recruit ambitious and forward-thinking individuals. We look for a minimum 2(1) degree and the relevant interpersonal skills for success as a commercial solicitor.

What you'll do: Trainees complete a six-seat training contract over the two-year period.

Perks: Pension, life assurance, medical insurance, subsidised gym membership, travel season ticket loans, volunteering days and sports and social club.

Sponsorship: All GDL and LPC fees plus £7,000 maintenance grant for each course.

Facts and figures

Total partners: 85
Other fee-earners: 270
Total trainees: 56

Trainee places available for 2019: 30
Applications received pa: 1,500

First year salary: £35,000
Second year salary: £36,000
Newly qualified salary: £47,000

Turnover in 2015: £80.8m (+6% from 2014)
Profits per equity partner: £484,000 (+11%)
(see legalbusiness.co.uk for full financial information)

Application process

Apply to: Frances Bennett.
How: Online application form.
When: By 31 July 2017 for 2019 contracts.
What's involved: Application form, assessment centre including group exercise, written exercise, psychometric testing and interview.

Vacation schemes

Winter: 12-16 December 2016 (apply by 4 November 2016)
Spring: 3-13 April 2017 (apply by 12 January 2017)
Summer: 12-23 June, 26 June-7 July 2017 (apply by 12 January 2017)

Burness Paull LLP

50 Lothian Road, Edinburgh EH3 9WJ

Survey results *(marks out of 100%)*

Satisfied in your job?	81
Firm living up to expectations?	85
High quality of work?	83
Enough client contact?	73
Stress-free?	60
Happy work/life balance?	69
Friendly firm?	89
Great social life?	88
Good vacation scheme?	90
Confident you'll be kept on?	73
Good remuneration?	78
Diverse firm?	83

 **verdict**

Burness Paull is a 'top-tier firm with a good strategy and great client contact' based solely in Scotland and with a focus on 'Scottish clientele'. This 'established firm' is 'forward-thinking' and 'well regarded in the industry', with a 'clear vision of where it wants to be in the legal market'. Well-known specialisms include oil and gas, corporate, infrastructure and real estate. There are 'great opportunities for trainees to get involved in', including 'exciting and challenging transactions'. Although there are 'occasional long hours and very late nights', the firm organises many 'social events' and encourages a 'healthy work/life balance' in order to 'set itself apart from other law firms', and trainee feedback has led to a **Lex 100 Winner** gong in our social life category. Trainees describe a 'thoroughly rewarding experience' and their best moments include 'working on a major case', 'receiving positive feedback' and 'being trusted with an NQ's work at an early stage'. Trainees also have the 'opportunity to make their mark' during the 'in-depth training'. Partners 'take the time' to build 'strong relationships' with the trainees and are 'receptive to new ideas'. But sometimes trainees report feeling under 'too much pressure' and being set 'unrealistic goals' while there is 'no certainty of receiving an NQ position'. However, newcomers have loved their secondments where they received 'significant responsibility and exposure to a wide variety of legal matters', which 'allowed trainees to prepare better advice and assistance for clients in the future'. Burness Paull has a 'social atmosphere' and puts trainees 'in a good position for their future career' in the legal profession.

If the firm were a fictional character it would be...

Riley (Inside Out) – lots of characters inside pull together to make it look like one from the outside

The firm

A market-leading firm in Scotland, Burness Paull has offices in Glasgow, Edinburgh and Aberdeen. The 250-strong team of lawyers is led by over 50 partners. Corporate, infrastructure and real estate matters are handled across the three offices, while Aberdeen is a key point of contact for clients in the oil and gas industry.

The deals

Acted for Standard Life during its acquisition of Pearson Jones from Skipton Building Society; represented Vodafone in litigation that has UK-wide ramifications for all telecoms operators working under the Telecommunications Code; assisted Bank of Scotland with the £30m financing to a consortium of investors for the acquisition of Tulloch Homes; advised ITN on its contracts with on-air talent; advised Canadian-listed oil company Sterling Resources on the $42.5m sale of its Romanian oil and gas interests to the Carlyle Group.

The clients

BlackRock; Ecotricity; Everton Football Club; Falkirk Council; KKR; Maersk; Santander; Scottish Enterprise; Stewart Milne Group; Technip.

The star performers

Top-ranking departments according to *The Legal 500* (see legal500.com for more details)
Banking and finance; Charities and not-for-profit; Commercial litigation; Commercial property; Corporate and commercial; Crime: fraud; EU and competition; Employment; Environment; Health and safety; IT and telecoms; Intellectual property; Local government; Media and entertainment; Oil and gas; Pensions; Planning; Property litigation; Sport; Unit trusts, OEICs, and investment trusts.

- **Why did you choose this firm over any others?** 'Sterling reputation'; 'performed well during recession'; 'opportunity to work closely with partners at the top of the game'; 'opportunity to be part of growth'; 'based solely in Scotland'; 'enjoyed the summer placement'; 'clear vision of where it wants to be in the legal market'; 'specialises in a number of areas'; 'positive feedback from trainees already at the firm'; 'I enjoyed my interview'

- **Best thing about the firm?** 'Social things going on'; 'absence of hierarchy'; 'sense of friendliness'; 'wide variety of seat opportunities'; 'inclusive atmosphere'; 'incredibly knowledgeable colleagues'; 'the lack of egos'; 'the culture of the firm lends itself to development'; 'fee-earners are not scared to give responsibility to trainees who show themselves to be competent'; 'generally brilliant colleagues'; 'the majority of management are accessible'

- **Worst thing about the firm?** 'Lack of international secondment opportunities'; 'departments are not all held to the same standard of trainee care and training'; 'not much team-building opportunities within your department'; 'working hours can be tough'; 'there seems to be a divide between the offices'; 'there are very limited opportunities for court experience for second-year trainees'

- **Best moment?** 'Receiving glowing feedback on a particular piece of work'; 'completing a large matter and receiving thanks from the client for doing so'; 'going on secondment to a major new client'; 'writing and publishing an IP blog'; 'being involved in a large property deal'; 'attending client meetings'; 'being involved in preparing for tribunal'; 'seeing a matter through to completion by myself'; 'being trusted by the partner in my team with a piece of detailed work'

- **Worst moment?** 'A string of 10pm and later finishes to complete a matter'; 'seat preferences submitted not always corresponding to seat moves'; 'spending days on end with only admin work in a particular division'; 'making a mistake and knowing it was due to my own hastiness'; 'preparing for an NQ interview was quite stressful'

A day in the life of...

... **Alexander Watt** trainee solicitor, Burness Paull

Departments to date: Banking; corporate finance; Standard Life secondment

University: University of Aberdeen

Degree and class: LLB (Hons), 1st

8.20am: I aim to get into the office for around 8.20 or 8.30am. This allows me to consider the list of tasks I have for the day and reread any emails I received on my BlackBerry the night before.

9.00am: I have been working on a large transaction involving the sale and purchase of a company. We are acting for the buyers and are therefore required to carry out due diligence. I had previously drafted the initial corporate aspect of the due diligence report which was then passed to my colleague for review. I spend most of the morning going through their comments and making the necessary changes. I then double-check the report to ensure that there are no mistakes.

11.00am: A colleague has asked me to research a specific point which may have an impact on a sale and purchase agreement we are negotiating. There is a relatively tight deadline on this, as one of the partners of the firm is required to get back to the client today on the point. As trainees, we are often required to research very specific queries and produce an answer in a relatively short space of time (while also concurrently dealing with all of our emails and other ongoing work)! I research the area and produce a note summarising my conclusion.

1.00pm: At lunchtime, I often meet up with the other trainees and discuss the different types of work going on in the firm and what everyone is up to in the evening.

2.00pm: Having completed the research task, a senior colleague has asked me to draft corporate ancillaries for an ongoing transaction. Again, the client has requested a quick turnaround. I consider what is required by searching our internal bank of pro forma documents and previous drafts on our system.

4.00pm: A colleague has asked me to complete a company search report on a target company. This involves reviewing information available on Companies House to gain an understanding of the company. It is an important task which can help flesh out any issues with the company's constitutional documents which can then have an impact on the deal structure. Having completed my most urgent tasks for the day,

> 'At lunchtime, I often meet up with the other trainees and discuss the different types of work going on in the firm.'

I start preparing a bible of documents for a completion that has recently completed.

6.00pm: I normally leave the office at around 6.00 or 7.00pm. We are sometimes required to stay longer but are encouraged to leave if there is nothing urgent. I make a list of actions for tomorrow before leaving for the night.

www.burnesspaullgraduates.com

About the firm

Address: 50 Lothian Road, Edinburgh EH3 9WJ
Telephone: 0131 473 6182
Website: www.burnesspaull.com
Email: hranddevelopment@burnesspaull.com
Twitter: @BurnessPaullHR

Managing partner: Ian Wattie

Other offices: Aberdeen, Glasgow.

Who we are: We are a top-tier commercial law firm serving a UK and international client base from Scotland. At the last count we were advising clients in more than 60 jurisdictions.

What we do: We work across sectors that are vital to our economy, with a focus on oil and gas, financial sector, property and infrastructure, and corporate Scotland.

What we're looking for: We're looking for academically excellent, well rounded, focused and sharp individuals.

What you'll do: During your two-year traineeship you will have four stimulating six-month seats in four practice areas. We are also recognised for the quality of our extensive training programme.

Perks: Competitive salary; holiday entitlement; contributory pension plan; bonus scheme; life assurance; legal discounts; healthcare benefits, including a health cash plan; interest-free season ticket loans for commuting; reduced rates for city-centre car parking; cycle-to-work scheme.

Sponsorship: Payment of Diploma of Legal Practice.

Facts and figures

Total partners: 59
Other fee-earners: 198
Total trainees: 42

Trainee places available for 2019: 16
Applications received pa: 290
Percentage interviewed: 20%

Turnover in 2015: £51.3m (+11% from 2014)
Profits per equity partner: £480,000 (+8%)
(see legalbusiness.co.uk for full financial information)

Application process

Apply to: Lorna Macaulay, graduate recruitment and development advisor.
How: Online.
When: See website for deadline dates.
What's involved: See website for application process details.

Vacation schemes

Spring: Insight day. See website for details.
Summer: Six weeks during June, July and August. See website for application process details.

Burness Paull

CMS Cameron McKenna LLP

Cannon Place, 78 Cannon Street, London EC4N 6AF

Lex 100 Winner

See categories below
and tables from page 69

Survey results *(marks out of 100%)*

Satisfied in your job?	83
Firm living up to expectations?	84
High quality of work?	79
Enough client contact?	73
Stress-free?	63
Happy work/life balance?	64
Friendly firm?	85
Great social life?	79
Good vacation scheme?	84
Confident you'll be kept on?	59
Good remuneration?	74
Diverse firm?	80
Good international secondments?	87

 **verdict**

'Forward-looking' CMS Cameron McKenna is an 'ambitious firm' with a vast 'international network' that is particularly 'strong in Europe'. The 'internationally-focused firm' is a **Lex 100 Winner** for its overseas opportunities and provides a 'unique hands-on experience' for trainees which is both 'very rewarding' and 'totally different' to that of peers. CMS is described as a 'top firm' that is a 'leader in natural resources' and also real estate. The 'commitment to investing in people' is evident as the firm offers 'first-class training opportunities' and 'quality training', though the 'poor trainee retention rates' are of concern to many new recruits. But it is a 'human firm', with trainees at the heart of it, and 'impressive clients and law firm rankings' go hand-in-hand. Notably, 'CMS seems to have the best of both worlds: the best work while maintaining its persona as personable and friendly'. 'Big egos' and 'arrogant staff' aren't a problem here as the atmosphere is 'very supportive and people are friendly'. There is 'great supervision' provided for the new recruits and the 'fee-earners are approachable' as there isn't a 'rigid hierarchy'. Nevertheless, trainees should expect nothing less than hard work and will be expected to handle City working hours, whether that is 'working weekends', 'managing a double all-nighter' or 'the unpredictability of hours'. But there is said to be 'no face-time culture'. Trainee highlights include 'sealing a deal', 'attending face-to-face client meetings' and 'being assigned a great deal of responsibility throughout a large project'. If you are looking for a challenge at a 'friendly firm' with a 'good reputation' and an 'international footprint', keep CMS Cameron McKenna in mind.

If the firm
were a fictional character
it would be...

Pikachu (Pokémon) – friendly, fierce, a winner
and a proven energy expert

The firm

CMS recorded an 8.4% revenue rise in 2015 for its ten member firms in Europe, and in February 2016 became the first international firm to launch in Iran. The firm is valued by clients for its leadership in real estate and natural resources. It was nominated for the CSR Team of the Year gong at the *Legal Business* Awards 2016.

The deals

Advised Belltown Power on its £66m acquisition of a 50% interest in the Frodsham Wind Farm project from Peel Energy; acted for HSBC and Bank of Scotland as lead arrangers in a £210m financing to Miller Homes and certain subsidiaries; acted for Standard Life Investments in a highly complex business integration with Ignis Asset Management; acted for Sovereign Capital during the £92m sale of Alcumus Group to Inflexion; advised Johnson & Johnson on the $1.9bn sale of Cordis in the UK and Ireland to Cardinal Health.

The clients

Chubb; Clydesdale Bank; Deloitte; Diageo; Goldman Sachs; QBE; Santander; Schlumberger; Skrill Group; Viatel.

The star performers

Top-ranking departments according to *The Legal 500* (see legal500.com for more details)
Banking and finance; Commercial contracts; Commercial litigation; Corporate tax; Crime: fraud; Debt capital markets; Derivatives and structured products; EU and competition; Employment; Equity capital markets; Financial services (non-contentious/regulatory); Flotations: small and mid-cap; Immigration; Insolvency and corporate recovery; Listed funds; M&A: upper mid-market and premium deals, £250m+; Pensions; Securitisation; Unit trusts, OEICs and investment trusts; Venture capital.

- **Why did you choose this firm over any others?** 'Excellent vacation scheme'; 'high-quality work'; 'secondment opportunities'; 'commitment to CSR'; 'I wanted to do energy law at a top firm'; 'widest European network of offices'; 'a top-ranked firm in Scotland'; 'sector group focus'; 'female managing partner and high proportion of female partners'; 'the compulsory secondment was a huge draw'; 'controlled expansion strategy'; 'the firm embraces technology'

- **Best thing about the firm?** 'The great new offices'; 'the relaxed atmosphere'; 'major clients in a range of sectors'; 'speed of growth'; 'open-plan offices are indicative of the firm's willingness to allow everybody to interact with each other'; 'the lack of commuting in the morning'; 'approachability of partners'; 'the trainees tend to be a little older'

- **Worst thing about the firm?** 'Very low retention rates'; 'the salary is particularly low in Scotland'; 'the lack of a proper induction'; 'perhaps the lack of cohesiveness between the UK offices'; 'lack of daylight in the offices'; 'all the fundraising updates'; 'the time recording software'

- **Best moment?** 'Seeing an extremely big deal come to full completion'; 'meeting my team and training during the banking away weekend'; 'my secondment to a client in Vienna'; 'training sessions weekly to build knowledge and understanding of the banking sector'; 'receiving positive feedback from a client on a particularly challenging matter'; 'the CMS football tour 2015'; 'being heavily involved in a multi-million pound transaction'

- **Worst moment?** 'Seeing a huge deal fall through and the client disappointed'; 'turning up to work after a 4am karaoke masterclass'; 'my seat in a small disputes team with heavy administration tasks'; 'the late nights where I was in on my own and felt like I was drowning'

A day in the life of...

... Adam Beach trainee solicitor, CMS London

Departments to date: Corporate, a secondment to CMS Mexico (City), oil and gas, and technology

University: Birmingham

Degree and class: Law, LLB, 2(1)

9.00am: I arrive at the office having been to the gym and have a hearty breakfast of poached eggs, avocado and smoked salmon from our staff canteen, Cannons. I watch the news and check my phone for any urgent emails, then head to my desk.

9.30am: Unless there is something urgent that has arrived overnight or that I have planned to do first thing, I arrive at my desk and have a look at my to-do list, which I have prepared the night before. One of the key aspects of being a trainee is keeping on top of various tasks and prioritising appropriately. I usually prepare a to-do list at the start of the week and add to it as things crop up, ranking the tasks in order of importance.

10.00am: We are currently advising one of the firm's key clients on a substantial asset sale in a multi-faceted deal covering several practice groups. I have a call with one of the senior associates in our Aberdeen office, who gives me instructions on drafting a term sheet for one aspect of the deal. The client is quite strict on fees, so I must make sure that I work efficiently in producing the draft.

11.30am: On the same deal, I am keeping track of the billing time recorded by all the lawyers involved, which is then sent to the

client on a weekly basis. One of the lawyers has not closed her time sheet, so I give her a call and remind her to do so (never a fun phone call!).

12.15pm: A partner in my team urgently needs a letter translated from Spanish to English for a transaction involving a Colombian client. Sensing the consequences for missing the deadline, I drop everything and use one of the office's quiet rooms to translate the letter without any interruptions.

1.00pm: Having managed to finish the translation on time, I meet some other trainees for lunch. We grab some sushi and sit by the Thames, enjoying the sunshine.

1.45pm: Feeling suitably refuelled, I get back to my desk and prepare for a meeting taking place at 3.00pm. Our client wants to start a joint venture in Africa, and I am meeting with him and a partner to discuss how the joint venture will be structured. I prepare a checklist that we will work through at the meeting, the answers to which will then be incorporated into a joint venture agreement.

3.00pm: The client arrives and we greet him in reception. He isn't interested in legal jargon, so we boil everything down to simplistic but

commercial terminology. After going through the questionnaire with the client, the partner asks me to draft the joint venture agreement and send him a first draft that afternoon. I go onto our system and find a precedent agreement, which I then tailor according to what the client spoke about during the meeting.

'Our client wants to start a joint venture in Africa, and I am meeting with him and a partner to discuss how it will be structured.'

6.00pm: I finish drafting and send my work over to the partner, whose initial reaction seems positive. We will go over the draft tomorrow and make any necessary amendments before sending out to the client for review.

6.30pm: I have a football match for CMS that kicks off at 7.30pm, so I cycle over to the pitches in Haggerston. It is our final league fixture before a break – hopefully we will finish the season well!

www.graduates.cms-cmck.com

About the firm

Address: Cannon Place, 78 Cannon Street, London EC4N 6AF
Telephone: 020 7367 3000 **Fax:** 020 7367 2000
Website: www.cms-cmck.com
Email: grad.rec@cms-cmck.com
Twitter: @cmsuk_graduates

Senior partner: Penelope Warne
Managing partner: Stephen Millar

Other offices: London, Bristol, Aberdeen, Edinburgh and Glasgow.

Who we are: CMS is a top global elite firm and the most modern with 60 offices in 34 countries.

What we do: Our lawyers advise international clients across all types of commercial law, including corporate, banking and finance, energy, intellectual property and real estate. We advise many of the world's leading corporations, financial institutions and government organisations.

What we're looking for: We welcome exceptional law and non-law graduates who can contribute fresh thinking, an international outlook and formidable analytical skills.

What you'll do: Our training contracts offer a variety of responsibilities and interesting work across four seats. You'll enjoy access to senior partners and the support and autonomy you need to develop your talent and expertise.

Perks: Gym membership/subsidy, life assurance, pension scheme with firm contributions, private healthcare, season ticket loan, confidential care line, subsidised restaurant and 25 days' holiday with options to buy a further five days. You are also guaranteed to spend a seat outside your home office on a client, regional or international secondment.

Sponsorship: All of our trainees receive sponsorship through the GDL and LPC (or PEAT for Scotland), including tuition fees, as well as a maintenance grant for each year of study.

Facts and figures

Total partners: 860
Other fee-earners: 3,200
Total trainees: 120

Trainee places available for 2019: 50+
Applications received pa: 1,500
Percentage interviewed: 15-20%

First year salary: £40,000
Second year salary: £45,000
Newly qualified salary: £67,500

Turnover in 2015: £753.3m (+6% from 2014)
Profits per equity partner: £469,000 (+3%)
(see legalbusiness.co.uk for full financial information)

Application process

Apply to: Danny Cash, graduate recruitment and development team leader.
How: Please visit website.
When: Please visit website.
What's involved: Stage one – online application and psychometric testing. Stage two – assessment day (commercial analysis, presentation, group exercise and partner interview).

Vacation schemes

Summer: Please visit our website.

CMS
Law . Tax

Charles Russell Speechlys

5 Fleet Place, London EC4M 7RD

Lex 100 Winner

See categories below
and tables from page 69

Survey results *(marks out of 100%)*

Satisfied in your job?	81
Firm living up to expectations?	85
High quality of work?	82
Enough client contact?	82
Stress-free?	67
Happy work/life balance?	75
Friendly firm?	87
Great social life?	75
Good vacation scheme?	88
Confident you'll be kept on?	68
Good remuneration?	75
Diverse firm?	81
Good international secondments?	67

 **verdict**

Although Charles Russell Speechlys feels like a 'mid-sized firm', it has 'international capacity' with offices in Europe and the Middle East. 'The firm is not so small that it can't attract high-calibre work while it is not so large that a trainee feels like just another face in the crowd,' one respondent summarised. The 'strong private client department' and 'commercial awareness' were 'very appealing' to its recent recruits. There are a 'wide variety of seat options available' for trainees to try out, which is great for aspiring lawyers who are unsure of where they would like to specialise. But inevitably there is 'competition for seat allocations' which 'creates uncertainty'. Newcomers were impressed by the 'good reputation, friendly atmosphere and strong career prospects' the firm offers. There is 'high-level work available to trainees from the outset'. Recent recruits reported 'direct client contact', 'completing a corporate deal' and 'achieving a good settlement for a claimant after a six-year battle'. Trainees feel frustrated sometimes by the 'long hours' and 'dull administration tasks'. But Charles Russell Speechlys' trainees are in for a steep 'learning curve' as they are 'instantly a trusted and integral part of the team'. Even though there are 'not enough social events', everyone at the firm is 'approachable, friendly and open', and the firm is a **Lex 100 Winner** for low stress levels. Trainees are keen to grasp the 'excellent opportunities' on offer, from client secondments to hands-on experience in different departments. People who 'work hard' at the firm 'achieve and are definitely rewarded'. For those looking for a 'very friendly firm, early responsibility and exciting work', take a closer look at Charles Russell Speechlys.

If the firm were a fictional character it would be...

Glenn (The Walking Dead) – confident, courageous and reliable, but still with a touch of character

The firm

Charles Russell Speechlys was formed in November 2014 following the merger of Speechly Bircham and Charles Russell. The new firm has 170 partners, over 500 lawyers in total and revenues of £135m, plus a collection of offices in Europe and the Middle East. Private wealth services are the firm's core focus, and in June 2016 it strengthened this offering in Switzerland with the hire of three experienced partners. Other areas of focus include corporate, real estate and TMT.

The deals

Advised Nike on the expiry of its sponsorship deal with Manchester United; acted for Celesio to obtain immunity from fines following a CMA investigation into an alleged care home medicines cartel; advised Morgan Stanley on the regulatory issues associated with access to new trading venues, new products and MiFID II; advised the management team of Blackrock Programme Management on an investment made into the business by Dunedin LLP; acted for MayAir on its admission to AIM.

The clients

Actis; Arqiva; Central Bank of Bahrain; ITV; Kreos Capital; Moneycorp; TTT; VinaCapital; W H Ireland; Westfield.

The star performers

Top-ranking departments according to *The Legal 500* (see legal500.com for more details)

Agriculture and estates; Art and cultural property; Commercial contracts; Commercial litigation; Corporate restructuring and insolvency; EU and competition; Emerging markets; Employment: employers; Financial services (non-contentious/regulatory); Flotations: small and mid-cap; Fraud: civil; Immigration: business; Listed funds; M&A: mid-market, £50m-£250m; Private equity: transactions: Mid-cap deal capability; Private funds; Professional discipline; Reputation management; Retail funds; Venture capital.

- **Why did you choose this firm over any others?** 'I wanted a full-service law firm that also offered a stand-alone private client department'; 'the opportunity to have exposure to London'; 'one of the top private client firms in the UK'; 'people are approachable and willing to involve junior members of the team'; 'office location'; 'opportunities for client secondments'; 'an interesting mix of clients'; 'strong regional presence'

- **Best thing about the firm?** 'Friendly people from all different walks of life'; 'the management do care about your welfare and are always putting on social events'; 'I feel my contributions are valued'; 'decent coffee machines on every floor'; 'many of the clients are household names'; 'the friendly and positive attitude'; 'the wide range of departments'

- **Worst thing about the firm?** 'The office currently being split across three buildings in London'; 'the printers always seem to be broken'; 'the seat rotation process isn't always as transparent as it could be'; 'the pay is not quite at the level of work that we do'; 'IT hiccups associated with merger'

- **Best moment?** 'Being praised by the partner and associate on a matter after I had done some crucial and very complex calculations'; 'assisting at an employment mediation'; 'I was involved in a high-profile unfair dismissal case in which I was part of the team involved in proving a surgeon was unfairly dismissed'; 'getting to draft an employment contract'

- **Worst moment?** 'Almost missing a 4pm court deadline'; 'having to do a verification statement'; 'being the last person left on the whole floor late on a Friday night'; 'printing documents from a data room'; 'a lengthy disclosure exercise'

A day in the life of...

... **Nathan Lightman** second-year trainee, Charles Russell Speechlys
Departments to date: Corporate recovery and insolvency, private client, Harrods secondment, corporate
University: University of Birmingham
Degree and class: Political Science, 2(1)

7.00am: If I'm doing particularly well, I leap out of bed at 7.00am and start my day. I usually like to cycle into work – it gets me going for the day and certainly keeps me sharp, especially cycling right along Aldwych!

9.00am: I arrive for work, fresh from running the gauntlet of the City on a bike. I usually have breakfast at my desk while reading through my emails and planning the structure of my day. I keep a (somewhat nerdy) electronic to-do list in spreadsheet form, which ranks my tasks in order of priority. I like to aim to make a start on new work as soon as possible after receiving instructions, so that I can get a good idea of how long the remainder of the task will take me. This really helps both in planning my own workload, and in letting the fee-earner know when they are likely to get the work back.

12.30pm: This is when I usually have lunch, which is a great chance to see the other trainees and to have a hearty lunch at 6@6, our excellent café. There are often training events at lunch as well, which could be anything from technical legal updates to CSR events.

1.30pm: I might start work on a piece of research which a partner has requested I look into. This can range from a very specific tax point (such as the rate at which corporate non-resident landlords are taxed on UK rental income) to a very general instruction to find out what I can about the entire tax system of Antigua and Barbuda. The variety of work available to trainees is very impressive, and means that no two days are ever truly alike.

4.30pm: Since it's a Thursday, all the trainees, paralegals and associates in the department meet to discuss any interesting or difficult cases or points of law which have come up that week. This is a brilliant opportunity to talk over anything you might have found interesting or challenging, and trainees are actively encouraged to contribute. It also offers a chance for everyone in the department to keep up with what everyone else is doing. The trainees form a supportive network across the firm, and are always a good first port of call for a quick question. It feels like I know everyone well, and we often cross paths at both official firm events and socially.

The merger has been a big positive from a trainee's point of view – it has opened up new secondment opportunities and strengthened various departments across the firm, which can only be beneficial. It feels like everyone is pulling together in the same direction. I have almost always left at a sociable hour

> **'The trainees form a supportive network across the firm, and are always a good first port of call for a quick question.'**

so far in my training contract. Trainees are not expected to stay late unless there is a big deal or case in the pipeline, and even when I have had to stay late there has always been someone staying with me. After work I often take part in sporting activities (hockey, football or cricket) with the firm, which is a great way to meet people and to engage with clients.

About the firm

Address: 5 Fleet Place, London EC4M 7RD
Telephone: 020 7203 5000   **Fax:** 020 7203 0200
Website: www.charlesrussellspeechlys.com

Senior partner: Christopher Page
Managing partner: James Carter

Other offices: Guildford, Cheltenham, Paris, Geneva, Luxembourg, Zurich, Manama, Doha.

Who we are: Charles Russell Speechlys is one of a small number of law firms which provides personalised, considered advice to dynamic and entrepreneurial organisations, as well as astutely commercial advice to individuals and their families.

What we do: We are uniquely positioned to provide comprehensive advice where these two sets of needs overlap and as a result we work with some of the world's most successful entrepreneurs, wealthy families and growth businesses.

What we're looking for: We require candidates to achieve a minimum of a 2(1) in their degree and be able to demonstrate

Facts and figures

Total partners: 152
Other fee-earners: 454
Total trainees: 48

Trainee places available for 2019: 24
Applications received pa: 900
Percentage interviewed: 9%

First year salary: £38,000 (London), £31,000 (Guildford), £27,500 (Cheltenham)
Second year salary: £40,000 (London), £32,000 (Guildford), £28,500 (Cheltenham)
Newly qualified salary: £63,000 (London), £48,000 (Guildford), £41,000 (Cheltenham)

other key attributes outside academia, such as teamwork, leadership, communication skills and initiative. People come to us from all backgrounds and degree disciplines, with a range of views that combine to give us our distinctive perspective on the law.

What you'll do: The two-year training contract at Charles Russell Speechlys is divided into four seats, giving trainees the opportunity to experience a range of different practice areas before qualification. Throughout the training contract, there are regular meetings and reviews between the trainees and their supervisors to ensure they are continuing to receive a broad range of quality work and that they are developing the required skills and knowledge as they progress through their seats.

Perks: Private medical care; PHI and life assurance; pension; season ticket loan; cycle to work; 25 days' holiday and a subsidised restaurant in the London offices.

Sponsorship: We undertake to pay GDL and/or LPC course fees together with a maintenance grant.

Turnover in 2015: £134.5m
Profits per equity partner: £325,000
(see legalbusiness.co.uk for full financial information)

Application process
Apply to: Hayley Halvatzis, HR advisor.
How: Online application via www.charlesrussellspeechlys.com.
When: By Summer 2017.
What's involved: Assessment day includes an interview and other exercises designed to assess identified performance criteria.

Vacation schemes
Summer: Summer schemes take place across June and July in our London and Guilford offices (apply by 31 January 2017).

CRS
Charles Russell
Speechlys

Cleary Gottlieb Steen & Hamilton

Lex 100 Winner

See categories below and tables from page 69

City Place House, 55 Basinghall Street, London EC2V 5EH

Survey results *(marks out of 100%)*

Satisfied in your job?	75
Firm living up to expectations?	80
High quality of work?	(88)
Enough client contact?	85
Stress-free?	65
Happy work/life balance?	56
Friendly firm?	93
Great social life?	67
Good vacation scheme?	(95)
Confident you'll be kept on?	81
Good remuneration?	(89)
Diverse firm?	88
Good international secondments?	(89)

 **verdict**

Cleary Gottlieb Steen & Hamilton has an 'incredible reputation', and the 'international dimension to the work' of this US firm makes it a 'very respected name' in the global legal market. It is said that 'the quality of cross-border and international work is second-to-none'. Trainees certainly appreciate the 'opportunity to work with very high-profile clients' and regularly 'work on deals which make the front pages of the FT'. The firm has claimed four **Lex 100 Winner** gongs, including for work quality and international opportunities. Recent highlights include 'working through the night with a great team on an M&A deal', 'being given a great deal of responsibility early on in a litigation matter' and 'closing a small transaction by myself'. A few respondents mention the 'unpredictability of the working hours', and there are examples of trainees working past midnight and at weekends, though the 'great salary and benefits' available goes some way to remedy this. A common theme in Cleary Gottlieb's feedback is the 'non-departmentalised structure', a 'flexible' approach that 'allows you to experience a breadth of practice which would not be possible elsewhere'. The 'quality of its training' is also acclaimed, and due to the 'lack of a formal training structure' it's 'all about practical learning'. A couple of respondents reflected fondly on their 'great experience' of the 'enjoyable' Cleary Gottlieb vacation scheme. Away from the office, trainees went on a weekend trip to Brussels where they 'got to meet colleagues from all the different offices across Europe', and this is indicative of the 'extensive cooperation across teams and offices worldwide'. To train at a 'meritocratic' firm where there is a culture of 'always trying your best', keep Cleary Gottlieb Steen & Hamilton on your radar.

If the firm were a fictional character it would be...

The BFG – a giant that can appear daunting at first, but it soon puts you at ease and makes you comfortable

The firm

With approximately 1,200 lawyers based in 16 offices worldwide, Cleary Gottlieb has long held a reputation as an elite international firm. The firm is lauded for its M&A, private equity and acquisition finance work, and was one of the first US firms to set up in London, opening an office over 40 years ago. The firm was nominated for Dispute Resolution Team of the Year at the *Legal Business* Awards 2016.

The deals

Advised Greece on a €7.16bn bridge loan from the European Union under the European Financial Stabilisation Fund; acted for Armenian bank Ardshinbank on a $100m offering of amortising notes; advised UBS and Deutsche Bank on Pershing Square's inaugural $1bn Rule 144a bond offering; advised America Movil on its €3bn exchangeable bond offering; advised the Republic of Côte d'Ivoire on English law aspects of its $1bn Eurobond.

The clients

ArcelorMittal; BNP Paribas; Citigroup; Coca-Cola Company; Crédit Agricole; Fiat; Goodyear; NBK Capital; TPG; Warburg Pincus.

The star performers

Top-ranking departments according to *The Legal 500* (see legal500.com for more details)
Acquisition finance; Bank lending – investment grade debt and syndicated loans; Banking litigation: investment and retail; Commercial litigation; Competition litigation; Debt capital markets; EU and competition; Emerging markets; Equity capital markets; High yield; International arbitration; M&A: upper mid-market and premium deals, £250m+; Private equity: transactions: Large-cap deal capability.

- **Why did you choose this firm over any others?** 'Great experience on the vacation scheme'; 'quality of work is high'; 'the people are incredibly friendly'; 'I wanted to work for an international firm, but in a smaller office environment'; 'the people are incredibly friendly'; 'flexible departments'; 'flat hierarchy'; 'very respected name'; 'great salary and benefits'

- **Best thing about the firm?** 'The atmosphere is great'; 'partners are very easy to talk to and avoid any enforcement of a hierarchical structure'; 'the work is really interesting'; 'there is a culture of everyone trying their best'; 'lock-step structure'; 'relaxed about working from home'; 'standard of the employees'; 'reading about your work in the Financial Times'

- **Worst thing about the firm?** 'Associate pay not equivalent to peer group'; 'the canteen could do with a bit of a revamp'; 'poor work/life balance'; 'it can be quite disorganised at times'; 'the lift can take ages'

- **Best moment?** 'Receiving good feedback'; 'we were recently taken to Brussels for a weekend'; 'the immediate client contact'; 'replacing the associate on a deal when he stepped down and completing the deal successfully'; 'getting a message from the other side telling me I had done a great job'

- **Worst moment?** 'Being stuck in the office doing due diligence on the weekend'; 'being left unsupported on a very large transaction'; 'working on an IPO'; 'writing something wrong in a large email chain'; '2am bundling'

A day in the life of…

Chloe Barrowman final seat trainee, currently on secondment to the Hong Kong office

Departments to date: Finance, Capital Markets, M&A
University: Durham
Degree and class: English Literature

7.00am: I get up early and take a hike up into the hills just behind my apartment – the views are beautiful and the walk sets me up for the day. I set off for work around 9.00am – it's a nice day this morning so I forego the minibus and walk there in about 25 minutes.

9.30am: I arrive at the office and catch up with my emails. I review the closing checklist for a finance deal I'm working on that's due to close at the end of the month, and check I'm up to date with all the documents I'm responsible for. The finance team has been really keen to give me responsibility and I've become particularly familiar with various types of security documentation, so I'm quite comfortable that I understand the ongoing issues. I send a couple of follow-up emails on documents I'm waiting for from clients and co-counsel and file my emails so only outstanding work is sitting in my inbox.

10.00am: I begin reviewing the latest draft of a subordination agreement we have received in connection with the finance deal. I mark up the document based on my previous discussions with my supervisor and some helpful precedents he has sent me, and make a list of points I need to discuss with him.

12.30pm: This lunchtime there is a training session on rights issues and open offers, which is relevant to the more general corporate work I'd like to do when I return to London. The Hong Kong office provides lunch for the training, and the sessions are really helpful for making sometimes complex subjects more accessible.

1.30pm: I turn to a pro bono matter I was involved with back in London. We are working with the International Refugee Assistance Programme, helping to produce submissions for refugee applications on behalf of Syrian and Lebanese refugees. It's a fascinating project, although our regular phonecalls with our client can sometimes be upsetting given the difficult situation he's in. I work with my co-trainee on the matter, who is also currently on secondment in the Hong Kong office, to incorporate the associate's comments on our submission.

2.30pm: I receive comments on some of the security documents I have been working on from local counsel. I review the comments, make a note of some points I want to check with my supervisor and check I've got everything ready ahead of our meeting at 3.00pm.

3.00pm: I meet with my supervisor to discuss the points I made on the subordination agreement. He gives me some helpful pointers to go away with. I also raise my queries on the security documents, which he talks through with me so I can go away and mark the document up. I go back to the subordination agreement and review again based on my discussion with my supervisor. I then incorporate my comments on the security documents and send back to my supervisor for his review.

5.00pm: I attend a meeting with one of the funds associates I've been working with. He briefs me on a deal he's currently involved with for a major client – it involves making a number

> '**We are working with the International Refugee Assistance Programme, helping to produce submissions for refugee applications**'

of filings in Japan and he needs me to review all the filings to check they are accurate and all the information is up to date. I familiarise myself with the documentation and make a start on my review.

7.30pm: Having completed the first draft of all the filings, I send them through to the associate with a few important points he might want to look at. I check through my inbox again to make sure I'm up to date with my other deals and head out to meet some of the trainees for dinner. The trainee network in Hong Kong is fantastic and there's always something going on if you've got the time to spare.

www.cgsh.com/careers/london

About the firm

Address: City Place House, 55 Basinghall Street , London EC2V 5EH
Telephone: 020 7847 6860
Website: www.cgsh.com/careers/london
Email: longraduaterecruit@cgsh.com

Managing partner: Mark Leddy

Other offices: New York, Washington DC, Paris, Brussels, Moscow, Frankfurt, Cologne, Rome, Milan, Hong Kong, Beijing, Buenos Aires, Sao Paulo, Abu Dhabi and Seoul.

Who we are: Cleary Gottlieb Steen & Hamilton LLP is a leading international law firm with 16 closely integrated offices located in major financial and political centres around the world.

What we do: Core areas of practice in London are M&A, financing and restructuring, capital markets, international litigation and arbitration, and competition. In addition there are successful self-standing practices in tax, financial regulation, and IP and IT.

What we're looking for: We look for candidates who are enthusiastic about the practice of law in a challenging and dynamic international setting. While academic excellence is a pre-requisite, we place particular emphasis on recruiting candidates with whom we and our clients enjoy working. A sense of humour is as important as the ability to think critically.

What you'll do: By recruiting 12-15 trainees each year we are able to offer bespoke training that is tailored to our trainees' interests, experience and aptitudes. We encourage our trainee solicitors to accept increased responsibility as soon as they are ready to do so.

Perks: 25 days' holiday, employer pension contribution, gym membership subsidy, private healthcare, life insurance, long-term disability insurance, dental insurance, employee assistance programme, childcare vouchers, Bright Horizons back-up care and subsidised staff restaurant.

Sponsorship: LPC and GDL funding. A maintenance grant of £8,000 is paid for each year of professional study.

Facts and figures

Total partners: 193 (global)
Other fee-earners: 1,200 lawyers globally
Total trainees: 20
Trainee places available for 2019: 12-15
Applications received pa: Approximately 2,000
Percentage interviewed: 5% of applicants are invited to attend an open day.

First year salary: £48,000
Second year salary: £52,000
Newly qualified salary: £105,000

Application process

Apply to: Claire Astbury
How: Cover letter and full CV via our website.

When: By 31 July, two years in advance of the year in which the training contract is due to commence.

What's involved: We recruit the vast majority of our future trainees from among our vacation scheme students. Selection for vacation placements is through an open day comprising presentations on the firm, case study workshops and interviews. Candidates applying outside the vacation scheme have two interviews with graduate recruitment, partners and associates.

Vacation schemes

Winter: 5-16 December 2016
Spring: 27 March–7 April 2017
Summer: 26 June–7 July 2017 and 10–21 July 2017

CLEARY GOTTLIEB

Clyde & Co LLP

The St Botolph Building, 138 Houndsditch, London EC3A 7AR

Survey results *(marks out of 100%)*

Satisfied in your job?	79
Firm living up to expectations?	77
High quality of work?	82
Enough client contact?	73
Stress-free?	59
Happy work/life balance?	79
Friendly firm?	85
Great social life?	74
Good vacation scheme?	82
Confident you'll be kept on?	72
Good remuneration?	61
Diverse firm?	78
Good international secondments?	65

 **verdict**

Clyde & Co is well-established as a 'large and very prestigious City firm', with a 'good reputation in shipping' and other areas of expertise including insurance and aviation. As well as offering 'great exposure to different areas of the law', the firm's 'global presence' and 'approach to international expansion has been particularly energetic'. The firm has a 'down-to-earth feel' and an 'open-door policy' which creates an 'inclusive and friendly atmosphere'. There is a 'fantastic work/life balance' as employees are 'treated like human beings'. Recruits train alongside 'smart, savvy lawyers who know what they are doing', and the 'mostly fair supervisors' are a 'privilege to work with'. 'Everyone is extremely welcoming, supportive and friendly' and the 'good quality of work' is coupled with a 'decent level of responsibility for trainees'. Trainees describe the work as 'hands-on', and best moments involve 'being heavily involved in a multi-billion pound deal', 'working on high-profile deals that make the news headlines' and the 'secondment in San Francisco'. An added bonus for new recruits is that when they join 'the firm pays for gym membership'. There are a few problems with the 'disorganised HR administration' which at times appears to 'lack direction and can be frustrating'. 'Unnecessary stress' can be placed on trainees when there is a 'late timing of announcements' and 'lack of clarity on how many seats are given'. Trainees report 'receiving responsibility from the start' and feel in control of 'managing small cases or issues, drafting documents and attending client meetings'. Take time to research Clyde & Co if you want a 'good training programme' with 'international opportunities'.

If the firm were a fictional character it would be...

Sinbad the Sailor – goes on many adventures around the world and manages to navigate some stormy seas

The firm

Clyde & Co is acclaimed for its insurance, aviation and shipping capabilities. The firm has continued its international expansion in 2016 by opening offices in Miami and Dusseldorf. In recognition of his role in Clyde & Co's continued success, senior partner James Burns won Management Partner of the Year at the *Legal Business* Awards 2016. The firm has also posted an impressive 13% revenue rise for the last financial year.

The deals

Advised West Africa Gas as project sponsors on the financing for the importation of LNG into Ghana for regasification and onward sale to the Ghanaian government; advised Pyranha Mouldings in corporate manslaughter proceedings; continued to act for Estée Lauder on all employment matters, with multiple tribunal claims and two potential acquisitions occurring in the last year; assisted Peterborough City Hospital with a number of matters regarding the £335m Greater Peterborough Health Investment Plan PFI project; advised DEG, FMO and Proparco on the financing of a 40MW solar photovoltaic plant in Kenya.

The clients

AIG; Airbus; Asda; Beehive Group; Glencore; Just Retirement; PetroSaudi; QBE; Qantas Airlines; Universal Music Group.

The star performers

Top-ranking departments according to *The Legal 500* (see legal500.com for more details)

Art and cultural property; Asset finance and leasing; Aviation; Commercial litigation; Commercial property; Commodities: physicals; Education; Employment; Environment; Health and safety; Immigration: business; Infrastructure (including PFI and PPP); Islamic finance; Mining and minerals; Oil and gas; Personal injury: defendant; Power (including electricity, nuclear and renewables); Rail; Shipping; Trade finance.

- **Why did you choose this firm over any others?** 'An interesting mix between tradition and innovation'; 'its international aspect'; 'Clydes is litigation focused, which was important to me'; 'industry specialisms'; 'insurance capabilities'; 'because of my experience on the vacation scheme'; 'presence in uncommon locations'; 'the friendliness of the staff'; 'because they specialised in marine and insurance'; 'use of languages'; 'leader in insurance law'; 'international secondment opportunities'

- **Best thing about the firm?** 'Calibre of the work'; 'the lawyers in many areas are the best at what they do'; 'it is very relaxed for an international law firm'; 'global nature of business'; 'the quality of work'; 'good trainee group'; 'the sectors that the firm specialises in'; 'very social'; 'the firm's collegiate nature'; 'the biscuits'

- **Worst thing about the firm?** 'Occasionally having to do relatively tedious work'; 'seat choices sometimes seem arbitrary'; 'low pay when an associate'; 'lack of pastoral care'; 'lack of dialogue between graduate recruitment and trainees'; 'not very good at communicating big changes'; 'it feels like it is lacking strategy in the London corporate teams'

- **Best moment?** 'Being given my own case to run by a partner during my second seat'; 'chairing a client meeting'; 'the banking and finance seat'; 'working on sanctions advice'; 'being given important work to complete independently'; 'doing a first draft of submissions in an arbitration'; 'winning several points in a hearing for a major shipping case'; 'working in San Francisco'

- **Worst moment?** 'Bundling for a week'; 'missing social engagements to stay at work'; 'being sent to the Guildford office for six months without prior notice'; 'the nerves when I rang the other side for the first time to demand payment'; 'having to take a note at a four-hour meeting where I had very limited understanding of the concepts involved'

A day in the life of...

... Jonathan Cockerill first-year trainee, Clyde & Co LLP

Departments to date: Marine and international trade, client secondment at the Automobile Association

University: Oxford University   **Degree and class:** BA History 2(1)

8.00am: Straight out of law school, I am a first-seat trainee within Clyde & Co's marine and international trade departments. My day begins early, as I head from the London suburbs into the centre of the city where Clyde & Co is based.

9.00am: I have been allocated a supervisor who is my day-to-day mentor and guides me in my work. Today, I've been asked to support on a demurrage case. Demurrage is a fine ship charterers pay if they are late loading or discharging their cargo. I am responsible for running each of the many claims in our demurrage file and on this occasion I need to call a ship charterer to discuss their payment of the demurrage that they owe.

10.00am: The ship charterers are based in Singapore, so I take account of the time difference and decide to call them around 10.00am so that I can ensure I speak to them before the end of their working day. The discussion is productive and we agree for the payment to be made as soon as possible. I follow up the call with an email to confirm the discussions and keep my supervisor informed of developments. This is just one example of the kinds of matters I am involved in across my department. They are truly global in scale and the degree of responsibility I am exposed to is great experience for me.

11.30am: Another project I am working on is the drafting of an arbitration notice and I work closely with my supervisor to discuss what I need to include. I have learnt that being communicative and staying organised are two key skills that enable me to manage my workload effectively.

12.30pm: By the time lunchtime comes around, I am eager to get together with the other trainees at Clyde & Co. We gather in the top floor cafeteria and discuss our experiences – it has been fantastic to get to know other trainees who are going through the same experience as me.

1.30pm: During the afternoon, I'm briefed by an associate solicitor who needs urgent help to file the skeleton argument of a case we have been working on at court. While the details of the case are confidential, I rush off to court and file the skeleton argument. I then serve a copy on the barristers involved at their chambers.

3.00pm: Returning to the office, I'm engaged with another urgent request, reflecting the timeliness of legal work. An associate solicitor needs an exhibit bundle for a witness statement he has drafted. I build the bundle using documents he has earmarked for copying and update the witness statement to reflect the document references. This could eventually end up in court so everything has to be just right and attention to detail is crucial.

> **'I've learnt that being communicative and staying organised are two key skills that enable me to manage my workload effectively.'**

5.00pm: I finish the afternoon by getting back to a research task I've been working on for a couple of days concerning a defective notice.

6.30pm: By the end of the day, my department heads out to enjoy a few drinks at a local wine bar. It is great to have the opportunity to socialise and get to know my colleagues better.

www.clydecograduates.com

About the firm

Address: The St Botolph Building, 138 Houndsditch, London EC3A 7AR
Telephone: 020 7876 5555
Website: www.clydeco.com
Email: graduaterecruitment@clydeco.com
Twitter: @ClydeCoGrads

Senior partner: James Burns

Other offices: 45 offices globally (see website for details).

Who we are: Clyde & Co is a dynamic, rapidly expanding global law firm focused on providing a complete legal service to clients in our core sectors. With over 1,800 lawyers operating from 45 offices and associated offices in six continents, we advise across a wide range of contentious and transactional matters.

What we do: Our five core global sectors: insurance, energy, trade and commodities, infrastructure, transportation. Other areas of expertise: banking and financing, corporate disputes, cyber security, education, emerging markets, employment, financial services, fraud, healthcare, hospitality, intellectual property, litigation, pensions, real estate, trade sanctions.

Facts and figures

Total partners: 350
Other fee-earners: 1,800
Total trainees: 100

Trainee places available for 2019: 45-50
Applications received pa: 2,000
Percentage interviewed: 10%

First year salary: £36,000
Second year salary: £38,000
Newly qualified salary: £63,000

Turnover in 2015: £395m (+8% from 2014)
Profits per equity partner: £660,000 (+10%)
(see legalbusiness.co.uk for full financial information)

What we're looking for: The firm is looking for candidates who combine excellent academic results with strong commercial acumen and a practical approach to problem-solving. Trainees need to communicate effectively and build relationships with clients and colleagues.

What you'll do: You will gain early responsibility with opportunities to develop your skills through close personal supervision and a wide range of training courses. You will undertake four six-month seats, which will cover both transactional and contentious work. You may also choose to be seconded to one of our overseas offices, or have the opportunity for a client secondment.

Perks: Private medical insurance, dental insurance, 25 days' holiday per year, life assurance, pension, interest-free season ticket loan, subsidised gym membership, employee assistance programme, cycle to work scheme and a subsidised restaurant.

Sponsorship: Full fees for GDL and LPC as well as a maintenance grant.

Application process

Apply to: Graduate recruitment team – graduaterecruitment@clydeco.com.
How: Online.
When: Please see our website.
What's involved: Interview, group exercise and written assessments.

Vacation schemes

Spring: Two-week Easter scheme, please visit our website for further details and closing dates.
Summer: Two summer London schemes as well as one Manchester summer vacation scheme, each for a period of two weeks. We also run a two-week summer vacation scheme each year in our Dubai office. Please visit our website for further details and closing dates.

CLYDE & CO

Cooley (UK) LLP

Dashwood, 69 Old Broad Street, London EC2M 1QS

Lex 100 Winner

See categories below
and tables from page 69

Survey results *(marks out of 100%)*

Satisfied in your job?	86
Firm living up to expectations?	89
High quality of work?	84
Enough client contact?	75
Stress-free?	60
Happy work/life balance?	72
Friendly firm?	91
Great social life?	86
Good vacation scheme?	91
Confident you'll be kept on?	58
Good remuneration?	93
Diverse firm?	88

 verdict

Having already earned an 'excellent reputation in the US', Cooley has 'clear objectives for the development of the London office' since entering the City in 2015. Current trainees applied to the now-defunct Edwards Wildman before Cooley hired the bulk of that firm's London staff, but the trainee cohort notes that Cooley 'provides many opportunities for trainees and associates'. Much of these are centred on the firm's 'areas of expertise', as it represents 'many high-profile and cutting-edge clients' in the 'technology, life sciences and venture capital' sectors. This leads to 'interesting work' and as the firm has a 'small trainee intake' there is 'a lot of exposure and responsibility on matters at an early stage'. Examples of this include 'discussion of case strategy with a QC' and 'being involved in a large-scale investigation process'. Despite working for an American firm with 'international scope', trainees complain that there are 'no international secondments'. The small office size is deemed advantageous as it 'creates a friendly, supportive and cooperative atmosphere' and means that 'moving to a new seat does not feel like moving to a new firm as in larger offices'. There can be a 'lack of transparency on seat rotations' and currently 'the choice of departments for your training contract is slightly restricted'. Partners and associates are 'really good about involving you on particular types of deals if you express an interest in them', and the 'frequent social events are attended by all employees, not just fee-earners'. The social life has earned the firm one of four **Lex 100 Winner** awards. To train at a firm newly-arrived in the City that boasts an 'entrepreneurial feel' and an 'excellent reputation in the technology sector', consider Cooley.

If the firm were a fictional character it would be...

Q (James Bond) – loves technology, and this behind-the-scenes creativity allows those in the spotlight to achieve their objectives

The firm

Cooley launched in London in January 2015, establishing the California-headquartered firm's 12th office and first in Europe. The firm is a global leader in the TMT and IP spaces, and is also respected for its litigation capabilities. In recognition of Cooley's impact on the City's legal scene, it was shortlisted for Legal Technology Team of the Year at the *Legal Business* Awards 2016.

The deals

Advised Anthos Capital and Index Ventures on a $15m Series A financing for FaceIt, an online eSport gaming platform based in London; acted for Bambino Holdings in defending proceedings relating to the sale of Formula 1 racing shares; advised the Federal Government of Nigeria on sovereign immunity issues arising from the attempted enforcement in England of a Nigerian judgment against the client; acted for Tesla Motors in a trade mark dispute with a Polish electric powerboat manufacturer; advised Warner Music International on various data protection issues.

The clients

Apollo Global Management; Betway Group; Citibank; Fox; Guardian Media Group; Igas Energy; Munich Re; Nikon Europe; Twitter; XL Catlin.

The star performers

Top-ranking departments according to *The Legal 500* (see legal500.com for more details)
Brand management; Commercial litigation; Corporate restructuring and insolvency; Data protection; EU and competition; Financial services (non-contentious/regulatory); Fraud: civil; IT and telecoms; Insurance and reinsurance litigation; Insurance: corporate and regulatory; Insurance: insolvency and restructuring; Intellectual property; International arbitration; M&A: mid-market, £50m-£250m; Media and entertainment (including media finance); Pharmaceuticals and biotechnology; Product liability: defendant; Public international law; Reputation management; Venture capital.

- **Why did you choose this firm over any others?** 'Everyone is very friendly'; 'great work'; 'I had a great experience on the vacation scheme and knew it was the right fit for me'; 'an American law firm that provided international opportunities'; 'Cooley stands out for having a fantastic corporate department'; 'quality of clients'; 'excellent reputation in the technology sector'; 'many high-profile and cutting-edge clients'

- **Best thing about the firm?** 'The welcoming atmosphere'; 'the variety of work available'; 'there is an open-door policy'; 'the remuneration is very generous and we recently received a salary increase'; 'the free fresh fruit'; 'Thursday cake trolley'; 'the quality of the work'; 'the fact that every tech and internet company wants to work with us'

- **Worst thing about the firm?** 'Limited international secondment opportunities'; 'lack of transparency on seat rotations and qualification positions'; 'as there are so many San Francisco clients, calls are often a bit later in the evening than would be desired'; 'the firm encourages participation in pro bono programmes'

- **Best moment?** 'A day-long mediation where the client often asked my advice'; 'being taken to several conferences with clients and counsel and asked for my own input'; 'being part of a team attending a hearing'; 'attending a very swanky completion dinner following the successful investment by a large Turkish conglomerate into a restaurant in Mayfair'; 'receiving good individual feedback from a key client'

- **Worst moment?** 'Meeting a tight deadline on document preparation'; 'when I got muddled up in a task and it was late in the day'; 'weeks spent in my commercial litigation seat reviewing transcripts'; 'late night pagination'; 'needing to get a partner signature for a court document when all of the partners were at a retreat'

A day in the life of...

... Laura Dietschy second-year trainee, Cooley (UK) LLP

Departments to date: Commercial litigation, insurance and reinsurance
University: Strasbourg, France
Degree: French law

9.00am: I sort through my emails and to-do list (and add to my diary the Cooley cocktails event organised by the firm for the next day). When my supervisor comes in a few minutes later, he gives the go-ahead on an injunction application we have been preparing for a few days.

10.15am: I have finalised the witness statement and its exhibit, and prepare to obtain the witness' signature on my way to counsel's chambers. I draft the covering letter for the opposing party so I can head to their offices as soon as the application has been heard at the RCJ. This is a time-sensitive matter, so preparation and planning is key.

10.45am: In the cab on my way to counsel, I get a call from the partner in charge of the matter, explaining that the hearing will not go ahead today because the opposing party has agreed to negotiate. I still head to chambers to update counsel's bundle in case the negotiations are unproductive and the application needs to be lodged later in the week. We still need to keep thinking ahead.

11.50am: I am back in the office in time for a corporate training session which is followed by my current department's marketing meeting. These types of lunch breaks provide me with the opportunity to not only have a sociable breather, but also to get updated on the firm's priorities, opportunities and new clients. These

meetings offer great exposure to different partners' approaches to business development and I appreciate being included.

2.00pm: A piece of advice I drafted for a pro bono matter has been amended by the partner I have been working with. I head to his office to discuss certain points. We discuss one problematic paragraph and he explains to me what the standard industry practices, in his experience, actually are. I am encouraged to form opinions and be ready to defend them, which is a by-product of the constant exposure I have to associates and partners alike.

4.20pm: I have now made the final changes to the memorandum of advice and the partner in charge has sent it to the client. I head to the canteen for some strawberries and cream, and meet with a couple of other trainees for an update on their day. One of them is very busy with a complex litigation matter, which I know a few of us will be helping with soon. I return to my desk to clear my diary for the coming days.

4.35pm: I have been toying with a complicated piece of research for a while and am determined to finish it. I call the information services team to see whether they have found any further jurisprudence on the question. They have found a very helpful case that confirms my findings and reassures me that I have taken the right approach so far.

5.30pm: Now that I know how to frame my research results, I amend the memorandum I have been drafting and add the case found earlier.

6.30pm: Another trainee kindly offers to proof-read my research memorandum

> **'I am encouraged to form opinions and be ready to defend them.'**

before I send it to the relevant associate; precise attention to detail is key here. In the meantime, I quickly set out the CPR procedure for applying to obtain default judgment in an email, as we haven't received the defence in one of our matters. I discuss it with my supervisor, who seems happy with the answer, and add the deadlines to the relevant team members' diaries.

7.40pm: The trainee who has helped proof-read my research memorandum is also done with her work for the day, so we head off to play our tennis fixture on the courts just beside our office.

www.cooley.com/uktrainee

About the firm

Address: Dashwood, 69 Old Broad Street, London EC2M 1QS
Telephone: 020 7556 4373   **Fax:** 020 7785 9355
Website: www.cooley.com
Email: uktrainee@cooley.com
Facebook: www.facebook.com/CooleyLLP
Twitter: @CooleyLLP

CEO: Joe Conroy
Managing partner (London): Justin Stock

Other offices: Boston, Colorado, Los Angeles, New York, Palo Alto, Reston, San Diego, San Francisco, Seattle, Shanghai and Washington DC.

Who we are: Cooley is an international, commercial law firm and is best known for its representation of high-growth companies, often on matters where technology and innovation meet the law.

What we do: We have pre-eminent technology, life sciences, venture capital and fund formation practices. We solve legal issues for entrepreneurs, investors, financial institutions and established companies.

What we're looking for: Individuals with incisive minds, who enjoy solving complex business and legal challenges. High levels of achievement, both academically and in activities beyond study are key.

What you'll do: Trainees rotate every six months through some of the firm's contentious and non-contentious areas. Many of our clients are household names and the quality of the work is extremely high. Our smaller working teams mean the level of exposure and ability to contribute in meaningful ways is significant. A development programme, including the professional skills course, supplements this hands-on approach.

Perks: Gym subsidy, fitness reimbursement, life assurance, pension scheme with company contribution, private healthcare, STL and social events.

Sponsorship: Course fees and a living allowance while studying: £8,000 if studying in London, £7,500 outside London.

Facts and figures

Total partners: 28
Other fee-earners: 63
Total trainees: 9

Trainee places available for 2019: 4
Applications received pa: 400

First year salary: £44,000
Second year salary: £48,000
Newly qualified salary: £90,000

Application process

Apply to: Sarah Warnes – trainee recruitment and legal talent manager.
How: Online via www.apply4law.com/cooley.
When: By 31 January 2017 for 2019 contacts.
What's involved: The main route to a trainee position is via our summer placements. Successful candidates undergo online critical appraisal exercises, then a morning assessment centre with group business case study, followed by selection through to interview in the afternoon on the same day.

Vacation schemes

Summer: 26 June-7 July 2017 and 17-28 July 2017 (apply by 31 January 2017).

www.cooley.com/uktrainee

Covington & Burling LLP

265 Strand, London WC2R 1BH

Lex 100 Winner

See categories below
and tables from page 69

Survey results *(marks out of 100%)*

Satisfied in your job?	84
Firm living up to expectations?	(87)
High quality of work?	84
Enough client contact?	81
Stress-free?	64
Happy work/life balance?	76
Friendly firm?	91
Great social life?	69
Good vacation scheme?	(95)
Confident you'll be kept on?	(84)
Good remuneration?	(87)
Diverse firm?	(93)

 **verdict**

Covington & Burling is singled out for its 'niche specialisms' in life sciences and insurance. The US-headquartered firm has a 'small intake' of recruits but this means there are 'great chances for early-on responsibilities' and 'client contact'. Trainees are given 'excellent support from the team' and receive 'feedback from senior associates and partners'. Colleagues are 'approachable and supportive rather than intimidating'. Best moments for trainees include 'taking the lead on a multi-million pound restructuring for one of the clients', 'working independently from early on in the training contract' and 'supervisors complimenting good work'. Trainees have found the 'workload can be unpredictable at times' with an unbalanced 'distribution of work – some people are very busy while others have nothing to do'. Trainees have attributed this to a 'lack of communication'. 'Long late nights and stress' can happen but newcomers report they feel 'always extremely well supported' by other team members. The 'excellent working environment' gives trainees an 'invaluable experience' and 'healthy work/life balance'. Five **Lex 100 Winner** gongs have been secured, including in the diversity and remuneration satisfaction categories. The firm 'regularly advises on high-profile matters', offering lots of opportunities for trainees if they are 'willing to put the time in'. 'Pro bono is encouraged', plus 'meaningful and interesting projects' give newcomers the opportunity to develop their 'drafting skills and further their understanding of various legal areas'. Trainees like the 'unique personalities and diverse working environment', so those who are looking for a challenge in a 'friendly and inclusive environment' should consider applying to Covington & Burling.

If the firm were a fictional character it would be...

Rory Gilmore (Gilmore Girls) – very clever but down-to-earth, and has a serious coffee addiction

The firm

US firm Covington & Burling has firmly established its market presence since setting up in London in 1988. The firm commands an enviable reputation for its work in the insurance and life sciences sectors. Covington is also well-respected for its broad TMT coverage, including data protection, IT, media and sport, and for offering corporate advice on matters pertaining to investment funds, flotations and venture capital.

The deals

Advised Indivior on the UK and US employment elements of its demerger from Reckitt Benckiser; advised Californian biotech company Verseon Corporation on the US law aspects of its £66m IPO; acted for Allergy Therapeutics on a £20m placing; assisted AstraZeneca with its $575m purchase of Takeda's respiratory medicines business; acted for FilmFlex Movies in a software contract dispute.

The clients

Consort Medical; Coty; Holland & Barrett; Howden Group; Imperial Innovations; Johnson & Johnson Limited; Microsoft; Monster Energy; National Grid; Sanofi.

The star performers

Top-ranking departments according to *The Legal 500* (see legal500.com for more details)
Commercial contracts; Commercial litigation; Corporate crime (including fraud, bribery and corruption); Data protection; EU and competition: Trade, WTO, anti-dumping and customs; Employment: employers; Equity capital markets; Financial services (non-contentious/regulatory); Flotations: small and mid-cap; IT and telecoms; Insurance litigation: for policyholders; International arbitration; M&A: upper mid-market and premium deals, £250m+; Pharmaceuticals and biotechnology; Private funds; Product liability: defendant; Sport; Venture capital.

- **Why did you choose this firm over any others?** 'Greater balance and variety within the training contract'; 'I really enjoyed the vacation scheme'; 'I felt that at Covington I would be able to receive the best possible training'; 'the excellent arbitration practice'; 'the small intake'; 'inclusive environment'; 'the international nature of the work'

- **Best thing about the firm?** 'Extremely high-quality standards expected'; 'excellent work environment'; 'the highly intelligent colleagues'; 'the interesting, high-profile matters the firm regularly advises on'; 'the collegiality'; 'unique personalities'; 'the people'; 'the diversity'; 'getting to understand how a deal works from start to finish'

- **Worst thing about the firm?** 'Possibly opaque at times'; 'unstructured training compared with other firms'; 'no food facilities'; 'no gym scheme'; 'the workload can be unpredictable at times'; 'the lack of communication'

- **Best moment?** 'Having the opportunity to do substantive work on a high-profile case'; 'hearing excellent feedback about my contribution'; 'taking the lead on a multi-million pound restructuring for one of our clients'; 'working independently on a matter from start to finish early on in the training contract'; 'doing a very difficult, complex piece of research'; 'preparing for a closing meeting'

- **Worst moment?** 'Receiving the mark-up of my first written piece of work'; 'a long night in the office followed by a very early start the next day'; 'I got stuck in the office by myself one night as my supervisor had gone home. A crisis with a client arose and I had to deal with it on my own'

A day in the life of...

... Ramon Luque second-year trainee, Covington & Burling LLP

Departments to date: Corporate; dispute resolution; client secondment; life sciences (current seat)
University: University of Warwick **Degree and class:** Philosophy, 1st

9.00am: Having scanned through my emails on the way to the office, I arrive with a rough plan for the day ahead, knowing that this may well change as matters develop throughout the day.

9.30am: I catch up with my supervisor, who mentions that our client has requested a call later today to update them on the due diligence we have been conducting on a business they plan to acquire. Covington trainees typically share an office with their supervisor, and as with my previous supervisors, the relationship is informal and relaxed.

9.45am: I head downstairs with my colleagues for our weekly catch-up meeting with the Brussels team by videoconference. The food and drug regulatory practice advises life sciences clients on the full range of regulatory, transactional and contentious matters that affect their operations. The meeting gives us time to update each other on our matters and to discuss any points of interest.

10.15am: I return to my desk and finalise an agreement that I have been drafting over the last several days concerning the sale of a pharmaceutical product. The regulatory aspects of the deal are complex and challenging, which makes it rewarding. Having spent six months on secondment at a multinational pharmaceutical company, my current seat has given me the opportunity to consolidate my experience in this area.

12.30pm: Having sent the agreement to my supervisor for his review, I make the short trip to Covent Garden for lunch with some of the trainees.

1.30pm: A partner briefs me on a new matter for a client who is developing a diagnostic medical device for the detection of certain types of cancer. He asks me to draft a note for the client to explain the regulatory and legal implications surrounding this innovative product. We briefly discuss the contents of the note, I research any outstanding issues, and draft an outline. I then pause at around 3.45pm to prepare for the upcoming call.

4.00pm: My supervisor and I attend the call with our US-based client. The due diligence exercise has lasted around a month and we are reaching the final stages. We update the client with any material findings that could affect their decision to purchase the company. Our client is happy to proceed, and we agree to send them a final report of our findings by the end of the week. I have a record of our findings to date, but make a note to consolidate these into the final report tomorrow to ensure that my supervisor has enough time to review it.

4.30pm: Each month, I compile a summary of news items that may be of interest to our clients in the life sciences sector. It is a good way of keeping up to date with the latest developments. I spend some time searching

> '**Covington trainees typically share an office with their supervisor, and the relationship is informal and relaxed.**'

for items of interest and begin to write these up.

7.00pm: Covington's associate advisory committee (AAC) meets regularly to discuss issues of interest and concern to the firm's associates. Trainees are welcome to all events, and as part of its social calendar, the AAC has organised a go-karting trip for this evening. I head off to the track with my colleagues for an evening of high-octane fun.

www.cov.com

About the firm

Address: 265 Strand, London WC2R 1BH
Telephone: 020 7067 2000
Website: www.cov.com/en/careers/lawyers/london-graduate-recruitment-programme
Email: graduate@cov.com

Managing partner: Chris Walter

Other offices: Beijing, Brussels, London, Los Angeles, New York, San Francisco, Seoul, Shanghai, Silicon Valley and Washington DC.

Who we are: Covington & Burling LLP was founded in Washington DC nearly a century ago. Today, the firm has over 900 lawyers globally. Covington's London office, overlooking the Royal Courts of Justice, was established over 25 years ago. Covington has been rated a Top Ranked Leading Law Firm in *Chambers UK 2016* and appears in *The Lawyer* Top 30 International Law Firm, as well as *Legal Business* Global 100 surveys.

What we do: At Covington, you will have an opportunity to work on cutting-edge deals for international and UK corporates such as Microsoft, Astra Zeneca and Facebook, Fortune 100 businesses and leading technology, life sciences and media companies. We offer services across a wide range of practice areas, advising clients on their most challenging and complex matters. Most of the work has an international element, and all our practice groups operate across borders.

What we're looking for: We are looking for consistently high academic results (on target for a 2:1 degree or above and with strong A level results), commercial awareness, strong interpersonal skills and ability to work well in a team.

What you'll do: You will do four six-month seats, rotating between departments. All trainees will undertake a seat in corporate and a seat in dispute resolution. We can offer optional seats in the following areas: employment, life sciences and technology and media. Client secondments may also be available.

Perks: Benefits include life assurance, pension, private healthcare and season ticket loan.

Sponsorship: Successful training contract applicants will receive payment of tuition fees for both the GDL and the LPC, as well as a maintenance grant of up to £8,000. We do not pay fees retrospectively for completed courses.

Facts and figures

Total partners: 275
Other fee-earners: 690
Total trainees: 11

Trainee places available for 2019: up to 7
Applications received pa: 400
Percentage interviewed: 10%

First year salary: £43,000
Second year salary: £47,000
Newly qualified salary: £85,000

Application process

Apply to: Alexandra Reddington.
How: Online application form.
When: By 17 July 2017 for 2019 contracts.

Vacation schemes

Summer: June/July 2017. Apply by 31 January 2017.

COVINGTON

DLA Piper UK LLP

3 Noble Street, London EC2V 7EE

Lex 100 Winner

See categories below
and tables from page 69

Survey results *(marks out of 100%)*

Satisfied in your job?	78
Firm living up to expectations?	80
High quality of work?	78
Enough client contact?	71
Stress-free?	62
Happy work/life balance?	70
Friendly firm?	86
Great social life?	80
Good vacation scheme?	87
Confident you'll be kept on?	70
Good remuneration?	73
Diverse firm?	79
Good international secondments?	(85)

 **verdict**

The 'international footprint' is a strong part of DLA Piper's makeup as the firm has offices in the UK, mainland Europe, Asia-Pacific, the Middle East and the Americas. Trainees love the 'global reach, breadth and scope' that goes hand-in-hand with an 'internationally-focused law firm'. Trainees have been 'blown away' by the 'high-quality training'. As a 'big firm', there are 'broad practice groups' so trainees are not obliged to 'specialise early on'. There is a 'warm, fostering and friendly culture' and 'senior members of the team are very approachable'. The firm 'invests a lot of time in training and offers exciting opportunities'. Top trainee moments include 'travelling to Moscow for an interview', 'taking responsibility for meeting a client unsupervised' and 'the sense of achievement after completing multiple deals back-to-back'. In particular, trainees treasure their experiences on international seats anywhere from Sydney to Singapore, and this has earned the firm a **Lex 100 Winner** medal. 'Over-competitive personalities' and 'all-nighters' can be part of the package. The 'long hours' are 'demanding and there are high expectations' of trainees. This certainly means that trainees are never bored and 'virtually never have nothing to do'. One struggle is that the sheer 'volume of lawyers employed can sometimes make it difficult to stand out from the crowd', but trainees are impressed by the 'extensive career opportunities' on offer. Since the 'turn of the century', the firm has 'undergone serious growth in comparison to its competitors' and has a 'clear objective in place' as it strives to achieve its 'potential and ambition'. Those looking for a 'leading law firm' with 'great potential' and 'worldwide scope' should seriously consider DLA Piper.

If the firm were a fictional character it would be...

Lucy Pevensie (The Chronicles of Narnia) – a bit of an upstart who never stopped believing and gave the big kids a run for their money

The firm

DLA Piper has continued its international expansion over the last 12 months, merging with firms in Sweden and Finland and setting up new offices in Morocco and South Africa as it bulks up its extensive global network. Nationally, DLA Piper is active across the full spectrum of high-value legal work, and is notably strong in the TMT, white-collar fraud, real estate and private equity spaces. One of its three nominations at the *Legal Business* Awards 2016 was for Legal Innovator of the Year.

The deals

Advised HCL Technologies on its acquisition of Volvo's IT services arm; advised Market Tech Holdings on the £900m refinancing of its Camden property portfolio; advised Ever Smart International Enterprise on the sanctions elements of its IPO on the Hong Kong Stock Exchange; advised Commonwealth Development Corporation in its cornerstone investment in Insitor Impact Asia Fund; assisted Discovery Communications with its £950m buyout of the remaining 49% shares in Eurosport.

The clients

Amec Foster Wheeler; Babcock International; Deutsche Bank; HSBC; Heineken; London Stock Exchange Group; PureTech Health; Reckitt Benckiser; Virgin Media; Visa UK.

The star performers

Top-ranking departments according to *The Legal 500* (see legal500.com for more details)
Acquisition finance; Asset based lending; Banking litigation: investment and retail; Commercial litigation; Competition litigation; Corporate tax; Corporate crime (including fraud, bribery and corruption); Commercial contracts; EU and competition; Equity capital markets; Financial services (contentious); Flotations: small and mid-cap; Fraud: civil; Gaming and betting; International arbitration; Private equity: transactions: Mid-cap deal capability; Private funds; Public international; Tax litigation and investigations; VAT and indirect tax.

- **Why did you choose this firm over any others?** 'The breadth of practice areas'; 'potential quality of work that I would be exposed to'; 'the people are really friendly'; 'international presence'; 'prestige'; 'firm with a strong strategy'; 'disrupting the big players in the market while maintaining its regional roots'; 'great pro bono opportunities'; 'the strength of the litigation and employment departments'; 'retrospective funding for GDL'; 'the vacation scheme was fantastic'

- **Best thing about the firm?** 'Down-to-earth people'; 'its strategy and constant growth'; 'ease of approaching more senior fee-earners to receive guidance'; 'does not rest on its laurels and is striving to be the biggest player in every market'; 'its progression in the recent past and vision to be the leading global business law firm'

- **Worst thing about the firm?** 'Seat allocation politics'; 'institutional mentality'; 'lack of trainee social events'; 'lack of brand awareness from peers'; 'doing lots of administrative tasks'; 'top-heavy in some departments'; 'computer system needs an upgrade'; 'there are few internal promotions to partnership'; 'pay gap between London and regional wages'

- **Best moment?** 'Completing a large outsourcing transaction which I had assisted on from start to finish'; 'making a successful application for a stay of proceedings in the High Court'; 'being involved with two IPOs'; 'travel to Moscow to interview clients'; 'drafted submissions for an arbitration case'

- **Worst moment?** 'Making a mistake'; 'the occasional 2am finishes'; 'some of the training'; 'having to run in a pencil skirt to deliver a bundle to a client on time'; 'working with a client, who was extremely difficult to deal with and very demanding'

A day in the life of...

... **Charlotte Woodfield** trainee solicitor, DLA Piper UK LLP

Departments to date: Finance and projects, employment
University: University of Leeds
Degree and class: French and Management, 2(1)

8.30am: I arrive at the office early to check my emails and review my to-do list for the day ahead. I have received an email overnight from a colleague in our New Zealand office – he has provided some advice on a global business outsourcing project I am assisting my supervisor with. I draft a summary of the advice to send to our client and send this to my supervisor.

9.00am: I receive an email from a client sending me some documents for disclosure on a case that I am working on. I send the documents to our reprographics team and ask for them to be printed out. I make a note to respond to the client this afternoon once I have had an opportunity to review the documents.

9.30am: My supervisor gives me her comments on the summary of advice I drafted and asks me to send this to the client. We have a meeting with another client at 10.00am, so I spend a few minutes reading up on the client's business in advance of the meeting.

10.00am: The client would like us to conduct a review of all of the company's international employment contracts. I take notes during the meeting and speak to my supervisor afterwards about the next steps. We will need assistance from several of our international offices, so she asks me to draft an email to brief

them on the matter and to ask them for fee estimates for the work required.

11.30am: I return to my desk to join a call between a senior associate and one of the witnesses in an unfair dismissal case. We go through the witness statement I have drafted for them and the witness expands on some points so that I can add further detail to their statement.

12.30pm: I meet another trainee for lunch to discuss a pro bono matter we are working on together. We are assisting an asylum seeker in making a claim for asylum. We divide the different areas of research between us and agree to meet again in a week's time to discuss our findings.

1.15pm: The documents that I sent to the reprographics team this morning have been printed and delivered to my desk. I review these and add them to the disclosure file. I update the senior associate and we agree on a list of outstanding documents we would like to ask the client to search for.

3.00pm: I attend a telephone preliminary hearing with an associate. The purpose of the hearing is to agree the issues to be decided in the case and to set the case management directions. The employment judge orders that certain aspects of the claimant's claim be struck out, which is good news for our

defendant client. I draft an email updating the client on the outcome of the hearing and send this to the associate.

4.00pm: I dial in to a think-tank call on gender pay gap reporting with a group of fee earners from different offices. I have been involved in giving training to clients on

> **'I return to my desk to join a call between a senior associate and one of the witnesses in an unfair dismissal case.'**

this topic, so I feed back to the group on the issues our clients have raised when discussing this with them.

5.00pm: I amend the witness statement we went through with a witness earlier today and send it to the senior associate for her to review before sending it to the client tomorrow.

6.30pm: I check with my supervisor that there isn't anything else I can help with this evening and then I head downstairs to meet some other trainees to attend a wine-tasting networking event at a hotel nearby.

www.dlapipergraduates.co.uk

About the firm

Address: 3 Noble Street, London EC2V 7EE
Telephone: 08700 111111   **Fax:** 020 7796 6666
Website: www.dlapiper.com
Email: recruitment_graduate@dlapiper.com
Twitter: @DLA_Piper
          @DLA_Piper_Grads
Facebook: DLA_PiperUKGraduates

Global co-chairman: Juan Picon
Managing partner: Simon Levine

Other offices: Birmingham, Edinburgh, Leeds, Liverpool, Manchester, Sheffield and international offices in over 30 countries worldwide.

Who we are: A leading global law firm, built to serve clients wherever in the world they do business.

What we do: Corporate; employment; finance and projects; intellectual property and technology; litigation and regulatory; real estate; restructuring; and tax.

What we're looking for: A diverse group of talented individuals who have a consistently strong academic performance, formidable commercial acumen, who are articulate, ambitious, driven, and have sharp minds, enthusiasm and intellectual curiosity.

What you'll do: Trainees complete four six-month seats, with an opportunity to express what areas of law they would like to experience during their training contracts. They also have the opportunity to do a seat abroad or a client secondment. Current international secondments include Bangkok, Dubai, Hong Kong, Madrid, Moscow and Sydney. They also benefit from high levels of responsibility and award-winning learning and development programmes.

Perks: 25 days' holiday, pension scheme, private medical insurance, permanent health insurance, life assurance, season ticket loan, cycle to work scheme, social club, sports teams, subsidised gym membership, subsidised restaurant and discounts at local retailers.

Sponsorship: Fees and maintenance grants paid for the GDL and LPC.

Facts and figures

Total partners: 1,300 globally
Other fee-earners: 2,800 globally
Total trainees: 170 in the UK

Trainee places available for 2019: up to 75
Applications received pa: 3,100
Percentage interviewed: 17%

First year salary: London £42,000; English regions £27,000; Scotland £24,000.
Second year salary: London £47,000; English regions £30,000; Scotland £26,000.
Newly qualified salary: London £70,000; English regions £41,000; Scotland £38,000.

Application process

Apply to: Linda Luong, senior graduate recruitment advisor.
How: Apply online.
When: By mid-July for 2019 contracts.
What's involved: Online application form, online psychometric test, assessment day.

Vacation schemes

Spring: London and Leeds only.
Summer: Two-week placements during various dates between June and August across the UK.

DWF LLP

1 Scott Place, 2 Hardman Street, Manchester M3 3AA

Survey results *(marks out of 100%)*

Satisfied in your job?	82
Firm living up to expectations?	80
High quality of work?	81
Enough client contact?	76
Stress-free?	65
Happy work/life balance?	77
Friendly firm?	87
Great social life?	79
Good vacation scheme?	86
Confident you'll be kept on?	76
Good remuneration?	76
Diverse firm?	86

 verdict

'Proactive and ambitious', DWF is a firm that promises 'forward momentum and growth in the market-place'. Trainees found the 'big national' firm 'particularly appealing' because of its 'constant progression and innovation'. The firm 'continues to grow and develop, pushing for more high-profile work while remaining committed to delivering great advice and client satisfaction'. One trainee reports that this can be a 'double-edged sword' as such momentum 'is hard to keep up'. Yet year-on-year, the firm is able to 'meet that growing ambition', and opened its first international office in Dubai in March 2015. Trainees agree it would be good to have 'international secondments' available. The 'four-month seat rotation' gives trainees a 'wide variety of experience in different areas of the legal industry'. It can be 'stressful and the hours can be long, depending on the seat'. DWF has a 'genuinely distinct identity' as a 'friendly firm' where all 'members of staff have a voice regardless of position or hierarchy'. Notably, trainees feel 'valued as employees and as members of the DWF family'. There are 'plenty of opportunities' on offer for new recruits as the firm provides 'good-quality work'. The 'level of support', 'client contact' and 'good responsibility' all make it a 'very inclusive workplace' for trainees. There is a 'friendly atmosphere' as 'colleagues of all seniority levels are very approachable'. Top moments include 'drafting the paperwork for a sale of a property more than £30m', 'working on a £70m refinancing deal' and 'attending a large multi-party mediation hearing until 1am and settling the case'. If you are looking for the 'chance to make a difference', look no further than DWF.

If the firm were a fictional character it would be...

Cole Trickle (Days of Thunder) – an ambitious and talented underdog that rose through the ranks to become a champion

The firm

DWF expanded into Europe in December 2015, first opening a Brussels office before adding bases in Cologne and Munich through a German tie-up. The full-service firm is an insurance leader, and also possesses highly regarded employment, private client and personal injury practices. DWF earned two nominations for the *Legal Business* Awards 2016, in the Insurance and Legal Technology Team of the Year categories.

The deals

Won a case for Trafigura concerning a $150m purchase of oil supplies from Malaysia; advised Tata Chemicals Europe on £140m of syndicated term and revolving credit facilities; advised The Authentic Food Group on its acquisition of a facility in Dundalk, Ireland from Heinz; advised the official receiver on the compulsory liquidation of Redcar Steelworks; advised Transport Scotland on the procurement of the Caledonian Sleeper and ScotRail franchise.

The clients

Birmingham City Council; Hovis; Liverpool FC; Lloyds Banking Group; Serco Group; Standard Life; Telefonica UK; UK Commission for Employment & Skills; United Utilities Water; Yodel.

The star performers

Top-ranking departments according to *The Legal 500* (see legal500.com for more details)

Banking and finance; Charities and not-for-profit; Commercial litigation; Commercial property; Contentious trusts and probate; Corporate and commercial; Corporate tax; EU and competition; Employment; Energy; Family; Health and safety; Immigration; Insolvency and corporate recovery; Intellectual property; Local government; Personal injury: defendant; Personal tax, trusts and probate; Property litigation; Social housing.

- **Why did you choose this firm over any others?** 'Excellent vacation scheme'; 'interesting work given to trainees'; 'the innovative products'; 'secondment opportunities'; 'brilliant people'; 'people have a voice at all levels'; 'the open day was the best'; 'I had worked here as a paralegal for two years before applying and wanted to stay'; 'good clients'; 'opportunity to do good work in the regions'; 'positive news coverage'; 'growing firm in London'

- **Best thing about the firm?** 'The opportunity to get involved in CSR activities'; 'great colleagues'; 'open-plan office'; 'ability to progress and chance to make a difference'; 'the leadership'; 'inclusiveness'; 'the calibre of people working in the teams'; 'expanding quickly'; 'social side'; 'the office views'

- **Worst thing about the firm?** 'The teabags'; 'vending machines are too tempting'; 'the lack of consistency with trainee supervisors'; 'focus on hours'; 'lack of international opportunities'; 'limited options in choosing seats'; 'sometimes the IT systems can have a bit of a meltdown'; 'the differences between offices'; 'expenses policy'

- **Best moment?** 'Attending client meetings'; 'attending court on a number of interesting matters'; 'receiving high praise on work that I had carried out'; 'secondment to a large outsourcing company so I had first-hand experience of what the client receives'; 'working with young and disadvantaged people to improve their career confidence'; 'completing a cross-jurisdictional deal in corporate'; 'managing my own load of case files in insurance'

- **Worst moment?** 'Undertaking a large disclosure exercise which took the best part of two-and-a-half months to complete'; 'staying extremely late to finish urgent work'; 'lugging a suitcase full of files around the RCJ'; 'informing the wrong Mr Jones he would be going to trial'; 'a lot of long days in real estate'; 'working late into the night at home'

A day in the life of...

... Joseph Hui second-year trainee solicitor, DWF LLP

Departments to date: Construction, corporate, pensions, employment, secondment to the Pension Protection Fund

University: The University of Melbourne   **Degree:** Bachelor of physiotherapy honours

8.30am: I arrive at the office after a 45 – minute commute while I review emails which have come in since I left the office last night. I make a quick mental note of my to-do list for the day before I arrive into the office and usually have just enough time to pop down into the bistro to grab some breakfast before I make a start on the day's work.

9.15am: I prepare the documents that we need for an 'all parties conference call' on a complex acquisition and ensure that all the required documents have been circulated to the project team ahead of the call.

9.30am: I attend the call with the rest of the corporate team working on the project which deals with any outstanding issues and actions. The client has asked that certain documents are provided by the end of the week and I prepare a detailed note of the meeting setting out the actions agreed.

10.30am: I resume work on a due diligence report that I was working on the previous day and check the electronic data room for additional information provided by the other party overnight. This involves reviewing any information disclosed against questions that we have submitted. I arrange a catch-up with my supervisor to discuss any relevant information disclosed and identify any additional points we will need to raise with the other party.

1.00pm: I attend the monthly 'corporate know how' session hosted by our professional support lawyer. The topic this week deals with the UK Takeover Code and the treatment of minority shareholders in a transaction. This training comes at quite a good time as we are currently advising a client on an issue involving difficult minority shareholders and I can apply this knowledge fairly promptly.

2.00pm: I have a quick lunch with some of my fellow trainees in the bistro to catch up on what they have been working on for the past few days. We also discuss the upcoming summer boat party and plans for the weekend.

2.30pm: I attend a meeting with my supervisor dealing with the reconstitution of some lost company statutory books. This exercise involves reviewing all the company filings on Companies House and gives me a good opportunity to practise my detective skills and not to mention my mathematical skills.

3.30pm: I attend a meeting with my supervisor with a potential new client who is looking to acquire a sports club overseas. The deal is top secret at present and has significant regulatory implications. The meeting gives me a good insight as to how sports clubs make decisions and the importance of communication and PR timing.

At the end of the meeting, my supervisor and I agree a set of actions and I set out to prepare a fee quote setting out our scope of work and potential costs.

5.30pm: Having recently returned from a secondment at The Pension Protection Fund, I email some of my old colleagues to arrange

> **'The deal is top secret at present and has significant regulatory implications.'**

the long-awaited after-work drinks in the Sky Gardens on the 35th floor of our office building.

6.00pm: I am asked by one of the partners to assist with drafting an urgent undertaking in relation to a joint venture which is needed before 8.00pm. Having located the relevant information, I set out to draft the relevant document and submit it to the supervisor for approval before sending it out to the client.

7.30pm: Having finished with the day's work, I catch up with some of my fellow colleagues and head off to a local drinking establishment for some well-earned rest.

www.dwf.law/join-us/graduate

About the firm

Address: 1 Scott Place, 2 Hardman Street, Manchester M3 3AA
Telephone: 03333 2022
Website: www.dwf.law
Email: trainees@dwf.co.uk
Twitter: twitter.com/DWF_graduate

Senior partner: Carl Graham
Managing partner: Andrew Leaitherland

Other offices: Birmingham, Edinburgh, Glasgow, Leeds, Liverpool, London, Newcastle.

Who we are: DWF is a national commercial legal business that offers clients excellent commercial guidance combined with sector specialist knowledge.

What we do: DWF has core strengths in insurance, corporate and banking, real estate and litigation, and in-depth industry expertise in six chosen sectors.

What we're looking for: We're looking for talented, ambitious people who are passionate about helping our clients achieve their commercial goals. You'll provide innovative solutions and think differently about their needs.

What you'll do: At DWF, we offer six four-month seats, giving you the opportunity to experience more practice areas than a traditional training contract.

Sponsorship: Full sponsorship of LPC.

Facts and figures

Total partners: 271
Other fee-earners: 1,164
Total trainees: 95

Trainee places available for 2019: c.50
Applications received pa: 1,500
Percentage interviewed: 20%

First year salary: £22,000-£36,000 (depending on location).
Second year salary: £25,000-£40,000 (depending on location).
Newly qualified salary: Varies depending on location and practice group.

Turnover in 2015: £191m (+0% from 2014)
Profits per equity partner: £325,000 (-16%)
(see legalbusiness.co.uk for full financial information)

Application process

Apply to: Emma Byers.
How: Online application form on website.
When: By 7 July 2017 for 2019 contracts.
What's involved: Online application, first stage interview and assessment centre.

Vacation schemes

Summer: Programmes in Summer 2017 (apply by 27 January 2017).

Debevoise & Plimpton LLP

65 Gresham Street, London EC2V 7NQ

Lex 100 Winner

See categories below and tables from page 69

Survey results *(marks out of 100%)*

Satisfied in your job? **91**

Firm living up to expectations? **91**

High quality of work? **91**

Enough client contact? **77**

Stress-free? **59**

Happy work/life balance? **58**

Friendly firm? **96**

Great social life? **67**

Good vacation scheme? **93**

Confident you'll be kept on? **84**

Good remuneration? **85**

Diverse firm? **96**

Good international secondments? **72**

 **verdict**

'Internationally-renowned' Debevoise & Plimpton is 'dedicated to investing vast amounts of time and resources in their trainees' and offers 'good remuneration'. The 'small trainee intake' means recruits are immersed in 'close-knit teams' and receive 'responsibility at an early stage', leading to 'great client contact'. The US firm has a 'collegiate and friendly atmosphere' where trainees are working alongside 'exceptional lawyers', and one of the best things is the 'quality of supervisors and other lawyers'. Everyone is 'very approachable and willing to spend time explaining complex aspects of deals or cases they are working on'. Trainees have the opportunity to 'make a significant contribution' and receive 'complex and sophisticated work'. Nevertheless, it is clear that there are 'high expectations' of trainees. Best moments for newcomers include being 'heavily involved in the hearing preparation for a high-profile, inspiring human rights matter' and 'being trusted to take charge of a due diligence report by myself, and coordinating the team's contributions'. Trainees love the 'frequent champagne tea parties for the whole office' and the 'business programme in the New York office'. Despite its 'array of international offices', a number of trainees report limited 'international secondment opportunities'. The 'excellent reputation', especially in litigation and arbitration, precedes the firm and there is a 'clear focus on growing the highly-regarded litigation department'. All told, the firm has won a very impressive seven **Lex 100 Winner** titles, including for job satisfaction and the vacation scheme. 'Prestigious' Debevoise & Plimpton is a great choice for trainees looking to get their hands on 'world-class work' in exchange for 'high levels of responsibility'.

If the firm were a fictional character it would be...

Jay Gatsby – a flash, ambitious American eager to impress, with honest motives

The firm

Debevoise & Plimpton's London base opened in 1989, and is the firm's second largest behind its New York headquarters. Strong performances in the funds and disputes space led to the London office posting a 20% revenue rise for 2015, breaking the $100m barrier. Debevoise opened an office in Tokyo in March 2016, its first global launch for 14 years.

The deals

Advised Clayton, Dubilier & Rice on £360m senior secured facilities to fund its acquisition of Motor Fuel Group; advised American Securities on the merger control aspects of its $855m acquisition of Blount International; advised TA Associates on its acquisition of a majority stake in Access Technology Group; advised Helios on its acquisition of Orange Group's 70% stake in Telkom Kenya; defended the Republic of Korea in an arbitration involving share disposals in an oil company.

The clients

AIA Group; Access Industries; American International Group; The Carlyle Group; Deutsche Bank; Dover Corporation; HarbourVest Partners; Mitsui & Co; Ontario Teachers' Pension Plan; Triton Partners.

The star performers

Top-ranking departments according to *The Legal 500* (see legal500.com for more details)
Acquisition finance; Corporate crime (including fraud, bribery and corruption); Corporate tax; EU and competition; Emerging markets; Insurance: corporate and regulatory; International arbitration; M&A: upper mid-market and premium deals, £250m+; Private equity: transactions: Large-cap deal capability; Private funds; Public international law.

- **Why did you choose this firm over any others?** 'The firm's support of pro bono opportunities spanning multiple types of legal assistance'; 'stellar international disputes practice'; 'excellent vacation scheme experience'; 'the quality of work'; 'friendly staff'; 'dedication to investing vast amounts of time and resources in their trainees'

- **Best thing about the firm?** 'Excellent support staff'; 'multiple opportunities for trainees to take a lead on certain work'; 'business programme in the New York office'; 'the quality of the work'; 'technology allowance'; 'frequent champagne tea parties for the whole office'; 'clear focus to grow the highly-regarded litigation department'

- **Worst thing about the firm?** 'The international secondment opportunities'; 'view from the office isn't great despite its central location'; 'lack of social activities organised by the firm'; 'the printers are hopeless'; 'decisions are often made in the NY office so they don't always make perfect sense for those working in the UK'

- **Best moment?** 'Closing a pro bono transaction in which I had a prominent role'; 'being given the responsibility to run a small deal myself'; 'working on genuinely interesting transactions'; 'being heavily involved in the hearing preparation for a high-profile, inspiring human rights matter'; 'being able to use foreign language skills'; 'being sent to New York for a three-week business education programme'

- **Worst moment?** 'Reorganising desk sets'; 'cancelling a weekend's worth of plans with visiting friends due to a closing being moved up'; 'delaying holiday due to an extended deadline'; 'running in the rain to file documents at court'; 'document system temporarily losing the last six versions of an agreement'

A day in the life of...

... Alice Hallewell trainee solicitor, Debevoise & Plimpton LLP

Departments to date: Corporate: insurance and financial institutions group; finance; Moscow finance and corporate
University: Balliol College, Oxford
Degree: Classics

9.30am: I am currently seconded to our Moscow office, sitting in the finance and corporate group. I walk to work and grab breakfast on my way in. Over breakfast I check through the emails that have come in overnight.

10.00am: Just prior to arriving in Moscow, I attended the UnLtd legal advice clinic in London with a corporate associate. I drafted a letter of advice based on our meeting, which covers different legal forms that a social enterprise could take. Overnight I received comments from the corporate associate, so I do some research and amend my draft to cover the additional points he suggested.

12.30pm: As I only recently arrived in Moscow, my supervisor and another associate take me out to lunch at a local restaurant to welcome me.

1.30pm: Our client is acquiring the remaining interest in a joint venture that we previously helped set up. I have been assisting with due diligence on the acquisition. I discuss the results of my review of the documents with the associate

I'm working with and he suggests that I prepare the first draft of the due diligence report summarising the issues we have found.

2.00pm: After our meeting I start drafting the due diligence report, based on precedents and our discussion of the reviewed documents. The client wants a short-form report on any 'red flags' we have found, so I condense my notes and ensure there is no repetition.

4.00pm: I co-ordinate with a Russian legal assistant who has been reviewing the Russian language documents for the due diligence exercise, and we agree the form in which she will summarise the issues that arose in the Russian documents so that I can incorporate her findings into the report.

5.00pm: We have a call with the client to discuss a few outstanding matters in relation to the acquisition before a call with the other side to negotiate these points. The call brings to light different interpretations of the underlying joint venture documentation. Both sides decide

to discuss further with their respective clients before coming to an agreement. I take detailed notes of what is discussed in the call. After the call we review the action points that arose and agree to discuss them further in the morning.

6.30pm: I return to my office and have received final comments from the corporate

> '**As I only recently arrived in Moscow, my supervisor and another associate take me out to lunch to welcome me.'**

associate in London on my pro bono advice letter. I proofread and finalise the letter before sending it out to the client.

7.30pm: As there is nothing else urgent for today, I head out for dinner with trainees from other firms who are also on secondment to Moscow.

www.debevoise.com/careers

About the firm

Address: 65 Gresham Street, London EC2V 7NQ
Telephone: 020 7786 9000   **Fax:** 020 7588 4180
Website: www.debevoise.com
Email: London-recruit@debevoise.com

Managing partners: Lord Goldsmith QC, Richard Ward

Other offices: New York, Washington DC, Paris, Frankfurt, Moscow, Hong Kong, Shanghai, Tokyo

Who we are: Debevoise is a leading international law firm. The London office works on many of the highest profile and most complex transactions in Europe and worldwide. We do this by virtue of our English and New York law expertise and our close integration with our other offices.

What we do: In developing our practice in London, we have sought to replicate the core strengths of our practice worldwide. Our focus is on private equity, insurance, international disputes and investigations, financial institutions, M&A, finance, capital markets and tax.

What we're looking for: Students whose personal qualities, academic record and other achievements demonstrate exceptional ability, motivation and potential. Applicants will make a significant contribution to our firm and thrive in our unique culture. We look for an ability to listen actively, think creatively and interact successfully. We also look for maturity and leadership qualities.

What you'll do: One of our basic principles is that each of our associates should become a 'well-rounded' lawyer – an effective counsellor, adviser and advocate – who can combine legal knowledge with the ability to deal with a range of situations. Trainees develop their skills through formal training and on-the-job experience. The two years are split into four six-month seats with an opportunity to gain experience in at least three distinct areas.

Perks: Bonus, private medical and dental insurance, life assurance, group income protection, pension, computer allowance, cycle scheme, interest-free season ticket loan and subsidised on-site café.

Sponsorship: Full tuition fees are paid for the GDL and LPC, together with a maintenance grant of £8,000 per year.

Facts and figures

Total partners: 18
Other fee-earners: 90
Total trainees: 15

Trainee places available for 2019: 8
Applications received pa: 400+
Percentage interviewed: 10%

First year salary: £50,000
Second year salary: £55,000
Newly qualified salary: £113,200

Application process

Apply to: London-recruit@debevoise.com
How: Online application form available on our website from 1 May 2017.
When: By 31 July 2017 for September 2019.
What's involved: Interview and written assessment. Attendance on our summer placement scheme is preferred but not compulsory.

Vacation schemes

Summer: June-August 2017 (apply between 1 December 2016-15 January 2017).

Debevoise
&Plimpton

Dechert LLP

160 Queen Victoria Street, London EC4V 4QQ

Survey results *(marks out of 100%)*

Satisfied in your job?	71
Firm living up to expectations?	71
High quality of work?	69
Enough client contact?	64
Stress-free?	62
Happy work/life balance?	65
Friendly firm?	72
Great social life?	55
Good vacation scheme?	68
Confident you'll be kept on?	53
Good remuneration?	86
Diverse firm?	70
Good international secondments?	37

 **verdict**

Trainees find the 'international opportunities' and six-seat rotation on offer at Dechert 'intriguing and unique'. There is a certain amount of 'flexibility with the training contract' as the HR team is 'accommodating of seat choices if particular desires are expressed'. The firm excels in a number of specialisms, including representing blue-chip clients on M&A deals, private equity transactions and investment fund matters, and is in a 'good place in the market'. This 'large US firm in the City' offers the 'small intake of trainees' a 'tailored training experience'. The 'learning is hands-on' as trainees are encouraged to develop as both 'individuals and team players'. Trainees have a 'chance to progress, gain responsibility and are involved at the heart of the firm rather than being stuck with document review'. There is a 'high level of direct work for partners', and new recruits work with 'supportive lawyers'. The firm has a 'strong ethos' whereby employees 'work hard and play hard', as Dechert aspires to get the best out of its trainees. There are a few grumbles about the 'air conditioning having a mind of its own' and the 'coffee machines'. More seriously, the 'lack of communication in terms of workload' can be frustrating, and 'occasional long hours' can be 'unpredictable in some departments', having a knock-on effect on the work/life balance. Highlights for trainees include being 'trusted to run a project without being micro-managed extensively', 'closing big deals for important clients' and 'working on a High Court injunction'. Dechert is a great option for those looking to advise 'excellent clients' on 'truly global deals'.

If the firm were a fictional character it would be...

Daddy Warbucks (Annie) – a hard-working American, generous with its charitable contributions and supportive of your career

The firm

Dechert performs strongly across the corporate and commercial disciplines, representing blue-chip clients on M&A deals, tax and investment funds matters and private equity transactions. The firm recently gained a Singaporean law licence, and also entered into an association with a Saudi firm in September 2015, two moves which have strengthened its already solid international credentials.

The deals

Advised Cenkos Securities on Highland Natural Resources' re-admission to the standard market; advised The Hunt Companies on its acquisition of a 50% stake in Amber Infrastructure Group; acted for NML Capital in claims against Argentina, following the latter's bond payment default; advised Azerbaijan's state-owned oil company on a $750m unsecured notes issue; advising AM-Pharma and its shareholders on the sale of a minority interest in the company to Pfizer.

The clients

AGC Equity Partners; Apollo Management International; BNY Mellon; Bank Audi; Barbican Insurance; Haymarket Media; OTE Group; Poxel; Weiss Korea; Wells Fargo Bank.

The star performers

Top-ranking departments according to *The Legal 500* (see legal500.com for more details)
Banking litigation: investment and retail; Commercial litigation; Corporate crime (including fraud, bribery and corruption); Debt capital markets; EU and competition: Trade, WTO, anti-dumping and customs; Emerging markets; Employment: employers; Equity capital markets; Flotations: small and mid-cap; Fraud: white-collar crime; International arbitration; Investment funds: Hedge funds; Listed funds; M&A: mid-market, £50m-£250m; Partnership; Private equity: transactions: Mid-cap deal capability; Private funds; Public international law; Retail funds; Securitisation.

- **Why did you choose this firm over any others?** 'I had worked with Dechert lawyers before'; 'smaller intake'; 'more hands-on learning'; 'many interesting departments to specialise in'; 'I got a very positive impression of the firm and the people I met'; 'good clients'; 'good salary'; 'large range of interesting work'; 'the office atmosphere'

- **Best thing about the firm?** 'It has a very strong financial services group'; 'the work-hard-play-hard ethos'; 'exposure to clients'; 'trainees are given a fair bit of responsibility'; 'people work together well'; 'a better work/life balance than most firms with a comparable salary'; 'flexibility to shape your training contract as you see fit'

- **Worst thing about the firm?** 'The air conditioning has a mind of its own'; 'having to tolerate the occasional bad jokes of our American colleagues'; 'very few international opportunities';

'certain partners can be difficult at times'; 'the coffee machines'; 'lack of communication in terms of expected workload'

- **Best moment?** 'Going to an off-site client meeting in Mayfair in the first week'; 'being given the opportunity to run the closing of a deal'; 'being given the responsibility of drafting a suspicious activity report having reviewed all of the relevant documents'; 'assisting with and attending a Supreme Court hearing'; 'taking part in a signing'

- **Worst moment?** 'Reviewing boxes of deeds'; 'any time I felt like I didn't have enough partner support on a matter'; 'arduous document review'; 'being left to deal with a case that was beyond my level of responsibility'; 'bundling documents under time-pressure'

A day in the life of...

... George Thompson third-seat trainee, Dechert LLP

Departments to date: Financial services (London), finance and real estate, financial services (Dublin)

University: Bristol

Degree: History

8.45am: I arrive into the office early to attend one of the department's regular training sessions. Today's training is being given in collaboration by partners in both the London and Singapore office; thanks to the firms updated video conferencing systems it feels like everyone is in the same room despite the distance. I am viewing it all from the Dublin office where I am currently on secondment. The training is focused on the structure and drafting of fee provisions in a private equity partnership agreement, a complicated and crucial aspect of the structure of a private equity fund and an area which is often heavily negotiated between the parties.

10.00am: I get to my desk and after a chat with my supervisor about ongoing work, priorities for the day and her cute puppy, I reply to emails that have come in overnight regarding ongoing matters on a number of files that I have been assisting on. I am given a lot of opportunity to work independently on a number of smaller files and assist them with general business work. This has allowed me to develop professionally and also see first-hand how my work can have a real impact on progressing a matter for a client.

11.00am: I attend a call with my supervisor, the partner running the matter and opposing counsel to negotiate the commercial and legal issues on a number of agreements which we are drafting for a US client. I have been involved in the drafting of these agreements from the outset so am asked to contribute to the discussion. I also take a detailed note of the points agreed and then finalise the drafting. My supervisor points out some precedents that can help but says that we will need to draft some of the amendments from scratch and asks me to have a go at putting some language together. This is a great opportunity for me to develop my drafting skills and put into practice what I've learnt thus far on the establishment and constitution of investment funds.

1.00pm: I head out to grab lunch with a colleague in one of Dublin's great eateries.

2.00pm: In advance of a weekly update call with a UK client who is looking to launch a new fund in the EU through Ireland, I review, update and issue the ongoing matters list for the project which forms the basis for discussion of progress on the project and will prompt the various parties of issues they need to keep abreast of. Running the list is a very important task and is a great way to get involved in a project as a trainee as it gives an insight into what it takes to get a multimillion-pound fund launched.

2.30pm: I attend the update call and take notes on the status of the various aspects of the project and a number of issues that I'll need to follow up on. I then have a quick discussion with the partner managing the matter as to how he wants me to proceed and then head back to my desk to draft and issue an email to all parties of the key action points that need to be accomplished in the coming weeks.

> 'Running an ongoing matters list is a very important task and is a great way to get involved in a project as a trainee.'

4.30pm: I receive an email from the Central Bank of Ireland, the regulator for all Irish-domiciled funds, asking for clarity on a fund which we recently submitted for authorisation. After researching the point and then chatting it over with my supervisor, I send a response before getting back to making final changes to the agreements I was amending earlier.

7.00pm: I review my to-do list and note things to get on with in the morning before heading off towards Temple Bar to meet friends for a drink.

www.dechert.com/careers

About the firm

Address: 160 Queen Victoria Street, London EC4V 4QQ
Telephone: 020 7184 7000   **Fax:** 020 7184 7001
Website: www.dechert.com
Email: graduate.recruitment@dechert.com

Managing partners: Camille Abousleiman, Gus Black, Jason Butwick, Miriam Gonzalez

Other offices: Almaty, Austin, Beijing, Boston, Brussels, Charlotte, Chicago, Dubai, Dublin, Frankfurt, Hartford, Hong Kong, Los Angeles, Luxembourg, Moscow, Munich, New York, Orange County, Paris, Philadelphia, Princeton, San Francisco, Silicon Valley, Singapore, Tbilisi, Washington.

Who we are: Dechert is a global specialist law firm with 900+ lawyers across 27 offices. Focused on sectors with the greatest complexities, legal intricacies and highest regulatory demands, we excel in delivering practical commercial judgement and deep legal expertise for high-stakes matters. In an increasingly challenging environment, clients look to us to serve them in ways that are faster, sharper and leaner without compromising excellence. We are relentless in serving our clients – delivering the best of the firm to them with entrepreneurial energy and seamless collaboration in a way that is distinctively Dechert.

What we do: Our lawyers in London are active in all Dechert's core practice areas of corporate and securities, financial services and investment management, finance and real estate, white-collar defence, complex commercial litigation, international arbitration and intellectual property, as well as business restructuring and reorganisation, employment, international trade and EU government affairs, EU and UK competition and tax. We are also one of the few law firms equipped with a full-service US corporate practice in London, with the capability to advise domestic and international clients on a broad spectrum of US regulatory and transactional issues.

What we're looking for: A genuine interest in business, commitment, personality and ambition.

What you'll do: Dechert trainees will complete the majority of the required PSC courses during their induction, as well as undertaking the firm's new hire induction and IT training programme. Trainees will also attend various talks from the firm's practice areas and soft skills sessions on a range of topics, such as legal writing and negotiation. At each seat rotation there is department-specific training giving you an introduction to the practice, the team and the work.

Perks: Gym membership/subsidy, life assurance, pension scheme with company contributions, private health and dental care, season ticket loan and subsidised restaurant.

Sponsorship: LPC and GDL full fees and £10,000 maintenance grant.

Facts and figures

Total partners: 40 (London)
Other fee-earners: 78 (London)
Total trainees: 20

Trainee places available for 2019: 8-12

First year salary: £45,000
Second year salary: £50,000
Newly qualified salary: £90,000

Application process

Apply to: Lara Machnicki, graduate recruitment manager.
How: Online application.
When: Please see our website for upcoming application deadlines.
What's involved: Online application form, video or telephone interview, face-to-face interview, written exercise and an office tour with a current trainee solicitor.

Vacation schemes

Spring: Apply by 31 December 2016.
Summer: Apply by 31 January 2017.

Dentons

1 Fleet Place, London EC4M 7WS

Survey results *(marks out of 100%)*

Satisfied in your job?	85
Firm living up to expectations?	83
High quality of work?	83
Enough client contact?	76
Stress-free?	63
Happy work/life balance?	71
Friendly firm?	83
Great social life?	78
Good vacation scheme?	89
Confident you'll be kept on?	76
Good remuneration?	81
Diverse firm?	86
Good international secondments?	40

 **verdict**

Dentons has an 'ambitious strategy' and a 'global vision' to build on its already significant 'international network'. The firm now has a Chinese presence following its 2015 merger with Dacheng, offering a 'strong reputation' plus 'international reach'. Recruits claim that the best thing about the firm is its 'global presence' and the resultant 'international opportunities', but there are complaints that 'some international secondment seats were axed'. Many trainees find the firm's 'strong reputation' for 'banking work' appealing. One trainee reported choosing Dentons purely because they could see themselves 'fitting in well'. There is 'excellent supervision' for new recruits who are given 'regular reviews' to track progress. The 'small trainee intake' means newcomers are given 'great responsibility', 'valuable work' and 'interaction with clients'. Trainees love their 'welcoming colleagues' and the 'incredible level of responsibility' means they are 'trusted to see clients' on their own. The 'friendly and inclusive culture' ensures 'no one is an anonymous face'. Top trainee moments include 'working on a deal for one of the biggest private equity firms in the world which made the headlines of the FT', 'spending an international secondment in San Francisco' and 'completing a complex transaction under high pressure to the delight of the client'. 'Late nights', 'very tight deadlines' and 'long hours come with the territory' but are 'no more' than trainees expected, and there are 'friendly and social activities run by the firm' to enable everyone to relax. Take a closer look at Dentons if you are looking for an 'ambitious global firm' that is going places.

If the firm were a fictional character it would be...

The Brain (Pinky and the Brain) – trying to take over the world

The firm

Since *Lex* last went to print, Dentons has continued its dizzying international expansion with openings in Europe, Asia-Pacific and Latin America, building on its landmark merger with China's Dacheng in 2015. Dispute resolution, M&A and finance are all staple practice areas. Dentons was also nominated for the TMT Team of the Year accolade at the *Legal Business* Awards 2016.

The deals

Acted for a lending syndicate on a $1.7bn revolving facility to Israel Chemicals; advised on the restructuring of LPN notes issued by Ukraine's PrivatBank; advised KSL Capital Partners on the pension elements of its acquisition of De Vere Village Hotels; advised Hong Kong-based transport operator MTR on all aspects of its successful bid to operate Crossrail; advised Virgin Atlantic on a high-profile IT project.

The clients

Citigroup Global Markets; Emirates; Enbridge International; Hatfield Colliery; Hyundai Capital; John Lewis Partnership; National Bank of Oman; Royal Mail Group; Société Générale; Statoil (UK) Trading.

The star performers

Top-ranking departments according to *The Legal 500* (see legal500.com for more details)
Acquisition finance; Asset finance and leasing; Aviation; Bank lending – investment grade debt and syndicated loans; Commodities: derivatives; Corporate restructuring and insolvency; Debt capital markets; Derivatives and structured products; Emerging markets; Health and safety; Infrastructure (including PFI and PPP); Islamic finance; Mining and minerals; Oil and gas; Pensions dispute resolution; Pensions (non-contentious); Power (including electricity, nuclear and renewables); Rail; Securitisation; Trade finance.

- **Why did you choose this firm over any others?** 'It gave me the opportunity to do City work without having to stay in London'; 'it was the only firm I saw whose offices outside London did the same work as the London office'; 'the range of practice areas'; 'the small number of trainees for such a big firm'; 'the recognised strengths of the firm in banking, energy and real estate fit with my interests'; 'excellent reputation in banking law'; 'the growing nature of the firm'

- **Best thing about the firm?** 'Good level of support and training'; 'name recognition'; 'excellent supervision'; 'the quality of work'; 'some great client secondments'; 'the high level of responsibility that you are given as a trainee'; 'the clients'; 'international work'

- **Worst thing about the firm?** 'Long hours at times', 'a lot us didn't get a seat we'd chosen until our fourth seat'; 'the trainee international secondments were cancelled at the last minute with no warning'; 'the building is too small for the firm's ambitions'; 'some people underestimating how little you know as a first-seat trainee'

- **Best moment?** 'Being sent to the employment tribunal by myself'; 'being flown abroad for a client event'; 'attending important signing meetings with clients on my own'; 'being congratulated on the work I had done on a deal by the partner and associate in charge'; 'drafting large sections of witness statements that made it to applications mainly unedited'

- **Worst moment?** '18-hour day in a department where I had an unsupportive supervisor'; 'staying in until 3am drafting notices of assignments'; 'post-completion bibles'; 'sending an email to the wrong people and it being too late to do anything about it'; 'being told off for making a mistake'; 'being asked to proofread a 1,000-page document'

Why Dentons?

Who we are: Dentons is the world's first polycentric global law firm. A top 20 firm on the Acritas 2015 Global Elite Brand Index, the firm is committed to challenging the status quo in delivering consistent and uncompromising quality and value in new and inventive ways. Driven to provide clients with a competitive edge, and connected to the communities where its clients want to do business, Dentons knows that understanding local cultures is crucial to successfully completing a deal, resolving a dispute or solving a business challenge. Now the world's largest law firm, Dentons' global team builds agile, tailored solutions to meet the local, national and global needs of private and public clients of any size in more than 125 locations serving 50-plus countries. www.dentons.com.

Dentons is a truly 'polycentric' international law firm that fully embraces the diversity of its geography, cultures and legal traditions. The firm has no headquarters, no dominant national culture, and proudly offers clients talent from diverse backgrounds and countries.

Training: As part of Dentons, you'll be given all the responsibility you can handle. You'll learn on the job by taking a real part in running deals and cases, meeting with real clients and taking your place in the fast-paced and increasingly global world of business. After all, it's this type of experience that makes great lawyers and prepares you for the daily pressures of your professional career. At Dentons, you'll get it almost from day one.

If commercial law is your ambition, beginning your career with us will help you fulfil it. You'll be welcomed into a team globally renowned for its expertise. We'll help you develop your skills and knowledge in an open and supportive environment.

London: A training contract in our City office in London will place you at the centre of one of the world's leading legal practices. In your first two years, you'll spend six-month seats in four of our practice areas. Along with a seat in our banking and finance practice and a contentious seat (or an external litigation course), you may also have the opportunity to work in one of our international offices, or to work directly with one of our clients within their team and office.

Milton Keynes and Watford: Our Milton Keynes and Watford training contract will see you rotate between these two offices where we are able to provide a City-level out-of-town legal service to many household name clients.

Our practice areas across the Milton Keynes and Watford training contract include corporate, dispute resolution, real estate, property litigation, financial litigation, construction and employment, and you'll spend six-month seats in four of them. You must complete one non-contentious transactional seat (eg, corporate or real estate) and one contentious seat.

Vacation placements: We offer two-week vacation schemes in London during the Easter and Summer vacations and in Milton Keynes and Watford during the Summer vacation.

These placements consist of business games, department visits and social events, giving potential trainees an insight into commercial law and our way of life at Dentons.

Social activities: You'll have plenty of time to socialise with your peers in activities organised by our trainee representatives.

> **'We believe social activities are vital to the happiness of our team, and they're an important part of our firm's culture.'**

It's not just our trainees who like to have fun, though. We believe social activities are vital to the happiness of our team, and they're an important part of our firm's culture.

You can participate in over 20 sports teams, including football, rugby, hockey and cricket. Or, if you prefer something less competitive, we offer aerobics, yoga and a choir. Our busy social committee organises firm-wide events like quiz nights, sponsored walks and drinks evenings, with all proceeds going to our nominated charity of the year.

www.dentons.com/uk-graduates

About the firm

Address: 1 Fleet Place, London EC4M 7WS
Telephone: 020 7242 1212   **Fax:** 020 7246 7777
Website: www.dentons.com/uk-graduates
Email: graduaterecruitment@dentons.com
Twitter: twitter.com/Dentons

Chief executive: Elliot Portnoy

Other offices: Please visit www.dentons.com/global-presence for a full list of offices.

What we do: We offer an international legal practice focused on quality in sectors such as: energy, transport and infrastructure, financial institutions and funds, government, insurance, manufacturing, real estate, retail and hotels, and TMT.

What we're looking for: There's no typical candidate for our training contract programme. The expertise within our firm is as diverse as the needs of our global clients. We look for people with a wide range of skills, aptitudes and personalities, with the potential to contribute to our growing success. Being a team player is important, as is having the drive and ambition to succeed in a highly demanding work environment.

What you'll do: You'll learn on the job by running parts of real cases, meeting with real clients and taking your place in the fast-paced and increasingly global world of business. We offer four six-month seats, which may include a seat in one of our international offices or with one of our clients. You will be given responsibility early on, working with your team and clients in real business situations.

Perks: Subsidised gym membership, season ticket loan, pension scheme and private medical insurance.

Sponsorship: GDL/LPC fees during actual years of study; study maintenance grants of £5,000 per year of study (£6,000 in London).

Facts and figures

Total partners: 2,892
Other fee-earners: 4,614
Total trainees: 47

Trainee places available for 2019: 30
Applications received pa: 1,600
Percentage interviewed: 20%

First year salary: £40,000 (London)/£27,200 (Milton Keynes/Watford)
Second year salary: £44,000 (London)/£29,750 (Milton Keynes/Watford)
Newly qualified salary: £65,000 (London)/£44,000 (Milton Keynes/Watford)

Turnover in 2015: £796m
Profits per equity partner: £625,000
(see legalbusiness.co.uk for full financial information)

Application process

Apply to: Graduate recruitment.
How: Online application form.
When: By 31 March 2017 for non-law applicants; by 31 July 2017 for law.
What's involved: Online application form, a critical thinking exercise, first interview with human resources, followed by an assessment day.

Vacation schemes

Spring: London (apply by 31 December 2016).
Summer: London, Milton Keynes and Watford (apply by 31 December 2016).

Farrer & Co

66 Lincoln's Inn Fields, London WC2A 3LH

Lex 100 Winner

See categories below
and tables from page 69

Survey results *(marks out of 100%)*

Satisfied in your job? **90**

Firm living up to expectations? **93**

High quality of work? **90**

Enough client contact? **83**

Stress-free? **72**

Happy work/life balance? **85**

Friendly firm? **96**

Great social life? **86**

Good vacation scheme? **95**

Confident you'll be kept on? **84**

Good remuneration? **80**

Diverse firm? **88**

 verdict

Trainees value the 'sense of history and longevity' at Farrer & Co. The firm has earned a 'reputation for excellence' because of its 'strength in certain practice areas', and respondents enjoy the 'kooky clients and unusual work' this brings. The 'quality and breadth of work' can lead to prominent tasks for trainees, including 'getting involved in a highly publicised and complex case', 'assisting in a high-profile litigation' and 'going for lunch with a celebrity at their country house'. When not undertaking 'interesting work', juniors can be handed 'monotonous tasks' which have led to 'Friday night bundling' and 'completing a file review for over a month'. The training contract is 'well-structured' as it provides 'great variety through the six-seat programme'. 'Working directly with partners' is another plus as it means recruits 'learn from and get one-to-one time with the best in their fields'. One recruit speaks of 'constant client contact', and this has led to welcome recognition for trainees whose highlight moments included 'getting praised by a client for my work'. Having a 'small intake of trainees' is also considered beneficial as 'you feel valued as an individual'. This notion is enhanced by the firm's 'genuine appreciation of your private life' and 'respect for work/life balance', and Farrer & Co is named a **Lex 100 Winner** for work/life balance, as well as in a staggering nine other categories. Minor grumbles are reserved for the 'lack of a communal eating area or place for everyone to congregate', but this doesn't hinder the 'good social atmosphere' as trainees label the 'working environment' as founded on 'friendliness' and 'inclusivity'. There is 'real investment in trainees as the future of the firm', so take a detailed look at a career with Farrer & Co.

If the firm were a fictional character it would be...

Mr Darcy (Pride and Prejudice) – has traditional values, but a warm heart

The firm

Farrer & Co has a 300-year heritage and has built its success through a focus on long-term client relationships. It has earned a reputation as one of the best all-round private client firms, plus has impressive corporate and commercial expertise, while maintaining outstanding charities and agriculture departments.

The deals

Instructed by a group of trustees regarding claims of more than $2bn against Sergei Pugachev; defended Axel Springer in libel proceedings pertaining to an article published in a German business magazine; advised the Duchy of Cornwall on its Poundbury Development; acted for Hub Group on the acquisition of an office block in Wembley; acted for the Institute of Cancer Research in a planning application for a new research building in Sutton.

The clients

The Art Fund; British Olympic Association; Deutsche Bank; Eton College; Imperial College; the Natural History Museum; RBS; Royal College of Surgeons of England; Save the Children; the Telegraph Media Group.

The star performers

Top-ranking departments according to *The Legal 500* (see legal500.com for more details)
Agriculture and estates; Art and cultural property; Contentious trusts and probate; Commercial litigation; Commercial property; Charities and not-for-profit; Education: institutions; Education: schools; Employment: employers; Employment: senior executives; Family; Fraud: civil; M&A: smaller deals, up to £50m; Media and entertainment (including media finance); Partnership; Personal tax, trusts and probate; Planning; Property finance; Reputation management; Sport.

- **Why did you choose this firm over any others?** 'Inclusive environment'; 'size of the trainee intake'; 'the emphasis on long-term relationships'; 'a recognition of life outside of work'; 'most fee-earners seem to enjoy their work'; 'the widely recognised quality of training'; 'top-class reputation'; 'unparalleled client contact'; 'fantastically friendly atmosphere'; 'get to work with top practitioners'; 'quality of clients'; 'variety of seats'

- **Best thing about the firm?** 'Accessible partners'; 'good training'; 'six-seat rotation'; 'not having to formally apply for an NQ position'; 'emphasis on respect for trainees'; 'no face-time culture'; 'no hierarchy'; 'very forward-thinking in its IT'; 'quality of work and clients'; 'friendliness'; 'trainees and fee-earners treat each other with respect'

- **Worst thing about the firm?** 'Lack of secondment opportunities'; 'bad coffee'; 'the firm can go further in terms of diversity'; 'the sandwiches'; 'lack of canteen space to eat lunch'; 'it's reputation with other lawyers because it's not stuffy at all'

- **Best moment?** 'Completing work for high-profile people'; 'getting excellent feedback on work that I did'; 'attending client meetings with partners'; 'completing a big transaction just before Christmas in the banking team'; 'seeing a whole matter through from start to finish and being mostly responsible for the research'

- **Worst moment?** 'Messing up early on in my first seat'; 'a rare 10pm finish finalising a court bundle'; 'forwarding an email to the wrong address'; 'being in a quiet seat'; 'bundling'; 'disclosure'

A day in the life of...

... David Morgan trainee, Farrer & Co

Departments to date: Residential property and secured lending, IP and commercial, reputation management and media disputes

University: Sheffield University, Kaplan Law School   **Degree and class:** Psychology (1st), LLM (Distinction)

8.30am: After braving the traffic on my new bike, I arrive at the office, shower and log on for about 8.45am. Throughout the year departments hold regular breakfast seminars which we are invited to attend; for example members of the family and private client teams hosted a recent event on mental capacity. As well as a good introduction to different areas of law it is also an opportunity to meet some of our clients.

9.30am: The reputation management team handles a range of interesting and high-profile matters. I get involved in a variety of tasks including: drafting instructions for counsel; writing letters to internet search providers to remove defamatory search results; and liaising with other professionals including PR advisors and forensic investigators. Defamation is a particularly exciting area of law and I have seen significant developments in case law since the introduction of the Defamation Act 2013. This morning I have been preparing trial bundles ahead of a hearing in which our client has been subjected to a malicious and damaging attack. I am scheduled to attend the hearing next month where we are seeking both damages and an injunction against the defendant.

11.00am: The team involves me in as many client meetings as possible and this is something I really enjoy as we have a wide range of engaging clients which include

sporting bodies, museums and galleries, entrepreneurs, families and individuals. I will be responsible for recording the key details of the meeting and will have a chance later today to practice my dictation skills to produce an attendance note.

1.00pm: On a sunny day, our location by Lincoln's Inn Fields is a great place to catch some fresh air or meet up for lunch with colleagues. There are often also lunchtime talks that we can attend. These may be specifically for our trainee intake or for wider firm attendance.

2.00pm: This afternoon I have been asked to produce the first draft of a letter before claim for an important client. As a trainee you are subject to a high level of supervision (particularly in litigation where mistakes can be costly) which took me a while to get used to but I do appreciate the support while I develop my own experience and judgement.

4.00pm: We represent a number of magazines and throughout the week our team provides pre-publication advice on articles and stories the journalists are working on. In addition to the law, I have had to develop a substantial amount of knowledge on certain reality tv celebrities and popstars! Yet while fun, this area of our work also engages some tricky and interesting questions on privacy rights and data protection.

5.00pm: Business development is an important part of fee-earners' time and you get involved as a trainee by attending functions or helping draft articles or newsletters that are published on the firm's website and circulated to interested clients. I have been asked to draft

> 'I have seen significant developments in case law since the introduction of the Defamation Act 2013.'

a short piece for the Farrer's sports group on the US PGA putting controversy. The firm has been involved in advising on sporting rules and the tournament provides a good opportunity to remind clients of the need to ensure their procedures are robust enough to withstand all scenarios.

6.00pm: I usually finish work between 6.00pm and 7.00pm. I will sometimes attend client functions or go for drinks with the various chambers we instruct. Farrers is a very sporty firm and I play for the Farrer and Co football and cricket teams which is a great way to get to know other people outside the office.

www.farrer.co.uk

About the firm

Address: 66 Lincoln's Inn Fields, London WC2A 3LH
Telephone: 020 3375 7000 **Fax:** 020 3375 7001
Website: www.farrer.co.uk
Email: graduaterecruitment@farrer.co.uk

Senior partner: Richard Parry

Who we are: Farrer & Co is a leading modern law firm with a distinguished history of providing expert advice to a diverse range of clients, both UK and international.

What we do: We are leaders in private client, agriculture, sports, defamation, heritage, family and charity law. Our IP and commercial practice, disputes and employment teams are also highly rated.

What we're looking for: Team spirit, leadership, dynamism, versatility, a questioning mind, great communication skills, commercial awareness and a sense of fun.

What you'll do: The trainee will experience six seats across the firm, handling 'real' work with early responsibility and an excellent legal and skills-based training programme.

Perks: Flexible benefits scheme, sporting teams/clubs, season ticket loan, 25 days' holiday, group income protection, group life assurance, company doctor, subsidised yoga/pilates, subsidised gym membership, pension scheme, private medical insurance after one year, wellwoman/wellman checks.

Sponsorship: We pay all LPC and GDL fees, plus a maintenance grant of £7,000 per year of study.

Facts and figures

Total partners: 73
Other fee-earners: 170
Total trainees: 20

Trainee places available for 2019: 10
Applications received pa: 800
Percentage interviewed: 6%

First year salary: £35,000
Second year salary: £38,000
Newly qualified salary: £59,000

Turnover in 2015/2016: £57.5m (+8.5%)
Profits per equity partner: £500,000 (+11.6%)

Application process

Apply to: Donna Davies, recruitment consultant.
How: Online via our website.
When: By 31 July 2017 for 2019 contracts.
What's involved: First interview with written exercise, second interview with a case study scenario.

Vacation schemes

Spring: 3-13 April 2017.
Summer: 26 June-7 July 2017; 17-28 July 2017.

FARRER&Co

Fieldfisher

Riverbank House, 2 Swan Lane, London EC4R 3TT

Survey results *(marks out of 100%)*

Satisfied in your job?	79
Firm living up to expectations?	79
High quality of work?	77
Enough client contact?	65
Stress-free?	62
Happy work/life balance?	75
Friendly firm?	88
Great social life?	77
Good vacation scheme?	90
Confident you'll be kept on?	76
Good remuneration?	75
Diverse firm?	78
Good international secondments?	48

 **verdict**

With a 'great reputation and breadth of clients', Fieldfisher offers an 'excellent environment to train in', plus a 'strong sector focus' on TMT. A few trainees applied to the firm after enjoying vacation schemes and many trainees love the 'killer riverside views' from the 'fancy London offices'. The 'flat hierarchy' is characterised by the 'friendly and approachable people' who are always 'helpful when you have queries'. The 'small trainee intake' immerses new recruits into 'friendly and sociable teams' where they have 'a lot of responsibility within a meritocratic atmosphere'. Although the responsibility can be 'stressful at times', it helps trainees 'learn and develop quickly'. The firm puts a 'strong emphasis on training and gives you training sessions' to ensure you succeed. Trainees have a 'great work/life balance' and receive 'plenty of independence plus interesting work' without 'being worked to the bone'. There are many different 'seats on offer' and although seat choices are 'not guaranteed', the team 'works hard to ensure everyone gets to work in the areas they have a strong preference for'. Trainees have 'lots of contact with big-name clients' and are 'encouraged to be individuals'. There are a few grumbles about the 'canteen food', 'coffee machines' and a 'lack of international secondment opportunities'. Top trainee moments include 'working through the weekend on a large deal and seeing how the contribution helped towards the larger goal', 'leading a settlement negotiation' and 'dealing with influential media clients'. For those looking for 'good opportunities to prove yourself' in a well-respected City firm, Fieldfisher could be the right choice.

If the firm were a fictional character it would be...

The Weasley Twins – runs a successful business, but is a great laugh and very personable

The firm

Tech specialist Fieldfisher has enjoyed another good year by posting a 7% increase in firmwide revenue for 2015/16. In June 2016, the firm entered Italy by merging with 21-partner firm SASPI, adding to its network of offices in France, Belgium, Germany, China and the US. Fieldfisher has also announced a new three-year plan to focus on the technology, energy and natural resources, and finance and financial services sectors.

The deals

Advised eBay on its joint venture with Argos for click and collect services; assisted Pearson VUE with its disposal of the Driving Theory Test service to Learndirect; advised Azibo Holdings on its sale of Currencies Direct in a £200m management buyout funded by Corsair Capital and Palamon Capital Partners; acted for Lehman Brothers Finance's liquidator in pursuing a breach of contract claim; advised Merkle Group on a $250m acquisition and working capital facility provided by a consortium of US banks.

The clients

Atalaya Mining; BBC Worldwide; British Medical Council; Cenkos Securities; Channel 4 Investments; Digital UK; Fuse Universal; John Lewis; RCI Europe; Time Warner.

The star performers

Top-ranking departments according to *The Legal 500* (see legal500.com for more details)
Administrative and public law; Banking litigation: investment and retail; Commercial contracts; Commodities: derivatives; Corporate crime (including fraud, bribery and corruption); Emerging markets; Financial services (contentious); Financial services (non-contentious/regulatory); Flotations: small and mid-cap; Fraud: civil; Healthcare; Listed funds; Mining and minerals; Personal injury: claimant; Professional discipline; Property finance; Reputation management; Retail funds; Tax litigation and investigations; Venture capital.

- **Why did you choose this firm over any others?** 'Strong commitment to pro bono work'; 'balance of being professional but not taking things too seriously'; 'offers a better work/life balance than a lot of other City firms'; 'the firm specialised in IP which was the key area I was interested in'; 'the work/life balance'; 'good reputation and breadth of clients'; 'smaller intake of trainees so more responsibility'

- **Best thing about the firm?** 'Expertise in IP and tech'; 'partners want to see you do well and give you good opportunities to prove yourself'; 'you can leave at 5.30 if your work is done'; 'the open-plan office means we don't have to knock on doors and partners are willing to answer questions and give advice'; 'the breadth of seats on offer'

- **Worst thing about the firm?** 'The approvals processes for IT or other equipment can be slow and lumbering'; 'gender bias in certain departments needs to be addressed'; 'bonus scheme not really accessible to trainees in reality'; 'news stories about how PEP has massively increased yet pay rises not reflected in staff'; 'rigidity of training'

- **Best moment?** 'Working on a large project and seeing it mentioned in the national and legal press'; 'being given the responsibility to complete a deal by myself'; 'presenting to 100+ people at our privacy summit'; 'meeting a client at their offices in my second week'; 'closing my first transaction'; 'being seconded to Brussels'

- **Worst moment?** 'Unclear expectations from partners'; 'feeling like the job I did was not good enough'; 'a three-hour Excel training session'; 'having to work a weekend'; 'racing to court to meet a deadline'; 'Friday nights catching up on the admin I've been too busy to sort earlier that week'

A day in the life of...

... **Bhavul Haria** first-year trainee solicitor, Fieldfisher

Departments to date: Corporate (M&A and equity capital markets), real estate finance

University: Durham

Degree and class: Classics, 2(1)

7.30am: I set off from my home to the gym. I find that a workout puts me in a calm and composed state for the working day ahead.

8.30am: I arrive at the office and have breakfast in our canteen downstairs. There is nowhere in the City that does better poached eggs on toast! I then get to my desk and scan the headlines of various news sites online.

8.45am: I check my emails to see if anything has arrived in my inbox which is urgent. I respond to the relevant emails and make a to-do list of my tasks for that day.

9.00am: My supervisor arrives and we talk through the day ahead and what tasks need to be done. I typically work with a variety of partners and associates in both M&A and equity capital markets. The whole team is very friendly, and the open-plan office means everyone is very approachable.

9.30am: I am currently working on a deal which is due to close by the end of the day. It is a big acquisition which inevitably involves a mountain of paperwork! I discuss the matter with the associate and partner working on the case and check that everything is in order.

10.00am: I arrange an all-parties call on another international acquisition. I have spent the past week conducting due diligence on the various contracts, checking for change of control and assignment provisions. The client has a number of questions.

11.00am: In corporate, there are regular training sessions in order to get trainees up to speed as quickly as possible. Today's training is on management buyouts – an incredibly fascinating subject matter.

12.00pm: It's time for our weekly corporate European call. The team gathers on the ninth-floor meeting room. Our other European offices dial into the meeting and partners give presentations on various updates in the market. An associate gives a talk on shareholder rights in a major High Court case recently concluded.

1.15pm: It is a rare sunny day! I venture to a swanky new salad bar near Cannon Street, and then eat outside with the other trainees. I did my vacation scheme with the majority of the trainees in my intake, as well as the LPC, so a lot of us are really good buddies.

1.45pm: I am assigned some research by a senior associate to confirm a position with our client. This involves browsing PLC and reading several articles. Once I find the answer, I prepare a note to summarise my findings, which I pass on to the senior associate.

3.00pm: Ahead of the closing, the partner calls me into a meeting room to run through our documents list and our closing checklist. Emails fly in from the client and the lawyers for the other side. It is my job to collate the documents and put in the respective signature pages. It looks like everything is in order and ready to go.

4.30pm: I run the firm's mixed touch rugby team, so I send out the weekly email. We are gunning for the Regent's Park Trophy!

> '**I did my vacation scheme with the majority of the trainees in my intake, so a lot of us are really good buddies.**'

5.00pm: Closing time. We have a conference call with all relevant parties and, much to my relief, all goes off without a hitch. It is now my job to send out copies of all executed documents to the parties involved, and to undertake the post-completion requirements, such as creating a bible of documents and registering charges and appointments/resignations on Companies House.

7.00pm: A number of the trainees head downstairs to the office bar on the ground floor. We catch up over drinks and then move on to a bar in the City. I savour my fruit juice, safe in the knowledge that it has been a good day.

About the firm

Address: Riverbank House, 2 Swan Lane, London EC4R 3TT
Telephone: 020 7861 4000   **Fax:** 020 7488 0084
Website: www.fieldfisher.com
Email: graduaterecruitment@fieldfisher.com
Facebook: www.facebook.com/FieldfisherGraduates/
Twitter: @FieldfisherGrad

Senior partner: Matthew Lohn
Managing partner: Michael Chissick

Other offices: Brussels, Düsseldorf, Hamburg, Paris, London, Munich, Manchester, Rome, Milan, Venice, Turin, Silicon Valley and Shanghai.

Who we are: Fieldfisher is a European law firm with market-leading practices in many of the world's most dynamic sectors. We are an approachable, forward-thinking organisation with a particular focus on technology, finance and financial services, and energy and natural resources among other sectors.

What we do: Our growing European network of offices supports an international client base alongside our Silicon Valley and Shanghai teams. Among our clients we count social media sites and high-street coffee chains as well as life sciences and medical devices companies, energy suppliers, financial institutions and government departments.

What we're looking for: We value more than just talent, ambition and great qualifications. We don't believe in developing legal clones; the people who do the best here have interests, experience and a life outside the office. We are a law firm built around people and we want you to be yourself.

What you'll do: We believe in giving you maximum exposure. That's why we offer more secondment opportunities than most law firms. On our training contract, you'll complete four six-month seats. But even before the contract starts, you'll benefit from our training and support.

Perks: We offer a full flexible benefit package that allows you to choose the benefits that suit you. Options include travel insurance, health insurance, gym membership and season ticket loans.

Sponsorship: We offer sponsorship through the GDL (if applicable) and the LPC; we provide our future trainees with a competitive maintenance grant during their studies.

Facts and figures

Total partners: 173
Other fee-earners: 253
Total trainees: 29

Trainee places available for 2019: 14
Applications received pa: c2,000
Percentage interviewed: 15%

First year salary: £37,000
Second year salary: £40,000
Newly qualified salary: £62,000

Turnover in 2015: £113.3m (+9% from 2014)
Profits per equity partner: £506,000 (+23%)
(see legalbusiness.co.uk for full financial information)

Application process

Apply to: Amelia Spinks.
How: Online at http://careers.fieldfisher.com/application-process.html.
When: By 31 July 2017 for 2019 contracts.
What's involved: Please see http://careers.fieldfisher.com/application-process.html.

Vacation schemes

Spring: Apply by 15 January 2017.
Summer: Apply by 15 January 2017.

fieldfisher

Foot Anstey LLP

Salt Quay House, 4 North East Quay, Sutton Harbour, Plymouth PL4 0BN

Lex 100 Winner

See categories below and tables from page 69

Survey results *(marks out of 100%)*

Satisfied in your job? **90**

Firm living up to expectations? **90**

High quality of work? **90**

Enough client contact? **85**

Stress-free? **68**

Happy work/life balance? **89**

Friendly firm? **96**

Great social life? **74**

Good vacation scheme? **84**

Confident you'll be kept on? **84**

Good remuneration? **83**

Diverse firm? **90**

 **verdict**

Foot Anstey is an 'entrepreneurial, expanding firm' which offers trainees the 'opportunity to work with regional, national and international clients while remaining true to its roots in the West Country'. Trainees found the 'personality and lifestyle combined with the reputation and growth' of the firm particularly appealing. The 'support network' is good as trainees are assigned a supervisor, a buddy and a separate mentor. Most trainees sit next to their supervising partner so the 'level and quality of supervision is very high'. As one trainee noted, 'I don't feel like I have people peering over my shoulder the whole time. I am simply allowed to get on with all the support I need.' The 'beginning of the training contract is always the hardest period' as newcomers go through the 'transition from student to trainee'. Trainees receive 'excellent training' and get a 'manageable amount of responsibility' including 'client contact from day one' and 'high-quality work', factors which have led to the firm winning a mightily impressive nine **Lex 100 Winner** medals. There is no 'stay-late culture' at Foot Anstey, and trainees are 'encouraged to manage their workloads' to ensure they can 'get out of the office'. The main criticism is the 'expectation to move every six months or so' and the 'geographical spread' of the offices across the UK 'can be a pain' and means trainees are 'required to travel'. But the trade-off is that trainees are not 'just a number but get to play a vital role in transactions'. Highlights include 'receiving favourable feedback' and 'completing my first Islamic finance transaction'. The 'down-to-earth lawyers' are 'keen to help out' and new recruits are made to 'feel included'. If you are looking for an 'ambitious firm' with a 'good reputation' and an 'excellent support network', take a closer look at Foot Anstey.

If the firm were a fictional character it would be...

Pongo (101 Dalmations) – loyal and intelligent, with a fun-loving side

The firm

Foot Anstey has a strong presence in the South West, with offices in Exeter, Plymouth, Taunton, Truro and Bristol. Firm strengths include agriculture and estates, corporate tax, TMT and insurance. Foot Anstey has an impressive list of clients, and was acknowledged for its performance by being shortlisted for National/Regional Team of the Year at the *Legal Business Awards 2016*.

The deals

Advised Greenridge Investment Management on the financing of its £70m acquisition of the National Air Traffic Control Services HQ; assisted Bristol University Student Union with the £30m redevelopment of its central building; advised longstanding client 90 North Real Estate Partners on an offshore equity structuring to facilitate a residential development; advised South Gloucestershire and Stroud College on the expansion of its facilities through the acquisition of the former Berkeley Nuclear Laboratory site; advised Aardman Animations on user and child friendly content licence terms and revising its download terms.

The clients

Age UK; Bristol City FC; the Business Growth Fund; Department of Health; Jelf Group; Lloyds Bank; Odeon Cinemas; Robert Dyas; the Royal Shakespeare Company; Warner Music Group.

The star performers

Top-ranking departments according to *The Legal 500* (see legal500.com for more details)

Agriculture and estates; Banking and finance; Charities and not-for-profit; Clinical negligence: claimant; Court of Protection; Corporate tax; Construction; Commercial litigation; Contentious trust and probate; Environment; EU and competition; Employment; Family; Islamic finance; Licensing; Media and entertainment; Pensions; Property litigation; Public sector: education; TMT: IT and telecoms.

- **Why did you choose this firm over any others?** 'I worked here as support staff for two years throughout undergraduate and postgraduate before becoming a trainee, and the firm was incredibly supportive of my career progression'; 'a friendly, inclusive environment and an excellent work/life balance'; 'based in the South West but with City-quality work'; 'open-plan offices'; 'the firm really values its employees'

- **Best thing about the firm?** 'All the staff are very helpful in supporting you'; 'very professional yet friendly'; 'the client contact from day one'; 'managed responsibility'; 'high-profile clients'; 'the trust that the firm places in its trainees'; 'you can have a sea view from your desk at the Plymouth office'; 'the newly-formed Bristol netball team'

- **Worst thing about the firm?** 'Trainees are expected to move between offices during the training contract'; 'sometimes teams are so busy that you get little chance for feedback on your work'; 'having to move location every six months'; 'lower remuneration'; 'few social activities within the firm'

- **Best moment?** 'Being heavily involved in an interesting dispute, including attending a High Court trial in London'; 'going to a round table settlement meeting'; 'attending mediation and short possession hearings'; 'being trusted to meet clients independently'; 'being given a complex case to handle practically on my own'

- **Worst moment?** 'Dealing with a difficult staff member'; 'being given lengthy tasks which someone without any legal experience or background could do'; 'working late between Christmas and New Year to prepare a due diligence report'; 'receiving feedback on my need to improve on accuracy'; 'managing normal seat workload around induction training'

A day in the life of...

... **Oli Macrae** second-year trainee solicitor, Foot Anstey

Departments to date: Construction, commercial, and media and IP litigation

University: University of Exeter

Degree and class: Law 2(1)

6.35am: I usually head to the gym (conveniently next to the office) at the start of my day. I find that it clears the mind and sets you up for a productive day.

8.00am: I arrive at the office, check my emails and browse the local news for the day. I then prepare my to-do list for the day.

9.00am: At our weekly huddle (an office-wide standing meeting during which we discuss cases, events and interesting topics) I present a short update on any relevant local news stories that may affect our services, clients or the wider business community. I present for up to five minutes and the meeting lasts no longer than 20 minutes.

9.30am: Having concluded the huddle, I return to my desk to an email from a senior associate in our Bristol office, enquiring as to my availability to assist with a distribution agreement review that requires turning around within 48 hours. I set aside time in my afternoon to begin the task.

10.15am: I meet a solicitor in the commercial team in our boardroom to practices a presentation I will be delivering the following day to the client I am on part-time secondment with. The presentation is on effective contract negotiations for the client, so I have a run through to ensure my timings are on point, and that the content is digestible.

11.00am: I spend the remainder of the morning finalising a client note on the obligations on banks when issuing payment instruments (bank cards). When completed and proof read, I send this to the partner in the financial services branch of the commercial team to consider before sending to the client.

12.45pm: I walk into town with some of the team to grab something to eat.

1.45pm: I start reviewing the distribution Agreement received this morning. My role is to review the document in full, highlighting any possible risks to our client and, where possible, suggesting places where we could reasonably improve their position. We aim to 'participate rather than commentate', which means going further than simply risk flagging – we look out for the client's best interests at all times, come off the fence and give our view on the best option for the client, and reflect this in our advice.

3.00pm: I take a five-minute break from the contract review, to check in with the other trainees regarding a CSR day we are arranging for the following month. I suggest a couple of local options and we agree to decide on our preference at our next meeting.

5.15pm: I send the completed first draft of the distribution agreement review back to my Bristol colleague for his input and comment. I have flagged a couple of areas I was unsure

of, but still tried to put forward my opinion and be proactive rather than immediately seeking guidance from others.

5.35pm: I sit down with the partner who reviewed the note prepared for the bank this morning. There were a couple of changes made to the note.

> **'My role is to review the document in full, highlighting any possible risks to our client.'**

5.45pm: Before heading off I ensure I have all my materials to hand for the presentation I will be delivering the following morning. I then head off to a Foot Anstey cricket match against an important referrer of the firm. This offers a good opportunity for trainees to network. During my time at Foot Anstey, I've had a fantastically varied workload, exposure to high-value matters, plenty of autonomous responsibility (while still feeling supported by those that supervise me) and an abundance of direct client contact – this is something that really makes Foot Anstey stand out as a prospective employer for applicants.

www.footansteycareers.com

About the firm

Address: Salt Quay House, 4 North East Quay, Sutton Harbour, Plymouth PL4 0BN
Telephone: 01752 675000 **Fax:** 01752 675500
Website: www.footanstey.com
Email: contact@footanstey.com
Twitter: @FootAnstey

Managing partner: John Westwell

Other offices: Bristol, Exeter, Plymouth, Taunton, Truro.

Who we are: A leading regional, top 100 law firm, Foot Anstey is a major presence in the South West. With five offices across the region, our lawyers offer a range of specialist legal services to our regional, national and international clients.

What we do: The firm is arranged into seven main groups: clinical negligence; real estate; commercial; corporate; dispute resolution; employment; and private wealth. We also have a niche expertise in Islamic finance.

What we're looking for: We welcome applications from all law and non-law graduates who have a strong academic background, exceptional communication skills, and the vision to be part of our future. We are an ambitious firm – we want people that will help take us there.

What you'll do: Our training programme is designed to help you reach your full potential. Our trainees undertake six seats of four months with regular, open communication between the trainees and supervisors as standard. You will get exposure to situations to develop your legal and commercial expertise, in an environment that is friendly and supportive.

Perks: All trainees are entitled to the flexible, forward-thinking 'choices' benefits package, which includes: 25 days' holiday, options to buy/sell holiday, contributory pension scheme, life assurance, cycle scheme and childcare vouchers. In addition we offer a popular 'lifestyle hour', the chance to take one hour off work each week to promote a healthy work/life balance.

Sponsorship: Grants available towards GDL, LPC and living expenses.

Facts and figures

Total partners: 49
Other fee-earners: 155
Total trainees: 21

Trainee places available for 2019: 12

First year salary: Competitive
Second year salary: Competitive
Newly qualified salary: Competitive

Application process

How: Online application.
When: By 1 June 2017.
What's involved: Group presentation, written exercise and interview.

Vacation schemes

Summer June/July 2017: apply by 1 April 2017

www.footansteycareers.com

Gibson, Dunn & Crutcher LLP

Telephone House, 2-4 Temple Avenue, London EC4Y 0HB

Survey results *(marks out of 100%)*

Satisfied in your job?	74
Firm living up to expectations?	59
High quality of work?	79
Enough client contact?	49
Stress-free?	34
Happy work/life balance?	64
Friendly firm?	74
Great social life?	64
Confident you'll be kept on?	74
Good remuneration?	(89)
Diverse firm?	84

 verdict

Gibson, Dunn & Crutcher is a new *Lex 100* entrant, and the LA-headquartered outfit runs one of the City's newest training programmes with the inaugural trainee cohort having started in September 2015. The early reports are promising, with one trainee stating that 'the people are very friendly and down-to-earth' while a peer agreed that 'the people who work here' is one of the best things about the firm. Favourable comparisons to other training contracts suggest there is 'a lot more partner contact' at Gibson Dunn, as well as 'very good hours in comparison'. As part of such a small intake, one recruit writes that they are 'not treated as a trainee' and 'do not feel like a number', adding 'my opinion is asked and I feel like part of the team'. Responsibility is forthcoming, and one respondent tells us 'I have had the chance to be involved in the management of a free legal advice clinic and its training sessions'. Perhaps understandably, 'as the training contract is not established there are a lot of changes as to what is being offered along the way', and therefore some 'seat and secondment options may not be available as originally thought'. Still, there are 'lots of opportunities' for trainees to get excited about, including 'attending the new lawyer's retreat in Arizona with everyone who is new to Gibson Dunn across all offices globally'. The pay is also excellent, giving the firm a **Lex 100 Winner** prize. Gibson Dunn will recruit larger intakes in the coming years, so to be among the first London trainees at the firm, keep your eyes peeled for further developments.

If the firm were a fictional character it would be...

Alice (Alice in Wonderland) – is still discovering its way here, and is on an adventure being shaped by lots of different personalities

The firm

The LA-headquartered Gibson Dunn has offices throughout the Americas, Asia, Europe and the Middle East, and excels across the full suite of corporate and financial practice areas. Having had a presence in London for over 30 years, the office's first trainee intake arrived in September 2015.

The deals

Advised Gala Coral on its £2.3bn merger with Ladbrokes; acted for Markit on the acquisition of three companies: CoreOne Technologies, DealHub and Information Mosaic; acted for Lone Star Funds in its $1.4bn acquisition of Hanson Building Products; acted for UBS regarding a number of global fraud investigations; advised Oaktree Capital Management on a number of deals, including the sale of a UK portfolio to Logicor.

The clients

Amazon; AnaCap; Apollo; HP; Kennedy Wilson Europe; Lone Star; Marriott International; Oaktree Capital; Schlumberger; UBS.

The star performers

Top-ranking departments according to *The Legal 500* (see legal500.com for more details)
Acquisition finance; Bank lending – investment grade debt and syndicated loans; Commercial litigation; Commercial property: general; Commercial property: hotels and leisure; Commercial property: investment; Competition litigation; Corporate crime (including fraud, bribery and corruption); EU and competition; International arbitration; M&A: upper mid-market and premium deals, £250m+; Private equity: transactions: Large-cap deal capability; Property finance.

- **Why did you choose this firm over any others?** 'The people are very friendly and down-to-earth'; 'lots of opportunities'

- **Best thing about the firm?** 'The people who work here'; 'I get a lot of partner contact and I am not treated as a trainee'; 'my opinion is asked and I feel like part of the team'; 'I do not feel like a number'; 'I have had very good hours'

- **Worst thing about the firm?** 'As the training contract is not established there are a lot of changes as to what is being offered along the way'

- **Best moment?** 'Attending the new lawyer's retreat in Arizona with everyone who is new to Gibson Dunn across all offices globally'; 'I have had the chance to be involved in the management of a free legal advice clinic and its training sessions'

- **Worst moment?** 'Finding out that the secondment options may not be available as originally thought'

Gibson, Dunn & Crutcher LLP

Telephone House, 2-4 Temple Avenue, London EC4Y 0HB

Three associates give their opinions on what it's like to work at Gibson, Dunn & Crutcher LLP.

Chris Loudon

I joined Gibson Dunn's disputes team immediately after training at a large UK firm because I wanted an opportunity to work on high-profile, cross-border litigation, to travel, and to work in foreign languages. All of these expectations have been more than fulfilled. In only my second week, I attended an appeal hearing before the highest court in Luxembourg and since then have spent a considerable amount of time working in Luxembourg, Paris and Zurich for a major international client.

At Gibson Dunn, junior associates are given levels of responsibility and client contact that they would not get at other firms. I work with and present to very senior individuals within the client company on a regular basis. The challenge of continually having to deal effectively with difficult and unfamiliar situations is one I relish.

Gibson Dunn also encourages associates to get involved in pro bono matters. I am part of a team, led by Gibson Dunn partner Lord Falconer, that represents the Hillsborough Family Support Group and I was present in Liverpool Cathedral to advise the families on the momentous day on which the Hillsborough Independent Panel delivered its report.

Although Gibson Dunn is a large international firm with all the attendant resources and support network, the London office is relatively small and close-knit, making it a very pleasant place to work.

Amy Sinclair

I joined Gibson Dunn's labour and employment team in January 2015. One of the key things that attracted me to the firm was the exposure to a diverse range of work with a truly international client base.

Any day, I might find myself advising a client on issues as diverse as collective consultation obligations in a redundancy scenario, the employment, pensions and data protection aspects of public and private mergers and acquisitions, or working on employment-related litigation.

This is challenging but exciting and is one of the main reasons why I enjoy working at Gibson Dunn so much.

Leila Greer-Stapleton

I joined Gibson Dunn in September 2012, seeking increased responsibility and exposure to a range of top-quality corporate deals at a diverse and ambitious international firm. Two years on, I have not been disappointed!

Gibson Dunn has given me the opportunity to get involved in an exciting range of international transactional work, ranging from aircraft financing, assisting a private equity fund to invest into a top luxury fashion brand, helping to set up investment funds in the Middle East, and helping English companies to list on NASDAQ and the New York Stock Exchange. I have also been seconded to our Dubai office, where I worked on a media M&A deal.

> **'At Gibson Dunn, junior associates are given levels of responsibility and client contact that they would not get at other firms.'**

Gibson Dunn is a growing and ambitious firm, and associates are encouraged to be like-minded. I have been given a lot of responsibility on my deals, having been required to take the lead in drafting transactional documents and liaising with the client and the other side's advisers. The partners and senior associates come from a range of diverse backgrounds, and so I am constantly learning from their wealth of experience too.

Gibson Dunn is genuinely collegiate and supportive. It has a mentoring scheme under which all associates are paired up with a partner who offers advice on professional and personal development.

About the firm

Address: Telephone House, 2-4 Temple Avenue, London EC4Y 0HB
Telephone: 020 7071 4000
Website: www.gibsondunn.com

Senior partners: Jeff Trinklein, James Cox (London)
Managing partner: Ken Doran

Other offices: Beijing, Brussels, Century City, Dallas, Denver, Dubai, Hong Kong, Los Angeles, Munich, New York, Orange County, Palo Alto, Paris, San Francisco, Sao Paulo, Singapore, Washington DC.

Who we are: One of the world's top law firms. Our lawyers provide legal advice on a wide range of business issues to internationally listed companies, large private companies and many other organisations with international operations and ambitions.

What we do: Our London office, founded more than 30 years ago, offers in-depth advice on all aspects of corporate work, including mergers and acquisitions, dispute resolution and international arbitration, private equity, commercial real estate, real estate private equity, finance, business restructuring and reorganisation, project finance, capital markets and taxation, competition, and labour and employment.

What we're looking for: Exceptional individuals from a wide range of backgrounds who are capable of taking the initiative and fulfilling our clients' needs, who have excellent academics as well as strong interpersonal and organisational skills, and who can rise to the challenge of working within small, focused teams and having client contact early in their careers.

What you'll do: Over two years, trainees will have the opportunity to work alongside and learn from some of the best lawyers in their fields. Trainees may also have the opportunity to choose a seat in one of our overseas offices.

Sponsorship: GDL and LPC fees and maintenance grants paid.

Facts and figures

Total partners: 367 worldwide, 24 in London
Other fee-earners: 913 worldwide, 53 in London

Total trainees: 4 (from September 2016)
Trainee places available for 2019: 6-8

First year salary: Competitive US rate

Application process

Apply to: Kathryn Edwards, London graduate recruitment manager.
How: Application form on website.
When: By July 2017 for training contracts commencing in September 2019
What's involved: Interview.

Vacation schemes

Summer: July 2017-July 2018 (apply by February 2017)

GIBSON DUNN

Hill Dickinson LLP

No 1 St Paul's Square, Liverpool L3 9SJ

Survey results *(marks out of 100%)*

Satisfied in your job?	75
Firm living up to expectations?	73
High quality of work?	79
Enough client contact?	79
Stress-free?	64
Happy work/life balance?	81
Friendly firm?	77
Great social life?	62
Good vacation scheme?	83
Confident you'll be kept on?	76
Good remuneration?	63
Diverse firm?	77
Good international secondments?	65

 **verdict**

The striking 'buzz and energy' and 'collegiate atmosphere' of Hill Dickinson are both widely praised. This 'friendly firm' is well known for its 'marine expertise' and enjoys a 'strong reputation in the North West'. A 'very attractive' stand-out factor is the 'friendly, relaxed atmosphere' as 'everyone on all levels is down-to-earth and approachable', although several respondents reported there are 'not enough opportunities for trainees across offices to come together'. The 'small trainee intake' of about four a year at the London office results in 'many opportunities for responsibility' as well as a 'large variety of work and exposure to big deals everyday'. The firm offers 'excellent training' so trainees are not 'stuck at the photocopier' but get their hands on 'good-quality work'. Some trainees grumbled about the 'lack of communication' and 'cost-cutting of items such as tea, coffee and stationery'. That said, supervisors deliver 'useful feedback to consistently improve the skills' of their new recruits, plus the firm has an 'international client base' with some opportunities for international secondments. Best trainee moments include 'being offered an NQ position', 'receiving a congratulatory email from a very important client' and 'making a without-prejudice call to negotiate with another solicitor early on'. Keep Hill Dickinson in mind if you are striving for a 'lot of early responsibility' at an 'ambitious firm'.

If the firm were a fictional character it would be...

Odysseus – wise, enduring and able to adapt to different situations

The firm

Hill Dickinson has developed its capabilities over 200 years. Offering the full gamut of legal services, the firm is renowned for its shipping expertise and also earns praise for its commercial litigation, insurance and real estate work. The firm has an impressive international reach, with over 1,350 lawyers stationed in offices across England and in Hong Kong, Monaco, Piraeus and Singapore.

The deals

Advised Nidera on a $3m GAFTA arbitration; acted for Cenkos Securities on Reneuron Group's £68.4m placing on the London Stock Exchange; acted for pharmaceutical manufacturer Nupharm Group on its sale to Quantum; advised Eddie Stobart Logistics on the sale of its UK automotive logistics business to BCA Market Place; advised Johnson Service Group on its £69.4m acquisition of London Linen Supply.

The clients

AstraZeneca; BNP Paribas; BP; Cargill; Europcar; JP Morgan; NHS England; Royal Caribbean Cruises; Swiss International Air Lines; Tradex.

The star performers

Top-ranking departments according to *The Legal 500* (see legal500.com for more details)
Aviation; Banking and finance; Charities and not-for-profit; Clinical negligence: defendant; Commercial litigation; Commodities: physicals; Crime: fraud; Debt recovery; Education; Employment; Family; Health and safety; Insolvency and corporate recovery; Licensing; Local government; Pensions; Professional negligence; Shipping; Travel: personal injury; Travel: regulatory and commercial.

- **Why did you choose this firm over any others?** 'Variety of seats'; 'location'; 'reputation'; 'prominence in North West'; 'high quality of work'; 'client contact'; 'worked as a paralegal previously'; 'partners of the firm were involved in the recruitment process'; 'marine law'; 'smaller trainee intake'; 'huge variety of seat choices'; 'international client base'; 'for its reputation in shipping law'; 'great levels of responsibility'

- **Best thing about the firm?** 'The people'; 'those I have worked with have been friendly'; 'buzz around business services group'; 'level of responsibility'; 'the supportive atmosphere which promotes development and helps me improve my skills and knowledge on a continual basis'

- **Worst thing about the firm?** 'Obsession with financials and belief that turnover is the be all and end all'; 'lack of transparency over career progression'; 'the Manchester office is a bit tired'; 'supervisor accountability'; 'no choice of seat in first year'; 'the pay'; 'not enough opportunities for trainees across the offices to come together'

- **Best moment?** 'Obtaining an administration order against a partnership where the corporate partners were based abroad'; 'producing a 50-page disclosure letter and due diligence exercise in three weeks'; 'visiting Lloyds of London'; 'working with the employment team'; 'managing my own cases during my first seat'; 'being thanked for doing a good job'

- **Worst moment?** 'Being berated for not doing something quickly enough'; 'not being able to qualify early'; 'having a limited time to turn around court documents'; 'not feeling supported'; 'when I made an error on some work for the head of the department'; 'having little to do'

A day in the life of...

... **Katie Somerville** trainee solicitor, Hill Dickinson LLP

Departments to date: Property, corporate, commercial litigation, Manchester

University: The University of Chester

Degree and class: Law and Journalism, 2(1)

The Manchester property team is a very busy department which has grown dramatically in size and expertise during my seat, creating an interesting and dynamic working environment which has provided me with a wealth of experience to stand me in excellent stead for my next seat and beyond.

My typical day starts at the office between 8am and 8.30am (depending on how disciplined I have been at getting out of bed that morning!). I begin my day by checking emails and prioritising my to-do list. I then double-check my diary for the day and for the rest of the week to make sure I am aware of any deadlines I have approaching. This seat has required sharp organisational skills as I have been responsible for assisting on live transactions whilst also managing post-completion tasks for a number of matters at any given time.

From the very beginning of my seat I was given the opportunity of drafting important transactional documents and as such my time in the property team has been significant in improving my drafting skills. I am regularly involved in drafting a wide variety of documents such as leases, licences for alterations, licences to assign and deeds of covenant.

I have recently assisted on a matter where our client was taking a lease of an office

premises in London and, as has been the case with a number of matters I have worked on, I was given the opportunity to be involved in the matter from inception to completion and encouraged to take ownership of the transaction. There were a number of 'sticking points' within the licence for alterations and the lease and I was responsible for negotiating these issues with the solicitor acting for the landlord, ensuring at that all times I was reporting back to the client and taking the client's instructions on how they wished me to proceed.

It is rare that a week passes where I am not assisting on a matter for which I am given responsibility for the due diligence side of the transaction. This entails carrying out a review of the title to the property or piece of land for which the client is taking an interest in, ordering and reviewing the appropriate searches and surveys and compiling a comprehensive yet succinct report for the client. I find this work particularly interesting as you gain an extensive in-depth knowledge of the property with which you are dealing.

The level of client contact during my property seat has been brilliant. As I have been allowed to take on the role of number one point of contact on several transactions, I am given the opportunity to liaise with clients over the phone and by email on a daily basis and this has served to enhance my

communication skills and let me build a good rapport with clients.

I have also been fortunate enough to work alongside the property finance team on a number of matters. This again has added further variety to my days. The team advises a number of leading banks on

> **'The level of client contact during my property seat has been brilliant.'**

secured lending transactions and as such the nature of the work forms a property/banking hybrid which I have found particularly interesting.

I would highly recommend this seat to the current and future trainees as in my experience the quality and variety of the work and clients and the responsibility afforded to trainees makes it a rewarding and valuable seat. I hope that this article has provided a useful insight into the day in the life of a property trainee. If you would like any further information about my time in this seat please feel free to contact me.

www.hilldickinsontrainees.com

About the firm

Address: No.1 St Paul's Square, Liverpool L3 9SJ
Telephone: 0151 600 8000
Website: www.hilldickinson.com
Email: recruitment@hilldickinson.com
Twitter: @HD_Trainees

Senior partner: David Wareing
Managing partner: Peter Jackson

Other offices: Manchester, London, Sheffield, Monaco, Piraeus, Singapore, Hong Kong.

Who we are: We're an award-winning, full service international law firm of around 1,150 people, including 190 partners and legal directors, with big clients, great people and fantastic opportunities.

What we do: We're a full-service commercial law firm, so we cover all areas of law across a number of sectors including insurance, retail, aviation, sports, media, health and marine.

What we're looking for: Academically, you'll need at least a 2(1) and ABB or equivalent. We want our trainees to show a commitment to learning and the insight and awareness to understand our clients' demands.

What you'll do: Due to our small intake (up to 12 trainees for 2019), there's lots of interesting work to go around and you will be given challenges from the start. Your mentor will be on hand throughout to offer advice, guidance and support.

Perks: As well as a host of fantastic training opportunities, we also provide some pretty good perks: pension, travel insurance, buying and selling holiday entitlement, permanent health insurance and life assurance, season ticket loans, BUPA cover, and we'll even give you your birthday off (paid).

Sponsorship: LPC fees paid and maintenance grants of £5,000 for the north and £7,000 for London.

Facts and figures

Total partners: 190 (including legal directors)
Other fee-earners: 732
Total trainees: 22

Trainee places available for 2019: 12
Applications received pa: 1,000 approx
Percentage interviewed: 10%

First year salary: £24,000 (Northern), £32,000 (London)
Second year salary: £26,000 (Northern), £34,000 (London)
Newly qualified salary: up to £40,000 (Northern), £58,000 (London)

Turnover in 2015: £104.4m (-6% from 2014)
Profits per equity partner: £261,000m (-4%)
(see legalbusiness.co.uk for full financial information)

Application process

Apply to: Emma McAvinchey-Roberts – talent and development manager, Jennifer Hulse – senior talent and development advisor.
How: Online via the website.
When: By 31 July 2017 for 2019 contracts.
What's involved: Online application, online video interview, Watson Glaser, assessment centre, partner interview.

Vacation schemes

Summer: Apply by 31 January 2017.

HILL DICKINSON

Hogan Lovells International LLP

Atlantic House, Holborn Viaduct, London EC1A 2FG

Survey results *(marks out of 100%)*

Satisfied in your job?	77
Firm living up to expectations?	80
High quality of work?	76
Enough client contact?	69
Stress-free?	60
Happy work/life balance?	69
Friendly firm?	86
Great social life?	77
Good vacation scheme?	84
Confident you'll be kept on?	75
Good remuneration?	86
Diverse firm?	84
Good international secondments?	78

 **verdict**

Trainees describe Hogan Lovells as operating at the 'top of the market' and a 'great alternative to the Magic Circle' because of its enviable 'international presence' and 'friendly atmosphere'. Several trainees were 'greatly influenced' by enjoyable vacation schemes at the firm through which they discovered an 'inclusive working environment'. There is a 'diverse range of legal departments', from energy to real estate, which gives trainees the 'opportunity to try out different areas of the law before qualifying'. Trainee highlights include 'completing a deal and seeing it make the FT' and 'being the main point of contact for one start-up client and helping them to establish their business'. The 'inevitable grunt work' of 'bundling under time pressure' and 'working late – whether that is all-nighters or weekends' can create 'stressful moments in some seats'. But overall the firm has a 'human approach' to working hours and there is 'no face-time culture, if you are busy you stay late and if you are not then you can go home'. This is a 'supportive culture' where everyone wants to 'encourage and help' trainees to succeed, and the firm has an 'ongoing commitment to improving diversity and wellbeing, listening to staff and what makes them tick'. Current trainees loved their international seats including in Hong Kong, reporting it was both a 'very rewarding' and 'fantastically different' working experience. The firm is a double **Lex 100 Winner** for international secondments and remuneration satisfaction. Keep Hogan Lovells in mind if you are looking for 'high-quality work' in the City and a 'broad range of clients'.

If the firm were a fictional character it would be...

Hawkeye (Avengers) – unpretentious, clever and an expert at what it does

The firm

Hogan Lovells has more than 2,500 lawyers based in 26 countries, and counts corporations, financial institutions and governments among its client base. The firm is highly regarded for its dispute resolution, IP, projects and real estate capabilities. Hogan Lovells secured an impressive three nominations for the *Legal Business* Awards 2016, in the Restructuring, Dispute Resolution and Real Estate Team of the Year categories.

The deals

Advised Vietnam Airlines on its debut $580m financing of four Boeing 787-9 Dreamliner aircraft provided by Exportimport Bank of the United States; acted for Natixis and ING on the provision of a $530m pre-export facility to Uralkali; advised AlixPartners as administrators and a syndicate of lenders on the asset sale of the Parabis Group; acted for BNP Paribas on its €20bn secured structured products programme; advised Volkswagen Financial Services on its £10bn securitisation programme and the £350m Driver UK deal.

The clients

Barclays; Citibank; eBay; Honeywell; London Metal Exchange; News Corporation; Pakistan International Airline; SABMiller; Santander; Virgin Media.

The star performers

Top-ranking departments according to *The Legal 500* (see legal500.com for more details)
Acquisition finance; Asset finance and leasing; Aviation; Bank lending – investment grade debt and syndicated loans; Commodities: derivatives; Corporate restructuring and insolvency; Debt capital markets; Derivatives and structured products; Emerging markets; Employee share schemes; Health and safety; High yield; Infrastructure (including PFI and PPP); Islamic finance; Mining and minerals; Oil and gas; Pensions dispute resolution; Rail; Securitisation; Trade finance.

- **Why did you choose this firm over any others?** 'Quality of vacation scheme'; 'broad range of practice areas'; 'international work'; 'inclusive culture'; 'people I met on my vacation scheme were very welcoming'; 'wide range of secondment opportunities'; 'broad range of clients'; 'great application process'; 'the expectation that you will be a human being and not a drone'; 'strong reputation for litigation'; 'good financial remuneration'; 'high-quality work and a global reach'

- **Best thing about the firm?** 'Good-quality training'; 'people are keen to help you learn'; 'international work'; 'the cookies'; 'associates and partners are happy to help and do so cheerfully'; 'excellent clients'; 'effort is made to put on interesting firm events and to set up societies'; 'great exposure in my first seat'; 'the breadth of practice areas'; 'lots of opportunities for trainees'; 'supportive culture'

- **Worst thing about the firm?** 'Bad hours in some seats'; 'sometimes workloads aren't spread evenly'; 'not being sure about getting a job after the training contract'; 'niche areas have few job openings'; 'no visibility higher up the hierarchy'; 'being made to do a finance seat in your training contract even when you know that you have no interest in qualifying there'

- **Best moment?** 'Taking on my own pro bono clients'; 'completing a deal which I had been involved in all the way through'; 'closing my own real estate deals'; 'involvement with organising an innovative new training scheme with partners'; 'personally being involved in a negotiation with the other side of a litigation dispute'; 'advising the general counsel of a FTSE100 company one-on-one'

- **Worst moment?** 'Working on the weekend'; 'endless bundling in a litigation seat'; 'an all-nighter just before Christmas'; 'making a mistake on a transaction'; 'clearing up lunch rubbish after a hearing for my supervisor and the barristers'; 'hours with little work to do'; 'stressful technical problems'; 'administrative tasks'

A day in the life of...

... Joshua Reynolds second-seat trainee solicitor, Hogan Lovells

Departments to date: Financial institutions, corporate litigation, investigations, contentious insolvency and fraud
University: University of Birmingham
Degree and class: Law with French, 2(1)

7.45am: I get in promptly so that I can spend 45 minutes or so in the firm's in-house gym. Starting my day this way means that I am fully awake and ready to go once I am at my desk.

9.15am: I check my emails and catch up with my supervisor about where we are with an internal investigation we have been working on for a client in the publishing industry. The client had contacted us in light of allegations that a group of its employees had pirated the client's products and sold them to customers for personal profit. My main role in the investigation has been to gather evidence of impropriety by looking through the employees' email correspondence with each other and third parties. I start to notice a pattern of emails with large attachments going to random email addresses. The attachments look like cheap knock-offs of some of the client's publications. I flag this to my supervisor who commends me for spotting the trend. We set up a call with the client to discuss this development.

10.00am: I have a meeting on the top floor of the office with a pro bono client, who I will be representing next week at a hearing. The government recently deemed her ineligible for Employment Support Allowance, a benefit which she has been claiming for over a decade. I spend a couple of hours with her, gathering the information I need so that I can write up my submissions to the Social Security Appeals Tribunal. Hogan Lovells strongly encourages trainee involvement in pro bono work. Apart from helping the firm to give back to the community and promote good citizenship, pro bono work gives trainees the opportunity to lead their own matters and gain invaluable experience of building and maintaining client relationships.

12.30pm: A number of our trainee intake have become connoisseurs of the many Mexican lunch venues around Holborn, so we take the opportunity to get out into the summer sun whenever we can and eat together in Lincoln's Inn Fields.

1.30pm: I join the client call with my supervisor and the partner on the matter. The client's MD mentions how he has recently come into possession of two of the pirated materials. The partner asks him to describe these and it quickly becomes clear that these texts are the same as those which were being distributed on the emails I had seen. The partner moves the phone in my direction and allows me to explain my earlier findings to the client.

2.30pm: I make a start on drafting a report for the client summarising the evidence we have gathered and potential next steps.

3.30pm: An associate asks me to do some urgent research into an area of law I am unfamiliar with. I know all of the other trainees in the department are busy on other matters, so I ask my supervisor if finishing the report to the client on the piracy issue can wait until later. He says it can. Managing your time

> '**Hogan Lovells strongly encourages trainee involvement in pro bono work.**'

and the expectations of your clients and colleagues is a key skill for any trainee.

5.30pm: Having consulted hard copy and online sources, I revert back to the associate with my research. I know I have nearly finished my report, so I spend the rest of my day getting it done so that my desk is clear for tomorrow morning.

7.00pm: On my way out of the office I pop my head into a fellow trainee's office. He is done for the day too, so we head down to the firm's wine bar for a drink.

www.hoganlovells.com/graduates

About the firm

Address: Atlantic House, Holborn Viaduct, London EC1A 2FG
Telephone: 020 7296 2000
Fax: 020 7296 2001
Website: www.hoganlovells.com/graduates
Email: graduate.recruitment@hoganlovells.com

Chair: Nicholas Cheffings
CEO: Steve Immelt **Deputy CEO:** David Hudd

Other offices: Alicante, Amsterdam, Baltimore, Beijing, Brussels, Budapest, Caracas, Colorado Springs, Denver, Dubai, Dusseldorf, Frankfurt, Hamburg, Hanoi, Ho Chi Minh City, Hong Kong, Houston, Jeddah, Johannesburg, London, Los Angeles, Luxembourg, Madrid, Mexico City, Miami, Milan, Minneapolis, Monterrey, Moscow, Munich, New York, Northern Virginia, Paris, Perth, Philadelphia, Riyadh, Rio de Janeiro, San Francisco, São Paulo, Shanghai, Silicon Valley, Singapore, Sydney, Tokyo, Ulaanbaatar, Warsaw and Zagreb.

Who we are: A practical, straight-talking approach to law. Open, honest and deep relationships with clients. Training that keeps on evolving. A global community where everyone is on the same wavelength – but always encouraged to be themselves. All of this gives Hogan Lovells a different dynamic to other global law firms.

Facts and figures

Total partners: Over 800
Other fee-earners: Over 2,500
Total trainees: 120

First year: £43,000
Second year: £48,000
Newly qualified: £71,500

What we do: The firm has a reputation not just for the consistently high quality of its 2,500 lawyers, but also for its sense of community. The network of 45 global offices collaborates closely and constructively. Together, our teams of corporate, finance, dispute resolution, government regulatory and intellectual property lawyers tackle some of the most intricate legal and commercial issues that businesses face.

What we're looking for: High-calibre candidates who can demonstrate strong academic and intellectual ability, ambition, resilience, strong communication and interpersonal skills, and a professional, commercial attitude.

What you'll do: Six months in four different practice areas, including corporate, finance and litigation. In the second year, there is the option to go on a client or international secondment.

Perks: Benefits include: 25 days' holiday, private medical insurance, life assurance, private health insurance, season ticket loan, in-house gym, subsidised staff restaurant, access to a dentist, doctor and physiotherapist, discounts at local retailers.

Sponsorship: Maintenance grants are available for GDL and accelerated LPC. GDL is £7,000 outside London and £8,000 within London.

Application process

Apply to: www.hoganlovells.com/graduates.
How: Online application form.
When: Non-law by 31 January 2017, law by 30 June 2017.
What's involved: Online application, online critical thinking test, telephone interview, assessment centre.

Vacation schemes

Spring: 27 March-7 April 2017.
Summer: 19 June-7 July 2017 and 17 July-4 August 2017.
Open days: 15-16 June 2017 (non-law); 27 June and 5 July 2017 (law).

Holman Fenwick Willan

Friary Court, 65 Crutched Friars, London EC3N 2AE

Lex 100 Winner

See categories below
and tables from page 69

Survey results *(marks out of 100%)*

Satisfied in your job?	**85**
Firm living up to expectations?	83
High quality of work?	82
Enough client contact?	71
Stress-free?	61
Happy work/life balance?	81
Friendly firm?	84
Great social life?	56
Good vacation scheme?	80
Confident you'll be kept on?	80
Good remuneration?	69
Diverse firm?	73
Good international secondments?	**97**

 **verdict**

Current trainees rave about the 'fantastic and highly-rewarding training experience' and the guaranteed international secondment opportunities on offer at Holman Fenwick Willan. Recruits can expect to go on 'at least one international secondment' during the training contract and the firm 'tries very hard to support trainees through these seats'. The firm is named a **Lex 100 Winner** in the international secondment and job satisfaction categories. The 'international scope' is impressive, with more than 450 HFW lawyers working across Asia, Australia, the Middle East, Europe and South America. The 'great set-up in the firm' offers trainees 'excellent opportunities' and exposes them to 'interesting tasks'. Therefore it is no surprise that international secondments top many trainees' favourite moments so far. Other notable mentions include 'working on a highly topical deal which made the newspaper headlines' and a 'welcome breakfast at the Sky Bar'. The 'vacation scheme' proved to be invaluable as it gave trainees a 'very useful insight into how the firm operates'. As it stands, the 'training programme is improving' and trainees receive 'personalised and trainee-focused contracts' rather than 'grunt work on a conveyor belt'. 'Supportive supervisors devote time to explain things to you' which trainees really appreciate. Although there is the occasional 'late-night bundling', the lawyers mainly keep 'reasonable hours'. At times trainees say the firm can feel 'disorganised' and the 'pay is not the best available', but the lack of a 'face-time culture' results in a 'good work/life balance' and the teams 'are extremely friendly and hardworking'. Apply to Holman Fenwick Willan if you want to travel during your training contract and work on global deals.

If the firm were a fictional character it would be...

Sean Maguire (Good Will Hunting) – friendly, extremely smart and unpretentious

The firm

Holman Fenwick Willan is renowned for its expertise in transportation law, most notably in the shipping industry. The firm's work is regularly on an international scale, and it offers advice to clients on issues pertaining to trade, commodities, fraud and competition law. Arbitration and commercial litigation are two other areas of strength. The firm recently entered into a formal association with Shanghai's Wintell & Co, creating a new outpost in an international network employing over 450 lawyers.

The deals

Advised Hong Kong Aircraft Engineering Company on competition clearance of the $328m restructuring of two joint-venture companies it had formed with Rolls-Royce and Singapore International Airlines; advised Cargill in a multi-million dollar Supreme Court case; acted for Novae in a matter concerning the liquidation of Glasgow Rangers FC; advised Asia Coal Energy Ventures on its $210m acquisition of Asia Resource Minerals; advised Hoegh Autoliners, Gard Marine & Energy and Gard P&I on the grounding of the Hoegh Osaka in January 2015.

The clients

BP; Cathay Pacific; Citigroup; DHL; Genting Hong Kong; Goldman Sachs; Lucozade Ribena Suntory; Maersk; Morgan Stanley; Nordea Bank.

The star performers

Top-ranking departments according to *The Legal 500* (see legal500.com for more details)
Asset finance and leasing; Aviation; Commercial contracts; Commercial litigation; Commodities: derivatives; Commodities: physicals; Construction: contentious; EU and competition; Fraud: civil; IT and telecoms; Insurance: corporate and regulatory; International arbitration; M&A: mid-market, £50m-£250m; Mining and minerals; Oil and gas; Professional negligence; Shipping; Trade finance; Travel: regulatory and commercial.

- **Why did you choose this firm over any others?** 'The medium size which would lead to greater responsibility'; 'the international opportunities'; 'its sector specialisms'; 'shipping specialisation'; 'working in interesting, tangible industries'; 'first-rate reputation in its core sectors'; 'vacation scheme was very useful insight of the firm'

- **Best thing about the firm?** 'The people within the firm know what they are doing inside out'; 'colleagues are highly-skilled and enthusiastic about what they do'; 'the fantastic learning environment'; 'friendly and collegiate atmosphere'; 'I get a lot of feedback on my work which is very helpful and useful'

- **Worst thing about the firm?** 'Sometimes it is not clear why certain decisions are made'; 'the pay is not the best available'; 'the seat change process'; 'general building facilities'; 'the logo is pretty bleak'

- **Best moment?** 'Settling a claim after negotiations with the other side'; 'assisting a successful settlement'; 'attending a five-day trial'; 'overseas secondment'; 'working on a highly topical deal and later seeing it in the papers'; 'working on a high-value oil and gas transaction'; 'getting deeply involved in interesting projects'

- **Worst moment?** 'Late-night disclosure'; 'working late to rectify a mistake I had made'; 'having to deal with a difficult partner'; 'preparing a bundle for court on a Sunday when all the printers decided to stop working'

A day in the life of...

... **Margarita Kato** trainee, Holman Fenwick Willan

Departments to date: Commodities
University: LSE
Degree: Law

9.00am: I get into the office and re-read several emails I received earlier in the morning. As we have a lot of clients based in Asia, we often receive emails overnight that I need to review in the morning. I then write a to-do list for the day.

9.30am: I receive a call from an associate based in the Singapore office in relation to a client who visited the London office the previous day and who had provided me with a large number of documents in relation to an ongoing arbitration. The associate asks me to work through them and pull out the emails flagged by the client and scan them to her so that she is able to review them in preparation for a call with the client. The time difference means I can work on them during the day and have them ready for her when the Singapore office opens the next day. I spend the next couple of hours locating emails on the itemised list provided by the client. I check their contents to ensure that the emails correspond to the list. The emails are to be used for drafting witness statements and submissions so the client has explained why she has flagged them and it is easy to double-check their contents.

10.30am: I take a break to read the 'Commodities News' bulletin that is sent to all fee-earners in the commodities department.

11.00am: Counsel has come in for a short internal meeting to discuss disclosure on a large mining case that we have been working on. I attend to give him an update on how matters are progressing and stay as the meeting turns into a discussion on strategy and the various applications that we will need to file in court.

1.00pm: I grab some lunch from the canteen and read the news before getting back to work as I have a busy day.

1.30pm: My supervisor asks me to undertake a research task in relation to using a third party debt order against a party who is not paying out against an award that has been given in our favour. He provides the background to the issue so that I can focus my research. I spend a few hours researching the matter and drafting an email summarising my research.

4.30pm: I send the research to my supervisor and we discuss. He queries an assumption that an arbitration award has to be turned into a judgment in order to obtain a third party debt order. He asks me to double-check this as well as the conversion procedure with the dispute resolution professional support lawyer (PSL). I speak to the PSL and explain the background and my research. She agrees with my conclusions and I revert to my supervisor. He summarises the research in a short email and sends it to the client.

7.00pm: I finalise the email task that I had been working on earlier in the day and produce a single PDF of all the emails that were flagged by the client. I double-check

> **'Counsel has come in for a short internal meeting to discuss disclosure on a large mining case that we have been working on.'**

the PDF and spot a few mistakes and ask for assistance from the document production team to make amendments and then I send it off to the associate in Singapore for her to review.

7.45pm: After checking my to-do list and clearing away my papers, I head home.

www.hfw.com/graduate-recruitment

About the firm

Address: Friary Court, 65 Crutched Friars, London EC3N 2AE
Telephone: 020 7264 8487
Website: www.hfw.com
Email: georgina.callwood@hfw.com
Twitter: @HFWGrads
Senior partner: Richard Crump
Managing partner: Marcus Bowman

Other offices: Paris, Brussels, Geneva, Piraeus, Dubai, Shanghai, Hong Kong, Singapore, Perth, Melbourne, Sydney and São Paulo. Associations: Abu Dhabi, Beirut, Kuwait, Riyadh, Shanghai, Singapore, Tianjin.

Who we are: We are an international law firm with over 450 lawyers worldwide and a market-leading reputation for advising businesses operating in a number of industry sectors, including aviation, commodities, construction, energy, financial institutions, insurance, mining, ports and terminals, shipping, space, yachts and travel, cruise and leisure, all of which are integral to the way international commerce works.

What we're looking for: We look for trainees who are bright, commercially focused and hard working. Strong communication skills and team working skills are a must. In addition, as our training contract is truly international we look for individuals who have a global perspective and an interest in completing international work.

What you'll do: Every year we recruit only a small number of trainees – 15 per year split across a September and March intake. This enables us to give every trainee our full attention, and means that your individual contribution makes a difference. A training contract at HFW consists of four six-month seats – typically three contentious seats and one transactional seat, with at least one seat spent outside London in an international office. Trainees are involved in a combination of workshops, departmental know-how sessions, mentoring by experienced lawyers and on-the-job training. Overall, we aim to provide you with a dynamic, supportive and varied environment in which you are challenged to become the best lawyer you can be.

Perks: Private medical insurance, subsidised gym membership, season ticket loan.

Sponsorship: GDL/LPC fees paid and a maintenance grant of £7,000 (£5,500 outside London) is available for each year of study.

Facts and figures

Total partners: 161
Other fee-earners: 520
Total trainees: 30

Trainee places available for 2019: 15
Applications received pa: 1,000
Percentage interviewed: 10%

First year salary: £37,000
Second year salary: £39,000
Newly qualified salary: £61,000

Turnover in 2015/16: £143.1m (+3% from 2014/15)
Profits per equity partner: £519,000

Application process

How: Online at www.training-contracts.com/Grad-Rec-Home
When: By 31 July 2017 for 2019 contracts
What's involved: Online application form, assessment centre, partner interview.

Vacation schemes

Spring: Apply by 14 February 2017.
Summer: Apply by 14 February 2017.

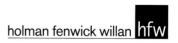

Ince & Co LLP

Aldgate Tower, 2 Leman Street, London E1 8QN

Survey results *(marks out of 100%)*

Satisfied in your job?	75
Firm living up to expectations?	67
High quality of work?	73
Enough client contact?	60
Stress-free?	52
Happy work/life balance?	73
Friendly firm?	78
Great social life?	70
Good vacation scheme?	83
Confident you'll be kept on?	65
Good remuneration?	60
Diverse firm?	70
Good international secondments?	39

 verdict

Ince & Co offers 'very good formal training sessions' which include 'weekly seminars and lectures' to help ease trainees into their training contracts. While being given 'independence', trainees feel 'very supported' and love how the firm is 'actively encouraging' their progression. The firm organises 'external speakers' to come in regularly and discuss a range of topics from the 'basics of contract law to the more intricate areas of law the firm specialises in'. The firm's 'strengths are in its core practices' including M&A, aviation and insurance, but it is internationally renowned for its shipping expertise. The 'flexible training system' allows trainees to 'pick up work from any of the firm's departments'. Recruits don't have to give up 'good-quality work' when they 'move seats' as each practice area is 'interesting and complex'. The firm has the 'winning combination' of 'incredibly approachable' partners who 'possess extensive knowledge and experience' and are 'willing to help'. Trainees grumble about 'uneven distribution of workload' as some are overwhelmed while others have 'periods of nothing to do'. Training highlights include 'playing a key role in a case', 'receiving positive client feedback' plus 'being given a high level of responsibility early on which was both encouraging and exciting'. Trainees love the 'friendly atmosphere', the 'people who work here' and the 'good work/life balance'. If you are looking for a personalised training contract at an expert shipping firm, why not add Ince & Co to the list.

If the firm were a fictional character it would be...

Violet Crawley (Downton Abbey) – a conservative character, but with an adventurous side

The firm

Founded in 1870, Ince & Co has established an international reputation for its shipping expertise, routinely advising ship-owners, charterers and insurers on a variety of issues. The firm set up a Cologne office in May 2016, its second in Germany after launching in Hamburg in 2001. Ince & Co now employs over 600 lawyers spread across 12 offices in Europe, Asia and the Middle East. The firm also has well-regarded practice groups covering M&A, aviation and personal injury.

The deals

Acted for DNB as a creditor on the restructuring of Italian shipping company RBD Armatori; defended Travelers, RSA, Novae, Canopius, Omega, Atrium and Markel as the insurers on proceedings by the assured owner of a superyacht following extensive fire damage; advised long-term client Golar LNG on a commercial agreement with Perenco Cameroon regarding the development of a floating LNG project; advised on the fire on board an Ethiopian Air Boeing 787 Dreamliner, caused by a lithium battery; acted for PST Energy 7 Shipping on the high-profile Supreme Court case relating to the collapse of the OW Group.

The clients

British Marine Mutual; Dragon Oil; Fred Olsen; GasLog; Gunvor; Hercules Offshore; Nordea; Petrofac; Vitol; XL Catlin.

The star performers

Top-ranking departments according to *The Legal 500* (see legal500.com for more details)
Asset finance and leasing; Aviation; Commercial litigation; Commodities: physicals; Fraud: civil; Insurance and reinsurance litigation; Insurance: corporate and regulatory; M&A: smaller deals, up to £50m; Oil and gas; Personal injury: defendant; Professional negligence; Shipping.

- **Why did you choose this firm over any others?** 'Litigation focus'; 'mid-sized firm'; 'the practice areas are exactly what I wanted to do'; 'the niche areas of law that this firm operated in really appealed to me'; 'interesting industry sectors'; 'flexible training system allowing you to pick up work from any firm department'; 'good experience on the vac scheme'

- **Best thing about the firm?** 'The work that we do'; 'the people'; 'good-quality work which you don't have to give up when you move seats'; 'friendly atmosphere'; 'complex and often very topical litigation'; 'ongoing training at least once a week on contract law and shipping law'; 'independence of trainees and informality'

- **Worst thing about the firm?** 'Could do with more structure to work allocation as some trainees are very quiet while others are given more work despite already being at full capacity'; 'nothing ever seems particularly well organised'; 'pay doesn't always reflect the longer hours worked'

- **Best moment?** 'Running a sizeable case single-handedly for a partner and coming up with a legal point which ultimately led to the client winning the dispute'; 'attending a hearing within a month of starting'; 'working on a high-profile ship casualty'; 'drafting a supplemental agreement to amend a facility agreement'

- **Worst moment?** 'Spending most of a seat doing very little for that department'; 'translating several hundred documents into English'; 'paginating trial bundles by hand'; 'writing a presentation to a tight deadline in an area I knew nothing about'

A day in the life of...

... Sang Joon Park second-year trainee, Ince & Co LLP

Departments to date: Trainees can work accross all of the firm's business groups in each of their seats

University: University College London **Degree:** Law LLB, International Business Law LLM

6.45am: I start the day early today as I have a squash match against a friend working in the City. We try to squeeze in a few games two to three times a week to keep relatively fit.

8.30am: I arrive at my desk, armed with some coffee, and check my to-do list. I am currently assisting a partner in preparing for an LMAA arbitration which is due to start in a matter of weeks. The case concerns corrosion damage to the tank tops after a cargo of wet sulphur was shipped on board. We are acting for the owner of the vessel claiming repair costs against the charterer who was contractually obliged to inform us about the nature of the cargo. I receive a call from counsel. We discuss what amendments need to be made to the hearing bundles, including a supplementary witness statement from one of our appointed experts. I prepare a number of inserts, and update the bundles and indices. Having checked for any errors, I draft a cover email, attaching the supplementary expert report and serve it to the solicitors acting for the other side.

10.30am: Ince's training contract does not restrict trainees to solely undertake work from the department in which they are sat. My current seat in the energy group has given me the opportunity to work on a dispute regarding an oil and gas project (an area of personal interest). Our client is owed a large sum of money for the work they performed under a contract to install, operate and maintain a production facility in Iraq for a large operator company. I have been asked to draft a letter before action to the other side. I draft the letter and send it to the partner for review and also send a brief email to the client informing them that by the end of the day they will receive the letter to review. I also start drafting the claim submissions in preparation for commencing proceedings.

12.30pm: I briefly stop for lunch in the firm's canteen. A lot of the trainees try to take lunch at about the same time each day as it's a good chance to catch up.

1.30pm: Returning to my desk, I review a number of new emails regarding the upcoming arbitration. Counsel has made a number of requests. I am asked to first draft a document which details all of the issues as set out in our pleadings, and summarise the differing opinions on these issues according to the various witnesses and experts. I work through the witness statements, taking note of their evidence and incorporating this into the document.

4.00pm: I continue drafting the claim submissions for the oil and gas dispute. This task can take time, depending on the complexity of the case. However, as this is a simple debt recovery claim, I can navigate through most of the documents fairly quickly and draft the particulars of claim accordingly.

The client has also sent through further relevant documents which will help me to plead their claim in full. I submit the draft to the lead partner for review.

6.00pm: Along with billable work, trainees are often tasked with writing articles about contemporaneous legal topics or cases which

> **'My current seat in the energy group has given me the opportunity to work on a dispute regarding an oil and gas project.'**

may be of interest to our clients. I receive an internal case update which mentions a Supreme Court decision in relation to contract law. I visit the office of the partner who is responsible for co-ordinating these articles for our clients, and have a discussion about the case and its relevance to our clients in the energy sector. She asks me to review the case and draft a case commentary tomorrow.

7.30pm: Tonight is Ince drinks. The firm regularly hosts drinks on the balcony of our offices. It is always a relaxed and enjoyable occasion (especially if the weather is nice).

graduates.incelaw.com

About the firm

Address: Aldgate Tower, 2 Leman Street, London E1 8QN
Telephone: 020 7481 0010   **Fax:** 020 7481 4968
Website: www.incelaw.com
Email: recruitment@incelaw.com
Twitter: @incelaw

International senior partner: Jan Heuvels

Other offices: Beijing, Cologne, Dubai, Hamburg, Hong Kong, Le Havre, Monaco, Paris, Piraeus, Shanghai, Singapore.

Who we are: With 140 years of experience we're one of the oldest law firms in the City, but we're not bound by tradition. We've built our success by always taking an innovative approach, looking for new ways to apply legal strategies and create new law.

What we do: Ince has five core business groups: aviation, energy, insurance and reinsurance, international trade and shipping. We are frequently at the forefront of developments in contract and tort law.

What we're looking for: 2(1) or equivalent at degree level, AAB or equivalent at A Level. Proactive, academic, enthusiastic about our practice areas and expertise.

What you'll do: From the moment you step through the door you'll be given real responsibility for real cases. Although your work will be supervised by partners, you'll also enjoy a high level of autonomy. Because we don't have rigid departmental structures, you're encouraged to approach partners and get involved in all aspects of our practice areas throughout your training contract.

Perks: Private healthcare scheme, permanent health insurance, interest-free season ticket loan, Ride 2 Work scheme, fitness subsidy (firm contributes up to £30p/mth for any gym or other fitness-related membership), InceFlex – flexible benefits scheme – offers additional benefits via salary sacrifice, such as dental, insurance, travel insurance, critical illness cover and buying/selling holiday.

Sponsorship: Fees for future trainees. GDL: £6,500 for study within London and Guildford and £6,000 for elsewhere. LPC: £7,000 for study within London and Guildford and £6,500 for elsewhere.

Facts and figures

Total partners: 90
Other fee-earners: 250
Total trainees: 18 (London)

Trainee places available for 2019: approximately 10
Applications received pa: 650
Percentage interviewed: 10%

First year salary: £37,000
Second year salary: £41,000
Newly qualified salary: £62,000

Turnover in 2015: £79.4m (-8% from 2014)
(see legalbusiness.co.uk for full financial information)

Application process

Apply to: Shalini Chawla, recruitment and resourcing manager.
How: Online application via graduates.incelaw.com.
When: By 31 July 2017.
What's involved: One interview with one member of HR and one partner. Before the interview commences, the candidate is asked to complete a spelling and grammar test, drafting exercise and prepare for an intray exercise. The intray exercise is then discussed during the interview, after the motivation/CV-type questions.

Vacation schemes

Spring: Apply by 31 January 2017.

INCE & CO | INTERNATIONAL LAW FIRM

Irwin Mitchell LLP

Riverside East, 2 Millsands, Sheffield S3 8DT

Survey results *(marks out of 100%)*

Satisfied in your job?	78
Firm living up to expectations?	78
High quality of work?	84
Enough client contact?	82
Stress-free?	60
Happy work/life balance?	78
Friendly firm?	88
Great social life?	76
Good vacation scheme?	77
Confident you'll be kept on?	72
Good remuneration?	66
Diverse firm?	83

 **verdict**

Irwin Mitchell offers a 'uniquely tailored training contract', with the 'two streams' of personal legal services and business legal services prompting one respondent to summarise that 'my training contract is focused on the type of work and clients I want to experience'. The firm attracts many recruits keen to 'focus on personal legal services at a top-tier national firm' with a 'market-leading position in 'family, personal injury and public law'. Trainees also note that 'the corporate side of the business is growing rapidly', and that Irwin Mitchell is an 'ambitious firm with a clear strategy'. We are told that 'the variety of clients makes for a well-rounded experience', and work highlights include 'seeing a transaction through to completion' and 'spotting an issue that ultimately knocked 50% off the value of a multi-million euro dispute'. The 'lack of communication from top-level management' is identified as a problem, as 'sometimes you are kept waiting for information in relation to the next seats that you are going to'. The 'approachability of staff at all levels' is appreciated, as is the fact that 'partners actually care about you and your development'. The 'comprehensive training' also ensures that trainees experience 'direct client contact and substantive work'. The 'emphasis on time recording' is a real drag for some trainees, and there is a perception that 'the NQ salary and employee benefits do not match the competitor firms that IM is trying to rival'. This is partially offset by the 'healthy attitude to work/life balance' and the 'good socials' enjoyed by the current intake. For the chance to experience a training contract at a firm with 'ambitious and acquisitive growth plans', head to Irwin Mitchell.

If the firm were a fictional character it would be...

Mace Windu (Star Wars) – calm and patient, but can quickly destroy obstacles when required

The firm

In November 2015, Irwin Mitchell announced the takeover of former *Lex 100* entrant Thomas Eggar, a £40m firm with six offices in the South East. The newly-expanded Irwin Mitchell has acquired several smaller firms in recent years, and has refreshed its brand to stress its credentials as a commercial firm and a market leader for personal injury and clinical negligence claims. The firm was crowned Private Client Team of the Year at the *Legal Business* Awards 2016.

The deals

Advised BlackRock Workspace Property Trust on its £32m disposal of a portfolio of four light industrial properties to Westbrook Partners; represented the Intrepid Brewing Company in a trade mark dispute with Greene King; advised ABN AMRO Commercial Finance on the provision of a funding package to Excel Components; advised EasyJet on a number of tribunal claims; represented the families of 16 British citizens who were killed, as well as many of the injured victims of the 2015 Tunisia terrorist attacks.

The clients

3 Sovereign Square; Canal & River Trust; Decathlon UK; General Medical Council; HSBC; Jones Lang LaSalle; Metro Bank; National Grid; Santander UK; Sheffield City Trust.

The star performers

Top-ranking departments according to *The Legal 500* (see legal500.com for more details)
Asset based lending; Charities and not-for-profit; Clinical negligence: claimant; Commercial property; Contentious trusts and probate; Corporate and commercial; Court of Protection; Crime: fraud; Education; Family; IT and telecoms; Insolvency and corporate recovery; Intellectual property; Local government; Pensions; Personal injury: claimant; Personal tax, trusts and probate; Professional negligence: claimant; Property litigation; Public sector: education.

- **Why did you choose this firm over any others?** 'Friendly atmosphere on vacation scheme and again at partner interview'; 'I wanted to work at a claimant firm'; 'I attended an open evening and found the firm friendly and welcoming'; 'full-service firm so lots of options for departments to train in'; 'excellent vacation scheme'; 'friendly and supportive staff'; 'unparalleled litigation experience'; 'the clear ambition to grow'; 'national firm with strong regional presence'

- **Best thing about the firm?** 'Focus on business development'; 'friendships that have grown from working relationships'; 'the quality and variety of work'; 'proactive and forward thinking'; 'being treated as a person with knowledge and skills'; 'snack trolley'; 'good socials'; 'genuine passion to get the best for their clients'; 'fruit bowl Monday and biscuit Thursdays is a nice bonus!'

- **Worst thing about the firm?** 'Trainees do not integrate between the north and south'; 'lack of supervision'; 'offices are not particularly glamorous'; 'no canteen'; 'limited international opportunities'; 'the IT system is pretty bad'; 'there is not a lot of choice about what seats you complete'; 'the TV adverts'

- **Best moment?** 'Telling a client his claim was successful'; 'when a case I was working on settled and appeared in the press'; 'running own files'; 'receiving good feedback from a notoriously tough partner'; 'a supervising fee-earner asking for and listening to comments on an area where I have previous industry experience'; attending an inquest'

- **Worst moment?** 'Struggling with time management'; 'messing up on seemingly simple tasks'; 'starting a research task for a partner at 9pm'; 'uncertainty around seat placements'; 'administrative work'; 'dealing with IT'; 'working very late on my second day'; 'having to spend four months in a seat I did not want to be in'

Why Irwin Mitchell?

Three associates share why they decided to join Irwin Mitchell

Hayley Johnson
BLS associate, banking and finance, Sheffield

I joined Irwin Mitchell to assist with setting up a new team at a time when many other law firms were not investing or recruiting in the business legal services space. The opportunity to join Irwin Mitchell presented an exciting challenge for me personally, as well as a really good way to progress my career with a major national law firm with a strong foundation and an established reputation. It was exciting to join a firm with a clear ambition to develop its business legal services division and a developed strategy to do so. I wanted to be part of a team working together on a national basis to provide the best possible service to business clients and joining Irwin Mitchell gave me the opportunity to achieve this.

Nicola Meier
PLS associate, personal injury, Southampton

I joined Irwin Mitchell back in 2010 from another firm and at the time I remember being attracted by the prospect of working for a market leader with a pioneering approach. I was also impressed by Irwin Mitchell's reputation as being an innovative and forward-thinking firm, with real expertise in personal injury work. Six and a half years on, I can say that joining Irwin Mitchell has given me a fantastic opportunity to specialise in a really rewarding area of law and to progress my career. I initially joined the London office, but relocated to head up a new team on the South coast in Southampton. The firm's commitment to delivering exceptional service to each and every client is impressive and the working environment is fantastic – my colleagues are all very friendly and a good work/life balance is actively encouraged.

Ravi Francis
private wealth associate, London

"My decision to join Irwin Mitchell was driven by a number of factors. The foremost of these was that it has such a strong and long-standing reputation for private client and tax. This has grown and improved further still since I joined, and the recent launch of Irwin Mitchell Private Wealth promises very exciting times ahead.

The second reason was that the firm has a large number of market-leading experts, both within my practice area and across the firm. This not only offers the best opportunities for learning, but that strength in depth also adds credibility and convenience to our offering to clients. Simply put, I wanted to be on the same team as these people.

Finally, the combination of the above means that the firm is able to attract some of the best clients out there; it is still very exciting

> '**It was exciting to join a firm with a clear ambition to develop its business legal services division and a developed strategy to do so.**'

and satisfying to work on such prominent, technically challenging and high-value client matters, and in a highly specialised area like international tax, those opportunities can only be found at a handful of firms.

www.irwinmitchell.com/graduates

About the firm

Address: Riverside East, 2 Millsands, Sheffield S3 8DT
Telephone: 0144 276 7777
Website: www.irwinmitchell.com
Email: graduaterecruitment@irwinmitchell.com
Twitter: @IMgraduates

Group chief executive: Andrew Tucker

Other offices: Birmingham, Bristol, Cambridge, Chichester, Gatwick, Leeds, London, Manchester, Newbury, Newcastle, Southampton.

Who we are: Irwin Mitchell is a national firm, and one of the few law firms to provide a diverse range of legal services to business and private clients.

What we do: We offer a broad range of personal and business legal services to a range of businesses and private individuals.

What we're looking for: Those who have the ability to work under pressure, be creatively minded, use their initiative and have strong problem-solving skills.

What you'll do: Trainees will have three training seats and a qualification seat, giving them the chance to gain practical experience in diverse areas of law, in their selected stream.

Perks: 25 days' holiday, contributory pension scheme, health plan, death in service cover, critical illness cover, recognition scheme, season ticket loan, two CSR days a year, sports team sponsorship.

Sponsorship: If your application is successful, we will meet all the fees associated with your LPC and, if applicable, your GDL if you have not started or completed your studies when offered a training contract. We also provide a maintenance grant to help you through your studies.

Facts and figures

Total partners: 293
Other fee-earners: 1,480
Total trainees: 122

Trainee places available for 2019: 50
Applications received pa: 2,000+
Percentage interviewed: 13.7%

First year salary: £25,000 (regional), £36,000 (London)
Second year salary: £27,000 (regional), £38,000 (London)
Newly qualified salary: Dependent on the office and division you qualify in.

Turnover in 2015: £210.6m (+4% from 2014)
Profits per equity partner: £600,000 (+5%)
(see legalbusiness.co.uk for full financial information)

Application process

Apply to: Nicola Stanley (graduate recruitment manager).
How: Online application form.
When: By 30 June 2017 for 2019 contracts.
What's involved: Online application, video interview and assessment centre.

Vacation schemes

Summer: 19-30 June and 3-14 July 2016 (apply by 15 January 2017).

Jones Day

21 Tudor Street, London EC4Y 0DJ

Lex 100 Winner

See categories below
and tables from page 69

Survey results *(marks out of 100%)*

Satisfied in your job?	85
Firm living up to expectations?	84
High quality of work?	85
Enough client contact?	83
Stress-free?	61
Happy work/life balance?	58
Friendly firm?	90
Great social life?	88
Good vacation scheme?	93
Confident you'll be kept on?	82
Good remuneration?	85
Diverse firm?	80

 verdict

The 'non-rotational training scheme' is the stand-out reason current trainees chose to pursue a training contract with Jones Day. The US firm has an 'individual and entrepreneurial approach to the training contract' which offers a different experience to the rest of the market. Trainees can test the water in a 'lot of different departments without the commitment of a six-month seat' so you 'never risk not getting the seat you want'. The 'unique training system' allows trainees to 'take control and tailor' their own training which is 'exciting, but clearly not for everyone'. It is also notable that many trainees who chose the firm completed their 'vacation scheme here and loved it', and the firm is a **Lex 100 Winner** in this category, securing a second win for social life. Trainees are not 'spoon-fed' but have the 'liberty' to take 'significant control over which department and individuals' they want to work for. The 'biggest challenge of this system is to ensure you get a structured training' so you must 'remain pro-active in seeking the appropriate training and ask relevant questions'. Trainees grumble about the normal training contract problems such as 'late nights', 'hard days' and 'creating bundles'. Top trainee moments include the 'week-long trainee trip to Washington DC for the new lawyers' academy', 'running an entire project for a bank under supervision of a partner' and 'a completion in Vienna'. The firm has a 'fierce global presence' with 43 offices worldwide from Tokyo to Madrid. Self-starters looking for a variety of departments and a different approach to training should take a closer look at Jones Day.

If the firm were a fictional character it would be...

Eli Gold (The Good Wife) – charismatic and confident, and means business

The firm

Jones Day employs over 4,200 lawyers in 42 offices around the world, marking it out as one of the world's largest law firms. The firm is a popular choice for blue-chip companies seeking advice on a range of corporate and commercial matters, including M&A, investment funds and restructurings. The firm's London office is its largest outside of the US and opened in 1986.

The deals

Advised Amdipharm Mercury on its $3.5bn divestiture by Cinven to Concordia Healthcare; advised Macquarie European Infrastructure Fund on the sale of Wightlink Ferries to Balfour Beatty Infrastructure Partners; defended MasterCard in the interchange fees litigation; assisted BNP Paribas with its acquisition of a £15bn equity derivatives portfolio from RBS, which involved a review of 900 transactions; advised Bité Finance on its outstanding €200m senior notes.

The clients

AB Electrolux; Bank of America Merrill Lynch; Blackstone; CBRE; Goldman Sachs; Greystar; Inflexion; Paperlinx; The Riverside Company; Standard Bank.

The star performers

Top-ranking departments according to *The Legal 500* (see legal500.com for more details)

Asset based lending; Bank lending – investment grade debt and syndicated loans; Banking litigation: investment and retail; Commercial contracts; Commercial litigation; Competition litigation; Corporate crime (including fraud, bribery and corruption); Corporate restructuring and insolvency; Corporate tax; Derivatives and structured products; EU and competition; Financial services (non-contentious/regulatory); Fraud: civil; International arbitration; M&A: upper mid-market and premium deals, £250m+; Private equity: transactions: Mid-cap deal capability; Private funds; Property finance; Real estate funds; Trade finance.

- **Why did you choose this firm over any others?** 'Suited to those who have experience from other industries'; 'non-rotational training system'; 'the atmosphere at the social events'; 'impressive partners at interview'; 'global presence'; 'the work trainees get involved with provides exposure to a high level of responsibility early on'

- **Best thing about the firm?** 'The respect with which you are treated as a trainee'; 'the week-long new lawyers' academy in Washington, D.C'; 'feeling free to manage your own work'; 'the quality of clients'; 'sharing an office with a fellow trainee'; 'the ease with which you can build relationships with lawyers at all levels of qualification'; 'the lack of hierarchy'

- **Worst thing about the firm?** 'Not having the experience to know when you should not take any more work on'; 'appraisal process'; 'the pay is starting to lag behind other US firms'; 'occasional lack of support'; 'feeling a little lost when there is no work'; 'lack of secondment opportunities for trainees'

- **Best moment?** 'Being personally rung up by the CEO of a client to congratulate me on a negotiation'; 'key role in a big M&A deal'; 'completing my first deal on my own'; 'following a certain litigation matter from the beginning to the end'; 'a completion in Vienna'

- **Worst moment?** 'Reviewing a prospectus until 4am'; 'the periods where you are searching for work'; 'eating lunch at the desk has to be the most miserable thing'; 'having two or three associates expect the majority of my time on any particular day and trying to make it work'

A day in the life of...

... Katie Brown first-year trainee, Jones Day

University: LSE
Degree: Law

8.30am: I cycle into work and arrive early to catch up on things before the office gets busy. I grab some breakfast from our in-house café, then head up to my office. I received some emails overnight from the other side (based in the Middle East) of a corporate restructuring I am working on. They raised queries on one of the transaction documents so I draft a response and make a note to speak to the supervising partner about it when he gets in.

9.30am: There is a bi-weekly team meeting at 10.00am for an initial public offering (IPO) I have just started working on. An IPO is the first sale of a company's shares to the public and leads to its flotation on a stock market such as the London Stock Exchange (LSE). My role is carrying out due diligence (reviewing lots of documents) on the company and drafting the prospectus for investors containing the company's financial and business information. I spend the next half hour reviewing drafts of our due diligence report and the prospectus and noting points to mention in the meeting.

10.30am: After the meeting I buy some homemade carrot cake from an internal bake sale raising money for Bravery Boxes (a charity founded by one of our lawyers) and spend the rest of the morning working on the IPO documents. This is my first ever experience working with our capital markets team so everything is new to me. I list my questions as I work on the drafts and pop in before lunch

to see the associate also working on the deal. He happily answers my questions and explains a bit more about the IPO.

12.30pm: The weather is great so a few of us trainees meet in the lobby and walk across to sit and eat lunch in the gardens of Inner Temple.

1.15pm: I catch the supervising partner on the Middle East deal and discuss my draft response with him. He agrees with my suggested position and asks me to run it by the client before I respond to the other side. I email the client when I get back to my desk. The client has some questions about the approach so calls me to discuss. I provide an explanation, the client confirms he is happy with my draft so I send this to the other side. I've been on the deal from the beginning and understand it well, so I have been given a lot of responsibility communicating both with the other side and the client, which makes the work really enjoyable.

3.30pm: Because of the firm's non-rotational system, I am working on a number of different matters across departments. I now receive an email from the seller on a real estate transaction I am working on with replies to our preliminary enquiries. I circulate them to the construction, environmental and planning specialists on the deal for their review. I then speak to the associate involved

about replies I think may be important. The seller has also sent through some tax documentation so I print this out and go to one of our tax associates to ask him about it. I am responsible for co-ordinating the Jones Day deal team and keeping all enquiries and responses recorded in a table, so I spend the rest of the afternoon making sure it's updated.

> 'This is my first ever experience working with our capital markets team so everything is new to me.'

6.00pm: The day is winding down so I make sure I've answered all emails arriving throughout the day and write a 'to-do' list for tomorrow. I check whether any of the associates I'm working with needs anything else doing.

6.30pm: A few of my colleagues are heading down to Tooting Bec lido tonight for a practice swim and run in preparation for the Jones Day triathlon in a few weeks. I've been roped into the relay team for the swimming leg, so I grab my wetsuit and head downstairs to meet my fellow triathletes.

www.jonesdaylondon.com

About the firm

Address: 21 Tudor Street, London EC4Y 0DJ
Telephone: 020 7039 5959   **Fax:** 020 7039 5999
Website: www.jonesdaylondon.com
Email: recruit.london@jonesday.com
Facebook: www.facebook.com/JonesDayGraduatesUK

Partner in charge – London: John Phillips

Other offices: Continental Europe, Asia, US, Latin America, Middle East, Asia Pacific.

Who we are: Jones Day is a truly global law firm, with 44 offices in major centres of business and finance throughout the world. Our 2,500 lawyers have vast transactional and contentious experience and our unique system of governance contributes to our perennial ranking as among the world's best in client service.

What we do: Our lawyers address demanding and complex global matters, including: cross-border M&A; real estate; finance transactions (banking, capital markets, investment funds, private equity and structured finance); global disputes; and regulatory matters.

Facts and figures

Total partners: 60 approx
Other fee-earners: 120 approx
Total trainees: 40 approx

Trainee places available for 2019: 20
Applications received pa: 1,600
Percentage interviewed: 20%

First year salary: £45,000 (2016)
Second year salary: £50,000 (2016)
Newly qualified salary: £85,000 (2016)

What we're looking for: Successful candidates want to work on global deals and become partners of the future – not just qualify with us; are predicted (or have gained) a 2(1) in any degree discipline; have strong intellectual and analytical ability as well as good communication skills; and demonstrate resourcefulness, drive and dedication. Over half our trainees are non-law graduates and 30% were graduates or postgraduates when they applied to us.

What you'll do: The firm operates a unique, non-rotational system of training in which trainees can work across different practice areas simultaneously. This allows for early responsibility and faster development of potential.

Perks: Private healthcare, season ticket loan, group life cover, salary sacrifice schemes and personal pension.

Sponsorship: GDL and LPC paid, plus £9,000 maintenance grant per year of study. Fast-track LPC for sponsored students (mid-August to end-February) with a six month gap thereafter before training starts in September.

Application process

Apply to: Manager, trainee recruitment/development.
How: Online at www.jonesdaylondon.com from 1 September 2016.
When: By 13 January 2017 for a placement and 2019 training contract. We expect to recruit all trainees from our placement candidates.
What's involved: Online application; academic reference; two-partner interview. (No assessment centre, no psychometric testing; no video interviews.)

Vacation schemes

Two week periods in each of:
Winter: December 2016 (apply by 28 October 2016).
Spring: March 2017 (apply by 16 December 2016).
Summer: July 2017 (apply by 13 January 2017).

K&L Gates LLP

One New Change, London EC4M 9AF

Lex 100 Winner

See categories below
and tables from page 69

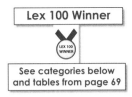

Survey results *(marks out of 100%)*

Satisfied in your job?	81
Firm living up to expectations?	83
High quality of work?	79
Enough client contact?	68
Stress-free?	63
Happy work/life balance?	86
Friendly firm?	89
Great social life?	73
Good vacation scheme?	69
Confident you'll be kept on?	74
Good remuneration?	77
Diverse firm?	83

 verdict

K&L Gates has earned 'international prestige' and is a 'rapidly expanding firm' with an 'inviting atmosphere'. The 'small trainee intake' results in 'early responsibility', 'good levels of client contact' and 'high-quality work'. Trainees can 'shape' their own 'contract experience' as their 'input and opinions are valued'. There are weekly training sessions that help guide the trainees, and supervisors provide an 'unrivalled level of support'. The 'friendly, inclusive approach' makes it 'very easy' for trainees to 'integrate into departments and the firm as a whole'. There is a 'real buzz in the meeting rooms with clients' but 'without the cut-throat atmosphere'. As a result of the 'flat hierarchy', this is a 'collegiate working environment' where 'partners are approachable and colleagues are friendly'. Top trainee moments involve 'sealing a £100m deal', 'receiving responsibility for key documents on a corporate deal' and 'working on a high-profile fraud case'. 'Working late on Fridays' and 'bundling' are problems that trainees sometimes face, but on the whole the US firm offers 'competitive hours' that provide a 'good work/life balance', leading to a **Lex 100 Winner** medal. While a few trainees found nothing much to complain about, some trainees grumbled about the fact that they can't choose the 'first seat', and less seriously a few lamented the 'standard of the coffee'. Despite the 'exposure and interaction with the international offices', there is also a 'disappointing lack of international opportunities' available. Still, for those looking for an international firm which maintains a 'nurturing and caring environment', K&L Gates could be the perfect fit.

If the firm were a fictional character it would be...

Nathan Drake (Uncharted) – funny, intelligent and very good at what it does

The firm

K&L Gates has gradually expanded from its US heartland to become a large international firm with offices in the Americas, Asia-Pacific, Europe and the Middle East. Munich became office number 46 in July 2016. The firm is full-service, an offering which includes representing major clients on an array of corporate, finance and property matters. In London, the firm has over 50 partners and over 100 fee-earners in total.

The deals

Advised CRH on its purchase of Lafarge's UK business, a necessary condition of the Holcim-Lafarge merger; acted for The Central Bank of Ecuador in Privy Council proceedings involving claims of $579m; advised LKQ Corporation on its €1bn acquisition of Rhiag-Inter Auto Parts Italia from Apax; advised Trinity Mirror on the highly publicised Operations Elveden and Golding; advised corporate service provider Capita on the restructuring of Ukrexim Bank's $1.48bn LPN programme.

The clients

3D Systems; Cenkos Securities; Deutsche Bank; Eaton Vance; Electrical Geodesics; Laing O'Rourke; Lucozade Ribena Suntory; Panmure Gordon; QInvest; William Hill.

The star performers

Top-ranking departments according to *The Legal 500* (see legal500.com for more details)
Commercial contracts; Corporate crime (including fraud, bribery and corruption); Debt capital markets; Derivatives and structured products; EU and competition; Financial services (contentious); Flotations: small and mid-cap; Fraud: civil; Fraud: white-collar crime; Gaming and betting; Health and safety; Infrastructure (including PFI and PPP); Investment funds: Hedge funds; International arbitration; Islamic finance; M&A: mid-market, £50-£250m; Partnership; Retail funds; Securitisation; Travel: regulatory and commercial.

- **Why did you choose this firm over any others?** 'The office has incredible views of London'; 'quality of training'; 'the variety of seats on offer'; 'international nature of the firm'; 'inviting atmosphere'; 'high level of responsibility'; 'familiarity with it from past experience'; 'American'; 'good levels of client contact'; 'a good balance of high-quality work without a cut-throat environment'; 'smaller trainee intake'

- **Best thing about the firm?** 'The firm is very inclusive'; 'friendly colleagues'; 'fantastic on-site canteen that makes delicious lunches'; 'international work'; 'friendly atmosphere makes it very easy to integrate into your department and the firm more widely'; 'the friendliness and camaraderie of its employees'; 'small trainee intake allows for good levels of responsibility'

- **Worst thing about the firm?** 'The coffee is quite possibly the worst thing I have ever tasted'; 'the firm's marketing is very poor'; 'you cannot choose your first seat'; 'lacks proper firm-organised events'; 'seat selection could be more transparent'; 'the lack of international seat opportunities'

- **Best moment?** 'Attending a client meeting with barristers'; 'attending a week-long inquest where I was able to meet the witnesses, barrister, and the client'; 'being praised for my contribution to a statement of reply'; 'closing a multi-jurisdictional deal that only myself and a senior associate had worked on'; 'involvement in drafting commercial contracts for an international client'

- **Worst moment?** 'Working late on the night of the Christmas party'; 'a trial in litigation that was severely understaffed due to costs restrictions'; 'PSC training'; 'having almost all the printers break while working on a weekend'; 'rushing last-minute work after having a whole free day'; 'IT training'

A day in the life of...

... Zara Din trainee, K&L Gates LLP

Departments to date: Commercial disputes, corporate
University: Warwick
Degree and class: Law, 2(1)

7.45am: I am in the middle of carrying out a due diligence exercise with a corporate associate. The deal is an exciting one, and relates to a share acquisition. On the way to work I check my BlackBerry, the associate has emailed asking me to update the master due diligence report with the findings from the department specialists. During a due diligence exercise, trainees manage the report: this involves communicating with the department specialists and feeding back to the team.

8.15am: I arrive at the office and make myself a coffee. I read the BBC news, check my emails and prioritise today's work. The same associate has asked me to review some documents in the data room. Some will need to be reviewed by specialists, so I speak to colleagues in other departments to arrange for this to be done.

8.30am: My supervising partner is in the middle of a deal, and asks if I can review a folder of ancillary documents sent by the other side. I print off the folder and discuss them with the partner. Once agreed and initialled, I scan them back to the associate on the other side.

9.30am: I update the due diligence report. It is my job to stay on top of updates and to be alert to any red flags that have been raised.

10.00am: I review some of the new documents in the data room, which I discuss with the associate and then summarise in the report.

10.30am: An email has come in from a client regarding an insolvency claim. Since this matter is a small one, the partner has given me the opportunity to directly liaise with the client. The firm try to give us as much responsibility as possible. The matter may involve a litigation claim, so the corporate partner asks if I can speak to a litigation partner. The firm's open-door policy means that I feel at ease when talking with colleagues from other departments, and partners are generous with their time. I draft an email to the client.

11.30am: We have recently been instructed by a Japanese client who is working on an intra-group re-organisation. An associate asks if I can assist with a share purchase agreement. A week earlier I produced the first draft of an asset purchase agreement, which was a great learning experience. As a trainee, you are rarely given a task that you have done before, but there is always someone willing to provide guidance. The associate asks me to produce a first draft of the share purchase agreement. This is also new to me but I am keen to have a go.

1.00pm: I grab lunch in the downstairs canteen and catch up with trainees and associates.

2.00pm: I send a copy of the first draft of the share purchase agreement to the associate. He asks if I can produce the stock transfer forms and the share certificates. I draft the forms and certificates and grab a tea from the kitchen.

3.30pm: The associate and I review my documents for the intra-group re-organisation.

4.15pm: A colleague in a US office informs me that a client is intending to do a rush equity offering. He asks for the board minutes in relation to the client's English subsidiary. I locate the minutes and send them to him.

> 'Since this matter is a small one, the partner has given me the opportunity to directly liaise with the client.'

4.30pm: The partner I sit with asks me to research electronic signatures. He needs to know when they are a valid method of executing documents. I look into Law Society guidance and read around the area.

5.30pm: I attend one of the regular seminars that the firm hosts with external speakers and current and prospective clients. The seminar is followed by drinks with the other attendees, which allows trainees to meet with clients.

6.45pm: I make sure that I am not needed for anything else, then I head over to Soho to meet friends. Later I check my BlackBerry and make a note of an email to deal with tomorrow.

www.klgates.com/careers

About the firm

Address: One New Change, London EC4M 9AF
Telephone: 020 7648 9000   **Fax:** 020 7648 9001
Website: www.klgates.com
Email: trainee.recruitment@klgates.com

Administrative partner: Antony Griffiths

Other offices: Anchorage, Austin, Beijing, Berlin, Boston, Brisbane, Brussels, Charlotte, Charleston, Chicago, Dallas, Doha, Dubai, Fort Worth, Frankfurt, Harrisburg, Hong Kong, Houston, Los Angeles, Melbourne, Miami, Milan, Munich, Newark, New York, Orange County, Palo Alto, Paris, Perth, Pittsburgh, Portland, Raleigh, Research Triangle Park, San Francisco, Sao Paulo, Seattle, Seoul, Shanghai, Singapore, Sydney, Taipei, Tokyo, Warsaw, Washington, Wilmington.

Who we are: K&L Gates represents leading global corporations, growth and middle-market companies, capital markets participants and entrepreneurs in every major industry group, as well as public sector entities, educational institutions, philanthropic organisations and individuals.

What we do: K&L Gates is active in the areas of corporate/M&A, capital markets, private equity, restructuring and insolvency, finance, derivatives, funds, antitrust, competition and trade regulation, real estate, planning and environment, intellectual property, media and sport, construction, insurance coverage, regulatory, tax, employment, litigation, international arbitration, white-collar crime and other forms of dispute resolution.

What we're looking for: We are looking for highly motivated, intellectually curious individuals with an interest in commercial law, looking for comprehensive training.

What you'll do: We have a thorough induction scheme consisting of weekly legal education seminars, workshops and a full programme of skills electives. Emphasis is placed on early responsibility and client contact. Pro bono and CSR activities are also encouraged.

Perks: Permanent health insurance, season ticket loan, 25 days of holiday, private health insurance, life insurance, subsidised sports club membership, pension, GP services.

Sponsorship: GDL fees paid, plus £5,000 maintenance grant, LPC fees paid plus £7,000 maintenance grant.

Facts and figures

Total partners: 55
Other fee-earners: 85
Total trainees: 17

Trainee places available for 2019: tbd
Applications received pa: 1,000
Percentage interviewed: 10

First year salary: £37,500 (2015)
Second year salary: £44,000 (2015)
Newly qualified salary: £68,000 (2015)

Application process

Apply to: Hayley Atherton, recruiting manager.
How: Online application.
When: Apply by 31 July 2017 for 2019 contracts.
What's involved: Online testing, full assessment centre and interview.

Vacation schemes

Summer: Apply by 31 January 2017.

Kennedys Law LLP

25 Fenchurch Avenue, London EC3M 5AD

Survey results *(marks out of 100%)*

Satisfied in your job?	76
Firm living up to expectations?	79
High quality of work?	82
Enough client contact?	77
Stress-free?	55
Happy work/life balance?	83
Friendly firm?	82
Great social life?	67
Good vacation scheme?	83
Confident you'll be kept on?	79
Good remuneration?	62
Diverse firm?	79
Good international secondments?	37

 verdict

Praised as 'one of the best insurance/reinsurance disputes firms in the City', Kennedys is considered a 'very reputable litigation firm' which offers trainees 'plenty of opportunities to do more than just sit at your desk with paperwork'. Examples of a 'good level of responsibility' handling 'high-quality work' include 'being able to run my own case from near start to finish, which ended up at trial', 'personally representing a client at an infant approval' and 'going to a settlement meeting in a multi-million pound case'. Tellingly, first experiences at the firm have been positive, as one respondent says 'I enjoyed the assessment day and felt that I fitted into the firm' while another tells us 'I did the vacation scheme here and loved it'. A complaint made is that the firm is 'quite London-centric', and that there can be a 'lack of interaction between offices'. Though the firm is primarily known for its insurance litigation work, respondents state that Kennedys 'has been growing rapidly for some time', is 'truly excellent in all divisions' and that 'high-quality work is available department-to-department'. Feedback reports that there can be a 'high-pressure environment' at times, perhaps due to 'billable targets for trainees being brought in'. Yet 'partners are willing to assist you with queries' and always 'let you know how well you did or what areas you need to improve on'. In this way, the firm 'really trusts its employees'. For the 'chance to work with people who are the best in the field' and to represent a 'wide client-base on high-profile matters', consider applying to Kennedys.

If the firm were a fictional character it would be...

Professor X (X-Men) – extremely intelligent, and an incorruptible force for good

The firm

Insurance specialist Kennedys has focused its international ambitions on Latin America and Scandinavia over the last twelve months. The firm has set up offices in Brazil, Peru and Denmark, and entered into local alliances in Argentina, Norway and Sweden. Kennedys posted a 7% revenue rise for the last financial year, and was named Legal Technology Team of the Year at the *Legal Business* Awards 2016.

The deals

Successfully defended a £5m birth injury claim against Barts Health NHS Trust; acted for Riverstone and Brit Insurance on behalf of an insured engineer, who allegedly negligently designed an industrial port development; advised Merlin Entertainment regarding the HSE investigation into an accident that occurred on a ride at Alton Towers theme park; represented Mitsui Insurance and Daiichi Sankyo in a class action concerning an alleged defect in a hypertension drug; advised key client Scarborough Group International on a major development near the centre of Manchester.

The clients

ACE; Chubb; Great Western Railway; Hilton Hotels; JD Wetherspoon; Medical Protection Society; Spire Healthcare; Touchstone Underwriting; Virgin Holidays; Volkerfitzpatrick.

The star performers

Top-ranking departments according to *The Legal 500* (see legal500.com for more details)
Aviation; Clinical negligence: defendant; Commercial litigation; Commercial property; Construction; Dispute resolution; Employment: employers; Environment; Health and safety; Insurance and reinsurance litigation; Licensing; Personal injury: defendant; Product liability: defendant; Professional negligence; Shipping; Sport; Rail; Travel: personal injury.

- **Why did you choose this firm over any others?** 'Due to the amount of insurance and litigation work'; 'great reputation'; 'clinical negligence team'; 'a leading insurance firm'; 'I did the vac scheme and enjoyed it hugely'; 'I had been a paralegal at the firm and really enjoyed it'; 'purely litigation-based practice'; 'the work/life balance is extremely good'; 'the opportunity to get involved work with top clients'

- **Best thing about the firm?** 'The range of clients'; 'the quality of work'; 'relaxed working environment'; 'people aren't stuffy'; 'free breakfast and fruit every day'; 'the working hours are fantastic'; 'high-end work'; 'good level of responsibility from the start'; 'the firm really trusts its employees'; 'I feel you can always ask someone for help'

- **Worst thing about the firm?** 'The amount of work is sometimes overwhelming'; 'lack of a regular international secondment'; 'lack of social events'; 'choosing seats can be a bit confusing as there is a lot of overlap in terms of work between the teams'; 'salary'; 'organisation'; 'poor IT system'; 'the great London/regional divide'

- **Best moment?** 'Spending three weeks at an inquest'; 'secondment opportunity and client contact following that'; 'visiting a major client to interview witnesses on my own'; 'running a file on my own and getting a great result for a client'; 'drafting and filing a last-minute application and winning it'; 'going to trial for a brilliant case which we won'

- **Worst moment?** 'Photocopying'; 'staying late at night to finish work'; 'preparing bundles for a trial'; 'having to work solidly over the course of a weekend to review a lengthy underwriting agreement'; 'sometimes having so much work that I've got very little feedback'

A day in the life of...

... Amber Jenner trainee, Kennedys Law LLP

Departments to date: Liability, healthcare
University: Reading University
Degree and class: Law, 2(1)

9.00am: I arrive at the office and check my emails. I respond to urgent messages and review my tasks for the day.

9.15am: A letter of response is due within two weeks. In order to allow sufficient time to obtain client approval, I review the evidence we have attained so far and decide what allegations from the letter of claim we should admit and which we should deny. Based on this, I then draft the letter of response and forward to the senior associate for approval.

11.30am: I draft a statement for a witness based on comments previously received from them and the documentation which supports their statement. After receiving approval from my supervisor, I forward it to the witness, asking them to review and comment as appropriate.

12.30pm: I am asked to review the proof provided by a claimant for the past losses they are claiming. I begin comparing the schedule of loss to the documents we have received, noting any issues along the way.

1.00pm: Over lunch, I attend a seminar on the recent advancements in prosthetics. The firm regularly organises lunchtime talks from barristers, experts and solicitors and

it is a great way to keep up with the latest developments in your practice area.

2.00pm: In an upcoming trial, we will be seeking permission from the courts to rely on witnesses via video links from various jurisdictions around the world. I review the CPR for the rules relating to video evidence and determine which authorities we require permission from to do this. I then start to contact these authorities to obtain such permission.

3.00pm: Authority has been received from a client to attend a settlement meeting with the claimant. I draft instructions to counsel to attend this meeting and ask them to provide updated guidance on their quantification of the claim.

3.30pm: I receive notification from chambers that the court has listed the trial in a matter. I note the date and draft witness summons for our experts and witnesses. I arrange for a cheque to be raised for the correct court fee and prepare the summons for hand delivery to court on the court run tomorrow.

4.45pm: The witness whose statement I drafted this morning calls me. They

wish to amend a small section of the statement but confirm they are happy with the remainder. I amend their statement and then resend it to the witness for final review and signature.

5.30pm: I am due to attend a conference with experts and counsel tomorrow morning. I therefore spend some time refreshing my

> 'I attend a seminar on the recent advancements in prosthetics. The firm regularly organises lunchtime talks.'

memory on the case and the key issues to be discussed. I then check my copy of the bundle for the conference, ensuring all documents required are included.

6.00pm: Drinks have been organised by some members of my team. I therefore leave the office and head to a bar in Leadenhall Market to meet my colleagues.

www.kennedyslaw.com/careers/graduates

About the firm

Address: 25 Fenchurch Avenue, London EC3M 5AD
Telephone: 020 7667 9667
Website: www.kennedyslaw.com
Email: hr.admin@kennedyslaw.com
Facebook: www.facebook.com/kennedystrainees
Twitter: https://twitter.com/KennedysLaw

Senior partner: Nick Thomas

Other offices: Auckland, Belfast, Birmingham, Brazil, Brussels, Cambridge, Chelmsford, Copenhagen, Dubai, Dublin, Edinburgh, Glasgow, Hong Kong, Lisbon, London, Madrid, Manchester, Miami, Moscow, Peru, Sheffield, Singapore, Sydney, Taunton.

Who we are: Kennedys is an international law firm with specialist expertise in litigation/dispute resolution and advisory services.

What we do: Our growing network of offices delivers straightforward legal solutions to the insurance, corporate and public sectors.

What we're looking for: As Kennedys has a vibrant and supportive working environment, we're looking for sociable and enthusiastic team players with commercial awareness.

What you'll do: You will be given a good level of responsibility early on, with support from a dedicated supervisor and formal training.

Perks: Permanent health insurance, pension, private medical insurance, life insurance, 25 days' holiday increasing to 27 after five years' service, interest-free season ticket loan, gym membership or subsidy, cycle-to-work scheme, childcare vouchers and an employee assistance programme.

Facts and figures

Total partners: 187
Other fee-earners: 646
Total trainees: 42

Trainee places available for 2019: 16
Applications received pa: 750
Percentage interviewed: 10%

First year salary: £25,000 – £34,000
Second year salary: £28,000 – £37,000
Newly qualified salary: Varied

Turnover in 2015: £129.9m (+1% from 2014)
Profits per equity partner: £410,000 (-2%)
(see legalbusiness.co.uk for full financial information)

Application process

Apply to: Nicola Standley.
How: Online application form.
When: By 31 July 2017 for 2019 contracts.
What's involved: Video interview, critical thinking test, assessment day.

Vacation schemes

Summer: Apply by 31 January 2017.

Kennedys
Legal advice in black and white

King & Wood Mallesons

10 Queen Street Place, London EC4R 1BE

Survey results *(marks out of 100%)*

Satisfied in your job?	69
Firm living up to expectations?	69
High quality of work?	72
Enough client contact?	62
Stress-free?	60
Happy work/life balance?	48
Friendly firm?	72
Great social life?	59
Good vacation scheme?	87
Confident you'll be kept on?	62
Good remuneration?	64
Diverse firm?	70
Good international secondments?	61

 **verdict**

King & Wood Mallesons combines 'great work' with clear 'areas of expertise'. The firm's 'corporate exposure' and 'prevalence in the international funds market' complement its 'global outlook' and this helps to ensure that trainees obtain a 'good level of responsibility'. Recruits report having 'a lot of client contact', and work highlights have included 'completing a large Chinese inbound investment deal', 'executing a faultless piece of complicated drafting' and 'playing a key part in a well-publicised and innovative deal'. Some respondents feel that the firm is 'still working out its direction post-combination', and while the 'legacy SJ Berwin work and clients' is a plus point, the 'flux due to the merger' results in a 'lack of firm-wide cohesiveness'. KWM's 'welcoming, interesting and enjoyable vacation scheme' earns plaudits, as do the 'approachable associates' who 'really care about your development as a trainee'. Indeed, the 'friendliness and approachability of all staff' is appreciated, and feedback states that 'some partners are truly fantastic' and 'the other trainees are a really good bunch of people'. A common complaint is that 'hours can be long' and 'sometimes face-time is necessary'. Trainees speak of 'leaving work at 2am on a Saturday', and 'being told off for leaving the office at 7pm the day before even though I had finished all my work.' The 'communication around seat allocations is poor' at times, but 'going on international secondment' is a 'brilliant opportunity' to 'gain exposure to another legal system'. The quality of training at the firm is deemed 'as good as, if not better than, market standards'. To experience life at a firm with a 'down-to-earth and modern feel', consider applying for a training contract at King & Wood Mallesons.

If the firm were a fictional character it would be...

Yan Naing Lee (Rush Hour) – has Hong Kong heritage, is full of courage and is famous around the world

The firm

King & Wood Mallesons is the first global law firm to be headquartered in Asia, and consists of more than 2,700 lawyers across 30 international offices. The London office is held in high regard for its real estate and finance practices. The firm opened a Cambridge office in March which will serve national and international clients. The firm was named TMT Team of the Year at the *Legal Business* Awards 2016.

The deals

Represented AA plc on the £1.1bn refinancing of its existing debt package; advised Morgan Stanley on updating its $5bn note, warrant and certificate programme; acted for Canadian convenience store chain Alimentation Couche-Tard on its NOK675m debut European bond; advised Golden Gate Capital on the non-US employment elements of its acquisition of The DOW Chemical Company's global Angus Chemicals business; assisted a consortium led by Macquarie with the refinancing of a portfolio of power projects comprising the Severn power plants, Baglan Bay and Sutton Bridge.

The clients

Amcor; Brit Group Services; British Land; China General Nuclear Power Group; FTI; Ladbrokes; Lion Capital; Morgan Stanley; Telstra; Universal Music Group.

The star performers

Top-ranking departments according to *The Legal 500* (see legal500.com for more details)

Brand management; Commercial contracts; Competition litigation; Commercial property; Corporate crime (including fraud, bribery and corruption); EU and competition; Environment; Equity capital markets; Financial services (contentious); Gaming and betting; M&A: upper mid-market and premium deals, £250m+; Planning; Property finance; Private equity: transactions: Mid-cap deal capability; Power (including electricity, nuclear and renewables); Private funds; Real estate funds; Securitisation; VAT and indirect tax; Venture capital.

- **Why did you choose this firm over any others?** 'Great vacation scheme'; 'international opportunities'; 'strong funds practice'; 'legacy SJ Berwin's reputation'; 'the firm's corporate focus'; 'not too big to be faceless'; 'the atmosphere of the London office'; 'corporate exposure'; prevalence in the international funds market'; 'down-to-earth and modern feel'; 'global outlook'

- **Best thing about the firm?** 'Generally friendly people'; 'free lunch'; 'the level of responsibility'; 'international opportunities'; 'the friendly environment'; 'some of the associates really care about your development as a trainee'; 'the other trainees are a really good bunch of people'; 'some partners are truly fantastic'; 'dynamic, modern firm'; 'a real open-door policy feel'; 'it's not overly hierarchical'; 'cohesive trainee cohort'; 'the training is excellent'

- **Worst thing about the firm?** 'Lack of firm-wide cohesiveness'; 'management of seat rotations'; 'trainee intakes were downsized a couple of years ago'; 'hours can be long'; 'certain seats are wildly over-subscribed and are impossible to get into'; 'some departments find it difficult to integrate trainees socially'; 'work is not always fairly distributed'; 'stressed and high-intensity people seem to abound'; 'limited secondment opportunities'

- **Best moment?** 'Being given the freedom to run my own closing'; 'getting some drafting experience'; 'stroking a penguin at a client event'; 'going on secondment to the Sydney office'; 'attending a client meeting'; 'the two-week induction'; 'completing an all-consuming deal'; 'the Christmas parties'; 'running small matters'; 'completing a deal which I had a lot of responsibility for'

- **Worst moment?** 'Too much work on too early'; 'having my offices hours fed back to me as not being long enough'; 'all-nighters'; 'missing most of the Christmas party'; 'getting in a taxi at 10.30pm to deliver board minutes'; 'large amounts of admin-heavy work'; 'the four-week induction period'

A day in the life of...

... David Richardson Corporate trainee, King & Wood Mallesons

University: Bristol
Degree: Philosophy

7.00am: The alarm clock goes off! I check my work email on my phone to see what has come in overnight, jump straight in the shower and have a bowl of porridge in front of BBC Breakfast.

8.45am: Arrive at my desk and begin actioning/responding to emails that came in since I left the office the night before. One of the emails is from lawyers in Hong Kong requesting information on the scope of work which I sent them last night. This has to be prioritised in order to ensure my response is received within normal business hours (Hong Kong is 7 hours ahead).

9.30am: My supervisor and I have a call with a major private equity client who is issuing instructions on a new acquisition. My responsibilities include taking detailed notes of the conversation and typing up into a file note that can be used for future reference.

10.45am: While on the earlier call, an associate I have been working for on another deal has emailed to ask if I can pop into her office to discuss due diligence. It turns out the client has now asked for an interim due diligence report to be provided to them by the end of the week. In addition, she asked me to prepare some corporate authorisation documents for a different matter that she can review later today. With little time to waste, I reach out to the other departments who feed in to the report letting them know of the new instructions, and set a deadline to receive their report input.

11.05am: Once I get back to my desk, my supervisor forwards me an email from a client asking some specific questions about one of their deals that completed 6 months ago. He asks me to urgently look through our archives and extract the relevant information in order to answer their queries.

11.45am: I begin drafting the corporate authorisations based on my associate's instructions with a view to getting the first drafts to her just after lunch.

12.30pm: Arrange to meet some of the trainees in my intake for lunch in Stanley's (the firm canteen), followed by a drink in the sun on the firm's roof garden terrace.

1.00pm: Get back to drafting the corporate authorisations that had been given to me in the morning.

2.00pm: I hand my draft corporate authorisations to my associate, and she reviews them. She makes some minor amendments to them before saying they are fine to send across to the other side's lawyers.

2.20pm: After sending off the corporate authorisations to the other side, I then print off 8 packs of documents required for a client meeting in our offices at 3.00pm.

2.50pm: I place the meeting bundles in the meeting room and wait at the first floor reception to greet the clients as they arrive.

3.00pm: Once everybody is here and the meeting has commenced, I take detailed

> 'I meet some of the trainees in my intake for lunch in Stanley's, followed by a drink in the sun on the firm's roof garden terrace.'

notes throughout. What was scheduled to be a two hour meeting turns out to be three.

6.15pm: Manage to get back to my desk to type up a file note on the meeting so it can be sent out to my supervisor and the client this same evening.

7.50pm: Rather than having free dinner in Stanley's, my arm is twisted by a couple of trainees in Finance to go out for Italian food and one or two glasses of claret.

http://careers.kwm.com/en-uk

About the firm

Address: 10 Queen Street Place, London EC4R 1BE
Telephone: 020 7111 2268 **Fax:** 020 7111 2000
Website: http://careers.kwm.com/en-uk
Email: graduate.recruitment@eu.kwm.com

Senior partner: Stephen Kon

Other offices: We have more than 30 offices worldwide across Asia, Hong Kong, Europe and the Middle East.

Who we are: King & Wood Mallesons is a new breed of law firm combining local depth with a global platform. Offering a different perspective to commercial thinking and the client experience, 2,700 lawyers across more than 30 international offices are working with clients every day to understand local challenges and navigate through regional complexity. With access to a global platform, we are providing commercial solutions and transforming the way legal services are delivered. How do we do this? By focusing not just on what you want, but how you want it. Working in close partnership with clients, our relationships are built on delivering a market-leading experience and providing access to deep legal insights and local connections, with the benefit of a global platform. As the only firm in the world able to practise PRC, Hong Kong, Australian, English, US and a significant range of European and Middle Eastern laws, we are opening doors and helping businesses to make smart choices to shape their future.

Facts and figures

Total partners: 84
Other fee-earners: 190
Total trainees: 60

Trainee places available for 2019/20: 30
Applications received pa: 1,600-2,000
Percentage interviewed: 20%

First year salary: £40,000
Second year salary: £44,000

What we do: Our ability to connect emerging opportunities with market-leading capability is pushing the frontiers of what can be achieved for our clients. We advise clients on the full spectrum of commercial, financial and specialist legal services, with a principle focus on: antitrust and regulatory, banking and finance, corporate M&A and securities, OR/litigation, projects (energy and resources), funds/private equity, real estate and tax.

What we're looking for: A strong academic record, an interest in law in a commercial context and a self-motivated team player with good analytical skills.

What you'll do: Training consists of four six-month seats in a variety of departments, including two corporate seats. Trainees will spend two seats (which may include a seat abroad) within the following areas: finance, mergers and acquisitions, equity capital markets, private equity, venture capital, investment funds and real estate.

Perks: Health insurance, season ticket loan, gym membership, pension scheme, free lunch, bicycle loan.

Sponsorship: Full fees paid for both GDL and LPC and a maintenance grant of up to £7,250 depending on location.

Application process

Apply to: Graduate recruitment team.
How: Online application via website.
When: By 31 July 2017 for contracts commencing September 2019/ March 2020.
What's involved: Two interviews and a case study.

Vacation schemes

Spring: Two weeks (apply by 31 January 2017).
Summer: Two-week schemes throughout the summer (apply by 31 January 2017).

KING & WOOD
MALLESONS

Kirkland & Ellis International LLP

30 St Mary Axe, London EC3A 8AF

Survey results *(marks out of 100%)*

Satisfied in your job?	80
Firm living up to expectations?	83
High quality of work?	87
Enough client contact?	79
Stress-free?	51
Happy work/life balance?	36
Friendly firm?	81
Great social life?	75
Good vacation scheme?	87
Confident you'll be kept on?	87
Good remuneration?	91
Diverse firm?	81
Good international secondments?	59

 **verdict**

A 'private equity specialist', Kirkland & Ellis represents 'some of the biggest and best fund managers in the global private equity industry', an industry which recruits believe to be 'very exciting to work in'. The vacation scheme served as a good introduction to the firm, with those who attended telling us of 'enjoyable work' within a 'welcoming atmosphere'. On the training contract there is 'early responsibility' in the form of 'exposure to real work', and the 'international transactions' are considered 'exciting deals' to be involved in. A 'fast learning curve' is to be expected with experiences including 'leading negotiations on a crucial point, and winning' and 'closing a complicated bespoke fund for a client under time pressure'. The firm's three **Lex 100 Winner** awards are for work quality, confidence in being kept on and remuneration satisfaction. Undoubtedly, the major criticism focuses on the 'long and unpredictable hours', which can translate into the 'expectation of 24/7 availability on BlackBerry'. Yet there is a 'laidback atmosphere' in the office, and lawyers are free to 'wear casual dress all day'. Respondents state that being part of a 'smaller intake' results in 'higher exposure to meaningful work' and the 'likelihood of quick progression'. This cause is aided by the firm's 'commitment to junior lawyers' who are 'treated as respected members of the team'. There is a 'work hard, play hard' philosophy at Kirkland & Ellis. 'Meeting clients for closing drinks' is a chance to unwind, as was the 'firm-wide dance at the Christmas party'. To work alongside 'brilliant and dynamic colleagues' at a firm with an 'entrepreneurial culture', apply to Kirkland & Ellis.

If the firm were a fictional character it would be...

Han Solo (Star Wars) – brash, supremely practical but is not afraid to take a risk

The firm

Kirkland & Ellis's London headcount has increased considerably in recent years. The US firm entered London in 1994, and earns plaudits for its private equity, investment funds, restructuring and litigation practices. The firm has a presence across Asia, North America and Europe.

The deals

Advised Bain Capital on the €485m financing of its acquisition of the Wittur Group; advised Pamplona Capital on the €315m financing of its acquisition of Partner in Pet Food from Advent International; advised Centerbridge Partners as majority lender on the debt-for-equity restructuring of Apcoa Car Parks; acted for TPG Growth on its buyout of Frank Recruitment Group; acted for Vista Equity Partners in the £725m acquisition of Advanced Computer Software Group.

The clients

Accenture; BNP Paribas; KKR Credit; Molson Coors Brewing; Montagu Private Equity; Oaktree Capital; Rhône Capital; Summit Partners; Teva Pharmaceuticals; Vitruvian.

The star performers

Top-ranking departments according to *The Legal 500* (see legal500.com for more details)
Acquisition finance; Commercial litigation; Corporate crime (including fraud, bribery and corruption); Corporate restructuring and insolvency; Corporate tax; EU and competition; Financial services (non-contentious/regulatory); High yield; International arbitration; M&A: upper mid-market and premium deals, £250m+; Private equity: transactions: Large-cap deal capability; Private funds.

- **Why did you choose this firm over any others?** 'Level of responsibility early on'; 'client base'; 'transactional nature of work'; 'small trainee intake'; 'lots of responsibility from the get-go'; 'exposure to big clients in the PE space'; 'smaller deal teams so you are integral to projects and given the opportunity to have a real voice'; 'the location is excellent'; 'no face-time'

- **Best thing about the firm?** 'There's always lots to do'; 'the firm is PE focused'; 'flexibility over training contract and ability to carve out your career'; 'being given a pay rise before even starting at the firm'; 'consistently approachable supervisors'; 'top-quality work'; 'minimal process-driven work'; 'lots of social events'; 'the friendly atmosphere'; 'the office'

- **Worst thing about the firm?** 'Unpredictable hours'; 'the work/life balance'; 'we don't have a gym in the office'; 'expectation that all emails should be responded to immediately'; 'the quality of the training can be a bit variable'; 'expectation of 24/7 availability on Blackberry'

- **Best moment?** 'Closing of global deal'; 'attending trial in the High Court and getting to sit on the benches, behind counsel, on a matter worth £7bn'; 'experiencing my first closing'; 'being an integral part of closing a big fund'; 'attending a ten-hour long negotiation meeting alongside a partner and an associate'

- **Worst moment?** 'High levels of work under time pressure'; 'the morning of an all-nighter proofing a skeleton argument'; 'working an all-nighter on a Sunday night'; 'unexpectedly closing a deal while abroad on holiday and ending up spending two days of my trip glued to my laptop'; 'post-midnight closing a nightmare deal'

A day in the life of...

... Yushra Raheem second-year trainee, Kirkland & Ellis
Departments to date: Debt finance, funds, regulatory
University: Queen Mary University
Degree and class: Law, 1st

8.50am: On my way to work I check my BlackBerry to sort through any emails that may have come in overnight. Due to the international reach of our deals, we often interact with parties located across multiple jurisdictions and time zones. Due to this, you can sometimes wake up to several emails from counterparties or foreign counsel.

9.20am: I arrive at the Gherkin and head to my desk. I check my emails and reply to any urgent correspondence requiring immediate attention. Having done this, I go to the kitchen to get some breakfast. Kirkland provides free breakfast every day, and the food on offer varies from pastries, to muffins, cereal and fruit.

9.45am: I check through my to-do list, adding anything additional that may have come in overnight, and prioritise my workload. Due to the transactional nature of the work, we often have catch-up meetings with the deal team to discuss ongoing items and priorities for the week. After the team catch-up, I begin drafting documents in relation to a fundraise we are shortly expecting to close, while responding to ongoing correspondence with the client and investors.

11.30am: Having completed that task, I turn next to another deal in its earlier stages. I review a draft of the private placement memorandum and investment advisory agreement, and add in any necessary updates based on correspondence with local counsel and changes to the parties involved, or the deal structure. As a trainee, you are a key part of the deal team and your role will often include tracking a document and/or closing checklist, to reflect updates in the deal and progress towards closing.

1.00pm: I meet some fellow trainees for lunch in our office restaurant on the 22nd floor, which has panoramic views of the City.

1.45pm: I sit in on a call with investors and take notes on the points of negotiation. The smaller trainee intake means that you are often one of two or three juniors on a deal, and are given the opportunity to produce the first draft of most documents. I head back to my desk and begin updating the fund documents to reflect the terms negotiated on the call.

3.30pm: I send my updated draft to the associate on the deal and we discuss any changes needed before sending out to the client for review. I email foreign counsel in various jurisdictions to request their input on the transaction. I sit in on a call and we get an update from the client informing us that the deal is progressing well and that things are likely to accelerate from next week onwards.

4.30pm: I go back to finalising my review of the private placement memorandum, having received further updates from the client and foreign counsel. At Kirkland, you are given a lot of responsibility and autonomy over your workload from an early stage. While this can be daunting, it is an invaluable experience and really enables you to develop your skills. I was responsible for assisting with drafting the ancillary fund documents, first drafts of investor side letters and helping to manage local

> **'At Kirkland, you are given a lot of responsibility and autonomy over your workload from an early stage.'**

counsel in the various jurisdictions involved; however, I was supported throughout the deal by my supervisor and the associate also working on the deal.

7.00pm: Having updated the documents in relation to the fundraise, I send a copy to the associate for her comments. I update the closing checklist and circulate to the team, summarising the deal progression for the day and key priorities for tomorrow.

7.45pm: After updating my to-do list for the following day, I head out to dinner with some friends.

www.kirkland.com/ukgraduate

About the firm

Address: 30 St Mary Axe, London EC3A 8AF
Telephone: 020 7469 2000 **Fax:** 020 7469 2001
Website: www.kirkland.com
Email: ukgraduaterecruitment@kirkland.com

Other offices: Beijing, Chicago, Hong Kong, Houston, London, Los Angeles, Munich, New York, Palo Alto, San Francisco, Shanghai, Washington DC

Who we are: Kirkland & Ellis is an international law firm with more than 1,700 lawyers representing global clients in offices worldwide.

What we do: In London we are renowned for providing multidisciplinary advice to our wide range of leading private equity clients. We also have a market-leading international arbitration and litigation practice which represents a large range of clients across all sectors globally.

What we're looking for: We are looking for intelligent, motivated, ambitious individuals who can bring a sense of initiative and commercial awareness to our teams.

What you'll do: Much of our training is on the job, working shoulder to shoulder with partners and associates. This is supplemented by our compulsory trainee training programme, designed to equip you with the skills required to succeed as a junior lawyer.

Perks: Offices in the Gherkin; discretionary bonus; gym membership; subsidy; life insurance; private healthcare; season ticket loan.

Sponsorship: All trainees are required to undertake their GDL and/or LPC at the University of Law. Full sponsorship and maintenance grant of £8,000 provided for both courses.

Facts and figures

Total partners: 793
Other fee-earners: 893
Total trainees: 19

Trainee places available for 2019: 10
Applications received pa: 1,000
Percentage interviewed: 6%

First year salary: £46,000
Second year salary: £50,000
Newly qualified salary: $180,000

Application process

Apply to: Rebecca McEwan, graduate recruitment specialist.
How: Online application form.
When: Apply by 14 July 2017 for 2019 contracts.
What's involved: Interviews with partners.

Vacation schemes
Summer: Apply by 13 January 2017.

KIRKLAND & ELLIS

Latham & Watkins

99 Bishopsgate, London EC2M 3XF

Lex 100 Winner

See categories below
and tables from page 69

Survey results *(marks out of 100%)*

Satisfied in your job?	82
Firm living up to expectations?	83
High quality of work?	83
Enough client contact?	73
Stress-free?	59
Happy work/life balance?	59
Friendly firm?	91
Great social life?	76
Good vacation scheme?	92
Confident you'll be kept on?	88
Good remuneration?	93
Diverse firm?	92
Good international secondments?	82

 **verdict**

US firm Latham & Watkins offers aspiring trainees fantastic 'international opportunities' and a 'competitive salary package', two of the five categories which have secured the firm **Lex 100 Winners** medals. Many of its current trainees decided to choose the 'expanding firm' after an 'excellent experience on the vacation scheme'. The 'quality of training' is reflected in 'top-quality work' and 'high levels of responsibility'. Although this responsibility is 'often frightening, especially at the beginning', trainees soon find it 'becomes exciting' as they have the chance to work on 'first-of-a-kind deals'. The 'incredible training programme' encourages trainees to be 'autonomous and responsible rather than just spoon-fed from the outset'. The 'small trainee intake' results in more 'diverse and challenging areas of work' to experience, and trainees 'benefit from a good support system', including an 'excellent mentoring system' which allows trainees to 'make some good friends in the close-knit teams'. Also, the 'open-door policy' creates a 'relaxed atmosphere' in the office where 'supervisors are happy to take a lot of time to go through both the basics and more complicated issues that arise'. At times you can expect 'demanding and unpredictable hours' which can be 'intense and quite exhausting'. Also, 'workloads can vary which means trainees are either extremely busy or very quiet'. Top trainee moments include 'travelling to Chicago for five days on a departmental retreat in the second week of training', 'closing a long and stressful deal' and the 'international secondment to New York'. This global firm provides services for 'first-rate clients', so if you want to excel and get your hands on 'exciting, headline-grabbing work' add Latham & Watkins to the list.

If the firm were a fictional character it would be...

Harry Hart (Kingsman: The Secret Service) – friendly and well-mannered, but not to be provoked

The firm

US firm Latham & Watkins has strengthened considerably in London in the last couple of years, with the office posting a 12% turnover rise last year. The firm has over 2,100 lawyers based in 13 countries, and is a pacesetter across a number of corporate and finance practice areas, including high yield and acquisition finance. Latham was nominated for Private Equity Team of the Year and US Law Firm of the Year at the *Legal Business* Awards 2016.

The deals

Advised Onex Partners on its $4.6bn acquisition of the SIG Combibloc Group; represented Travis Coal Restructured Holdings in an arbitration to enforce a loan repayment; advised JP Morgan as underwriter and arranger on the €6.8bn debt financing to facilitate ChemChina's acquisition of Pirelli; advised Vimpelcom on a cash tender offer for $2.1bn in outstanding dollar-denominated Eurobonds; advised banks including Goldman Sachs on three bonds for Altice related to its acquisition of PT Portugal.

The clients

Addison Lee; Aon; Aviva; The Carlyle Group; Deutsche Bank; Ernst & Young; Helios Investment Partners; London Metal Exchange; Nordic Capital; Sorin Group.

The star performers

Top-ranking departments according to *The Legal 500* (see legal500.com for more details)
Acquisition finance; Banking litigation: investment and retail; Corporate restructuring and insolvency; Commercial contracts; Commercial litigation; Corporate tax; Data protection; Debt capital markets; Derivatives and structured products; Emerging markets; Environment; Equity capital markets; Fraud: civil; High yield; International arbitration; M&A: upper mid-market and premium deals, £250m+; Mining and minerals; Oil and gas; Private equity: transactions: Large-cap deal capability; Private funds.

- **Why did you choose this firm over any others?** 'The friendliness of the people that I met during the vacation scheme'; 'American culture'; 'really international vibe'; 'the pay'; 'the vacation scheme was fulfilling'; 'straightforward recruitment process'; 'quality of work'; 'the firm is clearly in the ascendancy'; 'small intake and high levels of responsibility'

- **Best thing about the firm?** 'The high degree of responsibility given to trainees'; 'associates and partners always willing to answer questions'; 'the exposure to different work'; 'currently the largest firm in the world by revenue'; 'the fact the firm is so hungry to expand in London'; 'friendly and relaxed atmosphere'

- **Worst thing about the firm?** 'The unpredictable nature of the work'; 'lack of clarity regarding seat choices'; 'the elevators can be really slow in the morning'; 'demanding hours'; 'when you are the only trainee on a fairly high-stress deal stretching over several weeks it can be quite exhausting'

- **Best moment?** 'Being telephoned by a senior associate to congratulate me on a piece of work'; 'being part of a transaction from start to finish within the first few months of my first seat'; 'leading a closing in my first few weeks'; 'international secondment to New York'; 'speaking directly to GCs'; 'the banking retreat in Berlin'

- **Worst moment?** '18 days straight in the office'; 'having to page turn bundles'; 'being asked to research something and draft an email to a partner in ten minutes'; 'sitting around for hours just waiting for documents from the US to come in'

A day in the life of...

... Laura Connolly trainee, Latham & Watkins

Departments to date: Corporate, project finance
University: Oxford (St. Peter's)
Degree: Law

8.45am: I check my BlackBerry as I'm leaving the house to gauge the day's work load. A trainee from another law firm has sent me some documents that I had requested, so I quickly email back to thank him and we arrange a call for 4.00pm.

9.15am: I arrive in 'Red & White', the firm's restaurant. It's the monthly free breakfast day, so I have a bacon sandwich and sit down with a few associates and trainees. The trainee intake is small, and so we all became friends and mixed with the associates very quickly. There's no feeling of a social hierarchy or 'feeding chain' at Latham.

9.30am: I have a catch up with my supervisor about the emails that came in overnight and write a joint to-do list, splitting the tasks. My favourite thing about Latham is how much trust is placed in trainees: no task is too big for me to 'have a crack at'. As part of a corporate financing for a large listed company in the Middle East we're negotiating term sheet comments with over ten different banks, so I discuss with my supervisor which comments may not be acceptable to our client and why.

11.15am: I join my supervisor to take a call with one of the banks to discuss their comments. The call lasts 45 minutes, after which I update the documentation; I have to use a combination of free drafting (to reflect the bespoke positions agreed on) and use of precedents.

12.30pm: Project finance monthly team lunch: the whole team is provided with a hot buffet lunch. We talk about recent developments in the project finance world, the deals going on within the team and any business development initiatives. It's a great way to spend some time with the whole team, especially the people I haven't yet worked with. We discuss a team day out go-karting and plan the barbeque for afterwards.

2.00pm: Back to my desk to finish off my drafting task. I discuss it with my supervisor; he gives me helpful comments and explains how to best represent our client's position. I revise my draft based on his comments.

3.30pm: Another transaction we're working on, a Saudi Arabian project financing, is signing soon and so I update the CP (conditions precedent) checklist based on the documents I received this morning. I review the series of documents and send the checklist back before the call at 4.00pm. On the call we talk through the updated CP documents and make sure we are on the same page as to what is outstanding.

5.00pm: I meet some of the other trainees and associates downstairs and we head to a pro bono meeting. We're involved in a prisoners' advice service whereby we work with a charity that offers free legal advice and support to adult prisoners in England and Wales. Aside from being a great cause, this is a great opportunity to practise our drafting and research skills and to work with people in other departments.

5.45pm: I work through the rest of my to-do list. I write some notes from the call earlier so that there's a record of what was agreed. I begin drafting some signing instructions for the Saudi deal so that I can send them to my supervisor for review in the morning.

> 'My favourite thing about Latham is how much trust is placed in trainees: no task is too big for me to "have a crack at".'

6.45pm: One more thing left! For my next seat, I will be going to the Hong Kong office for six months, and so I have to send some forms to HR for my visa. The East is an increasingly important part of the global commercial platform and I'm really looking forward to experiencing life and business over there.

7.15pm: After asking my supervisor if there's anything else he needs help with, I pack up my stuff and head home for dinner.

www.lw.com

About the firm

Address: 99 Bishopsgate, London EC2M 3XF
Telephone: 020 7710 1000   **Fax:** 020 7374 4460
Website: www.lw.com
Email: londongraduates@lw.com

Managing partner: Jay Sadanandan

Other offices: Barcelona, Beijing, Boston, Brussels, Chicago, Dubai, Düsseldorf, Frankfurt, Hamburg, Hong Kong, Houston, Los Angeles, Madrid, Milan, Moscow, Munich, New Jersey, New York, Orange County, Paris, Rome, San Diego, San Francisco, Shanghai, Silicon Valley, Singapore, Tokyo, Washington DC.

Who we are: Latham & Watkins is an international law firm with more than 2,100 lawyers located in the world's major financial, business and regulatory centres.

What we do: The firm is recognised for its work advising some of the world's leading corporates, financial institutions and private equity firms on their most significant transactions and disputes.

What we're looking for: The firm looks for outstanding people who have the potential to become exceptional lawyers. Initiative, enthusiasm, ambition, intellectual rigour and teamwork are some of the traits particularly valued at Latham. Trainees who demonstrate their motivation and ability to excel will thrive in a first-class training experience and be rewarded with a brilliant career.

What you'll do: During their four six-month seats each trainee receives bespoke supervision and outstanding support while being afforded meaningful responsibility from the outset and significant legal experience on qualification. In addition to training organised by each department, trainees also benefit from a core 'trainee foundation' curriculum designed to bridge the gap between law school and practice.

Perks: Healthcare, dental, cycle-to-work and pension schemes, life assurance, subsidised café and gym membership.

Sponsorship: GDL and LPC course fees are paid by the firm and reimbursed in full if a successful applicant has completed their studies. A maintenance grant of £8,000 is paid in each year of study.

Facts and figures

Total partners: 66
Total trainees: 45

Trainee places available for 2019: 24
Applications received pa: 1,000
Percentage interviewed: 15%

First year salary: £45,000
Second year salary: £48,000
Newly qualified salary: Competitive

Application process

Apply to: Graduate recruitment team.
How: Online application form at www.lw.com/londongraduates

Vacation schemes

The firm runs two vacation schemes every year, each lasting two weeks. Participants spend time with different practice areas, gaining invaluable experience involving real work with real clients. Please visit the website for further details.

LATHAM&WATKINS

Leathes Prior

74 The Close, Norwich NR1 4DR

Lex 100 Winner

See categories below
and tables from page 69

Survey results *(marks out of 100%)*

Satisfied in your job?	74
Firm living up to expectations?	84
High quality of work?	74
Enough client contact?	82
Stress-free?	42
Happy work/life balance?	82
Friendly firm?	78
Great social life?	90
Good vacation scheme?	91
Confident you'll be kept on?	80
Good remuneration?	58
Diverse firm?	72

 **verdict**

A 'well-respected local firm with a long history', Norwich's Leathes Prior ensures trainees 'get early responsibility and involvement in valuable work right from day one'. This has led to stand-out experiences which include 'being able to manage my own case load' and 'drafting and advising on complex commercial software agreements, with limited supervision'. There is a 'genuine desire to accommodate the wishes of the trainee', as exemplified by one trainee who successfully obtained an international secondment with the 'joint UK Law Societies' office in Brussels'. Though this wasn't a Leathes Prior secondment, the trainee wrote that 'my firm has been very supportive while I've been out here'. The workload can be inconsistent, with experiences ranging from 'occasionally working long hours' and 'sitting for hours on end with nothing to do'. Respondents believe that they have 'more client contact' than peers working elsewhere. One recruit enjoyed 'receiving an email complimenting me on my service, where I had more or less run a matter by myself'. Praise is also forthcoming from partners, and 'receiving positive feedback when you have done a lot of work on a case' was another individual's favourite moment to date. One trainee moans that they 'do not get the chance to meet up with other trainees often as we all have busy schedules', but the 'friendly and flexible attitude' at the firm combined with the 'approachable staff' somewhat mitigates this and is enough to claim a **Lex 100 Winner** award for social life. 'Additional training opportunities' include 'volunteering for the Norfolk Community Legal Services organisation' and the 'charity events that the firm participates in'. To train at a medium-sized East Anglian firm 'with real personality', head to Leathes Prior.

If the firm were a fictional character it would be...

Fantastic Mr Fox – friendly, quick-witted and adaptable

The firm

Established in 1876, Leathes Prior is a leader in the East Anglia region. This 16-partner firm has four offices in the centre of Norwich, and specialisms include franchising, insolvency, intellectual property and sports law. The commercial property and agricultural teams have both recently expanded to meet client demand.

The deals

Advised AIM-listed CVS Ltd on numerous acquisitions; advised racing driver Seb Morris and rally driver Chris Ingram on contracts and sponsorship matters; represented a shareholder and director of UK and Spanish companies against allegations of fraud amounting to £9m; advised The Holkham Estate on tenancy matters; advises the British Horseracing Authority on all of its employment issues.

The clients

Air Livery, Banham Poultry, Countrywide Signs, Drain Doctor, Greensleeves Garden Care, Healthwatch Norwich, Intelligas, Norfolk Farm Produce Ltd, Senior Care at Home, Wok & Go.

The star performers

Top-ranking departments according to *The Legal 500* (see legal500.com for more details)
Agriculture and estates; Charities and not-for-profit; Commercial litigation; Commercial property; Contentious trusts and probate; Corporate and commercial; Crime: fraud; Debt recovery; Education; Employment; Family; Franchising; Health and safety; Intellectual Property; Personal injury: claimant; Personal tax, trusts and probate; Planning; Property litigation; Sport; Transport and shipping.

- **Why did you choose this firm over any others?** 'It is a well-respected firm locally with a long history'; 'it has a personality'; 'good work/life balance'; 'really friendly'; 'flexible attitude'; 'local, medium-sized and offers early responsibility'; 'quality of work experience programme'

- **Best thing about the firm?** 'There are lots of social events and activities to get involved with'; 'the genuine desire to accommodate the wishes of the trainee'; 'relaxed atmosphere'; 'responsibility is given early'; 'you get involved in valuable work right from day one'

- **Worst thing about the firm?** 'I am the first trainee to do an international secondment, and it took some convincing'; 'the lack of day-to-day feedback on how well you are doing'; 'lack of communication between management and rest of the firm'

- **Best moment?** 'Receiving an email complimenting me on my service, where I had more or less run a matter by myself'; 'drafting and advising on complex commercial software agreements, with limited supervision'; 'being able to manage my own caseload'; 'being granted the international secondment'

- **Worst moment?** 'When I was new to the firm and my immediate supervisor was on holiday'; 'lack of initial training meant that I was uncertain as to the financial processes in my first few months'; 'occasionally working long hours'

A day in the life of...

... **Alex Saunders** trainee solicitor, Leathes Prior

Departments to date: Corporate, employment, dispute resolution and commercial

University: Sheffield

Degree and class: English Literature, 2(1)

My day starts in typical fashion; I walk a few hundred yards from the car park up the historic, picturesque Cathedral Close to the office. The location of our offices was one of a number of reasons that I wanted to join Leathes Prior and gives a good indication of the character of the firm as a whole. After grabbing a coffee and catching up with colleagues in my team, I set myself down to plan for the day ahead.

I spend a large part of the morning assisting one of the partners with due diligence on a corporate transaction that is scheduled to complete over the next week or so. I assist in preparing the legal due diligence report to send to the client and send additional queries to the other side's solicitors. A point that will no doubt be echoed by the other trainees is that Leathes Prior offer and actively encourages trainees to take responsibility from an early stage.

While waiting for information that I need, I respond to a few emails and begin reviewing a sale and purchase agreement on a separate corporate transaction. I meet a few colleagues for lunch at a nearby café, where we catch up on our respective weekends, recent holidays and the more serious topic of the likely impact of Brexit on our various practice areas. I have noticed since joining that there is a real focus on socialising outside work at Leathes Prior – so whether it's meeting colleagues for lunch-drinks on a Friday or firm wide events, there is always plenty going on.

On my return from lunch, I turn my attention to a distribution agreement that I am preparing for a client in the manufacturing sector. I liaise with the client on a few tweaks and send a final copy to him for use.

As it approaches the end of the day, a few colleagues and I meet to discuss different ways of marketing the corporate and commercial team, in particular the legal services that we provide to businesses in the digital and technology sectors. It is a productive meeting and we agree on a number of ideas to focus on over the next month. The ability to market yourself and your firm are becoming increasingly central to the role of a junior lawyer, and the marketing team at Leathes Prior is always willing to support and facilitate ideas where possible.

Before I leave the office, I review my notes on a matter in preparation for a conference call with the client tomorrow and with that, I leave the office to play tennis with a few friends from other firms in the city.

Having initially undertaken a work experience placement at Leathes

> **'I have noticed since joining that there is a real focus on socialising outside of work at Leathes Prior.'**

Prior, and subsequently my training contract, I am looking forward to the prospect of embarking on the next stage of my career with the firm. If you are someone who enjoys client contact, thrives on early responsibility and is willing to put in hard work, I sincerely recommend applying for a training contract with Leathes Prior.

www.leathesprior.co.uk/careers

About the firm

Address: 74 The Close, Norwich NR1 4DR
Telephone: 01603 610911 **Fax:** 01603 610088
Website: www.leathesprior.co.uk
Email: info@leathesprior.co.uk
Facebook: www.facebook.com/LeathesPrior1876
Twitter: @leathesprior

Senior partner: William Riley

Other offices: Norwich

Who we are: Leathes Prior is a leading East Anglian firm operating from offices in the exceptionally attractive Cathedral Close and Tombland areas of Norwich

What we do: We provide a comprehensive legal service to a wide variety of commercial and private clients, as well as several niche areas including: Full Contact (Sports Law), Mediation 1st, Employmentor and Traffic Lawyers.

What we're looking for: Save for exceptional cases, we look for a minimum 2(1) degree (in any discipline), a genuine desire to practise law and a preponderance of A or A* grades at A level, as well as the ability to spell preponderance. You should possess good commercial awareness, marketing skills and a desire to work in an environment where initiative is rewarded and responsibility comes early.

What you'll do: We aim to compile training programmes to meet the wishes of individual trainees. The normal pattern is four six-month seats. All trainees will work closely with the firm's partners and will gain excellent hands-on experience of contentious and non-contentious work.

Perks: Trainees will benefit from health cover and the option to participate in various social and sporting events on behalf of the firm.

Sponsorship: Financial support by way of an interest-free loan to be used towards the LPC is available.

Facts and figures

Total partners: 13
Other fee-earners: 35
Total trainees: 8

Trainee places available for 2019: 3-4
Applications received pa: c 100
Percentage interviewed: 10-20%

First year salary: £20,500
Second year salary: £21,500
Newly qualified salary: c £30,000

Application process

Apply to: Lauren Smith, HR manager
How: Email to lsmith@leathesprior.co.uk
When: By 23 July 2017 for 2019 contracts.
What's involved: Successful applicants will be invited to attend an assessment day.

Vacation schemes

For 2017: deadline for applications is 31 January 2017, placements generally arranged for Spring/Summer with some exceptions made for those looking for Autumn/Winter placements.

LEATHES PRIOR
SOLICITORS

Macfarlanes LLP

20 Cursitor Street, London EC4A 1LT

Survey results *(marks out of 100%)*

Satisfied in your job?	83
Firm living up to expectations?	85
High quality of work?	86
Enough client contact?	76
Stress-free?	54
Happy work/life balance?	59
Friendly firm?	81
Great social life?	71
Good vacation scheme?	90
Confident you'll be kept on?	83
Good remuneration?	76
Diverse firm?	78

 **verdict**

Macfarlanes puts an 'emphasis on training and investing in people' which is reflected in the firm's 'high retention rates'. The 'first six weeks of each seat' provides trainees with 'roughly five hours of training, including workshops and seminars'. Trainees get 'lots of exposure to quality work', including 'premium transactions'. There is a 'high level of responsibility' as trainees are able to 'run matters with minimal supervision but at the same time still have the confidence to ask associates or partners for additional help'. Everyone is 'intelligent, engaged, ambitious and willing to help by answering questions'. The 'small teams are partner-led' and trainees gain the opportunity to learn from senior colleagues first-hand. Current trainees praised the 'individually-tailored training' as one of the 'strengths of the training contract'. 'High expectations and standards are set by many associates and partners', and the firm is 'well managed and benefits from having a clear sense of direction in the marketplace'. Top trainee moments include 'contributing to the structuring of an enormous deal which made the front page of the FT', 'closing a deal' and carrying out a 'last-minute interview with a high-profile client in relation to a news story that was hot off the press that day'. There were quite a few grumbles about 'long hours', including one trainee who worked a 'sixty-hour week in four days after returning from a holiday', but the firm does have a 'genuine desire for all employees to have a reasonable work/life balance'. Those looking for top-flight and intellectually challenging work in a 'nice environment' should consider applying to Macfarlanes.

If the firm were a fictional character it would be...

Ferdinand the Bull – doesn't follow the crowd as a default but treads its own path

The firm

Macfarlanes is an eminent UK firm and a favoured port of call for major national and international clients. An independent firm, Macfarlanes adopts a rare approach among top-tier City players by developing relations with expert foreign firms to represent clients on cross-border matters. The firm excels in M&A, private client and private equity activity.

The deals

Acted for Altria – the largest shareholder in SAB Miller – on the tax aspects of the brewing giant's £73bn merger with Anheuser-Busch InBev; acted for Pork Farms on the phase two merger clearance aspects of its acquisition of Kerry Foods' chilled savoury pastry business; advised Goldman Sachs and Deutsche Bank on the merger control aspects of their €288m purchase of the National Bank of Greece's private equity portfolio; acted for Elegant Hotels Group on its £100m AIM flotation; acted for Appleby on the sale of its fiduciary business, Appleby Fiduciary & Administration, to Bridgepoint.

The clients

3i; Canary Wharf Group; Exor; Finsavio; Graphite; International Game Technology; Legal & General; Lexington; Shawbrook; TPG.

The star performers

Top-ranking departments according to *The Legal 500* (see legal500.com for more details)
Acquisition finance; Commercial litigation; Contentious trusts and probate; Corporate tax; Debt capital markets; Derivatives and structured products; EU and competition; Equity capital markets; Financial services (contentious); Financial services (non-contentious/regulatory); Flotations: small and mid-cap; Fraud: civil; Investment funds: Hedge funds; M&A: upper mid-market and premium deals, £250m+; Personal tax, trusts and probate; Private equity: transactions: Mid-cap deal capability; Private funds; Real estate funds; Retail funds; Tax litigation and investigations.

- **Why did you choose this firm over any others?** 'Strong corporate practice'; 'reputation for quality'; 'independent firm'; 'quality of the training programme'; 'regular lunchtime seminars'; 'it's very profitable'; 'good-sized intake'; 'smaller firm with high-quality work'; 'has a reputation in the City as being one of the best places to train'; 'range of departments'; 'reputation in corporate areas'; 'top-tier private client practice'

- **Best thing about the firm?** 'Quality of the work'; 'the firm is very well managed and benefits from having a clear sense of direction in the marketplace'; 'ability to operate internationally from one office in London'; 'size of teams means your exposure to high-quality work is really good as a trainee'; 'my opinion is always valued'; 'the amount of client contact on a day-to-day basis'

- **Worst thing about the firm?** 'Pay is too low'; 'gender imbalance at partnership level'; 'seat selection process can be a little hit-and-miss'; 'trainees are sometimes kept in the dark about qualification spaces'; 'the offices are a bit outdated'; 'it can be difficult to get initiatives off the ground as people can be slow to change'

- **Best moment?** 'Completing a deal where I felt that I had added value to the outcome'; 'reading witness statements that had been produced using an evidence grid I had put together'; 'being able to give cogent advice to the managing partner of a private equity house'; 'running my own matter and being congratulated at the end'; 'being genuinely helpful to people'

- **Worst moment?** 'Spending all weekend doing verification for the deal to fall through on Monday'; 'reviewing litigation files'; 'bad feedback'; 'juggling five deals'; '19 solid lever-arch files of due diligence on one deal'; 'making a mistake and having to go cap-in-hand to the partner'

A day in the life of...

... Florence Barnes second-year trainee, Macfarlanes LLP

Departments to date: Tax, corporate M&A
University: Cardiff University
Degree and class: Law, first class honours

8.45am: I arrive at work in advance of the M&A practice group's weekly monitoring meeting. This week the meeting will focus on 'practice points' and all members of the group are asked to contribute with any interesting new points of legal knowledge they have come across in the last week. I spend a few minutes catching up on emails and preparing what I will say at the meeting.

9.30am: When the meeting is over I head to the firm's café for a quick coffee and catch up with fellow M&A trainees before returning to my desk.

10.00am: I have a call with a client. The client is a UK private equity firm who we acted for on a transaction recently where they were selling a large global group of companies. The transaction was completed three weeks ago but I still have a lot of ongoing work in relation to it, mostly involving distribution of the sale proceeds to a large number of shareholders who held shares through a nominee company. On the call, we discuss the next steps which need to be taken in relation to

this distribution of proceeds and agree to catch up again in a few days.

10.30am: I return to work on a research note I am producing for the partner I sit with. The note concerns the rights of shareholders to requisition meetings of a company and broader routes of action that activist shareholders can take. The note is to be given to the directors of a company involved in a large public takeover, and will require a lot of time and thought. It consumes the remainder of my morning.

1.00pm: I attend a lunchtime training session with the other M&A trainees. The training sessions we have internally are provided by solicitors or partners within the M&A group and we have them most weeks. The topic of this training session is an update on the new market abuse regime.

2.30pm: After our lunchtime training session, I spend a while discussing the research note I am working on with the partner who asked me to write it. A lot of further points for research come out of our discussion and I spend some time looking into these.

4.00pm: An associate comes to my office to brief me on a new matter we are starting work on. A client wishes to make interim dividend payments and is seeking our advice on how to go about this. The associate gives me several documents to draft, which includes sets of board minutes and consents.

'I have a call with a client. The client is a UK private equity firm who we acted for on a transaction recently.'

6.30pm: Having made a start on the interim dividend documents, I return to the work on the distribution of the proceeds of the sale that I discussed on the call earlier. I work through a few of the points discussed on the call and then make a list of what I need to finish in the morning. I leave the office and head home at about 7.30pm.

www.macfarlanes.com/careers

About the firm

Address: 20 Cursitor Street, London EC4A 1LT
Telephone: 020 7831 9222   **Fax:** 020 7831 9607
Website: www.macfarlanes.com
Email: gradrec@macfarlanes.com
Facebook: @MacfarlanesGrad
Twitter: @Macfarlanesgrad

Senior partner: Charles Martin
Managing partner: Julian Howard

Who we are: Macfarlanes is a leading City law firm with a straightforward, independently minded approach. The driving force behind the firm is an absolute commitment to delivering the right advice in the right way to our clients.

What we do: We are recognised for the quality of our work and people, not just in dealing with the full range of corporate and commercial matters, but in advising our clients on their private affairs.

What we're looking for: We look for a rare combination of character, drive and intellectual curiosity, along with strong interpersonal skills, an ambitious and commercial approach, drive, motivation and resilience.

What you'll do: A combination of hands-on experience with real responsibility and challenge with a first-class education programme and the support you would expect from a leading firm.

Perks: Flexible benefits package including life assurance, pension scheme, private healthcare, in addition to a discretionary performance-related bonus scheme, subsidised restaurant, season ticket loan and gym membership.

Sponsorship: LPC and CPE/GDL course fees, maintenance allowance for LPC students (£7,000) and GDL students (£7,000 in London, Guildford and Oxford, and £6,250 elsewhere).

Facts and figures

Total partners: 87
Other fee-earners: 262
Total trainees: 59

Trainee places available for 2019: up to 30
Applications received pa: 900
Percentage interviewed: 15%

First year salary: £42,000
Second year salary: £46,000
Newly qualified salary: £71,000

Turnover in 2016: £161.026m
Profits per equity partner: £1.29m

Application process

Apply to: Catherine Morgan-Guest, graduate recruitment manager.
How: Online application.
When: By 31 July 2017 for 2019 contracts.
What's involved: Case study, group exercise and presentation, interview and written exercise.

Vacation schemes

Spring: 3-13 April 2017 (apply by 31 January 2017).
Summer: 26 June-7 July 2017 and 10-21 July 2017 (apply by 31 January 2017).
First Year Insight Day: 30 March 2017 (apply by 28 February 2017).

MACFARLANES

Maples Teesdale LLP

30 King Street, London EC2V 8EE

Survey results *(marks out of 100%)*

Satisfied in your job?	82
Firm living up to expectations?	85
High quality of work?	82
Enough client contact?	85
Stress-free?	52
Happy work/life balance?	72
Friendly firm?	92
Great social life?	62
Confident you'll be kept on?	55
Good remuneration?	80
Diverse firm?	87

 verdict

Maples Teesdale 'has a fantastic reputation as a boutique commercial property law practice', and its training contract is therefore considered ideal for those keen to 'work with true property experts'. As a 'niche specialist property firm', Maples Teesdale 'attracts impressive clients' and represents them on 'really exciting projects and transactions', and survey feedback has secured a **Lex 100 Winner** award for client contact. Trainees 'get to experience all aspects of a property transaction', and highlight achievements include 'attending an all-day mediation where we secured a very favourable outcome for our client', 'working with my supervising partner on a commercial property auction purchase which had lease involvement' and 'managing the construction documents on a large development project'. There are complaints that 'trainees often do not get much secretarial support', and this can lead to 'being over-worked' and being tasked with various admin chores such as photocopying and bundling. The 'small trainee intake size' is popular as it means that recruits are given 'higher levels of responsibility early on'. The firm's 'hands-on approach to training' consists of 'very good training initiatives' such as 'external speakers and workshops developing your business skills, and internal training for trainees and NQs given by partners'. The 'lack of social events' is a minor gripe, but this doesn't prevent the 'friendly, inspirational and knowledgeable colleagues' from making it 'a nice environment to work in'. To work at a 'growing firm' in the City that combines 'expertise in commercial property law' with a 'great list of clients', consider applying to Maples Teesdale.

If the firm were a fictional character it would be...

Elizabeth Bennet (Pride and Prejudice) – articulate, intelligent and diligent

The firm

Maples Teesdale is a commercial property law specialist based in the City. Many of the firm's partners previously worked at large City firms. Maples Teesdale's impressive client base includes institutional investors, property developers, construction companies and multinationals.

The deals

Acted for Rockspring in the development, letting and sale of 24 Monument Street, London City; advising Legal & General on the redevelopment of the Grafton shopping centre in Cambridge; acting for Gatwick Obviously Not in relation to contesting an air space decision made by the Civil Aviation Authority.

The clients

Arcadia Developments; Avignon Capital; Legal & General; Lloyds Bank International; London Properties; Rockspring Asset Management.

The star performers

Top-ranking departments according to *The Legal 500* (see legal500.com for more details)
Commercial property: development;
Commercial property: general;
Commercial property: investment;
Construction: non-contentious; Planning;
Property finance; Property litigation.

- **Why did you choose this firm over any others?** 'Focus on commercial property law'; 'openness to career changers'; 'it's a really hands-on training contract'; 'the quality of work you get as a trainee is excellent'; 'exciting opportunity for anyone with an interest in property law'; 'the friendliness of the firm'; 'you are a valued member in each transaction'; 'rapidly expanding'

- **Best thing about the firm?** 'People are happy to share their experience'; 'the firm has a genuine desire for all employees to have a reasonable work/life balance'; 'work with varied and interesting clients'; 'everyone is approachable'; 'good client contact'; 'being able to run with matters with minimal supervision'; 'supervisors take the time to guide you through whatever you are working on'

- **Worst thing about the firm?** 'Needing partner approval to bring up deeds from storage'; 'the trainees can often be the last people left in the office at the end of the day'; 'lack of social events'; 'trainees often do not get much secretarial support'

- **Best moment?** 'The completion of the first real matter I ran on my own with very little supervision'; 'attending meetings with the client'; 'being involved with a large development project'; 'working with my supervising partner on a commercial property auction purchase'; 'attending an all-day mediation where we secured a very favourable outcome for our client'

- **Worst moment?** 'When the printer decided it didn't want to print and I had to produce over 40 documents to go out that evening'; 'photocopying for court bundles'; 'having to go through 39 boxes of property deeds and create a schedule of all the documents'; 'being over-worked in one department'

A day in the life of...

... Holly Watt first-year trainee, Maples Teesdale LLP

Departments to date: Construction, commercial property

University: Cardiff University

Degree and class: LLB, Law and German, 1st

9.00am: On my way into the office I use the train journey to check the news headlines. Working at a specialist property law firm, it's particularly important to keep up to date with what's happening in the UK real estate market, as well as the economy in general.

9.30am: I have a voicemail to go and speak to a senior associate who then explains the background to a long leasehold interest purchase we are currently acting on. We have received the searches back and now I am to draft the report on title for our client.

10.00am: I am negotiating a deed of variation and take a call from a client. I discuss this call with the partner I am working with on this matter and we decide on a course of action. I draft a response email. This is excellent experience of negotiating a document, communicating with our client and understanding our client's requirements so that we can best protect their interests.

10.45am: We have been asked to tender for a piece of work so my supervisor asks me to visit the site of the potential purchase. I take pictures of the site and the surrounding area to use in the tender pack that has to be sent out the same day. It's fantastic experience, going on site visits; you gain a better understanding of the property and any potential issues which may cause problems later on. It's also important to show the client

that we take the time to understand each matter we are instructed on.

12.00pm: As it is a Wednesday we have an internal know-how training session. These sessions are a great way to keep up to date with changes in the law and current issues.

1.00pm: I have lunch with the other trainees and associates. We are entering a team into the London Legal Walk so I have organised a charity bake sale.

2.00pm: I start to go through the searches and title documents in relation to the leasehold title purchase. I make a note of any enquiries to raise of the seller and start to draft the report on title. This is an important process as it informs the client of the key points in relation to the purchase which may affect their enjoyment/ownership of the property.

3.45pm: Trainees are in charge of Maples Teesdale's social media and so I check and update our Twitter account. I also proof read an article for our website and various media platforms. You are involved in marketing and promoting the firm's brand from a trainee, which really helps you feel part of the development of the brand and you form ideas as to how to raise awareness of the firm.

4.15pm: I sit in on a conference call with a client with the real estate finance department

regarding a large upcoming finance deal which I will be involved in. I take notes in the call and then type these up and distribute them among the team. Large property transactions often involve more than one department in the firm and they are a great opportunity to work with other teams and gain an understanding of what they do.

> '**It's fantastic experience, going on site visits; you gain a better understanding of the property and any potential issues.**'

4.50pm: My supervisor has finished checking a lease that I drafted the day before and I go through the amendments with him. It's a renewal lease so I have to check the terms of the existing lease and ensure the renewal lease is consistent. I make the amendments and draft an email sending the lease out to be negotiated. Being a trainee in commercial property means you get a lot of responsibility at an early stage but are still supported so it's a very hands-on learning experience.

6.00pm: I check my emails and make my to-do list for the next day, prioritising any urgent matters.

www.maplesteesdale.co.uk

About the firm

Address: 30 King Street, London EC2V 8EE
Telephone: 020 7600 3800   **Fax:** 020 3465 4400
Website: www.maplesteesdale.co.uk
Email: enq@maplesteesdale.co.uk
Twitter: @maplesteesdale

Managing partner: Mark Bryan

Who we are: Maples Teesdale are the UK's leading commercial real estate specialists, providing innovative, full service and truly partner-led services.

What we do: The core property practice is complemented by strong construction, planning, property litigation, finance and corporate teams. Our clients include large institutional investors, property developers and companies, construction companies, multinationals, banks, high-net-worth individuals and family offices, sole property traders and occupiers.

What we're looking for: We welcome applications from both law and non-law students. Among other things, we look for candidates with a strong academic background (minimum ABB at A Level (excluding general studies) and a 2(1) at degree level). When reviewing your application we also consider work experience (both legal and non-legal), sporting achievements and any positions of responsibility held. We also like to find out a little bit about you and your personality and what has inspired you into a career in the law.

What you'll do: Our trainees are the future of our business. You will receive the best training possible in a friendly and supportive environment. At the same time, we will ensure that your training contract is stimulating and rewarding. Our largest department is our commercial property department. This is supported by five other departments: construction, corporate, finance, litigation and planning. Our trainees have the opportunity to gain experience, skills and knowledge across these different departments in four, six-month seats and there may also be an opportunity to spend time on secondment with clients.

Perks: Pension, Ride2Work cycle loan scheme, interest free season ticket loans, life assurance.

Facts and figures

Total partners: 16
Other fee-earners: 32
Total trainees: 6

Trainee places available for 2018: 2 or 3
Applications received pa: 50
Percentage interviewed: 30%

First year salary: £35,000
Second year salary: £37,000
Newly qualified salary: £56,500

Application process

Apply to: Jon Blackburn, partner.
How: Online application form.
When: Applications should be submitted by no later than 19 August 2017 for 2018 training contracts.
What's involved: In your interview, two partners will ask you questions about your academic record, work experiences, interests and hobbies, and challenge you on a few commercial questions.

maples teesdale

Mayer Brown International LLP

201 Bishopsgate, London EC2M 3AF

Survey results *(marks out of 100%)*

Satisfied in your job?	75
Firm living up to expectations?	78
High quality of work?	77
Enough client contact?	70
Stress-free?	62
Happy work/life balance?	64
Friendly firm?	83
Great social life?	66
Good vacation scheme?	89
Confident you'll be kept on?	76
Good remuneration?	81
Diverse firm?	82
Good international secondments?	45

 verdict

Mayer Brown offers a 'range of international work' as a result of 21 'global offices'. The 'down-to-earth' firm is praised by trainees for offering 'top-class training' with 'lots of opportunities to attend talks and meetings'. The firm champions a 'strong work ethic' and its 'quality lawyers' give 'formal training sessions' to trainees. There is a 'small trainee intake' so all the trainees are 'good friends'. Recruits receive a 'lot of responsibility' and 'high-quality work' such as 'drafting agreements from scratch' and 'attending face-to-face meetings with clients'. The 'work is interesting', and trainees have the opportunity to take on more responsibility which can include 'running completions single-handedly'. As well as the understandable 'rookie mistakes', the 'very long hours, weeks and occasional all-nighters' is something trainees grumble about. Top trainee moments include 'running and completing a small real estate transaction from start to finish', 'successfully negotiating contract terms with lawyers from another firm on my own' and an 'international secondment to Hong Kong'. The firm has 'strong departments' in finance, insurance and projects. But some trainees feel there is a 'lack of scope to consider seats for qualification in non-core departments as they take on fewer qualifiers'. Notably, the 'open-door policy' encourages the 'friendliness and personalities of people' to shine, regardless of seniority. People have 'friendly conversations with each other', and trainees love the 'great characters in the office', but would like to see 'more social events arranged' by the firm. Those aspiring to 'learn a lot' in a top City firm should take a closer look at Mayer Brown.

If the firm were a fictional character it would be...

Marge Simpson – soft on the inside, but has a competitive exterior and can compete with the best

The firm

Mayer Brown has 90 partners based in London, and earns positive reviews in the City for its finance, insurance and projects practice groups. The firm opened an office in Dubai in June 2016 to add to its already extensive global network. Mayer Brown was shortlisted for Real Estate Team of the Year at the *Legal Business* Awards 2016.

The deals

Acted for Autopista del Sol, Concesionaria Española on the €570m Autosol project bond; advised arranger RBS on updating its €35bn programme for issuing notes governed by English and German law; advised Progroup on multi-jurisdictional aspects of its €400m inaugural bond issue; advised Bank of America Merrill Lynch as arranger on the €145m Taurus pan-European CMBS; advised Entertainment One on the implementation of an executive incentive plan.

The clients

CF Lending; Citigroup; Deutsche Bank; European Bank for Reconstruction and Development; HSBC; Hibu; ISDA; Liberty Speciality Markets; UniCredit; Wells Fargo.

The star performers

Top-ranking departments according to *The Legal 500* (see legal500.com for more details)
Acquisition finance; Asset based lending; Bank lending – investment grade debt and syndicated loans; Banking litigation: investment and retail; Commercial contracts; Corporate tax; Debt capital markets; Derivatives and structured products; EU and competition; Emerging markets; Employment: employers; Equity capital markets; Financial services (non-contentious/regulatory); Flotations: small and mid-cap; High yield; Infrastructure (including PFI and PPP); Mining and minerals; Pensions dispute resolution; Securitisation; VAT and indirect tax.

- **Why did you choose this firm over any others?** 'Experience on the vacation scheme'; 'I liked the variety of strong departments the firm has'; 'its global reputation'; 'the friendliness of the people'; 'secondment opportunities'; 'contentious work on offer'; 'the people I met at the assessment centre were very friendly and down-to-earth'; 'great clients'; 'global presence whilst retaining British working culture'; 'people I met at law fairs and recruitment events'

- **Best thing about the firm?** 'Great people'; 'some great characters in the office'; 'the location'; 'friendly atmosphere'; 'the range of international work available'; 'everyone is hard-working'; 'the level of work is really good'; 'good-quality clients'; 'the client secondments'

- **Worst thing about the firm?** 'It doesn't offer consistent qualification opportunities across all departments'; 'the long hours'; 'some departments have more demand for trainees than others'; 'lack of integration between trainee intakes';

'the social life'; 'lack of flexible working policy'; 'the fact that major decisions regarding the firm's direction still appear to come from the US'

- **Best moment?** 'Running completions single-handedly'; 'while on client secondment, successfully negotiating a deal with several partners at a large international law firm'; 'drafting transaction documents'; 'being on conference calls with the client and counsel'; 'the run up to Christmas involved a lot of dinners and drinks events'; 'running the due diligence for a deal in my first month'

- **Worst moment?** 'An extremely busy period in one of the transactional departments'; 'proofreading documents through the night'; 'being quiet during the day but busy in the evening'; 'having to work seven hours on a Saturday'; 'having to confess to a partner that I had made a typo on a document which had already been circulated'

Why Mayer Brown?

... Michelle Ansah first-seat trainee, Mayer Brown International LLP

Departments to date: Corporate
University: King's College London
Degree: Geography

The vacation scheme was a great opportunity for me to experience the day-to-day activities of lawyers at the firm. During my two-week Easter vacation scheme, I was exposed to two different practice areas and given tasks from my supervisor and other members of each department who were extremely helpful and took the time to explain tasks, projects they were working on and answer any general questions that I had. Our visit to the firm's Paris office during the vacation scheme was also a highlight and reinforced Mayer Brown's international presence.

After accepting my offer, I studied the LPC at law school alongside fellow future Mayer Brown trainees. This also provided a great opportunity to get to know my future colleagues. The firm was actively involved in our LPC course, which involved key modules and carefully selected electives in order to prepare us for working at Mayer Brown. Alongside the LPC, the firm offers a bespoke course tailored for Mayer Brown trainees which allows for regular visits to the firm, which meant that I was already familiar with the office before my first day of my training contract.

I am currently in my first seat in the corporate department where I share an office with my supervisor, a partner in the corporate practice. Before my seat, I expected most of my work to come from my supervisor. However, since starting, while my supervisor does give me work, I have also been encouraged to approach other members of the team and as a result have had exposure to a broad spectrum of corporate work (public and private M&A, capital markets, funds and outsourcing) and various types of corporate deals such as corporate real estate and corporate insurance. Sitting with my supervisor has also helped me build my confidence to discuss legal issues and how best to approach them with senior lawyers. The relatively smaller trainee intake has also been beneficial as this means more exposure to quality legal work. As my seat has progressed, I have been given more responsibility on deals I am working on.

The firm is committed to professional development and organises many training sessions by associates and partners for its trainees. Mayer Brown also offers secondment opportunities during your training contract either to international locations, such as New York and Hong Kong, or to established clients of the firm, which further enhances one's training and professional network.

While at Mayer Brown I have participated in some of the many pro bono initiatives the firm offers including volunteering at the Islington Law Centre and using my legal research skills to help draft reports for a recent pro bono research project. The firm also offers other activities including joining and playing with various sports teams, joining the Christmas choir and many charity events, such as the recent charity football tournament and an upcoming comedy night.

> **'Our visit to the firm's Paris office was a highlight and reinforced Mayer Brown's international presence.'**

I am glad that I am training at Mayer Brown as it provides a supportive and collaborative environment in which to do challenging, rewarding and quality legal work alongside lawyers who are instrumental in their respective fields. I would strongly recommend considering Mayer Brown if you want to work at a truly global law firm that is committed to investing in your professional development as a lawyer.

www.mayerbrownfutures.com

About the firm

Address: 201 Bishopsgate, London EC2M 3AF
Telephone: 020 3130 8621
Website: www.mayerbrownfutures.com
Email: graduaterecruitment@mayerbrown.com
Instagram: @mayerbrownfutures

Senior partner: Sean Connolly

Other offices: Bangkok, Beijing, Brussels, Charlotte, Chicago, Dubai, Dusseldorf, Frankfurt, Hanoi, Ho Chi Minh City, Hong Kong, Houston, London, Los Angeles, Mexico City, New York, Palo Alto, Paris, Rio de Janeiro, Sao Palo, Shanghai, Singapore and Washington.

Who we are: Mayer Brown was one of the first law firms to develop a global platform in recognition of the fact that many of its clients increasingly needed integrated, cross border legal advice. The firm is now one of the world's leading global law firms with offices in major cities across the Americas, Asia, Europe and the Middle East. In Brazil, the firm has an association with Tauil & Chequer Avogados. Through the association, the extensive international expertise of its lawyers and its presence in the leading financial centres around the world, Mayer Brown provides high quality legal advice and client-focused solutions to support many of the world's leading businesses.

What we do: Our lawyers practise in a wide range of areas, including corporate, finance, real estate, construction, litigation and dispute resolution, employment, pensions, antitrust and competition, insurance and reinsurance, tax, financial services regulatory and intellectual property.

What we're looking for: We are looking for candidates who not only have a consistently strong academic record, including a minimum of a 2(1) degree or equivalent and AAB at A Level or equivalent in any discipline, but who also have a wide range of interests and achievements outside their academic career.

What you'll do: Trainees can tailor their training contract from a range of different seats, including our main practice areas, and client and international secondments. Trainees will be given significant opportunities to assist on matters that may be multidisciplinary, cross-border and high-profile in nature.

Perks: Private healthcare scheme, subsidised gym membership, 25 days' holiday.

Sponsorship: The firm will cover the cost of the GDL and LPC and provide a maintenance grant of £7,000 in London and £6,500 elsewhere. The firm asks all LPC students to complete the LPC at BPP law school in London.

Facts and figures

Total partners: 87
Other fee-earners: 130
Total trainees: 30

Trainee places available for 2019: 15
Applications received pa: 1,500+

First year salary: £42,000
Second year salary: £47,000
Newly qualified salary: £71,500

Application process

Apply to: Danielle White.
How: Online via our graduate recruitment website.
When: By 31 July 2017 for 2019 contracts.
What's involved: Online application form, online tests and assessment centre.

MAYER·BROWN

Memery Crystal

44 Southampton Buildings, London WC2A 1AP

Survey results *(marks out of 100%)*

Satisfied in your job?	65
Firm living up to expectations?	64
High quality of work?	72
Enough client contact?	64
Stress-free?	41
Happy work/life balance?	71
Friendly firm?	84
Great social life?	52
Confident you'll be kept on?	35
Good remuneration?	55
Diverse firm?	67

 verdict

Memery Crystal offers trainees 'excellent exposure to quality work' in an 'inviting and friendly atmosphere'. It is a 'small firm' with some 'big clients', and trainees are given real responsibility as they are 'trusted to do work which is of a quality usually reserved for qualified solicitors'. This gives trainees 'hands-on' experience which allows them to 'progress and develop' during the training contract. It is evident that the London firm 'genuinely cares' as it offers 'sociable hours' and a 'decent work/life balance'. Notably, there is a lot of 'partner/trainee interaction' so trainees have the chance to build 'good relationships'. There is also 'good client contact' and the work on offer is 'varied and interesting'. There is the 'very occasional late night' and 'during the summer months' there can be 'incredibly quiet periods'. Best trainee moments include 'acting as a lead assistant preparing for a hearing and drafting witness statements', 'working on several multi-million pound re-financing deals' and 'drafting a niche legal document from scratch with no precedent, which received praise'. Trainees also report 'attending court hearings with clients' and 'running calls with clients'. One criticism is the perception that 'different departments operate independently with little interaction between them' which can lead to a 'lack of mixing'. Trainees suggest a communal area 'would help inter-departmental relations'. There is 'no face-time culture' and 'everyone is incredibly welcoming', so if you're on the lookout for a 'good/work life balance' without compromising on work quality, take the time to research Memery Crystal.

If the firm were a fictional character it would be...

Brian Griffin (Family Guy) – small but intelligent, with a good heart and a sense of humour

The firm

Headquartered in London, Memery Crystal is a single-office firm formed in 1978 and since developed into one of the country's leading independent firms, with a renowned dispute resolution team complementing the firm's work on small to mid-level commercial transactions. The firm is often called upon to represent international clients, and enhanced its profile in November 2015 by announcing an exclusive strategic partnership with China's Yingke.

The deals

Defended Gulfsands Petroleum in breach of contract and statutory claims brought by a former CEO; advised Pala Investments on the $10m bridge financing of Alufer Mining's bauxite project in Guinea; advised longstanding broker client Brandon Hill Capital on San Leon Energy's £29m fundraising; advised T.G. Acquisitions on the £90m acquisition of the Thomas Goode store in Mayfair; advised Electric Word on agency agreements in Italy and the UK, and assisted the client with a dispute in Australia.

The clients

African Thunder Platinum; Asda; BMJ Publishing Group; Beckman Group; Debenhams; Deloitte; Imperial Pharmaceuticals; Sapcote Developments; Shanta Gold; Ubiquitous.

The star performers

Top-ranking departments according to *The Legal 500* (see legal500.com for more details)
Commercial contracts; Commercial litigation; Commercial property: general; Commercial property: retail; Employment: employers; Flotations: small and mid-cap; M&A: smaller deals, up to £50m; Media and entertainment (including media finance); Mining and minerals; Property litigation; Property finance.

- **Why did you choose this firm over any others?** 'Good-quality work'; 'early responsibility'; 'excellent exposure to quality work'; 'decent work/life balance'; 'friendly atmosphere'; 'the type of work'; 'opportunity for client contact'; 'mid-size firm'; 'the firm genuinely cares about you and your progression and development'

- **Best thing about the firm?** 'Working closely with partners'; 'people are really approachable and friendly'; 'good interaction with all levels of fee-earners'; 'people will trust you to do meaty work which is of a level usually reserved for qualified solicitors'; 'small firm so more involvement in higher level work'

- **Worst thing about the firm?** 'Retention rate'; 'lack of secretarial support'; 'small firm, so smaller deals'; 'less well-known among

peers'; 'lack of mixing with other departments both socially and in the cross-selling of work'; 'no communal area'; 'split over six floors which doesn't help inter-departmental relations'

- **Best moment?** 'Running a call with a client to talk them through the warranties on a placing agreement'; 'getting the first go at writing long letters in complex litigation'; 'getting to attend court hearings with clients'; 'working on several multi-million pound re-financing deals'

- **Worst moment?** 'Putting the wrong letter in a bundle and having to re-paginate less than an hour before filing'; 'dealing with an aggressive fee-earner'; 'twiddling my thumbs over a very quiet summer period'

A day in the life of...

... Rebecca Mohan-Kenny second-seat trainee, Memery Crystal

Departments to date: Dispute resolution, real estate
University: King's College London
Degree and class: American Studies BA (Hons) 2(1)

8.30am: I arrive at work and check my inbox. The nature of the real estate department means that as a trainee you take ownership of many of your own files, as well as assisting on larger scale transactions, so it is important to take stock each day and prioritise matters so that nothing is overlooked.

9.00am: We have work experience students with us this week so I check with my colleagues to see if there is any work that the students can assist with, or hearings that they can attend to try and gain some experience during their week at the firm.

9.45am: My supervisor asks me if I have availability later in the day to attend a planning project team meeting at the offices of one of our client's project manager and take a note in the afternoon. After confirming that I do, I prepare copies of the necessary documents to bring to the meeting so that we are not unduly delayed. I then re-visit my to-do list to reorganise my day in light of the new meeting in the afternoon.

11.00am: I attend a meeting with the finance director and a representative from Thomson Reuters regarding the firm's use of online resources such as *Practical Law* and *Westlaw*. As trainees, we spend a large amount of time using these online resources in all departments. During the meeting we discussed a number of things including which features are and are not utilised, what potential training may be of assistance firm-wide and the development and progression of the online resources themselves.

12.15pm: When I return from my meeting, having bought some lunch, I see that I have received some documents back from the solicitors on the other side in a re-financing that I am working on. I review the documents in light of the previous correspondence and then send them on to my client for instructions.

1.00pm: We are struggling to obtain contact information for one of the neighbours on a development project as the property is owned by an international company. I complete an international company search directly with the relevant corporate registry but I am told that the results can take five-seven working days. I update the client accordingly in order to manage expectations.

2.30pm: My supervisor and I leave the office and travel to the planning project team meeting. There is a lot to discuss and the meeting is long and detailed, however ultimately very productive.

5.30pm: I get back to the office after the meeting and because it is relatively quiet I dictate my attendance note while the discussion is still fresh in my mind so as to ensure that it is an accurate, contemporaneous note.

6.15pm: I receive further drafts for a matter I have been involved in relating to the ongoing negotiations for an assignment which have

> **'I attend a meeting with the finance director and a representative from Thomson Reuters regarding the firm's use of online resources.'**

been progressing for a few months. I speak to the client on the telephone to discuss the developments in the latest draft and take their instructions. I then revert to the solicitors on the other side with comments.

7.00pm: I leave the office and make my way to join a few colleagues at the pub.

About the firm

Address: 44 Southampton Buildings, London WC2A 1AP
Telephone: 020 7242 5905   **Fax:** 020 7242 2058
Website: www.memerycrystal.com
Email: lbrett@memerycrystal.com
Twitter: @MemeryCrystal

Managing partner: Nick Davis

Who we are: Headquartered in London, Memery Crystal is a single-office firm which was formed in 1978 and has since developed into one of the country's finest independent firms, with a renowned dispute resolution team complementing the firm's work on small to mid-level commercial transactions.

What we do: Our main practice areas include equity capital markets, M&A, banking/debt finance, tax, employment, employee incentives, IP, commercial contracts, real estate and dispute resolution. Much of our work has an international dimension and we have a strong focus in key sectors including natural resources and technology. We are ranked among the leading firms acting for AIM-listed companies and we were named 'Dispute Resolution Team of the Year' at the 2014 *Legal Business* Awards and Litigation Team of the Year at the 2014 *Lawyer* Awards.

What we're looking for: We are looking for high-achieving individuals with a strong academic background, from any discipline, who are commercially minded. We welcome applications from ambitious, driven and enthusiastic candidates who demonstrate a willingness to take on responsibility.

What you'll do: Trainees will rotate seats every six months and we aim to give second-years their preference in seat choice. During their training contract trainees are given on-the-job training and mentoring and are invited to all sessions in the firm's internal training programme. Due to our partner-led service, trainees will work closely with partners from all departments, and will receive regular feedback in addition to their appraisals every three months with their supervisor and a member of HR.

Perks: 25 days' holiday (increases to 30 days with length of service), private medical insurance, life assurance, interest-free season ticket loan, subsidised gym membership, group pension scheme, travel insurance, childcare vouchers and cycle to work scheme.

Sponsorship: The firm funds the GDL and the LPC.

Facts and figures

Total partners: 27
Other fee-earners: 29
Total trainees: 8

Trainee places available for 2019: 8
Applications received pa: 300
Percentage interviewed: 15

First year salary: £35,000
Second year salary: £37,000
Newly qualified salary: Competitive

Application process

Apply to: Helen Seaward, human resources manager
How: Online application form.
When: By 31 July 2017 for 2019 training contracts.
What's involved: Two interviews following successful application.

MemeryCrystal

Michelmores LLP

Woodwater House, Pynes Hill, Exeter EX2 5WR

Survey results *(marks out of 100%)*

Satisfied in your job? 90

Firm living up to expectations? 90

High quality of work? 88

Enough client contact? 85

Stress-free? 70

Happy work/life balance? 84

Friendly firm? 94

Great social life? 86

Good vacation scheme? 83

Confident you'll be kept on? 92

Good remuneration? 78

Diverse firm? 90

 **verdict**

In the words of one respondent, Michelmores is an 'ambitious firm always seeking opportunities to grow and develop without compromising on the quality of services it provides'. Trainees are inspired to 'feel passionate about opportunities for the future' as the firm has an 'entrepreneurial approach' to expansion. The full-service firm is a 'good fit' for aspiring lawyers who are not 'set on a practice area' as it has 'strengths in several different areas', with the 'three core departments' being real estate, business and private client. Trainees enthuse about 'exposure to interesting cases and City-quality work while still maintaining a work/life balance'. Top trainee moments include 'taking ownership of a client matter' and 'being sent to the London office last-minute to assist on a large corporate deal'. Trainees love the 'level of responsibility' and have grown into their roles as a 'point of contact for many clients who rely directly on advice' from them. Client contact is one of the nine categories in which the firm is named **Lex 100 Winner**. Collectively, trainees report there is some 'uncertainty over seat choices' which can be 'stressful' as there isn't 'enough time for those who need to move offices without worry'. But trainees have noted 'there are conscious efforts to improve this area including regular discussions with HR'. Michelmores is a 'nice place to work' as there is a 'friendly, encouraging and genuinely helpful environment', plus trainees enjoy being 'challenged and receiving constant encouragement to strive to be a better lawyer'. For those looking for an 'ambitious firm' that will encourage you to develop as a lawyer, Michelmores 'outshines the competition'.

If the firm were a fictional character it would be...

R2-D2 (Star Wars) – practical and efficient, thought not afraid to make some big noise

The firm

Headquartered in Exeter and with additional offices in London and Bristol, Michelmores is a top 100 firm offering a broad range of business, real estate and private client services. The firm represents major clients across the full range of practice areas, including intellectual property, corporate tax and agriculture and estates.

The deals

Advised Ducalian Capital on fund incorporation and funding rounds for its investments; assisted Aero Stanrew on the sale of its shares to TT Electronics; advised York Global Finance on an application by Lehman's UK administrators for directions on the distribution of a £4bn surplus; advised Finnfund on a $30m debt facility for sustainable forestry development in Tanzania and Uganda; advised African Agriculture Fund on convertible debentures.

The clients

BDO; Deloitte; Flybe; HM Prison Service; KPMG; The Met Office; The Metropolitan Police Service; Mint Velvet; Port of London Authority; RNLI.

The star performers

Top-ranking departments according to *The Legal 500* (see legal500.com for more details)
Agriculture and estates; Charities and not-for-profit; Clinical negligence: claimant; Commercial litigation; Commercial property; Contentious trusts and probate; Corporate tax; Crime: fraud; Debt recovery; EU and competition; Employment; Family; Health and safety; Insolvency and corporate recovery; Intellectual property; Personal tax, trusts and probate; Planning; Project finance and PFI; Public sector: education; TMT: IT and telecoms.

- **Why did you choose this firm over any others?** 'Quality of work'; 'friendly atmosphere'; 'they made me feel passionate about the opportunities for the future'; 'ambitious firm situated in the South West'; 'a good fit for me at law fair and on the vacation scheme which was comprehensive'

- **Best thing about the firm?** 'Seeking entrepreneurial growth in a quietly determined manner'; 'it is very friendly and inclusive'; 'continuous efforts to improve service and national recognition of firm'; 'lots of junior lawyers who regularly get together outside of work'; 'level of responsibility from day one'

- **Worst thing about the firm?** 'Fighting for a car parking space'; 'out-of-town office location'; 'the firm's in-house café closes at 3pm'; 'sometimes there is a lack of communication between the three core departments'; 'lack of transparency regarding seat rotations'

- **Best moment?** 'Attending an eight-day trial'; 'being properly involved in high-profile matters'; 'attending the Royal Courts of Justice for a hearing'; 'attendance at conferences with counsel and medical experts in London'; 'being sent to our London office at the last minute to assist on a large corporate deal'

- **Worst moment?** 'Being the victim of a broken printer'; 'having a mediation postponed after prepping the bundles'; 'almost missing a court deadline'; 'trying to remember everyone's names when I first started'; 'you are expected to do a lot of marketing events'

A day in the life of...

... **Jasmine Davis** trainee, Michelmores LLP

Departments to date: Tax trusts and succession, planning and contentious probate/family

University: Cardiff University

Degree and class: BA History (Hons), 2(1)

8.00am: I live a few miles outside Exeter so my day starts with a short (traffic-dependent!) commute. I lift-share with another trainee and so we chat about how our week is going.

8.40am: I try to get to my desk a little before 9.00am. This gives me time to get a coffee from the onsite café before starting work.

9.00am: Before I start anything, I review my to-do list and see what I need to complete during the day. Typically an email will have arrived overnight which needs to be dealt with promptly. If my supervisor has been working late, I normally come in to find some additional tasks on my desk.

9.30am: I have a quick catch-up with my supervisor and another lawyer in my team. We regularly catch up so that we can discuss what we are all working on and it gives me an opportunity to ask any questions.

9.45am: Time for another coffee. The office is very social so whenever you make a coffee you generally end up having a quick chat with someone from another team.

10.00am: I am currently in the planning team and in this seat I have been given really good opportunities for client contact. This morning I am drafting a complex highways agreement, so I get my head down. I have to consider the instructions carefully, adapt a precedent to

make sure it fits the instructions and draft some bespoke clauses. This involves making a call to the client to clarify their instructions.

12.00pm: I step away from drafting and check my emails. I have been given responsibility for a number of small files and so I have a few emails from clients with queries. The benefit of running your own files is that it encourages you to really think about what the client wants to achieve and the service the client expects. It also gets you involved in billing, which is a key skill for qualification.

12.30pm: My supervisor and I review my drafting. He points out how to improve the draft and it is ready to send to the client for review.

1.00pm: Lunchtimes are often spent in our conservatory café. The trainees usually get together and chat. Somehow the chat always seems to come back to seat rotations!

2.00pm: Back at my desk and I am working on a sector report. Michelmores operates a sector approach and each trainee is assigned to one of the sectors. I am in the private wealth sector and attend regular meetings. I am responsible for drafting the meeting minutes and preparing the quarterly sector report, which updates the management team on our progress.

4.00pm: In the planning team I am often asked to help clients draft objection letters

in relation to planning applications. I have a telephone conference with a client and my supervisor to discuss a draft objection letter. As I have had a lot of involvement in the drafting process, my supervisor lets me lead the call. Michelmores is great for giving trainees direct exposure to clients and real

> '**The benefit of running your own files is that it encourages you to really think about what the client wants to achieve.'**

responsibility. The call goes well and this is a real confidence boost.

5.00pm: I review my to-do list and start to think about what I need to achieve tomorrow. I finish off a few tasks I have been working on during the day.

6.00pm: I normally leave the office around 6.00pm, though this can vary depending on what I have on. We have an in-house gym and so I try and use this when I can muster up the motivation. We are all currently training for the Michelmores 5k charity run! At the end of the week the junior lawyers usually get together for some informal drinks.

www.michelmores.com/recruitment/graduates

About the firm

Address: Woodwater House, Pynes Hill, Exeter EX2 5WR
Telephone: 01392 688688   **Fax:** 01392 360563
Website: www.michelmores.com
Email: gradrecruitment@michelmores.com
Facebook: MichelmoresCareers
Twitter: @mmcareers

Senior partner: Will Michelmore
Managing partner: Malcolm Dickinson

Other offices: Bristol, London

Who we are: Michelmores is an ambitious top 100 law firm, with over 450 staff, 67 partners and a turnover in excess of £30m.

What we do: We provide business, real estate and private client expertise to a wide range of local, national and international clients.

What we're looking for: We are looking for team players with real ambition, who relish responsibility and are as passionate about the success of the firm as we are.

What you'll do: We run a structured training and development programme, which aims to equip trainees with the key skills needed to be a successful solicitor, both technically and personally. Trainees spend six months in four different teams, working closely with a designated supervisor and receiving high levels of responsibility and client contact from an early stage.

Perks: Private medical insurance; season ticket loan; in-house gym, including access to an in-house personal trainer (Exeter only) or corporate membership at selected gyms (all offices); group personal pension plan; subsidised café (Exeter only); a day off for your birthday.

Sponsorship: We fully fund the LPC with the University of Law and offer a £5,000 bursary.

Facts and figures

Total partners: 67
Other fee-earners: 153
Total trainees: 15

Trainee places available for 2019: 8
Applications received pa: 250
Percentage interviewed: 15

First year salary: £24,000 (Exeter)
Second year salary: £26,000 (Exeter)
Newly qualified salary: £38,000 (Exeter)

Turnover in 2015: £30m (+15% from 2014)
Profits per equity partner: £295,000 (+4%)
(see legalbusiness.co.uk for full financial information)

Application process

Apply to: Gabby Essame, HR advisor.
How: Online application form.
When: By 31 July 2017 for 2019 training contracts.
What's involved: Video interview followed by an assessment day comprising an interview, verbal reasoning assessment, written assessment, group exercise and article discussion with a partner.

Vacation schemes

Summer: July 2017 (apply by 28 February 2017).

Mills & Reeve LLP

Botanic House, 100 Hills Road, Cambridge CB2 1PH

Lex 100 Winner

See categories below
and tables from page 69

Survey results *(marks out of 100%)*

Satisfied in your job?	85
Firm living up to expectations?	87
High quality of work?	86
Enough client contact?	85
Stress-free?	63
Happy work/life balance?	81
Friendly firm?	91
Great social life?	80
Good vacation scheme?	91
Confident you'll be kept on?	75
Good remuneration?	55
Diverse firm?	85

 verdict

Mills & Reeve's current trainees found the 'six-seat rotation contract particularly desirable'. The 'four-month seat system' allows trainees to make an 'informed decision' about the area of law they would 'like to qualify in'. Trainees are 'not a tiny cog in a massive machine but a valued member of the team' as the 'size and structure' of the firm allows trainees to take on 'proper work and responsibility'. One trainee enjoyed taking on a pro-active role rather than being 'just the note-taker'; instead they were 'trusted to attend meetings with clients unsupervised'. This has helped propel the firm to a **Lex 100 Winner** gong for client contact. Partners dedicate a 'lot of time' to supervising trainees carefully and giving them 'one-to-one training'. There isn't a 'hierarchal feel to the firm' and trainees are 'encouraged to engage with staff at all levels'. Moreover, the firm is 'attentive to the development' of trainees as they are given 'the best chance to learn'. The firm encourages a 'non-stressful and healthy approach to work/life balance' and several trainees report 'zero weekend office hours'. But there are still some 'long late nights' in store for trainees and at times there is 'inconsistency in the trainee workload'; some days they are 'very busy or have nothing to do'. Top trainee moments include 'running a £30m real estate finance matter with the necessary supervision of a partner', 'attending a three-day employment tribunal away from the office as the sole representative of the firm' and 'completing a deal late at night'. Grumbles centre on the salary and the fact that trainees 'are unable to specify a preference for their first seat'. But if you're looking to be 'intellectually challenged' with plenty of responsibility, Mills & Reeve could be the firm for you.

If the firm were a fictional character it would be...

Brock (Pokémon) – sometimes in the background, but arguably the best trainer of the group

The firm

Mills & Reeve is a top 50 LB100 firm, with its headquarters in London and five other office across the country giving the firm a national reach. It is renowned for having an excellent family law team and for its expertise in real estate, corporate and TMT law.

The deals

Advised shareholders of Brandbank Ltd on its multi-million pound acquisition by Nielsen Holdings; advised Coventry University on a £73m project to replace a former Royal Mail building with five 18-storey towers and a shopping centre; advised The British Library on EU procurement compliance for a multi-million pound development; advised Kingston Higher Education Corporation on a £77.7m term loan; advised the British Medical Association on the launch of its own ABS, named BMA Law Ltd.

The clients

Barclays Bank; Baxter Healthcare; Cambridge University Press; the Department of Health; Institution of Engineering Technology; LV Commercial Mortgage; Larking Gowen; PWC; QV Foods; Urban&Civic.

The star performers

Top-ranking departments according to *The Legal 500* (see legal500.com for more details)
Agriculture and estates; Banking and finance; Charities and not-for-profit; Commercial litigation; Contentious trusts and probate; Corporate and commercial; Corporate tax; Debt recovery; EU and competition; Education; Employment; Family; Health and safety; Immigration; Insolvency and corporate recovery; Licensing; Pensions; Personal injury: defendant; Professional negligence; Project finance and PFI.

- **Why did you choose this firm over any others?** 'High proportion of clients from the public sector'; 'excellent reputation'; 'blue-chip client list'; 'reputation as best firm in the region'; 'attentive to development of trainees'; 'secondment opportunities for the Ministry of Defence'; 'quality of work outside London'; 'wide variety of practice areas means you can try out lots of different fields'

- **Best thing about the firm?** 'You get a real sense that people enjoy working here'; 'there is a really warm atmosphere'; 'trainees are respected as full members of the team'; 'there is a lack of hierarchy'; 'high-profile clients'; 'the level of client contact'; 'variety of training opportunities'; 'our collaborative culture is something that we really value'

- **Worst thing about the firm?** 'The salary could be slightly higher'; 'there are pockets of the firm that don't share the same ethos'; 'IT systems'; 'inconsistency in trainee workload'; 'sometimes the temperature in the office can be a little cooler than I'd like'; 'not always able to get the seats requested'

- **Best moment?** 'The Christmas party'; 'being seconded to a pharmaceutical company in one of my seats'; 'getting involved straight away on a large project'; 'having a partner personally come up to me and congratulate me on the quality of my work'; 'the pod decorations at Christmas'; 'drafting an agreement for a client which required little amendments by my supervisor'

- **Worst moment?** 'Breaking a printer on day one'; 'when a client shouted at me'; 'accidentally shredding our only certified copy of a document'; 'attending a pub quiz with some very senior partners and not quite doing myself justice when answering the questions'; 'working until late at night long after the last person in the team has left'; 'not getting one of my requested seats'

A day in the life of...

... Sam Goldsmith first-year trainee, Mills & Reeve (Norwich)

Departments to date: Real estate disputes, family and corporate
University: University of East Anglia
Degree: Law LLB

8.30am: Like most people who work in the Norwich office, I live only a short walk away and can therefore leave home slightly later.

8.45am: I always start the day by checking my emails. This allows me to note any new tasks which have arrived in my inbox and plan my day.

9.30am: The work we complete as trainees varies depending on the seat; in corporate I would use the morning to ensure the data rooms and due diligence processes I was managing were ticking over smoothly, whereas in family I would usually attend a client meeting with my supervisor. In real estate disputes I use the morning to complete research. The team partially works as an in-house team as we receive various queries from property lawyers across the firm. These queries tend to relate to specific or technical questions of law, therefore I will often need to use a mix of offline and online resources to complete the research. I always produce an 'outcome of research' memo giving a short response to the question asked and a longer explanation.

11.00am: It is around this time I receive the majority of my work as the other fee-earners will have considered their own to-do lists and addressed any urgent tasks. I have always received work from across the teams I have sat with rather than working solely under my supervisor. There is no hierarchy within Mills &

Reeve; I am currently sitting next to a partner and am just as likely to receive work from him as I am from any associates within the team.

11.30am: Having received the additional work I will make a decision based upon urgency as to what task to do next. On this occasion I have been asked to draft possession proceedings on behalf of one of the firm's main clients but I have also drafted claims for relief from forfeiture, injunction applications and created trial bundles. In family I drafted cohabitation agreements, undertook financial disclosure for divorce proceedings and drafted court applications regarding child custody.

1.00pm: Mills & Reeve subsidises its canteen so, depending on the weather, I will often eat downstairs with the other trainees, NQs and paralegals. If the weather is nicer some of us will eat lunch in the grounds of the cathedral or take a walk along the river to a coffee shop to get our fix before the afternoon.

2.00pm: I attend many meetings in the afternoon; on this occasion it is to discuss recovering costs from the other side with a client who we successfully represented in the High Court. In corporate I was allowed to take the lead in eight of nineteen meetings we held when completing a subdivision.

3.30pm: As trainees we are encouraged to get involved in the firm as a whole. Some

trainees plan social events for the office while others contribute to the firm's newspaper, *Signpost*. I, along with three other trainees, put myself forward to organise the firm's annual charity challenge. I would use the afternoons to organise the logistics for the event by speaking to participants or challenge and accommodation providers.

> **'In corporate I was allowed to take the lead in eight of nineteen meetings we held when completing a subdivision.'**

5.30pm: My supervisor tends to leave around this time and will always tell me to go home too. At Mills & Reeve we are not expected to stay late simply for the sake of staying late – the work-life balance is another positive.

6.00pm: I usually leave around this time having given my to-do list one final glance to ensure I have finalised any tasks which need completing. There is a really good social scene in Norwich so usually at least twice a week I will either be playing football, going for a run with colleagues or attending a local young professional event.

www.mills-reeve.com/graduates

About the firm

Address: Botanic House, 100 Hills Road, Cambridge CB2 1PH
Telephone: 01223 222336   **Fax:** 01223 355848
Website: www.mills-reeve.com
Email: fiona.medlock@mills-reeve.com
Twitter: @MillsandReeve

Senior partner: Justin Ripman
Managing partner: Claire Clarke

Other offices: Birmingham, Cambridge, Leeds, London, Manchester and Norwich.

Who we are: Mills & Reeve is a major UK law firm renowned for its outstanding service to national and international clients, for its collaborative culture and deep sector expertise.

What we do: Core sectors are: corporate and commercial, banking and finance, education, family, food and agribusiness, healthcare, insurance, private wealth, real estate investment, sport and technology.

What we're looking for: We welcome candidates from both law and non-law disciplines who already have or expect a 2(1) degree or equivalent. You will need to be highly motivated with excellent interpersonal skills, confidence, commercial awareness, a professional attitude and be ready to accept early responsibility.

What you'll do: Trainees complete six four-month seats. An in-house training programme, developed by our team of professional support lawyers, supports the PSC. Performance is assessed by informal reviews during the seat and a more formal review at the end of each seat.

Perks: Flexible benefits scheme, pension scheme, life assurance, bonus scheme, 25 days' holiday a year, a sports and social committee, subsidised restaurant, season ticket loan, employee assistance programme.

Sponsorship: Full course fees for the LPC and GDL. Maintenance grant during the LPC year and GDL year.

Facts and figures

Total partners: 110
Other fee-earners: 440
Total trainees: 35

Trainee places available for 2019: 21
Applications received pa: 1,100
Percentage interviewed: 7%

First year salary: £25,000
Second year salary: £26,500
Newly qualified salary: £40,000

Turnover in 2015: £81.6m (+3% from 2014)
Profits per equity partner: £337,000 (+2%)
(see legalbusiness.co.uk for full financial information)

Application process

Apply to: Fiona Medlock, graduate recruitment manager.
How: Online.
When: By 31 July 2017 for September 2019 training contracts.
What's involved: Online application form, online critical thinking test, assessment centre involving a group exercise and interview.

Vacation schemes

Summer: Application deadline = 31 January 2017, Cambridge 19 June to 30 June 2017, Birmingham 3 July to 14 July 2017, Manchester 10 July to 21 July 2017, Norwich 17 July to 28 July 2017.

MILLS & REEVE

Mishcon de Reya

Africa House, 70 Kingsway, London WC2B 6AH

Survey results *(marks out of 100%)*

Satisfied in your job?	78
Firm living up to expectations?	82
High quality of work?	86
Enough client contact?	83
Stress-free?	58
Happy work/life balance?	59
Friendly firm?	86
Great social life?	74
Good vacation scheme?	75
Confident you'll be kept on?	79
Good remuneration?	46
Diverse firm?	79

 **verdict**

Mishcon de Reya is a 'creative firm' where trainees are offered the chance to 'experience high-powered corporate deals'. The 'small trainee intake' results in 'exposure to particularly high-quality work' and a 'good calibre of cases to get involved in'. Trainees are 'fully integrated' into teams and are 'exposed to lots of opportunities to be involved with the best deals'. Additionally, the firm encourages trainees to share 'ideas and suggestions', and these are then 'taken seriously'. Current trainees have built up a 'great working and socialising relationship', enjoying the 'ambitious ethos and spirit' as the 'forward-thinking' firm is 'getting larger'. You can expect a 'wide variety of seats in different departments' plus the 'niche offerings' work well alongside the 'strong core litigation practice'. The senior fee-earners understand 'you have a life outside of work and encourage you to live it', as everyone at the firm has a 'passion outside law'. That said, trainees complain about 'late-night bundling' and 'completing deals at 4am' when the firm is 'very busy' and employees keep 'very long hours'. But trainees report a 'satisfactory work/life balance' as although it is 'hard work at times' they are 'generally looked after'. Top trainee moments include 'having a co-authored article published externally', 'successfully reducing a sport player's ban for doping from four years to two', and 'obtaining a freezing injunction and search order without notice to the defendant'. Those looking for an 'innovative firm' which provides plenty of 'hands-on experience' should take a closer look at Mishcon de Reya.

If the firm were a fictional character it would be...

Donna Paulsen (Suits) – sleek, sassy and effective

The firm

With offices in London and New York, Mishcon de Reya is an independent firm with a strategic international presence. The top 40 LB100 firm is well-respected for its private client, real estate and TMT prowess, and was nominated for both Dispute Resolution Team of the Year and Law Firm of the Year at the *Legal Business* Awards 2016.

The deals

Advised the management team of Morgan Stanley on its exit from the company; represented Pimlico Plumbers in a dispute regarding employment status; advised Tottenham Hotspur Football Club on state aid issues relating to its proposed new stadium; acted for Woodford Investment Management in an investment into life sciences company Immunocore; acted for RBS Action Group members in litigation against RBS.

The clients

Arden Partners; Badoo; Bidvest Foodservice International; CBRE; Fox International; Gagosian Gallery; Hewlett-Packard; Microsoft; Sainsbury's; Woodford Investment Management.

The star performers

Top-ranking departments according to *The Legal 500* (see legal500.com for more details)
Art and cultural property; Banking litigation: investment and retail; Commercial litigation; Competition litigation; Contentious trusts and probate; Corporate crime (including fraud, bribery and corruption); Employment: employers; Employment: senior executives; Family; Financial services (contentious); Flotations: small and mid-cap; Fraud: white-collar crime; Gaming and betting; Immigration: business; Immigration: human rights, appeals and overstay; M&A: mid-market, £50m-£250m; Personal tax, trusts and probate; Private equity: transactions: Mid-cap deal capability; Reputation management; Tax litigation and investigations.

- **Why did you choose this firm over any others?** 'Mix of private work with corporate'; 'I felt part of the team even on the vacation scheme'; 'it is generally a very respectful firm both to its staff and the clients'; 'the firm appeared dynamic and on the up'; 'career advancement opportunities'; 'the sense that the firm was on an upward trajectory'; 'enjoyable interview process'

- **Best thing about the firm?** 'The variety of work'; 'excellent lawyers'; 'new office'; 'the people are very genuine, caring, supportive and fun'; 'trainees are deeply involved in the minutiae of the cases so you feel some ownership and pride in the outcome'; 'the quality of work is strong across a wider breadth of legal disciplines than most City firms'; 'spending time with the other trainees'

- **Worst thing about the firm?** 'The pay is still not at market standard'; 'it's a shame you can't leave via the lovely front doors after 7pm'; 'a political, opaque and tortuous seat move process'; 'slow internet'; 'they charge for chocolate'; 'can feel somewhat overstretched as support staff are not evenly distributed throughout teams'

- **Best moment?** 'Dressing up as an elf for the kids Christmas party'; 'organising and pulling off a successful pub quiz for 150 people in the firm'; 'feedback from a QC on the quality of a substantive letter entirely of my own drafting'; 'attending an important hearing on my first day'; 'my first completion on a banking deal'

- **Worst moment?** 'Bundling until the early hours'; 'getting some figures wrong for a document required for court'; 'realising that something I had been working on was based on totally the wrong information and having to redo it over the weekend'; 'lack of support from a supervisor'

A day in the life of...

... Millicent Freeman first-year trainee, Mishcon de Reya

Departments to date: Trusts and succession disputes, real estate
University: University of Edinburgh
Degree: German and European History

8.45am: I check my emails and write my to-do list as soon as I get in. I then head to a real estate 'know-how' update meeting with the rest of the department, where we are provided with recent case law updates and relevant commercial and legal news. We need to ensure our advice is current, commercially informed and relevant.

10.00am: We are acting for a tenant who requires a lease renewal over two properties. The major update is the inclusion of a landlord-only break clause which allows the landlord to terminate the lease early. We are encouraged to have hands-on responsibility in the team. As such, I deal directly with the landlord's solicitors and ensure the client is kept informed. One of the associates in the team is supervising me and we discuss a couple of queries before I email the amended draft lease to the landlord's solicitor.

11.00am: After a quick coffee run, I head to a meeting with the digital legacies working group, which I became involved with during my first seat. The DLWG meets to keep abreast of the law regarding digital legacies. There is widespread confusion over what happens to the content of your digital accounts, such as Facebook, Paypal and Bitcoin, after death. Top of today's agenda is the recent BBC interview with a partner at Mishcon which was aired last week. We discuss how to build on this publicity and what the next steps should be.

11.35am: I get back to my desk to an email from one of the associates in the team who has asked me to register a transfer of a property with the Land Registry. I submit the forms and mark in my diary to check the Land Registry portal for a response in two days' time.

12.15pm: I deliver a presentation about life as a trainee at Mishcon to work experience students. The students seem really engaged and it's good to be able to pass on some of what I have learnt.

1.00pm: I head out with some of the other trainees for lunch and a walk around Lincoln's Inn Fields. It's good to catch up with them and hear how they're getting on.

2.00pm: The team has been working on the sale of a huge estate for over six months, and I've been heavily involved since I started the seat. As well as assisting with various individual leases and licences, I have also been working on electronic and hardcopy disclosure. As it is such a large-scale case, I send regular emails to the team asking for updates on any ongoing management matters, so that I can keep our records up-to-date. Staying organised and being flexible enough to deal with last-minute developments is vital to the success of such a complex transaction.

3.30pm: I send an update email to the other first-year trainees regarding the Corporate

Challenge we are involved in. We have been tasked to raise £10,000 for Beanstalk, a charity which provides literary support for children. This weekend we have organised to do a collective 110 mile sponsored walk from Oxford to London along the Thames Path.

4.30pm: I receive a call from an associate in my former department, asking me to research

> **'We have been working on the sale of a huge estate for over six months, and I've been heavily involved since I started the seat.'**

the different restrictions available to be entered onto the title register of a property. Our client's relative has died, leaving three properties in his name. Our client has a claim over those properties and wants to ensure they are not sold without his knowledge. One of our strengths at Mishcon de Reya is the breadth of our practice, and we often call upon other departments for their advice and input. I do the research and write up a short memo.

6.45pm: I check my diary for tomorrow and then I head over to the Cow, a nearby favourite haunt, for a drink with colleagues in the sunshine.

www.mishcongraduates.com

About the firm

Address: Africa House, 70 Kingsway, London WC2B 6AH
Telephone: 020 3221 7000
Website: www.mishcon.com
Email: trainee.recruitment@mishcon.com
Twitter: @Mishcon_de_Reya, @mishcongrads

Managing partner: Kevin Gold

Other offices: Associated office in New York.

Who we are: Founded in 1937, Mishcon de Reya offers every legal service to companies and individuals and our expertise covers five areas: analysing risk, protection of assets, managing wealth, resolving disputes and building business.

What we do: We are organised internally into six different departments: corporate, employment, dispute resolution, family, Mishcon Private and real estate. The firm also has a growing number of specialist groups which include: art; betting and gaming; finance and banking; fraud; immigration; insolvency; and IP.

What we're looking for: Our trainees are typically high-achieving and intelligent individuals with good interpersonal skills and outgoing personalities. Strength of character and ability to think laterally are key.

What you'll do: Trainees gain experience, skills and knowledge from across the firm in four six-month seats. These include both contentious and non-contentious work. Because of the relatively few training contracts offered, trainees can be exposed to high-quality work with early responsibility. Trainees are supported with a training and development programme and extensive internal training, in addition to the Professional Skills Course. Trainee performance is monitored closely and trainees can expect to receive regular feedback in addition to mid- and end-of-seat appraisals.

Perks: 25 days' holiday, health screening, life assurance, dental insurance, group income protection, private medical insurance, travel insurance, critical illness cover, gym membership, season ticket loan, group pension scheme, yoga classes, childcare vouchers, cycle scheme, in-house doctor, bonus scheme and give-as-you-earn schemes.

Sponsorship: The firm provides full LPC and GDL funding, and a maintenance grant of £5,000 payable in the GDL and LPC year.

Facts and figures

Total partners: 114
Other fee-earners: 196
Total trainees: 24

Trainee places available for 2019: 15
Applications received pa: 1,500
Percentage interviewed: 5%

First year salary: £34,000
Second year salary: £36,000

Turnover in 2015: £116.7m (+12% from 2014)
Profits per equity partner: £897,000 (-8%)
(see legalbusiness.co.uk for full financial information)

Application process

Apply to: Charlotte Lynch, graduate recruitment and development advisor.
How: Apply online at www.mischongraduates.com.
When: By January 2017. Please see our website for earlier closing date for Winter vacation schemes.
What's involved: Applicants will be considered for a training contract once they have completed a vacation scheme.

Vacation schemes

Winter: December 2016
Spring: April 2017
Summer: July 2017.

Mishcon de Reya

Morgan, Lewis & Bockius

5-10 St Paul's Churchyard, London EC4M 8AL

Survey results *(marks out of 100%)*

Satisfied in your job?	79
Firm living up to expectations?	80
High quality of work?	78
Enough client contact?	66
Stress-free?	59
Happy work/life balance?	53
Friendly firm?	80
Great social life?	60
Good vacation scheme?	73
Confident you'll be kept on?	72
Good remuneration?	88
Diverse firm?	81
Good international secondments?	84

 **verdict**

'Down-to-earth' Morgan, Lewis & Bockius is an 'up-and-coming firm' that offers its trainees 'high-profile cross-border work'. It is known as a 'reputable international firm' and current trainees loved their international secondments from which they 'learnt a lot'. The firm is a **Lex 100 Winner** for its international secondments, and for salary satisfaction. There is a 'nurturing environment' as the 'friendly firm encourages people to talk to each other' and this helps 'in terms of professional and personal development'. Trainees love the 'firm socials' because it is great fun 'hanging out with associates and other trainees'. The firm has US-based offices and global clients so trainees 'regularly work to other people's time-zones' which can result in 'long hours' and 'stressful days'. But trainees are 'rewarded with interesting work, early responsibility and hands-on experience', a winning combination that 'prepares us for becoming successful qualified lawyers'. Top trainee moments include 'working in Dubai on a project finance deal including a site visit and drafting documentation' and 'acting as first point of contact on an M&A transaction'. Although the 'training contract is new', there are 'weekly lunchtime training sessions presented by various practice groups of the firm', plus the great opportunity to work within a 'diverse workforce' where every employee is 'different in their own way' with no set 'Morgan Lewis type'. The 'flexible firm' listens to its trainees and does its best to 'work around seat preferences' to ensure everyone is happy. Those looking for secondments abroad and the chance to tailor your seat choices should check out Morgan, Lewis & Bockius.

If the firm were a fictional character it would be...

Spock (Star Trek) – logical, thorough and dependable

The firm

Global law firm Morgan, Lewis & Bockius boasts 29 offices across the United States, Europe, Asia and the Middle East. The firm provides comprehensive corporate and finance counsel to its international clients, who range in size and can be found across all major industries.

The deals

Advised Natixis on a $750m pre-export finance syndicated facility to EuroChem; advised Pearson plc on its €500m issuance; acted for Russia's VTB Bank on tender offers for $3.9bn in bonds; advised Actavis on the reduction of its workforce across 70 countries following the client's acquisition of Allergan; advised BG Group as one of the lead sponsors on the development of a major LNG project in Tanzania.

The clients

AstraZeneca; Auden Mckenzie Holdings; Beazley Underwriting; Citigroup; Google; London Metal Exchange; Pantheon Ventures; Perrigo; Platinum Equity; Sanofi-Aventis.

The star performers

Top-ranking departments according to *The Legal 500* (see legal500.com for more details)
Bank lending – investment grade debt and syndicated loans; Commercial litigation; Competition litigation; Corporate tax; Debt capital markets; EU and competition; Emerging markets; Employment: employers; Equity capital markets; Immigration: business; Insurance and reinsurance litigation; International arbitration; M&A: mid-market, £50m-£250m; Oil and gas; Pharmaceuticals and biotechnology; Private equity: transactions: Mid-cap deal capability; Securitisation.

- **Why did you choose this firm over any others?** 'Friendly and down-to-earth interviewers'; 'smaller intake equals more responsibility and better training'; 'the international secondments'; 'massively high-profile in the US'; 'relatively small (but growing) office in a large firm'; 'you are able to get involved in high-profile cross-border work'; 'the quality of work delegated to the trainees was very appealing'

- **Best thing about the firm?** 'The people are very friendly and inclusive'; 'listens to the trainees to try and work around their seat preferences'; 'it's location is great – right next to St Paul's so the views are lovely'; 'a female chair who seems to know each of us, including trainees, and takes an interest'; 'the salary'; 'the anti-trust department'

- **Worst thing about the firm?** 'The lack of amenities within the building'; 'the training contract is relatively new'; 'most things need sign off from the US'; 'delays on information about what is happening generally, specifically in terms of next seats'; 'regularly working to other people's time zones'

- **Best moment?** 'Preparing a memo of advice for a haute couture designer'; 'closing a deal I was working on in my first seat'; 'client meetings with the managing partner of the office'; 'living and working abroad for six months'; 'attending court and arbitration hearings'; 'hanging out with the other trainees and associates'; 'working in Dubai on a project finance deal'

- **Worst moment?** 'Document review deadline'; 'staying up until 5am for a closing in the corporate department'; 'unnecessarily tight deadlines'; 'closing a deal when ill'; 'working into the early hours'

A day in the life of...

... **George Crosse** first-year trainee, Morgan Lewis

Departments to date: Corporate and business transactions
University: University of Nottingham
Degree and class: Law 2(1)

8.15am: I arrive at my desk a little earlier than usual, as I received an email overnight from a New Zealand-based client, requesting a copy of the company shareholder register which I had updated post-completion of a deal. I send a copy across, then review my inbox and quickly update my to-do list.

9.00am: I make my way to the monthly trainee breakfast meeting. It's a great opportunity to informally discuss our training contract and the different experiences we've had within our seats.

9.45am: I head back to my desk and catch up with my supervisor on the current matters we are working on and any impending work deadlines. We are currently assisting a large Australian media company on its planned initial public offering (IPO). This includes undertaking due-diligence of the company's material contracts which are governed by English law; and co-ordinating with our other global offices, when the governing law is from their respective jurisdiction.

1.00pm: I grab a quick lunch with one of the associates. Our office is based in St Paul's and there are many quirky independent cafes right behind our building. Today I buy a Vietnamese inspired salad and we decide to eat on the steps of St Paul's Cathedral.

1.30pm: When I get back from lunch, I have an email from an associate in my team asking if I could pop into her office. She is drafting a share purchase agreement (SPA) in relation to the acquisition of a telecommunications company and explains that the other side's lawyers are attempting to remove a clause in the SPA that would negatively impact our client.

3.00pm: I sit down with the associate and go over some of my findings. I highlight the relevant case law where a seller had succeeded in removing a clause of the SPA and the repercussions that ensued. The associate then invites me to join the conference call.

4.00pm: I attend the conference call and listen to the negotiations where it is decided that the clause will be left in the SPA. Listening in is a great way to experience first-hand how a lawyer can successfully negotiate.

5.00pm: Our labour and employment practice group is hosting a presentation for clients on recent developments in employment law. I ask the partner hosting the event if I could come along – he is more than happy for me to join. The collegiate atmosphere in the office encourages trainees to network amongst different practice groups. Getting involved with the various events and

initiatives that are held here is a great learning experience.

6.00pm: I come back to my desk to find an email from a pro bono client, who is having some difficulty understanding a consultancy agreement that I helped draft for her new business venture.

> **'Being given responsibility at such an early stage in my career helps me prepare for life as an associate.'**

6.30pm: I finish some non-urgent tasks that I need to complete this week, such as Companies House filings. As a trainee, I have to take responsibility for managing my tasks for the deals I am working on. Being given responsibility at such an early stage in my career helps me prepare for life as an associate.

7.30pm: Once I have checked there is nothing further I can assist my supervisor with, I leave the office. My next seat is on secondment to our Singapore office, so I head to a pub in Bank for a 'meet and greet' networking event with other Singapore-bound trainees from different firms in the City.

About the firm

Address: 5-10 St Paul's Churchyard, London EC4M 8AL
Telephone: 020 3201 5000 **Fax:** 020 3201 5001
Website: www.morganlewis.com
Email: londontrainingprogramme@morganlewis.com

Senior partner: Jami McKeon (global)
Managing partner: Peter Sharp (London)

Other offices: Almaty, Astana, Beijing, Boston, Brussels, Chicago, Dallas, Dubai, Frankfurt, Hartford, Houston, London, Los Angeles, Miami, Moscow, New York, Orange County, Paris, Philadelphia, Pittsburgh, Princeton, San Francisco, Santa Monica, Silicon Valley, Singapore, Tokyo, Washington DC, Wilmington.

Who we are: Morgan Lewis provides comprehensive corporate, transactional, regulatory and litigation services to clients of all sizes and across all major industries.

What we do: Antitrust, corporate, debt and equity capital markets; finance and restructuring; labour and employment, including employment litigation and immigration advice; private investment fund formation and operation; structured transactions, tax planning and structuring; international commercial disputes, arbitration, insurance recovery and white-collar matters. Morgan Lewis is also strong in certain business sectors, including life sciences, financial services, energy and technology.

What we're looking for: Strong interpersonal, communication and client service skills and analytical ability, as well as a proven ability to work effectively both independently and within a team.

What you'll do: Trainees will be faced with consistently high-quality, challenging assignments, working with senior lawyers on complex and frequently cross-border matters.

Perks: 25 days' holiday p/a, life assurance, health and travel insurance, dental insurance, long-term disability insurance, option to take up to four weeks qualification leave at the end of training contract, season ticket loan and pension.

Sponsorship: Sponsorship of LPC and GDL at BPP University in London. A maintainence grant of £8,000 will be provided.

Facts and figures

Total partners: 33
Other fee-earners: 34
Total trainees: 12

Trainee places available for 2019: 8 vacancies
Applications received pa: 300
Percentage interviewed: 10-15%

First year salary: £43,000
Second year salary: £48,000
Newly qualified salary: £90,000

Application process

Apply to: Graduate recruitment team.
How: Online application via the website.
When: Apply by 31 July 2017 for 2019 contract.
What's involved: Two back-to-back interviews, with two partner interviewers in each. A tour of the office by a trainee.

Vacation schemes

Summer: Apply by 31 January 2017.

Morgan Lewis

A day in the life of...

... Lara Sirimanne trainee, Morrison & Foerster (UK) LLP

Departments to date: Capital markets and corporate, sitting in litigation from September 2016 and undertaking final seat in Singapore.
University: Keble College, Oxford **Degree and class:** BA Jurisprudence; 2(1)

8.30am: On my way to work I check my emails and prioritise my morning accordingly, responding to urgent queries immediately.

9.00am: My first task for the day is from a Japanese client regarding a distribution from one of the group's UK subsidiaries. As longstanding UK advisers to this major corporation, we act for the group on both transactional work and general corporate matters on an almost daily basis. I discuss my proposed approach with a senior associate and draft the required corporate authorities.

10.30am: My focus then moves to a large ongoing acquisition by our client, a US public company, of a well-known sportswear brand. The target has a global presence and it has been great fun building relationships with colleagues in our US and European offices on this deal. I have been managing the due diligence process, so my first task is to allocate the new documents uploaded to the data room by the seller to the appropriate legal teams and update my colleagues across the globe. While reviewing the English law documents, I identify an issue which could affect the purchase. I update the due diligence report with this information and flag it to a senior associate.

12.00pm: The documents I drafted for the Japanese client have now been reviewed and, after a few edits, I send them to the

client's in-house counsel with a note outlining the next steps.

12.30pm: We now have a training session on UK insolvency procedures, delivered by partners in our business restructuring and insolvency group. We have regular training delivered by senior MoFo lawyers or external experts.

2.00pm: I receive a call from a client for whom we recently completed a €75m acquisition. I am usually their first point of contact on any European aspect of the deal, the small trainee intake means that I have an unbeatable amount of responsibility and client contact. On this deal, for example, I was the sole MoFo representative at the closing – a great experience as I was able to visit the main acquisition site and toast the successful completion with both parties! Today's call is to discuss the post-completion establishment of branch offices across Europe. I have been co-ordinating the administrative process for each jurisdiction and liaising with local counsel in the five countries, so I update the client on the progress made and advise on next steps.

3.30pm: As we have a spare moment, my supervisor and I head to the games room for a heated ping-pong match. We're a tight-knit firm but on the odd occasion we need to release our competitive spirits and the games room provides the perfect setting!

4.00pm: We turn our attention to an important client call we're about to host. A sporting client has come to us with an exciting proposal for a global competition involving eGaming. First, we have a preparatory call with the MoFo team, which includes colleagues from various practice groups across LA, Berlin and Hong

> **'The small trainee intake means that I have an unbeatable amount of responsibility and client contact.'**

Kong, and then, when the client joins the call, we discuss their vision for the competition and provide them with initial suggestions as to how best to run it. After a post-call debrief, I circulate a note to the MoFo team summarising the call and the next steps.

6.30pm: At the end of the day my attention returns to our Japanese client. This time it is for an office-wide celebration of the announcement of a landmark and transformative public takeover offer by the client. It is wonderful to see the hard work of the MoFo deal team being appreciated and the champagne flowing!

http://careers.mofo.com

About the firm

Address: CityPoint, One Ropemaker Street, London EC2Y 9AW
Telephone: 020 7920 4000   **Fax:** 020 7496 8500
Website: www.mofo.com
Email: lmccall@mofo.com
Twitter: @MoFoLLP

Managing partners: Alistair Maughan and Jonathan Wheeler

Other offices: Beijing, Berlin, Brussels, Denver, Hong Kong, Los Angeles, New York, Northern Virginia, Palo Alto, San Diego, San Francisco, Shanghai, Singapore, Tokyo, Washington DC.

Who we are: Morrison & Foerster is a global firm with over 1,000 lawyers in key technology and finance centres in the US; Europe and Asia.

What we do: We work on cutting-edge global transactions and high-profile litigation matters. Our work has a strong bias towards the technology and finance sectors.

What we're looking for: We are looking for individuals with a 'can do' attitude, a willingness to be challenged, openness to diverse perspectives and some real energy. A strong academic background is essential.

What you'll do: The training contract in London comprises four six-month seats, rotating between departments. Seats available include bankruptcy restructuring and insolvency; capital markets; corporate; finance; litigation; tax, and technology transactions.

Perks: 5% pension contribution, private medical insurance, Denplan, death in service and long-term disability insurance, childcare vouchers, cycle to work scheme, season ticket loans, payroll giving, subsidised gym membership.

Sponsorship: Full GDL and/or LPC fees paid after training contract offer acceptance, plus a maintenance grant of £8,000 per annum. Otherwise, 50% reimbursement of receipted course costs if exams have already been completed upon training contract offer.

Facts and figures

Total partners (London): 18
Other fee-earners (London): 29
Total trainees (London): 6

Trainee places available for 2018/2019: 2/4
Applications received pa: c.1,000
Percentage interviewed: 4.4%

First year salary: £38,500
Second year salary: £43,600
Newly qualified salary: £82,000

Application process

Apply via: www.careers.mofo.com.
How: Online application form for a vacation scheme placement. MoFo accepts candidates into the London trainee program on the basis of a successful performance during a summer vacation scheme.
When: From 1 October to 31 December 2016 for a summer scheme placement in 2017.
What's involved: First round interviews with associates and graduate recruitment. Second stage interviews include a case study and a presentation, and are conducted by two partners and a trainee.

Vacation schemes

Summer: 3-14 July 2017; and 17-28 July 2017. Apply by 31 December 2016.

Nabarro LLP

125 London Wall, London EC2Y 5AL

Survey results *(marks out of 100%)*

Satisfied in your job?	80
Firm living up to expectations?	82
High quality of work?	80
Enough client contact?	72
Stress-free?	54
Happy work/life balance?	67
Friendly firm?	89
Great social life?	82
Good vacation scheme?	97
Confident you'll be kept on?	83
Good remuneration?	71
Diverse firm?	81
Good international secondments?	40

 **verdict**

Respondents praise Nabarro's 'six-seat training contract' for offering a 'real range of good-quality work', plus the chance to gain such broad experience is also 'very helpful for those who are unsure about which areas they are interested in'. The firm's 'fantastic vacation scheme' also proved popular with current trainees, and merits a **Lex 100 Winner** award. Feedback also highlights the 'brilliant training' and how 'all trainee supervisors seem to be great role models'. Highlight achievements include 'attending a multi-million pound hearing in the international dispute resolution centre following months of preparation for the case' and 'being trusted to advise a client face-to-face in a meeting'. Trainees are disappointed about 'the lack of international opportunities' available, despite the 'overseas offices and European alliance', yet those who have been on international secondments speak of a 'really enjoyable' experience. The 'lack of cohesion between the different offices' can be a frustration, as 'sometimes as a member of the Sheffield office the London office can feel like a different firm'. Still, it is appreciated that the 'excellent support staff' are 'friendly and approachable', and as one respondent comments, 'the representatives that came to various law school events also really sold the firm'. Trainees are very pleased with the 'great offices', and cite the fantastically-stocked salad bar' and 'new fizzy-water tap' as favourite features. To train at a firm that commands a 'terrific reputation in the real estate market' and engenders 'a real sense of cohesiveness and support', apply to Nabarro.

If the firm were a fictional character it would be...

Mrs Patmore (Downton Abbey) – friendly and supportive, but pushes you when there's work to be done

The firm

London-headquartered Nabarro remains a market-leader in real estate, and was nominated for both Real Estate Team of the Year and Competition Team of the Year at the *Legal Business Awards 2016*. The firm has overseas offices in Brussels, Dubai and Singapore, and also has an alliance with other leading European firms. Aside from property law, the firm is active across the corporate and commercial practice areas.

The deals

Advised Redefine International on its £490m acquisition of AEGON's UK property fund; defended UK Coal in more than 70 unfair dismissal and disability discrimination claims; assisted Tarmac with the sale of its headquarters in Wolverhampton; successfully defended the State Bank of India in a race discrimination and whistleblowing claim brought by a former trader; advised the North York Moors National Park Authority on a planning agreement for a deep mine proposal.

The clients

BAE Systems; Biffa Waste Services; GE Capital; Henry Boot; Laing O'Rourke; Land Securities; Manchester Airport Group; Manchester City Council; Santander; Veolia Environmental.

The star performers

Top-ranking departments according to *The Legal 500* (see legal500.com for more details)

Banking and finance; Clinical negligence: defendant; Commercial litigation; Commercial property; Construction; Corporate and commercial; Corporate restructuring and insolvency; Employee share schemes; Employment: employers; Environment; Health and safety; Local government; Pensions dispute resolution; Pensions (non-contentious); Personal injury: defendant; Planning; Property litigation.

- **Why did you choose this firm over any others?** 'Friendly atmosphere'; 'specialisms in my area of interest'; 'the six-seat training contract'; 'good-quality work without the Magic Circle hours'; 'perceived friendly approach'; 'fantastic vacation scheme'; 'there is a good amount of trainee responsibility'; 'it is one of the best firms in Sheffield'; 'offered the opportunities of a large firm with the friendliness of a smaller firm'

- **Best thing about the firm?** 'The free dinners after 7pm'; 'workplace environment'; 'seniors' willingness to help you learn'; 'the quality of work in some departments is super exciting'; 'the quality and range of training available is outstanding'; 'there is a nice atmosphere in the office'; 'the responsibility you get given from your first day'; 'desire to be an attractive place to work'

- **Worst thing about the firm?** 'The lifts'; 'lack of international opportunities'; 'occasional lack of control over working hours'; 'some lack of transparency over qualification process'; 'it is still hard to see where the senior female role models are'; 'getting expenses signed off by finance'; 'many of the partners are still very old school'

- **Best moment?** 'Completing a deal by myself'; 'drafting my first lease'; 'the first day in every seat that you start feeling competent'; 'attending court hearings of matters in which I have been heavily involved'; 'being sent on secondment to Brussels'; 'receiving very positive feedback from a client early on following a piece of research'; 'researching for a BBC interview'

- **Worst moment?** 'Being told off by the partner for not posting my timesheet'; 'incorrectly executing and completing a £300m sale contract'; 'having to cross reference hundreds of documents in a schedule'; 'late nights in the office in the run up to Christmas'; 'realising an email sounded less polite than I intended and having a fee-earner pick up on this'

A day in the life of...

... George Mole first-year trainee, Nabarro LLP

Departments to date: Real estate, IP and IT
University: University of Birmingham
Degree and class: Political science 2(1)

9.00am: I arrive on the 16th floor where I share an office with one of the partners, and make myself a cuppa on the way to my desk. Once I'm sat down, the first thing I do is review my to-do list from yesterday and make a new list for today. This is one of the key things I learnt from my time in real estate, where trainees may be working on over 25 active matters – the only way to stay on top of it is to be organised!

9.15am: Last weekend I took a group of 26 of my colleagues to Liverpool to play touch rugby in the Corporate Games 2016 (which I am still aching from!). So I take the opportunity to write a small article with a few pictures to be posted on the social page of our intranet site. The firm is very sociable and throughout the rest of the day I receive a few compliments for organising the event.

9:35am: Time to start my billable work for the day and I've got some drafting to do which should take most of my morning. This involves drafting a letter to the third party to our client's sponsorship agreement with a global leader in cosmetics. The letter will explain the key clauses and importance of the warranties included in the licence that they are being asked to sign, which will give our client the right to use their intellectual property.

11.10am I get a call from my supervisor. He tells me he has been asked to update a number of sections in one of the main texts on IT law, *International Computer and Internet Contracts and Law* by Michele T Rennie. As his trainee, he asks me to help him. This is a massive undertaking that will give me work to do until the end of my seat, but I'm happy to get involved as it will give me a chance to gain greater insight into some very interesting and technical areas of law, such as computer software piracy and data licence agreements. I start on this research task straight away to get ahead of the curve.

12.45pm: I get a call from one of my fellow trainees who asks if I can join him for lunch. When we get to the canteen, despite having made my own lunch today, there is a fresh sushi pop-up stand that is just too tempting... double lunch it is.

1.15pm I return to my desk much fuller than when I left and my roommate invites me to attend three conference calls starting in 15 minutes with different legal counsel from Germany, Holland and Switzerland in relation to advertising standards in those countries. I take notes for all of the calls and am asked to summarise the advice for each jurisdiction into a file note which can be sent to the client.

3.30pm: I head to a meeting room for the monthly fund-raising committee meeting. Here we discuss the upcoming events and delegate roles among us. Our next event is our annual Battle of the Bands at the 100 Club on Oxford Street, and I have volunteered to order the food and attempt to source a drum kit, guitar and bass amps, if possible.

4.00pm: I check the emails I have received while in my meeting. There's a couple of notifications that new IP and IT documents

> '**Last weekend I took a group of 26 of my colleagues to Liverpool to play touch rugby in the Corporate Games 2016.**'

have been uploaded to the dataroom for one of the corporate deals I have been assisting on. I spend the next few hours reviewing these to highlight any areas of concern that I think should be highlighted to our client in the due diligence report.

6.55pm: I diarise a couple of events for tomorrow then head down to the canteen for (free!) dinner; my choice tonight is pollock with new potatoes and vegetables.

7:20pm: Having posted my time entries for the day, I log off and head to the pub with some friends to watch tonight's football match.

graduates.nabarro.com

About the firm

Address: 125 London Wall, London EC2Y 5AL
Telephone: 020 7524 6000
Website: www.nabarro.com
Email: graduateinfo@nabarro.com
Twitter: @nabarrograds

Senior partner: Ciaran Carvalho
Managing partner: Andrew Inkester

Other offices: Manchester, Sheffield, Brussels, Dubai and Singapore.

Who we are: Nabarro is an leading international law firm offering a broad range of legal services to major national and international clients in the public and private sectors. We deliver the highest quality, business-focused advice to clients, clearly and concisely, no matter how complex the situation.

What we do: The firm focuses on four key sectors: healthcare and life sciences, infrastructure, real estate and technology. Main areas of work include banking and finance, corporate, real estate, pensions and employment, funds and indirect real assets, IP/IT, dispute resolution, planning and environmental, construction and energy.

What we're looking for: You will be required to demonstrate strong academic achievement (a minimum 2(1) degree and AAB at A-level), commercial awareness, excellent interpersonal skills and teamwork, motivation and drive. Applications are welcomed from law and non-law students and we are committed to making the most of diverse skills, expertise and experience. Accordingly there is no typical Nabarro trainee and we aim to recruit from a wide range of universities. We offer training contracts in our London and Sheffield offices.

What you'll do: Trainees undertake six four-month seats to ensure maximum exposure to the firm's core practice areas, as well as the opportunity to spend time in more specialist areas, or possibly on secondment.

Perks: Private medical insurance, pension, life assurance, 26 days' holiday per year, season ticket loan, subsidised restaurant, GymFlex and occupational healthcare. Trainee salaries are reviewed annually.

Sponsorship: Full fees paid for the LPC and GDL plus a maintenance grant: LPC: £7,000 London, £6,000 regional; GDL: £6,000 London, £5,000 regional. We reimburse 50% of fees retrospectively if you have already completed the GDL or LPC.

Facts and figures

Total partners: 106
Other fee-earners: 266
Total trainees: 53

Trainee places available for 2019: 25
Applications received pa: 750
Percentage interviewed: 40% (videos plus assessment centre)

First year salary: London £38,000, Sheffield £26,000
Second year salary: London £42,000, Sheffield £29,000
Newly qualified salary: London £62,000, Sheffield £40,000

Turnover in 2015: £126.1m (+8%)
Profits per equity partner: £631,000 (+31%)

Application process

Apply to: Mirrick Koh, graduate recruitment and trainee development manager.
How: Online application only – graduates.nabarro.com.
When: Between 1 October 2016 and 3 January 2017 for 2019 training contracts.
What's involved: Video screening prior to an assessment day (which consists of an interview and a group and written assessment), followed by a summer vacation scheme.

Vacation schemes

We recruit all our trainees from our vacation scheme and offer 55 places a year.
Summer: June and July 2017 (apply between 1 October 2016 and 3 January 2017).

N A B A R R O

Norton Rose Fulbright

3 More London Riverside, London SE1 2AQ

Survey results *(marks out of 100%)*

Satisfied in your job?	76
Firm living up to expectations?	79
High quality of work?	74
Enough client contact?	67
Stress-free?	57
Happy work/life balance?	56
Friendly firm?	86
Great social life?	74
Good vacation scheme?	87
Confident you'll be kept on?	79
Good remuneration?	81
Diverse firm?	84
Good international secondments?	85

 **verdict**

The 'global prestige' and 'ambitious international outlook' of Norton Rose Fulbright is acclaimed by its trainees. There is an 'overwhelming international emphasis to the work', and the 'opportunity to go abroad' is a huge draw as an international seat 'is almost guaranteed'. Trainees praise the overseas secondments as 'extremely rewarding', which helped to secure a **Lex 100 Winner** title. Another common theme in the feedback is the 'industry group' approach at NRF, which allows trainees 'to become an expert in a business sector as well as a legal expert'. Recent trainee highlights include 'preparing witness statements for the High Court for a cross-border merger' and 'working on a complex arbitration'. Perhaps unsurprisingly, 'the hours could be better', and there are instances of 'staying up all night proofreading' and 'not leaving before midnight'. There is said to be a 'supportive atmosphere' on the vacation scheme, where the 'friendly nature of colleagues' is appreciated. There are some complaints about the structure of the training contract and a few respondents lament the 'loss of the six-seat rotation', while others refer to 'the lack of flexibility in seat rotations as we have to complete three compulsory seats'. NRF takes its pro bono work seriously, and as such 'it's obligatory for trainees to act as volunteer advisers at the Croydon and Tower Hamlets law centres'. Another plus point is that 'a great emphasis is placed on trainee development by team members of all levels', and the 'intellectual calibre of the associates and partners' certainly sets a good example. To train at a 'pre-eminent City firm' with an 'international outlook' and 'clear ambitions', apply to Norton Rose Fulbright.

If the firm were a fictional character it would be...

Mr Wemmick (Great Expectations) – very professional and busy during working hours, but friendly afterwards

The firm

Norton Rose Fulbright is a prominent City firm with more than 3,800 lawyers based in over 50 cities across the globe, and in June 2016 the firm set up a second base in California by opening a San Francisco office. The firm has one of the world's foremost projects, energy and natural resources groups, and the London office is particularly regarded for its work in this area.

The deals

Advised Bank of America as arranger on a $150m cross-border ABL facility for the Panavision group; advised Saga Cruises on the acquisition of a new 236-metre luxury cruise vessel; represented Citibank in a dispute over metals stored in Qingdao; advised Emirates Airlines on its $913m ECA-backed sukuk to fund the acquisition of four Airbus A380s; advised Amni International Petroleum Development Company on its $31m acquisition of Afren's interest in the Okoro oil field offshore Nigeria.

The clients

BMW; BP; Crown Estate Commissioners; Macquarie Group; Natixis; Pension Protection Fund; the Republic of Angola; Standard Chartered Bank; Sumitomo Mitsui Banking Corporation; Wells Fargo.

The star performers

Top-ranking departments according to *The Legal 500* (see legal500.com for more details)
Asset based lending; Asset finance and leasing; Aviation; Commodities: physicals; Debt capital markets; Derivatives and structured products; Emerging markets; Employee share schemes; Health and safety; Infrastructure (PFI and PPP); Islamic finance; Mining and minerals; Oil and gas; Pensions dispute resolution; Pensions (non-contentious); Power (including electricity, nuclear and renewables); Rail; Securitisation; Shipping; Trade finance.

- **Why did you choose this firm over any others?** 'Good culture'; 'the international secondment opportunities'; 'friendly ethos'; 'breadth of training'; 'really good client focus'; 'established firm with a long history'; 'its reputation in the City'; 'a lot of my fellow trainees have studied abroad and speak different languages'; 'I wanted to be a part of a trailblazing international law firm'; 'culture of the firm'; 'friendly and social'

- **Best thing about the firm?** 'You are really encouraged to seize secondment opportunities'; 'very broad spectrum of highly-regarded practices'; 'the location is lovely'; 'biscuit bars on the client floor'; 'location at London Bridge'; 'the personable people'; 'the emphasis on excellence'; 'the inclusive environment'

- **Worst thing about the firm?** 'Not enough space in offices'; 'there is currently no canteen'; 'the hours in certain teams'; 'the opacity of the seat selection process'; 'the wifi password requests'; 'it's a long way from the RCJ if you're on a court run'; 'the lack of a gym on site'; 'it would be nice if they offered language courses'

- **Best moment?** 'Seeing improvement in my abilities'; 'going to meet a CEO of a client on my own'; 'having an argument with opposing counsel on the telephone'; 'having a client say how impressed they were'; 'secondment to the Sydney office'; 'running a signing on my own and doing a good job'; 'going to New York for a month-long business trip'

- **Worst moment?** 'Not being able to handle my first real criticism'; 'working 30 hours straight on a corporate deal during closing'; 'spending three weeks with no work'; 'due diligence tasks'; 'client secondment to Citibank'; 'a very hard week working on a deal only to have it postponed'; 'being asked to make tea'; 'working all night three times in one week'

A day in the life of...

... **Constantine Markides** trainee, Norton Rose Fulbright

Departments to date: Environment, safety and planning
University: University of Cambridge
Degree: Land economy

8.30am: I arrive before 9.30am to give myself time to plan my day and deal with any outstanding matters. Trainees in the environment, safety and planning team have to be organised. A typical day will involve a variety of tasks ranging from stand-alone work to banking, corporate and property support work. I head to my desk where I separate my work into two lists, namely 'urgent' and 'less urgent'.

9.30am: I send a news bulletin to everyone in the real estate department, highlighting the most recent commercial property news.

10.00am: An associate is preparing a planning report for a property development in London and has asked me to review a new local land charges search sent by the Land Registry. This search indicates any changes in the planning conditions affecting the proposed use of a property. I compare the new search with the previous one, noting any differences and discussing these with the associate.

10.30am: I attend the weekly team meeting where each person summarises the projects they are working on, any developments since the last meeting, the training sessions they have attended and any marketing opportunities.

11.00am: I update the planning report to reflect my review of the local land charges search, which the associate then checks.

11.30am: I receive an email from an associate asking me to suggest topics for articles to be included in Practical Law Company's (PLC) monthly environmental bulletin, which provides environmental law know-how and market information for lawyers. I spend the next hour compiling a list of important topics and send these to the associate.

12.30pm: I have volunteered to help organise Norton Rose Fulbright's seven-a-side football tournament. I meet up with the football team's captain for lunch at the canteen downstairs to discuss what needs to be done. The canteen has recently been refurbished and provides a different range of food choices daily. The firm also regularly organises lunchtime training sessions and seminars which are generally very informative and well-attended.

2.00pm: I head back to my desk to continue working. I have volunteered to be a trainee buddy for one of the vacation scheme students, so I send her an email appointment to meet up for a coffee to discuss her experience at Norton Rose Fulbright so far. There is an extensive pastoral support system at the firm.

2.15pm: I am asked by an associate to provide a summary planning report for the refinancing of solar farms. I find the information in the planning decisions on various planning authority websites and send the complete summary to the associate for her to check.

3.15pm: The team has been involved with an environment deed apportioning liability for land contamination regarding the acquisition of a brownfield site by one of our major clients. My supervisor asks me to help manage

> **'The firm regularly organises lunchtime training sessions and seminars which are generally very informative and well-attended.'**

the transaction by preparing the schedules to the environment deed that will be signed on completion. I start reading the environment deed to familiarise myself with the details.

4.30pm: I head downstairs to catch up with the vacation scheme student over a coffee.

5.00pm: My supervisor asks me to research the grounds for which an interested party to a contentious dispute can apply for an expedited hearing and the process for this. I finish the research and send it to my supervisor.

6.30pm: I occasionally attend formal and informal social events which provide a great chance to meet other staff.

www.nortonrosefulbrightgraduates.com

About the firm

Address: 3 More London Riverside, London SE1 2AQ
Telephone: 020 7444 2113   **Fax:** 020 7283 6500
Website: www.nortonrosefulbright.com
Email: graduate.recruitment@nortonrosefulbright.com
Facebook: Norton Rose Fulbright Graduates UK
Twitter: NLawGrad

Managing partner: Martin Scott

Other offices: We have more than 3,800 lawyers and legal staff based in over 50 cities across Europe, the United States, Canada, Latin America, Asia, Australia, Africa, the Middle East and Central Asia.

Who we are: Norton Rose Fulbright is a global legal firm. We provide the world's pre-eminent corporations and financial institutions with a full business law service.

What we do: Recognised for our industry focus, we are strong across all the key industry sectors: financial institutions; energy; infrastructure, mining and commodities; transport; technology and innovation; as well as life sciences and healthcare.

What we're looking for: All applicants must have achieved at least AAB in their A levels or equivalent and be on course to achieve (or to have achieved already) a 2(1) degree or above.

What you'll do: Our four-seat training contract gives trainees an insight into our core practice areas and industry sectors. Trainees also have the opportunity to spend six months on international or client secondment.

Perks: Gym membership/subsidy, life assurance, pension scheme with company contributions, private healthcare, season ticket loan, subsidised restaurant, cycle-to-work scheme, private GP service, subsidised music programme.

Sponsorship: Financial support is provided for both GDL and LPC students. We will pay course fees and a maintenance grant to successful training contract applicants. We do not, however, offer retrospective funding if you have commenced the GDL or LPC prior to our offer. Our maintenance grants are £8,000 for GDL students and £7,000 for LPC students.

Facts and figures

Total partners: 1,100 (worldwide)
Other fee-earners: 3,800+ (worldwide)
Total trainees: 100+
Trainee places available for 2019: Up to 50

First year salary: £42,000
Second year salary: £47,000
Newly qualified salary: £72,000

Turnover in 2015: £1,118m (-3% from 2014)
Profits per equity partner: £394,000 (-6%)
(see legalbusiness.co.uk for full financial information)

Application process

How: Online application.
When: Finalists and graduates: 1 October 2016–29 January 2017. Penultimate-year undergraduates (law), finalists, graduates (law and non-law): 1 June–16 July 2017.
What's involved: Online application, assessment day.

Vacation schemes

Winter: Applications open: 1-30 October 2016 (finalists and graduates).
Summer: Applications open: 1 October 2016–8 January 2017 (penultimate-year undergraduates and finalists).

NORTON ROSE FULBRIGHT

Olswang

90 High Holborn, London WC1V 6XX

Survey results *(marks out of 100%)*

Satisfied in your job?	76
Firm living up to expectations?	76
High quality of work?	76
Enough client contact?	66
Stress-free?	56
Happy work/life balance?	67
Friendly firm?	82
Great social life?	69
Good vacation scheme?	87
Confident you'll be kept on?	64
Good remuneration?	72
Diverse firm?	77
Good international secondments?	40

 **verdict**

Olswang has an 'excellent reputation in media and TMT law' making it 'the place to be' if you want to work in these sectors. The 'interesting clients' are at 'the cutting-edge of their industries', and advising them can offer 'fantastic exposure to the in-house practices of large media organisations'. The impressive clients are considered one of the best things about the firm, but trainees note that sometimes there 'isn't much client contact'. Trainees are 'key members of the team' and are known as 'individuals rather than trainee number X'. There is 'zero expectation of face-time as everyone has side hobbies that keep them motivated and in touch with the outside world'. There have been a few grumbles from trainees about 'being over-loaded with work' and 'working long days and nights'. The 'very tight deadlines' result in trainees working 'under high pressure', though celebratory moments include 'a bottle of champagne after finishing the verification process for an investor presentation'. Also, trainees enjoy 'meeting famous people through the media practice', as well as 'completing deals for happy clients'. The 'firm is self-aware in trying to break down any hierarchy as much as possible', and as a result Olswang lawyers are 'friendly and inclusive'. Trainees get to work with 'different teams of people who are highly intelligent and have different working styles you can learn from'. This is 'good-quality training' which involves a 'combination of formal and informal training sessions'. Those who want to work with 'top clients' at an 'innovative firm' should take a look at Olswang.

If the firm were a fictional character it would be...

Danny Ocean (Ocean's Eleven) – chilled, stylish, delegates well and always gets the job done

The firm

Olswang is a popular choice for clients seeking advice on all matters relating to media, IT and telecoms law. The firm also contains a large corporate department which handles a variety of mid-market deals. Olswang enjoys an international reputation owing to its network of offices in Europe, and the firm announced non-exclusive associations with firms in Hong Kong and Singapore in December 2015.

The deals

Assisted Catalent with the proposed closure of its UK packaging facility site, affecting over 150 employees; acted for Surreal Vision during its sale to Facebook; advised Gamesys on its £425m sale of Jackpotjoy to Intertain Group; acted for key client UBS Global Asset Management on the £113m acquisition of New Brook buildings in London; defended Focus Pharmaceuticals in litigation against Novartis.

The clients

BP; Bloomberg; Cineworld; Groupon; Investec; Jeremy Clarkson; Marks & Spencer; Prezzo; Unilever; Vodafone.

The star performers

Top-ranking departments according to *The Legal 500* (see legal500.com for more details)
Brand management; Commercial property: hotels and leisure; Commercial contracts; Employment; Fraud: civil; Flotations: small and mid-cap; Franchising; Gaming and betting; IT and telecoms; Intellectual property; M&A: mid-market, £50m-£250m; Media and entertainment (including media finance); Property finance; PATMA: Patent attorneys; Pharmaceuticals and biotechnology; Property litigation; Reputation management; Sport; VAT and indirect tax; Venture capital.

- **Why did you choose this firm over any others?** 'The focus in TMT'; 'the great interview process'; 'interesting and diverse list of clients'; 'ability to compete with higher level firms'; 'the industry sectors the firm primarily works with'; 'the firm's non-hierarchical reputation'; 'I loved the vacation scheme'; 'client base in media and technology'; 'great reputation for being a top firm with interesting clients'

- **Best thing about the firm?** 'The clients'; 'the people'; 'a friendly place to work'; 'places a lot of trust in its trainees'; 'top-quality work across all the departments I have worked in'; 'the firm is very self-aware'; 'tries to break down any hierarchy as much as possible'; 'everyone is trying their best to be friendly and inclusive'

- **Worst thing about the firm?** 'Not meeting the cool clients'; 'lack of communication from HR'; 'international opportunities have been reined in hugely over the last few years', 'general belt-tightening is still evident'; 'some of the IT systems are starting to feel out of date'; 'difference in expectations of trainees across different departments'; 'sometimes initiatives quickly lose momentum and ideas are not followed through'

- **Best moment?** 'Client Christmas party'; '4am distressed loan negotiations'; 'going to court'; 'attending very interesting meetings with external counsel; 'getting good feedback from senior colleagues'; 'working as part of a team on a transaction which spanned corporate, finance and commercial departments'; 'compiling a regulatory report on a new Microsoft product in its desired territories and receiving great feedback'

- **Worst moment?** 'Leaving some documents for execution in a taxi'; 'working hard on a deal that didn't go ahead'; 'feeling over-loaded with work on occasion'; 'many long nights verifying an AIM admission document'; 'working late on the night of the Christmas party'

A day in the life of...

... David Whitehead trainee, Olswang

Departments to date: Corporate, commercial litigation
University: St Catharine's College, University of Cambridge
Degree: English

8.40am: I arrive at work after cycling in. After a shower and a quick check of my emails I grab a coffee and head up to the third floor.

9.15am: At my desk I draw up a to-do list prioritising my tasks for the day (I learned early on that being organised is the one of the key skills a trainee has to learn). I start by reviewing a bundle I prepared the previous evening for a court hearing the following week. Preparing bundles is an important (and sadly unavoidable) task for litigation trainees, and the rest of the team are relying on it having been checked thoroughly! Once I've checked that all the documents are properly referenced I send the bundle off to be copied.

10.15am: I attend a meeting with the rest of the team (a partner and two associates) ahead of the hearing and take a file note of a call with counsel. Strategy for the hearing is discussed, and I am assigned a number of follow-up tasks including drafting a letter to the court. I have been involved with this particular case since the beginning of my seat and have enjoyed my role within the team. One advantage of being part of a comparatively small intake of trainees is that you are given a fair amount of responsibility early on in your training contract.

11.30am: I have a brief chat with a partner about a smaller matter I'm working on, and I give him a witness statement I have drafted to

review. On this matter I'm working directly for the partner and have been trusted to carry out a lot of the work independently, which is great if a little nerve-wracking!

12.00pm: I get back to my desk to find an email from an associate asking if I'm available to carry out a discrete piece of research on a point of law before the end of the day. I don't have any other high-priority tasks to complete so I reply to say that I have capacity and make a start on the research (an ability to prioritise is the other key skill a trainee has to learn).

1.00pm: I head up to the canteen for lunch and catch up with a few of the other trainees. It's almost time for us to start thinking about our next seats, so the main topic of conversation is where everyone would like to go next.

2.00pm: I get back to my desk to find that the copies of the bundle have been delivered. I walk over to court (which is just around the corner) to file the bundle, and I arrange for other copies to be sent out.

2.45pm: I get a coffee on my way back into the office and start writing up my research note. An email is sent to all litigation trainees asking for someone to write a blog article on a recent case, for which I volunteer.

3.45pm: My supervisor asks me to update the costs budget on a case I am helping her with.

I'm familiar with the process, having worked on the case for a while, so it fortunately doesn't take me too long to complete. I finish my research note and send it back to the associate.

4.30pm: I head upstairs to join the student I am tutoring as part of The Access Project,

> 'On this matter I'm trusted to carry out a lot of the work independently, which is great if a little nerve-wracking!'

a volunteer organisation that provides academic support to a local school. I am helping my tutee prepare for her AS-level exams, which are fast approaching.

6.00pm: I type up my file note from the earlier meeting and circulate it to the team, and write myself a note detailing tasks that have to be completed the next day.

7.00pm: I leave the office and meet with some of my fellow trainees for a drink in the sunshine, including some who are currently on client secondments and I haven't seen for a while.

www.olswangtrainees.com

About the firm

Address: 90 High Holborn, London WC1V 6XX
Telephone: 020 7067 3000 **Fax:** 020 7067 3999
Website: www.olswang.com
Twitter: @Olswang **LinkedIn:** Olswang

Senior partner: Mark Devereux
CEO: Paul Stevens

Other offices: Belgium, France, Germany, Spain, Singapore, the UK.

Who we are: Olswang is an international law firm recognised for our deep industry expertise in technology, media and telecoms. We pride ourselves on our innovative approach to legal services and bringing insight and influence to our clients. Olswang manages to combine passion with a business-minded approach to the law. Our power is in our people: driven, highly-commercial and creative, they are committed to innovation and making an impact.

What we do: Olswang provides expertise across a wide range of practice areas including commercial contracts, competition and regulatory, corporate, employment, pensions and benefits, finance, intellectual property, litigation, real estate, sourcing, procurement and supply chain, restructuring and special situations, and tax.

What we're looking for: At the heart of Olswang are some truly talented people. Being a trainee at Olswang is both demanding and rewarding. The firm is interested in hearing from individuals who have achieved, or are on course for, a 2(1) degree or above, and are enthusiastic, energetic, confident and able to display a commitment to the law.

What you'll do: Training consists of four six-month seats in corporate, real estate, litigation, finance, commercial or IP. You will be assigned a mentor, usually a partner, to assist and advise you throughout your training contract. In-house lectures supplement training, three-monthly appraisals assess development and regular social events with the other trainees are encouraged to forge stronger, lasting relationships.

Perks: Childcare vouchers, dental, gym, healthcare, pension, PHI (after 12 months), STL, cycle to work scheme, life assurance, annual health screening, subsidised staff restaurant.

Sponsorship: GDL and LPC fees paid plus a maintenance grant.

Facts and figures

Total partners: 97
Other fee-earners: 301
Total trainees: 29

Trainee places available for 2019: 9
Applications received pa: 2,000
Percentage interviewed: 4%

First year salary: £37,000
Second year salary: £41,500
Newly qualified salary: £61,000

Turnover in 2015: £126.7m (+8% from 2014)
Profits per equity partner: £490,000 (+0%)
(see legalbusiness.co.uk for full financial information)

Application process

Apply to: Katharine Banbury, graduate recruitment and development manager.
How: Online: www.olswangtrainees.com.
When: By 31 July 2017 for September 2019 and March 2020 applications.
What's involved: Commercial exercise, competency-based interviews, psychometric tests and written exercises.

Vacation schemes

Spring and summer: We run a Summer work placement scheme for penultimate and final year law students, final year non-law students and graduates. We have 10 places on the Summer 2017 scheme and remuneration is £320pw. The closing date to apply is 15 January 2017.

OLSWANG

O'Melveny

Warwick Court, 5 Paternoster Square, London EC4M 7DX

Survey results *(marks out of 100%)*

Satisfied in your job?	70
Firm living up to expectations?	70
High quality of work?	68
Enough client contact?	70
Stress-free?	43
Happy work/life balance?	55
Friendly firm?	90
Great social life?	80
Good vacation scheme?	75
Confident you'll be kept on?	72
Good remuneration?	(88)
Diverse firm?	88
Good international secondments?	68

 **verdict**

The 'glamour of working for a US firm' appealed to O'Melveny trainees, who now enjoy 'great exposure to high-quality work' and representing 'sophisticated international clients'. The firm's London base is 'small enough that you can know everyone in the office', and the similarly small intake means the firm 'takes a real interest in your development'. We are told that 'a lot is expected of trainees' and that they are 'actively involved in deals'. There are some 'excellent supervisors' at O'Melveny who have offered welcome feedback to trainees and two highlight moments were 'getting a good review in my first mid-seat appraisal' and 'helping with a panel discussion and receiving a special mention from the associate in charge'. The 'workload is variable between different departments', and trainees have endured 'busy periods' as well as 'very little work' on occasion. One respondent writes that 'the breadth of training is limited' as compared to other large firms in the City, but this does not mean that opportunities are limited. Not only is there 'exposure to international work' while in London, but the international secondments provide 'a sense of the wider firm', and one lucky trainee gained 'excellent experience' in the Hong Kong office. O'Melveny is named a **Lex 100 Winner** in the remuneration satisfaction category. The 'social life' and 'genuinely friendly atmosphere' is lauded, and the trainee cohort has had 'fewer late nights compared to friends at Magic Circle firms'. 'If you make the effort, you can really progress' at O'Melveny, so consider applying to this 'fun and social' firm.

If the firm were a fictional character it would be...

Jess (New Girl) – a quirky American with a warm heart but a clear focus on its future career

The firm

L.A's O'Melveny has an international footprint of 16 international offices, including one of the largest Chinese practices of any US-headquartered law firm. The firm specialises in media, entertainment, investment funds, international arbitration and mid-market M&A deals. The London office is small, with around 20 qualified lawyers supported by seven trainees.

The deals

Acted for Asiana Airlines in the air cargo cartel litigation; represented ICAP plc in its appeal to the EC's finding of alleged complicity in the manipulation of interest rate benchmarks governing derivatives.

The clients

Actis; Coller Capital; GIC Private Limited; Goldman Sachs International; Greensphere Capital; Helios Investment Partners; Impax Asset Management; Livingbridge; Samsung Electronics; Vivendi.

The star performers

Top-ranking departments according to *The Legal 500* (see legal500.com for more details)
Competition litigation; International arbitration; Private funds.

- **Why did you choose this firm over any others?** 'Really enjoyed my time on the vacation scheme'; 'believed a smaller office environment would suit my personality'; 'good-quality work and clients'; 'genuinely friendly atmosphere'; 'international'; 'small enough to know everyone in the office'

- **Best thing about the firm?** 'The firm is really good at what it does'; 'because of the smaller intake, if you want to go on secondment you will be able to'; 'very little time is spent doing menial work'; 'great exposure to high-quality work'; 'international and sophisticated clients'

- **Worst thing about the firm?** 'A lot of people have never heard of OMM, which can be frustrating'; 'due to its small size, sometimes in busy periods training can slip in an effort to ensure work is completed'; 'periods of very little work'; 'the workloads are very variable between different departments'

- **Best moment?** 'Secondment in Hong Kong. Excellent, excellent experience'; 'getting a good review in my first mid-seat appraisal'; 'helping with a ICC YAF panel discussion and receiving a special mention from the associate in charge'

- **Worst moment?** 'Quiet periods'; 'people notice the bad things'; 'mixing up some MR01s and being shouted at'

A day in the life of...

... Fergus Grady second-year trainee solicitor, O'Melveny

Departments to date: Litigation, investment funds, transactions (secondment in Hong Kong) and corporate

University: Bristol

Degree and class: History, 2(1)

8.30am: I head to work and check emails on my BlackBerry to see what has come in overnight and if anything requires immediate attention. I grab a coffee in Paternoster Square (our office is right next to St Paul's) before entering the office. I have breakfast at my desk while reading the papers. I review my to-do list and prioritise my workload for the day.

9.15am: My supervisor, who I share a room with, arrives and we discuss the different tasks we need to get done today. I am currently sitting in the firm's corporate department. The main work stream involves M&A work, but we also advise clients on a wide range of corporate issues. One of the deals I have been working on involves a client selling a large number of share warrants it holds in a German company. This is a relatively small transaction and I have been given the responsibility of leading the process. We have a call with the client this morning in which we will update them on comments we have received from local counsel and run them through the final steps towards closing.

11.00am: A client has sent through a non-disclosure agreement they have received from the seller in respect of a potential acquisition. They have requested a markup by close of business. We often receive these from this client. They are sent to an internal mailing list and, subject to everyone's capacity,

trainees generally take it in turns to review them. I reply confirming that we will revert with comments. These documents are fairly short, but do often require substantive revisions before they are acceptable to the client. As a result, they are a really useful learning tool for trainees, especially when you first start. Once I have reviewed the document and made my amendments, I pass it on to an associate to check over what I have done.

12.30pm: I head to one of our meeting rooms for a training session on warranties and indemnities. Lunch is provided. One of the counsel runs us through a typical warranty schedule, explaining certain provisions and giving us some drafting advice. This session is part of an ongoing series of corporate training for trainees and other junior lawyers.

1.35pm: An associate has reviewed the markup of the non-disclosure agreement that I prepared this morning. He has made a few minor changes. I send out our revised version of the agreement to the client with a cover email explaining some of the key amendments we have made.

2.45pm: We receive a draft of a share purchase agreement from opposing counsel. This relates to another matter I have been working on. Our US client is acquiring a company in the UK. It is a heavy markup and

there appear to be a few re-trades on some commercial points. My supervisor and I prepare an issues list for the client summarising the changes. We split up the different sections that each of us will cover and get to work.

5.15pm: With the issues list sent to the client for their review, my supervisor and I challenge

> '**I challenge a newly qualified associate and one of my fellow second-year trainees to a quick game of table football. We win convincingly.**'

a newly qualified associate and one of my fellow second-year trainees to a quick game of table football. We win convincingly. The table is a great way to catch up with colleagues and enjoy some healthy competition in the office. I head back to my desk and start wrapping up the final tasks of the day.

6.30pm: With nothing urgent left to do, I prepare my to-do list for the next day. It is a beautiful sunny evening in the City so I decide to forgo the pub and run home down the Embankment.

www.omm.com/careers/london

About the firm

Address: Warwick Court, 5 Paternoster Square, London EC4M 7DX
Telephone: 020 7088 0000   **Fax:** 020 7088 0001
Website: www.omm.com
Email: graduate-recruitment@omm.com
Twitter: @omelvenymyers

Managing partner: Jan Birtwell

Other offices: Beijing, Brussels, Century City, Hong Kong, Los Angeles, Newport Beach, New York, San Francisco, Seoul, Shanghai, Silicon Valley, Singapore, Tokyo, Washington DC.

Who we are: O'Melveny is a leading international law firm with approximately 750 lawyers practising in 15 offices in the key US, Asian and European economic and political centres.

What we do: In London, we have both a transactions department – which advises on private equity, corporate finance, M&A and investment fund matters – as well as an international litigation department, with antitrust and competition services support provided through the Brussels office. London also has the key transitional support functions which are essential to a leading corporate practice, such as tax and regulatory.

What we're looking for: New recruits must have proven academic ability, sound commercial awareness, be keen team players and have the ability to carry real responsibility from the outset.

What you'll do: Trainees complete seats with partners/senior associates in each of our core practice areas. They receive regular formal and informal feedback, as well as legal and non-legal skills training. Trainees are also frequently seconded overseas to our Hong Kong, Singapore and Brussels offices.

Perks: 25 days' holiday, pension, life insurance, long-term disability insurance, private health insurance, travel insurance, interest-free season ticket loan, corporate rate gym membership.

Sponsorship: We sponsor GDL/LPC fees incurred post-recruitment and award a maintenance grant (currently £8,000 per annum).

Facts and figures

Total partners: 7
Other fee-earners: 19
Total trainees: 6

Trainee places available for 2019: Up to four
Applications received pa: Approximately 200
Percentage interviewed: 5-10%

First year salary: £41,000
Second year salary: £44,000
Newly qualified salary: Competitive

Application process

Apply to: Natalie Beacroft.
How: Apply online via www.apply4law.com/omm.
When: By 30 June 2017 for 2019 training contracts.
What's involved: Online application; interview with partners/senior associates, presentation, written exercise.

Vacation schemes

Summer: Summer 2017 (apply by 31 January 2017).

Osborne Clarke

One London Wall, London EC2Y 5EB

Lex 100 Winner

See categories below
and tables from page 69

Survey results *(marks out of 100%)*

Satisfied in your job? 87

Firm living up to expectations? 90

High quality of work? 89

Enough client contact? 76

Stress-free? 67

Happy work/life balance? 79

Friendly firm? 96

Great social life? 81

Good vacation scheme? 94

Confident you'll be kept on? 83

Good remuneration? 89

Diverse firm? 93

Good international secondments? 46

 verdict

'Down-to-earth' Osborne Clarke is deemed 'an exciting place to train', and following recent 'international growth' trainees tell us that the firm has 'big ambitions'. The 'great culture' and 'high-quality training' make the firm a 'friendly and supportive environment' where trainees work with 'some of the industry's finest lawyers'. Trainees 'dive in at the deep end' and receive a 'high level of responsibility from day one'. Top trainee moments include 'settling a dispute single-handedly', 'working on a multi-million pound acquisition finance deal' and 'seeing an important deal through to completion'. There is a downside to the busy workload, with a few grumbles about '2am finishes', 'tight deadlines' and 'all-nighters'. Senior members of staff demonstrate an 'investment in training' by focusing on the 'development of skills and mentoring'. Trainees, given the necessary support and guidance of other staff members, 'manage their own workload', giving them 'greater independence'. Osborne Clarke has secured eight **Lex 100 Winner** gongs, including in the job satisfaction and work quality categories. Colleagues are 'friendly and welcoming' here, which creates an 'open atmosphere' in which trainees feel that they can 'approach more senior lawyers' and 'learn a lot from colleagues through getting involved in a wide variety of work'. Also, trainees praise the 'range of top-quality clients'. There is a regrettable 'lack of international secondment opportunities' though one trainee reports being 'fortunate' to go on a client secondment to Microsoft. The firm is a 'great environment to work in' as it is 'entrepreneurial and constantly growing', so ambitious, aspiring trainees should take a closer look at Osborne Clarke.

If the firm were a fictional character it would be...

Alfred Borden (The Prestige) – has worked its way up from humble beginnings to rival the elite

The firm

Osborne Clarke continues to perform impressively, and posted a 17% rise in UK revenue over the last financial year, and a 23% increase in global turnover during the same period. The firm is renowned for its TMT, infrastructure and real estate knowledge, and was nominated for Legal Technology Firm of the Year at the *Legal Business* Awards 2016. Osborne Clarke has offices across mainland Europe as well as on both coasts of the US.

The deals

Advised RWE Innogy on the sale of a 50% stake in the Triton Knoll offshore wind farm to Statkraft and the negotiation of associated joint venture agreements; represented EE on commercial disputes and procurement litigation; acted for the UK's four leading high street banks – Barclays, RBS, Lloyds and HSBC – on a £250m loan to St James's Place; advised Majestic Wine on restructuring its board and senior management after acquiring Naked Wines; advised InfraRed on its debt and equity investment in the Tidal Lagoon Swansea Bay.

The clients

Balfour Beatty Investments; Danone; Dyson; Marks & Spencer; Mulberry; PricewaterhouseCoopers; Ralph Lauren; TalkTalk; Tata Technologies; Vodafone.

The star performers

Top-ranking departments according to *The Legal 500* (see legal500.com for more details)
Asset finance and leasing; Banking and finance; Commercial litigation; Construction; Corporate and commercial; Corporate tax; EU and competition; Energy; Employment; Environment; Health and safety; Insolvency and corporate recovery; Intellectual property; Media and entertainment; Planning; Professional negligence; Project finance and PFI; Property litigation; TMT: IT and telecoms; Transport: rail.

- **Why did you choose this firm over any others?** 'My interview was a great experience'; 'quality of the work'; 'non-stuffy'; 'its focus on technology'; 'strong performance'; 'exciting prospects'; 'recommendations from other solicitors'; 'I did a vacation scheme here, I felt very comfortable and included and loved how nice everybody was'; 'really exciting work'; 'big ambitions'; 'Bristol office'; 'supportive environment'

- **Best thing about the firm?** 'How friendly everyone is'; 'the firm is entrepreneurial and constantly growing'; 'excellent quality of work'; 'being given a high level of responsibility'; 'the open-plan office really sculpts and shapes the firm's attitude'; 'culture and leadership'; 'genuinely down-to-earth and friendly firm'; 'working with some of the industry's finest lawyers'

- **Worst thing about the firm?** 'There could be more flexibility around seat allocation'; 'missing the cake trolley'; 'would love an onsite gym'; 'they need to bring the Bristol cookies to the London office'; 'absence of a subsidised cafeteria'; 'others can underrate it'; 'trainee seat allocation needs to be readdressed'

- **Best moment?** 'Preparing and attending a mediation for a key client'; 'being given the opportunity to attend a business development event early on'; 'attending an employment tribunal'; 'being commended for work well done'; 'working with the international offices'; 'holding a conference call all on my own'; 'my first completion'; 'receiving praise from clients'

- **Worst moment?** 'Making a mistake and needing to fix it quickly'; 'when there was little to no work'; 'nearly missing the summer party'; 'slightly repetitive work'; 'completing a multi-million pound deal at 6am after an all-nighter'; 'the morning after the Christmas party'

A day in the life of...

... Kiera Taylor trainee, Osborne Clarke LLP

Departments to date: Corporate tax and incentives, real estate, projects, commercial litigation, competition

University: University of Kent (Canterbury) **Degree and class:** Law (first class)

8.40am: Coffee stop! After my train journey to work this is always a welcome treat – and it's en route to the office front door.

8.50am: I make a quick dash past the office café to pick up some breakfast before heading to my desk to start the day (on Fridays we have the Trainee Breakfast Club).

9.00am: The first thing I do after logging in (and starting my timer) is check my calendar. As trainees are so heavily involved in all areas of the firm it's really important to keep up-to-date with meetings, training sessions and work from your team. An average day is likely to include charity committee or team meetings and there are often lunch-time training sessions from various departments across the firm.

9.15am: The partner in my team asks for an update on our client's draft merger form which we need to submit as part of a merger filing. We have been working closely with the lawyers on the other side to complete the form which is incredibly detailed and requires very specific information from both entities. We set up a call with the other side for 11.15am so that we can talk through the highlighted queries.

10.00am: International competition team meeting by VC. This is a great opportunity to catch up with colleagues and discuss work in progress and in the pipeline. Working in the competition team gives me great exposure to the wider OCI community. The teams from Cologne, Paris, Brussels, Rome, London, Madrid and Bristol work closely together, both on cross-jurisdictional matters and the monthly OCI competition newsletter, a publication of recent competition issues for clients. I am responsible for co-ordinating the newsletter articles from all offices and I liaise with our international lawyers on their blog posts.

11.15am: I brief the team's partner ahead of our call with the other side's lawyers. During the call my chief task is to manually mark up our draft merger form in accordance with the new information being provided to us. I also note down additional queries which are raised and which we will need to revert to our client on. After the call I quickly draft a telephone attendance note for the file and email our client with the updated draft and new queries.

12.30pm: Summer is definitely here today and I am joining the rest of the trainees for lunch in the park across the road. We have some vacation scheme students with us this week and would like to show them a little of what the area around the office has to offer.

1.30pm: My supervisor emails me about a new matter with a longstanding client which concerns parallel trade. As this matter concerns both competition and IP issues we will work closely with our IP litigation team. I am asked to do some research on the company which is importing our client's products and to put together a note for my supervisor, which includes a summary of the relationship between exhaustion of trade mark rights and abuse of dominance.

4.00pm: Our health and wellbeing team has announced the weekly arrival of free fruit for

> **'As trainees are so heavily involved in all areas of the firm it's really important to keep up-to-date.'**

the office! I head over to the first-floor kitchen and collect some for the team.

4.30pm: Newsletter articles come in from our Paris and Madrid offices. I make a start on proof-reading and marking up the articles in line with OC house-style and to ensure there have been no glitches in translation (a task which sometimes involves amusing calls to my international colleagues).

6.00pm: Pens down and PCs off – it's time to join the other juniors in our first softball game of the season. We've teamed up with a local property firm for the annual league.

www.osborneclarke.com/trainees

About the firm

Address: One London Wall, London EC2Y 5EB
Telephone: 0117 917 3484 **Fax:** 0117 917 3485
Website: www.joinoc.com
Email: trainee.recruitment@osborneclarke.com
Twitter: @OC_trainee

Senior partner: Andrew Saul
Managing partner: Ray Berg

Other offices: Amsterdam, Barcelona, Brescia, Bristol, Brussels, Cologne, Hamburg, Madrid, Milan, Munich, New York, Padua, Paris, Rome, San Francisco, Silicon Valley, Thames Valley.

Who we are: Osborne Clarke is an award-winning multinational law firm. We've grown rapidly, and with 19 global offices we're proud to say that our influence and impact can now be applied almost anywhere.

What we do: We think sector first, organising ourselves around the current affairs and future challenges of the industries we serve, rather than traditional legal practice areas. It helps keep us one step ahead.

Our core services all thrive on innovation: digital business, energy, financial services, life sciences, real estate, recruitment and transport.

What we're looking for: Candidates who can: comunicate effectively; think commercially and practically; solve problems creatively; build effective relationships; and demonstrate initiative. Foreign language skills are also an advantage.

What you'll do: Trainees complete four six-month seats, typically in corporate or banking, real estate, litigation and one other area.

Perks: 25 days' holiday (plus a Christmas shopping day), pension, permanent health insurance, private medical insurance, life assurance and season ticket loan.

Sponsorship: We pay candidates' GDL and LPC tuition fees, provided that they are no more than half way through either course when they are recruited, along with a maintenance grant.

Facts and figures

Total partners: 213
Other fee-earners: 536

Trainee places available for 2019: 20
Applications received pa: approx 1,200
Percentage interviewed: approx 10%

First year salary: £34,000-£39,000 (varies on location)
Second year salary: £36,000-£41,000 (varies on location)
Newly qualified salary: £47,000-£62,500 (varies on location)

Turnover in 2015: £151m (+6% from 2014)
Profits per equity partner: £550,000 (+7%)
(see legalbusiness.co.uk for full financial information)

Application process

Apply to: Zoe Reid, recruitment officer.
How: Online application form.
When: By 15 January 2017 for 2019 contract.
What's involved: Online application form, online verbal reasoning test, assessment centre, interview.

Vacation schemes

Summer: July 2017 (apply by 15 January 2017).

PwC

1 Embankment Place, London WC2N 6DX

Survey results *(marks out of 100%)*

Satisfied in your job?	82
Firm living up to expectations?	84
High quality of work?	81
Enough client contact?	78
Stress-free?	48
Happy work/life balance?	64
Friendly firm?	91
Great social life?	73
Good vacation scheme?	87
Confident you'll be kept on?	75
Good remuneration?	81
Diverse firm?	90
Good international secondments?	70

 **verdict**

PwC's widely recognised membership of the 'PwC network' was a key factor for trainees in deciding to apply here, and there is a focus on trainees developing their 'commercial awareness' and grasping the 'vast opportunities' available to them. PwC excels at giving trainees direct contact with a 'phenomenal range of clients'. It is also noted by current trainees that the firm provides a 'brilliant vacation scheme' which is 'very structured and provided fun socials'. The firm is also named a **Lex 100 Winner** for its encouraging diversity levels. The 'culture of collaboration' is the 'biggest difference' with peers' training contracts, as PwC recruits have the 'opportunity to work with professionals other than lawyers'. Trainees work in 'small teams' where they gain 'hands-on experience' on 'exciting high-profile projects'. Top trainee moments include 'international trips', 'working on the largest corporate de-merger ever' and 'working on a high-profile financial services project'. The 'lack of recognition in the legal market' is disappointing for some trainees, but this is 'rapidly changing', and trainees have 'good opportunities to contribute to cases' where the 'senior level contact' is high. There is 'good supervision' and trainees receive 'encouragement, support and appreciation' from their seniors. The 'long hours, weekend-working and middle-of-the-night bundling' are notable concerns among current trainees, though on the whole respondents thrive in the 'vibrant environment'. Those looking to combine genuine responsibility with 'top-notch clients' in a non-traditional environment should consider PwC.

If the firm were a fictional character it would be...

Bruce Wayne (Batman) – all the investment and resources at its fingertips, but the public has yet to appreciate its true identity and capabilities

The firm

A member of Big Four accountancy firm PwC's wider network, PwC offers clients an integrated service of legal advice drawn from an international pool of over 2,500 lawyers based in over 85 countries. Through such connections the firm has a strong commercial focus, and is commended for its dispute resolution, human resources and corporate crime work. The firm's revenues rose by 15% in 2014/15.

The deals

Worked for Drax Power and Infinis Energy Holdings in a judicial review of the decision to remove a renewable energy tax exemption; advised the Dooba Group on the development of a brownfield site near Leeds; worked in a group litigation concerning a stamp duty reserve tax and challenge against HMRC; assisted a pharmaceutical company with a global compliance project; conducted a privacy impact assessment of connected cars for a manufacturer.

The clients

Bupa; Dreamjet; Eni International Resources; Kobalt; Phones4U.

The star performers

Top-ranking departments according to *The Legal 500* (see legal500.com for more details)
Commercial contracts; Commercial litigation; Commercial property; Corporate crime (including fraud, bribery and corruption); Data protection; Employment: employers; Fraud: civil; IT and telecoms; Immigration: business; Intellectual property; M&A: smaller deals, up to £50m; Pensions (non-contentious); Tax litigation and investigations.

- **Why did you choose this firm over any others?** 'It has a modern feel to it'; 'quality of the vacation scheme'; 'close links with PwC give the firm access to top-notch clients'; 'the firm's clear trajectory towards a multidisciplinary approach to legal services demonstrated its uniqueness'; 'PwC is consistently rated as the number 1 in The Times Top 100 Graduate Employers'

- **Best thing about the firm?** 'It's a relatively small firm with a huge clientele'; 'quality of clients for the size of the firm'; 'the culture of collaboration with PwC'; 'secondment opportunities to PwC and clients in both the UK and abroad'; 'vibrant environment'; 'I am encouraged to get to know other graduates and non-lawyers from PwC to grow my network'

- **Worst thing about the firm?** 'The uncertainty of being kept on'; 'lack of support structures'; 'audit rules restricting us from working with certain clients'; 'the expensive canteen'; 'constant confusion that PwC Legal is in-house'; 'the current lack of recognition in the legal market'

- **Best moment?** 'Working on a high-profile financial services project'; 'secondment to PwC'; 'being given responsibility for drafting an entire suite of restructuring documents'; 'working on the largest corporate de-merger ever'; 'receiving positive feedback from a senior partner'

- **Worst moment?** 'Bundling in the middle of the night'; 'staying late to review thousands of emails'; 'some consistently long hours in my second seat'; 'the long hours and the stress'; 'being called into work on a Saturday and Sunday'

A day in the life of...

... **Anita Shah** second-year trainee, PwC

Departments to date: Tax disputes, commercial and regulatory disputes, corporate and pensions
University: Bristol
Degree and class: Politics, 2(1) Hons

8.30am: I'm currently in the pensions department and with an eventful day ahead of me I get in early to prepare for the fortnightly team know-how breakfast. This session is where the team get together to discuss technical updates. I'm presenting on a recent Court of Appeal case and we spend the session discussing the impact of the judgment, and what this may mean for our clients.

9.30am: Back at my desk, I review the emails that have come in overnight and update my to-do list in order of priority. One of the emails raises a query from the other side's lawyers on a tripartite agreement. I draft a response and make a note to speak to the partner about it when he returns from his meeting.

10.00am: I join another partner on a conference call with our client based in Bermuda. He has overseas assets in the British Virgin Islands, Miami and France and wants our advice on the implications of the assets being transferred into his pension scheme. I make a note of everything that was discussed on the call.

10.30am: I begin doing the initial research for our Bermudan client. Being part of an international network in over 85 countries, I pick up the phone to our colleagues in various overseas firms and talk through some of my initial thoughts. My overseas colleagues talk me through local law and the formalities required

in their jurisdictions for transferring the assets. I feed these points into my initial report for the partner to review and provide his comments.

12.30pm: It's a beautiful day so I meet some of the other trainees to grab lunch from the live kitchen in the canteen and we head up to the roof terrace to enjoy the sunshine overlooking the London Eye. It's not long before we need some cooling off and we stroll across to Covent Garden for some ice cream before heading back to the office.

1.15pm: This afternoon we have a conference with leading counsel on a question of law relating to the equitable remedy of rectification. Our client wants to know whether a mistake in their historic pension scheme deed can be rectified and I look over the instructions to counsel which I helped prepare a few weeks ago. I finalise the bundles containing the trust deeds and documentation and get our files ready for the conference.

2.00pm: A partner in my team and I are joined by two of our colleagues from our regional Tax team, and we walk down the Strand to counsel's chambers. Our conference is lively and engaging and counsel talks us through the intricate points of law and the prospects of success for our client.

5.00pm: I return back to the office and start the follow-up from the conference. I'm

responsible for producing the conference notes, an important task as it will be referred to constantly as the matter progresses and it's essential for capturing every point that was discussed. I record all my hand-written notes into a dictaphone, while everything is still fresh in my mind, so that I can recall the specific context of the technical points.

'Being part of an international network across more than 85 countries, I pick up the phone to our colleagues in various overseas firms.'

6.30pm: The day is winding down, so I make sure that I've responded to all my emails and check whether there is anything else that needs to be done this evening. After confirming with my team members, I write my to-do list for tomorrow.

7.00pm: It's been a busy day, but tonight is the NextGen pizza making and wine tasting with other juniors from different business areas coming together. I pack up my things, meet some of the other trainees in Embankment Gardens and we head over to Soho!

www.pwc.com/uk/work-in-legal

About the firm

Address: 1 Embankment Place, London WC2N 6DX
Telephone: 0808 100 1500
Website: www.pwc.com/uk/work-in-legal
Facebook: facebook.com/PwCCareersUK
Twitter: @PwC_UK_Careers

Who we are: PwC is an exciting place to launch your legal career. With more than 2,500 lawyers over 85 countries, we have the most extensive legal services network in the world.

What we do: Practice groups include mergers and acquisitions, banking, commercial litigation, commercial fraud, corporate structuring, employment, intellectual property and information, pensions, real estate and tax litigation.

What we're looking for: We look for ambitious, motivated people with the drive to become the leading lawyers of the future, then help them commit to realising that potential.

What you'll do: You'll quickly gain practical, hands-on experience and lateral thinking skills as part of a team, generating creative ways to tackle complex problems and receiving support to gain a professional qualification.

Perks: Holiday entitlement, bike scheme, discounted gym membership, healthcare scheme, interest-free loan, life assurance, pension scheme, season ticket loan and study support.

Sponsorship: Trainees can apply for a scholarship award to help with the costs of the Graduate Diploma and the Legal Practice Course. If successful, you'll receive the total cost of the tuition and examination fees plus a significant contribution towards living expenses.

Facts and figures

Total partners: 26
Other fee-earners: 260
Total trainees: 19

Trainee places available for 2019: 25

First year salary: £39,000

Application process

How: www.pwc.com/uk/work-in-legal
When: By 27 January 2017 for 2019 contracts.
What's involved: The initial stages of the application include career focus questions and online psychometric tests (logical and verbal), after which will be a first-round competency-based interview, then an assessment centre (written exercise, logical and verbal psychometric tests, and group exercise), then finally the senior interview, which is again competency-based.

Vacation schemes

Summer: June 2017 and July 2017 (apply by 27 January 2017).

Pemberton Greenish

45 Cadogan Gardens, London SW3 2AQ

Lex 100 Winner

See categories below and tables from page 69

Survey results *(marks out of 100%)*

Satisfied in your job?	79
Firm living up to expectations?	83
High quality of work?	79
Enough client contact?	69
Stress-free?	(73)
Happy work/life balance?	(86)
Friendly firm?	86
Great social life?	76
Confident you'll be kept on?	63
Good remuneration?	66
Diverse firm?	73

 **verdict**

Pemberton Greenish is commended by trainees for its 'excellence in property and private wealth'. Survey respondents enthuse about the 'level of responsibility' they are given, and a training contract highlight for one member of the cohort was 'a client meeting in which I was given the go-ahead by a partner to take an actively vocal role and to lead the questioning'. Sloane Square is considered a 'perfect location' to work in, and the firm's links with the nearby Saatchi Gallery are great news for one 'art-loving' trainee. There are complaints about a 'lack of secondments', and of 'some seats being four months long as it would be nice to have the full six months in each department', particularly with one trainee finding 'the first day of a new seat' to be a daunting moment. There is 'less fierce competition between trainees' at this 'friendly firm', and the 'supportiveness of staff' is equally appreciated. 'Taking ten days out to complete the PSC exams' wasn't fun, yet Pemberton Greenish takes care to ensure trainees enjoy a 'good work/life balance', which leads to **Lex 100 Winner** medals in the stress-free and work/life balance categories. Aside from the regular caseload, trainees are encouraged to undertake pro bono work, and for one respondent this led to 'a project which was very interesting and very different to other work I have undertaken here'. To train at a small London firm with a 'superb reputation' and clear areas of specialism, take a closer look at Pemberton Greenish.

If the firm were a fictional character it would be...

George Smiley (Tinker Tailor Soldier Spy) – amiable, intelligent, trustworthy

The firm

Pemberton Greenish focuses on the three core areas of corporate, private wealth and real estate, carving out an enviable reputation in these areas for over 200 years. Clients include real estate businesses, domestic and international private individuals and charitable foundations and trusts.

The deals

Pemberton Greenish advises clients on a range of investment and development mandates, and is the firm of choice for conflict work from many larger practices.

The clients

Birchall Properties; Helical Bar; Native Land.

The star performers

Top-ranking departments according to *The Legal 500* (see legal500.com for more details)
Commercial property: general;
Commercial property: investment;
Property litigation.

- **Why did you choose this firm over any others?** 'Excellence in property and private wealth'; 'good work/life balance'; 'the practice areas were perfect for me'; 'location'; 'reputation'

- **Best thing about the firm?** 'Location'; 'work/life balance'; 'friendliness'; 'supportiveness of staff'

- **Worst thing about the firm?** 'No secondment opportunities'; 'three out of five seats are only four months long – it would be nice to have the full six months in each department'

- **Best moment?** 'A client meeting in which I was given the go-ahead by a partner to take an actively vocal role and to lead the questioning'

- **Worst moment?** 'Probably the first day of a new seat'; 'taking ten days out to complete the PSC exams'

A day in the life of...

... Rebecca Day first-year trainee, Pemberton Greenish LLP
Departments to date: Corporate, private wealth and residential real estate
University: Lincoln
Degree: LLB Law

9.00am: I sit down at my desk after an early-morning gym workout. I eat my breakfast at my desk while I review my emails and prioritise my task list for the day ahead.

9.30am: This morning I am reviewing a new matter which I am taking over from one of my colleagues. I spend some time reviewing the file. Trainees have the opportunity to run their own files, as well as assisting other fee-earners, in the residential real estate team. This really helps to improve my communication, drafting and research skills. On this particular matter the client has asked us to draft a deed of variation to vary his lease. Once I have finished drafting the document, my supervisor gives me helpful feedback and explains the next stage of the process so I can take the matter forward.

11.30am: I receive a memo from a partner in the team asking me to submit Land Registry applications to tidy up the register of the property he is working on. I ask one of my colleagues for assistance where I am not sure but I am otherwise able to complete and submit these applications on my own. I make a diary note to check the progress of the application in two weeks.

1.00pm: At lunch I have a fundraising and events committee (FAEC) meeting. The FAEC arranges social events for staff and fundraises for the firm's chosen charity. Previous events have included a staff quiz, Bake-Off competition and Just-A-Minute game show! Trainees are involved with organising events throughout their training contract and chair the committee in their second year of training. Trainees are also responsible for arranging the staff Christmas party, which is a brilliant opportunity to interact and socialise with people from across all departments.

2.00pm: In the afternoon I accompany a partner to a meeting at the client's address. Trainees in residential real estate often get the opportunity to attend meetings, conferences with counsel and hearings at court or the tribunal. Afterwards I draft an attendance note of the meeting for the file and discuss the next steps with my supervisor. The client has asked us to prepare a note of our formal legal advice and to draft several documents.

3.30pm: Before I can make a start on drafting, I have a telephone call from a solicitor on another matter. We have been in negotiations over a licence for alterations to a flat which has finally been agreed. He informs me that he would like to complete the licence today. Once off the phone, I review the file and contact my client to take instructions on completion. My client agrees and I telephone the solicitor back to complete the licence. Afterwards I arrange for the necessary documents to be sent to the other side.

4.00pm: I pick up where I left off following my meeting this afternoon. Drafting the advice memo involves carrying out research and reviewing the deeds packets. My first draft takes an hour and a half. Once I have completed it I give it to the partner to review.

> '**Trainees have the opportunity to run their own files, as well as assisting other fee-earners.**'

5.30pm: I receive an email from the Land Registry informing me that registration of a property I am dealing with has now been completed. I print the necessary documents and update the file. I also inform the matter partner of the progress and draft a letter to the client to inform them that their property has now been registered.

6.00pm: I meet my colleagues in the local pub for a drink before heading home.

www.pglaw.co.uk/recruitment

About the firm

Address: 45 Cadogan Gardens, London SW3 2AQ
Telephone: 020 7591 3333   **Fax:** 020 7591 3300
Website: www.pglaw.co.uk
Email: law@pglaw.co.uk

Senior partner: Robert Barham
CEO: Robert Graham-Campbell

Who we are: We are a central London law firm with over 200 years' experience specialising in the property, private wealth and SME sectors. We provide our clients with 'big firm' expertise, but with an individual approach and personal service which only specialist firms can provide.

What we do: Our core practice areas are real estate, private wealth and corporate. Our clients include domestic and international private individuals, real estate and entrepreneurial businesses, and charitable foundations and trusts.

What we're looking for: We look for candidates who are bright and able to think commercially and practically. We want a team player and someone who will actively contribute to the firm's social activities. We are also looking for candidates with a genuine interest in the firm's practice areas who are looking to develop their careers at the firm.

What you'll do: Trainees will rotate through five seats during a two-year period: residential real estate, commercial real estate, private wealth, corporate and real estate disputes. Trainees will handle 'real work' with early responsibility and will receive legal and skills-based training, and ongoing support and feedback.

Perks: 25 days' holiday, pension scheme, season ticket loan.

Sponsorship: Details upon application.

Facts and figures

Total partners: 19
Other fee-earners: 36
Total trainees: 5

Trainee places available for 2019: Up to 3

First year salary: £31,750 (September 2017)
Second year salary: £33,250

Application process

Apply to: www.pglaw.co.uk/recruitment/trainee-solicitor-scheme.
How: Online only.
When: By 30 June 2017 for 2019 contracts.
What's involved: Interview.

Penningtons Manches LLP

125 Wood Street, London EC2V 7AW

Survey results *(marks out of 100%)*

Satisfied in your job?	79
Firm living up to expectations?	74
High quality of work?	83
Enough client contact?	85
Stress-free?	60
Happy work/life balance?	81
Friendly firm?	84
Great social life?	65
Good vacation scheme?	85
Confident you'll be kept on?	74
Good remuneration?	62
Diverse firm?	77

 **verdict**

'Individual training and great responsibility' are stand-out factors for Penningtons Manches' current trainees. This 'social firm' offers trainees a 'good amount of client contact and lots of supervision' in a 'friendly environment', and is named a **Lex 100 Winner** for its impressive client contact levels. Some respondents found the 'great vacation scheme' an invaluable insight into how the firm operates. The 'small intake of trainees' and 'hands-on experience' result in a 'high level of responsibility' and 'good work' being distributed to trainees. Colleagues are 'extremely approachable, friendly and supportive', and the 'work/life balance' is good. Senior colleagues 'care about the training' the firm offers, resulting in trainees getting their hands on 'challenging and important work'. Although the pay 'could be higher', one of the best things about the firm is its 'upwards trajectory in the market'. Top trainee moments include 'settling part of a small case', 'securing payment of the client's costs' and 'attending a hearing at the Royal Courts of Justice'. Rookie mistakes, 'late nights with little warning' and 'juggling the workload' appear to be the most common problems for the firm's trainees. There are mixed responses about the 'social events'; one trainee reports a 'lack of sporting events for women' while another says that they love 'getting involved'. Sometimes the 'seat availability can be quite hit-and-miss', but trainees enthuse about the scope and the 'wide range of practice areas', with specialisms ranging from M&A to personal injury. Penningtons Manches provides a 'very rewarding' training contract; if this sounds appealing, look no further.

If the firm were a fictional character it would be...

Reginald Jeeves (PG Wodehouse) – good-humoured and able to offer practical solutions

The firm

Penningtons Manches has established a strong UK presence with offices in London, Basingstoke, Cambridge, Guildford, Oxford and Reading. In addition to this nationwide coverage, the firm opened an office in San Francisco in December 2014 through which it offers English law advice to established clients. M&A, personal injury and private client are three of the firm's well-known practices, with the latter earning a Private Client Team of the Year nomination at the *Legal Business* Awards 2016.

The deals

Acted for Bush & Co Rehabilitation on the £28m sale of share capital to NAHL Group; advised Veryan Holdings on an £18m fundraising by a syndicate of international investors; advised LG Motion on its acquisition of a 65% controlling interest in Precision Acoustics; advised Sun Life of Canada on the operation of its historic pension products; instructed by Frontier Estates in connection with the £40m redevelopment of Epping Town Centre.

The clients

BBC Worldwide; Bell Educational Services; EDF Energy Nuclear Generation; Facenda Group; Handelsbanken; Manx Tidal Energy; Oxera Consulting; Oxford University Press; PRP Architects; Santander UK.

The star performers

Top-ranking departments according to *The Legal 500* (see legal500.com for more details)
Banking and finance; Clinical negligence: claimant; Commercial litigation; Commercial property; Corporate and commercial; Education; Employment; Environment; Family; IT and telecoms; Immigration; Intellectual property; Pensions; Personal injury: claimant; Personal tax, trusts and probate; Property litigation; Social housing.

- **Why did you choose this firm over any others?** 'Its IP and life sciences reputation in Oxford'; 'because of my interest in family law'; 'the reputation of friendliness'; 'cohesive atmosphere'; 'lots of supervision'; 'strength in work for private individuals and on the real estate/commercial/corporate side'; 'the variety of practice areas'

- **Best thing about the firm?** 'High quality of work'; 'responsibility given to trainees'; 'upwards trajectory in the market'; 'wide range of practice areas'; 'generally only one trainee per seat so all work filters down even to first years'

- **Worst thing about the firm?** 'Trainee pay could be higher'; 'administrative support is not that good'; 'seat availability can be quite hit-and-miss'; 'lack of social events for trainees'; 'lack of biscuits in internal meetings'; 'little opportunity to get involved in business development events'

- **Best moment?** 'Managing a transaction from start to finish'; 'seeing a will from instructions to signing for a lovely client'; 'being complimented for a big, difficult task has been very rewarding'; 'holding my own client meeting, albeit with supervision'; 'preparing for and attending a hearing at the Royal Courts of Justice'; 'settling part of a small case I had been handling throughout my seat'

- **Worst moment?** 'Bibling 30 files for a client'; 'preparing court bundles under strict time constraints'; 'late nights with little warning'; 'staying late to prepare urgent bundles'; 'making a mistake with the execution of some documents'; 'dealing with juggling work and stress'

A day in the life of...

... Katie-Claire Lloyd second-year trainee, Penningtons Manches LLP

Departments to date: Commercial dispute resolution, clinical negligence, family, commercial, IP and IT

University: Cambridge

Degree: Natural sciences

8.30am: I arrive at the office and grab a coffee and some breakfast on my way past the kitchen. I prefer to arrive when it's still quiet to give myself some time to review my task list for the day and work out what I need to prioritise. It also helps to have an idea of what meetings and appointments the partners and associates that I am working with have scheduled, so I find it useful to quickly check our calendars.

9.00am: I take a look through my emails and deal with any urgent matters that I am able to attend to straight away. Today, a client has emailed requesting clarity on a competition law query. Before my supervising partner arrives, I consider the position and prepare a draft response. I am mindful to run all advice and decisions past those supervising me to ensure they are legally and commercially sound. The team gives me as much support as I need and, as I develop, I am given more responsibility.

10.00am: The commercial, IP and IT team has a weekly telephone conference call across all of the firm's offices on a Monday morning in which we discuss the work that we anticipate being involved in that week and allocate tasks accordingly. It's a good opportunity to learn more about the matters that other members of the team are working on and to offer assistance where it is needed.

10.20am: After the team call, a partner asks if I would mind assisting him with an urgent commercial matter. I grab my notepad and head into a client meeting with him. Following the meeting, the partner and I discuss the matter further and consider what steps we should take next. As this is a relatively new area for me, I ask the partner to clarify any points that were raised in the meeting that I was unsure of.

12.30pm: Today we have a lunchtime drafting workshop which is run by one of our partners. It's an interactive session and so as a group (over sandwiches and cake!) we consider a draft agreement and discuss modifications and improvements that can be made to a number of the clauses.

1.30pm: After catching up with a few of the trainees on my way back to my desk, I check my emails and get back to my task list for the day. I have been asked to consider whether our client's trade mark is potentially being infringed by a third party and if it is, to draft a cease and desist letter accordingly.

3.45pm: An associate asks if I can help her with a research task on a specific tech query. I have a chat with our knowledge lawyer to get some background in the area and to ensure that I can focus my research. In light of my research findings, I have a discussion with the associate and draft an advice note to the client. We have a team 'know how' session in a couple of days and I will use my research to form the basis of my presentation, which will be a great opportunity to practise my advocacy skills and raise my profile.

> **'The team gives me as much support as I need and, as I develop, I am given more responsibility.'**

5.30pm: I dictate my meeting notes from the client meeting earlier today, in case we need to refer to them later.

6.00pm: Tonight, the employment department has challenged the commercial, IP and IT team to a game of ping pong. The firm encourages a good work/life balance to help build our professional networks. Before I log off, I update my task list and ensure that my time recording for the day is complete.

www.penningtons.co.uk/careers

About the firm

Address: 125 Wood Street, London EC2V 7AW
Telephone: 020 7457 3000 **Fax:** 020 7457 3240
Website: www.penningtons.co.uk
Email: traineepost@penningtons.co.uk

Chief executive: David Raine

Other offices: Basingstoke, Cambridge, Guildford, Oxford, Reading and San Francisco.

Who we are: Penningtons Manches LLP is a leading UK law firm which provides high-quality legal advice tailored to both businesses and individuals.

What we do: We offer a broad range of legal advice including dispute resolution, corporate, commercial/IP/IT, real estate, employment, private client and family. We also have some highly respected niche practice areas such as professional regulation, immigration and clinical negligence.

What we're looking for: A high standard of academic achievement is expected. Clarity of expression, written and oral, and reliability in research are important to us. There should be mental flair and flexibility, and on the personal side, we look for self-confidence without arrogance, good humour, openness with discretion, a good team spirit and integrity.

What you'll do: Our trainees complete four six-month seats across the firm's three divisions and receive high levels of responsiblity and client contact. On a quarterly basis, trainees attend a day-long training session.

Perks: Flexible benefits including health insurance, travel loan and flexible holidays.

Sponsorship: We sponsor the LPC and provide a maintenance grant of £5,000.

Facts and figures

Total partners: 108
Other fee-earners: 231
Total trainees: 25

Trainee places available for 2019: Approx 12-14
Applications received pa: 700
Percentage interviewed: 5%

First year salary: £33,500 (London)
Second year salary: £35,500 (London)
Newly qualified salary: £55,000 (London)

Turnover in 2015: £57.5m (+2.3% from 2014)
Profits per equity partner: £319,000 (+19%)
(see legalbusiness.co.uk for full financial information)

Application process

Apply to: Helen Lewis, graduate recruitment manager.
How: Online application form, via our website.
When: By 31 July 2017 for 2019 training contracts.
What's involved: Interview(s), online critical thinking test, written exercise and presentation.

Vacation schemes

Summer: Week-long placements throughout July, (apply by 31 January 2017)

PENNINGTONS MANCHES

RPC

Tower Bridge House, St Katharine's Way, London E1W 1AA

Survey results *(marks out of 100%)*

Satisfied in your job?	81
Firm living up to expectations?	83
High quality of work?	80
Enough client contact?	72
Stress-free?	59
Happy work/life balance?	76
Friendly firm?	92
Great social life?	(82)
Good vacation scheme?	85
Confident you'll be kept on?	73
Good remuneration?	67
Diverse firm?	75

 **verdict**

RPC has an 'ambitious nature' and a 'pioneering spirit' that really appeal to trainees. The firm is 'paving the way for a modern, creative and commercially savvy way of practising law'. Senior management oozes with 'entrepreneurial spirit', adding to the 'refreshing modern outlook'. Trainees praise the 'inclusive culture', which 'lived up to expectations', and the trainee WhatsApp group is 'constantly active', befitting a firm named a **Lex 100 Winner** for social life. There is a degree of uncertainty around the number of NQ positions as they 'vary year-on-year', but top trainee moments include 'twice travelling to Russia with partners', 'attending a criminal trial undercover' and 'working on high-profile trials in the High Court'. The 'personality and environment' of the firm encourages a 'strong work/life balance', and trainees report being involved in 'cutting-edge work' whether that is working on 'high-profile cases or alongside well-known clients'. Current trainees are also impressed with the 'quality of work' they received on the firm's vacation schemes. The 'structured training programme' results in 'recognition of hard work' and 'high levels of responsibility'. There have been a few grumbles about 'bundling on weekends' and 'late nights', though one trainee describes how 'the team rewarded me for my individual working style and the quality of work by upping my responsibility'. Supervisors give trainees work that is 'challenging and interesting' but there is a 'great support network' so you don't feel overwhelmed. If you are looking to get your hands on 'good-quality work' at a pioneering firm that 'punches above its weight', take a closer look at RPC.

If the firm were a fictional character it would be...

Viola (Twelfth Night) – has a practical resourcefulness, an engaging wit, and a native intelligence

The firm

RPC posted a 6% rise in turnover for 2015/16, and is highly-regarded for its dispute resolution, insurance and media law capabilities. In May 2016 it launched RPC Perform, a consultancy for in-house lawyers. The firm was shortlisted for the Insurance & Legal Technology Team of the Year crowns at the *Legal Business* Awards 2016. RPC has UK bases in London and Bristol, as well as overseas offices in Hong Kong and Singapore.

The deals

Defended the Royal Embassy of Saudi Arabia before the Court of Appeal in a claim concerning the application of diplomatic immunity; advised Independent Print on the competition aspects of its £24m sale of the i newspaper to Johnston Press; acted for RFIB Holdings on the sale of its business to Calera Capital; advised Zeno Capital on the £90m sale of the London Fire Brigade's headquarters; advised International Brand Management Limited on a global endorsement deal with British band Little Mix.

The clients

Bellway Homes; Betfair; Ernst & Young; Faraday; Imperial College London; Lyceum Capital; RSA; Sports Direct; Taylor Wimpey; XL Caitlin.

The star performers

Top-ranking departments according to *The Legal 500* (see legal500.com for more details)
Banking litigation: investment and retail; Brand management; Commercial contracts; Commercial property; Competition litigation; Construction: contentious; Corporate crime (including fraud, bribery and corruption); Health and safety; Insurance: insolvency and restructuring; M&A: mid-market, £50m-£250m; Media and entertainment (including media finance); Personal injury: defendant; Private equity: transactions: Mid-cap deal capability; Product liability: defendant; Professional discipline; Professional negligence.

- **Why did you choose this firm over any others?** 'Potential for growth with the firm'; 'the trainee intake is just the right size'; 'the friendly reputation of the firm is something that greatly appealed to me'; 'they tried to make themselves sound different from the status quo'; 'extremely friendly culture'; 'City work but small-firm feel'; variety of seat offerings'; 'great vacation scheme'; 'genuinely seemed to do things differently'; 'multiple industry awards'; 'great offices'

- **Best thing about the firm?** 'Office overlooking the Tower of London'; 'lawyers who all get on with one another'; 'interesting departments'; 'house system'; 'getting involved in interesting work'; 'everyone is genuinely friendly'; 'high levels of responsibility in some departments'; 'free breakfast and dinner'; 'modern open-plan offices with lots of natural light and good views'; 'numerous clubs and societies'

- **Worst thing about the firm?** 'Limited non-contentious seat choices'; 'no microwaves or fridges'; 'flexible working infrastructure is behind the times'; 'competition for particularly popular seats'; 'NQ process is opaque'; 'the relatively low pay particularly after qualification'; 'not many international secondments'; 'that it is getting rid of having trainees in the Bristol office'; 'financial remuneration doesn't reflect how well the firm is doing'; 'not many international secondments'

- **Best moment?** 'Securing an instruction for the firm during my first seat'; 'finding out I am going to Hong Kong for my final seat'; 'excellent mid-seat review feedback'; 'carrying out research for counsel and having him reference me in his opinion'; 'presenting to a public company as part of a pitch'; 'organising a commercial awareness event for students'

- **Worst moment?** 'Infuriating IT crashes'; 'feeling like I don't understand a lot of the cases I am working on'; 'when the goalposts keep changing in a case'; 'dealing with a client in a difficult personal situation'; 'when I realised that I had failed to make a payment of tax for a client that might incur penalties'

A day in the life of...

... Chloe Johnston first-year trainee, RPC

Departments to date: IP litigation, professional and financial risks
University: Exeter
Degree and class: Philosophy and Political Economy, 2(1)

8.00am: I arrive at the office and take my things up to my desk. Usually I'd be heading to the café to get my breakfast but this morning the editors of the 'Trainees Take on Business' blog are hosting a breakfast event so I head to the client lounge to help set up.

8.30am: The 'Brexit Breakfast' kicks off and there is lots of discussion about the upcoming vote. We have laid out a selection of today's newspapers to inform the debates going on around the client lounge.

9.30am: I head back upstairs and check my emails. One of our clients has emailed requesting a consultation with counsel next week to discuss strategy for an upcoming hearing. I check the availability of the partner and associate on the matter, then call the clerk at chambers to request corresponding dates to put to the client.

9.45am: I write my daily to-do list and then pick up where I left off last night on a longstanding chronology task. I've been tasked with creating a chronology of all the documents we have and these span more than a five year period. This type of task is a great way to become familiar with a new matter and, as I will be involved with this case throughout my seat, it's crucial to get to grips with the background and facts.

11.30am: I take a call from an associate in the commercial disputes team who has a bundle which needs to be lodged at court urgently. Each of the first-year trainees in a contentious seat is on a rota in case our outdoor clerk is unavailable and this morning is my slot!

1.00pm: I arrive back from court just in time to catch some of the trainees at lunch in the café.

1.30pm: Back at my desk, a partner comes over to ask if I can assist on a matter which is potentially heading towards a judicial review. I prepare a memo which sets out a detailed analysis of which grounds we could rely on and the procedure for issuing a judicial review.

4.00pm: I have my weekly catch up with my supervisor. We grab a coffee and discuss my current workload, any challenges I'm facing and if I have any ideas about other work I'd like to get involved with.

4.30pm: During our catch up my supervisor briefed me on a new matter and asked me to research potential barristers that we could instruct. I review the CVs of various barristers and put together a list of those with the requisite expertise and experience and email it to my supervisor.

5.30pm: I attend a conference call which is between a partner, the clients and counsel, and take a thorough note. The purpose of the call is to discuss the claimant's disclosure that we have recently inspected and our strategy going forward. I type up the attendance note and speak to the partner about a task I

> 'I have my weekly catch up with my supervisor. We grab a coffee and discuss my current workload.'

have been set for tomorrow, which is to begin analysing the disclosure to determine if there are any gaps in what we have been provided with.

6.45pm: I leave the office and meet up with some of my GDL classmates for drinks and dinner on the docks!

www.rpc.co.uk/manifesto

About the firm

Address: Tower Bridge House, St Katharine's Way, London E1W 1AA
Telephone: 020 3060 6000
Website: www.rpc.co.uk/manifesto
Twitter: twitter.com/LifeinaLawFirm

Other offices: Bristol, Hong Kong, Singapore.

Who we are: If you're looking for a predictable career in a traditional firm, then please stop reading now. At RPC you'll get a whole lot more. Of course clients expect their lawyers to understand the law. But what they really want is advice from smart people who get the commercial context and can spot the business implications. On this measure, you won't find better than RPC; in 2015 the UK's leading client satisfaction report placed us in the top spot overall out of 383 firms benchmarked, and ranked us number one for quality of commercial advice. Not for the first time.

What we do: Combining this commercial outlook with some of the leading lawyers in their fields and great clients, we offer a depth of knowledge and creative approach to problem solving that few firms can rival. It's no surprise, then, that we're regularly praised in the leading directories for the quality of our training programmes.

What we're looking for: Although proven academic ability is important (we require a 2 (1) degree or above, not necessarily in law) we value energy, enthusiasm, business sense, commitment and the ability to relate well to others just as highly. Recruitment usually takes place in either July or August, two years before the training contract begins. Shortlisted candidates will be invited to one of our assessment days during which they will meet our existing trainees, associates and partners.

What you'll do: As a trainee you will receive first-rate training in a supportive working environment. You will collaborate closely with a partner and will be given real responsibility as soon as you are ready to handle it. At least six months will be spent in four areas of our practice. We encourage our trainees to express preferences for the areas in which they would like to train. In addition to the Professional Skills Course, we provide a complementary programme of in-house training. When you qualify we hope you will stay with us and we always do our best to place you in the area of law that suits you most.

Sponsorship: Bursaries are available for the GDL, if applicable, and the LPC. Bursaries comprise course and examination fees and maintenance grants of up to £7,000. We request that all our trainees complete their LPC and GDL at BPP Law School.

Facts and figures

Partners: 81
Other fee-earners: 345
Total trainees: 37

Trainee places available for 2019: 15
Applications received pa: 600

First year salary: £37,000
Second year salary: £40,000
Newly qualified salary: Merit-based

Turnover in 2015: £94.4m (+12% from 2014)

Profits per equity partner: £403,000 (+19%)
(see legalbusiness.co.uk for full financial information)

Application process

Apply to: Trainee recruitment team.
How: Online at www.rpc.co.uk/manifesto.
When: By 31 July 2017 for 2019 training contracts.

Vacation schemes

Summer: Apply by 31 January 2017.

Reed Smith LLP

The Broadgate Tower, 20 Primrose Street, London EC2A 2RS

Lex 100 Winner

See categories below
and tables from page 69

Survey results *(marks out of 100%)*

Satisfied in your job?	81
Firm living up to expectations?	82
High quality of work?	83
Enough client contact?	77
Stress-free?	69
Happy work/life balance?	68
Friendly firm?	90
Great social life?	70
Good vacation scheme?	87
Confident you'll be kept on?	78
Good remuneration?	67
Diverse firm?	84
Good international secondments?	43

 **verdict**

Reed Smith has an 'excellent reputation' for its 'specialised niche practice areas including shipping and media' which have established a 'global reach', and offices spanning the US, Europe, Asia and the Middle East. This gives trainees the opportunity to gain 'good exposure to international work' and generally work at trainee level is 'excellent, challenging and varied' as seniors take a 'genuine interest in your learning and development'. There is no 'glass ceiling or limit to the type of work you can do as a trainee, as long as you are capable and enthusiastic'. The 'small intake size' results in trainees getting 'more responsibility early on'. Trainees are rewarded with a 'good work/life balance' as they manage their own time and are consequently able to work generally 'better hours', which will have contributed to the **Lex 100 Winner** prize for low stress levels. There are no 'compulsory seat options' and trainees are given 'great influence' over which seats they get, therefore recruits are free to pursue their own areas of interest, 'particularly towards the end of their training contract'. Trainees grumble about 'compiling bundles', 'late-night admin' and, at the other extreme, sometimes 'not always having enough work to do'. Top trainee moments include 'completing the sale of a company which contributed to saving 400 jobs' and 'helping to close a transaction with parties from New York, Hong Kong and Paris at 4am in the morning, followed by a champagne lunch'. Trainees would love 'better coffee' and an 'in-house gym', though on the plus side the firm is 'very social' and there are a 'number of team- and firm-wide events'. It is 'truly a great place to train as everyone enjoys working with each other'. If this sounds appealing, get Reed Smith on your radar.

If the firm were a fictional character it would be...

Elastagirl (The Incredibles) – flexible and resourceful when required

The firm

Reed Smith secured a nomination for CSR Programme of the Year at the *Legal Business Awards 2016*, an accolade it won in 2015. Departments of note include the M&A, real estate and commodities groups. The firm has 26 offices across Europe, Asia, the US and the Middle East.

The deals

Advised the Côte Restaurant Group on the £78m refinancing of its credit facilities; successfully acted for Bunge in a Supreme Court case against Nidera; advised the Ministry of Finance of the Republic of Kazakhstan on a $4bn notes issuance under its MTN programme; acted for Wilmington Trust on the restructuring of a $750m RMBS; acted for Deutsche Bank on a $150m pre-payment facility for zinc smelter Nyrstar.

The clients

Barclays; Chevron; Citibank; DNB; European Federation of Energy Traders; Glencore; Hyundai Samho Heavy Industries; Instiglio; Oak Hill Advisors; Sovcomflot.

The star performers

Top-ranking departments according to *The Legal 500* (see legal500.com for more details)
Asset based lending; Asset finance and leasing; Bank lending – investment grade debt and syndicated loans; Commodities: derivatives; Commodities: physicals; Corporate restructuring and insolvency; Debt capital markets; Derivatives and structured products; Emerging markets; Employment: employers; Mining and minerals; Pensions (non-contentious); Securitisation; Shipping; Trade finance.

- **Why did you choose this firm over any others?** 'Friendliness of fee-earners'; 'a medium-sized intake'; 'it valued quality of training'; 'distinct mix of core practice areas'; 'I completed a vacation scheme here'; 'spectacular offices'; 'friendly interviewers'; 'best variety of seat choices during training contract'; 'it invests in the trainees'; 'a wide range of highly rated practice areas'; 'global reach of the firm'; 'I like the variety of high-profile work on offer'; 'number of trainees'

- **Best thing about the firm?** 'The view from London office'; 'the quality of work'; 'level of responsibility given to trainees'; 'everyone is approachable'; 'variety of work and seat choices'; 'the views from Broadgate Tower'; 'friendly culture'; 'pro bono opportunities'

- **Worst thing about the firm?** 'Late notification as to what your next department will be'; 'tends to follow other firms regarding salary'; 'the exposure to the other offices via secondments or travel is limited'; 'unpredictable hours at times'; 'no in-house gym'; 'the coffee is dreadful'

- **Best moment?** 'Completing the sale of a company, which otherwise would have been put into administration'; 'being asked to take the lead on a restructuring deal and successfully closing it'; 'managing my own cases'; 'completion drinks with the client when in my corporate seat'; 'being given my own files'; 'running conference calls with the client and their tax advisers'; 'being able to work on high-profile deals'

- **Worst moment?** 'Staying in the office until 2am compiling documents which we were then told were no longer required'; 'being overworked and underappreciated in one seat'; 'indexing an end-of-transaction bible'; 'organising original documents following a double fund launch'; 'working very late without being given any recognition for it'

An interview with...

... **Matthew Norman** trainee solicitor, Reed Smith LLP

University: University of Kent/Hong Kong University

Degree and class: LLB Law with a year abroad in Hong Kong

Why did you choose Reed Smith?

I chose Reed Smith for its diverse range of leading practice groups. Along with strong offerings in litigation, corporate and finance, Reed Smith also boasts a market-leading presence in shipping, media, and energy and natural resources. I very much wanted to gain international experience and Reed Smith offers this through its network of 26 international offices and secondment opportunities. Furthermore, I value the emphasis the firm puts on building and maintaining strong client relationships. This approach has afforded me the opportunity to undertake secondments at two different retail banks.

Which skills/attributes are key for your role? As a trainee, you can expect to be involved in a number of tasks for various supervisors at any given time. Luckily, this means no two days are the same, however it does require a high level of time management and organisation to successfully meet your deadlines. To achieve this you must be able to communicate effectively with your colleagues to determine which tasks to prioritise and what your supervisor expects from the final product.

Legal practice is driven by deadlines and thus you must be able to work under pressure, while maintaining keen attention to detail. Being a trainee can involve working long hours and continuous/constructive feedback as to areas you can improve. The key is to proactively seek

work and approach each task with enthusiasm and a positive attitude.

What are the best and most challenging things about your job? By far, the best part of my job has been getting involved in complex transactions that require completion within a tight deadline. Although enormously challenging, these situations bring out the best in you and provide a huge amount of satisfaction and confidence when completed. Similarly, trainees at Reed Smith receive a substantial amount of early responsibility, which can be daunting at first but highly rewarding from a development perspective.

What sets your company apart from its competitors as a top graduate employer? What sets Reed Smith apart is the firm's investment in you from an early stage. Before starting your training contract, the firm provides the opportunity to gain a master's degree in business and secondment to a client. This is an invaluable experience and provides a core commercial grounding and high level of client contact. Moreover, with a small intake of around 25 trainees each year, you are able to form strong relationships with graduate recruitment.

What is the culture like at Reed Smith?

The clichés of a 'collegiate' and 'open door' culture are wide spread, however I can say with honesty that Reed Smith has a

wonderfully friendly culture. The firm benefits from a genuinely flat hierarchy and interaction with senior colleagues and management is common-place. Furthermore, there isn't a 'Reed Smith' type and consequently this has fostered an inclusive environment where you are encouraged to be yourself.

> **'The firm benefits from a genuinely flat hierarchy and interaction with senior colleagues and management is common-place.'**

What advice would you give to someone applying for a role with Reed Smith? I cannot stress enough how important it is to be yourself! By letting your personality come through in your application and at interview stage, you will be better placed to display your interests and motivations for pursuing a career in commercial law. Thoroughly research the firm beyond brochures and the website. More importantly, convey this in your application. Many applicants fall into the trap of telling Reed Smith about Reed Smith. Instead, carefully consider what the application question is asking you and then demonstrate your knowledge by weaving it into your answer.

www.reedsmith.com/ukgraduates

About the firm

Address: The Broadgate Tower, 20 Primrose Street, London EC2A 2RS
Telephone: 020 3116 3000 **Fax:** 020 3116 3999
Website: www.reedsmith.com
Email: graduate.recruitment@reedsmith.com

Managing partner: Andrew Jenkinson

Other offices: Abu Dhabi, Athens, Beijing, Century City, Chicago, Dubai, Frankfurt, Hong Kong, Houston, Kazakhstan, London, Los Angeles, Munich, New York, Paris, Philadelphia, Pittsburgh, Princeton, Richmond, San Francisco, Shanghai, Silicon Valley, Singapore, Tysons, Washington DC, Wilmington.

Who we are: Reed Smith is a global law firm, with more than 1,700 lawyers in 26 offices throughout Europe, the Middle East, Asia and the United States. .

What we do: The firm represents leading international businesses, from FTSE 100 corporations to dynamic mid-market and emerging enterprises. Our lawyers provide litigation and other dispute resolution services, regulatory counsel, and legal advice on the full range of strategic domestic and cross-border transactions.

What we're looking for: We are looking for you to demonstrate that you have the skills and behaviours which would expect from our trainees which are: legal skills (such as research and analysis, and communication skills), citizenship (teamwork, developing self and others), business skills (leadership and matter and financial management) and client skills (client relationships and business development).

What you'll do: Trainees undertake four seats of six months duration and you will be able to choose from this wide range of disciplines as well as international and client secondments.

Perks: 25 days' annual holiday, permanent health insurance, subsidised cafeteria, life insurance, lifestyle discounts and concierge service, contributory pension scheme, season ticket loan, staff introduction bonus, conveyance fees reimbursed for domestic conveyance

Sponsorship: Full course fees for both the GDL and LPC, plus maintenance grants of £6,000 during your GDL study year and £7,000 through your LPC study year.

Facts and figures

Total partners (London): 116
Other fee-earners (London): 190

Trainee places available for 2019: 25
Applications received pa: 700
Percentage interviewed: 10%

First year salary: £38,500
Second year salary: £40,000
Newly qualified salary: £63,000

Application process

Apply to: Chloe Muir, graduate recruitment co-ordinator.
How: apply4law.com/reedsmith
When: By 30 June 2017.
What's involved: Case study, interview and group exercise.

Vacation schemes

Summer: June and July 2017 (applications open on 1 November 2016 and close on 31 January 2017).

Roythornes Solicitors

Enterprise Way, Pinchbeck, Spalding PE11 3YR

Lex 100 Winner

LEX 100 WINNER

See categories below and tables from page 69

Survey results *(marks out of 100%)*

Satisfied in your job?	**85**
Firm living up to expectations?	87
High quality of work?	82
Enough client contact?	70
Stress-free?	53
Happy work/life balance?	77
Friendly firm?	83
Great social life?	67
Good vacation scheme?	**97**
Confident you'll be kept on?	82
Good remuneration?	77
Diverse firm?	80

 verdict

Roythornes Solicitors has four offices across East Anglia and the East Midlands, and is labelled a 'regional heavyweight with a personal feel'. This 'medium-sized firm' can offer recruits a 'breadth of complex work', and there are 'lots of varied departments to get experience in' with the 'significant property department' earning a special mention. This year, the firm is named a **Lex 100 Winner** in the job satisfaction and vacation scheme categories. The 'trust and respect the partners place in you' is clear, and trainees appreciate the 'involvement with high-profile cases' and the 'ability from early on to be responsible for file-handling'. Trainee highlights have included 'preparing for and attending a huge trial on a long-running case', 'attending a joint settlement meeting with counsel and one of the firm's partners' and 'running and completing a high-value banking transaction'. There are instances of 'staying late' and being required to 'keep an eye on files during annual leave', and one respondent complains of 'stress from taking on too much work'. That said, Roythornes 'invests in trainees and all staff', and colleagues ensure that 'great weight is given to your personal preference of seats' – a sign of the 'friendly and helpful atmosphere in the office'. There are minor gripes about the 'location of head office' which 'could be closer to the town centre', an inconvenience which 'makes going to the pub after work a little more difficult when everyone drives home'. It is good for those who 'love the countryside' though, plus there are still 'plenty of opportunities to visit clients, go to court and attend hearings'. For an 'overwhelmingly positive experience' where you can 'work closely with partners on complex files', add Roythornes Solicitors to your shortlist.

If the firm were a fictional character it would be...

Old MacDonald – has long-standing expertise in the agricultural sector

The firm

Roythornes Solicitors' primary area of expertise is in representing clients in the agriculture sector, with renewable energy and property being complementary practice groups. The firm's headquarters is in Spalding, while the support of the Nottingham, Peterborough and Newmarket offices enables Roythornes to service clients on a national scale.

The deals

Acted for an investor on £14m-worth of agricultural land acquisitions; advising on divorce cases related to the division of agricultural assets; worked on the re-organisations of large estates and farming groups; advises on military accident, sports and travel injury claims.

The clients

Clients include family businesses, major blue-chip companies and private individuals based locally, nationally and internationally.

The star performers

Top-ranking departments according to *The Legal 500* (see legal500.com for more details)
Agriculture and estates; Contentious trusts and probate; Corporate and commercial; Family; Personal injury: claimant; Personal tax, trusts and probate.

- **Why did you choose this firm over any others?** 'Local reputation'; 'the expertise of those at the firm'; 'breadth of departments'; 'significant property department'; 'had a really friendly feel when I came for interview'; 'regional heavyweight with a personal feel'; 'the overwhelmingly positive experience I had on the vacation scheme'; 'breadth of departments'

- **Best thing about the firm?** 'The friendliness'; 'the trust and respect the partners place in you'; 'the breadth and range of work'; 'the inclusivity of the working environment'; 'I have found my niche'; 'the firm's friendly but professional attitude'; 'the atmosphere in the office – really friendly and helpful'; 'level of work available'

- **Worst thing about the firm?** 'Could be closer to town centre'; 'location of head office'; although I enjoy the countryside, it makes going to the pub after work a little more difficult when everyone drives home'

- **Best moment?** 'Attending a joint settlement meeting with counsel and one of the firm's partners'; 'preparing for and attending a huge trial on long-running case'; 'running and completing a high-value banking transaction'; 'working closely with partners on complex files'

- **Worst moment?** 'Billing'; 'conflicting priorities'; 'stress from taking on too much work'

A day in the life of...

... **Natasha Bicknell** first-year trainee, Roythornes Solicitors (Spalding)

Departments to date: Property/planning

University: University of East Anglia and BBP Law School, Holborn

Degree and class: Law 2(1), LPC: Distinction

8.35am: I arrive in the office and head to the kitchen where there is always a friendly face to talk to and have a quick catch up while making a coffee. It is not long before I am at my desk, reviewing my emails and calendar to see what tasks, deadlines and meetings there are today and looking ahead. I then write myself a to-do list which helps me set out what tasks need to be completed and prioritise accordingly.

9.10am: Morning catch up with my supervisor. Working in a busy and fast-paced planning department, communication is key to ensuring that deadlines are met and clients' expectations are exceeded with enquiries being handled in good time and effectively. Roythornes places an emphasis on ensuring that trainees are involved as a valued member of the team at every stage. This daily catch up gives me a great opportunity to speak one-on-one and review any work I have done the day before and ask any questions or queries that I may have.

10.00am: I am now planning the rest of my morning around a meeting at 12.30pm – a developer client phoned earlier this week as an application for planning permission was refused for residential development. We have arranged a meeting to discuss the strength of a potential appeal application. My supervisor has asked me to do some background research on the planning application and find out the reasons for refusal in light of the local and national planning policy.

11.30am: Catch up with my supervisor to evaluate the information I have found, as well as discussing my supervisor's thoughts and knowledge on this matter. We discuss the reasons for the refusal and the potential grounds of appeal, especially in light of the lack of a five-year housing land supply in the area concerned.

12.30pm: At the client meeting, my role is to take notes of the key issues and to gain an understanding of what is required, as I will be assisting with drafting the written representations for the appeal if the client wishes to proceed. Sitting in on meetings allows me to have a real insight and involvement in each matter, and also gives the client comfort in knowing who will be dealing and assisting with their case.

1.30pm: This lunchtime I head to Costa with a colleague who is also a fellow trainee and started at the same time as me.

2.30pm: Back at my desk, I dictate the attendance note for the appeal meeting, and then focus on urgent enquiries that need to be dealt with today. I receive an email from the council with proposed amendments to the draft s106 agreement which I issued to them earlier this week. After reviewing the changes, I telephone the client and discuss each amendment and we agree a strategy for responding. I then spend time drafting the client's proposals and run through them with my supervisor before reverting back to the council.

> **'Roythornes places an emphasis on ensuring that trainees are involved as a valued member of the team at every stage.'**

4.00pm: I ensure all urgent tasks have been completed and I start reviewing an infrastructure agreement and preparing a report which is to be issued to the client tomorrow.

5.40pm: It's Wednesday evening so it means only one thing, a badminton tournament with work. Tonight there are eight of us, one partner, a solicitor, and a few trainees and paralegals. I hope my team wins... again!

www.roythorne.co.uk/site/careers/trainees

About the firm

Address: Enterprise Way, Pinchbeck, Spalding, PE11 3YR
Telephone: 01775 842500   **Fax:** 01775 725736
Website: www.roythornes.co.uk
Email: recruitment@roythornes.co.uk
Twitter: @roythornes

Senior partner: Paul Osborne
Managing director: Vember Mortlock

Other offices: Nottingham, Peterborough and Newmarket.

Who we are: At Roythornes, we have been putting our clients first for over 80 years. By really getting to know their strengths, ambitions and concerns, we are better able to support and guide them, becoming their trusted advisors. We offer a powerful breadth and depth of legal expertise; we look at the big picture while getting the detail right. We embrace our individual talents while operating as one team.

What we do: Our clients include major blue-chip companies, family businesses and private estates and high-net-worth individuals, based locally, nationally and internationally. Our expertise spans the agricultural, food, property and energy sectors, as well as having exceptionally strong private client and commercial/corporate law departments.

Facts and figures

Total partners: 27
Other fee-earners: 81
Total trainees: 10

Trainee places available for 2019: 5
Applications received pa: 90
Percentage interviewed: 33%

First year salary: £23,500
Second year salary: £24,500
Newly qualified salary: £33,500

What we're looking for: We are looking for bright individuals who want a great career in law with Roythornes, who want to do exceptional work rather than just the everyday. They need to have the ambition and drive to make it happen. We are looking for trainees who will care about our clients and want to make long-term relationships, growing their work through referrals.

What you'll do: We are a partner-led firm and the trainees will have exceptional learning and development and supervision. Working alongside some of the leading experts in their fields the trainees will be exposed to complex, challenging work that will help them grow into the best they can be. We have our own agri-academy, regular lunch and learn, at home with... alongside many external training providers. We are also growing our mentoring scheme and fully committed to the blended learning approach.

Perks: Pension, health and life insurance, 24-days holiday per annum.

Sponsorship: We offer sponsorship of up to £10,000 for the LPC whether the trainee wishes to do the course full time or whether they wish to do their LPC part time while doing their training contract. We have trainees following both paths. We also run a bursary scheme for local students to support them entering the profession.

Application process

Apply to: Gillian Nash-Kennell, HR director.
How: We would like a covering letter and a CV sent to recruitment@roythornes.co.uk.
When: By 31 January 2017.
What's involved: Stage one: face-to-face interview with two partners. Stage two: full day, an assessment exercise in the morning followed by two different panel interviews.

Vacation schemes

Summer: Two weeks from 10 July 2017 (apply by 28 February 2017).

Russell-Cooke LLP

2 Putney Hill, London SW15 6AB

Survey results *(marks out of 100%)*

Satisfied in your job?	76
Firm living up to expectations?	75
High quality of work?	83
Enough client contact?	82
Stress-free?	60
Happy work/life balance?	79
Friendly firm?	92
Great social life?	70
Confident you'll be kept on?	52
Good remuneration?	69
Diverse firm?	86

 **verdict**

Russell-Cooke has a 'breadth of practice areas across commercial, private client and the third sector', so the work on offer is 'high-profile and interesting'. Trainees are 'encouraged to run their own small files' and to be the 'main point of contact for their clients'. The 'supervision from partners is fantastic and there is lots of confidence placed in trainees'. This trust placed in trainees results in a 'breadth of work', but trainees would like 'more mentoring' rather than relying on 'individual departments for informal support'. Staff are 'friendly and approachable', which creates a 'relaxed environment' as 'everyone is treated with respect on all levels of the organisation'. There are 'plenty of opportunities to get involved in cases in a meaningful way and to contribute to their outcome'. Top trainee moments include 'attending a nine-day trial', 'helping clients achieve the settlement they deserved in personal injury proceedings' and 'running files in every seat from portal claims in PI to estate administration in private client to small disputes in commercial litigation'. Notably, current trainees comment on the 'stressful competition for a single seat in popular departments' which results in some not being able to complete their 'preferred seats'. However, the 'variety of seats' on offer results in a 'useful learning experience' for trainees 'even if you do not get your first choice'. Trainees work 'reasonable hours' so they have a 'good work/life balance'. Those seeking 'responsibility' within a 'wide range of practice areas' should consider Russell-Cooke.

If the firm were a fictional character it would be...

Santiago (The Old Man and the Sea) – an experienced and intrepid campaigner with unexpected strength and genuine compassion

The firm

Russell-Cooke offers the full range of legal services out of its network of offices across London. The firm has a diverse mix of commercial, private and public sector clients, and is also noted for its abilities in family, clinic negligence and real estate law. The firm employs approximately 170 lawyers.

The deals

Advised the British Heart Foundation on a comprehensive governance review; acted for the Solicitors Regulation Authority against two individuals in relation to the collapse of a litigation finance fund and the misapplication of nearly £5m; acted for Petros London on the purchase and development of student accommodation at Canterbury Christ Church University; represented Woodcock Holdings in an appeal to the Secretary of State relating to a mixed-use project at West Sussex; acted for Sky UK in various proceedings pertaining to intellectual property rights.

The clients

Action for Children; Bar Standards Board; Farriers Registration Council; the International Protection of Adults; Just Healthcare; Kasada UK; Orderella; Rockshore Group; SportsDirect; Voluntary Service Overseas.

The star performers

Top-ranking departments according to *The Legal 500* (see legal500.com for more details)

Charities and not-for-profit; Clinical negligence: claimant; Commercial litigation; Commercial property: general; Contentious trusts and probate; Court of Protection; Crime: general; Employment: senior executives; Family; Fraud: white-collar crime; Immigration: business; M&A: smaller deals, up to £50m; Personal injury: claimant; Personal tax, trusts and probate; Planning; Professional discipline; Property litigation; Social housing: tenant.

- **Why did you choose this firm over any others?** 'Range of seats on offer'; 'good work/life balance'; 'variety of departments'; 'opportunity to do legal aid work'; 'firm values'; 'disputes and charities departments in combination with more common areas of practice like private client and commercial property'; 'quality of the training'; 'responsibility given to trainees'

- **Best thing about the firm?** 'Plenty of opportunities to get involved in cases in a meaningful way and contribute to their outcome'; 'everyone has been very welcoming and supportive in my first seat'; 'quality of the solicitors'; 'everybody is treated with respect and consideration at all levels of the organisation'

- **Worst thing about the firm?** 'Lack of transparency on qualification process'; 'trainees are worried about retention prospects'; 'multiple locations sometimes make it more difficult to socialise'; 'IT systems are a bit archaic'; 'limited trainee seats in some areas, particularly private client and family'

- **Best moment?** 'Getting good feedback for a complex piece of legal research'; 'securing a liability admission for a long-standing client'; 'helping clients to achieve the settlement they deserved in personal injury proceedings'; 'positive feedback from clients'

- **Worst moment?** 'Dealing with an incredibly rude client'; 'disclosure tasks'; 'making minor unforced errors'; 'not getting the seat I wanted for several rounds, which was quite stressful, and competing with several other trainees for a single seat in popular departments'

A day in the life of…

… Amina Al Hashim first-year trainee, Russell-Cooke LLP

Departments to date: Property; trust and estate disputes
University: London School of Economics and Political Science
Degree and class: LLB, 2(1)

9.00am: I arrive in the office and head to the kitchen to make my habitual coffee. While I'm waiting, I chat with my colleagues about the day ahead. I then settle myself at my desk and check my emails. I have a simultaneous sale and purchase completion to work on this morning; I email the accounts team to let them know I'm expecting our client's sale monies to come in. Once monies have arrived, I send the completion monies for our client's purchase.

10.00am: I receive a telephone call from the seller's solicitors to say that completion funds have been received and the keys have been released. I inform my clients who are delighted; they make their way to their lovely new home in the country and thank me for all my help. I'm pleased everything was done efficiently.

11.00am: I walk to East Putney station and take the tube into central London. I'm meeting a longstanding writer/director client while he's filming on set. His schedule is tight so I wait for a pause in filming, witness his signature on various deeds and head back to the office. As part of a small trainee intake I enjoy meeting with clients on a regular basis and very early on in my first seat.

1.00pm: A work friend and I walk to a local Italian restaurant which bakes authentic Italian pizza. We relax and catch up over lunch before heading back to the office.

1.45pm: Having finished the completions this morning, I research stamp duty and collective enfranchisement so I can advise a residents' association.

3.00pm: I make some amendments to an option agreement I've been drafting for a landowner client. My supervisor and I discuss it at length until we are happy that we've represented our client's requirements and interests fully. We meet with the client and discuss our amendments; he's happy with our work and asks our advice on another matter.

4.30pm: I tie up some loose ends at my desk and reply to some requisitions from the Land Registry. I review my calendar and flag the matters I will need to follow up within the next few days.

5.00pm: I fill in my trainee diary and make a record of everything I've done today. I have a discussion with my supervisor about tomorrow's matters; he's out of the office tomorrow and I'm holding down the fort. I work on some post-completion forms that need to be submitted to the Land Registry.

'As part of a small trainee intake I enjoy meeting with clients on a regular basis and very early on in my first seat.'

5.45pm: Satisfied that I've resolved everything that needs to be completed, I head to an inter-departmental event with the other trainees. We meet there and spend a couple of hours mingling and sampling the various cheeses on offer. I win a camembert in the quiz and head home with my prize!

www.russell-cooke.co.uk

lex100.com

About the firm

Address: 2 Putney Hill, London SW15 6AB
Telephone: 020 8789 9111   **Fax:** 020 8780 1194
Website: www.russell-cooke.co.uk
Email: graduate.recruitment@russell-cooke.co.uk
Twitter: twitter.com/RussellCooke

Senior partner: John Gould
Managing partner: Jonathan Thornton

Other offices: London (Bedford Row) and Kingston-upon-Thames.

Who we are: A broad London-based firm with a contemporary outlook, and strength in depth. Departments include charities, clinical negligence, commercial litigation, commercial property, corporate and commercial, cross-border estates and tax planning, employment, family, private client, professional regulation, and trust and estates disputes. Key clients include the Solicitors Regulation Authority, the Architects Registration Board, BSkyB, Pret a Manger and Sports Direct.

What we're looking for: An intellectually rigorous, independently minded trainee with a broad range of skills, both technical and personal.

What you'll do: Trainees sit in four departments across our offices with two formal reviews during each seat.

Sponsorship: LPC fees capped at £8,000.

Facts and figures

Total partners: 59
Other fee-earners: 130
Total trainees: 19

Trainee places available for 2019: 7
Applications received pa: Approximately 500
Percentage interviewed: 10%

First year salary: £34,000
Second year salary: £36,000
Newly qualified salary: Market rate for the area into which the trainee qualifies

Turnover in 2015: £32.6m
Profits per equity partner: £202,000

Application process

Apply to: Tess Morley.
How: Apply online at www.russell-cooke.co.uk/trainees
When: By 31 July 2017 for 2019 contracts.
What's involved: If you are invited for the first interview, it will be with a single partner. If you are invited for a second interview, it will involve a letter writing exercise, a group facilitated case study and discussion, a lunch with the current trainees and an individual interview.

RUSSELL-COOKE | SOLICITORS

Shearman & Sterling LLP

9 Appold Street, London EC2A 2AP

Lex 100 Winner

See categories below
and tables from page 69

Survey results *(marks out of 100%)*

Satisfied in your job?	80
Firm living up to expectations?	85
High quality of work?	87
Enough client contact?	72
Stress-free?	55
Happy work/life balance?	55
Friendly firm?	87
Great social life?	75
Good vacation scheme?	88
Confident you'll be kept on?	79
Good remuneration?	87
Diverse firm?	83
Good international secondments?	77

 **verdict**

The US-headquartered Shearman & Sterling is a 'truly global firm' undertaking 'cutting-edge work'. Trainees in London speak fondly of 'working alongside recognised experts and being able to learn from them'. In this way, 'the training is stellar', and the 'lack of hierarchy' and 'collegiate approach' makes for an 'excellent learning experience'. Respondents have gathered 'hands-on experience' across a 'variety of work', 'working on drafting complex legal submissions', 'being involved in an equity issuance of a major bank' and 'signing an extremely important transaction that made the cover of business papers'. The office itself receives a fair amount of criticism as 'the view from the building isn't very good' and 'a firm canteen would be nice', though one respondent is pleased to be working 'close to Shoreditch'. The 'professional but relaxed vibe' is a plus point, despite the 'lack of organised social events within departments'. As well as the 'exposure to global deals' enjoyed in London, international secondments are also available to trainees. Those who have completed overseas seats comment on the 'great quality of work' accompanied by the 'right amount of supervision', and Shearman is a **Lex 100 Winner** in the international secondments and remuneration satisfaction categories. Though some departments have 'consistently long hours', trainees are 'valuable members of the team and are made to feel appreciated', as exemplified by the '£30 dinner allowance and taxi home' for late finishes. Respondents treasure 'the respect you get for having trained at Shearman & Sterling', so if you're looking to join an international law firm with 'great prestige', add this firm to you shortlist.

If the firm were a fictional character it would be...

Indiana Jones – intelligent yet casual, it likes an adventure with calculated risks

The firm

Shearman & Sterling employs approximately 850 lawyers in 20 offices across Europe, Asia, North and Latin America and the Middle East. The London office has a reputation for handling high-profile banking, finance and energy work, as well as for strong performances from its commodities, M&A, and litigation teams. Shearman & Sterling was named Corporate Team of the Year at the *Legal Business* Awards 2016.

The deals

Acted on Liberty Global's $8.2bn acquisition of Cable & Wireless Communications; acted on the underwriter side on the multi-billion euro IPO and privatisation of ABN AMRO Group; assisted International Finance Corporation with launching private equity fund IFC Financial Institutions Growth Fund; acted for Electra as a co-investor alongside Patron Capital in the £325m acquisition of Grainger Retirement Solutions; advised Credit Suisse and others on a €239m offering by Dakar Finance.

The clients

Abu Dhabi Global Market; ArcelorMittal; Bank of America; Barclays; Bridgepoint; Citigroup; Engie; Intercontinental Exchange; Investcorp; Vitruvian.

The star performers

Top-ranking departments according to *The Legal 500* (see legal500.com for more details)
Acquisition finance; Banking litigation: investment and retail; Commercial litigation; Commodities: derivatives; Corporate tax; Debt capital markets; Derivatives and structured products; EU and competition; Emerging markets; Equity capital markets; Financial services (contentious); Financial services (non-contentious/regulatory); High yield; International arbitration; Investment funds: Hedge funds; Islamic finance; M&A: upper mid-market and premium deals, £250m+; Oil and gas.

- **Why did you choose this firm over any others?** 'Easy-going and friendly people'; 'quality of work and training experience'; 'international aspects'; 'the pay is very competitive'; 'small trainee intake'; 'friendliness of people on the vac scheme'; 'specialised in areas of law I was interested in'; 'future prospects'; 'top-quality work combined with a friendly atmosphere'

- **Best thing about the firm?** 'The senior lawyers all take the time to talk to you'; 'the trainees are all very friendly and there is a real sense of teamwork'; 'people appreciate the work you do'; 'working with top clients'; 'people are calm under pressure and great to learn from'; 'the buzzing working atmosphere surrounding doing great deals'

- **Worst thing about the firm?** 'Relentlessly long hours at times'; 'somewhat lacking in diversity'; 'some deals are simply not resourced well, and juniors get overloaded'; 'the air con switches off at 9pm'; 'the office isn't the most beautiful'; 'the learning curve is rather steep and at times quite scary'

- **Best moment?** 'Getting to do a seat in New York City'; 'being given responsibility on drafting a submission'; 'being recognised by a very senior partner for all my efforts'; 'getting recognition for a job well done'; 'attending management presentations with a client in Paris'; 'getting my section of a draft pleadings submitted to the tribunal in a major multi-billion dollar arbitration'

- **Worst moment?** 'The many times I haven't had time to get a bite to eat because I have been so busy'; 'attempting the Sisyphean task of tracing all of the intercompany obligations of a global banking group'; 'signing a document on the signature block rather than witnessing it. Twice.'

A day in the life of...

... Theodora Dimitrova second-seat trainee, Shearman & Sterling (London) LLP

Departments to date: Mergers and acquisition, financial institutions advisory
University: University of Cambridge
Degree: Law

9.20am: I arrive at the office, grab a cup of coffee and spend 15-20 minutes reading the BBC or the *FT*. I am currently involved in several public takeovers so it is useful to know what is going on in the business world.

9.40am: I take a look at my to-do list and order the tasks I need to complete according to priority. I have recently been involved in a fast-paced acquisition of a group of companies. My role has been to research points of law, draft ancillary documents and manage correspondence with various parties involved. I discuss with my supervisor, who is a counsel in the M&A department, whether I should prioritise reviewing and amending the shareholders' agreement or focus on drafting the board minutes approving the transaction. We discuss the structure and parties involved in the transaction and agree that it is better to press on with the shareholders' agreement as that involves obtaining information from the bankers and the corporate services provider.

11.20pm: I have also been involved in the sale of a mortgage portfolio involving a large financial institution. The parties to the transaction are supposed to sign the documents some time this week. I receive an email from one of the M&A associates asking if I could prepare signature pages to be signed at the client's board meeting today. During the afternoon I would have to head over to the client's offices to pick up the signed originals. I make myself a list of the documents for which I need to prepare signature pages and check the execution mechanics for contracts and deeds. I then give my PA the client's address so she can arrange a cab.

12.30pm: I attend a training session by Erskine Chambers on the common pitfalls in corporate transactions. It is one of many training events organised by Shearman's professional development team.

1.30pm: I get back to my desk and check my emails. One of the partners in M&A has asked me to check the Prospectus Rules and confirm the requirements in relation to financial information which needs to be included in a prospectus. Once I have pieced together the requirements, I draft an email to the partner who needs to go on a call with the client later in the afternoon on the same topic.

2.45pm: My taxi is here. I get to the client's office and check the signature pages to ensure that they have been signed correctly. I then head back to our office where I scan and organise the originals.

4.00pm: My supervisor asks if I would like to join a call in relation to the shareholders' agreement I reviewed this morning. The call identifies additional aspects of the transaction which I will need to capture in the board minutes. Afterwards we plan together how to reflect the new points discussed on the call in the minutes and I start working on my first draft.

5.40pm: We receive a request from one of our private equity clients to review and agree a non-disclosure agreement. I review and mark the document up. I send an email to the lawyers on the other side summarising

> '**I receive feedback from my supervisor on my draft board minutes and we come up with an action plan for the following day.**'

my comments and attaching my mark-up. I then receive a call from the associate on the other side and we arrange a call for tomorrow morning to discuss the outstanding points.

7.00pm: I receive feedback from my supervisor on my draft board minutes and we come up with an action plan for the following day.

7.20pm: I write tomorrow's to do list. Then I change into a cocktail dress and head out to the Financial News Awards dinner. It's a great opportunity to chat with colleagues in other departments at Shearman and meet lawyers from other firms.

ukgraduates.shearman.com

About the firm

Address: 9 Appold Street, London EC2A 2AP
Telephone: 020 7655 5000
Fax: 020 7655 5500
Website: ukgraduates.shearman.com
Email: graduates@shearman.com

Senior partners: Creighton Condon and Dave Beveridge
Managing partner (London): Nicholas Buckworth

Other offices: Abu Dhabi, Beijing, Brussels, Frankfurt, Hong Kong, London, Menlo Park, Milan, New York, Paris, Rome, San Francisco, Sao Paulo, Saudi Arabia*, Shanghai, Singapore, Tokyo, Toronto and Washington DC. *Abdulaziz Alassaf & Partners in association with Shearman & Sterling LLP

Who we are: Shearman and Sterling LLP is one of the world's leading premier global law firms and was established over a century ago. The London office opened in 1972, and quickly became one of the leading practices, covering all aspects of English, European and US corporate and finance law. Globally there are c900 lawyers, including around 200 partners.

What we do: Our main areas of work include finance, corporate (including mergers and acquisitions, private equity, equity capital markets and US capital markets), project development and finance, international arbitration and litigation, antitrust, tax, financial institutions advisory and asset management, real estate, and executive compensation and employee benefits.

What we're looking for: We are looking for trainees who are ambitious, relish intellectual challenge, and who want to be a success throughout their career.

What you'll do: During the two-year training contract, trainees have four seat rotations, with six months spent in each seat. One of these rotations may be completed overseas, in offices such as New York, Brussels, Abu Dhabi or Singapore. Trainees are fully integrated into the teams they work with and add significant value to the deals they are part of. From day one trainees are given a high level of responsibility, working with a range of individuals at all levels, from partners to associates. Trainees learn directly from the best in the industry, not just in the UK, but across a spread of jurisdictions.

Perks: Subsidised gym membership, private medical insurance, travel insurance, private dental insurance, BlackBerry, season ticket loans, annual eye test, matched pension contribution, life assurance, long-term disability insurance.

Sponsorship: Trainees are sponsored through the GDL and LPC, as well as receiving a maintenance grant.

Facts and figures

Total partners: 42
Other fee-earners: 142
Total trainees: 30

Trainee places available for 2019: 17
Applications received pa: Approx 900
Percentage interviewed: 6%

First year salary: £45,000
Second year salary: £50,000
Newly qualified salary: £95,000

Application process

Apply to: Online.
How: Online application via our website: ukgraduates.shearman.com
When: By 31 July 2017.
What's involved: Application form, interview and assessment centre.

Vacation schemes

Winter: Apply by 4 November 2016.
Spring: Apply by 20 January 2017.
Summer: Apply by 20 January 2017.

SHEARMAN & STERLING LLP

Shoosmiths LLP

The Lakes, Bedford Road, Northampton NN4 7SH

Lex 100 Winner

See categories below
and tables from page 69

Survey results *(marks out of 100%)*

Satisfied in your job?	85
Firm living up to expectations?	87
High quality of work?	82
Enough client contact?	80
Stress-free?	62
Happy work/life balance?	78
Friendly firm?	92
Great social life?	78
Good vacation scheme?	88
Confident you'll be kept on?	69
Good remuneration?	58
Diverse firm?	87
Good international secondments?	47

 **verdict**

Shoosmiths is a firm with a 'sizeable national presence' where trainees receive a 'good level of client contact'. Examples of current work highlights include a 'client meeting in the Isle of Man', 'attending a six-party mediation in London' and 'assisting in an all-party meeting for a potential development site'. Client secondments have also been popular, as they are a 'really valuable insight into what clients want from their lawyers', and one respondent was seconded to 'one of the largest vehicle manufacturers in the world'. The firm has secured **Lex 100 Winner** gongs for job satisfaction and living up to expectations. Indeed, the 'friendly environment' at the firm 'enables trainees to thrive', and Shoosmiths is 'very supportive of your career development'. Respondents cite a 'lack of choice' regarding seat rotations, and two trainees have commented on being given seats that they did not want, though with mixed results. One says that their 'opinion didn't change' after completing the seat, while the other says it 'ended up as a very positive experience'. The pay 'could be better', and 'salaries are not different according to the office location', though on the flip-side you can look forward to a 'good work/life balance'. Shoosmiths has a 'reputation for excellent training', and there is a clear 'emphasis on learning and developing'. Highlight moments enjoyed by the current cohort include 'completing my first transaction' and a 'nerve-wracking but thrilling urgent action for a large nationwide retailer days before Christmas'. To represent 'high-calibre clients' at a national firm that 'continues to grow and develop', consider applying to Shoosmiths.

If the firm were a fictional character it would be...

Columbo – under the friendly, unassuming façade is an astute and relentless character

The firm

Shoosmiths set up its eleventh office in July 2016, adding a base in Leeds to its extensive UK network. The firm offers a full service to its clients, and is particularly noted for its debt recovery, employment, commercial property and property litigation departments. It was shortlisted for National/Regional Firm of the Year at the *Legal Business* Awards 2016.

The deals

Acted as lead adviser to British American Tobacco in a supply chain and logistics project with DHL; advised Porterbrook Leasing on the procurement and leasing of new fleets of rolling stock for use by the Southern, Thameslink and Great Western franchises; advised MML Capital Partners on a term loan facility to finance the acquisition of the Learning Curve Group; continues to act for IKEA on a range of property mandates, including the disposal of two undeveloped sites and the purchase of a new potential store site; advised Truworths International on the £256m acquisition of the UK footwear retailer Office Retail Group.

The clients

Aldermore Invoice Finance; Bibby Financial Services; Coca-Cola Enterprises; DB Schenker; Gourmet Burger Kitchen; Hitachi Rail Europe; Honda; McDonald's; Thomas Cook; Thorntons.

The star performers

Top-ranking departments according to *The Legal 500* (see legal500.com for more details)
Banking and finance; Banking litigation; Clinical negligence: claimant; Commercial contracts; Commercial property; Corporate and commercial; Court of Protection; Debt recovery; Employment; Immigration; Insolvency and corporate recovery; Licensing; Media and entertainment; Pensions; Personal injury: claimant; Personal tax, trusts and probate; Planning and environment; Professional negligence; Product liability: defendant; Rail.

- **Why did you choose this firm over any others?** 'Personality-focused'; 'the calibre of clients'; 'very friendly and welcoming'; 'because I had worked here as a paralegal and therefore had experienced the relaxed and friendly culture here'; 'enjoyable assessment day'; 'the firm always ranks highly for client and employee satisfaction'; 'exposure to a broad range of work'

- **Best thing about the firm?** 'Friendly and supportive co-workers'; 'little hierarchy'; 'the culture'; 'work/life balance'; 'friendly team'; 'good supervision'; 'everyone works hard and expects you to put the effort in but is also very supportive of your career development, no matter what level they are'

- **Worst thing about the firm?** 'Not being able to choose first seat'; 'lack of transparency about seats and NQ positions'; 'the remuneration for the training contract is not the best';

'outdated IT systems'; 'hidden hierarchy'; 'international ventures are not an immediate focus'; 'Solent office location'; 'no opportunity to work in London'

- **Best moment?** 'Secondment opportunity'; 'face-to-face client meeting'; 'settling a case with 100% recovery and feeling like I could do the job'; 'first deal completion'; 'visit to European HQ of international company'; 'client secondment to a leading car manufacturer'; 'I was involved in an urgent action for a large nationwide retailer days before Christmas'

- **Worst moment?** 'Stressful times with not enough guidance from the person delegating the task'; 'taking my first PSC exam'; 'supplemental office duties'; 'not getting out to see clients as much as I would like'; 'typing up notes from a meeting with counsel'

A day in the life of...

... Tom Newborough newly-qualified solicitor, Shoosmiths (Nottingham)

Departments to date: Real estate litigation, corporate, banking, commercial real estate

University: Leeds

Degree and class: Psychology 2(1)

8.45am: I arrive at the office and go through my morning routine of checking/responding to emails. At Shoosmiths the focus is always on delivering a first-class client experience, so listening to and providing a prompt response to client enquiries is an important part of maintaining client satisfaction. Once my inbox is up to date, I keep on top of current affairs by browsing the internet. I also subscribe to email alerts from *The Lawyer*, so I aim to read these to keep up with the legal market specifically.

9.15am: I receive an email from a client requesting an update on the status of an engagement letter for which we need to agree terms with the solicitors on the other side. I have been trusted with the responsibility of taking the lead on this one, which means I am the client's first point of contact. I respond promptly, advising that we are awaiting a response from the solicitor on the other side, but it's important to be proactive so I inform him that I will chase this up. I email the solicitor involved to see if they've reviewed the document and if so whether there are any outstanding issues.

10.00am: I've been assisting my supervisor on an asset sale transaction which involves a Danish buyer and a UK seller. We are involved in the UK aspects of the transaction through our connections with a Danish law firm, via the World Services Group. The team are working to tight time-scales and I am asked by the client partner to co-ordinate a list of enquiries

to go to the seller for tomorrow afternoon. The transaction involves input from specialists across various departments, including pensions, regulatory, employment and commercial contracts. My role is to project manage this aspect of the transaction, to ensure all the necessary information is collated. I receive a call from one of the Danish lawyers leading the transaction to update me on the scope of work that is needed on the UK aspects of the deal. I then liaise with the relevant people involved and pass on this information.

12.30pm: I receive an email from the solicitor on the other side regarding the engagement from earlier in the day. There are still a few outstanding issues so we arrange to have a call later to discuss these further.

2.00pm: After lunch, one of the commercial partners involved in the asset sale transaction is in the Nottingham area and pops in to discuss the contract due diligence. I ask if I can assist further and it's decided that, as a training exercise, I will also review the relevant contracts and feed back my findings. I'm pleased to have been given the opportunity to take on more responsibility and that I have the support of my supervisor and colleagues.

4.00pm: I prepare for my negotiation call as arranged earlier. This is the first contractual negotiation I've had over the phone, so I'm keen to ensure I have prepared arguments

for the main contentious points that are likely to be raised. Everyone in the team is very approachable so I run this by a colleague who will be sitting in on the call as a silent observer and he gives me some final tips. The call goes relatively smoothly and we agree most of the points; however there are a couple of things which require further instructions from the client.

> **'I'm pleased to have been given the opportunity to take on more responsibility and the support of my supervisor.'**

I call the client and explain the key points and he gives me the go-ahead to go back to the other side and get everything agreed.

6.00pm: I send an updated version of the engagement letter to the solicitor, incorporating the changes discussed. This version is agreed and we arrange for execution of the document by the relevant parties. The client is pleased that this was finalised swiftly following his email this morning. I make a to-do list for tomorrow, prioritising the asset sale transaction work which needs to be checked by the partner in the morning, then meet a few colleagues for dinner and a couple of drinks.

www.shoosmiths.co.uk/graduates

lex100.com

About the firm

Address: The Lakes, Bedford Road, Northampton NN4 7SH
Telephone: 03700 863075
Website: www.shoosmiths.co.uk
Email: joinus@shoosmiths.co.uk
Twitter: @shoosmithsgrads

CEO: Claire Rowe
Chairman: Peter Duff

Other offices: Basingstoke, Birmingham, Edinburgh, Leeds, London, Manchester, Milton Keynes, Nottingham, Reading, Solent. Check our website for offices we are currently recruiting to.

Who we are: Shoosmiths is a major national UK law firm which is known for providing a consistently superb client experience. Our focus on people, relationships and results has defined our achievements for 170 years.

What we do: We offer training across five core practice areas. These include commercial, employment, regulatory, litigation, real estate, corporate, tax, private client and asset finance.

What we're looking for: You should be able to take initiative and talk business sense. You will have the drive and desire to learn quickly and develop your skills with high levels of client contact.

What you'll do: You will complete four six-month seats, one of which could be a secondment to a client's in-house legal team. You'll train in a supportive environment with the freedom to manage your own caseload and deal with clients on a daily basis.

Perks: Membership costs for local young lawyer groups, 23 days' flexible holiday, pension, life assurance, private medical insurance, dental plan, corporate discounts, £50 and a day off on your birthday.

Sponsorship: We will fund your GDL and/or LPC while you are studying, as well as providing a living allowance. We do not specify which provider you should complete your GDL and LPC at.

Facts and figures

Total partners: 155
Other fee-earners: 750
Total trainees: 42

Trainee places available for 2019: 25
Applications received pa: 2,000+
Percentage interviewed: 10%

First year salary: £26,000
Second year salary: £27,000
Newly qualified salary: £40,000

Turnover in 2015: £103m (+11% from 2014)
Profits per equity partner: £386,000 (33%)
(see legalbusiness.co.uk for full financial information)

Application process

Apply to: Samantha Hope, graduate recruitment manager.
How: Online application only.
When: By 30 June 2017.
What's involved: If successful at application stage, you will be invited to attend an assessment day in Autumn 2017.

Vacation schemes
Summer: June/July 2017 (apply by February 2017).

Simmons & Simmons

CityPoint, One Ropemaker Street, London EC2Y 9SS

Survey results *(marks out of 100%)*

Satisfied in your job?	77
Firm living up to expectations?	78
High quality of work?	82
Enough client contact?	75
Stress-free?	62
Happy work/life balance?	59
Friendly firm?	84
Great social life?	72
Good vacation scheme?	89
Confident you'll be kept on?	67
Good remuneration?	71
Diverse firm?	83
Good international secondments?	43

 verdict

Trainees are attracted to Simmons & Simmons for its 'good practice areas'. 'Certain departments have very good reputations in the market', with plaudits reserved for the firm's 'finance focus' and 'expertise in the IP and TMT sectors'. Examples of 'quality work' undertaken by trainees include 'negotiating contracts directly with the other side', 'being able to take the lead on a small project' and 'working on a large multi-national acquisition, and being fully involved in all aspects of that transaction'. A 'high-performance culture' is evident, and there is a 'genuine feeling that you can approach all people' with any queries. The firm enrols trainees on an MBA programme, and while it is deemed a 'clear illustration of the firm's commitment to us as individuals', others feel it can 'ruin the work/life balance' by 'combining studying with the demanding working hours of a trainee'. Colleagues are 'friendly and inclusive', and the firm itself runs 'market-leading LGBT initiatives'. The trainees are a 'really close' group, and many respondents also cite the 'great team atmosphere' that they have experienced in their respective departments. There are frustrations about the 'restricted seat choices', and also about the 'lack of transparency around qualification' as 'variable retention figures' have recently been an issue. Still, the 'training is very good' and as a result 'you really feel like part of the firm'. Several trainees have waxed lyrical about the firm's 'awesome' client secondments as they are not only a 'great experience' but also 'impressive on the CV'. To train at a firm which is 'well-placed in the market' where you can work alongside lawyers 'at the top of their game', consider Simmons & Simmons.

If the firm were a fictional character it would be...

Rudy Baylor (The Rainmaker) – intelligent, driven and very principled

The firm

Simmons & Simmons has grown from its London origins to be a major international firm across Asia, Europe and the Middle East. The firm has one of the largest full-service dispute resolution practices in the City, and also ably represents its clients on employment, investment funds and TMT work. In recognition of the breadth of its expertise, Simmons notched three nominations at the *Legal Business* Awards 2016.

The deals

Advised Chiltern International Group on its $447m financing for the acquisition of Theorem Clinical Research; advised the board of GHG Property Group on its proposed £2.1bn restructuring; advised lenders on the refinancing of a fleet of Airbus aircraft owned by LatAm Airlines; advised AIG Trade Finance on a novel $125m supply chain finance platform for the sub-investment grade market; assisted NextEnergy Solar Fund with the £290m acquisition and development of a number of solar assets in the UK.

The clients

Avenue Capital; Deloitte; the Department for Transport; Deutsche Bank; DONG Energy; Moody's; Morgan Stanley; Schlumberger; Shawbrook Bank; Swiss Re.

The star performers

Top-ranking departments according to *The Legal 500* (see legal500.com for more details)
Acquisition finance; Aviation; Bank lending – investment grade debt and syndicated loans; Commodities: derivatives; Corporate restructuring and insolvency; Debt capital markets; Derivatives and structured products; Emerging markets; Employee share schemes; Employment: employers; Infrastructure (including PFI and PPP); Islamic finance; Mining and minerals; Oil and gas; Pensions (non-contentious); Power (including electricity, nuclear and renewables); Rail; Trade finance.

- **Why did you choose this firm over any others?** 'The inclusive atmosphere'; 'positive experience on vacation scheme'; 'sector-focus appealed to me'; 'the famous collection of young British art'; 'its expertise in practice areas that I was interested in'; 'its reputation for friendliness'; 'sensible people'; 'many international opportunities'; 'free language lessons'; 'reputation for financial services'; 'the people at the law fair that I attended were really friendly and honest'

- **Best thing about the firm?** 'The people are very social and don't take themselves too seriously'; 'the profile of work'; 'very keen to support us'; 'the inclusive atmosphere'; 'secondments'; 'the quality of work'; 'expertise in IP'; 'the fudge in the meeting rooms'; 'very good on understanding and rewarding merit where it is deserved'

- **Worst thing about the firm?** 'Communication isn't very good'; 'partners asking for personal non-billable favours'; 'our in-firm canteen can be really hit-and-miss'; 'the international offices don't seem very integrated'; 'they could provide more support for first-seat trainees'; 'pay and incentives'; 'asset finance department'

- **Best moment?** 'Being invited to a fancy client dinner'; 'my client secondment bringing in work for the firm'; 'my performance review'; 'running my own transaction'; 'winning a pro bono case for a client which I conducted unsupervised'; 'having more senior members of staff genuinely ask me for my opinion on matters'; 'preparing for court'; 'effectively being left to deal with low-value matters alone'; 'winning the department Christmas party best-dressed prize'

- **Worst moment?** 'Page-turning piles and piles of hard copy documents in litigation'; 'adjusting to the change from student life to work life'; 'cancelling my holiday for a closing'; 'being shouted at'; 'the first time I worked past midnight'; 'one particularly gruelling 92-hour week'; 're-writing the same letter five times after getting different comments on each successive draft'

A day in the life of...

... **Suleyman Siddiqui** second-seat trainee, Simmons & Simmons
Departments to date: Litigation, real estate
University: University College London
Degree: History

9.00am: I get to my office and review emails that have come in overnight. I then begin writing a task list for the day in descending order of priority. I am currently sat in real estate, a busy department with many discrete tasks, and I find it's easier to keep on top of work by tracking the progress of each task individually.

9.15am: I begin to draft responses to emails, some of which are from our clients requesting advice on aspects of landlord and tenant law and others are from solicitors representing counterparties in transactions in which we are involved. I receive some comments on several documents so I review these and mark up the documents for discussion with my supervisor.

11.00am: I go for a coffee and catch-up with my supervisor to discuss our current case load. We review my mark ups from this morning and make some further changes, which I incorporate and send to the other side when I get back to my desk.

11.30am: I review two leases and make notes on their provisions. Then I draft a response to a client who has requested advice on the rent review provisions of each lease.

12.15pm: I prepare engrossed copies of a licence I have been involved in negotiating for the past two weeks, as well as covering letters to our client and the tenant. It's satisfying to have the final document in an agreed form.

1.00pm: I head down to our firm's canteen, Ampersands, and have lunch with some fellow trainees. It's a good opportunity to catch up with friends and I get to hear all about the banking department's training session this morning. We all tend to socialise together and it's a great way to find out what other departments are like, which helps with picking seat choices!

2.00pm: I am a member of the firm's environment committee which operates firm wide and is staffed by partners, associates and trainees who are interested in environmental issues. My trainee colleagues and I have been asked to write a column for the quarterly newsletter and we discuss some ideas for the column and allocate tasks.

3.00pm: An urgent client query has come through requesting advice on the enforceability of certain real estate instruments against a prospective buyer who has diplomatic immunity. I use the research resources on our intranet to look at this topic and begin drafting a memo for review by the matter partner. In our real estate department, trainees are given a lot of hands-on experience and client contact and are often expected to prepare first drafts of advice and some transactional documents.

> 'In our real estate department, trainees are given a lot of hands-on experience and client contact.'

6.00pm: A client (tenant) calls me and instructs us to provide our comments on a licence for alteration they have received from their landlord. I review the licence and mark it up with my comments for review by an associate in the team.

6.45pm: I check my task list and see nothing outstanding so I head out to watch a movie with some friends.

www.simmons-simmons.com/graduates

lex100.com

About the firm

Address: CityPoint, One Ropemaker Street, London EC2Y 9SS
Telephone: 020 7628 2020 **Fax:** 020 7628 2070
Website: www.simmons-simmons.com/graduates
Email: recruitment@simmons-simmons.com
Facebook: www.facebook.com/simmonsgraduates
Twitter: @SimmonsGrads

Senior partner: Colin Passmore
Managing partner: Jeremy Hoyland

Other offices: Amsterdam, Beijing, Bristol, Brussels, Doha, Dubai, Düsseldorf, Frankfurt, Hong Kong, Jeddah*, Lisbon*, Luxembourg, Madrid, Milan, Munich, Paris, Riyadh*, Shanghai, Singapore, Tokyo (*associated offices).

Who we are: Simmons & Simmons is a leading international law firm with fully integrated teams working throughout Europe, the Middle East and Asia.

What we do: We view the world through the lens of our key sectors: asset management and investment funds, financial institutions, life sciences and technology, media and telecommunications.

Facts and figures

Total partners: 250+
Other fee-earners: 800+
Total trainees: 80+

Trainee places available for 2019: approx 35
Applications received pa: approx 2,500

London/Bristol first year salary: £40,000/£36,000
London/Bristol second year salary: £45,000/£37,000
London/Bristol newly qualified salary: £68,000/£49,000

Turnover in 2015: £290.1m (+8% from 2014)
Profits per equity partner: £649,000 (+17%)
(see legalbusiness.co.uk for full financial information)

What we're looking for: We're looking for trainees who have great intellectual abilities, but who can also show they have initiative and drive. So whether you join us in London or Bristol, while we're interested in your academic successes, we also want to see your potential.

What you'll do: Alongside high-quality, international experience, our bespoke training programme helps you develop all the legal, commercial and personal skills you'll need to hit the ground running.

Perks: Benefits included are 25 days' holiday entitlement, life assurance, income protection insurance, medical insurance, gym subsidy, free GP visits, assistance if working late, back-up care service, music/singing lessons, season ticket loan, subsidised staff restaurant, travel insurance and pension contributions.

Sponsorship: We will cover full tuition fees for law school and offer a maintenance grant of £7,000 for the GDL and £7,500 for the LPC.

Application process

Apply to: Graduate recruitment team.
How: Online application.
When: By 15 January 2017 for London and Bristol training contracts.
What's involved: Online application form, online judgement and ability tests, video interview and assessment day.

Vacation schemes

Winter: Apply from 1 October 2016.
Spring: Apply form 1 January 2017.
Summer (London and Bristol): Apply from 15 October 2016.

Please note we recruit on a first come first served basis. We therefore advise you to apply as soon as possible to avoid disappointment.

Simmons & Simmons

Skadden, Arps, Slate, Meagher & Flom (UK) LLP

40 Bank Street, Canary Wharf, London E14 5DS

Survey results *(marks out of 100%)*

Satisfied in your job?	83
Firm living up to expectations?	85
High quality of work?	(90)
Enough client contact?	77
Stress-free?	(67)
Happy work/life balance?	55
Friendly firm?	77
Great social life?	77
Good vacation scheme?	92
Confident you'll be kept on?	80
Good remuneration?	(90)
Diverse firm?	83
Good international secondments?	77

 **verdict**

Commanding an 'unsurpassed reputation' as 'the leading global M&A practice', Skadden impresses trainees because of the 'size of corporate transactions that the London office works on and their cross-border nature'. Described by one trainee as 'the Goldman Sachs of law', Skadden works on 'huge deals' and is named a **Lex 100 Winner** for work quality, along with salary satisfaction and low-stress levels. Fittingly, one trainee's highlight moment to date was 'being delegated considerable control over an EU merger control process for a multi-billion dollar transaction'. Because of the firm's top-of-the-market stature, there is a 'good qualification salary', though the 'competitive culture' is tough as trainees work 'long hours' and 'often have to work during weekends'. The 'level of responsibility' in representing the 'excellent US client base' leads to hands-on work, and early stand-out achievements include 'being given responsibility for handling a small part of a deal almost independently after only a few weeks in the seat' and 'going on business trips abroad'. One person commented on the 'excellent exposure and responsibility on secondment in Brussels', though another recruit believes 'international secondment opportunities could be greater'. There is a 'personal touch to recruitment' at Skadden, which is first observed on the 'thoroughly enjoyable vacation scheme'. The 'turnover of associates' is a worry, and may be explained by the 'high expectations', but hard work 'is recognised' by senior colleagues. To train at a firm with a 'long-standing commitment to excellence' and a reputation that is 'second-to-none in the City and the US', send an application to Skadden, Arps, Slate, Meagher and Flom.

If the firm were a fictional character it would be...

Severus Snape (Harry Potter) – very powerful, has a reputation for being aloof but is actually quite nice

The firm

Reputable US firm Skadden, Arps, Slate, Meagher and Flom has grown exponentially since its conception in New York and now boasts 1,700 lawyers and 22 offices across the globe, including Beijing, Moscow, Hong Kong and Tokyo. The firm is an acknowledged expert in M&A, international arbitration and tax, and also possesses a strong reputation for litigation.

The deals

Advised the underwriters to Lenta's £275m public offering of GDRs listed on the LSE; acted for Israel Corporation on its spin-off of Kenon Holdings, which involved a dual listing of ordinary shares on the Tel Aviv and New York stock exchanges; advised Merck KGaA on its $17bn purchase of Sigma-Aldrich; acted for Nikkei in its $1.3bn acquisition of FT Group from Pearson; represented Vodafone in an investment treaty dispute against the government of India.

The clients

BNP Paribas; Ball Corporation; Capgemini; The Coca-Cola Company; Colony Capital; Crédit Agricole; Highbridge Capital; Mitsui Sumitomo; Mylan; Permira.

The star performers

Top-ranking departments according to *The Legal 500* (see legal500.com for more details)
Acquisition finance; Bank lending – investment grade debt and syndicated loans; Commercial litigation; Corporate crime (including fraud, bribery and corruption); Corporate restructuring and insolvency; Corporate tax; Debt capital markets; Equity capital markets; Financial services (non-contentious/regulatory); High yield; Insurance: corporate and regulatory; International arbitration; M&A: upper mid-market and premium deals, £250m+; Oil and gas; Pharmaceuticals and biotechnology; Private funds; Public international law.

- **Why did you choose this firm over any others?** 'Very highly ranked'; 'globally recognised'; 'high quality of work'; 'good pay'; 'the quality of the training'; 'at Skadden, as a corporate trainee, you are a general corporate trainee and can get involved in any aspect of an M&A deal that might interest you in any industry you want to'; 'reputation'; 'small trainee intake'; 'the quality of the work is top-notch'

- **Best thing about the firm?** 'The social side is great'; 'the firm's unsurpassed global reputation for corporate transactions'; 'from day one you are treated like an associate'; 'swanky offices'; 'its flat structure'; 'the huge deals are very impressive'; 'I have often been working on a matter solely with a partner'

- **Worst thing about the firm?** 'The high turnover rate of associates'; 'sandwiches during lunch presentations'; 'the hours'; 'the brutal culture'; 'the lack of respect for work/life balance'; 'international secondment opportunities could be greater'

- **Best moment?** 'Having my hard work recognised by my supervisor and the partner in my department'; 'seeing an extensive piece of work that I had worked on for months from the very beginning finally come together'; 'closing a deal all on my own three months into my training contract'

- **Worst moment?** 'The initial couple of weeks of not understanding what was going on'; 'hearing about my antics the day following the Christmas Ball'; 'spending days reformatting tables of financials'

A day in the life of…

… Ben Davies second-year trainee, Skadden, Arps, Slate, Meagher & Flom (UK) LLP
Departments to date: Litigation and international arbitration, capital markets, banking, corporate M&A (New York)
University: Exeter   **Degree and class:** BA Politics, First Class Hons

9.30am: I arrive at work, say hello to my secretary Lorraine and sit down at my desk. I am currently sitting in the corporate department with associate Claire Cahoon. I have spent the last five months focusing on capital markets work, but I also voiced an interest in M&A work so I have had the opportunity to do that also. I am currently working on four different matters so I make sure each day to make a list of the tasks that I need to complete so that I am organised and manage my time effectively.

10.00am: First things first, Claire and I have a call with Skadden attorneys in the Chicago office about a potential new deal that has come in over the weekend. Skadden has offices all over the world and I have worked with attorneys in the New York, Paris, Tokyo and Hong Kong offices to date. I make a note of the call and circulate to the participants a summary of what was said, including a list of action points going forward, once the call has finished.

11.00am: Danny Tricot, a partner in the capital markets group, calls me and asks me to prepare a set of board minutes in preparation for a client's board meeting in a few days. Danny is also the partner who oversees my training contract and after he's finished giving me instructions we discuss my proposed secondment the following March to Skadden's New York office. As a trainee I

have the option to spend six months in either Hong Kong, Brussels or New York and I am really excited about working abroad.

12.45pm: After spending several hours drafting the board minutes, it is time for lunch. There's no shortage of good restaurants and bars in Canary Wharf and lunch is spent getting to know the vacation students better in a more relaxed atmosphere.

2.00pm: Back in the office, I finish the board minutes and go and see Danny. He provides me with some minor comments and tells me to circulate the amended minutes to the client for their review. Danny is great to work for and has given me a quite a lot of responsibility on this matter while still being available in case I need to ask questions. I circulate the draft to the group and then get back to my to-do list.

2.30pm: I begin to incorporate comments that I have received from Claire on a prospectus for a Portuguese client of ours. In the last two months, I have visited this client twice in Portugal with Claire. Working for a firm with so many international clients definitely has its perks! Other tasks on my list include preparing some slides in preparation for a partner's pitch to a potential new client, updating a due diligence report, proof-reading an announcement of a client's proposed takeover of another company and

researching that client's disclosure obligations under the Takeover Code. I stay on task with these for the rest of the afternoon.

5.30pm: After I have finished my list of work for the day, I head to the monthly corporate department meeting which is chaired by the head of the group, Michael Hatchard. This

> **'I have worked with attorneys in the New York, Paris, Tokyo and Hong Kong offices to date.'**

meeting provides a forum for members of the department to discuss particular challenges that have arisen on their recent deals and how they were successfully tackled, and it's also a great opportunity for a trainee to meet and interact with the whole department.

6.15pm: After the meeting has finished I head to a vacation scheme event at a rooftop bar near St Pauls. There's plenty of vacation scheme events over the summer and they are always well attended by a wide range of Skadden attorneys. The social scene at Skadden is great.

recruit.skadden.com

About the firm

Address: 40 Bank Street, Canary Wharf, London E14 5DS
Telephone: 020 7519 7000
Fax: 020 7519 7070
Website: www.skadden.com
Email: aidan.connor@skadden.com

Managing partner: Pranav Trivedi (UK)

Other offices: Beijing, Boston, Brussels, Chicago, Frankfurt, Hong Kong, Houston, Los Angeles, Moscow, Munich, New York, Palo Alto, Paris, San Francisco, São Paulo, Shanghai, Singapore, Tokyo, Toronto, Vienna, Washington DC, Wilmington.

Who we are: Skadden is one of the leading law firms in the world with approximately 1,600 lawyers across the globe.

What we do: Our clients include corporate, industrial and financial institutions, and government entities. Lawyers across the European network focus primarily on corporate transactions, including domestic and cross-border mergers and acquisitions, private equity, capital markets, leveraged finance and banking, tax, corporate restructuring, and energy and projects.

What we're looking for: We seek to recruit a small number of high- calibre graduates from any discipline to join our highly successful London office as trainee solicitors. We are looking for candidates who combine intellectual ability with enthusiasm, creativity and a demonstrable ability to rise to a challenge and to work with others towards a common goal.

What you'll do: The firm can offer you the chance to develop your career in a uniquely rewarding and professional environment. You will join a close-knit and diverse team in which you will be given ample opportunity to work on complex matters, almost all with an international aspect, while benefiting from highly personalised training in an informal and friendly environment. The first year of your training contract will be divided into two six-month seats where you will gain experience in corporate transactions and international arbitration and litigation. In the second year of your training contract you will have the opportunity to discuss with us your preferences for your remaining two seats. We also offer our second-year trainees the opportunity to complete a seat in our Hong Kong or New York offices.

Perks: Bonus scheme, gym, membership, subsidy, life assurance, private healthcare, season ticket loan, subsidised restaurant.

Sponsorship: Full fees and £8,000 maintenance.

Facts and figures

Other fee-earners: 119 (London office)
Total trainees: 20 (London office)

Trainee places available for 2019: 10/12

First year salary: £45,000
Second year salary: £50,000
Newly qualified salary: £118,000

Application process

Apply to: Aidan Connor.
How: On website.
When: By 31 July 2017.
What's involved: Interview and case study.

Vacation schemes

Spring: 31 March-11 April (apply by 12 January 2017).
Summer: 16-27 June 2017, 30 June-11 July 2017, 14-26 July 2017 (apply by 12 January 2017).

Slaughter and May

One Bunhill Row, London EC1Y 8YY

Survey results *(marks out of 100%)*

Satisfied in your job?	79
Firm living up to expectations?	83
High quality of work?	81
Enough client contact?	67
Stress-free?	53
Happy work/life balance?	60
Friendly firm?	74
Great social life?	58
Good vacation scheme?	80
Confident you'll be kept on?	88
Good remuneration?	81
Diverse firm?	76
Good international secondments?	48

 **verdict**

Trainees are proud to work at Slaughter and May due to the firm's 'Magic Circle prestige' and 'reputation for excellence'. The firm is 'regarded highly among businesses', so it is no surprise that 'the quality of the clients is fantastic'. The 'multi-specialist approach' ensures trainees 'get to work on a much wider range of legal issues', rather than focusing on one particular area of law in each seat. Work highlights include 'working as part of a small team on a very large and high-profile corporate restructuring of an overseas company' and 'closing the second largest restructuring in European history'. Trainees sometimes struggle as 'standards are relentlessly high', and respondents comment that they have felt 'under intense pressure' and 'over-burdened' during their training contract. That said, the 'lack of billing targets' is a plus point. Hours can be 'unpredictable', and this can include 'working bank holidays' and some 'all-nighters', but respondents identify the 'lack of a face-time culture'. There is an 'intellectual' strain running through Slaughter and May, and you can look forward to 'working with incredibly bright people from a variety of different backgrounds'. **Lex 100 Winner** status has been secured in the confidence in being kept on category. The firm 'can be very hierarchical', and it is reported that there is 'little social interaction outside of working hours', but colleagues are 'personable and friendly'. The training is 'excellent', as 'associates make an effort to give us good, substantive work' and 'partners often get involved in training'. As such, trainees 'learn from partners and senior associates who are at the top of their fields'. For 'the chance to work with some of the finest legal brains in the City', apply to Slaughter and May.

If the firm were a fictional character it would be...

Frasier Crane – charismatic and highly intelligent, but amusingly self-regarding

The firm

Slaughter and May regularly handles some of the largest and most complex corporate and finance deals. A member of the City's elite group of Magic Circle firms, it has a brilliant reputation for its M&A, corporate tax and commercial litigation teams. The firm has strategically placed offices in Hong Kong, Brussels and Beijing, and also has a network of 'best friend' relationships with a number of top corporate firms around the world.

The deals

Advised Cable & Wireless Communications on the financing of its $1.85bn acquisition of Columbus International; acted on the winding-up of former Icelandic bank, Glitnir; advised Philips International on the de-risking of its pension fund in a £3.5bn buy-out; advised Ladbrokes on the employment elements of its merger with Gala Coral; advising Rolls-Royce on SFO and DoJ investigations into alleged bribery and corruption in overseas markets.

The clients

3i Group; BT Pension Scheme; British Airways; Cable & Wireless Communications; Carillion; Centrica; Ocado; Premier Oil; Santander; Standard Chartered.

The star performers

Top-ranking departments according to *The Legal 500* (see legal500.com for more details)
Acquisition finance; Aviation; Pensions (non-contentious); Employment: employers; Power (including electricity, nuclear and renewables); Employee share schemes; Oil and gas; Infrastructure (including PFI and PPP); Asset finance and leasing; Bank lending – investment grade debt and syndicated loans; Corporate restructuring and insolvency; Debt capital markets; Derivatives and structured products; Securitisation.

- **Why did you choose this firm over any others?** 'I admired its ethos in supporting the local community'; 'brilliant reputation'; 'quality of the work'; 'Magic Circle'; 'primarily its reputation in the market'; 'the quality of its client base and work'; 'I really enjoyed my interview'; 'I like their generalist approach'; 'prestige'; 'the multi-specialist approach enabling me to work in different areas'; 'good training'; 'no target hours or face-time culture'; 'future career opportunities'

- **Best thing about the firm?** 'The variety of work'; 'the friendliness of the people that work here'; 'some of the most challenging work in the City'; 'you get to work on some really exciting, difficult and high-profile transactions'; 'professionalism of people'; 'people take immense pride in what they do'; 'great training'; 'sitting with partners allows you to learn a lot very quickly'

- **Worst thing about the firm?** 'The hours'; 'the amount of stress that comes from working on such important, high-value deals'; 'can be quite opaque'; 'old-fashioned'; 'it can be exhausting during periods of intense work'; 'perfectionism'; 'the social side'; 'not many international secondment opportunities'; 'a lack of investment in IT infrastructure'; 'uncompetitive pay compared to American firms'; 'lack of diversity in trainees'

- **Best moment?** 'Seeing a project through from engagement to post-completion'; 'being given a lot of responsibility on a deal and my contribution being valued'; 'attending client meetings on multi-billion dollar deals'; 'being allowed to run my own deals'; 'attending a big client meeting'; 'working abroad in the UAE for three weeks'; 'getting good feedback'; 'involvement in a programme for visiting African lawyers'; 'representing the firm on a client call'

- **Worst moment?** 'Archiving'; 'being sent abroad unexpectedly and on reasonably short notice'; 'working on three consecutive weekends'; 'feeling out of my depth on a tough research task'; 'creating a table of emails'; 'preparing documents for submission in the early hours of the morning'; 'fighting an uphill struggle with our antiquated IT system'

A day in the life of...

... Kathryn Warden trainee solicitor, Slaughter and May

Departments to date: Financing, dispute resolution, pensions and employment, corporate
University: Aberdeen
Degree: Law LLB (Hons)

9.30am: My typical day starts at this time but I don't usually get busy until 10.00am, so I have time to catch up with the latest news.

10.30am: I join a conference call about the takeover I am working on and I am charged with taking a note of the call. We discuss the progress of the transaction documents and the next steps required with the client and its financial advisors. On these types of transactions, I have been included on every call and email, a process which allowed me to become familiar with other advisors and better understand the transaction as a whole.

11.45am: The associates and I sit down to discuss our 'to-do' list for today. My main task is completing verification of the scheme document and amending it to reflect the changes discussed on this morning's call.

12.00pm: I get an email from the target company's lawyers asking us for comments by 3.00pm on an announcement. I read the announcement and mark it up with minor comments. I give my comments to one of the associates to approve.

12.30pm: I attend a lunchtime trainee training session on private equity led by a partner in my group. Trainee training sessions are very practical. The sessions are based on the groups that you sit in, so they are really helpful in providing you with a good grasp of

the areas that you may come across during your time in that particular seat.

2.00pm: I join a presentation meeting with two other trainees from my corporate group. Most of our groups encourage trainees to develop their presentation skills. As a result, I sometimes find myself giving a presentation to partners who are experts in that particular field – a prospect that is slightly intimidating but one to which you grow accustomed.

2.30pm: Returning to my office, I find that the associate has approved my comments on the announcement and has given me his mark-up of the scheme document.

3.00pm: I send our revised drafts to the other side. The associate and I agree that the best approach is to call our client and its financial advisors in order to finalise the verification process. I have been given a great deal of responsibility from the outset on this transaction.

3.45pm: My supervisor asks me to carry out some research for him on the application of the class tests under the listing rules.

4.00pm: I have offered to take an interviewee on a tour of our office. I often get involved in recruitment events and am frequently asked about travel and secondment opportunities at the firm. During my training contract, I have been fortunate enough to spend time working

in Dubai for a client, and I have recently been offered the opportunity to go on secondment to Barcelona for my final seat.

5.30pm: I send the finalised verification notes to the other side. I call the associates to make sure there is nothing more they need from me tonight and I am asked to check out a point on the takeover code before I leave.

> **'I have been fortunate enough to spend time working in Dubai for a client and have recently been offered a secondment to Barcelona.'**

6.00pm: My supervisor asks me to join a call he has with a client to further my understanding of the impact of a new regulation which will come into force soon.

7.00pm: I head to my group's summer party with a few of the summer work experience scheme students. Each group has two big parties a year and there are other great events throughout the year. One memorable event I recently attended was a women's committee event for International Women's Day with a celebrity guest speaker.

www.slaughterandmay.com

About the firm

Address: One Bunhill Row, London EC1Y 8YY
Telephone: 020 7090 4454
Website: www.slaughterandmay.com
Email: trainee.recruit@slaughterandmay.com

Senior partner: Chris Saul
Practice partner: David Wittmann
Executive partner: Richard Clark

Other offices: Beijing, Brussels, Hong Kong, plus 'best friend' relationships around the world.

Who we are: Slaughter and May is one of the most prestigious law firms in the world. We advise on high-profile and often landmark international transactions. Our excellent and varied client list ranges from governments to entrepreneurs, from retailers to entertainment companies and from conglomerates to Premier League football clubs.

What we do: We are a full-service law firm to corporate clients and have leading practitioners across a wide range of practice areas including mergers and acquisitions, corporate and commercial, financing, tax, competition, dispute resolution, real estate, pensions and employment, financial regulation, information technology and intellectual property.

Facts and figures

Total partners: 114 worldwide
Other fee-earners: 400+
Total trainees: 141 worldwide

Trainee places available for 2019: 80

First year salary: £43,000
Second year salary: £48,000
Newly qualified salary: £71,500

Turnover in 2015: £504.5m (+7% from 2014)
Profits per equity partner: £2.229m (+9% from 2014)
(see legalbusiness.co.uk for full financial information)

What we're looking for: A strong academic background (good 2(1)), plenty of common sense and the willingness to accept responsibility. We are interested in applications from any source – 84 universities are represented among our lawyers.

What you'll do: During the two-year training contract, trainees turn their hand to a broad range of work, taking an active role in four, five or six groups while sharing an office with a partner or experienced associate. Most trainees spend at least two six-month seats in our market-leading corporate, commercial and financing groups. Subject to gaining some contentious experience, they choose how to spend the remaining time.

Perks: Private medical insurance, money purchase pension scheme with life cover, interest-free loan, childcare vouchers, interest-free season ticket loans, personal accident cover, subsidised staff restaurant and coffee bar, special membership terms for health club, corporate entertainment benefits, cycle to work scheme, qualification leave, enhanced family leave pay.

Sponsorship: The firm pays for tuition and examination fees for both the GDL and LPC courses and also provides a maintenance grant.

Application process

Apply to: Janine Arnold, trainee recruitment manager.
How: Through our online system (www.slaughterandmay.com.)
When: See website for deadline dates.
What's involved: As part of the application process, you will be asked to complete a short form and attach your covering letter and CV.

Vacation schemes

We offer open days, workshops and work experience schemes to enable you to gain an insight into life as a City lawyer. Full details of these opportunities can be found on our website.

SLAUGHTER AND MAY

Stephens Scown LLP

Curzon House, Southernhay West, Exeter EX1 1RS

Lex 100 Winner

See categories below
and tables from page 69

Survey results *(marks out of 100%)*

Satisfied in your job?	83
Firm living up to expectations?	85
High quality of work?	85
Enough client contact?	77
Stress-free?	67
Happy work/life balance?	85
Friendly firm?	88
Great social life?	80
Good vacation scheme?	73
Confident you'll be kept on?	79
Good remuneration?	70
Diverse firm?	84

 verdict

Stephens Scown is commended for its 'exceptional reputation in the South West and unashamed regional focus'. Respondents appreciate that the firm 'demonstrates authenticity and a clear vision' as it 'has its focus on the South West and on winning key clients based in the South West, unlike its competitors'. 'People are incredibly friendly' at Stephens Scown and 'you feel really valued' as a trainee. This is partly attributed to the size of the firm, as it is 'large enough to attract big cases and interesting work, but small enough for teams to be close and for trainees to play an important role'. Examples of the 'very high quality of work' include 'my first time completing advocacy at court on my own' and 'going to San Diego for an international event'. The training contract's structure of three eight-month seats splits opinion, as it 'provides ample time to really get to grips with the area of law, but then equally you do not get as much diversity'. There is also 'limited seat choice for trainees', as one respondent says 'I would find it beneficial to undertake a seat in an area of law that is not one of the traditional core areas'. Feedback does praise the quality of training at Stephens Scown, described as 'very structured with regular reviews to help me make and achieve targets', while also being 'intensive and detailed', which enables 'trainees to carry out real responsibilities'. While there can be some 'very tight client deadlines' and 'long days', it is not stressful as there is 'plenty of support for those who need it', leading to a **Lex 100 Winner** medal in this category. To train at a 'forward-thinking firm' that delivers 'outstanding client service', apply to Stephens Scown.

If the firm were a fictional character it would be...

Paddington Bear – liked by all, remembers where it came from and is passionate about food

The firm

With 270 staff and 50 partners across its three offices in Exeter, Truro and St Austell, Stephens Scown is a well-regarded South West firm. Its range of practice areas includes commercial litigation, intellectual property and social housing.

The deals

Advised Hastoe Housing Association on a number of site acquisitions, as well as right to acquire and enfranchisement issues; advised Wolf Minerals on a number of high-value transactions; acting for the liquidators in a claim under section 214 of the Insolvency Act 1986 against the former directors of a company; works on disputes arising from mis-sold interest rate swaps; acts on the sale and purchase of caravan parks for clients in the holiday and residential parks sector.

The clients

Arden International Motor Sport; Green Nation; Mongoose Energy; Orchard Pig; Vogt Solar.

The star performers

Top-ranking departments according to *The Legal 500* (see legal500.com for more details)
Agriculture and estates; Charities and not-for-profit; Commercial litigation; Commercial property; Contentious trusts and probate; Corporate and commercial; Employment; Energy; Environment; Family; Insolvency and corporate recovery; Intellectual property; Personal tax, trusts and probate; Planning; Professional negligence; Property litigation; Social housing; TMT: IT and telecoms.

- **Why did you choose this firm over any others?** 'The firm was very obviously friendly and sociable'; 'strong reputation in the South West'; 'good mix of seats and clients'; 'recommended by another trainee'; 'location in Cornwall'; 'Stephens Scown has a good reputation for its training'; 'an unrivalled reputation'

- **Best thing about the firm?** 'Teams work well together'; 'there is an awareness of what other team members are working on'; 'approachable partners who are happy for you to ask questions'; 'the work/life balance'; 'the people are all really friendly and helpful'; 'entrepreneurial flavour'; 'at the cutting edge in terms of use of technology'

- **Worst thing about the firm?** 'The IT system'; 'the limitations in available seats'; 'the fact that you are based in one office and it is hard to get seats in other offices that have different specialisms'; 'having call-centre desks, where you all work in a line'

- **Best moment?** 'Completing the first matter for which I had been the main point of contact for the client throughout'; 'having a consent order I drafted approved by the court'; 'the firm's annual away day was amazing – glorious weather, touch rugby, cake decorating, a hog roast, ice-cream van and tug-of-war between the different offices'

- **Worst moment?** 'Visiting a very frail man to complete a will who passed away the following day'; 'when I have to work a long day'; 'a day where there was a lot of deadlines which needed to be completed'; 'failing to spot an incorrect calculation in a document'

A day in the life of...

... Dan Partridge first-year trainee, Stephens Scown LLP

Departments to date: Family and commercial property
University: University of Exeter
Degree: Law

8.45am: After a short walk I arrive in the office and say hello to my colleagues. I've just moved to the commercial property department and I'm enjoying getting to know the team. Various emails have come in overnight and I start putting together my to-do list for the day.

9.00am: Andrew Knox, a partner in our insolvency team, has just obtained a final charging order from the High Court of Justice. He asks me to update the relevant paperwork and register the charge with the Land Registry. This is a straightforward task (!) but it's the first time I've registered a charge and it takes some time to work through the file and draft the relevant documents.

10.00am: Having recently moved seats I have assumed responsibility for various smaller matters that my predecessor, Jamie Bartlett, had been running. I draft various emails throughout the day and leave these with my supervisor, Nigel Coveney, for him to authorise. One of my favourite things about being a trainee is that we're given significant levels of responsibility very early on but we're also supervised very closely which helps keep stress to a minimum. I draft responses to the requisitions and file these on the Land Registry portal.

11.15am: One of the partners in the team asks me to do some research into the SRA accounts rules. I draft a quick email to him confirming the position.

12.00pm: The team heads up to the boardroom for our monthly team meeting. This month we're joined by Jim Gorrod, a member of the construction team, who gives us a brief legal update and explains typical scenarios in which we could use his experience to improve the service that we're offering to clients.

1.00pm: Lunchtime. There's a street food market on the green outside our office and I head out with another trainee to grab a burrito.

2.00pm: Back in the office, we've received various requisitions from the Land Registry in relation to the registration of a group of deeds of covenant for a developer client. While most of the registrations have gone through without any problems, inevitably some require further investigation. As a trainee you have more time than other fee-earners and so a common task is being asked to review a file and work out what's going on.

3.00pm: Toby Poole, a partner in our commercial property team, has asked me to assist him on the sale of a group of six flats. I've drafted completion statements and various emails which I work through with Toby and send off to the client for authorisation.

4.00pm: Trainees at Stephens Scown are strongly encouraged to get involved with as many networking and marketing opportunities as possible. I'm heading up a team which has entered a '£50 Challenge' to try and raise funds for a local children's hospice so I crack on with some administration. The trainees in our Cornish offices have recently raised the

> **'I'm heading up a team which has entered a "£50 Challenge" to try and raise funds for a local children's hospice.'**

bar by persuading the partners in their offices to perform 'YMCA' by the Village People so we're trying to up our game in response.

4.30pm: At the end of the working day I scan my task list again, making sure that I have completed everything that requires action. I will then file away emails and other paperwork that I have generated during the day.

5.30pm: Tonight we're taking part in the final round of the Exeter business games, which involves racing bell boats down the Exe. I'm looking forward to a great evening in the sun with friends and colleagues.

www.stephens-scown.co.uk

About the firm

Address: Curzon House, Southernhay West, Exeter, EX1 1RS
Telephone: 01392 210700   **Fax:** 01392 274010
Website: www.stephens-scown.co.uk
Email: graduaterecruitment@stephens-scown.co.uk
Facebook: www.facebook.com/stephensscown
Twitter: @stephensscown

Managing partner: Robert Camp

Other offices: Truro, St Austell

Who we are: We are proud to be the highest ranked law firm in *The Sunday Times* Best Companies to Work For. We're a law firm with a regional focus, but all the benefits of a big city rival. Passionate about the South West, we specialise in industries common throughout the region – green energy, food and drink, tourism, mining and more. But we also help businesses with a whole range of corporate and commercial affairs, as well as having a major private client and family law practice. As a firm we worked on over 100 deals last year and have band 1 Chambers rankings across four practice areas. We take great pride in our corporate responsibility and our commitment to the local communities in which we work guides our approach to business. Our people worked with around 60 different fantastic local charities and causes last year.

What we're looking for: We look for individuals who can demonstrate the drive, enthusiasm and ambition to be our future lawyers and partners. Applications are encouraged from both law and non-law graduates with a strong commercial and business awareness. You'll also need great personal and communication skills, as well as creativity and a sense of fun.

What you'll do: Your training contract with us will be fulfilling, challenging and rewarding. Undertaking three seats in a variety of contentious and non-contentious areas, you will be able to discuss your preferred choices and be actively involved in your development and progression. High-profile and challenging work, extensive client exposure and important responsibilities will all come your way. You will be part of our young marketing group where you will share ideas, learn new skills and be a part of the firm's marketing and business development plan.

Perks: PMI, group life assurance, pension scheme, employee assistance programme, 25 days holiday, day off for your birthday, unique shared ownership & bonus scheme, performance related bonus scheme, flexible working and family friendly policies, childcare vouchers, cycle to work scheme, enhanced maternity pay.

Sponsorship: Full funding provided where the LPC has not already been undertaken.

Facts and figures

Total partners: 50+
Other fee-earners: 115+
Total trainees: 20+

Trainee places available for 2019: 10+
Applications received pa: 350
Percentage interviewed: 20%

First year salary: Regionally competitive
Second year salary: Regionally competitive
Newly qualified salary: Regionally competitive

Application process

How: Online application.
When: Ongoing – check website for details
What's involved: Panel interview and assessment day.

Vacation schemes

Vacation scheme available over the summer and early autumn; applicants are encouraged to apply by April of the year they wish to participate.

Stephenson Harwood

1 Finsbury Circus, London EC2M 7SH

Survey results *(marks out of 100%)*

Satisfied in your job?	76
Firm living up to expectations?	79
High quality of work?	82
Enough client contact?	79
Stress-free?	60
Happy work/life balance?	65
Friendly firm?	86
Great social life?	66
Good vacation scheme?	80
Confident you'll be kept on?	74
Good remuneration?	66
Diverse firm?	77
Good international secondments?	(88)

 verdict

A 'firm with international offices, and therefore a player on the global stage', City firm Stephenson Harwood has clear 'areas of expertise' that include the shipping and aviation industries. The firm is 'strong in litigation' across various sectors, and commands a 'reputation as a top firm for arbitration'. Trainees speak glowingly of the 'strong client base' and 'good quality of work'. Stand-out trainee moments include 'completing the financing of six aircraft with little supervision' and 'celebrating with clients on a deal for a £90m residential property mortgage which I took the lead role on'. We hear that the 'seat allocation process is opaque' and some seats have proven less popular than others, yet the 'range of departments available was a big attraction' and the smaller size of teams creates a 'genuinely collegiate feel'. Respondents say that 'the people at Stephenson Harwood are its best asset', and you will receive 'straightforward feedback from supervisors' who 'do not take themselves too seriously'. Such a 'friendly environment' is appreciated, particularly as busy periods can involve 'unreasonably short and stressful deadlines' and 'working until the early hours on a deal'. A strength of the Stephenson Harwood training contract is the knowledge that 'if you express an interest in doing a secondment you are very likely to get it'. Trainees have worked in Dubai, Singapore and Hong Kong, and overseas seats are an 'exceptional chance to see another side of the firm' and to 'get involved in some exciting projects'. The firm is a **Lex 100 Winner** for international secondments. To train alongside 'friendly fee-earners' and undertake 'high-quality international work', consider Stephenson Harwood.

If the firm were a fictional character it would be...

Rafiki (The Lion King) – calm, experienced, and ready to guide you onto the right path

The firm

Stephenson Harwood goes from strength to strength. The firm entered into a formal relationship with China's Wei Tu in March 2016 to effectively practice in China, and then in June announced a 9% rise in revenues for 2015/16. The firm has over 900 staff and more than 140 partners based in ten offices across Asia, Europe and the Middle East. Traditional strengths include asset finance, real estate and commercial litigation.

The deals

Assisted North London Waste Authority with the development of an energy recovery facility valued at over £450m; advised Winsway Enterprises on its $350m cross-border bond restructuring; advised AIM-listed client Focusrite on the implementation of a management incentive plan following the client's IPO; advised Arriva UK Trains on its bid for the concession to operate London Overground services; advised Ryanair on litigation and arbitration in the UK and Europe.

The clients

Abellio Transport Holdings; Christie's; City of Cape Town; DNB Bank; Deutsche Bank; Hitachi Rail Europe; Interserve; Mercuria Energy Trading; The Royal College of Art; The Society of Art Dealers.

The star performers

Top-ranking departments according to *The Legal 500* (see legal500.com for more details)
Art and cultural property; Asset finance and leasing; Aviation; Bank lending – investment grade debt and syndicated loans; Commodities: physicals; Contentious trusts and probate; Corporate restructuring and insolvency; Employee share schemes; Employment: employers; Infrastructure (including PFI and PPP); Oil and gas; Pensions dispute resolution; Pensions (non-contentious); Personal tax, trusts and probate; Rail; Shipping; Trade finance.

- **Why did you choose this firm over any others?** 'International profile'; 'type of clients'; 'litigation-heavy'; 'good reputation'; 'small intake'; 'collegiate atmosphere'; 'well-recognised in the shipping industry'; 'international secondment opportunities'; 'reputation of commercial litigation department'; 'impressive vacation scheme'; 'reasonable hours'; 'the level of responsibility and exposure that trainees get'; 'has a great top-tier reputation in many areas'; 'good-sized firm where I wouldn't feel like I was just a part in a big machine'

- **Best thing about the firm?** 'It is involved in high-profile cases that can make the headlines sometimes'; 'you have the correct level of support throughout'; 'it seems to have got its approach to business and strategy spot on'; 'high degree of client contact from day one'; 'there is a genuine friendship between peers rather than any feeling of rivalry'

- **Worst thing about the firm?** 'Communication between departments'; 'qualification process is gruelling'; 'our marketing is not fantastic'; 'lack of social events'; 'no complementary dinner if you work late'; 'the IT systems'; 'some departments do not have a very good gender balance'; 'our junior salaries have hardly increased for quite a few years'

- **Best moment?** 'Being congratulated by a client at the end of the deal was a highlight'; 'a trip to Trinidad and Tobago for a week'; 'secondment to Singapore'; 'participating actively in meetings'; 'taking my own new instruction direct from a client'; 'securing a settlement in a small case that I had been working on with just my supervisor'

- **Worst moment?** 'Falling off a yoga ball'; 'finding myself out of my depth on a deal and getting frustrated'; 'bibling'; 'working seven days a week for over a month and having to ask for my birthday off!'; 'receiving an unreasonably short and stressful deadline on a major piece of document analysis'

A day in the life of...

... Calum Cheyne trainee, Stephenson Harwood LLP

Departments to date: Real estate, secondment to Seoul, rail finance, and marine and international trade

University: Durham **Degree and class:** History 2(1)

7.30am: I arrive at the (subsidised) gym across the road from the office for a pre-work swim.

9.00am: When I get to my desk I notice an email which came in overnight from the American lawyers we have been acting with on a recent case. They are looking to amend our pleadings in London in order to add weight to another aspect of the case in America. It's a tricky matter, requiring a delicate balance, so I crack on with a detailed review.

9.40am: An email goes around the trainees requesting assistance with an urgent deadline to get documents to court. They are hoping to line up a without notice hearing for a freezing injunction that afternoon, so I grab a jacket and a tie and dive in a taxi to the Strand.

11.10am: Having returned to the office and finished my review of the American documents, I drop off a mark-up with my comments on my supervisor's desk for him to review. He's locked in a heated conference call to a foreign client, so I slip out again quietly and leave it for him to look at.

11.15am: There's been a birthday in the group and accordingly a delicious array of cakes are on offer in the kitchen. I sample one of these and grab a coffee.

11.30am: My supervisor calls me in to discuss the American amendments. There are a few

points that I overlooked, but thankfully nothing too fundamental. We discuss his suggested amendments and I head back to my desk to draft a response to American counsel.

12.25pm: I head up to the seventh floor for a lunchtime training session. Today's talk is on difficulties with ship-to-ship transfers and has attracted a remarkable turnout; perhaps due to the accompanying buffet lunch.

2.00pm: An associate forwards me a query relating to ship sales. It appears to be a simple question, and the client has requested a response urgently. A skim of the relevant documents reveals that it may be more complicated than first anticipated, so I negotiate a two-hour window for research.

2.45pm: Having exhausted the relevant online materials, I move on to the library, convinced that the big red book on sale of ships is hiding the answer. Remarkably, it appears that I was in luck, and I return to discuss my findings with the associate. Thankfully she agrees, so I can begin drafting the note.

3.30pm: I send a copy of the finished product and await her further comments. There are a few drafting points for me to take on board but fortunately no major problems with the advice. I type up the amendments and send through the final draft. I use my spare 30 minutes to make some arrangements for an

upcoming placement scheme drinks evening that I have volunteered to help with.

4.30pm: I receive a call from a partner for whom I do not usually work. An arbitration hearing is taking place tomorrow and the trainee who usually sits with him is on holiday. He asks if I'd mind stepping in. I look up the

> **'Today's talk is on difficulties with ship-to-ship transfers and has attracted a remarkable turnout; perhaps due to the accompanying buffet lunch.'**

pleadings on the system and read them thoroughly to get fully up to speed, and then I start checking the bundles.

6.45pm: After a productive hour's prep, I dash down to the print room with the bundles and arrange for copies to be left on my desk in the morning. I'm playing tag rugby with the firm at 7.30pm, so I clear out my inbox, polish off my time-sheets and head for Shoreditch Park.

9.30pm: Following another famous victory for the Stephenson Harwood tag rugby team, and the beers that tend to follow, I take myself home.

www.shlegal.com/graduate

lex100.com

About the firm

Address: 1 Finsbury Circus, London EC2M 7SH
Telephone: 020 7809 2812
Website: www.shlegal.com
Email: graduate.recruitment@shlegal.com

Senior partner: Roland Foord
Managing partner: Sharon White

Other offices: Beijing, Dubai, Hong Kong, London, Paris, Piraeus, Seoul, Shanghai, Singapore.

Who we are: Join a firm that's ambitious, growing and delivering ground-breaking international deals. For our size, our global reach and client base are exceptional. That's why with us you can expect to work in tight, focused teams alongside associates and partners, where you'll always be right at the heart of the action.

What we do: Our strengths lie across five key practice areas – asset finance, marine and international trade, corporate finance, real estate, and commercial litigation and arbitration. These areas aren't just high-performing by internal standards, but are recognised as being among the best in the world.

Facts and figures

Total partners: 150
Other fee-earners: 400+
Total trainees: 36

Trainee places available for 2019: 18
Applications received pa: 1,300
Percentage interviewed: 10%

First year salary: £38,500
Second year salary: £42,500
Newly qualified salary: £65,000

Turnover in 2015: £145.2m (+20% from 2014)
Profits per equity partner: £746,000 (+40%)
(see legalbusiness.co.uk for full financial information)

What we're looking for: As well as at least a 2:1 in any subject area plus 320 UCAS points or equivalent, you'll need strong analytical skills, sound judgment, imagination and meticulous attention to detail. Also vital are the communication skills to be persuasive and build rapport, plenty of drive and determination, plus a keen interest in business.

What you'll do: There's a lot to look forward to as a trainee at Stephenson Harwood. Top-quality international work across a range of sectors is just the start. An environment that balances cutting-edge work with a respectful, friendly culture is also a huge plus; as is the chance to prove yourself on client secondment and make a name for yourself from day one.

Perks: Here's a snapshot of the flexible benefits you can choose from: childcare vouchers, critical illness cover, cycle2work loan, dental health scheme, give as you earn, gym membership subsidy, health screening, holiday (purchase and sale), life assurance, pension, private GP services, private medical insurance, retail vouchers, subsidised staff café, travel to work loan.

Sponsorship: We'll pay for your fees for the GDL and LPC at BPP London and offer maintenance awards of up to £6,000, if you're still studying.

Application process

Apply to: Sarah Jackson – graduate recruitment, CSR and D&I manager.
How: Online application form via the website: www.shlegal.com/graduate.
When: By 31 July 2017.
What's involved: Online application form, online numerical and verbal reasoning testing, face-to-face interview and assessment centre.

Vacation schemes

Winter: 12-16 December 2016 (apply by 12 November 2016).
Spring: 27 March-7 April 2017 (apply by 31 January 2017).
Summer: 12-23 June 2017, 26 June-7 July 2017, 10-21 July 2017 (apply by 31 January 2017).

STEPHENSON HARWOOD

Taylor Vinters

Merlin Place, Milton Road, Cambridge CB4 0DP

Survey results *(marks out of 100%)*

Satisfied in your job?	83
Firm living up to expectations?	83
High quality of work?	81
Enough client contact?	82
Stress-free?	57
Happy work/life balance?	78
Friendly firm?	91
Great social life?	70
Good vacation scheme?	62
Confident you'll be kept on?	63
Good remuneration?	54
Diverse firm?	83

 **verdict**

Lured by Taylor Vinters' 'longstanding reputation in Cambridge as a well-respected firm offering a range of expertise', respondents report that the 'six four-month seats' allow for 'exposure to a wide variety of matters' across 'exciting practice areas'. The firm is 'ambitious and expanding', and possesses a 'growing commercial technology department'. Many of the firm's clients are 'on the cutting edge of the technology sector'; one trainee says 'I know that the work I am carrying out is indirectly shaping the future'. It is clear that the firm 'really cares about its trainees and your career progression'. The 'training supervisors take the time to give constructive feedback on the work you perform', while for its part Taylor Vinters 'encourages feedback about the training process'. Stand-out examples of 'good-quality work' include 'running the negotiation and completion of a lease for one of the firm's key clients', 'direct involvement in a multi-million pound litigation' and 'dealing from start to finish with a complex re-mortgage of a several hundred-acre estate'. Trainees sometimes 'feel overwhelmed with work' as particular seats 'can be quite stressful' and demand 'working until the early hours'. The firm's 'clear strategy' has led to the growth of the London and Singapore offices, though trainees complain that there is 'no opportunity to travel' to the latter. The 'friendly atmosphere' at the firm means that 'personality is encouraged', and this welcoming environment is complemented by the fee-earners who 'support and assist you throughout your training'. To join a firm that is 'going in a very good direction' and which 'allows you to forge your own relationships directly with the clients', head to Taylor Vinters.

If the firm were a fictional character it would be...

Willy Wonka – has been successful by doing things its own way

The firm

Taylor Vinters is headquartered in Cambridge, and has two other offices in London and Singapore. The firm's threefold focus lies in the technology, investment and private client sectors, through which it represents an impressive list of entrepreneurial clients based in the UK and abroad.

The deals

Advised Atlas Genetics on a $20m fundraising from a new Russian VC investor; acted for Carter Jonas on its acquisition of New Square Holdings; advised the administrator of Orb Estates and Mitre Property Management on a complex group fraud case involving creditors' claims in excess of $160m; advised ARM Holdings on its workforce expansion; advised the British Pharmacological Society on a seven-year contract to publish two leading journals.

The clients

AgReserves Ltd; Carter Backer Winter; Elgin Energy; Ensors; Featurespace; Jockey Club Racecourses; Merz Pharma; Moore Stephens; Professor Stephen Hawking; University of Leicester.

The star performers

Top-ranking departments according to *The Legal 500* (see legal500.com for more details)
Agriculture and estates; Biotechnology; Bloodstock; Charities and not-for-profit; Commercial litigation; Commercial property; Corporate and commercial; Education; Employment; Family; IT and telecoms; Insolvency and corporate recovery; Intellectual property; Personal tax, trusts and probate.

- **Why did you choose this firm over any others?** 'Growing commercial technology department'; 'there is scope, not just for large responsibility, but also for fast promotions if kept on'; 'increased responsibility compared to other firms'; 'I did not want to move to London'; 'very friendly during vacation scheme'; 'feels like it is going in a very good direction'; 'has a good niche and reputation within that niche'

- **Best thing about the firm?** 'There is a friendly atmosphere about the office'; 'the work you are given during your training seat is meaningful'; 'quality of work and responsibility'; 'personality is encouraged'; 'I have been given plenty of client contact'; 'our clients are on the cutting edge of the technology sector'

- **Worst thing about the firm?** 'Lack of transparency at times'; 'the location is not great as there is not much to see or do at lunchtime'; 'can sometimes be overstretched and work long hours repeating the same tasks'; 'levels of remuneration and lack of bonus scheme'

- **Best moment?** 'Working in the private client wing'; 'running and completing a multi-million pound investment deal on my own with only the minimum amount of supervision required'; attending the Court of Appeal for a multi-million pound fraud claim'; 'handling my own files and running my own client meetings'

- **Worst moment?** 'Working in the commercial property team'; 'not getting to do more work in an area the firm specialises in that I would like to qualify into'; 'working for hours on several contracts that were never billed'; 'secondment to PI team at Slater and Gordon'

A day in the life of...

... **Sam Minshall** second-year trainee, Taylor Vinters

Departments to date: Commercial technology, private real estate, commercial disputes

University: University of Exeter

Degree: History with proficiency in Japanese

8.30am: A short cycle down the guided bus way in the sunshine is a great way to start the day. When I arrive at work, I load my computer, make a cup of coffee and catch up with my colleagues in the commercial disputes team. Then, after reading any new emails, I prioritise my tasks for the day ahead.

9.00am: An urgent matter concerning an important client arises, so I am called into a meeting to discuss how our team will tackle it. I am asked to conduct some research on some points of jurisdiction and to obtain a number of quotes from legal translation companies. One of the exciting things about this department is that they like to involve trainees in a range of matters, so you never know what kind of work will land on your desk.

10.00am: After completing my initial research, I report back to my team and ask how I can assist further. As we await further instructions from the client, I make a few calls to see how my property matters are progressing. Liaising with the Land Registry and banks can be time-consuming, so it definitely pays off to know the best times to call. After getting the confirmation I wanted, I email the client to keep them up-to-date.

12.00pm: As our important client decided to hold back on any further action, I turn my attention to the list of tasks I have prepared for the day. After sending a few chaser emails to other firms, I spend some time drafting instructions to counsel for advice in relation to an upcoming arbitration matter. This leaves me just enough time to finish a letter before lunch.

1.00pm: The firm regularly holds 'lunch and learn' sessions, which always draw in people interested in the topic (as well as those keen for a free lunch). Today's session is on data protection law in an employment context. Sessions like these are particularly helpful for the trainees at the firm, as they give us an insight into the type of work we can expect in other seats.

3.00pm: I meet with one of the newly qualified solicitors in the team to discuss a new matter. She gives me a brief summary of the client's business, a history of the litigation to date and a number of points that need clarifying. Armed with a list of questions to answer, I go back to my desk and begin my research.

5.00pm: After reporting back to my colleague with my research findings, I spend some time filling in my training contract record, responding to my latest emails and working through my list of tasks. As litigation is so time-critical, I always make sure that I

> 'The firm regularly holds "lunch and learn" sessions, which always draw in people interested in the topic (as well as those keen for a free lunch).'

am on top of key dates, so I look ahead to tomorrow to see what I have diarised.

6.30pm: I leave work in time to play football with my colleagues from across the firm. We manage to organise friendly games throughout the year with other firms but this week it is just a regular kick-about. It is great to meet up with my colleagues from across the firm and to get some much-needed practice in ahead of a 'footgolf' away day with some clients next week.

www.taylorvinters.com

About the firm

Address: Merlin Place, Milton Road, Cambridge CB4 0DP
Telephone: 01223 423444
Website: www.taylorvinters.com
Email: recruitment@taylorvinters.com

Managing partner: Ed Turner

Other offices: London, Singapore

Who we are: Taylor Vinters is not your typical law firm. We're excited by our clients, how their organisations and lives progress and how we can use our experience, networks and technical expertise to support them. Operating through our European hubs in London and Cambridge and Asia hub in Singapore, Taylor Vinters is a leading international law firm supporting innovative businesses and entrepreneurially minded people to make great things happen.

What we do: We understand that our clients are not only looking for a focus on their legal issues but also strong commercial acumen from their legal partner. We help our clients manage risk, make informed decisions and leverage networks to achieve their personal and business goals, by bringing together cross-disciplinary teams to address complex and multi-faceted issues and offer intelligent, joined-up solutions.

What we're looking for: Candidates should have energy, enthusiasm and a willingness to be the very best. We look for people that are not only technically excellent, but also have commerciality and a genuine desire to put the client at the heart of everything they do. We hire directly from our vacation scheme which runs in June/July 2017.

What you'll do: Trainees undertake seats across the business and will be given responsibility from day one. Trainees work closely with their training supervisor in each seat, learning on the job. This is complemented by other formal learning and development opportunities.

Perks: Health insurance, life insurance, pension, season ticket loan, competitive holiday allowance and the option to buy additional holiday, recognition scheme, health cash plan, range of social activities.

Sponsorship: Full sponsorship for the LPC.

Facts and figures

Total partners: 22
Other fee-earners: 63
Total trainees: 8

Trainee places available for 2019: 4
Applications received pa: 234
Percentage interviewed: 23%

First year salary: £26,000
Second year salary: £28,000
Newly qualified salary: £39,500 (Cambridge), £59,000 (London)

Application process

Apply to: Alix Balfe-Skinner, HR manager
How: Online via Apply for Law
When: By 31 January 2017 for 2019 contracts.
What's involved: Interview, vacation scheme, presentation.

Taylor Vintersˣ

Taylor Wessing LLP

5 New Street Square, London EC4A 3TW

Lex 100 Winner

LEX 100 WINNER

See categories below
and tables from page 69

Survey results *(marks out of 100%)*

Satisfied in your job? 85

Firm living up to expectations? 90

High quality of work? 84

Enough client contact? 76

Stress-free? 62

Happy work/life balance? 67

Friendly firm? 91

Great social life? 79

Good vacation scheme? 89

Confident you'll be kept on? 74

Good remuneration? 76

Diverse firm? 85

Good international secondments? 49

 **verdict**

Trainees applied to Taylor Wessing because of its 'reputation in the marketplace as being an innovator'. This reputation is in part due to the firm's 'focus on interesting core practice areas that are the industries of the future'. Respondents reserve acclaim for Taylor Wessing's 'specialist IP and media department', and also the firm's 'technology/life sciences industry focus'. Such 'varied work' brings with it the opportunity to work on behalf of a 'diverse range of interesting clients', and there is 'potential for early client contact'. Stand-out trainee moments have included 'working on a copyright case for a high-profile music event' and 'leading the negotiation with the other side in an employment settlement'. There are 'occasional late nights' and one trainee spoke of 'being overwhelmed with work and trying to manage expectations of clients and senior fee-earners', but there is a 'supportive workforce' and one respondent says that 'any time I have stayed late it has been noted by partners within my department and they have thanked me'. There are complaints that 'seat allocation could potentially be a more transparent process', and that 'you are not guaranteed your top choice of seat during your training contract'. Trainees appreciate that the 'offices are very modern and in a great location', and the firm's 'involvement with the arts' through its National Portrait Gallery sponsorship is a clear point of difference. **Lex 100 Winner** medals are secured for job satisfaction and living up to expectations. Outside of the office, trainees have undertaken 'very rewarding' client secondments. To train at a firm with a 'vision for the future' that involves 'striving for excellence and developing its talent', consider applying to Taylor Wessing.

If the firm were a fictional character it would be...

C-3PO (Star Wars) – technologically advanced, yet possessing charm and wit

The firm

Taylor Wessing has expanded its international network over the last 12 months, entering an association in Hong Kong, merging with its former ally in Vietnam and combining with a Dutch firm to add offices in Amsterdam and Eindhoven. The firm is an authority on venture capital and real estate law, and also has a dynamic TMT practice. It earned a nomination for Private Client Team of the Year at the *Legal Business* Awards 2016.

The deals

Advised Amino Technologies on a secured loan facility provided by Barclays to facilitate its acquisition of Entone; acted for Lloyds Bank on a £225m letter of credit and standby facility for companies owned by Trafigura; advised Unruly Media on cross-border invoice discounting agreements; represented easyJet in tribunal litigation relating to holiday pay; advised Pan Macmillan on various employment issues arising from its demerger from Macmillan Publishers.

The clients

AlixPartners; Amadeus Capital Partners; Bank of America; CVR Global; Deutsche Bank; Google; Index Ventures; Mimecast; PricewaterhouseCoopers; Tamar Energy.

The star performers

Top-ranking departments according to *The Legal 500* (see legal500.com for more details)
Acquisition finance; Agriculture and estates; Biotechnology; Contentious trust and probate; Corporate and commercial; Corporate restructuring and insolvency; Employment: employers; Employee share schemes; Immigration: business; Intellectual property; Islamic finance; Pensions dispute resolution; Pensions (non-contentious); Personal tax, trusts and probate; Power (including electricity, nuclear and renewables); Trade finance.

- **Why did you choose this firm over any others?** 'Because of its reputation for IP law'; 'for being a friendly firm'; 'quality of the work'; 'an innovative, forward-thinking and efficient law firm'; 'being involved in exciting, high-profile work'; 'good training'; 'forward-focused'; 'impressive clients'; 'excellent vacation scheme'; 'broad range of practice areas'; 'the friendly atmosphere'; 'the early level of responsibility'

- **Best thing about the firm?** 'Quality of the work'; 'the biscuits in the meeting rooms are excellent'; 'the lunch in Cloud 9 is very good and heavily subsidised'; 'supportive nature of trainee network'; 'a broad range of practice areas outside the city's core practices'; 'the extremely friendly and fun trainee cohort'; 'interesting range of practice areas'

- **Worst thing about the firm?** 'I don't think trainees are given enough training during each seat'; 'emphasis on IP during application process but small chance of sitting in that seat';

'lack of organisation and speed when determining seat choices'; 'lack of international secondments'; 'small number of female partners and female board members'

- **Best moment?** 'Acting for a high-profile client'; 'interesting client meetings'; 'team away days'; 'running the Prague marathon with my trainee intake'; 'working on a trial'; 'being involved in a high-profile patent litigation against a huge mobile phone manufacturer'; 'seeing a transaction through from start to finish'; 'having autonomy on my own matters'

- **Worst moment?** 'Reviewing evidence until the early hours of the morning'; 'working a weekend'; 'feeling under a large amount of stress to meet a deadline'; 'the IT training was rather dull'; 'checking deed schedules for an entire day and night'; 'feeling unsupported by my supervisor on a difficult matter'

A day in the life of...

... Tom Connock first-year trainee, Taylor Wessing LLP

Departments to date: Finance (second seat)
University: Bristol
Degree: Law (LLB)

8.30am: I arrive at the office early and head up to Cloud 9, our staff restaurant, to enjoy a cooked breakfast with some of the other trainees. The sun is shining so we sit on the terrace and enjoy the views across London. We all try to meet regularly to catch up and discuss our various seats.

9.15am: I head down to my office, make myself a coffee and begin making a to-do list for the day. My supervisor has scheduled a meeting with me at 9.30am to discuss a new deal and set me some tasks.

9.30am: After checking my emails, I am asked by my supervisor to produce a first draft of a legal charge for a new matter. We discuss the structure of the deal and the issues that will need to be addressed. As part of the team, trainees are given a high level of responsibility and are expected to assist in drafting important documents. I download the Taylor Wessing legal charge precedent and begin making the necessary amendments.

11.00am: I attend a short training session which is delivered by our professional support lawyer. Regular training sessions are important to ensure the team is always aware of new developments in the law.

11.45am: I continue with my drafting of the legal charge. As the deal involves some development work, I speak to an associate in the construction and engineering department for assistance. Taylor Wessing has a great collegiate atmosphere and departments often work closely with each other.

1.00pm: I head outside the office to grab some lunch in the sunshine. A large temporary screen has been installed in the square outside where I can watch Wimbledon while reclining in a deckchair!

1.45pm: I arrive back at my desk and have a voicemail message from a trainee at another firm wanting to discuss some amendments to draft board minutes. I call her back and we negotiate some wording to be inserted. I check this with the supervising associate who agrees it is appropriate. I email the trainee to confirm the board minutes are agreed.

2.30pm: On a separate matter, I attend a brief conference call with a client to discuss some outstanding points in a draft loan agreement and take detailed notes. Following the call, I assist my supervisor in incorporating these points into the document. Many of the outstanding points are commercial (rather than legal), however it is important that everyone understands the client's concerns.

4.00pm: I sit down with my supervisor to discuss my draft legal charge. He makes some amendments to ensure the document is more favourable to our client. We then send the document to the borrower's solicitors for their review.

5.00pm: I update the 'CP checklist' for another matter that I have been working on. The CP checklist records the progress of the 'conditions precedent'. I collect updates from the various departments working on the matter. I also speak to our counterparts

> **'A large temporary screen has been installed in the square outside where I can watch Wimbledon while reclining in a deckchair!'**

at a law firm in New York who are advising the client on aspects of US law. The multi-jurisdictional nature of the work can be very interesting and trainees are often the main point of contact for foreign counsel.

6.30pm: The firm is hosting a client summer drinks event and I have volunteered to assist with welcoming the guests and handing out name badges. When all of the guests have arrived, I grab a cold beer and network. Events like this are a great opportunity to meet and speak with clients in a friendly environment.

www.taylorwessing.com/graduate

About the firm

Address: 5 New Street Square, London EC4A 3TW
Telephone: 020 7300 7000 **Fax:** 020 7300 7100
Website: www.taylorwessing.com/graduate
Email: graduate@taylorwessing.com **Twitter:** @TaylorWessing

Senior partner: Adam Marks
Managing partner: Tim Eyles

Other offices: Amsterdam, Berlin, Bratislava, Brussels, Budapest, Cambridge, Dubai, Düsseldorf, Eindhoven, Frankfurt, Indonesia, Hamburg, Hanoi, Hong Kong, Ho Chi Minh City, Jeddah, Kiev, London – Tech City, Munich, New York, Palo Alto, Paris, Prague, Riyadh, Singapore, South Korea, Vienna and Warsaw. Representative offices: Beijing, Brno, Klagenfurt and Shanghai.

Who we are: Taylor Wessing is a full-service international law firm, standing at the forefront of the industries of tomorrow. Acting as legal advisors to well-known clients in progressive and cutting-edge sectors, we're a firm for ground breakers, the smart thinkers and the trail blazers. Our spark, focus and lateral thinking make us exceptional legal advisors.

What we do: Taylor Wessing offers industry-focused advice and in-depth sector experience including: banking and finance; capital markets; copyright and media law; corporate; commercial agreements; construction and engineering; employment and pensions; EU competition, IT and telecoms; litigation and dispute resolution; patents; planning and environment; private client; projects; real estate; restructuring and corporate recovery; tax; trade marks and designs.

What we're looking for: We look for team players with a minimum of ABB grades at A-level and a 2(1) degree in any discipline. You'll need to be confident and enthusiastic with the communication skills to build vibrant relationships with our clients. You'll have the energy, ambition and creativity to take early responsibility and make a real impact.

What you'll do: Our award-winning training (we won lawcareers.net best trainer – larger city firm in 2014) combines our in-house Professional Skills Course with six-month seats in four different practice groups, including one contentious seat and one in our corporate or finance areas. You will get regular partner contact and will work closely with associates on high-quality work from the outset. Frequent client contact and secondment opportunities to their offices are also offered.

Perks: Private medical care, pension scheme, life assurance, season ticket loan for travel, 25 days' holiday (with an extra day at Christmas), discounted gym membership and employee assistance programme.

Sponsorship: GDL and MA (LPC with Business) sponsored. A maintenance grant is provided.

Facts and figures

Total partners: 400
Total trainees: 47
Trainee places available for 2019: 24
Applications received pa: 800
Percentage interviewed: 3%

First year salary: £40,000
Second year salary: £44,000
Newly qualified salary: £63,000

Application process

Apply to: Sarah Harte, graduate talent advisor.
How: Online application form at graduate.taylorwessing.com
When: Closing date for 2019 is 30 April 2017.
What's involved: Assessment centre including a group exercise and commercial awareness, competency-based interview.

Vacation schemes

Summer: June and July 2017 (40 places available (2 x 20); 2 weeks' duration; remuneration of £275 per week). Apply by 30 January 2017.
First year open day: April 2017. Apply online by 1 March 2017.

TaylorWessing

Thrings LLP

6 Drakes Meadow, Penny Lane, Swindon SN3 3LL

Lex 100 Winner

See categories below
and tables from page 69

Survey results *(marks out of 100%)*

Satisfied in your job?	80
Firm living up to expectations?	81
High quality of work?	82
Enough client contact?	81
Stress-free?	61
Happy work/life balance?	86
Friendly firm?	89
Great social life?	68
Good vacation scheme?	63
Confident you'll be kept on?	62
Good remuneration?	55
Diverse firm?	80
Good international secondments?	49

 **verdict**

Trainees were impressed by the 'range of departments and sectors' covered by Thrings, as there is a 'wide variety of seats which maximises options for qualification'. The 'work is great', and in the words of one respondent tasks 'vary from the very basic to the most complex, enabling me to learn and develop as much as possible during my training contract'. Stand-out moments have included 'completing my first lease after difficulties in the lead up to completion', 'attending a multi-million pound settlement hearing three days before a trial at the Royal Courts of Justice' and 'being heavily involved in a very large property transaction worth £26.1m'. There can be some 'quiet periods', and a 'lack of work often leads to a lack of motivation', yet trainees are 'encouraged to attend networking and other client development events', and it is clear from the feedback that recruits can look forward to 'meeting clients face-to-face'. Trainees 'get moved around a lot' as seats are offered in Bath, Bristol, London and Swindon, and frustratingly there is 'no financial remuneration despite the fact you have to spend a small fortune on agency fees, flat deposits etc.' Despite this hassle, 'each office has a different character' and trainees enjoy Thrings' 'good regional links combined with the opportunity of working in London'. The firm-wide 'friendly atmosphere' means 'you are valued as an integral part of the team', and it is noted that 'the partners are very approachable'. The 'fantastic work/ life balance' is also mentioned and earns a **Lex 100 Winner** award. To train at a 'growing firm' which offers 'lots of potential for career progression', consider applying to Thrings.

If the firm were a fictional character it would be...

Matilda – gutsy, intelligent and loyal

The firm

A national firm with offices in London, Bristol and Bath, Thrings has undergone impressive strategic growth over the last few years, doubling its number of partners and building on its commercial focus. The firm is highly-regarded for its real estate, agriculture and private client practice groups. It also handles high-value family matters and has an expanding international client base.

The deals

Assisted the shareholders of Mainline Employment with the sale of the company to First Holdings; represented high-net-worth individuals in a High Court farm ownership and inheritance dispute; advised Castletown Estates on the negotiation of a Section 106 agreement with Carmarthenshire County Council concerning a mixed-use development; advised Uniform Wares on it global brand protection strategy.

The clients

Anthony Best Dynamics; The Badminton Estate; Bristol Water; Centurycomm; Countrywide Estate Agents; Dynamatic; Juicy Couture; National Farmers Union; Teleperformance; Waitrose.

The star performers

Top-ranking departments according to *The Legal 500* (see legal500.com for more details)
Agriculture and estates; Commercial litigation; Commercial property; Construction; Corporate and commercial; Employment; Environment; Family; Insolvency and corporate recovery; Intellectual property; Media and entertainment; Personal tax, trusts and probate; Planning; Property litigation; Real estate: commercial property; Sport; TMT: IT and telecoms.

- **Why did you choose this firm over any others?** 'The firm specialises in a variety of areas of law'; 'top 100 law firm'; 'corporate and commercial options'; 'London presence'; 'friendliness of the firm'; 'work/life balance'; 'provided you with invaluable training in an exceptional environment'; 'the firm's website'; 'the firm deals with both private client and commercial work'; 'the work is great'; 'opportunities with a range of clients'

- **Best thing about the firm?** 'I can approach any team if I have any queries'; 'senior fee-earners are friendly and approachable'; 'the work is interesting and varied'; 'trainees are involved in all aspects of the firm'; 'the level of work is fantastic'; 'everyone is so nice'; 'welcoming atmosphere'; 'good-quality work'

- **Worst thing about the firm?** 'The lack of parking available at the Swindon office'; 'the data management system'; 'you do not get to choose what location you do your seats in'; 'the pay in London is not fantastic for a trainee'; 'low retention from previous intake'

- **Best moment?** 'Attending a conference with counsel and a client regarding an upcoming trial'; 'independently dealing with a matter from start to finish'; 'being given full responsibility for a new client'; 'going out with the team for drinks'; 'getting to go to court to represent a client and see them win'; 'being involved in some high-profile cases'

- **Worst moment?** 'Having to review boxes of documents'; 'trying to balance organising the Christmas party for the whole firm while working on a huge corporate transaction'; 'not obtaining the seat I wanted from the very start of my training contract until my final seat choice'; 'having to make a huge court bundle'

A day in the life of...

... Megan Prideaux trainee solicitor, Thrings LLP

Departments to date: family, commercial property

University: Cardiff

Degree and class: Law, 1st

8.00am: A typical day starts with a walk from the train station, through Bath city centre, to the office situated on Queens Square over looking the park. I get into the office at about 8.15am and check through my emails. Each team sits in a group of desks called 'pods' and this is very useful for getting involved in different fee-earners work and for when you need to check something or ask a question. As trainees, we are given the responsibility of running our own files with supervision, and I usually start by prioritising my tasks for the day, as well as going through any work that my team would like me to take on. Each day is different and each client is different, leading to a varied seat with lots of new things to learn.

9.00am: Working in commercial property, there is usually a document to draft including leases, licences, wayleave agreements, contracts, transfers and Land Registry forms. Alternatively, I review documents that the other side's solicitor has drafted and make amendments/comments from our client's perspective. We act for a number of different types of businesses and individuals, so one minute I can be dealing with a lease of a dental surgery, and the next I can be assisting on a multimillion-pound sale of retail premises.

11.30am: I refer queries to colleagues in other departments as issues arise on files,

including our property dispute resolution team regarding security of tenure and lease validity issues and the planning team regarding permitted use queries. I also carry out legal research for the team eg relating to SDLT calculations on reverse premiums and water authority requirements where a building was constructed over a public sewer in the 1980s.

12.30pm: As trainees we have the responsibility of organising the firm's Christmas party so it is all things Christmas, even in July. I am also responsible for organising team meetings to make sure the fee-earners stay up-to-date with the market and changes in the law. Once a month we watch webinars together over lunch and review update notes.

2.00pm: I attend client meetings with the fee-earners including advising on replies to CPSE documents and signing completion documentation. I usually take a note of the meeting and produce an attendance note for the file.

3.30pm: I liaise with clients via telephone, email and letter providing advice on their matters, including explaining any documents and processes and answering any queries. It is good experience to have hands on direct contact with clients and to be able to build a relationship during the transaction.

4.30pm: I deal with post-completion steps at the end of matters. I monitor my Land Registry portal and deal with requisitions and applications to register transfers, leases and legal charges. I also liaise with the clients to make sure that their SDLT payments and returns are submitted within the deadlines.

> **'Each day is different and each client is different, leading to a varied seat with lots of new things to learn.'**

5.30/6.00pm: As trainees, we are encouraged to get involved with business development, both inside and outside the firm. I am a member of Bath Young Professionals, who organise fun networking events such as cocktail making and a night at the Bath Race Course. These events allow me to meet other young people working in different professions.

www.thrings.com

About the firm

Address: 6 Drakes Meadow, Penny Lane, Swindon, SN3 3LL
Telephone: 01793 410800 **Fax:** 01793 539040
Website: www.thrings.com
Email: solicitors@thrings.com
Facebook: Thrings
Twitter: @ThringsLaw

Senior partner: Jonathan Payne
Managing partner: Simon Holdsworth

Other offices: Bristol, Bath, Swindon, London.

Who we are: A vibrant, expanding top 100 UK law firm with a diverse client base, offering excellent career prospects to ambitious trainees. We operate from offices in Bristol, Bath, Swindon and London.

What we do: Thrings offers specialist advice in sectors such as aerospace and defence, agriculture, energy and waste, innovation and technology, and financial services from partner-led teams whose expertise matches that found in much larger City firms.

What we're looking for: You're bright and proactive, with a real commercial awareness. You're enthusiastic, dedicated and able to think independently. You hold a minimum 2(1) degree, possess strong 'A' levels and relevant work or life experience. You grasp facts well and work out solutions quickly. You're sitting here nodding your head, agreeing as you read this? We want to hear from you.

What you'll do: We operate a structured two-year training contract split into four six-month seats. You can expect to gain experience within at least three different practice areas, with a balance of contentious and non-contentious work types.

Perks: There are regular office organised social events and the firm offers a competitive salary and benefits package including private medical, life assurance, 25 days holiday and discounted shopping.

Facts and figures

Total partners: 61
Total trainees: 13

Trainee places available for 2019: 9
Applications received pa: 800
Percentage interviewed: 10%

First year salary: £26,000
Second year salary: £27,000
Newly qualified salary: £38,000

Turnover in 2015: £27.5m (+10% from 2014)
Profits per equity partner: £160,000

Application process

Apply to: hr@thrings.com
How: Via our website using the online application form on our careers page.
When: 2nd June 2017 for 2019 contracts.
What's involved: Initial telephone interview followed by an assessment day including interview, presentations and group activities.

THRINGS
SOLICITORS

Travers Smith LLP

10 Snow Hill, London EC1A 2AL

Survey results *(marks out of 100%)*

Satisfied in your job?	85
Firm living up to expectations?	86
High quality of work?	83
Enough client contact?	79
Stress-free?	65
Happy work/life balance?	72
Friendly firm?	94
Great social life?	88
Good vacation scheme?	92
Confident you'll be kept on?	82
Good remuneration?	85
Diverse firm?	83
Good international secondments?	54

verdict

Trainees applied to 'prestigious' Travers Smith in large part due to the City firm's 'excellent reputation for training'. A key aspect of this is the 'unique room-sharing system', where a 'trainee sits in a room with two to four associates and a partner'. We are told that this 'makes a huge impact on learning through observation', and partners 'take a keen interest in the professional development of their trainees' and are 'involved in your training every step of the way'. Partners also conducted the recruitment interviews, and were labelled 'impressive and the kind of people I want to emulate' by one respondent. This was one stage of the 'straightforward and personal application process' which introduced applicants to the 'collegiate and supportive atmosphere' at Travers Smith. The firm is a triple **Lex 100 Winner** this year. The 'quality of the work and the comparatively smaller size of the trainee intake' means that there are 'opportunities to take on responsibility at an early stage'. Highlight work moments to date include 'leading a board meeting for a listed company' and 'signing a very large transaction after the sale process accelerated rapidly'. When it gets busy the 'hours can be brutal', and this has resulted in 'working on a deal until 7am' and 'working overnight to complete a piece of research'. Trainees also criticise the 'lack of transparency regarding seat choices and qualification', though the 'retention rates are impressive'. Secondments are available in the Paris office, and for one recruit this was an 'excellent opportunity to challenge myself and improve my language skills'. To represent 'blue-chip clients' while working with 'extremely talented lawyers' in a 'team-oriented' environment, take a closer look at Travers Smith.

If the firm were a fictional character it would be...

Sandy Cohen (The OC) – sharp, calm and down-to-earth

The firm

City firm Travers Smith retained its Private Equity Team of the Year title at the *Legal Business* Awards 2016. It was also nominated for Law Firm of the Year, and has since published an excellent 13% rise in turnover for the latest financial year. The firm is widely respected for its finance expertise, and has a second office in Paris.

The deals

Advised Bridgepoint Development Capital on the financing of its acquisitions of tastecard and Gourmet Society; advised Investec Bank on a £15m revolving facility to fund investments made by Downing; assisted Nikkei with the incentive aspects of its £844m acquisition of The Financial Times Group; acted for Brewin Dolphin on the employment elements of the sale of its Stockade business to Alliance Trust Savings; acted for the British Steel Pension Scheme on a package of benefit changes to manage a substantial increase in the scheme's funding deficit.

The clients

AIG; Bank Negara Indonesia; The Carlyle Group; Deloitte; Exponent Private Equity; Monarch Alternative Capital; Pinewood Studios; RBS; Virgin Active; Western Union.

The star performers

Top-ranking departments according to *The Legal 500* (see legal500.com for more details)
Acquisition finance; Banking litigation: investment and retail; Commercial contracts; Competition litigation; Corporate restructuring and insolvency; Corporate tax; Data protection; Derivatives and structured products; EU and competition; Employee share schemes; Equity capital markets; Financial services (contentious); Flotations: small and mid-cap; Franchising; Fraud: civil; Investment funds: Hedge funds; M&A: upper mid-market and premium deals, £250m+; Pensions dispute resolution; Private equity: transactions: Mid-cap deal capability; Property finance.

- **Why did you choose this firm over any others?** 'Unique trainee-associate-partner seating arrangement'; 'brilliant colleagues'; 'a genuinely friendly working environment'; 'quality of training'; 'number of trainees'; 'the early responsibility given to trainees'; 'collegiate working environment'; 'the easy application process'; 'exposure to clients'; 'independent firm'; 'I loved the vacation scheme'; '100% equity partnership'; 'excellent reputation'

- **Best thing about the firm?** 'Sitting with the partners and learning that way'; 'everyone is very open to answering questions which helps greatly with development'; 'the importance placed on maintaining a good working culture'; 'always someone to go for a drink with'; 'outstanding quality of work of a small enough scale that you get real exposure'; 'impressive social calendar'

- **Worst thing about the firm?** 'Lack of diversity'; 'the IT system could be improved'; 'the condition of the offices'; 'lack of

biscuits'; 'no gym membership'; 'no international offices'; 'some of the more popular departments are not big enough to take all of the trainees who want to work there'; 'the qualification process is not particularly transparent'

- **Best moment?** 'Conducting interviews at a bank with a senior associate'; 'seeing my research impact the advice given to a client'; 'completing my first transaction in which I was the primary contact for the client'; 'getting a good review in my first seat'; 'attending an employment tribunal hearing'; 'tasked with drafting correspondence to opposing party'

- **Worst moment?** 'Bundling against the clock'; 'experiencing my first mistake'; 'working until 4am while in corporate'; 'watching a deal that I had worked on fall over'; 'making a silly mistake'; 'verification for an IPO'; 'having to juggle PSC commitments with a very busy period in the office'; 'making a silly mistake'

A day in the life of...

... Tom Lloyd trainee solicitor, Travers Smith LLP
Departments to date: Employment, finance, corporate (private equity group) and commercial, IP and technology
University: St Peter's College, Oxford University
Degree: Geography

7.30am: I get up early and make my way to the gym (taking advantage of the subsidised membership provided by the firm!) before grabbing a coffee and some breakfast as I head into the office. The firm's canteen is typically the go-to place for breakfast, providing a social hub where people congregate for a morning catch up.

9.15am: When I arrive at my desk I catch up with my supervising partner and associates. The graduate recruitment partners hosted a dinner for the trainees last night, so my room is inevitably keen to hear how this went. I then read through my emails, replying to any that can be dealt with quickly, before prioritising my tasks for the day.

9.30am: We have been carrying out a vendor due diligence exercise for the share sale of a company owned by one of our private equity clients. We are working towards a tight deadline as our private equity team is looking to send out a revised draft of the report by the end of today. The lead associate and I divide up the tasks: I am responsible for processing (where possible) the client's comments into the report and, where further information is required, preparing questions in advance of a call with the client this afternoon.

11.30am: I take a break from my due diligence work. A well-known high-street client is looking to enter into an arrangement with a counter-party for the delivery of its sandwiches around London, and has sent us a draft agreement to be reviewed. While I am supported by my supervising partner, I am encouraged to lead on drafting an email of advice to the client. Having scoured through the document, centring my review on the specific business needs of the client, I discuss my comments with the partner and send my email of advice to the client.

1.00pm: Lunchtime provides a good opportunity to get some fresh air. Being located no more than a five-minute walk from Farringdon, St Paul's or Chancery Lane, there is never a shortage of lunch options. Today I, and a few other trainees, choose to wander through Leather Lane Market, before settling in Smithfield Garden to eat our lunch in the sun.

1.50pm: When I get back to my desk, I respond to any emails that have come in while I was at lunch. Just before the due diligence call, the two associates and I sit down to decide who will be discussing each item on the agenda and the order in which this will occur.

2.30pm: We dial into the call with the client. I take notes and answer any questions on the sections of the report which I have been looking after. The call goes well and we now have enough information to finalise our section of the report. Following the call, I incorporate my notes into the report, before sending it to the associate for review. Having processed their comments, I liaise with the private equity team in relation to any outstanding points, before sending over our revised draft before the deadline.

> '**The 5-a-side football legal league is in the final stages of the season and the Travers Smith team has a title-deciding match tonight.**'

4.30pm: I receive some follow-up questions from the client on the email of advice I sent out earlier. I delve back into the agreement and discuss my proposed responses with the partner, before replying to the client.

6.30pm: The 5-a-side football legal league is in the final stages of the season and the Travers Smith team has a title-deciding match tonight. I look through my to-do list, checking I have finished everything that I had planned to do today. Having closed down my timers for the day and changed into Travers Smith football colours, I head off to the game (and the beers that often follow) with my teammates.

www.traverssmith.com

About the firm

Address: 10 Snow Hill, London EC1A 2AL
Telephone: 020 7295 3000   **Fax:** 020 7295 3500
Website: www.traverssmith.com
Email: graduate.recruitment@traverssmith.com
Twitter: @traverssmith
Facebook: TraversSmithGraduates

Senior partner: Chris Hale
Managing partner: David Patient

Other offices: Paris. Our strategy of establishing close ties with international law firms means we work with over 100 firms worldwide.

Who we are: Travers Smith is an award-winning City law firm with a reputation for enterprising thinking and uncompromising quality. Competing directly with the largest City firms, we attract top-quality work and provide a professional yet relaxed working environment. It is this that has led to one of the highest staff retention rates in the City.

What we do: The main areas of our practice are commercial (including IP and IT), corporate, employment, employee incentives, environment and operational regulatory, competition, dispute resolution, finance, financial services and markets, pensions, real estate, restructuring and insolvency, and tax.

Facts and figures

Total partners: 76
Other fee-earners: 245
Total trainees: 50

Trainee places available for 2019: 25
Applications received pa: 1,000

First year salary: £42,500
Second year salary: £47,500
Newly qualified salary: £71,500

Turnover in 2014/15: £106m
Profits per equity partner: £939,000

What we're looking for: We'll give you responsibility from day one – you will quickly find yourself on the phone to clients, in meetings and handling your own work (with guidance where needed). As such the firm looks for people who can combine academic excellence with common sense; who are determined, articulate and able to think on their feet; and who take their work but not themselves seriously.

What you'll do: The firm's comprehensive training programme ensures that trainees experience a broad range of work. All trainee solicitors sit with partners and associates, which ensures a refreshing lack of hierarchy. Trainees spend six months in our corporate department and another six months in a contentious seat. The firm offers you a choice for your other two seats in two of our other departments. Trainees may also have the opportunity to spend six months in the firm's Paris office.

Perks: Private health and permanent health insurance, life assurance, health screening programme, GP service, pension scheme, 25 days' holiday, cycle to work scheme, subsidised bistro, childcare vouchers, season ticket and corporate health club membership loans.

Sponsorship: Payment of GDL and LPC fees, plus maintenance grant.

Application process

Apply to: Germaine VanGeyzel, graduate recruitment manager.
How: CV and covering letter online via cvMail.
When: By 31 July 2017 for training contracts commencing in September 2019 and March 2020.
What's involved: Two interviews for training contracts. One interview for a vacation scheme place.

Vacation schemes

Winter: 5-16 December 2016. Rolling application from 1 October 2016.
Summer: 19-30 June 2017; 3-14 July 2017; 17-28 July 2017. Application deadline is 31 January 2017.

TRAVERS SMITH

Watson Farley & Williams LLP

15 Appold Street, London EC2A 2HB

Lex 100 Winner

See categories below
and tables from page 69

Survey results *(marks out of 100%)*

Satisfied in your job?	77
Firm living up to expectations?	81
High quality of work?	78
Enough client contact?	74
Stress-free?	63
Happy work/life balance?	66
Friendly firm?	84
Great social life?	70
Good vacation scheme?	79
Confident you'll be kept on?	73
Good remuneration?	83
Diverse firm?	77
Good international secondments?	95

 verdict

A 'good-sized City firm with an excellent reputation', Watson Farley & Williams handles 'high-quality work'. Trainees see the firm as 'top of the class in finance and projects work', while its 'reputation in shipping' is that of a market leader. Respondents cite this 'sector focus' as a 'key factor' in their decision to join. The 'six-seat rotation' has also proved popular, as it 'provides for greater opportunities to experience different departments'. Stand-out trainee moments include 'being involved in the closing of a huge deal', 'completing a corporate deal for a portfolio of over 30 hotels' and 'assisting on large-scale renewable deals and receiving recognition for my role'. At times there can be a 'lack of secretarial support for trainees', and this can lead to 'some very late nights doing menial tasks'. On the plus side, WFW is one of the few City firms to offer a 'guaranteed international secondment', and this is identified as one of the best things about the training contract and earns a **Lex 100 Winner** medal. Seats abroad have given recruits access to 'challenging work' and the opportunity to 'run your own matters', all while experiencing 'a lot of fun living somewhere completely new'. There is a 'friendly atmosphere' at WFW and a 'supportive work environment', as exemplified by the 'approachable partners'. Yet some trainees grumble about the lack of a 'social aspect' to the training contract, with one respondent saying 'it would be nice if there were more organised departmental social events'. But the current trainee cohort is buoyed by the firm's 'continued organic growth'. To experience life at a 'truly international' firm which offers 'high levels of responsibility at an early stage', consider Watson Farley & Williams.

If the firm
were a fictional character
it would be...

Aragorn (The Lord of the Rings) – human, will fight your corner and likes to travel

The firm

International firm Watson Farley & Williams has established an impressive network of 14 offices in 11 jurisdictions through Europe, Asia and the US. It is an undisputed leader in maritime law, and also advises UK and overseas clients on litigation, projects and real estate issues. The firm's revenue rose by 5% over 2015/16, in part due to a spate of lateral hires in New York and London.

The deals

Advised Citibank as co-ordinator for a syndicate of lenders on a $357m term loan facility for Subsea 7, to fund the construction of two new oilfield service vessels; acted for lenders including HSBC on a $500m reserve-based lending facility for Petroceltic International; assisted Mariana Resources with a number of mandates, including its acquisition of Aegean Metals; assisted PNE Wind with the £100m sale of its UK wind farm project pipeline to Brookfield Asset Management; advised CACEIS on the £6m financing of the acquisition of residential real estate in Holland Park.

The clients

88 Energy; All Leisure Group; Ascendos Rail Leasing; Budapest Airport; Flybe; MSC Cruises; Maas Capital Investments; Nacco; Nordea Bank; Swiss International Air Lines.

The star performers

Top-ranking departments according to *The Legal 500* (see legal500.com for more details)
Asset finance and leasing; Banking litigation: investment and retail; Commercial litigation; Commercial property; Commodities: physicals; Corporate tax; EU and competition; Employment: employers; Flotations: small and mid-cap; Immigration: business; International arbitration; M&A: mid-market, £50m-£250m; Mining and minerals; Planning; Power (including electricity, nuclear and renewables); Private equity: transactions: Mid-cap deal capability; Property finance; Rail; Shipping; Trade finance.

- **Why did you choose this firm over any others?** 'Very warm and friendly from the beginning of the application process'; 'guaranteed overseas secondments'; 'previous experience with the firm as a paralegal'; 'Asia presence'; 'excellent vacation scheme'; 'growing and continuing to do well despite the economic crisis'; 'one firm worldwide'; 'six-seat rotation'; 'interest in its core sectors'

- **Best thing about the firm?** 'International aspect in terms of the work'; 'the people you interact with everyday'; the guarantee of an overseas seat'; 'the restaurant'; 'working in small teams'; 'exposure to interesting work'; 'generally no face-time requirement'; 'increasing revenue year-on-year'

- **Worst thing about the firm?** 'The ongoing office refurbishment is making life quite difficult'; 'lack of transparency with respect to seat rotations'; 'not sure how the firm is trying to market itself'; 'the new IT system is still suffering from teething

problems'; 'there are some really old-fashioned partners who need to retire so the younger partners can freshen the firm up a bit'; 'the new carpet'

- **Best moment?** 'Bangkok secondment'; 'closing my first transaction'; 'succeeding at a very difficult task'; 'having the opportunity to work abroad for four months'; 'handling my own transactions in my first seat'; 'experiencing a diverse range of work'; 'managing ship deliveries'; 'seeing deals run from start to finish and being actively involved with the closing'; 'being trusted to attend the first part of a large closing meeting on my own'

- **Worst moment?** 'Late nights in the office'; 'spilling wine on a senior colleague'; 'the department during my second seat was too quiet'; '5am closing meeting'; 'having to re-paginate a bundle late on a Friday night when everyone else had gone home'

A day in the life of...

... Natasha Seel trainee, Watson Farley & Williams

Departments to date: Finance (London and Paris), litigation (London)

University: St Andrews

Degree and class: French and Social Anthropology 2(1)

9.00am: When I get to my desk, I check the emails that have come in overnight and prioritise those which require immediate attention. While preparing my 'to-do' list for the day my supervisor, a partner and head of the English law practice in the Paris office, brings in fresh orange juice and we discuss how I will apportion my time today and throughout the week. I will be preparing for an aviation closing scheduled for this afternoon as well as ensuring I keep progressing the shipping transaction I am currently working on. I try to work as efficiently and proactively as possible given the busy nature of the department, but in a small, supportive team such as this one I don't hesitate to check with a colleague if I am unsure about a task.

9.30am: I attend a conference call in respect of the conditions precedent to this afternoon's closing. The transaction is an international, innovative and complex aircraft financing involving numerous parties, so organisation is key. I take notes of points to be followed up on and after the call, I action these – including keeping track of the signed counterparts we receive, assessing when conditions precedent have been satisfied, and making amendments to documents that have been agreed pre-closing. As one of the parties is based in Malaysia, six hours ahead of Paris, I telephone local counsel to ensure the relevant documents are signed and circulated to us before the end of their working day.

11.30am: I turn to focus on a separate transaction that I am working on, an international shipping deal involving the financing of two large tankers currently under construction – I have been tasked with drafting corporate authorities and security documents. I discuss the drafts with the senior associate who is overseeing the work and make the suggested amendments.

1.30pm: I head out to one of the local cafés for some lunch with the associates and as I often do, return with a pistachio macaroon from my favourite pâtisserie!

2.30pm: I continue working on the shipping deal and after having reviewed the documents again and having checked with the senior associate and matter partner I am working with, I prepare to circulate them to our client, the financing bank. Given the international nature of this transaction, I also liaise with local counsel in different jurisdictions, including our New York office, in respect of the corporate authorities for the relevant entities.

3.30pm: I return to the aviation transaction and carry out final preparations for the closing meeting. This involves ensuring all the documents are in order and that that there are no outstanding items which could cause a delay.

4.30pm: The closing call, led by my supervisor, begins with all parties joining from across Europe and Asia. There is a tight timeframe for the closing to take place so we track the plane taking off on Flightradar24 (a live flight tracking website). Throughout the call I take notes of the key issues, including the exact times that need to be recorded on certain documents.

'In a small, supportive team such as this one I don't hesitate to check with a colleague if I am unsure about a task.'

5.30pm: After a successful closing, I collate, date and circulate the executed documents to all relevant parties. I also liaise with local counsel, providing them with all necessary documents in order for their legal opinions to be issued.

7.30pm: I reply to the emails that have come through while I've been away from my desk and then speak to my supervisor and finance team colleagues regarding upcoming tasks and matters. I then double-check I have completed all the necessary tasks for the day and plan for tomorrow, preparing an updated list.

www.wfw.com/trainee

About the firm

Address: 15 Appold Street, London EC2A 2HB
Telephone: 020 7814 8000   **Fax:** 020 7814 8017
Website: www.wfw.com
Email: uktrainees@wfw.com
Twitter: @WFW_UKTrainees

Managing partners: Chris Lowe, Lothar Wegener

Other offices: Athens, Bangkok, Dubai, Frankfurt, Hamburg, Hong Kong, Madrid, Milan, Munich, New York, Paris, Rome, Singapore.

Who we are: WFW was founded in 1982 in London. It has since grown to over 150 partners and a staff of over 800.

What we do: WFW is a distinctive law firm with a leading market position in international finance and investment, maritime and energy. We also specialise in natural resources, transport, real estate and technology.

What we're looking for: You will need a 2(1) or above. We also ask for at least ABB from A-level results, or their equivalent. As well as academic achievement, we particularly value applicants with initiative, drive and commercial awareness.

What you'll do: At WFW we deal with training and ongoing development in an individual way. During each seat, we discuss with you plans for the next one, encouraging a two-way conversation about areas you are interested in. Each trainee undertakes six four-month seats, sitting with a partner or a senior associate. Trainees spend one of those seats in an overseas office.

Perks: 25 days' holiday plus public and bank holidays, income protection scheme, life assurance, employee assistance scheme, group personal pension scheme, annual interest-free season ticket loan, £250 contribution towards a sports club membership or exercise classes of your choice, private medical insurance, flexible benefits scheme.

Sponsorship: Fees paid for both the GDL and the LPC, depending on the point of offer, plus a maintenance grant.

Facts and figures

Total partners: 151
Other fee-earners: 412
Total trainees: 36

Trainee places available for 2019: 18
Applications received pa: c600
Percentage interviewed: 30%

First year salary: £42,000
Second year salary: £46,000
Newly qualified salary: £68,000

Turnover in 2015: £125.2m (+7% from 2014)
Profits per equity partner: £520,000 (+7%)
(see legalbusiness.co.uk for full financial information)

Application process

Apply to: Lucie Rees, graduate recruitment and development manager.
How: Online application form.
When: By 28 July 2017 for 2019 training contracts.
What's involved: Online application form followed by a video interview, an assessment centre and a partner interview.

Vacation schemes

Spring: 27 March-7 April 2017 (apply by 27 January 2017).
Summer: 12-23 June 2017 and 10-21 July 2017 (apply by 27 January 2017).

WATSON FARLEY & WILLIAMS

Wedlake Bell LLP

71 Queen Victoria Street, London EC4V 4AY

Lex 100 Winner

See categories below
and tables from page 69

Survey results *(marks out of 100%)*

Satisfied in your job?	81
Firm living up to expectations?	83
High quality of work?	82
Enough client contact?	76
Stress-free?	61
Happy work/life balance?	66
Friendly firm?	92
Great social life?	82
Good vacation scheme?	92
Confident you'll be kept on?	58
Good remuneration?	65
Diverse firm?	81

 **verdict**

Trainees were enticed by the 'variety of practice areas' and 'broad range of departments' at Wedlake Bell. The 'mix of private client and corporate/commercial work' proved attractive, as did the fact that the firm 'offered expertise in the property field'. The 'small trainee intake' means that 'lots of responsibility is given out early on', and this entails 'writing and research, as well as chargeable work'. Trainee highlights include 'being involved in a big corporate transaction from start to finish', 'getting good feedback from a partner' and 'completing the first transaction I worked on, after it had already fallen through once'. At Wedlake Bell 'there is a culture of working hard but also respecting the importance of life outside of work', so while 'the hours can be long when it gets busy', feedback also mentions the 'good work/life balance'. The firm's vacation scheme is praised and merits a **Lex 100 Winner** medal, with two recruits separately describing it as a 'friendly and welcoming' experience. There is a 'focus on training' at the firm, and respondents appreciate the 'outstanding supervision' of 'very talented lawyers who genuinely care about your training'. There are complaints about the 'lack of transparency on qualification' and the resultant 'worry about not being retained', but the firm makes clear that it 'values each of its trainees' and is 'supportive of social events including the Christmas party and the ski trip'. Additionally, trainees get involved in the firm's business development work, an experience which affords a 'real understanding as to how the business as a whole works'. To train at a firm where trainees are 'trusted with great responsibility' and are given 'exposure to a variety of work', take a closer look at Wedlake Bell.

If the firm were a fictional character it would be...

Tyrion Lannister (A Game of Thrones) – has a good sense of humour and is extremely bright

The firm

London-based Wedlake Bell is renowned for its private client and family law practice, as well as for its work on mid-market M&A, brand protection, commercial property and probate cases. The LB100 firm has affiliations throughout Europe, Asia, South Africa and the US, strengthening its international capabilities.

The deals

Acted for Bio-Rad Laboratories on employment issues across 22 EMEA jurisdictions; assisted Hugo Boss with a proposed Black Friday promotion; advised William Nash on its £15m refinancing of an 18-property portfolio through Santander; advised Axpo on commercial arrangements for the cross-border transportation of nuclear waste; acted for Messila House on the £30m financing of the development of Montrose Square and 47 Belgrave Square.

The clients

British Journal of Urology; Care UK Community Partnerships; The Chartered Insurance Institute; Hargreaves Developments; Heron International; Jumeirah Carlton Tower; Lufthansa; Melford Capital Partners; Residential Land; Warburg HIH Investment Estate.

The star performers

Top-ranking departments according to *The Legal 500* (see legal500.com for more details)
Bank lending – investment grade debt and syndicated loans; Brand management; Commercial contracts; Commercial litigation; Commercial property; Construction: contentious; Data protection; Employment: employers; Family; IT and telecoms; Intellectual property; M&A: smaller deals, up to £50m; Pensions (non-contentious); Personal tax, trusts and probate; Property finance; Property litigation; VAT and indirect tax.

- **Why did you choose this firm over any others?** 'Mix of practice areas in which I have an interest'; 'size of trainee intake'; 'the offices are in a great location'; 'there is a genuine open-door policy'; 'very positive experience on the vacation scheme'; 'expertise in property and private client'; 'smaller firm'

- **Best thing about the firm?** 'Quality of work'; 'the people'; 'everyone is extremely approachable'; 'there is no hierarchy meaning the partners are just as easy to speak to'; 'there is a friendly atmosphere which radiates throughout the firm'; 'the sociability'

- **Worst thing about the firm?** 'IT systems'; 'pressure to work long hours'; 'the communal areas are on the small side'; 'the toilets'; 'lack of transparency on qualification'

- **Best moment?** 'The firm ski trip'; 'the feeling of satisfaction when completing a licence in a short time-frame for a client'; 'working to negotiate and settle a claim the day before the hearing'; 'dealing with a possession claim against trespassers under Part 55 of the Civil Procedure Rules'

- **Worst moment?** 'Photocopying'; 'organising documents'; '14 hours in a meeting to close a deal, and it falling through the next day'; 'spotting a mouse roaming the corridor'; 'being blamed for something I did not do'; 'dealing with grumpy clients'

A day in the life of...

... Chris Nelson trainee solicitor, Wedlake Bell LLP

Departments to date: Commercial litigation, corporate (current seat)
University: Brunel University
Degree and class: Law, 1st

9.00am: Having battled my way through London's bustling streets, I settle down at my desk in the corporate team. I check my to-do list, run through my priority tasks for the day with my supervisor and respond to a few emails.

9.30am: An associate asks me to determine how many days' notice our client, a publicly listed and traded company, must give to its shareholders ahead of an AGM. I turn to the Companies Act 2006 and check the articles of association of the company before drafting a brief research note.

10.00am: I have been assisting my supervisor on the buyback, by our client (a private limited company), of shares held by a departing shareholder. One of the directors is attending our offices this afternoon, so I print the final form documents that I helped prepare, double check the documents with my supervisor and flag where signatures are required.

10.30am: A partner has requested that I prepare documentation required for a client to comply with the new PSC regulations. I analyse the ownership structure of the company to determine the ultimate beneficial owner and prepare a draft set of board minutes, a board memorandum and a PSC register. My supervisor and I discuss and amend the documents before they are emailed to the client for approval.

11.30am: Since the start of my seat, I have assisted an associate on a client's proposed acquisition of another company. As part of the share purchase agreement (the 'SPA' – you quickly become familiar with acronyms!) I have been asked to prepare profiles for subsidiaries of the target. I prepare the profiles and update the SPA.

12.45pm: A senior associate in the commercial litigation team calls asking me to verify details of a company registered in Guernsey. I perform the search and note my findings in an email.

2.00pm: The director arrives at our offices to sign the buyback documents. I take notes of the meeting, witness the signatures and, when I return to my desk, scan the documents which I then send to the selling shareholder's solicitors in advance of completion.

2.30pm: I have been assisting an associate on the sale of two separate businesses. The client has provided a number of documents to be supplied to the buyers for their due diligence review. I redact commercially sensitive information before the documents are circulated to the buyer's solicitors.

3.30pm: I have been asked to review and sense-check the SPA that I updated this morning. I conduct a cross-reference check to ensure all references are accurate as well as a

definitions check to ensure that all definitions are correct and, importantly, that there are no duplicate definitions.

6.00pm: As it is month end, I assist my supervisor in running through WIP (work in progress) on various matters to determine what should be billed this month.

> **'Every month the corporate team has a know-how lunch meeting. I have been asked to give a presentation at the next meeting.'**

6.30pm: Every month the corporate team has a know-how lunch meeting. As I have been asked to give a presentation at the next meeting, I update my notes on recent decisions regarding variations to contracts, fiduciary duties of directors in joint ventures and the construction of exclusion clauses in warranty claims.

7.00pm: A few of the corporate team are heading to the local watering hole. I update my time recording and calendar and join the rest of the team for a few drinks in the sun.

www.wedlakebell.com/careers

About the firm

Address: 71 Queen Victoria Street, London EC4V 4AY
Telephone: 020 7395 3178
Website: www.wedlakebell.com
Email: recruitment@wedlakebell.com

Twitter: @WedlakeBell
Senior partner: Simon de Galleani
Managing partner: Martin Arnold

Who we are: Wedlake Bell LLP is a leading London law firm. We provide a full service to UK and international corporate and private clients.

What we do: Our expert teams cover the following core areas: commercial; IP and IT; corporate; dispute resolution; employment; pensions and employee benefits; private client; property and construction; banking; projects and infrastructure.

What we're looking for: Academic excellence together with commercial aptitude, common sense, enthusiasm and a personable nature.

What you'll do: Six months in four different practice areas. Trainee solicitors are closely supervised but have client contact and responsibility from day one.

Perks: Pension, health insurance, life assurance, season ticket loan, corporate gym membership, cycle to work scheme.

Sponsorship: LPC funding available, subject to the terms and conditions of any offer.

Facts and figures

Total partners: 59
Other fee-earners: 89
Total trainees: 12

Trainee places available for 2019: 6
Applications received pa: 250-300
Percentage interviewed: 15%

Turnover in 2015: £31.1m (+13% From 2014)
Profits per equity partner: £352,000 (+10%)
(see legalbusiness.co.uk for full financial information)

Application process

Apply to: The graduate recruitment department.
How: Online application.
When: By 31 July 2017 for September 2019 start.

Vacation schemes

Summer: First three weeks of July 2017 (apply by end of January 2017).

Wedlake Bell

www.wedlakebell.com/careers

Weil, Gotshal & Manges

110 Fetter Lane, London EC4A 1AY

Lex 100 Winner

See categories below
and tables from page 69

Survey results *(marks out of 100%)*

Satisfied in your job?	81
Firm living up to expectations?	83
High quality of work?	82
Enough client contact?	71
Stress-free?	58
Happy work/life balance?	53
Friendly firm?	81
Great social life?	61
Good vacation scheme?	90
Confident you'll be kept on?	90
Good remuneration?	90
Diverse firm?	78
Good international secondments?	57

 **verdict**

Weil, Gotshal & Manges enjoys a 'pre-eminent international reputation' for its 'cutting-edge work', and the firm 'strikes a great balance between private equity and restructuring' matters. Members of the 'small trainee intake' in the 'growing and ambitious London office' speak of a 'rewarding and challenging culture' within which they are exposed to 'top-tier clients'. Stand-out moments for the current trainee cohort include 'working directly with a partner to close a complex transaction', 'closing a mega banking deal' and 'assisting with the sale of a client's interest in a set of high-profile West End hotels'. Trainees gain satisfaction from the 'prestige' associated with market-leading deals, and the pay 'doesn't get much better at a law firm', earning a **Lex 100 Winner** prize for remuneration satisfaction. A downside to this enticing package is the 'unpredictable hours' which can result in 'doing an all-nighter' and 'cancelling on friends when work gets hectic'. Weil Gotshal has an 'excellent training programme' which is 'very hands-on', and one respondent to our survey adds that 'though the people we work with everyday are amongst the best in the industry, they are still very approachable and friendly'. There is a 'tendency for certain departments to dominate the firm environment', and one trainee describes how 'the firm is run by corporate so any other practice areas are usually secondary concerns', yet the firm is lauded for its 'ambition' and for providing a 'quality of work not offered to trainees elsewhere in the City'. A **Lex 100 Winner** gong for confidence of being kept on has also been secured. To join 'lean teams doing high-quality work' at an international firm which offers a 'clear path for career progression', consider applying to Weil, Gotshal & Manges.

If the firm were a fictional character it would be...

Don Corleone – creates a strong family culture and rewards its people very well

The firm

US firm Weil, Gotshal & Manges employs 1,100 lawyers in 20 offices around the world, and is often called upon to advise blue-chip companies on private equity and restructuring cases. The firm is strong across corporate and finance, and its excellence was recognised with nominations in the Finance and Restructuring Team of the Year categories at the *Legal Business* Awards 2016.

The deals

Acted for Hellman & Friedman on the multi-billion euro bank and bond financing of its acquisition of Bain Capital's stake in Securitas Direct; advised Blackstone/GSO on the first CLO platform to be compliant with new US and European risk retention rules; advised banks including Goldman Sachs on the high yield financing of Hellman & Friedman's acquisition of Securitas Direct, which was Europe's largest LBO in 2015; advised Barclays on restructuring two CMBS deals originated by General Healthcare Group totalling £2bn; acted for Equiniti Group on the pension plan elements of its IPO.

The clients

Advent International; Bain Capital; The Carlyle Group; Centerbridge; Deutsche Bank Asset Management; GE Capital; HNA Group; KPMG; Providence Equity; Weetabix.

The star performers

Top-ranking departments according to *The Legal 500* (see legal500.com for more details)
Acquisition finance; Commercial litigation; Commercial property; Corporate restructuring and insolvency; Corporate tax; Derivatives and structured products; Equity capital markets; High yield; Insurance: insolvency and restructuring; International arbitration; M&A: upper mid-market and premium deals, £250m+; Media and entertainment (including media finance); Pensions (non-contentious); Private equity: transactions: Large-cap deal capability; Private funds; Real estate funds; Securitisation; Tax litigation and investigations.

- **Why did you choose this firm over any others?** 'The focus on private equity'; 'I completed a vacation scheme at the firm and was won over by the quality of the work given to trainees and the friendly culture'; 'type of clients'; 'size of office and trainee intake'; 'the remuneration'; 'the retention rates'; 'excellent long-term career prospects'; 'excellent training'; 'high levels of responsibility'; 'particular strength in key areas'

- **Best thing about the firm?** 'Quality of work'; 'top reputation'; 'the size means you get comfortable very quickly'; 'the support from colleagues and staff really helps'; 'there seems to be a clear path for career progression'; lean teams doing high-quality work'; 'the people we work with everyday are amongst the best in the industry'

- **Worst thing about the firm?** 'Cliquishness'; 'inability to adapt to change or listen to employee concerns'; 'poor bonus structure'; 'strange culture'; 'the opaque procedures for trainee seat rotation allocations'; 'no structured trainee social events'; 'the outdated BlackBerrys that we are given'; 'unpredictable hours in transactional teams'

- **Best moment?** 'Direct negotiations with other side'; 'being given the opportunity to work on a deal independently'; 'going to Brussels to file a document'; 'reading about a deal in the press'; 'being singled out by the partner for special praise after completing the verification process for an IPO prospectus'; 'leading a conference call with a client'

- **Worst moment?** 'Being micromanaged by a junior associate with no people skills'; 'a few late nights during the week'; 'working on a closing over a very intense two-week period'; 'single-handedly completing the verification of an entire prospectus over the course of a weekend'; 'late-night proofreading'

A day in the life of...

... **Grace Smith** fourth-seat trainee, Weil, Gotshal & Manges
Departments to date: Corporate, banking, corporate secondment to New York, private funds
University: University of Oxford
Degree: Law

9.00am: I arrive at my desk and review my to-do lists prior to starting my work for the day. I find it particularly useful to have a list of my ongoing tasks so I can keep track of the progress of each of my matters. As a trainee, you can often be involved in a large number of matters at any one time and it is important to be on top of things. I talk to my supervisor about what he has on today and which tasks I can get involved with.

9.30am: Overnight, we received further comments on a private placement memorandum (PPM) we have been working on. I take a first look at the comments and discuss them with my supervisor before inputting them into our master version. We will be sending out a near-final draft this afternoon.

11.45am: I attend a meeting with my team to discuss a business development presentation we are working on. Weil encourages trainees and associates at all levels to get involved with business development. It is important to understand at an early stage the needs of our clients and how to best meet these.

12.30pm: I decide to take advantage of the good weather and head outside with a few of the other trainees to grab an early lunch. A select trainee intake is one of the things that attracted me to Weil. The relatively smaller intake is great from a social perspective and also means that as a trainee you are more

visible within the departments, and within the firm itself.

1.30pm: I attend a training session on funds tax basics, presented by a partner and an associate in the tax team. I find this session very useful as it is vital to have at least a basic understanding of why certain funds are structured in the way that they are, as well as how the laws in this area are changing and how tax structuring will need to adapt to this.

2.30pm: I continue my work on the PPM to ensure that we are in a position to send this out shortly. My supervisor has asked me to help out with a billing task for a large client of the firm. It is important as a trainee to have an awareness of the billing process and what our clients expect to see in terms of accounting for the work undertaken. At 3.00pm the weekly cake trolley stops by the office, so my supervisor and I take a quick break.

4.00pm: On a separate matter, a fund review, I join a call with our client to discuss the response we have received from the fund's counsel. In advance of the call, I review the relevant side letter so I am able to discuss which points have been accepted or included in the revised draft. We decide that it will be best to arrange for a call with the fund's counsel to discuss their approach and highlight the points which are of high importance to our client.

6.00pm: I speak to the partner and the rest of the team about the current status of one of my ongoing matters. We discuss the updates that have occurred in the last week, and what else needs to be done. Following the meeting, I update the steps paper to reflect the status of each task and

> **'A select trainee intake is one of the things that attracted me to Weil.'**

any additional steps to be taken. This is then circulated to the team, and later on to the client.

7.30pm: Before leaving the office, I go through my email inbox from the day and make sure I am up to speed with everything. I file each of my emails with respect to each matter, and flag those emails which require following up. I then join the rest of the team as we head off for our bi-monthly drinks social which is held at Flight Club on this occasion, and shortly descends into a full-blown darts rivalry!

www.weil.com/ukrecruiting

About the firm

Address: 110 Fetter Lane, London EC4A 1AY
Telephone: 020 7903 1042
Website: www.weil.com
Email: graduate.recruitment@weil.com
Facebook: Weil-Gotshal-Manges-UK-Graduates

Managing partner: Michael Francies

Other offices: Beijing, Boston, Budapest, Dallas, Dubai, Frankfurt, Hong Kong, Houston, Miami, Munich, New York, Paris, Prague, Princeton, Providence, Shanghai, Silicon Valley, Warsaw and Washington DC.

Who we are: With approximately 1,100 lawyers in 20 offices across the US, Europe, Asia and the Middle East, Weil operates according to the 'one firm' principle, allowing it to bring the right mix of firm-wide skill and local market presence to deliver co-ordinated legal advice to help its clients achieve their sophisticated goals and objectives.

What we do: Weil provides clients with legal expertise at the highest level across its key practices of private equity, corporate/M&A, funds, banking and finance, structured finance, restructuring and dispute resolution, and has been involved in some of the most significant, high-profile and prestigious mandates across all its legal specialisms.

Facts and figures

Total partners (London): 31
Other fee-earners (London): 100+
Total trainees (London): 24

Trainee places available for 2019: 15
Applications received pa: 1,500
Percentage interviewed: 10% for both vacation schemes and training contracts

First year: £46,000
Second year: £50,000
Newly qualified: £100,000

What we're looking for: Weil is looking for business-minded high achievers with confidence and self-belief. Individuals that will always push themselves to keep developing and improving and who can work effectively in a team. Entry requirements are AAB at A Level (or equivalent), excluding general studies, and a 2(1) at degree level.

What you'll do: Weil offers a comprehensive and sophisticated training programme with direct input from leading partners alongside a tailor-made approach to mentoring, career progression and development for each lawyer. Working in close-knit partner-led teams provides much greater responsibility and early exposure to the firm's global network of clients and contacts.

Perks: Private health cover; permanent health insurance; life assurance; pension (the firm will contribute to the group personal pension plan at the rate of 5% of basic salary); birthday holiday; health screening; 23 days' holiday, with holiday entitlement increasing by one year after each year of service, up to 28 days; £500 annual wellbeing allowance; two annual volunteering days; and an annual eye test with £50 towards glasses.

Sponsorship: Full GDL and LPC fees paid, plus a maintenance grant of £8,000 per annum.

Application process

Apply to: Lisa Powell, graduate recruitment and development manager.
How: Online application via www.weil.com/ukrecruiting.
When: By 31 July 2017 for 2019 training contracts.
What's involved: All applications are reviewed by the graduate recruitment team and a partner. Successful candidates will complete the Watson Glaser critical reasoning test, a video interview and a face-to-face interview with a partner and associate.

Vacation schemes

Spring: 3-13 April 2017 (apply by 13 January 2017).
Summer: 26 June-7 July 2017, 17-28 July 2017 (apply by 13 January 2017).

Weil

White & Case LLP

5 Old Broad Street, London EC2N 1DW

Survey results *(marks out of 100%)*

Satisfied in your job?	78
Firm living up to expectations?	82
High quality of work?	76
Enough client contact?	62
Stress-free?	58
Happy work/life balance?	57
Friendly firm?	84
Great social life?	81
Good vacation scheme?	79
Confident you'll be kept on?	86
Good remuneration?	91
Diverse firm?	85
Good international secondments?	96

 **verdict**

The 'international opportunities' available at White & Case feature heavily throughout the firm's feedback. The 'truly global approach to legal matters' ensures that trainees regularly work on 'large cross-border transactions', and the 'emerging markets focus' earns particular plaudits. The 'guaranteed overseas seat' is very popular, with destinations as varied as Tokyo, Paris and New York offering 'a brilliant opportunity for trainees to enjoy a new culture'. The **Lex 100 Winner** award for international secondments comes as no surprise. Back in London, trainees rave about White & Case's status as 'project finance market leaders', and about the 'high-quality, prestigious work' on offer. Trainee work highlights include 'having a lead role in the closing of a large deal involving 16 aircraft', 'drafting an underwriting agreement from scratch' and 'playing an important part in a huge cross-border deal with a high-profile client and reading about it in the FT'. Respondents report that there is a 'lack of consistency between different departments in terms of the quality of work given to trainees', and though there is a 'diverse range of departments', it is regrettable that 'some of the smaller practice groups take on few trainees'. Trainees lament that the 'long hours' often mean that 'weekends are no longer your own', but having 'one of the best trainee salaries in the City' helps to make up for this and secures a **Lex 100 Winner** spot for salary satisfaction. Recruits have entered into a 'very warm and team-oriented culture' as the firm 'considers its people as key to success of the business', earning a third **Lex 100 Winner** gong for confidence in being kept on. To train at a firm with a 'truly global profile' and a 'particular focus on career progression of junior lawyers', apply to White & Case.

If the firm were a fictional character it would be...

Philip Marlowe (The Big Sleep) – tenacious and a sharp talker, with a big heart

The firm

Global heavyweight White & Case is among the largest law firms in the City, and has 39 offices across the world, the latest being Cairo which opened in June 2016. The firm is a leader in the finance and energy spaces with a longstanding presence in the market, earning an enviable list of clients. It was nominated twice at the *Legal Business* Awards 2016, in the Restructuring and Private Equity Team of the Year categories.

The deals

Acted for the government of Ukraine on its $15bn sovereign Eurobond restructuring; represented CIT Group on the ECA-supported financing of over 50 Airbus aircraft on lease to various airlines; advised Trafigura's oil business Puma Energy on a $1.25bn term loan and revolving credit facility; advised GTECH on a multi-billion dollar covenant-lite issuance to fund its acquisition of International Game Technology; acted for Cabot Credit Management on a €310m offering.

The clients

Aliaxis Group; Barclays Bank; Deutsche Bank; GSO Capital Partners; Goldman Sachs; JPMorgan; Jackson Square Aviation; Qatar Rail; Standard Chartered; Thomas Cook Group; UK Export Finance.

The star performers

Top-ranking departments according to *The Legal 500* (see legal500.com for more details)
Acquisition finance; Asset finance and leasing; Bank lending – investment grade debt and syndicated loans; Debt capital markets; Derivatives and structured products; Emerging markets; Employee share schemes; Employment: employers; High yield; Infrastructure (including PFI and PPP); Islamic finance; Mining and minerals; Oil and gas; Power (including electricity, nuclear and renewables); Rail; Securitisation; Trade finance.

- **Why did you choose this firm over any others?** 'Guaranteed international seat'; 'high quality of work'; 'it is not a network of satellite offices, it is one firm globally'; 'sociable atmosphere'; 'early responsibility'; 'work in emerging markets'; 'strong practice in dispute resolution'; 'the firm had massive potential for growth in the next few years'; the approachability of everyone I met at interviews'

- **Best thing about the firm?** 'High levels of responsibility at an early stage of your career'; 'the people working here'; 'cookies'; 'partners take a keen interest in trainee development'; 'very international'; 'in any given time I can pick up a phone and speak with my colleagues in other parts of the world to consult them on work'; 'decent pay'

- **Worst thing about the firm?** 'The hours get pretty bad'; 'collating signature pages'; 'lack of communication from HR'; 'there is a lack of transparency when it comes to seat rotations'; 'graduate recruitment are not the most responsive bunch'; 'the lack of interactive training'; 'work/life balance is not ideal'; 'the canteen isn't great'

- **Best moment?** 'Being left in charge of communicating with the other side on a smaller matter'; 'helping with a closing and being able to go out for lunch afterwards with the client'; 'trainee induction days were extremely good fun'; 'flying to a meeting in West Africa to attend an interview with a witness'; 'attending very interesting hearings'

- **Worst moment?** 'Moving departments and trying to settle in new environments is always challenging'; 'dealing with printer issues'; 'being told off for very minor things that I would not have known as a first-seat trainee'; 'a particularly stressful deal'; 'some very tedious induction sessions'; 'long deal for asset finance'; 'huge administrative-style tasks'

A day in the life of…

… Amelia Smith fourth-seat trainee, White & Case LLP

Departments to date: Capital markets, litigation, project finance
University: Edinburgh
Degree and class: Middle Eastern Studies; 2(1)

8.45am: I get into the office pretty early to go through any emails that have come through since last night (and eat some breakfast). I am currently on secondment in our Singapore office and many of the transactions are spread across time zones so there is quite a bit of overnight email traffic.

9.15am: Having dealt with any urgent emails needing only a quick response, I check in with the project finance associates on the main deal I am working on, to get a feel for what deadlines are coming up this week and which tasks need to be done today. I get started on the most urgent task first, which involves comparing various precedent master services agreements to determine which we should use as our base document, and whether that base document is missing any important clauses. This agreement will set out how all utilities and services will be sourced and provided to an oil and gas project.

11.00am: A coffee break is needed so I head downstairs with a couple of associates and along the way we discuss the different aspects of the deal we are all working on – this can be a good way to find out a bit more about the context of the deal and to ask questions informally.

1.30pm: After reviewing one of the master services agreements and running through the morning's emails, I head to a nearby food market (one of the benefits of a secondment to Singapore) with another trainee for some lunch.

2.15pm: I get back from lunch and check through my emails, dealing with a few less urgent tasks left over from this morning.

2.30pm: A short but more urgent task comes in so the master services agreements have to wait while I deal with that. The request is from the capital markets team and involves proofreading a short agreement and updating the definitions and cross-references.

3.40pm: Proofreading done, I send a quick chaser email to one of my colleagues in the Jakarta office regarding the hard copy originals of various non-disclosure agreements, which need to be compiled into full sets of originals and sent out to our client.

5.45pm: The master services agreements are all reviewed so I put together an email explaining the most pertinent differences between the agreements, and hand over my mark-ups to the senior associate (making copies for myself and the rest of the team). I then catch up on some time entries from earlier in the week.

6.00pm: A new task comes in which involves preparing a time line setting out the conditions precedent documents for a share purchase agreement – this will help the team see which documents will need to be delivered prior to closing and which should be conditions subsequent.

> **'Many of the transactions are spread across time zones.'**

7.10pm: I do one final check through my emails and file anything which has been dealt with. There is a small, but not urgent, task which involves pulling together a few articles from various legal search engines. I have training tomorrow morning on contract drafting so I get these together before I head home and send them off to the associate who requested them.

7.40pm: I meet up with some trainees from another firm for drinks and dinner, making the most of a relatively quiet week!

www.whitecasetrainee.com

About the firm

Address: 5 Old Broad Street, London EC2N 1DW
Telephone: 020 7532 2899   **Fax:** 020 7532 1001
Website: www.whitecasetrainee.com
Email: londontrainee@whitecase.com
Facebook: WhiteCase   **Twitter:** @WhiteCase

Managing partner: Oliver Brettle

Other offices: Abu Dhabi, Astana, Beijing, Berlin, Boston, Bratislava, Brussels, Doha, Dubai, Düsseldorf, Frankfurt, Geneva, Hamburg, Helsinki, Hong Kong, Istanbul, Jakarta, Johannesburg, Los Angeles, Madrid, Mexico City, Miami, Milan, Moscow, New York, Paris, Prague, Riyadh, São Paulo, Seoul, Silicon Valley, Singapore, Shanghai, Stockholm, Tokyo, Warsaw, Washington DC.

Who we are: White & Case is a global law firm with nearly 2,000 lawyers worldwide. Our network of 38 offices provide the full range of legal services of the highest quality in almost every major commercial centre and emerging market.

What we do: We are proud to represent some of the world's longest established and most respected names alongside many start-up visionaries.

What we're looking for: White & Case is looking to recruit ambitious trainees who have a desire to gain hands-on practical experience from day one. They should have an understanding of international commercial issues and an interest in working on big-ticket, cross-border work. We recruit both law and non-law students and owing to the nature of our work, language skills are of interest.

What you'll do: The training contract consists of four six-month seats, one of which is guaranteed to be spent in one of our overseas offices. Our vacation schemes introduce candidates to the type of work our lawyers are involved in on a day-to-day basis.

Perks: We offer core benefits (including a personal pension plan, private medical insurance and life insurance) and flexible benefits (including cycle to work scheme, season ticket loan and dental insurance).

Sponsorship: Course fees paid for GDL and LPC. Maintenance grant for each full-time law school year.

Facts and figures

Total partners: 95
Other fee-earners: 293
Total trainees: 73

Trainee places available for 2019: 50
Applications received pa: 3,000
Percentage interviewed: 10-15% (video interviewed)

First year salary: £44,000
Second year salary: £48,000
Newly qualified salary: £90,000

Application process

How: Apply online at www.whitecasetrainee.com.
When: By 31 July 2017 for training contracts to commence in September 2019 or March 2020.
What's involved: Please visit our website for more details.

Vacation schemes

Winter: 12-21 December 2016 (apply by 2 November 2016).
Spring: 3-13 April 2017 (apply by 31 January 2017).
Summer: 19-30 June 2017 and 10-21 July 2017
(apply by 31 January 2017).
Open days: 24 November 2016 (apply by 10 November 2016) and 12 January 2017 (apply by 14 December 2016).
First-year two-day insight scheme: 17-18 May 2017
(apply by 31 March 2017).

WHITE & CASE

The Lex 100 survey

Featured firms:
part 2

Arnold & Porter (UK) LLP

Survey results *(marks out of 100%)*

Satisfied in your job?	87
Firm living up to expectations?	87
High quality of work?	87
Enough client contact?	87
Stress-free?	22
Happy work/life balance?	82
Friendly firm?	87
Great social life?	77
Confident you'll be kept on?	82
Good remuneration?	87
Diverse firm?	87

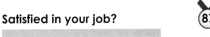

 **verdict**

A 'huge American outfit with a small office' in London, trainees appreciate how Arnold & Porter manages to 'attract headline-making clients and yet retains the feeling of a small City firm'. The fact that there are small teams 'gives trainees a greater opportunity to gain exposure to clients, work and business development programmes'. Furthermore, because there is only ever two trainees it means that 'the firm is able to really focus on our personal development'. Arnold & Porter is named a **Lex 100 Winner** in the job satisfaction category, and also for client contact, remuneration satisfaction and living up to expectations. The 'quality of work' attracts praise. One respondent is happy to be working alongside 'experts in life sciences', while a 'business trip to Zurich' is evidence of Arnold & Porter's international credentials. Another major trainee highlight was 'observing one of the litigation partners represent a trans-woman in a first-tier tribunal hearing after she had been denied her pension at the age of female entitlement, despite living as a woman for over 20 years'. On top of this, the 'committed pro bono practice advises extremely interesting clients'. It is quite telling that the most heavily criticised aspect of life at the firm is 'the coffee', and other fairly minor gripes are the 'nerves on day one' and the 'commute in rush hour'. Commutes are never fun, but you can look forward to 'stunning panoramic views of London' from the office. Recruits believe that they have a 'better work/life balance' than many of their peers as they train at an 'American firm, but without the American hours'. Consider applying to Arnold & Porter as 'everyone is very friendly, and even the busiest partners will make time to sit down with you and discuss your work'.

If the firm were a fictional character it would be...

Neo (The Matrix) – a bit of a nerd, enigmatic and possessing incredible ability

B P Collins LLP

 **verdict**

Trainees at Buckinghamshire's B P Collins comment favourably on the firm's 'location' and 'size', two characteristics which seem conducive to the 'good work/life balance' enjoyed by the current trainee cohort. The firm has 'particular expertise' in a 'range of practice areas', including private client and employment. There is 'lots of client contact' available, as trainees are 'encouraged to come up with solutions of their own' and to 'run client files in some departments'. Recent stand-out moments include 'completion days on corporate transactions', 'unexpectedly having to do my own advocacy for an application at court and succeeding' and 'successfully helping a father secure custody of his children in a case that really seemed like it was against the odds'. The 'lack of clarity regarding post-qualification retention' leads to some 'uncertainty', and though this is the main frustration there are also a couple of complaints that 'the pay could be better'. Still, feedback commends the 'inclusive culture'; there is a 'really great set of trainees' and also 'the fee-earners are very welcoming and have been fantastic to learn from'. Positive comments such as 'when I came in for my assessment day everyone was really friendly' and 'the good feel I got for the firm when I came in for an interview' suggest that B P Collins welcomes candidates throughout the recruitment process and the training contract. To join a 'great bunch of people' and 'get stuck into cases' at a firm which obtains work of a 'really high standard', make a note of B P Collins.

If the firm were a fictional character it would be...

Sulley (Monsters, Inc.) – friendly and caring, but can roar loudly when needed

Survey results *(marks out of 100%)*

Satisfied in your job?	79
Firm living up to expectations?	79
High quality of work?	79
Enough client contact?	77
Stress-free?	52
Happy work/life balance?	82
Friendly firm?	90
Great social life?	62
Good vacation scheme?	77
Confident you'll be kept on?	60
Good remuneration?	47
Diverse firm?	85

BTMK Solicitors LLP

Survey results *(marks out of 100%)*

Satisfied in your job?	75
Firm living up to expectations?	77
High quality of work?	72
Enough client contact?	77
Stress-free?	57
Happy work/life balance?	80
Friendly firm?	90
Great social life?	80
Confident you'll be kept on?	78
Good remuneration?	50
Diverse firm?	80

 **verdict**

Southend's BTMK Solicitors 'has a big presence in the community' and is deemed a 'reputable local firm' in a 'good location'. One satisfied respondent tells us 'I had completed work experience at the firm previously so I knew that I wanted to train here due to the high level of work provided and the people working here'. As the firm 'specialises in a number of different practice areas' there are 'opportunities to gain experience in many different areas of law'. This helps to ensure that 'no two days are the same', and trainees relish 'obtaining a variety of skills by working within a number of departments'. Highlights have included 'meetings with counsel' and 'attending a mediation in London where we secured an excellent settlement for our client'. The workload seems to vary as 'it can be stressful at times' while 'some days and weeks are slower than others'. The firm provides 'early responsibility', and 'having the opportunity to run cases under supervision and being able to successfully conclude those cases' is greatly appreciated by the entire trainee cohort. We are told that 'the training at the firm is very good' as the 'committed supervisors are very approachable and willing to help as they want me to succeed'. That said, there are a couple of gripes about there being 'no formal induction period'. BTMK 'really is a great place to work' owing to its 'relaxed atmosphere' and the 'favourable working hours'. Everyone is 'very welcoming' in this 'friendly environment', and one recruits writes that 'the Christmas meal was very fun'. For a 'steep learning curve and good experience in a variety of fields', consider training at BTMK Solicitors.

If the firm were a fictional character it would be...

Mark Darcy (Bridget Jones's Diary) – has integrity but is also down-to-earth and willing to get into the thick of it

Beale & Company Solicitors LLP

 **verdict**

An 'ambitious' firm whose work has made a 'notable difference' to its clients, Beale & Company Solicitors 'rivals top international firms' in the market in terms of the 'quality and value of work'. The practice is well known for 'dealing with construction and insurance', offering trainees the chance to 'specialise early on in their career'. Beale & Company 'invests in the future' of its trainees and treats them as 'future leaders'. Trainees hit the ground running 'with great responsibility' and 'decent tasks from the outset'. Although it is 'hard work' and trainees must remain 'switched on', there is a perception of 'much more client exposure' than experienced by peers at other firms. The 'small firm' has a 'friendly environment' that is 'relaxed and inclusive', resulting in a 'supportive atmosphere in the office'. It is 'very social', with Friday night outings on offer, and the firm puts an emphasis on a 'good work/life balance'. One trainee suggested the firm could adopt a 'more aggressive' stance to 'market itself' as it can be 'modest about what it can offer', but Beale & Company has 'sensible plans for growth'. Current trainees have gained 'invaluable experience' acting as a 'first point of contact' for a number of 'important clients and attending trials for an international arbitration worth over $100m'. Contributions made by trainees are 'valued' and 'taken on board' by the firm, so trainees develop the confidence they need to 'deal with clients' and as a result become 'much more confident and competent' lawyers. They regularly fundraise and are internationally 'well-connected', especially in the Middle East. Those seeking a 'niche firm' and a 'supportive atmosphere in the office' should check out Beale & Company Solicitors.

If the firm were a fictional character it would be...

Genie (Aladdin) – wise, gives excellent advice and is well connected in the Middle East

Survey results *(marks out of 100%)*

Satisfied in your job?	78
Firm living up to expectations?	82
High quality of work?	79
Enough client contact?	76
Stress-free?	55
Happy work/life balance?	83
Friendly firm?	82
Great social life?	72
Good vacation scheme?	73
Confident you'll be kept on?	65
Good remuneration?	62
Diverse firm?	75

Bevan Brittan LLP

For further information about Bevan Brittan, please visit lex100.com

Survey results *(marks out of 100%)*

Satisfied in your job?	75
Firm living up to expectations?	77
High quality of work?	83
Enough client contact?	74
Stress-free?	61
Happy work/life balance?	71
Friendly firm?	86
Great social life?	68
Good vacation scheme?	83
Confident you'll be kept on?	53
Good remuneration?	53
Diverse firm?	79

 **verdict**

The 'very strong' focus on the public sector at Bevan Brittan makes for 'interesting clients and working opportunities', as trainees work alongside 'leaders in their specialist fields' where the 'reputation and strength' of the clinical negligence department is particularly well known. There is the chance for trainees to get involved in a 'diverse range of work' and gain 'very valuable experience with a great deal of responsibility'. There are 'good quality' files for trainees to get their hands on and as the firm only takes on a 'small group' of trainees each year, this allows you to gain a 'fuller' experience. 'Good exposure' allows trainees to develop and 'learn quickly' with 'more client contact and responsibility', plus the 'no long-hours culture' and 'openness and inclusivity' is much appreciated. Trainees' top moments include 'closing a PFI deal', 'attending inquests and court' and 'tackling a hearing and telephone conference'. One trainee remarked that the firm is a 'good size' so trainees get to know all the people in the office 'very well', and the 'friendliness of people' is highly commended by respondents. Many trainees reported that 'failings' with IT is a real problem. Although trainees are 'thrown in the deep end', Bevan Brittan offers recruits a 'positive supportive environment' and the chance to learn on the job, thus trainees naturally feel 'appreciated and valued'. Bevan Brittan is the perfect choice for those interested in working for a leading public sector firm.

If the firm were a fictional character it would be...

The Hulk (Marvel Comics) – green, expanding and packs a punch

Bindmans LLP

 **verdict**

As a firm highly respected for its 'excellent reputation in civil liberties and human rights work', Bindmans' lawyers routinely take on 'important cases' and tackle 'interesting issues in the legal system and society as a whole'. The trainees work alongside 'some of the leading lawyers in their respective fields', and report experiencing a 'lot of client contact' and being given 'high levels of responsibility'. As an example of the 'interesting work' undertaken, one respondent mentioned 'working on the David Miranda case', while others speak of 'running my own fast-track case' and 'working closely with supervisors on a number of cases'. The combination of a 'good level of one-on-one support from a senior partner' and 'being allowed to develop quite a high degree of responsibility and autonomy in relation to some cases' is representative of the feedback we received. The main concern that trainees raised is the 'job availability post-training contract', as the 'lack of career certainty can leave paralegals and trainees feeling like temporary staff'. On a positive note, the 'friendliness of colleagues' as exemplified by the firm's 'open-door policy' helps to create a welcoming environment for trainees. Though there are times when you may find yourself 'copying documents at 9.30pm' or 'staying past midnight on a Friday to finish urgent bundling', Bindmans' 'standing in the legal sphere on human rights and legal aid' ensures the firm's popularity. To 'learn from and work with a lot of very talented lawyers in a broad spectrum of areas', apply to Bindmans.

Survey results *(marks out of 100%)*

Satisfied in your job?	77
Firm living up to expectations?	73
High quality of work?	79
Enough client contact?	83
Stress-free?	47
Happy work/life balance?	75
Friendly firm?	81
Great social life?	63
Confident you'll be kept on?	19
Good remuneration?	34
Diverse firm?	77

If the firm were a fictional character it would be...

Albus Dumbledore – old and wise, unrivalled in its field and committed to fighting against injustice and evil

Bircham Dyson Bell

Survey results *(marks out of 100%)*

Satisfied in your job?   78

Firm living up to expectations?   82

High quality of work?   82

Enough client contact?   76

Stress-free?   60

Happy work/life balance?   80

Friendly firm?   82

Great social life?   68

Confident you'll be kept on?   51

Good remuneration?   64

Diverse firm?   74

 **verdict**

Trainees applied to Bircham Dyson Bell after being inspired by the 'interesting range of niche practice areas' available, including 'private client, family, charities and public law'. These seats 'aren't available at many City firms', which helps to mark the firm out as a 'well-respected London firm that isn't too corporate'. The 'small departments' also ensure that trainees receive 'great responsibility', 'client contact' and 'the opportunity to get involved in high-quality work'. Stand-out work highlights have included 'attending high-profile board meetings and being able to contribute to them', 'going to a mediation and drafting the settlement at the end' and 'helping complete a very significant transaction which had several novel features'. The workload can be erratic, as respondents report both the 'occasional late night' and 'not having enough to do sometimes', but on the whole you can look forward to 'reasonable working hours'. Furthermore, the 'high quality of training' stems from 'close attention being given to trainee supervision and development', and there is a concerted effort to ensure that the trainee workload is 'not just admin' but also 'more interesting tasks such as drafting'. It is a shame that 'lots of perks have been cut back', including 'social events and CSR'. On the plus side, trainee opportunities include client secondments which are 'very good' and 'a rewarding experience'. Similarly, though the 'poor communal area' is raised, respondents commend the 'very nice and friendly people' for instilling a 'relaxed atmosphere'. To train alongside 'knowledgeable colleagues' at a London firm with niche areas of focus, conduct further research into Bircham Dyson Bell.

If the firm were a fictional character it would be...

The Fairy Godmother (Cinderella) – listens to and advises those in need of its wise counsel

Bird & Bird LLP

 verdict

Renowned for its clear sector focus, especially for its 'expertise in intellectual property', Bird & Bird has an 'excellent reputation' for offering 'expert legal services'. The 'positive ethos' at the heart of the firm creates a 'friendly environment' and 'healthy work/life balance', so much so that Bird & Bird is labelled 'probably the friendliest firm in the UK' and is named a **Lex 100 Winner** in the friendliness, social life and vacation scheme categories. There is a 'willingness to get trainees involved at all levels' through exposure to 'high-quality clients', plus 'everyone is approachable and responsible'. The 'quality of work' available means first-year trainees have already 'worked on high-profile, high-value deals', 'advised on highly sensitive communication projects' and 'drafted a witness statement for a client in an international arbitration worth over $50m'. There are a few grumbles about 'very late nights', seen as a 'rite of passage for litigation'. Other lows included 'flying to Majorca for an hour' and 'getting told off by a Master of the Queen's Bench for appearing before him without a tie'. But trainees recognise that 'lots of responsibility' and the 'opportunity to get to know a client and business well' creates 'better lawyers' and a 'better training experience'. There is the opportunity to get an 'invaluable insight into the client's perspective' with trainees 'involved in the wider team on deals'. The firm has a 'real open-door policy' where colleagues 'take the time to explain complex tasks so trainees can understand and gain further insight'. It has a 'more relaxed culture' and also can offer trainees 'international scope' with 27 offices worldwide. Bird & Bird is an excellent choice for those interested in 'lots of responsibility' and 'developing your skills as a lawyer'.

If the firm were a fictional character it would be...

Tweetie Pie – chilled out and charming, but always thrashes the competition!

Survey results (marks out of 100%)

Satisfied in your job?	84
Firm living up to expectations?	85
High quality of work?	84
Enough client contact?	72
Stress-free?	58
Happy work/life balance?	69
Friendly firm?	94
Great social life?	86
Good vacation scheme?	92
Confident you'll be kept on?	79
Good remuneration?	63
Diverse firm?	86
Good international secondments?	64

Blake Morgan LLP

Survey results *(marks out of 100%)*

Satisfied in your job?	80
Firm living up to expectations?	75
High quality of work?	82
Enough client contact?	79
Stress-free?	59
Happy work/life balance?	78
Friendly firm?	83
Great social life?	64
Good vacation scheme?	69
Confident you'll be kept on?	70
Good remuneration?	60
Diverse firm?	70

 verdict

Blake Morgan offers the best of both worlds as it is 'large enough to provide a breadth and depth of high-quality work', but small enough to provide a 'significant degree of responsibility'. Trainees 'do not get lost in an enormous corporate structure', and have 'great exposure' to a 'broad spectrum of work for high-level and prestigious clients', as well as a 'good level of responsibility and support'. So 'learning is very much on the job' for Blake Morgan's trainees who have 'lots of client contact'. There is the usual trainee gripe of 'photocopying, printing and preparing bundles', and 'more could be done to integrate trainees within the firm across different offices', but the 'collegiate atmosphere' is a plus. The 'relief and excitement of completing a deal', 'assisting the team with a deal involving a famous London landmark' and 'receiving a bonus' are current trainee highlights. Staff are 'very laidback' and 'genuinely willing to help', making training a 'superb experience'. The 'fantastic lawyers' who work here are 'inspiring' and if a trainee is up to the challenge, 'senior colleagues will let you take on as much responsibility as possible'. As a 'smaller firm', there is a 'better work/life balance' and trainees are offered a 'variety of practice areas' to try out. Blake Morgan offers a 'distinct and welcoming culture' and a 'strong regional presence' for ambitious trainees.

If the firm were a fictional character it would be...

The Hogwarts founders – talented people who have come together to create an amazing centre of learning

Blandy & Blandy LLP

 verdict

Blandy & Blandy's trainees consider the firm's Thames Valley base to be a strong point as the firm is 'close to London and often does London-quality work, but without the pressure and hard-nosed attitude of a City firm'. Respondents note that the pay is 'lower than usual for firms in the area', but the 'better work/life balance' helps to mitigate this and earns the firm a **Lex 100 Winner** award, with one also secured for client contact. As a mid-sized outfit, the firm is 'small enough so that you can get to know the people that you work with but big enough to offer quality work in a range of practice areas'. Both of these points are stressed throughout the feedback received from current trainees. The firm provides an 'inclusive culture from the very beginning' as the 'friendly and down-to-earth people' help to generate a 'collegiate atmosphere' at work. Blandy & Blandy also commands a good reputation locally, as one future joiner was 'recommended the firm by a solicitor friend for being excellent at what it does'. There are moments when trainees have 'little to do', with one adding that 'the amount of work is not as high as I expected'. On the whole though, the 'great training' ensures trainees obtain 'hands-on experience' such as 'direct correspondence with corporate clients'. Work highlights have included 'completion of the £100m sale of the Shinfield West site by the University of Reading', 'receiving appreciation from clients for the work I have completed for them' and 'attending the Royal Courts of Justice for a Court of Appeal case'. To represent a 'good range of clients' at a well-respected Reading firm which 'trusts trainees to handle matters', remember Blandy & Blandy.

If the firm were a fictional character it would be...

Aslan (Chronicles of Narnia) – has the power to tackle any opposition, and the ability to care for those in need

Survey results (marks out of 100%)

Satisfied in your job?	77
Firm living up to expectations?	77
High quality of work?	85
Enough client contact?	85
Stress-free?	65
Happy work/life balance?	87
Friendly firm?	90
Great social life?	75
Good vacation scheme?	65
Confident you'll be kept on?	60
Good remuneration?	47
Diverse firm?	82

Boodle Hatfield LLP

Survey results *(marks out of 100%)*

Satisfied in your job?	77
Firm living up to expectations?	83
High quality of work?	82
Enough client contact?	73
Stress-free?	53
Happy work/life balance?	82
Friendly firm?	85
Great social life?	71
Good vacation scheme?	73
Confident you'll be kept on?	55
Good remuneration?	70
Diverse firm?	81

 **verdict**

Boodle Hatfield's 'winning combination of high-quality work and a friendly approach' creates a 'buzzing atmosphere' for trainees. The firm has an 'amazing reputation in property and private client law' and the 'excellent quality of clients is matched by the reputation of the firm'. 'Good hours, more client contact, supervision and better quality work' are part of the deal here. The 'small intake' of trainees is at the heart of the firm and they are valued as 'important members of the team'. Trainees are able to gain 'real responsibility' and are 'really valued, plus encouraged to get involved in as much as possible' including 'lots of social things from yoga to charity events'. The partners, who are 'very generous with their time', 'acknowledge trainees have a life outside of work'. There are 'consistent working hours' which provides newcomers with a good 'work/life balance'. Although there are 'obviously moments where work is less interesting, these moments are not frequent'. So as opposed to 'carrying out simple transaction management', trainees 'draft interesting and varied documents'. Respondents' best moments so far include 'completing an assignment of a lease worth £35m', 'running possession claims' and 'strong appraisal feedback after three months in the litigation seat'. This 'small firm' may have 'no international offices' but Boodle Hatfield will suit trainees who want to receive superb personalised training but still 'go home at a 'normal' time'.

If the firm were a fictional character it would be...

M (James Bond) – demands very high standards, yet takes care of its employees

Boyes Turner

Lex 100 Winner

See categories below
and tables from page 69

 verdict

Selected by trainees for its 'location' and 'reputation', Reading's Boyes Turner is a 'forward-thinking' firm that can boast a 'variety of practice areas' and an 'impressive client list'. Considered a 'good size' by current trainees, Boyes Turner has a 'friendly environment' as 'everyone is approachable'. Trainees therefore have the confidence to embrace the 'high level of responsibility' that the training contract offers. 'Personally delivering talks and training to clients' and 'assisting on the sale of an £80m London development site' are just two examples of 'high-quality work with client exposure'. Respondents complain about the 'low pay', though they do appreciate the 'good work/life balance'. Performing the 'trainee sketch at the Christmas party' split opinion as it was cited as both a best moment and a worst moment to date, though it is a clear example of the firm's commitment to an 'excellent social life' which secures one of three **Lex 100 Winner** accolades. There are sometimes mundane tasks, including 'compiling disclosure lists', but the generally positive levels of client contact make up for this. So too do the 'very good' pro bono opportunities, as there is 'always lots going on' and the firm 'makes a concerted and conscious effort to support both local and national causes'. Recruits place great value on the 'recognition of their efforts by peers', and this is a further sign of the approachable nature of senior colleagues. To receive 'hands-on work' and healthy levels of client contact at a Reading firm with 'broad areas of practice', make a note of Boyes Turner.

If the firm were a fictional character it would be...

Dr Watson (Sherlock Holmes) – a faithful friend, modest yet intelligent with a keen eye for detail

Survey results *(marks out of 100%)*

Satisfied in your job?	77
Firm living up to expectations?	87
High quality of work?	80
Enough client contact?	77
Stress-free?	40
Happy work/life balance?	80
Friendly firm?	90
Great social life?	90
Good vacation scheme?	95
Confident you'll be kept on?	82
Good remuneration?	42
Diverse firm?	80

Brodies LLP

Survey results *(marks out of 100%)*

Satisfied in your job?	73
Firm living up to expectations?	79
High quality of work?	79
Enough client contact?	68
Stress-free?	57
Happy work/life balance?	69
Friendly firm?	82
Great social life?	57
Good vacation scheme?	83
Confident you'll be kept on?	79
Good remuneration?	46
Diverse firm?	78

 **verdict**

As one of the biggest firms in Scotland, Brodies has a 'great reputation' for having 'fantastic clients' and 'interesting work opportunities'. The firm is 'very inclusive' and there is a 'real collegiate atmosphere'. The 'extremely friendly and supportive character of the firm' was appealing to many newcomers. Trainees are not 'thrown in at the deep end' but are given 'quite a lot of support' from supervisors. One trainee described how the 'level of training and support is phenomenal'. Many trainees report hitting the ground running with 'lots of hands-on experience in court drafting' and running their 'own cases a few weeks into the traineeship'. Memorable moments for trainees include 'lots of responsibility in a multi-million pound refinance of a property portfolio', 'negotiating a lease transaction from start to finish for the first time' and 'managing to get an account of expense that was 100% correct'. There is a 'work hard, play hard' ethos at Brodies whereby trainees are sometimes expected to 'work late' to manage a 'stressful volume of work', including some 'dull administration'. Trainees have reported that the 'high expectations' can feel 'unmanageable at times', and inevitably 'long hours' are in store, but recruits are 'trusted' and 'develop the confidence needed to be a lawyer'. Although there are currently no international opportunities, the firm's 'big advantage' is that it offers a 'wide choice of training opportunities' as there is a 'variety of work' trainees can get involved in. For those looking to work at a Scottish firm respected for its 'expertise and reputation', Brodies is a great choice.

If the firm were a fictional character it would be...

Minerva McGonagall (Harry Potter) – a powerful, authoritative Scot

Bryan Cave

Lex100 verdict

US firm Bryan Cave earns plenty of positive feedback for its efforts at making candidates welcome. One trainee 'completed work experience here and loved every second of it', while peers praise the 'very friendly interview process' in which the firm 'focused on applicants being able to impress with actual experience and knowledge'. The 'relatively small London office takes on complex, cross-border work', and a benefit of the small trainee intake is that 'you become an integral part of the team and have the opportunity to make a real difference and get noticed'. Work highlights include 'closing two deals in one week', 'attending an international arbitration hearing in Paris' and 'the opportunity to participate in various pro bono tasks'. The current intake whinges about the 'unstructured approach to training seats' and the fact that there is 'no real chance to influence which seats you take and the duration of them'. What is encouraging is the 'number of departments willing to teach trainees', exposing them to a 'variety of work'. There can be 'periods of being extremely busy and then very quiet', but time is set aside for the 'new conscious push for lawyer and trainee development via training sessions'. There is a 'supportive and close-knit working environment' at Bryan Cave, epitomised by the intake 'working directly under partners' and the fact that 'all fee-earners are very approachable and happy to answer questions'. For a chance to unwind, the 'Friday evening drinks trolley' is a welcome tradition. To experience a 'small-office environment' while working for a 'global firm with some impressive clients', add Bryan Cave to your shortlist.

Survey results *(marks out of 100%)*

Satisfied in your job?	79
Firm living up to expectations?	79
High quality of work?	73
Enough client contact?	69
Stress-free?	45
Happy work/life balance?	45
Friendly firm?	87
Great social life?	55
Confident you'll be kept on?	51
Good remuneration?	57
Diverse firm?	75

If the firm were a fictional character it would be...

Tigger – wonderfully unpredictable, energetic and kind

Capsticks LLP

Survey results *(marks out of 100%)*

Satisfied in your job?	74
Firm living up to expectations?	71
High quality of work?	78
Enough client contact?	69
Stress-free?	58
Happy work/life balance?	72
Friendly firm?	81
Great social life?	57
Good vacation scheme?	81
Confident you'll be kept on?	67
Good remuneration?	61
Diverse firm?	77

 **verdict**

Capsticks Solicitors is a London-based firm that has 'niche specialisms and expertise' in healthcare, ranging from commercial work to charities. There is a 'friendly team environment' and 'everyone knows each other' as there are only 30 fee-earners spread over one floor. The seats rotate every four months and there is a 'lot of responsibility' for trainees as they 'draft case plans and advise clients'. The hours are 'sometimes long' but overall there is a 'good work/life balance' and supervisors are happy for trainees to leave at 5.30pm if 'everything is finished'. Generally the 'supervision is good' but some trainees report feeling 'thrown in at the deep end', and trainees complain about the 'pressure to hit weekly chargeable hours targets'. That said, colleagues are 'supportive and friendly' and the work is 'varied and interesting', as trainees are 'working with lawyers who are the best in their field'. Top moments for trainees include 'drafting advice to a client with minimal supervision', 'winning a case' and 'attending the Royal Courts of Justice on cases'. There is 'great CSR commitment' at the firm, and 'increasing opportunities to get involved with local voluntary work'. Trainees also appreciate the 'free breakfasts' and 'modern offices'. Keep Capsticks in mind if you want a 'great place to work' and a 'high level of responsibility'.

If the firm were a fictional character it would be...

Merida (Brave) – daring, compassionate, loyal and does not fit the stereotype

Cartmell Shepherd

 verdict

Cartmell Shepherd is praised for its 'outstanding local reputation and authenticity' as a long-established firm in Cumbria and Northumberland which 'has been able to modernise while staying true to its roots'. The firm is 'very friendly with an open-door policy', and this is complemented by Cartmell Shepherd's size which is summarised by one person as 'large enough to make me feel part of a big organisation boasting several regional offices but small enough to almost know everyone by name'. The 'varied workload' has produced highlight moments which include 'a defendant increasing their offer of settlement from £17,500 to £33,000 in a personal injury matter based on my quantum report', and 'being asked to get to grips with an agricultural sale file of two lots of farmland and to attend the auction the following week on my own'. The firm is a two-time **Lex 100 Winner** for work quality and living up to expectations. There is 'bags of client contact' which involves 'running meetings by myself and more responsibility for running files'. In this 'modern learning environment' supervisors are 'happy to spend time explaining things if you're not sure what you are doing', so you can expect 'lots of feedback on work, both positive and constructive'. That said, 'you can sometimes get conflicting advice on how to do things from different fee-earners, particularly when your supervisor is on annual leave'. There are retention concerns as 'being kept on is a complete unknown and doesn't really follow any pattern from previous years', but 'the firm says that it likes to keep all trainees' when possible. For 'responsibility from day one' and the chance to 'quickly get to grips' with work, remember Cartmell Shepherd.

Survey results *(marks out of 100%)*

Satisfied in your job?	83
Firm living up to expectations?	88
High quality of work?	88
Enough client contact?	83
Stress-free?	43
Happy work/life balance?	83
Friendly firm?	88
Great social life?	58
Confident you'll be kept on?	63
Good remuneration?	58
Diverse firm?	78

If the firm were a fictional character it would be...

Bob the Builder – has an array of tools at the ready to fix any problem

Coffin Mew LLP

Lex 100 Winner

See categories below
and tables from page 69

Survey results *(marks out of 100%)*

Satisfied in your job?	82
Firm living up to expectations?	84
High quality of work?	80
Enough client contact?	84
Stress-free?	58
Happy work/life balance?	90
Friendly firm?	88
Great social life?	76
Confident you'll be kept on?	84
Good remuneration?	72
Diverse firm?	78

 verdict

Coffin Mew is identified by current trainees as a 'South Coast leader' that is 'financially secure' and 'keen to expand and develop'. This optimism is evident in the firm's 'recognition that we are not just lawyers but the future of the business', and the firm 'actively encourages' trainees to get involved in business development efforts and to network widely. Trainees report being given 'plenty of responsibility'. Examples of 'high-quality work' have included 'being trusted to undertake and manage a demerger of two companies', 'attending a hearing at the bankruptcy court' and 'completing a multi-million pound deal at midnight and drinking champagne with the clients to celebrate'. At Coffin Mew you 'feel valued as a member of the team', and the firm has attained **Lex 100 Winner** medals in the confidence of being kept on and work/life balance categories. As well as having 'lots of input on seat choices', trainees work 'very good hours' and can always call on 'friendly colleagues' for assistance. Trainees do complain about 'having to do lots of admin' and sometimes 'dealing with copious amounts of paper'. There can also be a 'lack of feedback', though this does vary between departments. On a positive note, the 'hands-on training' is enthusiastically praised, and one respondent writes that each trainee is given 'the scope to make the most of your seat'. Illustrating the value placed on trainees at Coffin Mew, the firm's managing partner 'has been involved with our recruitment and training from day one', and 'takes an active interest in who is taken on and how we progress'. To receive 'lots of client contact' at a highly-regarded South Coast firm, get in touch with Coffin Mew.

If the firm were a fictional character it would be...

Mary Poppins – nurturing, but with high expectations

Collyer Bristow LLP

Lex 100 Winner

See categories below
and tables from page 69

 verdict

At Collyer Bristow there is a 'friendly and collegiate atmosphere' where 'everyone knows everyone'. 'Small team sizes' come hand-in-hand with 'high-value and interesting work' for trainees. The 'size of the firm' means that it has a 'smaller trainee intake' and therefore can 'focus on trainees' so new recruits are given 'a lot of responsibility early on'. Trainees report a 'healthy work/life balance' and 'good working hours', and Collyer Bristow is named a **Lex 100 Winner** in this category. There are 'monthly social events' which are great fun but more would be appreciated. Newcomers are 'encouraged to take part in networking events' which is 'good practice' and the firm offers a 'supportive environment' for trainees to grow, with a 'no-blame culture'. Best trainee moments include 'partners expressing appreciation for work', 'advising an off-site client' and 'working on a high-profile trial over a period of several months and seeing it through to fruition'. The 'welcoming atmosphere' creates an environment where partners 'value the opinions' of trainees. There are of course 'stressful busy days' when trainees have been 'too busy to have lunch' or 'spending virtually an entire week of days and nights working on a disclosure bundle'. As a 'small firm', there is a 'lack of international opportunities' but the training contract is the 'start of a learning curve' as 'approachable staff' help make the trainee experience 'exciting and challenging' with newcomers given 'client contact and responsibility'. If you are looking for a 'small firm' and a high level of responsibility, Collyer Bristow could be a great choice.

Survey results *(marks out of 100%)*

Satisfied in your job?	79
Firm living up to expectations?	76
High quality of work?	79
Enough client contact?	79
Stress-free?	46
Happy work/life balance?	87
Friendly firm?	86
Great social life?	76
Confident you'll be kept on?	65
Good remuneration?	59
Diverse firm?	79

If the firm were a fictional character it would be...

Ant Man – small but very capable, and punching above its weight

Cripps LLP

Survey results *(marks out of 100%)*

Satisfied in your job? 74

Firm living up to expectations? 79

High quality of work? 80

Enough client contact? 71

Stress-free? 65

Happy work/life balance? 81

Friendly firm? 89

Great social life? 77

Confident you'll be kept on? 76

Good remuneration? 45

Diverse firm? 84

 **verdict**

A 'strong regional firm with ambitions to grow', the Tunbridge Wells-based Cripps attracts trainees 'as you get to handle London-quality work while living in a nice town'. The 'six-seat rotation' proves incredibly popular as it 'allows for greater variety' and as one trainee tells us, 'if you don't know what you want to qualify in, this is really helpful'. Trainees are given 'genuine responsibility and the opportunity to be involved with high-quality work and clients'. Some of their favourite moments to date include 'dealing with an auction sale from start to finish, including the opportunity to attend the auction and being actively involved with the transaction', 'being tasked with co-ordinating the sale of a pharmacy and seeing it through to completion' and 'having an eight-page report on a complex area of law reviewed and sent on to the client with no alterations'. Trainees complain that their remuneration is 'disappointing' and has been 'frozen for several years'. On a more positive note, the 'healthy work/life balance' is appreciated as trainees are 'not treated like pack horses', and this is complemented by Cripps' staff being 'incredibly warm and accepting' and regularly 'socialising outside of work hours'. Though there can be a 'lack of consistency regarding the quality of supervision' between departments, respondents generally praise the 'opportunity to take ownership of your work'. Clients and senior colleagues have also been forthcoming in their praise for Cripps' trainees, with two highlight moments being 'when a client emailed my supervisor describing me as 'a keeper'' and 'receiving positive feedback from fee-earners at my end-of-seat appraisal'. To train at a 'regional heavyweight' which fosters a 'genuinely friendly and supportive atmosphere', apply to Cripps.

If the firm were a fictional character it would be...

Charmander (Pokémon) – orange, mild-mannered and evolving into something very powerful

Curtis, Mallet-Prevost, Colt & Mosle LLP

 verdict

New Lex 100 entrant Curtis, Mallet-Prevost, Colt & Mosle offers trainees the attractive combination of 'international work' and 'good exposure to clients'. The firm showed great 'flexibility' in recruiting a trainee from their paralegal pool, as this individual 'had given up on becoming a trainee after loads of rejections, but I managed to prove my worth as a paralegal and simply asked the question and got a yes!' Respondents report a 'wide variety of interesting and challenging work', and it is felt that the 'small number of trainees' leads to an 'increased level of responsibility and trust placed in you'. The 'litigation experience' is excellent, while on the non-contentious side one person's highlight was 'celebrating the completion of a complex loan agreement with opposing counsel at a champagne bar!' The levels of communication have been criticised as trainees cite a 'lack of feedback' during the training contract. Though there is 'generally a good work/life balance', we hear that there are instances of 'working a number of very late nights during the week and working on the weekend'. The 'opportunity to go to New York' was of course a big draw for trainees, as second-year trainees traditionally head to the firm's headquarters in the summer months. One respondent identifies 'the people' as the best thing about the firm, and employees find time to unwind away from the office with 'five-a-side football on a Monday'. To join a small team in the City without compromising on large international work, head to Curtis, Mallet-Prevost, Colt & Mosle.

If the firm were a fictional character it would be...

Hermione Granger – very smart, works hard and has its heart in the right place

Survey results (marks out of 100%)

Satisfied in your job?	67
Firm living up to expectations?	60
High quality of work?	67
Enough client contact?	77
Stress-free?	57
Happy work/life balance?	60
Friendly firm?	74
Great social life?	50
Confident you'll be kept on?	70
Good remuneration?	67
Diverse firm?	64
Good international secondments?	67

DAC Beachcroft LLP

Survey results *(marks out of 100%)*

Satisfied in your job?	75
Firm living up to expectations?	75
High quality of work?	79
Enough client contact?	67
Stress-free?	58
Happy work/life balance?	71
Friendly firm?	89
Great social life?	67
Good vacation scheme?	79
Confident you'll be kept on?	78
Good remuneration?	63
Diverse firm?	78
Good international secondments?	49

 **verdict**

The 'excellent standard of work' available at DAC Beachcroft impresses the current cohort of trainees. As a firm with 'national and international capabilities', DAC Beachcroft represents a 'diverse client base' and there is therefore scope to handle a 'variety' of different cases. This broad range of experiences has so far included 'attending a hearing at the Supreme Court for a matter I worked on', 'drafting a manufacturing/production and sale agreement for a client's new product' and 'running two big cases by myself while my supervisor was on paternity leave'. One criticism is that there is a perceived divide between the insurance and commercial departments, with the former being the firm's traditional strength. In the words of one respondent, 'as with any firm specialised in a certain sector, this specialism frequently becomes the focus of senior management'. It is a healthy sign that a few respondents mentioned previously being paralegals at the firm. One such trainee tells us 'I was impressed by the support and encouragement I received' as a paralegal, while another recounts that the experience 'reaffirmed my ambition to train with the firm'. While the salary is said to be 'quite low', trainees report a 'decent work/life balance'. Moreover, feedback champions the 'supportive environment' as exemplified by 'friendly' colleagues who 'support your development as much as they possibly can'. It is certainly appreciated that 'most partners are approachable and willing to discuss work and career progression'. To join a firm where trainees are given 'a lot of responsibility and the opportunity to express ourselves', add DAC Beachcroft to your list.

If the firm were a fictional character it would be...

Daenerys Targaryen (A Game of Thrones) – respected, and expanding in influence and reach

DMH Stallard LLP

 **verdict**

With a 'strong reputation in the South East', DMH Stallard makes a 'good impression' on its new recruits as a 'friendly firm'. It is the 'ideal place to train' as the firm is 'big enough to have good clients and complex work but also small enough to give trainees a high level of responsibility and client contact'. Trainees get 'good exposure to a wide range of matters within the legal sector they practise in' and are encouraged to take leading roles on deals. The 'training received from the partners' and 'friendly atmosphere' are praised by trainees as the best things about the firm. There is a 'personal approach' to training and the firm has an 'open culture'. Trainees are also given the 'opportunity to experience work in both Brighton and Crawley as well as the City during the training contract'. But there is 'limited seat choice', and some grumble about feeling 'steered towards becoming property or corporate solicitors'. Trainees also complain about the 'salary and photocopying'. However, highlight moments include one trainee being 'nominated "star of the quarter" by a senior partner for work on a difficult sale of a business to a FTSE 100 company', 'attending a 16-hour mediation and assisting in drafting the settlement agreement' and 'completing a corporate acquisition for two shareholders'. If you want to work at a firm with a 'relaxed environment' but which has a 'clear vision for its future', take a closer look at DHM Stallard.

If the firm were a fictional character it would be...

Gandalf (Lord of the Rings) – wise, a bit eccentric but can always be counted on

Survey results *(marks out of 100%)*

Satisfied in your job?	72
Firm living up to expectations?	77
High quality of work?	82
Enough client contact?	84
Stress-free?	45
Happy work/life balance?	84
Friendly firm?	85
Great social life?	50
Good vacation scheme?	67
Confident you'll be kept on?	67
Good remuneration?	37
Diverse firm?	79

Devonshires Solicitors LLP

Survey results *(marks out of 100%)*

Satisfied in your job? 71

Firm living up to expectations? 68

High quality of work? 78

Enough client contact? 68

Stress-free? 64

Happy work/life balance? 69

Friendly firm? 87

Great social life? (84)

Confident you'll be kept on? 48

Good remuneration? 32

Diverse firm? 73

 **verdict**

Devonshires Solicitors is a 'friendly' City firm that provides new recruits with a 'good variety of work'. One trainee 'worked here as a paralegal for a number of years prior to applying for my training contract' and was impressed by the 'environment, the people and the interesting departments'. Trainees are 'not consistently overworked and usually have a relatively good work/life balance' as the 'hours are sociable', leading to a **Lex 100 Winner** mention in the social life category. The firm is 'medium-sized', so everyone 'gets to know everyone'. The 'quality of work' is good, as highlights for trainees include 'being heavily involved in a £10m adjudication that lasted two months', 'experiencing contentious work', 'being part of an extremely high-level transaction' and 'going to a completion meeting with a variety of interesting parties'. One newcomer reported 'feeling out of my depth at the start of every seat', but the fact that 'everyone is lovely' suggests that colleagues are approachable and always keen to help out. Another recruit commented how the 'training given to trainees can be inconsistent between departments, and the partners aren't always the best at explaining what they want from you', but 'that moment in each seat when it all clicks together and you know what you're doing' is a real joy. Respondents believe that in CSR the firm 'consistently punches above its weight and is doing a fantastic job', and one trainee has spent time assisting local schoolchildren on their maths work. For 'lots of hands-on experience' at a small City firm renowned for its friendliness, head to Devonshires Solicitors.

If the firm were a fictional character it would be...

Alyosha (The Brothers Karamazov) – optimistic and keen to grow and improve

Dorsey & Whitney

Lex100 verdict

Dorsey & Whitney is a US law firm with a 'small office' in London where trainees 'fit in well'. The firm offers a 'training-focused' programme because trainees are 'one in four rather than one in 100' here. The 'excellent quality of training' is 'extremely hands-on' and the work/life balance is 'great, especially for an American law firm'. Trainees are given 'varied work, a good level of client exposure and real responsibility', with the tasks available to trainees deemed both 'substantial and high-quality'. There is an 'open-door policy' and an 'opportunity to work directly for partners'. Everyone is 'approachable and friendly' and the 'atmosphere is great'. There is 'no pressure to hang around and look busy' and there are 'no problems when asking for help because everyone is happy to provide it'. Trainee highlights include 'being involved in a high-profile deal', 'drafting the full set of closing documents' and 'getting recognition from all the partners for my hard work'. Several trainees grumble about the lifts because they are 'always so busy'. It is also noted that there are 'not enough options for training seats'. That said, there are 'plenty of pro bono opportunities' on offer which are 'very rewarding'. If you are looking for a 'friendly and approachable' US firm, keep Dorsey & Whitney in mind.

Survey results *(marks out of 100%)*

Satisfied in your job?	75
Firm living up to expectations?	75
High quality of work?	72
Enough client contact?	72
Stress-free?	52
Happy work/life balance?	77
Friendly firm?	87
Great social life?	57
Confident you'll be kept on?	82
Good remuneration?	65
Diverse firm?	87

If the firm were a fictional character it would be...

Leonard Hofstadter (The Big Bang Theory) – extremely smart and switched-on, but knows the importance of a life outside of work

Druces LLP

Survey results *(marks out of 100%)*

Satisfied in your job?	61
Firm living up to expectations?	63
High quality of work?	78
Enough client contact?	58
Stress-free?	51
Happy work/life balance?	76
Friendly firm?	63
Great social life?	69
Good vacation scheme?	46
Confident you'll be kept on?	46
Good remuneration?	38
Diverse firm?	68

 verdict

A 'well-established City firm with a great history', Druces is an 'ambitious firm' that has 'recently expanded' and is 'growing across all departments'. A new *Lex 100 entrant*, the firm is acclaimed by trainees for its 'excellent reputation for commercial property work', and there are also opportunities to 'gain in-depth experience in specialist areas such as employment and intellectual property'. One recruit 'wanted to work for a City firm but have a life outside work', and another writes that there is 'definitely no face-time culture here', though one respondent moans that the 'salary could be more in line with other City firms'. It is considered an advantage that 'there isn't the competitiveness that comes with a big trainee intake', and having 'one trainee per department means you get a lot of support and high-quality work'. Stand-out work highlights have included 'attending cross examination at a High Court trial', 'being trusted to run small matters' and 'giving a presentation to the department which received positive feedback'. The small size of the firm means that 'you really get the chance to get to know people', and this is complemented by the 'open-plan offices and friendly partners'. One minor complaint is that 'more socials need to be organised'. The London firm 'boasts a very impressive list' of 'high-profile clients', and there is 'exposure to a wide variety of work' as trainees are given access to 'several specialisms in each department'. The current cohort reports being 'involved in real matters from start to finish throughout the training contract'. For 'hands-on experience' at a growing City firm, apply to Druces.

If the firm were a fictional character it would be...

Pac-Man – old school, but still hungry

EMW Law LLP

Lex 100 Winner

See categories below
and tables from page 69

 verdict

EMW Law has an 'excellent reputation for its training'. The firm 'markets itself as dynamic and different' and provides trainees with a 'good standard of work and client exposure'. It is 'small enough to offer hands-on training yet large enough to have access to international clients and an excellent quality of work', and is named a **Lex 100 Winner** in the client contact and work quality categories. There are two offices, one in the City and one in Milton Keynes. The working hours are 'reasonable, predictable and not excessive' so recruits are 'not disappointed' and can enjoy a 'great work/life balance'. Trainees 'appear to be given lots of responsibility' as they are in control of running their 'own files and get involved in a lot of high-profile work'. Recruits are never 'made to feel like junior members of staff' and 'everyone is approachable and friendly on all levels'. Newcomers are 'lucky to interact and work with partners closely on a daily basis, which allows trainees to develop quickly and effectively'. There is a 'work hard, play hard attitude' and overall EMW Law is a 'lovely place to work' where recruits are 'rarely expected to carry out admin tasks'. The firm has a 'strong client base', and trainee highlights include 'running a case for one of the firm's biggest international clients' and 'closing a corporate deal'. Training contracts are inevitably 'very different from university' and one trainee comments on the culture shock. Although 'the level of responsibility is daunting', it is the 'best way to learn' as one trainee reports running their own files for big clients four months into the training contract. If you are looking for a firm with an 'inclusive and friendly atmosphere', add EMW Law to the list.

If the firm were a fictional character it would be...

Mighty Mouse – relatively small but represents big clients on important work

Survey results *(marks out of 100%)*

Satisfied in your job? 85

Firm living up to expectations? 83

High quality of work? (90)

Enough client contact? (87)

Stress-free? 59

Happy work/life balance? 77

Friendly firm? 90

Great social life? 79

Good vacation scheme? 57

Confident you'll be kept on? 59

Good remuneration? 60

Diverse firm? 86

Eversheds LLP

Lex 100 Winner

See categories below and tables from page 69

Survey results *(marks out of 100%)*

Satisfied in your job? 85

Firm living up to expectations? 87

High quality of work? 85

Enough client contact? 76

Stress-free? 55

Happy work/life balance? 69

Friendly firm? 95

Great social life? 81

Good vacation scheme? 87

Confident you'll be kept on? 83

Good remuneration? 76

Diverse firm? 91

Good international secondments? 87

 **verdict**

Eversheds is 'friendly and forthcoming' while maintaining its reputation as a 'leading national and international' law firm. There is a 'focus on innovation' and a constant 'awareness to improve and refresh'. The 'employees are valued as people' and they are 'not expected to be in the office at all times'. The firm has a 'realistic attitude to life as a trainee'; 'although late nights and long hours are unavoidable for big projects, they are not a daily fact of life'. Trainees report being 'treated well' and describe it as 'generally a great place to work', so it comes as no surprise to see the firm secure five **Lex 100 Winner** awards, including in the job satisfaction and friendliness categories. Also, newcomers are 'trusted with responsibility', 'rewarded with client contact' and receive 'interesting work'. There is a 'friendly, supportive culture' as 'everyone makes time to support and advise' trainees, who are always 'encouraged to ask questions'. The firm has a 'positive attitude towards inclusiveness at all levels from partners to trainees and other members of staff'. New recruits report 'there is a lack of hierarchy' and 'a flat structure is encouraged by the brilliant partners'. Trainees are 'rewarded with client contact' and their 'input is valued by senior staff'. There are 'unpredictable hours' and the 'workload can be quite high at times', but respondents tell us they 'never feel overwhelmed'. Trainees reveal they are given a 'good level of responsibility', and top trainee moments include 'receiving awards recognising good work', 'drafting a closure deed for a multi-million pound pension scheme' and 'sealing an international deal'. If you are looking for a 'down-to-earth' firm with international capabilities, take a closer look at Eversheds.

If the firm were a fictional character it would be...

Alicia Florrick (The Good Wife) – has excellent legal knowledge, is well-respected by peers and is ready to fight when required

FBC Manby Bowdler LLP

Lex 100 Winner

See categories below and tables from page 69

 verdict

New Lex 100 entrant FBC Manby Bowdler attracts many candidates due to its 'good reputation in the West Midlands and Shropshire'. Being part of a 'mid-sized firm' is considered advantageous as there are a 'number of different areas of law' available, and an accompanying 'lack of the presenteeism culture which seems to exist at bigger firms'. The firm runs a 'diverse training contract', and its 'specialist agricultural team' is noted for its 'high rating in *The Legal 500*'. The 'very positive training contract experience' reported by one respondent is backed up by fellow trainees who speak of a 'strong emphasis on professional development' and the 'good support network in place so that you are not left in an uncomfortable position where you feel out of your depth'. Examples of 'great client contact and responsibility' include 'going to the Royal Courts of Justice on an important case', 'being given responsibility to run smaller files under supervision of partner' and 'settling at a mediation where the client was delighted with the outcome'. The firm is a **Lex 100 Winner** in the client contact category. It is felt that the 'induction process for new employees could be improved' as the firm 'relies on a lot of complicated procedures and software which are difficult to navigate at first'. Though 'the salary is lower than at other regional firms of a similar size', praise is reserved for the 'great work/life balance' and trainees also enjoy the 'social events organised by the firm'. The 'strong support network of supervisors' is boosted by the 'open-door policy among partners and senior staff', resulting in an 'inclusive environment'. To train at a well-regarded West Midlands player which handles 'interesting work' and where 'everyone supports one another', consider FBC Manby Bowdler.

Survey results *(marks out of 100%)*

Satisfied in your job? 82

Firm living up to expectations? 78

High quality of work? 84

Enough client contact? 86

Stress-free? 50

Happy work/life balance? 82

Friendly firm? 80

Great social life? 68

Confident you'll be kept on? 72

Good remuneration? 38

Diverse firm? 76

If the firm were a fictional character it would be...

The Pink Panther – cool, calm and collected – and is able to improvise when the situation warrants it

Fisher Meredith LLP

Survey results *(marks out of 100%)*

Satisfied in your job? 54

Firm living up to expectations? 42

High quality of work? 57

Enough client contact? 67

Stress-free? 57

Happy work/life balance? 72

Friendly firm? 47

Great social life? 34

Confident you'll be kept on? 24

Good remuneration? 32

Diverse firm? 64

 **verdict**

Holborn-based Fisher Meredith is a *new Lex 100 entrant* and attracted its current intake because of the 'firm ethos' and the 'areas of law it specialises in'. Its 'reputation for legal aid and human rights work' were frequently cited in the feedback. The 'exposure to clients is much higher than average', and respondents speak of 'meeting wonderful clients', with one describing how 'my supervisor let me deliver some good news to a client recently and the client cried with happiness. Her son sent me a thank you card'. This is symptomatic of the life-changing nature of some of the work that Fisher Meredith carries out. But one trainee laments how 'the strong legal aid background of the firm is no longer welcome in the markets we work in; it's a situation that is undermining our reputation'. Being a 'small firm' allows for a certain level of flexibility, and one recruit tells us 'I interviewed in July and they offered me a training contract starting two months later, which was very attractive as I had done my LPC and was ready to go'. Things can be 'chaotic', and the training experience 'greatly varies from department to department' as 'in some you are given a lot of responsibility and have a lot of face-face contact with clients, while in others you have much less'. Respondents praise the 'supportive group of trainees and NQs' in the office, as well as the 'approachable pastoral carers'. The firm impresses due to the 'rankings of senior solicitors at the firm', and the fact that there are 'lots of women in senior positions'. To train at a highly-regarded London firm with a focus on human rights cases that ensures 'you will be given the opportunity to take on high-level work', remember Fisher Meredith.

If the firm were a fictional character it would be...

Mushu (Mulan) – small in size but is smart and caring

Fladgate LLP

 **verdict**

Trainees chose Fladgate for its 'entrepreneurial client base' and 'strong property and corporate departments'. There are 'not terrible hours' and 'no one expects' trainees to 'cancel plans unless it is absolutely necessary' so a 'good work/life balance' is possible. The 'small intake' of new recruits means trainees are 'given a lot of responsibility, especially in the property department'. Moreover, trainees are 'always given the opportunity to take on as much responsibility as they can handle'. One trainee reports being the 'main point of contact for clients' and being tasked with running their own files. The 'structured training' means recruits can get their hands on 'very high-quality work', and trainees love the 'collegiate atmosphere and friendly nature of all the staff, including partners'. Also, the firm offers 'training sessions' which give the trainees the 'opportunity to meet everyone from around the firm'. There are 'limited seat choices' and a 'limited opportunity for qualifying into the more niche departments'. Another issue is that trainees occasionally face 'boring tasks such as indexing, bundling and bible production' which makes trainees 'hungry for more challenging work'. Best moments include 'completing the sale of a property on a file run almost entirely by myself', 'assisting with the completion of the high-profile multi-million pound acquisition of a chain of convenience stores for a client' and 'drafting the documents on a large corporate restructure with a partner'. The 'expanding firm' has 'clear goals and has planned sensibly to achieve them'. If you want to work with 'talented people' and earn 'good remuneration', look no further than Fladgate.

Survey results *(marks out of 100%)*

Satisfied in your job? — 84

Firm living up to expectations? — 85

High quality of work? — 75

Enough client contact? — 72

Stress-free? — 59

Happy work/life balance? — 82

Friendly firm? — 84

Great social life? — 64

Confident you'll be kept on? — 74

Good remuneration? — 80

Diverse firm? — 80

If the firm were a fictional character it would be...

Bilbo Baggins (Lord of the Rings) – smaller than many, but should not be underestimated as it has achieved great things

Forbes Solicitors

Lex 100 Winner

LEX 100 WINNER

See categories below
and tables from page 69

Survey results *(marks out of 100%)*

Satisfied in your job? 83

Firm living up to expectations? 86

High quality of work? (89)

Enough client contact? (94)

Stress-free? (66)

Happy work/life balance? 77

Friendly firm? 90

Great social life? (83)

Good vacation scheme? 80

Confident you'll be kept on? (84)

Good remuneration? 49

Diverse firm? (89)

 **verdict**

Forbes Solicitors has a 'wide variety of departments' which means the 'training contract is diverse'. This is a great advantage and an 'important factor' for aspiring lawyers who are 'unsure' of which area they would like to 'specialise in and pursue long-term'. The firm is 'large enough to provide a good range of work' but small enough to be able to 'cater to individual trainee needs'. There is a good job satisfaction at the firm as trainees report a 'high retention rate', and the firm is duly named a **Lex 100 Winner** in the confidence in being kept on category, along with scooping five other gongs. The 'supportive staff' create a 'friendly environment' where trainees are 'treated as individuals rather than as cogs in the machine'. Another positive is the firm's 'work environment and culture', as it is 'highly competitive' and there is 'quality work' available to trainees. Calling all 'keen sportsmen and women', the firm offers 'opportunities to play football and cricket, both socially and as a networking tool'. Highlights for trainees include 'winning a possession hearing for a 70-year-old widow', 'receiving excellent client feedback which makes the job feel worthwhile' and 'taking part in commercial team-building events' which are 'great fun!' 'First day nerves' are inevitable for newcomers and trainees grumble that the 'first year salary' isn't much of an incentive and 'makes it difficult to live independently'. That said, it 'significantly improves in the second year which makes it seem worth biting the bullet'. Trainees feel 'very rewarded' by the 'professional, approachable and friendly atmosphere' the firm has to offer. If you are looking for a 'forward-thinking' firm across the North of England, keep Forbes Solicitors in mind.

If the firm were a fictional character it would be...

DI Jack Frost (A Touch of Frost) – very professional, diligent in its investigations, and with a dose of dry humour

Forsters LLP

 **verdict**

Trainees found Forsters' 'six-seat training contract' and 'West End location' 'big attractions' which 'separated it from other firms'. Forsters offers 'comprehensive training in all areas', and trainees get 'a lot of responsibility' such as 'going to client meetings' and 'running files under close supervision'. One trainee reports the 'training so far has been fairly informal, on-the-job style learning with a number of in-house seminars on legal know-how'. The 'positive training atmosphere' is sustained by the 'excellent standard of supervision'. It is an 'open and non-hierarchal working environment', aided by the 'cleverly laid out open-plan office', and recruits can 'happily ask questions or advice from partners'. Trainees are 'strongly encouraged to use support services and are rarely stuck with tedious tasks such as administration and photocopying'. Although the 'work could be more varied', there are no 'crazy hours' and trainees are 'treated like human beings'. There is 'no face-time culture' which means a 'good work/life balance', and seven **Lex 100 Winner** medals are proof of trainees' contentment. One trainee suggested the 'downside of having a four month seat meant you have to move seats just as you are getting settled in' but inevitably 'there are upsides too'. Best moments for trainees so far include 'working on a high-profile divorce case', 'accompanying a partner and solicitor on a business trip to Singapore' and a supervisor telling one trainee he would like to see them 'qualify into his department'. If you are looking for a 'supportive environment' and a 'good work/life balance' look no further than Forsters.

Survey results (marks out of 100%)

Satisfied in your job?	87
Firm living up to expectations?	89
High quality of work?	85
Enough client contact?	80
Stress-free?	65
Happy work/life balance?	90
Friendly firm?	95
Great social life?	84
Good vacation scheme?	99
Confident you'll be kept on?	80
Good remuneration?	83
Diverse firm?	91

If the firm were a fictional character it would be...

Kevin McAllister (Home Alone) – shows initiative, is highly effective and has a lot of fun

Fox Williams LLP

Survey results *(marks out of 100%)*

Satisfied in your job?	78
Firm living up to expectations?	78
High quality of work?	76
Enough client contact?	68
Stress-free?	62
Happy work/life balance?	62
Friendly firm?	82
Great social life?	66
Good vacation scheme?	76
Confident you'll be kept on?	50
Good remuneration?	70
Diverse firm?	74

 **verdict**

Fox Williams clearly makes a good first impression; one trainee says 'I was extremely impressed by the firm and the people I met during the vacation scheme', while another tells us that 'on my first assessment day I was really impressed with how friendly and welcoming everyone was'. The medium-sized firm's 'excellent lawyers' are 'individuals with genuine expertise', and the 'approachable partners' ensure that trainees 'feel supported'. Respondents speak keenly about carrying out 'quality work' on behalf of 'good clients'. Commenting on a Fox Williams niche, one new recruit says 'I was particularly interested in the firm's focus on fashion law'. Work highlights include a 'long but successful mediation with a very interesting client', 'winning at court', 'seeing M&A deals through from beginning to end' and a 'trial at the Privy Council'. Trainees are 'generally concerned about retention' as 'NQ opportunities seem quite limited', but there is a 'culture of friendliness' and a 'relaxed atmosphere' at work, despite the 'training contract being hands-on' and full of 'academic rigour'. The 'hours are much better than at the bigger firms', and feedback references the 'good work/life balance'. It is a sign of the trust the firm places in its trainees that you will 'attend client meetings on your own'. There is sometimes 'uncertainty around seat allocation', but opportunities abound as besides fee-earning work, one respondent informs us that 'we do a lot of charity fundraising'. For a 'great deal of responsibility at an early stage' alongside 'people who are really great to work with and for', add Fox Williams to your shortlist.

If the firm were a fictional character it would be...

Veronica Mars – relatively small and young, but punches well above its weight

Freeths

 verdict

A 'friendly and forward-thinking firm', Freeths has an 'entrepreneurial approach, willingness to innovate and a desire to adopt a fresh approach to everything'. The firm also takes a 'different approach to recruitment and utilises its legal assistant programme as the primary source of trainees'. This 'alternative route' allows the firm to 'look at a graduate's work ethic during the six-month legal assistant role' and assess whether graduates are a 'good fit'. Top trainee moments include a 'trip on a private jet to Jersey to complete a reverse takeover' and 'completing a major deal'. Trainees 'feel trusted', 'get stuck into legal work at an early stage' and receive 'fantastic training from partners'. The 'training is hands-on' and supervisors tend to make 'a real effort to give you tasks that help you learn' with plenty of 'client contact and responsibility', and the firm is named a **Lex 100 Winner** for work quality. There is a 'great emphasis on real world training and developing helpful lawyers', and trainees report feeling 'looked after'. The firm 'values each member of staff as an important member of the team'. The chairman 'knows the name of every trainee' and trainees get to know 'partners on a personal level'. This 'social firm' also recognises the importance of a healthy work/life balance' so it sets 'realistic, achievable goals' and is 'excellent at organising events' which give trainees 'good exposure to wider social networks', all of which secures a **Lex 100 Winner** award for social life. Trainees grumble about some 'extremely late nights' or 'all-nighters' which can be 'challenging', though the 'interesting choice of seats' was particularly appealing to current trainees. Those looking for a 'high standard of work', 'good pay' and a firm that is a 'privilege to work for' may wish to consider Freeths.

If the firm were a fictional character it would be...

Chewbacca (Star Wars) – friendly and loyal, but a force to be reckoned with

Survey results (marks out of 100%)

Satisfied in your job? 84

Firm living up to expectations? 86

High quality of work? (87)

Enough client contact? 82

Stress-free? 61

Happy work/life balance? 67

Friendly firm? 92

Great social life? (88)

Good vacation scheme? 60

Confident you'll be kept on? 82

Good remuneration? 75

Diverse firm? 86

Freshfields Bruckhaus Deringer LLP

Lex 100 Winner

See categories below
and tables from page 69

Survey results *(marks out of 100%)*

Satisfied in your job? 72

Firm living up to expectations? 78

High quality of work? 72

Enough client contact? 59

Stress-free? 59

Happy work/life balance? 47

Friendly firm? 82

Great social life? 72

Good vacation scheme? 84

Confident you'll be kept on? 79

Good remuneration? 70

Diverse firm? 78

Good international secondments? (77)

 **verdict**

'Market-leading' Magic Circle firm Freshfields Bruckhaus Deringer is a favourite because of its 'international reputation' and 'corporate focus' with a 'track record for advising on important deals and disputes all over the world'. Many trainees' 'absolute deciding factor' is the 'flexible three-month seat rotation' which gives them an insight into a 'range of departments' across eight seats. Freshfields' training contracts are enviable because the 'elite firm' offers 'good pay', 'quality training' and a 'great calibre of clients'. Many trainees have secured their places here on the back of their 'fun vacation schemes'. This 'powerhouse' offers 'intense training', a 'collegiate culture' and 'high-profile deals'. The 'varied work' trainees can experience often 'appears in headlines' of national newspapers. Top trainee moments include 'travelling to Milan for deal negotiations', 'competition law training in Brussels' and 'closing a multi-billion deal in a short timeframe'. The 'global dimensions' of the firm allow trainees to complete international secondments in New York, Paris and Dubai, and this earns a **Lex 100 Winner** medal. The 'large intake', 'good dinners and team events' help make trainees 'feel welcomed as part of the team'. Inevitably there are 'hectic, unpredictable hours' as a few trainees reported working 'double all-nighters and not sleeping for 72 hours', plus others note the 'administrative nature of some work'. But many trainees love working alongside the 'brightest people' who are 'fiercely intelligent high-achievers' and who offer the 'best instructions'. Ambitious trainees should look no further than the 'inclusive and diverse' Freshfields because its 'reputation and quality of work is unrivalled'.

If the firm were a fictional character it would be...

Yoda (Star Wars) – a powerful master that has trained some of the best practitioners around

Gateley Plc

 verdict

Current trainees like Gateley because of its 'friendly working environment' and the 'strong social aspect' to life at the firm, two of the three characteristics which have led to **Lex 100 Winner** triumphs. A few trainees applied for the training contract after 'really enjoying the vacation scheme'. Senior staff are 'approachable', 'recognise potential' and value employees as 'individuals', and everyone is 'so friendly and always willing to help'. Trainees are 'exposed to big clients, high-value transactions and a variety of departments'. Top moments include a 'secondment at a Premier League Football club', 'completing a £30m deal with the corporate recovery team in the space of four weeks' and 'running a share buyback transaction from start to finish'. Although trainees report the job is 'sometimes stressful when you feel out of your depth', the 'varied high-level work' on offer means trainees don't feel like 'burdensome students' but a 'useful team member'. At the heart of the training contract, there is a lot of 'client interaction' and 'hands-on training', and from the outset trainees are given a 'good level of responsibility'. This is both a 'positive and a negative', though it creates the 'best environment to develop key legal and soft skills'. A few drawbacks trainees mentioned were 'not being asked for seat preferences in the first year', a 'lack of international opportunities' despite the office in Dubai, and 'no canteen to socialise with colleagues'. The 'open-plan layout is great because it lends itself to an inclusive culture' so trainees 'can pick up subtler elements of the job such as observing partners communicate with their clients on a day-to-day basis'. Those looking for a 'social and dynamic work culture' should consider Gateley.

If the firm were a fictional character it would be...

Deadpool – charismatic, entertaining and not afraid to break the mould

Survey results *(marks out of 100%)*

Satisfied in your job?	83
Firm living up to expectations?	85
High quality of work?	88
Enough client contact?	82
Stress-free?	53
Happy work/life balance?	75
Friendly firm?	95
Great social life?	88
Good vacation scheme?	87
Confident you'll be kept on?	78
Good remuneration?	65
Diverse firm?	86

Geldards LLP

Survey results *(marks out of 100%)*

Satisfied in your job?   82

Firm living up to expectations?   80

High quality of work?   78

Enough client contact?   71

Stress-free?   62

Happy work/life balance?   78

Friendly firm?   87

Great social life?   63

Good vacation scheme?   79

Confident you'll be kept on?   75

Good remuneration?   76

Diverse firm?   83

 **verdict**

As a 'well-respected regional firm' headquartered in Cardiff, Geldards has a 'very good reputation' in Wales, while the offices in Derby and Nottingham earn it additional recognition as 'one of the best in the East Midlands'. Trainees cite these regional bases as 'an immediate draw' because they offer 'the opportunity to work on interesting cases without having to be in the City'. The firm has created a 'friendly and welcoming environment', so it is not surprising that the current trainee cohort includes former paralegals who 'really liked the firm's ethos and personality' and who felt that staying was the 'obvious choice'. Trainees have enjoyed 'great experience in a range of legal teams', and instances of 'quality work' include 'advocacy at the Cardiff Civil Justice Centre during a breach of contract trial', 'assisting on large corporate completions' and 'attending an onsite client meeting at a quarry'. Hours can be erratic, as feedback relates 'some very late nights' and also 'not having anything to do'. Respondents believe that Geldards strikes a healthy balance in its 'excellent training programme'; though 'support is in place within the training contract structure', it is also essential that trainees adopt a 'proactive approach and use their initiative'. The Nottingham office is situated in an industrial park, so this can mean that 'the social side is very quiet' and there are also 'no convenience stores within walking distance'. More generally, respondents state that the firm's size is a major plus point as it is 'small enough to be able to know partners and solicitors by name, but large enough to draw in interesting work from major clients'. To handle 'complex and demanding' work and to learn from 'very knowledgeable' senior lawyers, add Geldards to your shortlist.

If the firm were a fictional character it would be...

Fireman Sam – can be relied upon in an emergency, and has a great reputation in Wales

Gide Loyrette Nouel LLP

 verdict

France's Gide Loyrette Nouel naturally provides trainees with 'international opportunities', and its London office offers a nice balance between the 'City experience and the intimacy of a smaller firm'. Gide's 'stand-out reputation as an international player' brings with it the 'opportunity to travel with work'. One trainee who was seconded abroad appreciated that 'I was able to use my foreign language skills', while others who have worked in overseas offices tell us 'the local office was very supportive and helped me to settle quickly', and that 'getting to know colleagues in person has made subsequent collaboration much easier'. Unfortunately, the firm has scaled back the number of international secondments it offers. Recruits have been given 'quite high-level work', including 'filing a huge arbitration' and 'taking responsibility for all contact with a high-profile client while working closely with the Paris office'. There are concerns about the 'lack of opportunities at qualification' and even about 'job security', and some trainees feel that 'talent has left the firm' in recent years. That said, there is 'great access to partners' in the office, 'senior associates are approachable', and one individual's favourite moment to date was 'having a great mid-seat appraisal where the level of my work was praised'. There is 'no face-time culture' and trainees 'can generally finish at 6pm most days'. 'I know all my colleagues by name' says one respondent, and the 'small trainee intake' and 'friendly colleagues' no doubt helped. To represent 'Francophone clientele' from a small office connected to a wider international network, consider a career at Gide Loyrette Nouel.

If the firm were a fictional character it would be...

Dexter (Dexter's Laboratory) – an expert in the field, bringing a fresh perspective to Anglo-American peers

Survey results *(marks out of 100%)*

Satisfied in your job?	**54**
Firm living up to expectations?	**42**
High quality of work?	**72**
Enough client contact?	**47**
Stress-free?	**59**
Happy work/life balance?	**59**
Friendly firm?	**64**
Great social life?	**24**
Confident you'll be kept on?	**29**
Good remuneration?	**64**
Diverse firm?	**39**
Good international secondments?	**47**

Gordon Dadds

Survey results *(marks out of 100%)*

Satisfied in your job?	**66**
Firm living up to expectations?	**69**
High quality of work?	**61**
Enough client contact?	**54**
Stress-free?	**61**
Happy work/life balance?	**64**
Friendly firm?	**68**
Great social life?	**46**
Confident you'll be kept on?	**51**
Good remuneration?	**54**
Diverse firm?	**56**

 **verdict**

The 'entrepreneurial, aggressively acquisitive' Gordon Dadds acquired firms Davenport Lyons and Jeffrey Green Russell in April 2014 and October 2015 respectively. Trainees chose the firm because of its 'full-service and expanding nature'. We are told that the 'managing partner is business-savvy and it shows in the management of the firm and the work'. A *new Lex 100 entrant*, the firm offers a 'varied training contract with corporate, commercial, private client and family work'. The still 'relatively small size' is a strength as 'greater responsibility' is offered to trainees from an 'early stage' and there are 'smaller teams'. The 'location is great' as the central London office, near Covent Garden, is 'really convenient and has lots to offer in the evenings'. The other office is in the heart of Cardiff. Partners are 'really approachable' and there are some 'great personalities who have interesting stories to tell'. Notably, trainees would like a 'communal dining area' because it would be 'good to have a break-out area for informal meetings and lunch'. One trainee reported the 'very poor retention rates' and a perceived 'lack of opportunity for career progression'. Top trainee moments include 'involvement in a noted case worth more than $500m', 'making a Court of Appeal application' and 'being actively involved in drafting a witness statement with a client and counsel'. Mostly there are 'reasonable hours' and the 'healthcare benefits' are popular. Keep Gordon Dadds in mind if you are looking for a full-service 'expanding firm'.

If the firm were a fictional character it would be...

Aladdin – eager to prove its worth, and goes about its business with charm and a sense of humour

Gordons LLP

 **verdict**

Gordons is a 'medium-sized, friendly, Yorkshire-based firm' that offers new recruits a 'good work/life balance'. The atmosphere at the regional firm is 'relaxed and not too intense'. Notably, the 'people' are the best thing about the firm because they are always so 'friendly and willing to help'. The 'approachable solicitors and partners' are 'willing to ensure' that trainees are 'progressing and learning as much as possible about an area of the law'. It is evident that the firm puts an 'emphasis on developing' trainees' knowledge in a seat rather than pushing them to 'meet time and billing targets'. Therefore, trainees have the 'opportunity to learn instead of having to constantly time record and rush matters'. Highlights for newcomers include 'praise from highly-rated partners', 'receiving lots of positive feedback' and always being able to 'approach anyone at the firm for help or guidance'. There are opportunities to 'play football and netball', but one trainee commented there 'isn't a great social scene'. Trainees are required to 'do the post on a rota basis throughout the training', which is unpopular. Gordons is a great alternative for prospective lawyers who live in Yorkshire and wish to 'train and ultimately qualify there', so if you are looking for a 'relaxed firm', this would be a good choice.

If the firm were a fictional character it would be...

Katniss Everdeen (The Hunger Games) – smart, strong and a strategic thinker

Survey results *(marks out of 100%)*

Satisfied in your job?	75
Firm living up to expectations?	72
High quality of work?	70
Enough client contact?	60
Stress-free?	52
Happy work/life balance?	77
Friendly firm?	77
Great social life?	55
Good vacation scheme?	67
Confident you'll be kept on?	73
Good remuneration?	67
Diverse firm?	70

Gowling WLG

Survey results *(marks out of 100%)*

Satisfied in your job?	79
Firm living up to expectations?	85
High quality of work?	80
Enough client contact?	70
Stress-free?	64
Happy work/life balance?	71
Friendly firm?	88
Great social life?	73
Good vacation scheme?	94
Confident you'll be kept on?	81
Good remuneration?	75
Diverse firm?	86
Good international secondments?	71

 verdict

Gowling WLG formed in February 2016 following the merger of Wragge Lawrence Graham & Co with the Ottawa-headquartered Gowling. The combination 'is good for the firm and shows we are definitely going places', says one trainee, and it is evidence of the 'ambition' cited by others in the intake. There are a 'number of leading practice areas' to experience at the firm, and those mentioned by trainees include AIM-focused capital markets, IP, M&A and real estate. Trainees are 'given the autonomy to manage our own files', and examples of 'good-quality work' have included 'assisting on a large refinancing in my real estate seat' and 'handling three complex completions on my own in one day with a combined value of around £25m'. A complaint aired by one respondent is that 'the spread of workload is perhaps not managed fairly'. The 'good level of client contact' can see you 'leading a client meeting', and one trainee justly felt proud when 'a client called me specifically to thank me for my work'. There is some criticism of the 'qualification wage' and the apparent 'disparity in pay in Birmingham compared to London'. To counter this there is 'good work/life balance', and though 'hours can be long' on occasion, there is 'no pressure for face-time if you have completed your tasks for the day'. The firm is named a **Lex 100 Winner** for its vacation scheme. Recruits speak glowingly about the 'friendliness of the firm and its people', and because 'partners and supervisors make sure that you are always given work that will be a learning experience', one respondent wrote that 'everyone is valued for their contribution, and you feel a part of the team from day one'. For a firm that ensures 'high value is placed on good training and development', apply to Gowling WLG.

If the firm were a fictional character it would be...

Adrian Mole – intelligent and capable, and growing up quickly in a complicated landscape

Harbottle & Lewis LLP

 **verdict**

Harbottle & Lewis's 'reputation in the media and entertainment sectors' draws trainees to this 'small, niche London firm'. Owing to the firm's 'industry expertise', it commands a 'very strong market share in the media industries' and represents 'high-profile clients who are at the top of their fields'. Highlight moments for trainees have included 'taking the lead, with good supervision, on a number of minor transactions towards the end of my first seat while colleagues were on holiday' and 'working alone with a partner on a client's issue from beginning to end, reaching a settlement of in excess of £120,000'. The 'friendliness of the people working here' is another big plus, and the lack of hierarchy is evident in 'everyone eating together every day in the lunch room'. This negates the fact that the 'layout of the office sometimes limits the people you come into contact with'. Though Harbottle & Lewis is 'an all-service firm', and one respondent mentions 'running my own property deal from start to finish', it is felt that 'most trainees are here for the media work'. Because of this, retention rates in the media department are said to be 'notoriously bad', and 'most trainees are therefore resigned to the fact that it is very unlikely they will be offered employment in that department at the end of the training contract'. On the bright side, trainees report working fewer hours than peers, and say that they are 'not encouraged to stay late for the sake of it'. Client secondments are available, and they are a 'fantastic opportunity to gain valuable commercial experience'. To train at a firm which even receives 'good word-of-mouth praise from ex-employees', apply to Harbottle & Lewis.

If the firm were a fictional character it would be...

Miss Honey (Matilda) – friendly and caring, and takes a nurturing approach to training

Survey results *(marks out of 100%)*

Satisfied in your job?	78
Firm living up to expectations?	79
High quality of work?	78
Enough client contact?	70
Stress-free?	65
Happy work/life balance?	65
Friendly firm?	90
Great social life?	73
Good vacation scheme?	88
Confident you'll be kept on?	58
Good remuneration?	58
Diverse firm?	80

Harrison Clark Rickerbys

Survey results *(marks out of 100%)*

Satisfied in your job?	75
Firm living up to expectations?	74
High quality of work?	77
Enough client contact?	76
Stress-free?	51
Happy work/life balance?	55
Friendly firm?	79
Great social life?	73
Confident you'll be kept on?	71
Good remuneration?	67
Diverse firm?	78

 **verdict**

Harrison Clark Rickerbys is an 'inclusive firm' in the Three Counties with the 'potential to grow and expand'. Keen trainees therefore 'have every opportunity to progress' as hard work 'doesn't go unnoticed'. The 'invaluable training' offers 'immersive experience from the outset' as there is 'quality work' available rather than 'mere photocopying and tea-run duties'. The 'diversity of work and clients' is a consequence of a 'variety of different practice areas' from corporate law to family and divorce. There is a 'highly-structured support network' but supervisors are 'more than happy to trust trainees with responsibility early on'. Current trainees loved the 'supportive, progressive and excellent environment' and have been 'rewarded' with 'client face-time'. The 'supervision is good' and there is no shortage of 'excellent lawyers to learn from'. 'Long hours' or 'quiet days' are both part of the job but trainees recognise 'staying late to get an important deal done is both exciting and exhausting'. Top trainee moments include being 'awarded trainee solicitor of the year in-house', 'spending the day at the headquarters of one of the world's leading Formula One teams' and 'attending court to issue an urgent injunction'. Perks of the firm include 'subsidised gym membership, Christmas bonuses in M&S vouchers and an attendance bonus'. Trainees are 'not always guaranteed your seat preference' and one recruit reported there is a 'lack of keeping trainees in the loop regarding rotations and NQ jobs'. The firm is 'still developing and improving at a high rate', but those looking for a firm which offers 'hands-on experience' and 'invaluable training' should explore Harrison Clark Rickerbys.

If the firm were a fictional character it would be...

Thor (Marvel Comics) – strong, and with a single-minded drive to help those who need it

Hempsons

 **verdict**

Hempsons is lauded as a 'leader in the healthcare law field', and the 'prestige' associated with this market standing ensures that 'high-quality work' regularly comes through the door. Trainees take on 'lots of responsibility' and are 'given the opportunity to assist with important cases and make a real contribution'. The 'variety of work is arguably limited', and one respondent adds that 'there are limited seats available within the Manchester office'. Trainees are undoubtedly busy, and this is reflected in one recruit's training contract highlight being 'praise from a partner for settling a case cheaply and quickly', and in another trainee's worst moment to date, which was 'missing serving a defence by three minutes'. Despite the high volume of work, a 'friendly and relaxed environment' is firmly established at Hempsons, and the 'very good work/life balance' ensures for one trainee that the heavy workload is 'not to the detriment of my social and home life'. The 'interesting work' extends to client secondments and pro bono initiatives. We hear from one source that the former 'allowed me to gain insight into the goals, objectives and difficulties clients have', while the 'very good' pro bono opportunities include 'involvement with Pathways to Law, which provides help and guidance to young people considering a legal career'. If you are interested in the healthcare industry and would like to commence your career at a firm with a 'good reputation' that is 'well known as a market leader', you should look no further than Hempsons.

Survey results *(marks out of 100%)*

Satisfied in your job? 83

Firm living up to expectations? 79

High quality of work? 86

Enough client contact? 66

Stress-free? 56

Happy work/life balance? 79

Friendly firm? 89

Great social life? 66

Confident you'll be kept on? 79

Good remuneration? 63

Diverse firm? 66

If the firm were a fictional character it would be...

Alfred (Batman) – offers unfailing support, with intelligence, integrity and compassion

Herbert Smith Freehills LLP

Lex 100 Winner

See categories below
and tables from page 69

Survey results *(marks out of 100%)*

Satisfied in your job?	76
Firm living up to expectations?	81
High quality of work?	77
Enough client contact?	69
Stress-free?	57
Happy work/life balance?	53
Friendly firm?	84
Great social life?	74
Good vacation scheme?	89
Confident you'll be kept on?	85
Good remuneration?	80
Diverse firm?	84
Good international secondments?	92

 verdict

With 24 offices worldwide, Herbert Smith Freehills can boast of 'FTSE 100 clients' plus 'international opportunities' and 'work in emerging markets such as Africa'. Co-headquartered in London and Sydney, the firm has a 'hunger for growth', 'well thought-out future plans' and offers a 'different perspective from other firms'. It is felt that the 'investment the firm puts into its trainees bodes well for retention rates', and HSF duly earns a **Lex 100 Winner** award for confidence of being kept on. In a team of 'friendly, excellent lawyers', 'everyone is keen to help trainees learn and get the most out of their training contracts'. Trainees get their hands on 'complex and challenging work' which is at the 'cutting edge of the legal industry'. There are a few grumbles about the 'rite of passage for any true litigator' of 'bundling at 2am and having to work some weekends'. That said, there is a 'strong network of people', including 'most partners' who have an 'open-door policy' and supervisors who give 'positive feedback'. Trainees are 'encouraged to leave at a normal time' where possible as supervisors 'respect personal time' and recognise there is a 'life outside work'. As a result, trainees feel 'highly valued as individuals', despite the fact that sometimes 'hours can be unpredictable' and the 'work isn't evenly spread between trainees'. Trainee highlights include 'flying out to Amsterdam for a three-day closing', a 'secondment in Dubai' and 'flying to India for an exciting 24 hours in relation to a deal' (a second **Lex 100 Winner** medal is pocketed for international secondments). If you are looking for exciting work at a top City firm, look no further than Herbert Smith Freehills.

If the firm were a fictional character it would be...

Edna Mode (The Incredibles) – a thought leader that offers practical solutions

Higgs & Sons

 **verdict**

The 'wide diversity of practice areas' and 'range of sectors' that Higgs & Sons works in was of great interest to applicants, as was the fact that the firm has an 'excellent reputation' for having 'great links with clients'. There are 'opportunities to learn' because the firm 'places a lot of emphasis on trainees' development and takes a keen interest in their future ambitions'. The 'interesting and varied work' has included 'attending a five-day trial in Birmingham', while an example of the 'good level of responsibility' for one respondent was 'getting to conduct my own meeting with clients'. The main focus of discontent centres on the firm's Dudley location as 'public transport links to the firm are poor' and 'it can be hard to get to events in Birmingham', but we are told that trainees 'can leave work a little early if you need to get to an event'. Higgs & Sons is praised for 'the emphasis it places on the community', and through the 'strong focus on CSR' trainees are 'encouraged to take a lead in community projects'. The 'down-to-earth environment' is typified by the 'lack of barriers between junior and senior members of staff'. It is clear that trainees are trusted with 'the independence to run case files', and their input is clearly valued as the firm is 'flexible in terms of preferred seats'. The 'friendly working environment' means Higgs & Sons is 'an enjoyable place to work', and recruits also appreciate the 'good work/life balance'. With 'opportunities to get involved in projects across the firm', the Higgs & Sons training contract is 'an excellent way to learn and develop my skills'.

Survey results *(marks out of 100%)*

Satisfied in your job?	**75**
Firm living up to expectations?	**80**
High quality of work?	**73**
Enough client contact?	**68**
Stress-free?	**55**
Happy work/life balance?	**75**
Friendly firm?	**88**
Great social life?	**68**
Confident you'll be kept on?	**55**
Good remuneration?	**63**
Diverse firm?	**85**

If the firm were a fictional character it would be...

Sir Lancelot – a noble aide who fights valiantly for the cause

Hodge Jones & Allen LLP

Lex 100 Winner

See categories below
and tables from page 69

Survey results *(marks out of 100%)*

Satisfied in your job?	86
Firm living up to expectations?	85
High quality of work?	89
Enough client contact?	92
Stress-free?	50
Happy work/life balance?	73
Friendly firm?	83
Great social life?	76
Good vacation scheme?	48
Confident you'll be kept on?	63
Good remuneration?	46
Diverse firm?	83

 **verdict**

A common theme in the feedback gathered on London's Hodge Jones & Allen is the firm's 'strong ethos' and 'commitment to justice'. The firm takes on a lot of legal aid work, and coupled with its 'specialist departments, such as civil liberties', this demonstrates HJA's determination to 'work with and help vulnerable individuals'. Hodge Jones & Allen enjoys a 'great reputation', and the 'work that comes through the door' results in trainees being given a 'lot of client contact and responsibilities'. The firm is a triple **Lex 100 Winner** this year in our client contact, job satisfaction and work quality categories. Recent highlights enjoyed by current trainees include 'successfully representing a client at a prison adjudication in the second month of my seat' and 'winning a case at the Supreme Court'. Due to the nature of the firm's work, some moments can be particularly tough, for instance when one trainee 'informed a client that as a result of a court judgement he would be homeless'. One gripe is that there 'needs to be more interaction between the different departments/teams', though we are also told that 'everybody is friendly and approachable'. One respondent says that 'my supervisor treats me like an adult and there is mutual respect between us', while another tells us that 'the training principal listens to the needs of the trainees and puts this first'. HJA truly wants to provide you with good training'. The main criticism centres on the 'low trainee salary', though a 'good work/life balance' is also reported. Befitting the firm's social ethos, there are 'great opportunities to attend the Citizens Advice Bureau in Camden for advice sessions'. To 'help clients in difficult situations and see the difference it makes to them', take a look at Hodge Jones & Allen.

If the firm were a fictional character it would be...

Winston Smith (1984) – always finding ways to challenge the government

Howard Kennedy LLP

 **verdict**

'Not too big and not too small', Howard Kennedy is a 'growing, forward-thinking firm' that has 'ambitious aspirations for the future'. It is a 'strong City firm' with expertise in a range of sectors including corporate, retail and leisure. A 'friendly firm' with 'big-name clients', it is 'developing into a bigger name itself'. The firm has 'pretty epic office views' based in London Bridge right on the Thames. People are 'extremely friendly, genuinely welcoming and are keen to get to know you as an individual'. Supervisors make a 'conscious effort to pass on work' that will 'develop skills' and challenge trainees. The 'small trainee intake' means recruits get their hands on 'sophisticated and interesting high-profile deals'. The 'staff at all levels are approachable' and there isn't a shortage of 'high-quality lawyers to learn from'. Trainee highlights include 'completion drinks with clients', 'attending lavish and fun client events' and 'taking on more responsibility by walking a client through a share purchase agreement'. There have been a few grumbles about the 'stress when working to tight deadlines'. Also, one trainee suggested the 'seat selection process could be more transparent' as there is some 'uncertainty regarding the seat rotations'. Respondents praise the 'diverse recruitment' as trainees come 'from varied backgrounds'; as well as recent university graduates, the firm is keen to employ individuals who have had a 'previous career'. Keep Howard Kennedy in mind if you are looking to work at a mid-size firm that offers a 'good work/life balance' but plenty of challenges.

Survey results *(marks out of 100%)*

Satisfied in your job?	77
Firm living up to expectations?	78
High quality of work?	75
Enough client contact?	76
Stress-free?	59
Happy work/life balance?	70
Friendly firm?	84
Great social life?	74
Good vacation scheme?	89
Confident you'll be kept on?	60
Good remuneration?	64
Diverse firm?	73

If the firm were a fictional character it would be...

Arya Stark (A Game of Thrones) – friendly and sweet, but also strong and fierce when it needs to be

Howes Percival LLP

Survey results *(marks out of 100%)*

Satisfied in your job?	81
Firm living up to expectations?	86
High quality of work?	83
Enough client contact?	79
Stress-free?	61
Happy work/life balance?	81
Friendly firm?	88
Great social life?	56
Good vacation scheme?	75
Confident you'll be kept on?	68
Good remuneration?	68
Diverse firm?	77

 **verdict**

With its 'good support network', Howes Percival is a 'progressive regional firm' with a 'team-oriented atmosphere'. At the heart of the training, 'supervisors are very supportive in helping you progress'. The 'team sizes are not too big or too small' but just right to form a 'close-knit team'. 'Everyone knows everyone in the office' but the firm is still 'big enough to attract large international clients'. Trainees are 'exposed to high-quality work and are given expert supervision'. Although 'hierarchy is in place, senior staff have an open-door policy and are approachable'. Trainees are 'encouraged to attend internal and external events of all kinds, including meals at Michelin-starred restaurants and award ceremonies'. Top trainee moments include 'managing a high-value property transaction under supervision', 'receiving a gift from a client' and 'attending the Royal Courts of Justice'. There are 'busy spells' at the office where trainees are given 'demanding work', and although there are times when trainees are 'overloaded with work', there is 'no pressure to work 60+ hours a week'. Trainees comment on the 'lack of social opportunities outside work' as the firm is 'split across a number of offices', and feedback suggests it would be 'nice to spend more time with other trainees'. But trainees appreciate the 'high level of client contact', including working with clients on your own, and a 'friendly working atmosphere'. Those looking for a regional firm with a 'positive outlook' should consider Howes Percival.

If the firm were a fictional character it would be...

Alan Partridge – the consummate professional, and big in Norwich

Ison Harrison

New Lex 100 entrant Ison Harrison has ten offices in and around Leeds, and survey respondents were initially attracted to the firm because of its 'good reputation' in the area. 'I felt like I fitted in', says one recruit who 'did a work experience placement at this firm through BPP University, where I did my GDL'. Trainees greatly enjoy the 'areas of law practised', though regrettably 'you don't get much choice when it comes to seats'. 'Working in the family department' has been one respondent's favourite experience to date. There is also 'plenty of advocacy experience', and highlights have included 'issuing my first judicial review claim' and 'meeting a client in the morning, preparing her statements and applications and then going to court with her in the afternoon'. The firm also 'provides legal advice clinics on a weekly basis' from every office. The salary is criticised by the intake, but there is recognition from some that they have 'more responsibility than peers', and additionally there is widespread agreement that the Ison Harrison training contract offers 'very good hands-on training'. Recruits feel that the 'variety of training' is preparing them well for life as a qualified lawyer. 'Support is available' when needed, and the 'friendliness of the staff' means trainees can count on a 'very cooperative environment'. If you are looking for a training contract in the Leeds area, remember that Ison Harrison's trainees are given plenty of responsibility, while working alongside 'likeable people'.

Survey results *(marks out of 100%)*

Satisfied in your job? 78

Firm living up to expectations? 75

High quality of work? 78

Enough client contact? 70

Stress-free? 58

Happy work/life balance? 83

Friendly firm? 90

Great social life? 80

Confident you'll be kept on? 73

Good remuneration? 22

Diverse firm? 83

If the firm were a fictional character it would be...

Dr Doug Ross (ER) – professional, able, likeable and cool

Kingsley Napley LLP

Survey results *(marks out of 100%)*

Satisfied in your job?	83
Firm living up to expectations?	92
High quality of work?	87
Enough client contact?	85
Stress-free?	47
Happy work/life balance?	72
Friendly firm?	92
Great social life?	77
Confident you'll be kept on?	83
Good remuneration?	83
Diverse firm?	87

 **verdict**

From the outset, Kingsley Napley adopted a 'unique and friendly approach during the recruitment process'. Applicants met a 'large number of partners' during this time, which left a 'good impression' that the firm was 'friendly and welcoming'. The firm is named a **Lex 100 Winner** for living up to expectations and client contact, showing that this favourable first impression was accurate. The firm's 'reputation in the market in comparison to its size' also impresses, and it carries out a 'broad range of exciting and cutting-edge work', though the criminal team earns particular praise. Trainees at Kingsley Napley can look forward to 'work which is both interesting and challenging', and 'you are quickly dealing with your own cases, assisting with real tasks on large cases and speaking to clients'. Highlight moments include 'attending a three-day final hearing with counsel', 'site visits with clients' and 'a situation where I produced good and thorough research in a short space of time'. Minor gripes centre on 'the IT system' and that 'the offices are in need of a refurbishment', though respondents generally enthuse about 'coming to work every Monday and feeling good about it'. The 'small intake of trainees' is identified as a plus point and, more widely, 'Kingsley Napley is still small enough that everyone knows everyone'. Trainees appreciate having a 'great work/life balance and flexible opportunities', and note that the 'large number of socials is not restricted to your department'. Helpfully, the firm's 'role model lawyers have an open-door policy', allowing trainees to 'learn from the best' and to 'feel comfortable asking questions'. To join a firm that 'punches well above its weight while maintaining a good atmosphere', consider Kingsley Napley's training contract.

If the firm were a fictional character it would be...

Sherlock Holmes – delivers classic expertise, with style

Lester Aldridge LLP

Lex 100 Winner

See categories below and tables from page 69

 verdict

Lester Aldridge is 'ideal for training as it is a well-respected firm in many areas of the law' and offers trainees a great 'variety of work'. Trainees take on a 'high level of responsibility' as they get 'involved running cases' and carry out 'very little photocopying or filing'. The firm ensures a 'great learning process' which trainees really appreciate, even if at times the 'high-quality work' requires trainees 'to learn quickly'. There is a 'strong network of support' as trainees attend 'regular meetings and receive feedback' on their performance. This helps to ensure low stress levels, which along with work/life balance and confidence of being kept on has secured Lester Aldridge **Lex 100 Winner** accolades. The 'high-quality training is delivered from approachable and experienced supervisors at the forefront of their fields' plus the 'partners are approachable' and 'colleagues are always willing to provide help and guidance'. Also, respondents feel they can 'talk to most people' as the 'friendly atmosphere does not feel hierarchal' and trainees comment on the 'diversity of the firm'. The 'small trainee intake' results in trainees being 'challenged with new matters and clients'. Trainees have the 'freedom to do and learn' while gaining 'direct client contact and interesting work'. There is some 'uncertainty' regarding the 'allocation of the seats' and there were a few grumbles about the 'modest pay'. Best trainee moments include 'being offered a job on qualification at the end of my second seat', 'completing a large property transaction after many months of work' and 'being personally thanked for hard work by a client'. Take a closer look at Lester Aldridge if you are looking to sink your teeth into lots of 'proper work and responsibility'.

If the firm were a fictional character it would be...

John McClane (Die Hard) – an indefatigable fighter

Survey results (marks out of 100%)

Satisfied in your job?	82
Firm living up to expectations?	80
High quality of work?	85
Enough client contact?	75
Stress-free?	76
Happy work/life balance?	91
Friendly firm?	86
Great social life?	77
Good vacation scheme?	76
Confident you'll be kept on?	85
Good remuneration?	59
Diverse firm?	78

Lewis Silkin LLP

Survey results *(marks out of 100%)*

Satisfied in your job? 69

Firm living up to expectations? 68

High quality of work? 69

Enough client contact? 63

Stress-free? 58

Happy work/life balance? 70

Friendly firm? 80

Great social life? 75

Good vacation scheme? 83

Confident you'll be kept on? 65

Good remuneration? 59

Diverse firm? 76

 verdict

Lewis Silkin was chosen by trainees 'because of its particular practice areas', and the firm is well regarded for its expertise in TMT and IP as well as for its 'excellent reputation in employment law'. From its 'desirable location' in Chancery Lane, the firm's trainees handle 'really interesting work' which, given Lewis Silkin's position at the forefront of media law, can include 'very high-profile matters'. Individuals speak of 'having responsibility for small matters' and 'being responsible for my own clients'. Stand out moments thus far for trainees have included being tasked with 'tackling large transactions', 'winning in court' and 'preparing an analysis that a partner used in a client meeting'. The cohort appreciates that colleagues 'take the time to develop you as a lawyer', and recruits are aided by the 'well thought-out training sessions'. That said, the 'variation in the quality of supervision' is a complaint raised by a few survey respondents, with some stating their displeasure with 'the way supervision is managed by HR'. For one recruit, the 'friendliness' of the firm was first on display when they met 'representatives at City Law Live who made a really positive impression'. Those trainees who completed client secondments spoke glowingly of the 'great opportunity' and 'invaluable experience', but all also mentioned feeling 'isolated from the firm' as it 'didn't keep in touch' during this time. One person states that Lewis Silkin lives up to its 'rather more human law firm' branding, and we hear that a 'work/life balance is encouraged' and that trainees enjoy the 'social events' laid on by the firm. For a 'challenging but not exploitative' training contract at a London firm with widely respected departments, conduct further research into Lewis Silkin.

If the firm were a fictional character it would be...

Black Widow (Marvel Comics) – clever, attractive, can slip under the radar but proves highly effective

Linklaters LLP

 **verdict**

'Prestigious' firm Linklaters sets the 'benchmark for quality'. There is a 'focus on teaching trainees to become good lawyers in a supportive environment where questions are welcomed'. The firm has a 'clear commitment to training young lawyers' – earning **Lex 100 Winner** status for confidence of being kept on – and provides a 'friendly working environment' where colleagues are described as 'intellectual, talented and inspiring'. This 'top-of-the-market firm' provides a 'solid training base for the start of your legal career' which stands recruits in good stead for their future after the 'well-rounded', 'robust' and 'tailored experience'. One trainee describes the 'adrenaline from running around from pillar to post for 36 hours which only stopped once the champagne trolley was rolled in!' Other top trainee moments include 'signing a deal worth £25m', the 'incredible feeling when your work is commended in front of the whole team by a partner' and 'closing a long-running transaction which made the headlines of the FT'. Recruits grumble about the 'demanding and stressful hours' but they qualify that this was what they 'expected' from a Magic Circle firm. Despite the complaints about the 'work/life balance', trainees recognise the firm's efforts to 'improve and encourage more flexible working'. Recruits love the 'incredible international seats' which include Amsterdam, Tokyo and Hong Kong, plus the firm has a 'strong reputation in all of its departments', especially corporate, which makes it a 'great place to start your career'. Trainees also appreciate the range of facilities on offer, including on-site doctors. Ambitious individuals who want to be intellectually challenged and rewarded for plenty of hard work at a 'top-tier firm' should set their sights on Linklaters.

If the firm were a fictional character it would be...

Maximus Decimus Meridius (Gladiator) – strong and powerful with a strategic mind, but kind to those in its care

Survey results *(marks out of 100%)*

Satisfied in your job?	70
Firm living up to expectations?	76
High quality of work?	74
Enough client contact?	66
Stress-free?	57
Happy work/life balance?	44
Friendly firm?	77
Great social life?	71
Good vacation scheme?	88
Confident you'll be kept on?	86
Good remuneration?	66
Diverse firm?	77
Good international secondments?	70

MFG Solicitors LLP

Survey results *(marks out of 100%)*

Satisfied in your job?	82
Firm living up to expectations?	86
High quality of work?	82
Enough client contact?	72
Stress-free?	48
Happy work/life balance?	68
Friendly firm?	90
Great social life?	58
Good vacation scheme?	81
Confident you'll be kept on?	64
Good remuneration?	30
Diverse firm?	81

 **verdict**

New Lex 100 entrant MFG Solicitors is neatly summarised by one of its trainees as a 'successful firm which provides a fantastic opportunity to work alongside well-respected lawyers'. A regional firm with offices across the West Midlands, it can boast of a 'very tight base of substantial clients', and though it offers a wide range of legal services, it is notably a 'market-leading specialist in niche areas of law, including agriculture'. Trainee accomplishments include 'completing my first £1.5m transaction', 'attending client meetings' and 'reaching settlement in a family property dispute'. The 'pay rates for trainees' are criticised, but the work/ life balance is praised and the 'social and professional networking opportunities' are another plus point. One trainee who did two weeks' work experience with MFG Solicitors before joining the firm 'really enjoyed my time and the staff made me feel really welcome', while another current trainee 'had been working at the firm for three years as a paralegal'. Respondents elaborate on the 'friendliness of staff who put you at ease, which in turn means that you are not afraid to ask questions'. The 'direct contact with the partners' is evidence of a 'cohesive, well-integrated group of fee-earners who work well together and encourage an environment where learning and development is natural'. There may be periods of 'copying bundles into the late evening', but you can look forward to 'hands-on experience' because the firm 'trusts your ability to carry out a task rather than spoon-feeding you'. To 'see matters from instruction through to completion' and to thrive within a 'friendly environment' at a Midlands firm which demonstrates 'reciprocity between departments', head to MFG Solicitors.

If the firm were a fictional character it would be...

Del Boy (Only Fools and Horses) – has fewer resources than others, but maintains a spirit and tenacity which continues to make its clients smile

McMillan Williams

Lex 100 Winner

See categories below
and tables from page 69

 verdict

New Lex 100 entrant McMillan Williams adopts a unique approach in 'recruiting all trainees internally from the paralegal pool'. Successful applicants first work as paralegals for a year, with the firm planning from the outset to transfer all candidates to a training contract. The 'prospects for securing a training contract' are very good and even considered 'guaranteed' by survey respondents, and the added fact that 'the firm retains most of their trainees as NQs' furthers the belief in a firm offering 'career progression' to its employees. There are a 'large number of areas to work in', and highlight moments have included 'being involved in high-value transactions' and 'my first win in a family law matter'. The cohort reports a 'high quality of training' and appreciate that 'seat preferences are taken into account', but it is said that 'the training programme is not as structured as elsewhere' as 'seat lengths vary depending on business needs'. Though the 'salary is a little low in comparison to other firms of same size', McMillan Williams offers its trainees several advantages. As well as the impressive aforementioned retention rates, there is also an 'annual advocacy competition' that 'allows trainees and paralegals to build experience in what is possibly the most daunting thing that someone in a legal career can do'. Other plus points are the 'good peer support' among trainees, the firm's 'positive impact within the local community' and the 'exposure to client contact' which helped secure **Lex 100 Winner** status. With over 20 offices across the South of England, McMillan Williams offers trainees 'hands-on work to really thrive on'.

If the firm were a fictional character it would be...

Cinderella – it has big aspirations

Survey results *(marks out of 100%)*

Satisfied in your job? 77

Firm living up to expectations? 78

High quality of work? 85

Enough client contact? 90

Stress-free? 53

Happy work/life balance? 56

Friendly firm? 79

Great social life? 63

Good vacation scheme? 81

Confident you'll be kept on? 74

Good remuneration? 36

Diverse firm? 76

Milbank, Tweed, Hadley & McCloy LLP

Survey results *(marks out of 100%)*

Satisfied in your job?	83
Firm living up to expectations?	87
High quality of work?	88
Enough client contact?	80
Stress-free?	62
Happy work/life balance?	58
Friendly firm?	83
Great social life?	63
Good vacation scheme?	92
Confident you'll be kept on?	82
Good remuneration?	90
Diverse firm?	88

 **verdict**

A US-headquartered firm that is 'seen as among the best', trainees were lured by Milbank, Tweed, Hadley & McCloy's 'global brand'. There is a 'high level of responsibility' and 'interesting work' at the firm, with 'hands-on' tasks including 'speaking on all-parties conference calls about the part of the deal I'm responsible for', 'getting involved with two deals when they first came in and getting to assist in the planning and development of those cases' and 'working on a pro bono project and spending a lot of time developing a piece of work with the client'. The ability to provide such 'exposure to good work' prompted one trainee to label Milbank 'the best overall package' out of the firms that they had researched, and the four **Lex 100 Winner** gongs impress. The 'hierarchical structure is a bit daunting at times', and one respondent tells us 'I felt there was not a lot of support in the early days'. That said, the 'friendliness of the people and willingness to help' is noted. There is also a strong sense of teamwork during the training contract, as recruits speak fondly of 'feeling a key part of the team', with one adding that 'the team made a lot of time to explain the structure and documents to me'. The 'lack of a social life' is a minor grumble, but at least 'there is no face-time culture'. One advantage of a 'small intake' is that the trainees are 'involved with a more diverse range of work and given more responsibility' than their peers in larger cohorts elsewhere. To engage in 'top work' while learning alongside 'quality lawyers' at an international law firm, consider applying to Milbank, Tweed, Hadley & McCloy.

If the firm were a fictional character it would be...

Josiah Bartlet (The West Wing) – fiercely intellectual and with a humour-filled, calm delivery

Muckle LLP

 verdict

Acknowledged as 'one of the top firms' in Newcastle, Muckle has an 'excellent local reputation' and 'makes a real difference to the local area', so in the words of one trainee 'you can see the improvements and successes that you are a part of'. Though a regional firm, Muckle has 'excellent national and international clients', and has developed 'great relationships' with them over time. Trainees praise the levels of 'client contact and responsibility', and speak of 'involvement in the day-to-day running of files'. Stand-out moments include 'getting a result on a big dispute which made the client happy', 'attending a High Court trial for a high-profile client' and 'getting to work on a huge transaction in the corporate team and seeing it through from start to finish'. Complaints are few and far between. One person says that 'communication isn't always very good from management', and another tells us that 'the air conditioning in winter' is unpopular. Overall, commentary reveals that current trainees consider colleagues to be 'friendly and approachable', and that the firm 'places a strong importance on people'. One response is 'I like the fact that Muckle is a single-site firm', and this ensures 'everyone knows each other and it is really easy to work with other teams'. Trainees will sometimes 'work into the small hours', though this is said to be a 'rare event'. Muckle's staff work well together 'professionally and socially' and the firm is a **Lex 100 Winner** for social life. The 'tea trolley', 'Friday fizz' and 'Christmas party' are all greatly appreciated. To train at a North East firm with 'quality clients', remember Muckle.

If the firm were a fictional character it would be...

Mma Ramotswe (The No. 1 Ladies' Detective Agency) – honest, sorts out problems and loves the local community

Survey results *(marks out of 100%)*

Satisfied in your job?	84
Firm living up to expectations?	84
High quality of work?	82
Enough client contact?	77
Stress-free?	63
Happy work/life balance?	84
Friendly firm?	92
Great social life?	84
Good vacation scheme?	89
Confident you'll be kept on?	73
Good remuneration?	70
Diverse firm?	86

Mundays LLP

Lex 100 Winner

See categories below
and tables from page 69

Survey results *(marks out of 100%)*

Satisfied in your job?	80
Firm living up to expectations?	80
High quality of work?	84
Enough client contact?	89
Stress-free?	50
Happy work/life balance?	87
Friendly firm?	89
Great social life?	64
Confident you'll be kept on?	62
Good remuneration?	64
Diverse firm?	75

 verdict

The 'availability of City-quality work coupled with a good work/life balance' is a theme that strongly emerges in the survey feedback for Mundays. Respondents state that the Surrey-based firm is 'very good at entrusting trainees with proper responsibility for legal work', proving to those who 'didn't want to join the rat race' that 'good-quality work is not confined to London'. The 'level of work provided' across a 'variety of departments' is considered 'drastically better' when compared to peers' experiences at other firms. Highlights have included 'handing my supervisor some drafting and it coming back with no red pen on it' and 'attending court with a fee-earner on a dispute relating to matters of international arbitration law'. As mentioned above, the good work/life balance means recruits 'don't have to be seen to be working all hours', and the firm is named a **Lex 100 Winner** in this category, as well as for client contact. Mundays has a 'friendly atmosphere', though it is regrettable that 'there is not much scope for many social activities given the comparatively isolated location of the firm'. One respondent was 'very impressed by the friendliness of firm members when attending an open day', and this positive first impression is echoed by a peer who 'genuinely enjoyed the interview process'. There are concerns about 'not knowing if there is a job at the end', as it 'very much depends on if there is room in the department that you would want to qualify in'. Trainees 'feel like part of a team' as they 'often work alongside a partner or senior associate on key deals' and 'share an office with a senior fee-earner'. To experience 'high levels of client contact at an early stage without needing to sign your life away', consider applying to Mundays.

If the firm were a fictional character it would be...

Buttons (Cinderella) – straightforward, reliable and goes out of its way to please

Nockolds Solicitors

Lex 100 Winner

See categories below
and tables from page 69

 verdict

One respondent praises the 'approachable and supportive partners' at Nockolds, with another adding that 'they are always there to answer any questions we have and make sure we are okay with the workload'. The Bishop's Stortford firm offers trainees 'a large amount of responsibility and client contact', and one person is proud of the time 'when my client thanked me for my hard work'. One recruit says 'I have had a number of files which I have run all the way through', and some of the cohort's highlight achievements include 'seeing an estate administration file through from start to finish', 'drafting witness statements and attending settlement meetings' and 'the sale and purchase of my first property from beginning to end'. Admin tasks such as 'routine bundling' and 'looking for financial documents in a property that had been unoccupied for 18 months' have proved to be less stimulating work. One trainee tells us 'I was asked to choose my seats before my training contract commenced', and this is a sign of the 'inclusivity' of Nockolds' training contract. One complaint is 'having a London office but currently no London-based trainee seat', because if this was remedied it 'would provide a different environment to train in'. The atmosphere in the office is 'less stressful' than that reported by peers at other firms, and this may partly be due to the 'great social events' laid on. Indeed, these are two of the seven areas in which the firm is named a **Lex 100 Winner**. To join a firm which insists on an 'open-door policy' and a 'willingness to help and teach trainees', consider Nockolds Solicitors.

Survey results *(marks out of 100%)*

Satisfied in your job?	92
Firm living up to expectations?	92
High quality of work?	87
Enough client contact?	94
Stress-free?	69
Happy work/life balance?	94
Friendly firm?	94
Great social life?	94
Confident you'll be kept on?	79
Good remuneration?	64
Diverse firm?	87

If the firm were a fictional character it would be...

Dobby (Harry Potter) – is with you to the end and always happy to help

Paul Hastings LLP

Survey results *(marks out of 100%)*

Satisfied in your job? 80

Firm living up to expectations? 80

High quality of work? 66

Enough client contact? 50

Stress-free? 62

Happy work/life balance? 54

Friendly firm? 92

Great social life? 78

Confident you'll be kept on? 68

Good remuneration? 78

Diverse firm? 84

 **verdict**

A 'reputable name in the US', Paul Hastings is a *new Lex 100 entrant* and boasts a 'small London office with a great ambition for growth'. Trainees report that this 'small office size' allows for 'greater exposure to client work than you would get at a Magic Circle firm', and the 'high level of responsibility' that trainees are entrusted with results in 'great involvement in deals'. Examples include 'working on two simultaneous large investment fund closings on the Friday before Christmas', 'being very involved in closing a deal in the first few months of my training contract' and 'drafting a high-level client memorandum alongside a partner'. One respondent warns that 'the quality of trainee work can vary', and there are times when you are 'not being used enough for the more important projects' and instead tasked with admin duties. There are 'high expectations' of new recruits at this 'fast-paced' firm populated by 'hard-working people', but trainees benefit from the 'teamwork ethic' that thrives in the 'friendly, non-aggressive atmosphere' at Paul Hastings. It 'can be daunting' that 'a lot of the training is done on the job rather than formal training sessions', but the 'true open-door policy' prompts one trainee to tell us that 'I have never felt I could not approach a partner and ask for help or further guidance'. Trainees appreciate the 'good training contract salary', and there is also recognition that 'the hours are not as long here in comparison to other US firms'. Trainees speak glowingly of 'working with leading lawyers who are specialists in their fields'. To work at firm with a 'global reach' that 'advises the biggest international clients', consider an application to Paul Hastings.

If the firm were a fictional character it would be...

James Bond – internationally recognised and respected, and a highly-skilled operator

Payne Hicks Beach

 **verdict**

Payne Hicks Beach's 'reputation in private client and family work particularly appealed' to the firm's trainees. The 'quality of work' is lauded and earns one of two **Lex 100 Winner** titles, and the firm's 'commitment to providing a personal service to its clients' also merits praise. Trainees receive 'very thorough training' as there is 'one trainee per department'. This 'small intake size' leads to trainees taking on 'more responsibility than peers at different firms'. One respondent tells us 'it was rather overwhelming being told to run my own files from day one, but now I see the benefit of being forced to jump in at the deep end'. Highlight work moments for the current trainee cohort include 'drafting a lengthy statement which earned positive feedback from counsel', 'handling and completing my first property transaction' and 'going to a hearing with counsel but without supervision and getting the best possible result'. The 'occasional afternoons stuck doing enormous quantities of administrative work' aren't fun, and the firm's 'somewhat old-fashioned reliance on paper and hard copies' has proven to be a frustration, though we are told that 'this is soon to be greatly improved with the introduction of a new paperless system'. The 'stunning offices' and 'beautiful location' in Lincoln's Inn are very impressive – 'I don't think anyone could tire of walking into New Square'. One complaint is that 'there could be more social events', though 'staff have a good work/life balance' and trainees report 'more reasonable hours' than their peers at other firms. For a 'generous level of client contact' at a small firm renowned for its private client and family expertise, apply to Payne Hicks Beach.

If the firm
were a fictional character
it would be...

The Scarlet Pimpernel – a stickler for tradition

Survey results *(marks out of 100%)*

Satisfied in your job?	**85**
Firm living up to expectations?	**87**
High quality of work?	**90**
Enough client contact?	**75**
Stress-free?	**65**
Happy work/life balance?	**82**
Friendly firm?	**87**
Great social life?	**62**
Confident you'll be kept on?	**50**
Good remuneration?	**77**
Diverse firm?	**72**

Peters & Peters Solicitors LLP

Survey results *(marks out of 100%)*

Satisfied in your job?	76
Firm living up to expectations?	76
High quality of work?	73
Enough client contact?	83
Stress-free?	56
Happy work/life balance?	60
Friendly firm?	83
Great social life?	80
Confident you'll be kept on?	70
Good remuneration?	73
Diverse firm?	83

 **verdict**

One trainee describes Peters & Peters Solicitors as 'small enough to be friendly and personable but big enough to allow me to work with a range of people at any given point'. The firm has a 'good mix of areas of law' for those who want a training contract 'solely focused on contentious matters', and this 'variety of work' includes white-collar crime, general crime, extradition and civil litigation. These specialisms produce 'fascinating cases' and great trainee experiences, including 'contributing to the launch of a large action', 'assisting on an extradition and mutual legal assistance matter when a client was released from custody after two months in an overseas prison' and 'going to the police station to represent a client'. There are opportunities for 'personal interaction with clients' and this requires 'communication skills and tactical thinking, not just a knowledge of technical stuff or black-letter law'. Having 'no formal feedback process apart from end-of-seat appraisals so you often have to seek out feedback after a piece of work' is a minor gripe. Perks of the 'small trainee intake' include 'hands-on experience, working with partners directly and getting responsibilities early on', but one respondent complains of 'no financial assistance for the LPC'. The people at Peters & Peters are 'friendly and down-to-earth', and 'there is always someone to have lunch with or a chat over tea', while 'some people are particularly fond of karaoke at the end of a night out'. To 'specialise in niche practice areas' while you are 'surrounded by very clever people' and 'challenged every day', look into Peters & Peters Solicitors.

If the firm were a fictional character it would be...

Winston Wolfe (Pulp Fiction) – a stylish problem solver

Pinsent Masons LLP

 **verdict**

The 'appeal of international secondments', 'challenging work' and the firm's 'organic growth' all helped to seal the deal for current Pinsent Masons' trainees. 'Visible opportunities for career progression' are great for trainees' confidence in being kept on after the training contract. The firm is a **Lex 100 Winner** in the diversity and vacation scheme categories. Trainees praise the 'wide variety of seat options', but have found that 'niche areas such as financial regulation are only offered in London'. Highlights include 'travelling from Doha to Abu Dhabi to attend client meetings', 'reviewing the contracts of a Premier League football team' and 'having champagne after everything was signed off in a completion meeting'. 'All-nighters', 'occasional long hours' and 'administrative tasks' are all problems that trainees grumble about, but they also report getting a 'buzz' from the 'atmosphere and involvement in the team'. The 'work/life balance is good' as the firm offers a 'great social life and free dinners after 7pm'. The firm 'invests in trainees' and provides 'excellent introductory training sessions'. Supervisors have an 'open-door policy' and are 'genuinely interested in the ongoing progression and development' of their trainees. Furthermore, 'training is excellent every time you move into a new seat' and trainees are 'supported professionally and personally' by 'willing people' throughout the firm. You are 'frequently encouraged to observe qualified lawyers which is useful for learning how to handle matters that fall outside the scope of academic education, such as dealing with clients on the phone and at court'. Those looking for 'client exposure' within a supportive yet challenging environment will not be disappointed by Pinsent Masons.

If the firm were a fictional character it would be...

Carmen Sandiego – you never know where in the world it will turn up next

Survey results *(marks out of 100%)*

Satisfied in your job?	81
Firm living up to expectations?	82
High quality of work?	81
Enough client contact?	72
Stress-free?	65
Happy work/life balance?	72
Friendly firm?	93
Great social life?	81
Good vacation scheme?	92
Confident you'll be kept on?	77
Good remuneration?	74
Diverse firm?	89

Pitmans LLP

Survey results *(marks out of 100%)*

Satisfied in your job?	80
Firm living up to expectations?	80
High quality of work?	78
Enough client contact?	83
Stress-free?	60
Happy work/life balance?	86
Friendly firm?	90
Great social life?	69
Good vacation scheme?	84
Confident you'll be kept on?	72
Good remuneration?	60
Diverse firm?	80

 **verdict**

Trainees love Pitmans' 'impressive continued growth' as a result of its acquisitions over the last few years. This *new Lex 100 entrant* has established a 'great reputation' so can count on 'high-profile regional and national clients'. Trainees work alongside 'highly intelligent and experienced partners who are friendly, down-to-earth and not intimidating'. This results in an 'inclusive atmosphere as all partners are approachable'. You are 'never a cog in a big machine' as everyone is treated equally, and trainees are 'encouraged to attend client drinks events'. There are 'excellent opportunities for client contact and running files' only a few months into the training contract. It is not an environment in which people 'clock-watch', but equally there is 'no expectation of staying late just for the sake of it'. Pitmans is therefore named a **Lex 100 Winner** in the work/life balance category. Trainees are 'given the responsibility' to manage their own time as long as they 'produce high-quality work' and meet deadlines. The 'lack of international secondment opportunities' is disappointing for current trainees, but there is a 'broad range of matters' for trainees to get involved in. 'Support is always available' for those who want it, but the training is already very 'hands-on' as trainees 'receive a lot of client contact'. There are a few grumbles about 'tiring and tedious work, including filing', but highlights for trainees include 'drafting important agreements', 'being trusted to look after a client while liaising with counsel' and 'being involved in a key tribunal case which will set new law'. Those looking for a 'hands-on training experience' in a down-to-earth environment should add Pitmans to the list.

If the firm were a fictional character it would be...

Jiminy Cricket – a fun but wise partner to accompany you on your adventures

Prettys

 **verdict**

Praised as a 'local, well-established and friendly' firm, Prettys has offices in Ipswich and Chelmsford and offers a 'good quality of work outside of London'. One trainee who undertook work experience at Prettys was 'encouraged by the quality of the clients using the firm', while another reported being provided with 'interesting tasks that demonstrated the type of work a trainee would be involved in'. The firm is a **Lex 100 Winner** for client contact and work/life balance. There continues to be 'quality work for fee-earners', and highlights from the current cohort include 'assisting a fee-earner on a £250,000 personal injury settlement' and 'working directly with a partner on the disposal of a cleaning company'. There can be difficult times, as one recruit 'stayed late for several hours in case I was needed for the completion of a deal' while another 'felt out of my depth in the first week when I inherited numerous personal injury files from the previous trainee'. Yet the firm has a 'good reputation for training', as 'partners and senior fee-earners really invest time in the trainees'. Recruits have the 'opportunity to be an individual', and staff 'always try and place you in the seat you want rather than the seat they want you to be in'. A limitation of the 'dated offices' is the 'lack of a canteen or social area', but this doesn't hinder the 'friendly environment' and 'inclusive culture' of the office. Respondents comment favourably on the 'opportunity to work on interesting matters with experienced senior members of the firm in a friendly environment', and say that the firm is 'keen for trainees to get involved in pro bono work to help them develop as a solicitor'. For a 'high level of responsibility while also maintaining a good work/life balance', apply to Prettys.

If the firm were a fictional character it would be...

Velma Dinkley (Scooby-Doo) – always finds a solution, even when others fail

Survey results *(marks out of 100%)*

Satisfied in your job?	75
Firm living up to expectations?	75
High quality of work?	82
Enough client contact?	87
Stress-free?	62
Happy work/life balance?	88
Friendly firm?	92
Great social life?	78
Good vacation scheme?	77
Confident you'll be kept on?	83
Good remuneration?	65
Diverse firm?	80

RadcliffesLeBrasseur

Lex 100 Winner

See categories below
and tables from page 69

Survey results *(marks out of 100%)*

Satisfied in your job?	82
Firm living up to expectations?	82
High quality of work?	86
Enough client contact?	84
Stress-free?	60
Happy work/life balance?	90
Friendly firm?	90
Great social life?	54
Good vacation scheme?	63
Confident you'll be kept on?	57
Good remuneration?	43
Diverse firm?	74

 verdict

RadcliffesLeBrasseur is 'large enough to attract high-quality work from really interesting clients, but small enough to ensure that trainees are really well integrated'. The firm 'truly delivered' on providing current trainees with 'high levels of client contact and real responsibility from an early stage', one of the most important considerations when searching for a training contract. 'On-the-ground training' results in trainees being 'trusted and empowered to make real decisions on live cases' as they 'manage files, instruct counsel and liaise directly with clients'. The 'work/life balance is hard to beat as trainees will rarely be in the office past 6.30pm' – leading to a **Lex 100 Winner** prize in that category – though one trainee grumbled about 'staying late to produce a bundle for a hearing taking place the following morning'. The firm is a 'good all-rounder' as it has a 'decent breadth of practice areas to choose from'. Top trainee moments include 'effectively running a multi-million pound trust settlement case', 'attending a Crown Court hearing for gross negligence manslaughter' and 'sitting in on a huge four-week trial which attracted national press attention'. The people at RadcliffesLeBrasseur 'are friendly and the partners are very approachable', but trainees feel that some associates can be 'really demanding', resulting in a lot of pressure to meet 'unrealistic deadlines'. Thankfully there is an 'open-door policy' so 'everyone has time for you whether it is support staff or a senior equity partner'. Those looking for high levels of client contact and responsibility at a firm with a 'culture of hard work' should take a closer look at RadcliffesLeBrasseur.

If the firm were a fictional character it would be...

Robert Crawley (Downton Abbey) – has a penchant for tradition yet is friendly, open-minded and forward-thinking

Riverview Law

 **verdict**

Trainees explain that *new Lex 100 entrant* Riverview Law – which launched in 2012 – is 'different from a traditional law firm' as 'the culture of the business is that of an in-house environment'. In shedding the industry's normal 'seniority structure', Wirral-based Riverview impresses with 'the way the business treats all members of staff, and how open, friendly and supportive everyone is', characteristics which have led to **Lex 100 Winner** medals for, among others, low stress levels and friendliness. Trainees are 'recruited internally', so have already 'bought into the values of the firm' and know that it is a 'fun and relaxed place to work'. 'Trainees are entrusted with complex work', with stand-out achievements including 'settling my first mediation' and 'advising on a multi-million pound contract'. One complaint is that 'each working day can be quite similar in content and work', and can 'limit trainees' ability to develop legal skills across the board'. That said, the 'training is fantastic', and one respondent writes: 'I have weekly meetings with my trainee supervisor to go through any complex matters, but I also have the benefit of asking them anything at any time I want'. The workload can be inconsistent, as one trainee cites 'the volume of work in my third seat' as the worst moment to date, while another laments 'I have had times where I had very little work to do and had to assist other teams at short notice'. Still, trainees 'run their own matters and deal with clients on a daily basis', but 'the classic levels of stress and pressure don't exist at Riverview as questions are encouraged and support is never-ending'. To join a young firm which offers recruits exposure to 'varying types of commercial legal work', add Riverview Law to your shortlist.

If the firm were a fictional character it would be...

Holly (Red Dwarf) – offers sound advice through developments in artificial intelligence

Survey results *(marks out of 100%)*

Satisfied in your job? 81

Firm living up to expectations? 81

High quality of work? 78

Enough client contact? 80

Stress-free? (74)

Happy work/life balance? (91)

Friendly firm? (94)

Great social life? 81

Good vacation scheme? 75

Confident you'll be kept on? (90)

Good remuneration? 46

Diverse firm? 83

Royds Withy King

Lex 100 Winner

See categories below
and tables from page 69

Survey results *(marks out of 100%)*

Satisfied in your job? 87

Firm living up to expectations? 85

High quality of work? 87

Enough client contact? 81

Stress-free? 57

Happy work/life balance? 86

Friendly firm? 95

Great social life? 80

Confident you'll be kept on? 82

Good remuneration? 42

Diverse firm? 87

 **verdict**

Recruits were impressed by Royds Withy King even before the training contract started. One trainee 'joined as a paralegal and realised I didn't want to work anywhere else', despite having previously worked at others firms. Another survey respondent was prompted to apply to Withy King by word-of-mouth having been 'told about the excellent training from a friend who had also trained with the firm'. The firm 'specialises in niche practice areas', and the fact that trainees are 'consulted on seat choices' is greatly appreciated by the current cohort. Trainees have experienced work highlights that include 'completing a large corporate transaction on my own in the second week of my corporate seat', 'attending the Royal Courts of Justice on a personal injury case' and 'completing option agreements for landowners with a developer'. There are moans about the pay, and though the trainee salary has 'recently been increased', the 'salary for an NQ position' is still considered on the low side. Every trainee is 'treated like a proper fee-earner', as 'Withy King gives you the freedom to do what you want and find your feet early in your career'. One of the firm's four **Lex 100 Winner** awards is for job satisfaction. As they are given 'responsibility and opportunities from day one', each trainee is 'expected to be involved with everything from legal advice to business development'. There is also 'very good partner contact' and 'trainees are given a lot of support' when required. One criticism is that 'there aren't many occasions for the whole firm to socialise', though there is a 'friendly culture' and a 'relaxed, open atmosphere'. For a career at a firm renowned for 'excellent training' and for listening to its trainees' preferences, head to Royds Withy King.

If the firm were a fictional character it would be...

The Force (Star Wars) – complex, enduring and wielded for good

SAS Daniels LLP

Lex 100 Winner

See categories below
and tables from page 69

 **verdict**

Recruits were impressed by SAS Daniels straightaway. One former paralegal 'enjoyed the work' at the North West firm, while another trainee tells us 'I had done a work placement while in university, and then again at the end of my degree, and my perception of the firm only got better'. A third respondent writes 'following the assessment day I got a great impression of the firm', so it is clear that the firm is staffed by 'welcoming and friendly people'. SAS Daniels is a double **Lex 100 Winner** due to its impressive diversity and stress-free scores. There are a 'number of different departments' and 'each trainee is given an opportunity to explore different areas of law and express their preference'. The 'varied work' experiences have included 'attending an employment tribunal with a partner' and 'working on a multi-million commercial property transaction'. The major criticism mentioned by survey respondents is the 'low trainee wage', but a counter-point to this is the 'high retention rate' which provides a feeling of security. The 'networking opportunities' at SAS Daniels are appreciated, as is the fact that 'everyone in the firm is invited to get involved' in CSR efforts. Trainees 'can be placed in any office without very much notice', and this can require 'getting used to longer commutes'. This issue aside, the structure of the training contract is praised. The six-month rotations are popular, and respondents believe 'working closely with partners' to be a plus point. If you're looking to train alongside 'helpful colleagues' at a North West firm which offers 'quality work' across a 'good choice of seats', conduct further research into SAS Daniels.

If the firm were a fictional character it would be…

Lisa Simpson – intelligent, kind and hard-working

Survey results *(marks out of 100%)*

Satisfied in your job?	76
Firm living up to expectations?	86
High quality of work?	82
Enough client contact?	76
Stress-free?	70
Happy work/life balance?	84
Friendly firm?	92
Great social life?	82
Good vacation scheme?	81
Confident you'll be kept on?	82
Good remuneration?	36
Diverse firm?	91

Shakespeare Martineau LLP

Survey results *(marks out of 100%)*

Satisfied in your job?	76
Firm living up to expectations?	72
High quality of work?	78
Enough client contact?	76
Stress-free?	52
Happy work/life balance?	67
Friendly firm?	80
Great social life?	67
Good vacation scheme?	80
Confident you'll be kept on?	72
Good remuneration?	55
Diverse firm?	75

 verdict

Shakespeare Martineau is 'renowned for being ambitious', and offers trainees 'lots of opportunity for future progression'. In the wake of the June 2015 merger, one trainee applied because, in their words, 'I knew it would be a firm to watch in the next couple of years!' With its 'London office', 'strong Midlands presence' and 'unique mix of practice areas', Shakespeare Martineau commands 'good quality clients' and a 'variety of work'. Highlights among current trainees include 'working on big-value deals with high-profile clients', 'running files with minimal supervision' and 'working on a massively complex restructure of a group of companies and being able to understand the process'. There is criticism of the 'two-tier trainee salaries' and the 'lack of organisation when it comes to dealing with trainees', both of which have been identified as post-merger teething problems. The firm is 'dedicated to recruiting from within' as evident in the 'large number of partners who trained with the firm and have worked their way up'. A 'lack of transparency in the NQ application process' has been noted, though ultimately we hear that the newly-merged firm is 'really dedicated to making sure they retain their trainees and talent as a whole'. Respondents are impressed by the 'really knowledgeable' supervising partners who are 'experts in their respective fields'. The firm is considered 'more flexible than others in relation to considering early qualification'. The 'networking opportunities' are popular too, and trainees are encouraged to 'visit and work in other offices' and to develop their individual profiles within the firm. To experience 'excellent client contact' at a firm known for its 'friendliness and positive attitude', consider applying to Shakespeare Martineau.

If the firm were a fictional character it would be...

Rey (Star Wars) – new, exciting and great at what it does

Shulmans

 **verdict**

Leeds-based Shulmans is a 'medium-sized firm' that is 'big enough to provide quality training but small enough to give trainees real responsibility'. Respondents enthuse about the 'commercial client base' of this *new Lex 100 entrant*, which encompasses 'big household names and high-profile A-listers'. The 'good level of responsibility and client contact' leads to 'hands-on experience' with 'involvement in large cases'. Highlights include 'completing a complicated commercial property sale where I had been the lead fee-earner and main point of contact for the client', 'being involved in a mediation with a high-profile individual' and 'being given the responsibility to advise a sport's national governing body in relation to their consumer credit and commercial documentation'. Trainees complain about the 'uncertainty' created by the 'lack of a fixed policy on how to deal with trainees coming up to qualification'. That said, commentary also praises the 'friendly ethos' which means 'not being treated as a number'. 'Training is structured' so that 'in each seat we are allocated key learning objectives, and supervisors ensure that those objectives are met'. Furthermore, partners 'will find time to sit with you and provide you with feedback, regardless of how busy they are'. The social life is 'not the best'. We are told that 'the main events each year are a quiz night and the Christmas party', and that most staff leave both events quite early. Not only is there a good work/life balance, with trainees working 'predictable hours', but there is also a 'healthy balance of transactional work against admin tasks'. For a 'broad range of clients' and 'excellent work', this is an 'exciting time to join' Shulmans.

Survey results *(marks out of 100%)*

Satisfied in your job?	75
Firm living up to expectations?	75
High quality of work?	85
Enough client contact?	79
Stress-free?	50
Happy work/life balance?	60
Friendly firm?	82
Great social life?	39
Confident you'll be kept on?	74
Good remuneration?	75
Diverse firm?	74

If the firm were a fictional character it would be...

Princess Leia (Star Wars) – diplomatic, spirited and not afraid to fight

Sidley Austin LLP

Survey results *(marks out of 100%)*

Satisfied in your job?	75
Firm living up to expectations?	74
High quality of work?	89
Enough client contact?	71
Stress-free?	52
Happy work/life balance?	51
Friendly firm?	80
Great social life?	63
Good vacation scheme?	76
Confident you'll be kept on?	66
Good remuneration?	86
Diverse firm?	73
Good international secondments?	59

 verdict

A popular destination owing to its 'excellent and respected finance practice', US firm Sidley Austin commands an 'excellent global reputation' and handles 'great quality work', enabling trainees to execute 'highly complex deals' across the firm's 'impressive departments'. The firm is named a **Lex 100 Winner** in the work quality category. The 'small trainee intake' is seen as an advantage as, in the words of one respondent, 'I get great experience and become really relied upon and can become a valued member of the team'. Examples of 'lots of responsibility' include 'participating in every aspect of a large cross-border acquisition which closed within two months', 'closing a deal that I had been allowed to run' and 'drafting the employment warranties in a share and asset purchase agreement'. The 'very unpredictable hours' can make 'planning evenings and weekends difficult', but 'nobody expects face-time' and the pay is 'higher than at the Magic Circle', with this meriting a **Lex 100 Winner** medal. The 'approachability of partners' is appreciated, and senior colleagues are 'very giving with their time when it comes to explaining things and providing feedback to trainees'. This helps to ensure that 'trainees are very rarely made to feel commoditised'. As 'everything is run out of Chicago' it can feel like there is a 'lack of communication', and therefore a perceived 'lack of strategic direction'. Sidley Austin runs an 'enjoyable' vacation scheme which is a 'really good experience', and the 'very friendly and welcoming' staff epitomise the firm's 'laid-back work culture'. To train at a firm with an 'international outlook but with a smaller, more intimate office atmosphere', apply to Sidley Austin.

If the firm were a fictional character it would be...

Marty (Madagascar) – adventurous, and stands out from the herd

Spearing Waite LLP

 verdict

Leicester's Spearing Waite attracts trainees due to its 'good reputation in the area'. New recruits 'get to be part of an expanding firm', as evident in the 'move into a brand new office'. Trainees enjoy 'hands-on experience' and are given access to a 'wide variety of work'. Examples of trainees 'running their own case-loads' include 'the preparation of an injunction application, which I was allowed to see through to the end', 'helping successfully defend a claim of passing off which was dismissed at trial' and 'completing on a matter I handled from the beginning and receiving praise directly from the client'. These are clear examples of 'lots of client contact', though 'being unable to assist potential clients' in areas of law that Spearing Waite does not practice is a frustration. The firm's 'warm approach to recruitment', and 'praise for the management style of the partners', are examples of its 'dedication and loyalty to its staff'. It earns a **Lex 100 Winner** award in our friendliness category, and also wins for client contact, social life and work/life balance. Trainees work closely with their supervisors, and 'partners are genuinely keen to offer a positive learning experience'; one survey respondent speaks of 'opportunities to think outside the box and share my ideas with my senior colleagues'. We are told that the 'pay for trainees is low compared to others', and another criticism is that the firm 'does not fund the LPC as part of the training contract'. Still, Spearing Waite instils a 'supportive culture of high achievement' and 'encourages the growth and development' of its staff, who are treated as individuals. For 'lots of responsibility' working on 'high-value deals' at a firm which is undergoing 'exciting overall growth', consider applying to Spearing Waite.

If the firm were a fictional character it would be...

Filbert Fox – loyal to Leicester, and enjoying great success

Survey results *(marks out of 100%)*

Satisfied in your job?	82
Firm living up to expectations?	80
High quality of work?	80
Enough client contact?	92
Stress-free?	52
Happy work/life balance?	87
Friendly firm?	95
Great social life?	87
Good vacation scheme?	75
Confident you'll be kept on?	65
Good remuneration?	55
Diverse firm?	85

Squire Patton Boggs

Survey results *(marks out of 100%)*

Satisfied in your job?	83
Firm living up to expectations?	85
High quality of work?	83
Enough client contact?	78
Stress-free?	65
Happy work/life balance?	79
Friendly firm?	91
Great social life?	80
Good vacation scheme?	89
Confident you'll be kept on?	76
Good remuneration?	71
Diverse firm?	87
Good international secondments?	66

 **verdict**

The US-headquartered Squire Patton Boggs offers newcomers 'the great combination of being a strong international firm' with a base in London, while 'retaining its regional links' through offices in Birmingham, Leeds and Manchester. 'Long-established' as a 'big legal player in the UK', the impressive 'global footprint' that the firm now possesses ensures that trainees have 'opportunities to be involved in high-profile local, national and international matters'. A representative range of trainee work highlights includes 'helping with the completion of a £30m manufacturing transaction which was covered on the regional television news', 'attending a mediation in London' and 'being at the heart of a large, cross border M&A deal'. The firm is lauded for its 'enjoyable vacation scheme', during which the 'friendliness of partners and associates' left a good impression. There are complaints that the 'pay is slightly below similar firms and there is no bonus scheme for trainees', but respondents do praise the firm's 'very good focus on extracurricular activities, which makes for very well-rounded trainees'. Though the 'seat allocation can often feel very out of your hands' and 'trainees' preferences are not always met', the firm's popular six-seat training contract 'gives you more flexibility and the chance to get a very broad experience' across the 'range of different departments' at Squire Patton Boggs. Befitting a global firm, international secondments are available, and favourite moments included 'completing a seat in Paris', 'my international secondment to Saudi Arabia' and 'gaining an international secondment to the Brussels office'. For 'access to top-quality work' at a firm that can boast of 'big-name clients', consider Squire Patton Boggs.

If the firm were a fictional character it would be...

Buffy (Buffy the Vampire Slayer) – hard-working and a force to be reckoned with, but a great team player and really good fun

Steele Raymond LLP

 verdict

Trusted as a 'reputable firm in the area', Dorset's Steele Raymond is a *new Lex 100 entrant*. One trainee who initially undertook a university placement at the firm was 'impressed by the friendliness in the office' and also 'enjoyed the practice areas offered'. The 'dispute resolution and company and commercial departments are excellent', and respondents appreciate 'being given good work' which includes 'working on three trials' and 'assisting on a number of high-profile company transactions'. These are examples of the 'good opportunities to undertake interesting work' at Steele Raymond, and trainees are adamant that such levels of client contact 'assist in your development'. The 'lack of organisation for trainees' and 'poor communication in some departments' frustrate, with one respondent criticising the seat rotation process while another complains of 'feeling out of my depth with little assistance in a department that I was not overly familiar with'. The firm offers a degree of flexibility in its recruitment practices, as one recruit explains how they were able to join the firm because 'I was moving to the area and there was a position available'. There are inevitably instances of 'photocopying bundles', and also some quiet spells in the office, but the 'good work' that trainees enjoy proves to be fulfilling, and one person chose 'being told that I am being retained' as their best training contract moment. Every survey respondent wrote that 'the people' are the best thing about the Steele Raymond training experience, so if you are looking for a rounded training experience in Dorset, look no further.

If the firm were a fictional character it would be...

Popeye – small in size but punching well above its weight

Survey results *(marks out of 100%)*

Satisfied in your job? 64

Firm living up to expectations? 64

High quality of work? 58

Enough client contact? 31

Stress-free? 48

Happy work/life balance? 84

Friendly firm? 84

Great social life? 38

Confident you'll be kept on? 59

Good remuneration? 28

Diverse firm? 74

Stevens & Bolton LLP

Survey results *(marks out of 100%)*

Satisfied in your job? 80

Firm living up to expectations? 80

High quality of work? 78

Enough client contact? 67

Stress-free? 62

Happy work/life balance? 74

Friendly firm? 88

Great social life? 74

Good vacation scheme? 75

Confident you'll be kept on? 70

Good remuneration? 76

Diverse firm? 86

 verdict

'The clients and the nature of the work' at Guildford's Stevens & Bolton 'is analogous to that of a corporate firm in the City'. This *new Lex 100 entrant* has a 'reputation for high-quality work', and highlight moments mentioned in the feedback include 'working on a corporate deal from the very beginning to the very end', 'attending a four-day commercial litigation trial in London' and 'being given the opportunity to analyse complex legal issues on an international transaction'. The trainee cohort is excited by the firm's 'commitment to innovation', seeing it as 'very forward-focused and constantly looking for ways to improve'. One trainee says that 'the training contract has a good structure', as six four-month seats mean 'we're able to have a much more rounded experience, going to different departments and working on various areas of the law'. On the down side there is a 'lack of clarity over seat rotations' and 'trainees are not asked about seat changes'. Recruits mention the 'friendly and welcoming nature' of Stevens & Bolton, and that the firm is 'incredibly sociable and inclusive', but the 'lack of canteen/realistic breakout facilities' is a minor gripe. Having a 'small number of trainees' affords the intake 'more responsibility', and it is appreciated that 'even the managing partner and heads of department will always stop to chat and are keen to get to know us'. Indeed, one aspect of the 'great training' is being able to 'gain experience by working alongside high-calibre lawyers'. In addition, the 'high levels of client contact' are advantageous, and the few client secondments available 'really help trainees to understand what clients' priorities are'. To train at a 'reputable firm outside of London with big clients and highly-regarded partners', head to Stevens & Bolton.

If the firm were a fictional character it would be...

Elinor Dashwood (Sense and Sensibility) – classy, multi-talented and calm in a crisis

Sullivan & Cromwell LLP

 verdict

In London, Sullivan & Cromwell 'combines a small office environment with an outstanding client portfolio', and trainees report that the 'quality of work far outweighs the size' of the US firm's roughly 70-lawyer City base. Respondents appreciate that the firm 'treats each employee as a human being, rather than one of hundreds of disposable resources', so having a 'small number of trainees' in the intake is seen as a plus. The training itself is 'very hands-on', ensuring trainees 'learn through exposure'. Many respondents like this approach, but some feel that 'more formal training sessions would increase the breadth of topics covered by our training'. The firm's 'generalist approach' to training is praised, as trainees 'did not want to be pigeon-holed into a specific practice area on qualification'. As one recruit explains, 'on any given day I might be typing up notes of a conference with counsel on a financial regulatory point, preparing for an M&A closing, and speaking to lender's counsel on a debt issue'. There is 'room to improve the management of the workforce to ensure greater balance' as 'hours can be long', which can include 'working on a bank holiday' and 'a week of receiving urgent work at 5pm every day'. But London trainees feel the benefits of Sullivan & Cromwell's 'international nature', with experiences including 'going to New York for the firm-wide induction', 'going to Paris with a senior associate to complete a signing' and 'being told that I could go to Melbourne for my seat abroad'. Understandably, **Lex 100 Winner** status is secured for international secondments, and six other categories besides. For 'close contact with clients' and 'real responsibility from day one', Sullivan & Cromwell is a 'wonderful place to learn'.

If the firm were a fictional character it would be...

Jack Bauer (24) – quickly assesses all options and finds a way to get the job done

Survey results (marks out of 100%)

Satisfied in your job?	78
Firm living up to expectations?	83
High quality of work?	85
Enough client contact?	83
Stress-free?	68
Happy work/life balance?	58
Friendly firm?	93
Great social life?	77
Good vacation scheme?	95
Confident you'll be kept on?	92
Good remuneration?	95
Diverse firm?	92
Good international secondments?	93

TLT

Survey results *(marks out of 100%)*

Satisfied in your job?	83
Firm living up to expectations?	84
High quality of work?	86
Enough client contact?	89
Stress-free?	62
Happy work/life balance?	76
Friendly firm?	93
Great social life?	66
Good vacation scheme?	88
Confident you'll be kept on?	88
Good remuneration?	75
Diverse firm?	85

 verdict

TLT is identified by its trainees as a 'modern, forward-thinking firm' that is 'growing rapidly' in an 'ambitious but considered' manner. Training contracts are offered in Bristol, London and Manchester, and the 'opportunity to work with other offices' is considered a strength. The 'open-plan office' and 'lack of hierarchy' results in 'trainees sitting alongside partners', and as a result 'trainees seem like valued members of the team'. Indeed, the firm is this year named a **Lex 100 Winner** in both the confidence in being kept on and the client contact categories. Recruits get involved in an 'excellent level of work', often in 'niche areas of law', and recent highlights have included 'working on and attending a judicial review hearing at the High Court in my first seat' and 'completing a £12m transaction'. Respondents enthuse about TLT's 'pastoral approach to supervision', with one saying 'I can approach anyone in the firm if I have a question or a problem' and another adding that supervisors are 'focused on trainees gaining wide exposure to work and really preparing you for qualification'. This 'excellent support network' is no doubt made simpler because of the 'small trainee intake'. There are gripes about the 'lack of annual bonus scheme' and 'poor salary progression', particularly in contrast to 'the firms we want to compete with'. Despite the odd 'late and stressful night', the 'really good work/life balance' at TLT is generally praised. 'Being the primary contact for large clients' is a real thrill, and the 'opportunity to visit clients in London' is clear evidence of the 'great deal of responsibility' that TLT trainees enjoy. To embark upon a training contract at a 'progressive and innovative' firm which is 'always winning new and exciting work', make a note of TLT.

If the firm were a fictional character it would be...

Ginny Weasley (Harry Potter) – a relatively young player, but forward-thinking and innovative

Tees Law

 **verdict**

East Anglia's Tees Law has a 'good local reputation' and is located 'in a lovely part of the country'. Trainees were keen to 'experience a range of practice areas' at a 'rapidly growing law firm with great potential for future growth and prospects'. The 'friendly and welcoming atmosphere' is apparent from the 'excellent vacation scheme' and continues throughout the training contract. Trainees 'learn quickly in a supportive environment' where 'everyone is very approachable', and Tees Law 'encourages career progression'. One criticism is that 'the systems and accounts training could have been more detailed at the start of the training contract', though another respondent notes that 'the induction for trainees has improved'. Recruits enthuse about the 'broad exposure' and 'good involvement in a variety of different cases'. Highlight work experiences have included 'successfully obtaining a probate having been involved in the matter from the first meeting', 'completing on an extremely high-value commercial property' and 'my first settlement of a clinical negligence case on which I had conduct of the file with only light-touch supervision'. The 'offices are quite spread out and trainees are expected to move between them', which can lead to a 'bit of a commute for some seats'. Though this can eat into one's time, the firm 'promotes a fantastic work/life balance'. The 'support from training supervisors' is appreciated, as is the 'amount of responsibility given to trainees'. Not only is the client contact 'beneficial when it comes to qualification', it is also appreciated at trainee level as it 'always gives a feel-good factor'. If you're looking for a welcoming firm outside London which handles 'interesting work' and offers 'responsibility from the start', remember Tees Law.

If the firm were a fictional character it would be...

Derek Zoolander – has moved with the times to succeed in a tough industry

Survey results *(marks out of 100%)*

Satisfied in your job?	84
Firm living up to expectations?	80
High quality of work?	87
Enough client contact?	84
Stress-free?	40
Happy work/life balance?	67
Friendly firm?	90
Great social life?	65
Good vacation scheme?	77
Confident you'll be kept on?	79
Good remuneration?	70
Diverse firm?	84

Thomas Cooper LLP

Lex 100 Winner

See categories below
and tables from page 69

Survey results *(marks out of 100%)*

Satisfied in your job?	82
Firm living up to expectations?	83
High quality of work?	77
Enough client contact?	72
Stress-free?	57
Happy work/life balance?	92
Friendly firm?	87
Great social life?	66
Good vacation scheme?	54
Confident you'll be kept on?	76
Good remuneration?	82
Diverse firm?	82
Good international secondments?	92

 verdict

Thomas Cooper is 'among the best firms for shipping law', and this 'expertise' affords the firm an 'international status' which clearly appealed to current trainees. Recruits praise this 'medium-sized firm' as 'it is not so big that you feel like just a number, though it is still a City firm competing with much larger firms'. This market prominence is bolstered by the fact that there is a 'guaranteed international seat' for those who want to complete part of their training abroad, something that Thomas Cooper 'actively encourages'. These secondments are an 'excellent personal and professional experience', and one respondent enthuses about their 'exciting' time in Singapore. The firm is named a **Lex 100 Winner** for international secondments. Trainees undertake 'interesting work', and highlights have included 'attending a hearing at the Court of Appeal' and 'working alongside partners, associates, and counsel on a very complicated and developing point of tort law'. The firm is a 'little disorganised on the admin side' as trainees 'often get told only a month before rotation where we're sitting next', even if that is an international seat. Even though there are instances of 'weekend photocopying' and 'working until 10.30pm on a Friday', it is clear from the feedback that these are rare occurrences, and that the 'excellent work/ life balance' means trainees are 'usually out of the office by 6.30pm', earning another **Lex 100 Winner** award. Senior colleagues are 'supportive and generous with their knowledge and expertise', and this complements the 'friendly, down-to-earth' vibe at the firm. For a 'high level of responsibility' and the chance to work with renowned colleagues at an expert shipping firm, remember Thomas Cooper.

If the firm were a fictional character it would be...

Will Turner (Pirates of the Caribbean) – has a good heart, but gets its hands dirty

Tollers LLP

 **verdict**

A 'regional commercial firm' with a 'good reputation' across Northamptonshire and Buckinghamshire, Tollers 'provides a number of different services, meaning there is potential to experience a range of areas'. One respondent applied to the firm as it 'gave the opportunity to experience more hands-on work than at larger firms'. Examples include 'attending trials and mediations', 'taking the lead on my own files' and 'the completion of a complex refinancing matter', and a trainee speaks with pride about 'feeling useful and knowledgeable after only four months here'. The 'communication within and between departments' is criticised as there is a perceived lack of 'unity between some teams', and an absence of 'social/team-building events'. That said, there is an 'inclusive culture' at Tollers, and a new joiner noticed early on that 'the other trainees at the firm seemed genuinely happy'. This is no doubt partly explained by the 'good work/life balance'. Trainees sometimes 'undertake less attractive work', including 'slightly more administrative tasks' such as bundling. However, the trainee cohort is also tasked with 'more responsibility', and in the words of one person 'I have good people training me and got client contact from day one'. The 'multi-faceted' training contract also includes 'regular trainee meetings to organise charity events'. To 'learn a lot' at a respected regional firm which provides trainees with hands-on work and a well-structured training contract, consider applying to Tollers.

Survey results *(marks out of 100%)*

Satisfied in your job?	72
Firm living up to expectations?	71
High quality of work?	72
Enough client contact?	72
Stress-free?	49
Happy work/life balance?	76
Friendly firm?	87
Great social life?	49
Confident you'll be kept on?	62
Good remuneration?	51
Diverse firm?	62

If the firm were a fictional character it would be...

Johnny English – perhaps underestimated, it is actually highly effective

Trethowans LLP

Lex 100 Winner

See categories below
and tables from page 69

Survey results *(marks out of 100%)*

Satisfied in your job?	83
Firm living up to expectations?	85
High quality of work?	83
Enough client contact?	83
Stress-free?	60
Happy work/life balance?	73
Friendly firm?	95
Great social life?	82
Confident you'll be kept on?	67
Good remuneration?	53
Diverse firm?	80

 **verdict**

Trethowans is commended for its 'good reputation in the local area', and in October 2015 the firm merged with Dickinson Manser to add the latter's Poole base to offices in Salisbury and Southampton. Trainees remembered the Trethowans' application process as a positive experience, as one respondent to our survey was 'treated as someone who could contribute to the overall success of the firm'. Another reported feeling a 'good connection upon interview', while a separate trainee found the people at the assessment day to be 'really friendly and welcoming'. The 'quality of work' carried out by Trethowans is praised, as are the 'areas of practice' which the firm focuses on, and one trainee was grateful for 'the ability to do a seat in family law'. Highlight moments have included 'attending a trial', 'working on the administration of a multi-million pound estate' and 'settling a client's case over the phone, and managing to increase the defendant's final offer'. That 'some seats could have been better structured' is a frustration, as is the fact that 'being required to work in more than one office means a lot of commuting', but it is a good sign when one respondent states 'the firm takes my views into account when discussing my future seat options'. This is proof that the firm 'cares about training' as it 'goes out of its way to include trainees', and 'friendly and supportive' colleagues are all 'approachable and willing to answer questions', a trait which has helped the firm to secure a **Lex 100 Winner** award for friendliness. To work alongside 'exceptional lawyers' at a firm where you can receive 'an excellent level of client contact' and 'high levels of exposure to varied work', look into Trethowans.

If the firm were a fictional character it would be...

Penelope Pitstop (Wacky Races) – competitive, and going places

Trowers & Hamlins LLP

 verdict

A 'mid-size firm with international reach', Trowers & Hamlins offers 'excellent-quality work' to trainees 'wanting to gain exposure to markets outside of the UK'. The 'Middle Eastern presence' means that recruits have 'the opportunity to do a seat abroad', and the firm is a **Lex 100 Winner** for international secondments. These are said to be a 'great experience', and one trainee tells us that their secondment provided 'good exposure for my development within the firm'. A significant proportion of the survey feedback focuses on the firm's 'specialisms in property and the public sector'. Trainees also get a lot of 'hands-on experience', with one respondent stating that 'from the start of my training contract I have been given a high level of responsibility and been involved in live transactions'. Work highlights include 'being flown out to Switzerland for a client meeting' and 'being trusted to negotiate changes to ancillary banking documents'. One frustration aired by a few recruits is the perceived 'lack of brand recognition' and that Trowers 'doesn't get the recognition that I think we deserve'. The 'reputation for good training' is an accurate one, as 'graduate recruitment are approachable' while 'most partners will be more than happy to take time out to talk you through any issues or questions you may have'. The 'seat rotation process can be opaque' and trainees are 'made to wait a long time to find out where they will go next'. Still, 'the retention rates offer a level of security', and the fact that 'people want to stay on here and create a long-term career' is a result of the 'supportive environment' at the firm. For a 'very good mix of public and private sector work' at a firm experiencing 'organic growth', apply to Trowers & Hamlins.

If the firm were a fictional character it would be...

Princess Jasmine (Aladdin) – headstrong, full of vigour, and not afraid of an adventure

Survey results (marks out of 100%)

Satisfied in your job?	82
Firm living up to expectations?	84
High quality of work?	83
Enough client contact?	75
Stress-free?	61
Happy work/life balance?	75
Friendly firm?	88
Great social life?	71
Good vacation scheme?	77
Confident you'll be kept on?	77
Good remuneration?	84
Diverse firm?	85
Good international secondments?	82

Vinson & Elkins RLLP

Lex 100 Winner

See categories below
and tables from page 69

Survey results *(marks out of 100%)*

Satisfied in your job?	80
Firm living up to expectations?	83
High quality of work?	82
Enough client contact?	69
Stress-free?	49
Happy work/life balance?	56
Friendly firm?	89
Great social life?	66
Good vacation scheme?	85
Confident you'll be kept on?	73
Good remuneration?	83
Diverse firm?	87
Good international secondments?	79

 **verdict**

One respondent writes 'I was always drawn to US firms for the big-ticket work with high levels of responsibility', and that neatly summarises the feedback for Vinson & Elkins. The 'promise of working on wholly international deals and cases' was a 'major driver' for one trainee, and the firm's international secondment opportunities 'are very attractive'. Six months at the firm's Houston headquarters were considered 'one of my favourite parts of the training contract' by one lucky recruit, while a fellow trainee divided six months across the Hong Kong and Beijing offices, a combined stint which 'really put into perspective the offering this firm has across the world'. The firm is a **Lex 100 Winner** for international secondments. One negative result of being headquartered in the US is the perceived 'lack of transparency in decision making'. Back in London, the 'non-rotational system means that you are always challenged with varied work', examples of which include 'assisting with the signing of two deals in the M&A team in one week' and 'running the first stage of corporate restructuring, prior to the start of an investment by a major banking institution'. Trainees admit it is 'challenging juggling work from two or three departments' at one time, but they relish this 'sink or swim' reality. Vinson & Elkins offers a 'very niche set of specialisms' including arbitration, project finance and telecoms infrastructure, and this entails 'exciting work'. The 'long hours' mean the 'inability to make fixed plans during the week', though the 'great benefits' and the 'excellent salary' help to make up for this. To train alongside 'friendly, down-to-earth and driven' lawyers at a US firm in London, consider Vinson & Elkins.

If the firm were a fictional character it would be...

Sasha Fierce – hails from Houston, Texas and slays everything it turns its focus on

Walker Morris LLP

 **verdict**

'Based in Leeds' and with a 'clear focus on the region', Walker Morris is a single-site firm whose 'wide range of work' still enables trainees to 'get involved with 'large national and international' matters. The 'quality of clients' is impressive, as is the opportunity to 'be engaged in meaningful work right from the start'; trainees report 'running successful completions on large corporate deals'. The 'opportunity to go on secondments' is also appreciated, as they offer 'excellent exposure to work and the client' and are therefore 'extremely valuable and rewarding'. The 'quality of training' is lauded, and the 'six-seat training contract was also attractive' as it means trainees 'experience more areas of the law'. There is 'significant partner contact' at Walker Morris, and having the 'expertise of partners at a single site' is seen as an advantage for the firm. Respondents complain that the 'pay is no longer in line with the other big firms in Leeds'. Trainees can still be required to 'be in the office at 4am' and to do 'consecutive late nights while sitting in corporate', though it must be said that other recruits praise the 'realistic and reasonable work/life balance'. The 'friendly and approachable' nature of colleagues makes for a 'great working environment'. Trainees report feeling appreciated, with one citing 'the feedback I received from my first seat' and another being told by a partner that the quality of their work was what they 'would expect from a qualified solicitor'. To learn from 'talented and experienced lawyers' at a Leeds firm that is 'small enough so that your voice is heard but big enough to have an impressive client list', look no further than Walker Morris.

Survey results *(marks out of 100%)*

Satisfied in your job?	**76**
Firm living up to expectations?	**74**
High quality of work?	**83**
Enough client contact?	**82**
Stress-free?	**53**
Happy work/life balance?	**62**
Friendly firm?	**81**
Great social life?	**80**
Good vacation scheme?	**74**
Confident you'll be kept on?	**64**
Good remuneration?	**69**
Diverse firm?	**71**

If the firm were a fictional character it would be...

Roy Race (Roy of the Rovers) – consistently gets results no matter what the circumstances are

Ward Hadaway

Survey results *(marks out of 100%)*

Satisfied in your job?	77
Firm living up to expectations?	80
High quality of work?	79
Enough client contact?	74
Stress-free?	59
Happy work/life balance?	66
Friendly firm?	87
Great social life?	76
Good vacation scheme?	70
Confident you'll be kept on?	70
Good remuneration?	66
Diverse firm?	81

 verdict

Newcastle-headquartered Ward Hadaway's 'commitment to the north of England' appeals to trainees, and for those keen to work in the area the firm's 'excellent regional reputation' is bolstered by its 'large national and international clients'. Respondents report taking on 'interesting and challenging work' of 'great quality', and some favourite moments so far include 'attending two trials', 'completing my first transaction in property' and 'being given claim forms in my employment seat and being allowed to run the claim from start to finish'. Many recent recruits had a relationship with the firm prior to commencing their training contract, indicated by the following feedback: 'I worked at Ward Hadaway as a paralegal and enjoyed the working environment', 'I received a scholarship from the firm during university' and 'I did lots of work experience here which I really enjoyed'. This all points to a firm with a 'great working atmosphere' that encourages a 'friendly, open, and supportive culture'. Though trainees are 'able to give preferences about seats even in the first year', these aren't necessarily reflected in seat allocation. 'Occasional long hours' can mean 'dealing with a deadline for a court bundle late at night' and '1.30am finishes', though the 'high-quality supervision' ensures that trainees don't get stressed out and also aren't given admin tasks 'unless absolutely necessary'. There is a feeling that 'the integration could be better', as 'departments are fairly autonomous' and 'propagate different cultures across the firm', however one trainee feels that the latter point has its advantages in catering for 'different trainee personalities'. To train at a 'well-respected firm' which can offer 'great exposure to good quality work and clients', apply to Ward Hadaway.

If the firm were a fictional character it would be...

Milk Tray Man – always delivers the goods in style

Warner Goodman LLP

Lex 100 Winner

See categories below
and tables from page 69

 verdict

New Lex 100 entrant Warner Goodman is commended for its 'local reputation' across Hampshire. The firm 'has a family-like feel about it' and 'it does not work you into the ground but allows a very good work/life balance'. It is therefore no surprise that one trainee who was already working at the firm 'knew the systems, the people and the sort of work environment it was' and 'wanted to carry on being part of that'. Another respondent with 'previous work experience with the firm' spoke of the 'approachable and friendly' nature of colleagues. One trainee reports having 'more responsibility and better quality of work' than peers elsewhere, while another recruit writes that 'the firm treats you as part of the team rather than a 'junior''. Trainee work highlights include 'doing a transaction on my own' and 'getting good feedback from my clients on the first file in my name'. The feedback has propelled the firm to **Lex 100 Winner** status in the client contact category. Warner Goodman can be 'quite disorganised when it comes to deadlines for moving seats and giving information', and 'not getting training on new skills from the beginning of each seat' is a particular complaint in this regard. It is conceded, though, that 'this is due to the firm being small and flexible'. The 'relaxed training' is lauded, and a genuine sense of teamwork is instilled in each department. It is also evident to the current cohort that the firm is 'keen for individuals to progress', and naturally the survey respondents appreciate the investment made in them. To commence your legal career at a well-respected firm in the South of England, head for Warner Goodman.

Survey results *(marks out of 100%)*

Satisfied in your job?	76
Firm living up to expectations?	83
High quality of work?	79
Enough client contact?	89
Stress-free?	63
Happy work/life balance?	73
Friendly firm?	89
Great social life?	66
Confident you'll be kept on?	76
Good remuneration?	43
Diverse firm?	83

If the firm were a fictional character it would be...

Haymitch Abernathy (The Hunger Games) – is able to think extremely clearly about the long term

Weightmans LLP

Survey results *(marks out of 100%)*

Satisfied in your job? 74

Firm living up to expectations? 73

High quality of work? 81

Enough client contact? 74

Stress-free? 62

Happy work/life balance? 73

Friendly firm? 80

Great social life? 64

Good vacation scheme? 82

Confident you'll be kept on? 68

Good remuneration? 48

Diverse firm? 73

 **verdict**

A firm with a 'good reputation in the legal market', Weightmans is 'forward-thinking and dynamic', and its merger with Ford & Warren in July 2015 added a Leeds office to its national network. The firm is commended by trainees for its 'public sector work and expertise'. There is also 'exposure to good-quality work' across a 'wide range of areas', and recruits acknowledge that while 'insurance is the biggest business line', the firm is also busy representing 'large corporations' in the commercial sector. Three respondents volunteered that they were previously paralegals at Weightmans, with one adding that the 'ethos and work ethic appealed to me'. The firm is identified as being 'really down-to-earth and friendly', and is 'attentive to staff needs'. We are told that 'good people are running the firm', and there is 'a decent level of partner interaction and guidance'. There are complaints that 'it can seem a bit more centred towards its head office which means other offices can feel a bit isolated sometimes', and that because the 'HR side is run from Liverpool it means that it is difficult for HR to be completely approachable'. Representative work highlights include 'dealing with a high-profile litigation case and ten-day trial involving corrupt police officers' and 'hearing the news that one of our clients would no longer face police action in relation to a serious road traffic collision'. Respondents report a 'lack of organisation in respect of seat rotations', and it is not ideal that 'you could be expected to travel to other offices in the region for seats'. Still, the 'good work/life balance' is appreciated, as is the generally 'sociable office environment'. To train at a 'growing firm' which offers 'hands-on experience' and 'exposure to complex matters', remember Weightmans.

If the firm were a fictional character it would be...

Luther – is both pragmatic and inventive, and solves every problem it faces

Wilkin Chapman LLP

 **verdict**

Wilkin Chapman has a 'very good reputation' in Lincolnshire and East Yorkshire, and is labelled by one of its trainees as the 'best option in the region'. The firm has 'lots of practice areas', and the 'large number of departments allows for greater variety in seat choices'. The 'standard of work is good' as 'fewer trainees' means that there are 'opportunities to get involved with cases rather than undertaking administrative work'. Trainee highlights include 'getting your own first file', 'attending a trial where our client got the best possible outcome' and 'being given relatively high levels of responsibility and client contact in my current seat'. A minor gripe is that 'work can be intermittent', and as some supervisors are 'not good at delegating tasks' there is a 'lack of consistency in training between departments'. Despite this grievance, 'people are friendly and helpful' and trainees feel able to 'speak freely' to their colleagues. This 'welcoming atmosphere' means that trainees 'feel like a valued member of the team'. Some respondents have experienced 'uncertainty surrounding seat moves', and a belief persists that 'other firms seem far more structured in their approach to seat rotations'. On the plus side, there is 'good trainee retention' at the firm, and trainees report a 'better work/life balance' and a 'less stressful' training contract than some of their peers, and a **Lex 100 Winner** title is duly awarded for low-stress levels. Wilkin Chapman is a 'growing firm' that offers trainees 'challenging work', so research the firm further if you wish to train at a 'personable' regional outfit.

Survey results *(marks out of 100%)*

Satisfied in your job?	73
Firm living up to expectations?	72
High quality of work?	76
Enough client contact?	73
Stress-free?	76
Happy work/life balance?	82
Friendly firm?	83
Great social life?	78
Good vacation scheme?	68
Confident you'll be kept on?	71
Good remuneration?	49
Diverse firm?	75

If the firm were a fictional character it would be...

Michael Schofield (Prison Break) – determined, thinks under pressure and cares about others

Wilsons

Lex 100 Winner

See categories below
and tables from page 69

Survey results *(marks out of 100%)*

Satisfied in your job?	72
Firm living up to expectations?	75
High quality of work?	77
Enough client contact?	74
Stress-free?	47
Happy work/life balance?	(85)
Friendly firm?	75
Great social life?	65
Good vacation scheme?	70
Confident you'll be kept on?	64
Good remuneration?	60
Diverse firm?	79

 verdict

The combination of 'London quality of work outside London' and a 'fantastic work/life balance living in Salisbury' makes Wilsons an attractive proposition. Some recruits were first exposed to the 'good-quality work' on the 'enjoyable vacation scheme', during which the 'people were very friendly'. Being part of a small intake is considered advantageous, with one person saying 'we are a select few and I feel that we are recruited with a view to being future leaders in the company'. Wilsons 'offers excellent private client and charity work, with incredible clients in both areas'. Training contract highlights include 'working on a multi-million pound case', 'being involved in a big employment tribunal matter' and 'working in the charities department on contentious matters'. Trainees whinge that Wilsons is 'not always very transparent in decision-making'. This extends to the recruitment of trainees and seat moves, and one respondent complains of 'not being given the seat I wanted'. That said, the training contract is 'well structured' and the 'hands-on partner-led supervision' aids trainees' development. We are told that the 'salary could be better' and that 'the firm does not sponsor you for the GDL or LPC', but do bear in mind the aforementioned 'brilliant work/life balance' which earned a **Lex 100 Winner** gong for Wilsons. The current cohort praises the 'great experience' and 'incredibly rewarding' cases available, and favourite memories include 'visiting clients across the South of England' and 'receiving a thank you card from a client'. For one trainee who sought 'quality work and impressive clients', the opportunity to work for Wilsons 'was one I could not pass up'.

If the firm were a fictional character it would be...

Hercule Poirot – discreet, hard-working and immensely intelligent

Withers LLP

 **verdict**

A 'leading firm in its practice areas', Withers is 'top-ranked for its family and private client work', and trainees 'relish the opportunity to work in departments which are rated at the top of the field'. As a result of the 'interesting spread of work' in these practice areas, trainees enjoy representing a 'variety of clients' and feel that this work sets Withers apart from 'ordinary City firms'. Praise is reserved for the 'impressive application process', as one recruit says 'I enjoyed the interviews and found the people I met very engaging'. The 'small trainee intake is an attraction', as one respondent 'felt that the firm was more interested in recruiting engaging individuals rather than a mass of trainees where no one would know who you were'. An additional benefit of the small trainee cohort is that 'you can take on quite a lot of responsibility if you want it', and there is a concerted effort to ensure trainees experience 'quality work'. Work highlights to date include 'attending the High Court on a major divorce case', 'my international secondment to the Milan office' and 'reaching an agreement on a family matter after an all-day settlement meeting'. There are complaints that 'remuneration is less than at other City firms of a comparable size'. Colleagues are a 'very friendly bunch', though the 'lack of social events put on by the firm' is another gripe. That said, trainees greatly appreciate that Withers 'treats you as a valuable member of the team and takes a real interest in your career progression'. For a training contract that combines 'high-profile work' with the 'opportunity to work with practitioners at the forefront of their field', learn more about Withers.

If the firm were a fictional character it would be...

Mycroft Holmes – multi-talented, ambitious but utterly discreet

Survey results *(marks out of 100%)*

Satisfied in your job?   83

Firm living up to expectations?   83

High quality of work?   86

Enough client contact?   77

Stress-free?   63

Happy work/life balance?   70

Friendly firm?   86

Great social life?   63

Good vacation scheme?   85

Confident you'll be kept on?   64

Good remuneration?   67

Diverse firm?   80

Good international secondments?   63

Woodfines LLP

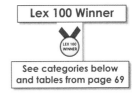
Survey results *(marks out of 100%)*

Satisfied in your job? (88)

Firm living up to expectations? 84

High quality of work? 84

Enough client contact? (86)

Stress-free? 60

Happy work/life balance? 84

Friendly firm? (94)

Great social life? 70

Good vacation scheme? 61

Confident you'll be kept on? 52

Good remuneration? 72

Diverse firm? (90)

 **verdict**

A 'regional firm with aspirations of further growth in the coming years', Bedford-headquartered Woodfines is well placed to offer its trainee cohort 'a lot of first-hand experience early on'. Survey respondents feel that they have 'benefitted from a dynamic training contract', with 'varied and engaging seats' spanning 'all areas of general practice along with crime and regulatory'. Work highlights include 'attending the High Court and making representations in front of the Master of the day' and 'the first time we secured an unlikely result for a client'. There are 'plenty of opportunities to move offices' during training, though we hear that there can be a 'lack of consistency and communication between the four offices', and one trainee moans of 'being stuck in traffic between the Bedford and Cambridge office for hours on end'. Feedback praises 'the level of work and responsibility you are given', which includes the much-cherished 'good amount of client contact'. It is felt that 'the pay could be slightly higher', but the 'workload seems to be reasonable and there isn't any pressure to stay late into the evening'. One recruit chooses 'the work atmosphere' as the best thing about the firm, as the 'friendly' staff 'seem to care about each other and take pride in their work'. It is therefore no surprise that the firm is a **Lex 100 Winner** in the friendliness category, and in three others. With the support of this internal network as required, respondents are trusted with 'hands-on work experience managing our own files'. To work at a full-service firm with offices across Bedfordshire, Buckinghamshire and Cambridgeshire and which provides its lawyers with 'scope to develop your career', take a closer look at Woodfines.

If the firm were a fictional character it would be...

Sir Topham Hatt (The Fat Controller) – takes a keen interest in the running of transport

Wright Hassall LLP

 verdict

New Lex 100 entrant Wright Hassall offers its trainees 'a good quality of work and a high level of responsibility'. The Warwickshire firm is praised for having 'the feel of a smaller-sized firm while being large enough to hold its own with much larger, multi-office firms'. This is demonstrated by the 'impressive client base' and the 'interesting work' which entails 'involvement with big projects'. Work highlights include 'successfully delivering a three-hour presentation to a key target client on the basics of contract law', 'attending the Royal Courts of Justice' and 'being involved with a very substantial strategic land transaction with a multitude of layers of complexity'. A 'friendly and welcoming' firm, Wright Hassall has an open-plan office which means 'it is easy to get to know people, including partners and the senior management team'. Despite this, there can be a 'lack of communication from partners to the rest of the firm'. The levels of client contact are enviable, and one recruit's stand-out moment was 'receiving client feedback on a successful deal'. Client secondments are available during the training contract, and these have been defined as a 'superb opportunity to learn and develop'. The small intake is one reason for the 'high-quality training' which 'appears to be more diverse and more structured than at other firms'. It is just as well, because one survey respondent believes that the LPC 'doesn't help that much in practice'. To commence your training at a 'good-sized regional firm with quality clients and work', make an application to Wright Hassall.

Survey results *(marks out of 100%)*

Satisfied in your job?	79
Firm living up to expectations?	85
High quality of work?	80
Enough client contact?	75
Stress-free?	54
Happy work/life balance?	75
Friendly firm?	79
Great social life?	72
Confident you'll be kept on?	84
Good remuneration?	70
Diverse firm?	77

If the firm were a fictional character it would be...

Jonathan Creek – enigmatic, unorthodox, but succeeds when others can't

Notes

Notes

Index to The Lex 100 firms

Index

Index to The Lex 100 firms continued

LPC providers